Religion Today

Religion Today

A Critical Thinking Approach to Religious Studies

Ross Aden

ROWMAN & LITTLEFIELD PUBLISHERS, INC.
Lanham • Boulder • New York • Toronto • Plymouth, UK

Published by Rowman & Littlefield Publishers, Inc.
A wholly owned subsidiary of The Rowman & Littlefield Publishing Group, Inc.
4501 Forbes Boulevard, Suite 200, Lanham, Maryland 20706
www.rowman.com

10 Thornbury Road, Plymouth PL6 7PP, United Kingdom

British Library Cataloguing in Publication Information Available

Library of Congress Cataloging-in-Publication Data

Aden, Ross, 1946–
  Religion today : a critical thinking approach to religious studies / Ross Aden.
    p. cm.
  Includes bibliographical references and index.
  ISBN 978-0-7425-6371-1 (cloth : alk. paper) — ISBN 978-0-7425-6372-8 (pbk. : alk.
paper) — ISBN 978-1-4422-1961-8 (electronic)
  1. Religions—Textbooks. 2. Religion—Textbooks. I. Title.
  BL80.3.A34 2013
  200.71—dc23   2012021964

∞™ The paper used in this publication meets the minimum requirements
of American National Standard for Information Sciences—Permanence of
Paper for Printed Library Materials, ANSI/NISO Z39.48-1992.

Printed in the United States of America

Contents

1

Introducing a Critical Thinking
Approach to Religious Studies

CHAPTER SUMMARY

1. How Religion Complicates Life in the Twenty-First Century

The growing role of religion in this century is making public life complicated. Even Mc-Donald's discovered its complexity when it tried to be sensitive to the new religious climate. To respect religious diversity in Singapore, the fast food chain substituted another symbol for the pig in its promotion of the Chinese New Year. The management had to quickly reverse course when its action caused an uproar.

The McDonald's misstep is a sign of the new religious situation in the twenty-first century. In today's global society, religion is not fading away as many predicted. Religion is vigorously asserting itself in all aspects of public as well as private life. Modern society is struggling to come to terms with its growing influence in international relationships, economics, politics, and culture. But dealing with the complications of religion is not easy.

2. The Widespread Ignorance of Religion and Its Consequence

For centuries, public higher education neglected the study of religion because it was thought to be irrelevant to modern life. Consequently, most Americans know little about these religious systems of meaning. Most failed a simple test on the basics of religion. This ignorance has negative consequences for foreign policy and international relations abroad and religious tolerance at home. Religious illiteracy makes it impossible for a full understanding of history, politics, and the Humanities. And such lack of knowledge makes it impossible to participate in the world's religious conversation about meaning in life. Education may have neglected religion to avoid controversy and affirm the separation of church and state. But now that solution no longer works, because religion will no longer be put down.

3. Religious Studies: Avoiding Hazards and Gaining Benefits

Since its development in the 1960s, the field of religious studies has worked hard to build up the content and develop the methods of the academic study about religion. The field defines itself as academic, multidisciplinary, and cross-cultural. These characteristics make its content and methods uniquely suited for learning about the current dynamics of religion while avoiding the hazards of religious study. The events of 9/11 stimulated some of the scholars in the field to propose a wider and more public role for religious studies. They realized that it had resources to offer to the public discussion of the pressing issues surrounding religion in today's world. This textbook explores the way that scholars in the field are contributing to the understanding of the issues of religion in this century. It relies on sources from this century.

4. A Textbook for the Twenty-First Century

This textbook is written in the twenty-first century from the viewpoint that religion has an emerging, enhanced status and critical role in this century. In the same way, religious studies has the new role of interpreting this renewed place of religion in human life. Scholars are developing new approaches to meet this challenge.

The purpose of this textbook is to give the reader the tools for the continuing study of religion in its contemporary context. The book will use the problem-solving process as an overall framework for each chapter. Problem solving focuses research and learning and integrates many skills of critical thinking. According to the theory of C. S. Peirce, problem solving is the fundamental process of learning. Each chapter will explore one of the broad areas of study within the field of religious studies.

5. The Advantages of Studying Religion

This section lists the benefits of studying religion: (a) it is interesting; (b) it helps one learn how to relate to other peoples and cultures; (c) it helps one learn to apply the perspectives of other academic disciplines; (d) it helps one understand the ways that humans have contended with questions of ultimate meaning, value, and destiny; and (e) it offers the satisfaction of finding solutions to problems and gaining new understanding. In summary, complexity can lead to understanding. The questions of religious studies are more important than the answers because they lead to fresh insight.

HOW RELIGION COMPLICATES LIFE IN THE TWENTY-FIRST CENTURY

Life is complicated. The increasing role of religion in the national and global affairs of the twenty-first century seems to be making it worse.

The international McDonald's hamburger chain found this out. For the Chinese New Year, McDonald's distributed soft plastic toy figures representing the animals of the Chinese zodiac. It left out the pig. It substituted a Doraemon Cupid toy instead. The chain thought including the pig would be insensitive to Muslims, who are not allowed to eat pork.[1]

Some people in Singapore immediately protested because the pig is one of the traditional cultural symbols of the zodiac. Surprisingly, some Muslims also reacted. They thought the substitution made them out to be overly sensitive. It is only eating pork that is *haraam*—that is, forbidden by Islamic law. Others joined in the complaint, calling the omission of one of the zodiac animals "self-censorship."[2]

In response to the protest, McDonald's apologized and put the pig back into the promotion. Communications director Linda Ming said, "We seek our customers' understanding that it has never been our intention to be disrespectful towards any religion or culture."[3]

Others besides MacDonald's have found the same difficulties. Observers say that religion complicates such aspects of life as American politics, gender issues, relationships with neighbors, ethnic and nationalistic conflicts, foreign policy

This wheel shows the symbols of the Chinese zodiac. When McDonald's Singapore removed the pig and substituted another character, controversy ensued.

and international relations, intelligence gathering, end-of-life decisions, and just about everything else.

Some people might believe that the world could get along without the complexity of religion and wish that religion would simply vanish. In fact, for more than two centuries, most academic scholars held that governments, schools, and other public institutions would not have to bother about religion. They taught that as the world became more modern and people became more educated, religion would soon become a harmless throwback to the past. After all, religions were merely collections of superstitions, fantasies, and unproven opinions. Religious belief had no place in the developing world of science and technology.

At the turn of the twenty-first century, the attacks of September 11, 2001, awakened everyone to the mounting importance of religion. Religion had not faded away. It was intruding into world affairs with new vitality.

International relations scholars Andrew J. Bacevich and Elizabeth H. Prodromou explain that since the end of the Cold War in 1991, religion has become more, not less, involved in world events. Noting its increasing visibility in world affairs, some scholars began to question the predicted demise of religion. They observed that religion was not conforming to the secular idea that the world could get along without it. It was showing surprising staying power even in the modern world.

The Importance of Religion in Today's World

A white paper of the American Academy of Religion (AAR) sums up the view of those who call attention to the new importance of religion in today's world: "World events have led Americans to a new appreciation of the importance of knowledge about religion and to a vivid awareness of the dangers that emerge when we fail to recognize religion as a potent source of motivation and behavior."[4] Broadcaster and journalist Krista Tippett agrees with the AAR statement. She states, "Religion has moved from the sidelines to the center of world affairs and American life . . . it remains a force that animates lives and nations and history—for better or for worse."[5] In her book on why religion still matters in the twenty-first century, Tippett describes her own personal discovery of the enduring power of religion. She recalls that her own spiritual search convinced her that modern thinking is weak and limited. She came to see that the reasoning that controls our law, politics, economics, and science cannot answer the deeper questions of meaning and morality.[6] Religion is an indomitable force in human life because it addresses these questions.

Chief Rabbi of the United Kingdom Jonathan Sachs agrees that today's scientific, economic, and political systems fail to answer the burning questions of human life. According to Sachs, at its best, the modern world offers countless choices of things to buy for those who have money to pay for them. But Sachs asserts that human beings are more than consumers that drive the global economic engine. Human persons are creatures who seek meaning. Unless we can find out who we are, why we are here on Earth, and what things have lasting worth, our lives will seem meaningless, no matter how many gadgets we have.[7]

In Sachs's view, the twentieth century was a time of warring political ideologies, including fascism, socialism, communism, and nationalism. Now in the twenty-first century, global capitalism has replaced these belief systems. Yet, in Sachs's view, the promises of the global marketplace are as empty as the philosophies that it has overpowered. Sensing what global capitalism lacks, many have never left religion. Others are turning to religion to reclaim the sense of identity and purpose that the mass society seems to steal from them.[8]

What Religion Does Better Than Anything Else

According to Sachs, "Religions, as total systems of meaning, create totalities."[9] Sachs points out that the term *religion* comes from the Latin word *religare*, meaning "to bind." Religions tie human persons to a reality that is infinitely greater than themselves. Religions, therefore, unite all the pieces of human life into an all-encompassing whole. Religious adherents believe that there is "something more" than the physical world and that "something more" is transcendent. This means that it is a reality that is much greater and more valuable than the material universe.

Individuals find meaning in this transcendent whole in two ways. First, religious adherents believe that all they know and experience in life fits into the wholeness of the infinite reality. This gives everything that exists and everything that happens profound meaning. Second, belief in this "greater whole" shapes the lives of the religious into a complete and purposeful way of life.

Thus, in Sachs's view, nothing else in human experience can do what religions do so well. Religions involve human beings in a community of transcendent meaning. Within the circle of their shared beliefs and sacred way of life, humans know their place in the universe, the significance of their lives, and the ultimate meaning of the events of human history.[10]

THE WIDESPREAD IGNORANCE OF RELIGION AND ITS CONSEQUENCE

Dealing with religious systems of meaning, however, is not easy, as McDonald's found out. Belief systems are complex networks of interrelated ideas, attitudes, and patterns of action. They have their own vocabulary, logic, and sentiments. For example, like Muslims, Jews do not eat pork. In Judaism, this prohibition is set within the framework of an intricate web of ideas about what is kosher according to the extensive set of Jewish dietary rules called *kashrut*. These laws, in turn, are based on the Torah, the Law of God. These dietary mandates are so complex that typically in Judaism, trained rabbis must teach and interpret them.

In summary, religions are systems of meaning that inform, shape, and enrich the lives of billions of people throughout the world. But the complexity of these webs of belief and practice makes them difficult to understand. Widening religious diversity has made this task even more challenging. Unfortunately, recent studies have shown that most Americans lack the basic knowledge that would help them meet the challenge of avoiding confusion and misunderstanding of religions in today's global society.

Americans Flunk a Simple Religion Test

For decades, American education, government, diplomacy, and business did not take the study of religion seriously. After all, many scholars thought that religion would soon disappear. As a result of the lack of attention, the public is religiously illiterate. The Pew Forum recently gave Americans a thirty-two-question test on religious knowledge. It covered basics of the Bible, historical figures, and world religions. Overall, Americans flunked the test, scoring 50 percent. Atheists and agnostics scored the highest at 65 percent, a "D." Jews and Mormons did almost as well at 64 percent. White evangelical Protestants scored 55 percent, while black Protestants scored 42 percent. White Catholics scored 50 percent, and Hispanic Catholics scored 36 percent.[11]

The results show that more education about religion would help improve the scores. Those who had taken a religion course in college scored 69 percent, almost the same as those with graduate degrees. College graduates scored ten points lower at 59 percent. High school graduates who did not go to college scored 43 percent. On the other hand, attending a private religious school helps somewhat. Graduates of private religious schools scored 55.6 percent in comparison with those who attended public schools, who scored 48.5 percent.

Interestingly, those who attended nonreligious private schools did better at 58 percent, but that is still ten points lower than the scores of college students who took a religion course.[12]

However, the study showed that the religious education of children and youth is failing: Even those who attended religious education programs at least once a week failed the test. Their score was 52 percent, only two points above the average of all Americans.[13]

The Consequences of Religious Ignorance

McDonald's had no intention of upsetting the sensitivities of either the Chinese who were celebrating their New Year or the Muslims who do not eat pork. It knew something about the religions involved. But not enough to avoid the misstep.

Ignorance of religion has consequences. For example, a study of the Chicago Council on Global Affairs advised President Barack Obama that American foreign policy must overcome its ignorance of religion. According to the summary of its findings, "American foreign policy is handicapped by a God gap, a narrow, ill-informed and 'uncompromising Western secularism' that feeds religious extremism, threatens traditional cultures, and fails to engage and encourage religious groups that promote peace, human rights, and the general welfare of their communities."[14]

When the Council referred to this "uncompromising Western secularism," it noted the prevailing idea in Western culture that religion only belongs in the private sphere, not in the public life of politics, economics, and social affairs. In this secular view, Westerners do not have to bother finding out about religion because it has nothing to do with life in society. However, the Council noted that much of the world does not have this idea of the separation of religion from the social order. For them, religion matters in the public as well as private sphere. The study stressed that the remedy for the short-sightedness of American foreign policy is to come to terms with the critical role of religion in this new century, especially in non-Western countries. This means taking the study of religion seriously.[15]

Religion not only complicates our relations with other countries and cultures, but, closer to home, religious illiteracy also makes people clumsy in their dealings with believers of other religions who live in their own communities. Religious ignorance often leads to prejudice as people compare the sacred ways of others unfavorably with their own.

Religion also permeates the course of human history, world politics, and the development of art, music, and literature. Religious ignorance makes it impossible to understand these spheres of human life.

Perhaps most important is the point that those who are ignorant of religion cannot understand the ongoing human conversation about meaning, a discussion that speaks the languages of the world's religions. Those who know these religious languages have access to the storehouses of the world's most profound wisdom. Those who are religiously illiterate cannot make use of these sources of profound understanding of their world, their neighbors, and themselves.

Neglect of Teaching about Religion No Longer Works

Yet learning about religion is complicated. Those who hoped that modern thinking would replace religion had a practical reason for believing that religion and public life should be separated. To understand, one must go back 500 years to the time of the Protestant Reformation in Europe and religious wars in England. In 1517, Martin Luther, a German monk, sparked a wholesale protest against what Luther and his sympathizers saw as the abuses of the Catholic Church. This Protestant Reformation resulted in the separation of Protestant churches from the Roman Catholic Church. Eventually, it resulted in a devastating period of warfare known as the Thirty Years War.

In 1534 CE, King Henry VIII declared that he was the head of the Church of England, not the pope in Rome. After that, the monarchy vacillated between sovereigns who favored the Protestant cause, those who wanted to return to Catholicism, and those who wanted to continue Henry VIII's program of a "Church of England." Eventually, a civil war arose and, for a time, the Protestants (Calvinists) held the upper hand. Finally, the monarchists were able to restore the monarchy and with it the "Church of England," which was neither Calvinist nor Catholic but under the king of England.

In the aftermath of these battles in the name of religion, certain philosophers arrived at a solution that would reduce the chances of religious war. The solution was to strip religion of its political power and take away its influence in public life. Then, relegated to the private sphere of individuals, it would be harmless.

In the "Western" cultures of Europe and North America, the idea of banishing religion from public life evolved into different forms of "secularism" based on the principle that religious institutions and influence should have no part to play in the public arena of politics, government, economics, and social affairs. In America, the prevailing form is the notion of "separation of church and state." In other parts of the Western world, it takes different forms.

Events since the turn of the century demonstrate that this "Western" idea of the role of religion in life is increasingly under challenge. In "non-Western" cultures outside of Europe and North America, many do not accept it, but see religion as a total way of life that encompasses the public as well as private sphere. Yet even in "Western" societies such as the United States, religious groups are testing the line between religion and government. Since religion believes in a transcendent reality that gives meaning to human life, it does not easily accept the confines of the private sphere. Believers tend to apply their beliefs and practices to all of their lives, whether public or private.

As religion breaks out of its secular limits and assumes a leading role on the world stage, it is becoming even more controversial. For example, this textbook will contain a chapter on the religious violence that regrettably is part of the emerging dynamics of religion in this century. But even if it is not a spark to actual violence, it is often a source of division and conflict, just as it often is a source of unity and reconciliation among peoples.

The controversial and complex nature of religion has been used as a reason for neglecting religion in the schools. Religious studies scholar Diane L. Moore observes that teachers often avoid the topic to prevent problems.[16] It is as if religion were too volatile a topic to handle in public schools.

But this strategy of dodging the difficulties of teaching religion has led to the proven religious illiteracy of the American public, and mistakes like the one McDonald's made. This is a new century when religion will no longer be put down. On the national and international level, religion is rising to confront the very secularism that put it in its place. The religious dynamics of this new global context may be distressing, but they are all the more reason for promoting the understanding of religion. As Moore states, the current ignorance of religion makes the "misunderstanding and exploitation" of religion likely, as the "culture wars" of America's current politics shows.[17]

RELIGIOUS STUDIES: AVOIDING HAZARDS AND GAINING BENEFITS

This textbook introduces the field of religious studies and how it is addressing the new religious situation of the twenty-first century. The field of religious studies offers ways to avoid hazards of studying religion while gaining the benefits of learning about it. One of the founders of this field, Ninian Smart (1927–2001), stated that the field as we know it today was established in the 1960s. Since then, scholars in the field have worked hard to devise ways of studying religion in the public arena. The fruit of their work is seen in the content and methods of religious studies that this book introduces.

The field of religious studies has built up an extensive store of knowledge about all aspects of religion. More important, the scholars of religious studies have discovered effective ways of studying religion without taking sides in the controversies between the religions.

Smart summarized the field's timely approach. He stated that the field is founded on a set of academic, multidisciplinary, and cross-cultural ways of studying all aspects of religions.[18]

The *academic* nature of the field means that religious studies can teach about religion without endorsing religion or any of the religions. The emphasis is on sound scholarship in the academic setting. It seeks to avoid the bias of *sectarian* as well as skeptical views. Of course, the sacred ways that religious studies explores are built on the belief in a transcendent reality or consciousness. However, the study of these ways does not depend on any extraordinary tools of insight, only human intelligence.

The Characteristics of Religious Studies

1. Academic
2. Multidisciplinary
3. Cross-cultural
4. Relevant to public life

In addition, the field of religious studies is a *multidisciplinary* field that treats religion as a factor in many aspects of human life. Religious studies expert William Beal explains the multidisciplinary approach: "We are about the *academic study of religion*, exploring and interpreting various religious beliefs, ideas, texts, practices, and institutions from a variety of scholarly perspectives—comparative, historical, cognitive, literary, sociological, anthropological, and philosophical, among others."[19]

The multidisciplinary aspect of religious studies goes in two directions. On the one hand, the field of study believes religion plays a part in practically all arenas of human life. It holds that it is difficult to study history, sociology, political science, psychology, and the arts and humanities without taking religion into account. Thus, religious studies offers essential insight into the dynamics of religion in these spheres of human life.[20] On the other hand, the field of religious studies views religion from the perspective of the wide range of academic disciplines that Beal mentions. The field of religious studies, therefore, offers ways for students to use what they know from other academic disciplines. As they apply the perspectives of chosen areas of study like psychology to the study of religion, students can learn more about both the chosen field of study and religion.

Finally, the *cross-cultural* nature of religious studies makes it especially suited for promoting the appreciation of religious diversity. Students in religious studies learn about the world's cultures as they study the religions at their core. In addition to this knowledge, however, religious studies helps students learn how to treat other cultures and their peoples with respect as well as critical thought. As we will see in the next chapter, the field has especially developed ways of breaking out of the Western ways of viewing religion. Because it is cross-cultural, the field of religious studies teaches students the important skill of how to view human life from the perspectives of cultures that are different than their own. They also learn to think critically about their own culture from these different viewpoints. As a cross-cultural field, religious students can help students learn how to engage with people of diverse backgrounds to achieve mutual understanding.

Religious Studies Assumes a Public Role

Religious studies evolved as an academic effort to make sense of the complexity of the tightly woven networks of meaning called "religions." Rebecca S. Chopp observes that throughout the latter part of the twentieth century, scholars of religion concentrated on the development of the field as a profession. The field divided into specialties, and scholars devoted themselves to internal matters within these distinctive areas of study.[21]

The result of this intense period of work was a substantial collection of content and methods described in the last section. The field had these to offer its students for overcoming the problems of studying religion. But its impact was still confined to academic circles.

In response to the events of 9/11, however, the professional association for religious studies broadened the stated mission of the field. Soon after the suicide attacks, the board of the American Academy of Religion (AAR) issued a statement. Scholars were now "to serve as resources" for ongoing discussions of the issues that the assaults had exposed. In particular, scholars of religion were to initiate conversations against religious discrimination and to "foster reflection on and understanding of religious traditions, issues, questions, and values." The members of the AAR were now urged to apply their scholarship to the "public understanding of religion and religions."[22]

Thus, 9/11 represents a turning point for the study of religion. The attacks proved what had been going on since the latter part of the twentieth century: religion was reclaiming its vital role in world and national affairs. In response to this new awareness of the public impact of religion, Chopp declared that the scholarship of religion was to "serve the public." The field of religious studies would address questions that people outside the walls of the university and college were asking.[23] Regarding its other characteristics, the field would not be relevant to current global affairs and public life.

Since 9/11, the field of religious studies has risen to the challenge of interpreting the complexity of religion and its role in the global society. More than a decade after 9/11, the field of religious studies continues to develop and grow. *Newsweek* magazine reports that the number of graduates with majors in religious studies or philosophy has doubled since the 1970s. Moreover, in 2009 "his-

Construction site at Ground Zero in New York City. The 9/11 attacks proved to be a turning point in the study of religion.

tory of religions" had become the most popular specialty of professional scholars in the field of history. Religious studies scholar Jeanne Kilde summarizes, "The study of religion has become a growth industry."[24]

A TEXTBOOK FOR THE TWENTY-FIRST CENTURY

This textbook takes into account the new religious situation since the turn of the century. It explores the efforts of scholars to make a public contribution to the emerging issues that are arising as religion asserts itself in the twenty-first century. Some of these issues involve religious violence, religious diversity and tolerance, the treatment of religious minorities, and ways to understand the beliefs and practices of other religions. It also addresses other questions that are discussed inside and outside the classroom such as the ownership of artifacts from Native American graves, the essential role of the brain in religious experience, and the future of religion in the global society. This book is written from the perspective of the new century, and in most cases, it uses sources from this time frame.

In summary, this textbook is written from the viewpoint that religion has an emerging status and enhanced role in the twenty-first century. Moreover, this book assumes that religion is complex and controversial, especially in today's world, when it is asserting itself in the public sphere. Because of its contemporary viewpoint, most of its sources are from this new century.

The Problem-Solving Approach as an Overall Method of Study

The initial problem of the book is to find a way of making rational sense out of the dynamics of religion in the twenty-first century. A satisfactory method would avoid the prejudice that favors one religious faith over another. It would aim at an impartial, fair, and reasonable understanding of the topics and issues of religion in today's world.

This textbook assumes that to meet this challenge, scholars must use the best of human reason, critical thinking. Critical thinking sorts out reliable evidence from uninformed opinion. It avoids hasty judgments based on ignorance or prejudice. In addition, it gains a more comprehensive understanding of the object of its study by looking at it from different points of view.

How Problem Solving Integrates the Skills of Critical Thinking

Scholars have developed an impressive number of ways to apply critical thinking to the topics and issues of religion. This book chooses to organize these ways in an overall process of thinking that is repeated in every chapter. This is the method of problem solving. It follows from the observation that religion poses complex problems and controversial issues in today's world. Yet the advantage of this overall method is that it challenges students to use a wide range of skills of critical thinking.

For example, suppose Ben is handed a narrow box divided in two. It has two marbles, one on each side of the divide. The challenge is to move the marbles so that both are on the opposite sides of the box. The box is covered, so one cannot place the marbles on each side. Can Ben do it in a few seconds?

Here is where critical thinking skills come into play. Ben *observes* the box, but probably does not immediately turn it over. He *analyzes* the forces operating on the marbles and their movement by tipping and shaking the box. He might read the directions again to see if one has made the correct *interpretation* of the problem. He *tests some alternatives* of manipulating the box and evaluates them. When all the options are exhausted, he looks for *more evidence.*

Suppose that eventually Ben turns the box over. He finds a sharp point on the bottom in the middle of the box. This pivot prompts him to make a *guess.* The point has to be there for a reason. Ah, he remembers the idea of centrifugal force. He makes the *inference* that the point is there to spin the box. He goes on to make the *deduction* that spinning things exert centrifugal force. The box is made to be a "spinning thing." Therefore, it will exert centrifugal force. Furthermore, he reasons that it follows that when the box is spinning and exerting centrifugal force, the loose marbles will go outward to the opposite sides of the box. Sure enough, Ben *evaluates* the tentative conclusion by spinning the box. It works. A simple wooden puzzle has stimulated the use of a wide variety of critical thinking skills.

The Learning Theory That Shapes the Outline of the Chapters

This text's use of the problem-solving method is founded on the thought of American philosopher C. S. Peirce (1839–1914). Peirce believed that all learning involves problem solving. He held that everyone holds on to their preferred ideas and habits of thought until they run across something that does not fit their normal ways of thinking. The gap between what they think they know and what they experience poses a problem that requires problem solvers to look for more information or a different viewpoint to find a reasonable solution.[25]

Effective problem solvers then sort out alternatives.[26] For example, they may tip the box of marbles from one side to the other in a futile attempt to make the marbles go where they want. Finally, an idea strikes them. A possible answer to the dilemma clicks in their mind like an electric plug in a wall socket—they may observe the sharp point on the bottom of the puzzle box and connect it with what they know about centrifugal force. This hunch is the first stage of inquiry. But the investigation is not complete until they test their hunch. They spin the box to confirm their hypothetical guess. When both marbles move to the outside of the box, they have solved the puzzle and learned something.[27]

The method of this textbook follows the process of thinking that Peirce described. But it refines it by using the ideas of Wayne Booth (1921–2005) and Peter Lipton (1954–2007). In *The Craft of Research*, Booth and his colleagues advised that a research project should start with the selection of a topic of interest. It should then frame questions that lead to a better understanding of the topic.[28] From there, researchers should search out problems that need to be solved to fill the gaps in their knowledge or to overcome the blocks in their understanding of the questions.

In keeping with this suggestion, each chapter will begin with an exploration of an interesting event or issue. Then we will stop to investigate the dynamics of this topic. This will lead to a discovery of a thought-provoking puzzle. This is a problem that challenges the way we think about the subject.

Once we discover the "research problem," the approach will take a cue from the research strategy of Peter Lipton called *inference to the best explanation* (*IBE*). Lipton proposed that the process of problem solving involves an examination of a number of alternative solutions to the problem. Problem solvers then choose to test the solution that they consider to be most likely.[29]

The reworking of Lipton's method will enable this book to review the options for thinking about questions of religion. It will survey the alternatives, before deciding which one might be most satisfactory. Thus the working strategy will help us learn an array of opinions on major topics of religious studies. Finally, the use of the modified IBE method will lead to the evaluation of different solutions, because it will ask us to choose the "best" alternative among options.

The Basic Outline of Each Chapter: The Problem-Solving Process

1. Defining the Problem
2. Focusing the Problem
3. Surveying the Alternative Approaches
4. Proposing the Most Promising Solution
5. Evaluating the Most Promising Solution

Here is the problem-solving process that frames the basic outline of each chapter:

1. *Defining the Problem*: Each chapter of the textbook will begin with an exploration of the topic starting with a current event or issue. We will locate the places where the common assumptions, knowledge, or viewpoints no longer seem adequate.
2. *Focusing the Problem*: Once we have found a gap between our prior way of thinking and what we encounter in today's world, the method will use thoughtful investigation and critical thinking to focus the question on a manageable problem.
3. *Surveying the Alternative Approaches*: When we have a clear understanding of the puzzle to be solved, we will survey a number of different ways out of the dilemma. This section will offer several different choices for consideration of the chapter topic under the section.
4. *Proposing the Most Promising Solution*: After we have laid out some significant options for working on our problem, we will select the most promising solution to it. The purpose of this section is not to give a full answer to our query about a topic. It is to suggest what a satisfactory solution might look like. The aim is to outline the proposal with enough detail so that we can evaluate it.

5. *Evaluating the Most Promising Solution*: This section will test the proposed solution in various ways. In doing so, it will clarify what an adequate answer to the puzzle might be. The evaluation might expose some remaining hidden assumptions. Finally, it will raise more questions for further study.

In summary, this problem-solving approach offers a single, easily applied method for studying religion and its role in the twenty-first century. It offers students of religion a discipline of thinking that yields sound, logical conclusions. Moreover, the problem-solving method engages students in active learning. In problem solving, students cannot merely absorb information. They must think through the case. The problem-solving methods help students learn how to find, evaluate, and use information for a focused purpose.

The Basic Information and Ideas for Study Found *within* the Outline of the Chapters

Note that this book presents the key terms, information, ideas, and methods for a foundation in the field of religious studies. It is important to remember that these essential tools for the academic study of religion are found *within* the outline of each chapter's problem-solving process. This means that this textbook is not a catalog of information about world religions. The chapters will cover the material that is typically required in introductory courses. However, the problem-solving outline of the chapters will help students understand the *relevance* of the terms, information, ideas, and approaches to the chapter topics as they work through the steps of the problem-solving process.

In summary, this book aims to help students learn tools and methods for applying critical thinking to the topics and issues of religion in the twenty-first century. The book aims to provide enough information and viewpoints to enable students to spend their time thinking through the ideas of the chapter.

The Questions Are More Important Than the Answers

Walter Capps (1934–1997) observed that religious studies is an "academic discipline" that uses "rules and methods" of scholarly study to make the subject of religion "intelligible."[30] This book will introduce students to current "rules and methods" of the academic study of religion. Yet these "rules and methods" are under development. They are changing just as the role of religion is changing, and religions are changing.

In summary, when we study religion in the twenty-first century, religion is a dynamic, changing, and often perplexing force in today's world. Trying to study it in all its complexity is like trying to hit a moving target in the dark. The field of religious studies is not static. It is shifting with the changing times. Therefore, the answers that scholars have given to academic questions about religion are important. More important, though, are the questions that point us to new vistas of insight into the dynamics of religion in the global society.

In this vein, journalist and broadcaster Krista Tippett provides the starting thoughts of this textbook. According to Tippett, "Religion is as visible and vital a part of global life now as it has been in any time in living memory." She adds that probing the rich topic of religion involves questions as well as answers because "our questions cleanse our answers and enliven our world."[31] Scholars of religion are not afraid to tackle complexity, even when it comes in the form of religion. To them, complications are puzzles to be solved, not frustrations to be avoided.

THE ADVANTAGES OF STUDYING RELIGION

Five Advantages of Studying Religion

1. It is interesting to investigate profound ideas, deep meanings, powerful experiences, and strange behaviors.
2. It helps students gain a wider view of human life and capacity to relate to other people and cultures.
3. It teaches students to use a number of academic disciplines.
4. It explores the ways that people address the ultimate questions of meaning, value, and destiny.
5. It is fun to work out problems as complicated as those of the role of religion in today's world.

Studying religion in the twenty-first century has many advantages. First, it is interesting. Exploring religion means investigating profound ideas, deep meanings, and powerful experiences, together with some of the strangest behavior imaginable. Taking religion classes means confronting challenging ideas and disconcerting practices. Studying religions means encountering forces that can build up human life in peace or tear it down in war.

Second, in the global society, studying religion is one of the best ways to develop a wider view of human life and a greater capacity to relate positively to other people and cultures. It is unlikely that one can become a responsible, contributing global citizen of today's world without a basic understanding of religion.

Third, students in religious studies learn to use a number of other academic disciplines for the investigation of religion. Religion provides the focus, but the fields of philosophy, psychology, sociology, anthropology, cultural studies, political science, history, art, literature, music, and even science have a place in the study of religion.

Fourth, to study religion is to explore the ways that human beings contend with such ultimate questions as meaning, value, and destiny. Whether one is a believer or not, it enriches one's life to understand how other people search for answers to the dilemmas of existence. Journalist Lisa Miller sums it up as follows: "For students earnestly interested in the Meaning of Life, religious studies is the way to go."[32]

Finally, solving puzzles is fun. When we work through a problem, we sharpen our powers of critical reasoning. And when we find a solution, we get a satisfying feeling. Religion is complicated, but wresting understanding out of this complexity gives one a feeling of accomplishment. Moreover, the insight we gain is useful for understanding ourselves, the world around us, and the role of religion in today's global society.

The academic study of religion is sometimes confusing. It is often challenging. But it is always an adventure. Traveling into the domain of religion means probing into the diverse beliefs, practices, and ways of life that continue to shape the lives of countless people across the planet. Increasingly, as religion asserts itself in today's world, these sacred ways also are making a decisive difference in the affairs of our global society.

Those who join in the exploration of religion will discover intriguing worlds of human meaning and experience. This textbook is meant to present the tools and resources that the field of religious studies has developed for the impartial investigation of these religions. But the book will add the further challenge of engaging students in critical thinking about the complex but critical issues of the considerable impact of religion and its current role in the twenty-first century.

KEY TERMS

Academic study of religion: the investigation of religion in educational settings dedicated to the advancement of learning. It treats religion as a human endeavor in contrast to theological study that accepts the premises of a particular religion.

Critical thinking: the thoughtful process of reasoning using the skills of logic to reach sound conclusions based on evidence.

Cross-cultural: dealing with more than one culture, usually by comparison or interaction of cultures.

Deduction: a conclusion reached by reasoning from a premise. The premise is a statement that is assumed to be true and on which the argument is founded; the process of reasoning from a premise going from a general statement to a specific conclusion.

Haraam: prohibited for Muslims by Islamic law, in contrast to halal, which is permitted for Muslims by Islamic law.

Inference: a conclusion reached by reasoning about what is thought to be true whether it is factual evidence or assumptions of truth.

"Inference to the best explanation": a problem-solving method that chooses the most likely explanation or solution to a problem and goes on to test it.

Multidisciplinary: using several academic disciplines that are distinctive branches of knowledge and scholarship in colleges and universities.

Religious studies: a contemporary academic field of scholarship that examines and interprets religion and religions from a wide range of perspectives.

Sectarian: narrowly restricted within the boundaries of a particular religious view or organization.

KEY QUESTIONS

1. How might McDonald's have handled the case of the promotional toys for the Chinese New Year in a way that was sensitive to religious diversity?
2. Considering how this chapter has defined religious studies, how would religious studies have helped guide McDonald's in its promotion for the Chinese New Year?
3. Why should religious illiteracy be a significant concern for society? Should teaching about religion be required in public secondary schools? In public colleges and universities? Defend your answer.
4. Outline the steps of the problem-solving process given in this chapter. According to C. S. Peirce, what is the role of surprise in the process? Why is it necessary to try to explore different options for the solution to a problem? How does one arrive at the "most promising" solution?
5. Identify and explain at least three of the critical thinking skills that problem solving uses.
6. List some of the benefits of studying religion and choose one or two that are most important to you.

2

Methods of Studying Religion

CHAPTER SUMMARY

1. Defining the Problem: The Muslim Headscarf in Personal Experience
Students at the University of Maryland and California State University–San Bernardino accepted the "Hijab Challenge" to wear the Muslim headscarf around campus. They personally experienced the discrimination that Muslims face in American society and elsewhere. These experiments showed the difference between the prejudice and hostility that the *hijab* ("cover") evokes and the motives and experiences of those who wear it. This difference raises the question of how to study issues like the Muslim "cover" in ways that will shed light on the current dynamics of religion and its role in the twenty-first century.

2. Focusing the Problem: Assumptions, Frames of Reference, and Associations of Ideas
We can analyze the conflicting viewpoints of the "cover" of Muslim women by using critical thinking to analyze their assumptions, frames of reference, and webs of associations. Assumptions are embedded in frames of reference. These frames are networks of associations of ideas that interpret events and shape the response to them. The associations of ideas are habits of connecting ideas together in clusters or categories.

According to the learning theory of William James, in order to learn anything new we must place it in a web of associations of things we already know. The challenge of this chapter is to find an approach to the study of religion that will overcome the limitations of preconceived webs of associations. To do this, we must find ways to break apart the old associations of ideas to make room for new evidence, new ways of thinking, and new understandings of religion. As we do this, we will develop new, more informed, and more intricate webs of interconnected ideas in wider frames of reference.

3. Surveying the Alternative Approaches: The Development of Religious Studies
This section outlines the development of the idea of religion and its associations from the Western Enlightenment of the eighteenth century. It finds that the Western idea of religion developed on the basis of the Enlightenment's separation of the religious from the secular. The separation of religion from public life protected society from religious conflict and established the freedom of individuals to believe according to their conscience.

The chapter then reviews the history of the academic study of religion. Scholars tried to develop theories of the basic nature and function of religion as they encountered new cultures and evidence. The principal method has been the *naturalist* approach. It has studied religion without the theological assumptions of a source in the supernatural.

The naturalist study of religion has three tracks. The anthropological found the essence of religion in its origin in nature gods, animism, or magic. The sociological found the essence of religion in its function of maintaining unity and the social order in human communities. The psychological found the essence of religion in the projection of psychological needs and fantasies on the screen of supernatural beings.

The evaluation of these approaches concludes that all of these approaches to study attempted to explain religion without accepting the doctrines of any specific religion. However, they accepted the biases of the Enlightenment view of religion and its separation from the secular as well as the assumptions and methods of science.

4. Proposing the Most Promising Solution: Strategies to Avoid Bias

The problem of freeing oneself from assumed associations while constructing new webs of meaning will, perhaps, never be fully solved. This chapter proposes three general strategies to deal with assumptions and illustrates these with representative scholars. The first is to try to eliminate any associations of ideas whatsoever (Yogacara Buddhism and J. Krishnamurti). Another is to study each religion as its own subject without comparing it to any others (Wilfred Cantwell Smith). The third is to study religion as a separate and unique subject that has to be studied on its own terms (Rudolf Otto).

5. Evaluating the Most Promising Solution: No Easy Way Out

This section presents the case of the repeal of a State of Oregon law that prohibited public school teachers from wearing religious clothing in the classroom. The analysis of this case will uncover several frames of reference. These associations of ideas help us understand the dynamics of the issue of religious clothing in Oregon. The case also helps us test the three proposed strategies of the unbiased study of religion.

The chapter ends with the thought that religious studies can contribute fair, informed, reasonable, and insightful understandings of religion and its role in world affairs. This goal depends on overcoming the predetermined habits of thought, especially those of the Western idea of religion. The evaluation of the three strategies for unbiased study concludes that all fall short of achieving this aim. The section asserts that the best way to overcome bias is to study religion the subject matter from "multiple perspectives" that correct and complement one another.

DEFINING THE PROBLEM: THE MUSLIM HEADSCARF IN PERSONAL EXPERIENCE

In classrooms across America, it is no longer surprising to see women wearing headscarves. The headscarf, popularly named the "hijab," identifies those who wear it as Muslim. According to the Pew Research Center, more than half of Muslim women under thirty say that they wear the hijab most of the time.[1] Many of these women are attending colleges and universities throughout the country.

Wearing the hijab makes a Muslim woman an easy target for mistreatment. Although seven in ten of Muslim women in America say that they wear the hijab frequently, 44 percent worry that they will be mistreated because of it. In contrast, 58 percent who do not wear the hijab worry about what would happen if they did.[2]

A study by the Pew Forum shows that their worries are well founded. One in three Muslims says that they have experienced acts of prejudice in the past year. The abuse ranges from being treated with suspicion (26 percent) and being called offensive names (15 percent) to being singled out by the police (9 percent) and being physically attacked or threatened (4 percent). The danger is worse for young adult Muslims. Four in ten young adult Muslims say that they have been mistreated in the past year because of their religion.[3]

Non-Muslim students in Maryland and California found out what it is like to face the likelihood of discrimination as a Muslim. All they needed to do was to put on the "cover." At the University of Maryland, for example, the Muslim Student Association handed out ninety headscarves. As "undercover Muslims," they experienced the attitudes of their fellow students toward the religion firsthand.[4]

At the university, a survey had already identified the stereotypes and mis-understandings on campus. Wearing the "cover" made these attitudes personal. One student received a hateful e-mail. Some of the others felt some subtle preju-dice. Most of the students simply noticed that the "cover" made their fellow students uncomfortable. When other students saw what they were wearing, they quickly looked away from them.[5]

Surprisingly, the participants said that wearing the hijab was a positive ex-perience despite the negative or uncomfortable reactions of students on campus. For example, they reported that the experience strengthened their self-acceptance and commitment to equality.

Over two hundred students tried the same experiment at California State University–San Bernardino. The Internet responses to the report of the experi-ment contained numerous crude comments that linked the Muslim "cover" with terrorism, Hitler, the blood of innocent people, unwillingness to assimilate to American ways, and intolerance in Muslim countries.[6]

Both groups were aware of the assumption that the hijab is a sign of the op-pression of women. In contrast, the women insisted that they chose to wear the scarf as a "cover" when they were teenagers or in their early twenties.[7]

On the one hand, the hijab stirs hostile looks, derogatory comments, or, at least, uncomfortable feelings. On the other hand, those who wear it in the United States say that it has nothing to do with terrorism, 9/11, or male domination of women. Rather, it has to do with commitment to the Muslim faith, religious duty, modesty, freedom from treatment as a sex object, and personal identity.

The negative reactions to the cover do not match the intentions and experi-ence of those who wear it. The varied responses to the hijab raise the question of how to make sense of these differing viewpoints. This collision of ideas about an article of clothing leads to the thought that controversies about the hijab require further exploration if we are to understand them. The initial question is how to study matters of religion like the "cover" in ways that shed light on the current dynamics of religion and its role in the twenty-first century.

A young woman wears a headscarf. The Muslim hijab, or "cover," is often a headscarf similar to the one seen here. It has created great controversy— some see it as a symbol of being a faithful Muslim, while others see it as oppression of women.

FOCUSING THE PROBLEM: ASSUMPTIONS, FRAMES OF REFERENCE, AND ASSOCIATIONS OF IDEAS

Internet articles like the reports of the campus hijab experiments are meant to stir an instant reaction. The reader feels compelled to jump to one side or the other. But the academic study of religion uses the discipline of critical thinking to step back and consider the case and its context before coming to a conclusion. The first chapter introduced the learning theory of C. S. Peirce. This American philosopher proposed that learning begins with something that does not fit our usual habits of thinking. In Peirce's view, an *anomaly* provokes us to search for new understanding. This glitch in our view of the world is something that does not conform to what we expect.

In this century after 9/11, the claims and counterclaims about the nature of Islam and the intentions of Muslims may be so familiar that we may not notice what is surprising about the matter of the hijab. It seems to be a simple, harmless piece of cloth. Yet it evokes powerful gut reactions for or against it. Instead of allowing these reactions to carry us away, we might ask *why* one thing can stir up so much raw feeling.

Red Flags for Critical Thinking about Religion

1. Assumptions
2. Associations of Ideas
3. Frames of Reference

One of the skills of critical thinking is to identify and evaluate the hidden assumptions lying behind statements that claim to be true. An *assumption* is something that people take for granted to be true and on which they base their reasons for what they believe. For example, when Muslim women wear the scarf as a religious practice, they assume that their religion teaches that women should wear a "cover" for the sake of modesty. To check out this assumption, they find instructions about women's clothing and modesty in the Qur'an, the sacred scriptures of Islam, and its interpretation in the example of the Prophet Muhammad.

On the other hand, what is the hidden assumption for the statement that Muslims are following their leaders like the Nazis followed Hitler? The key word is "like." The twisted thinking is that as the Nazis followed Hitler blindly, so Muslims are blindly following their murderous leaders.

But what is the evidence for this assumption? A survey of the Pew Research Center found that two in three citizens of the United States, Britain, France, Germany, and Russia are worried about Islamic extremists in their country. This concern seems to lie behind the assumption of the analogy between Hitler and Muslims. However, the Pew Center also found that the majority of Muslims in their countries also are concerned about extremism. For example, 73 percent of Lebanese Muslims and 64 percent of Egyptian Muslims share this concern. Moreover, the research found that 86 percent of American Muslims say that suicide bombing for the defense of Islam is rarely, if ever, justified. Scarcely 1 percent says that it is often justified.[8]

The critics charge that Muslims do not want to become assimilated into American society. The Pew Research found that 56 percent of Muslims want to adapt to the American way of life while 20 percent want to be distinct from American ways. But that is not what over one in two Americans think: they suppose that Muslims do *not* want to be integrated into American society.[9]

Understanding the Controversy over the Muslim "Cover": Competing Frames of Reference

We have come closer to the problem of this chapter, the challenge of using critical thinking to study religion in an impartial way that will lead to sound conclusions and deeper insights into religion.

So far, we have identified some assumptions of the responses to the hijab experiments, and we have evaluated them with the evidence of a survey of Muslims. To go deeper into the discussion requires another key understanding. Assumptions normally do not stand alone. They are part of a cluster of ideas.

We can call these *frames of reference*. Frames of reference are sets of ideas and attitudes into which we fit the facts we find and the experiences we have. For example, the members of a group such as a Muslim Student Association share a common framework into which all the beliefs fit. The group shares a unique vocabulary by which they all understand their world and themselves. Especially at first, "outsiders" to this frame of reference may not understand this way of speaking about experience or how the terms fit together as a whole.

Religious studies scholar Walter H. Capps states that we can only understand a word if we know what it means in its frame of reference. This framework of meaning is the word's context, its "world of discourse."[10] Capps states that the task of religious studies is to identify such frameworks of meaning. For example, if we want to understand the hijab in the way that Muslim women understand it, we will have to understand its frame of reference, the context of its use in the religion.

With this in mind, we can see that the responses to the hijab experiment can be set into two frames of reference. This first is the framework of meaning of the Muslim Student Association. According to Capp's principle, the non-Muslim students in the hijab experiment had a distinct advantage over the other students because the campus Muslim Student Association oriented them to its meaning for them.

The other frame of reference by which we can understand the Internet responses to the experience was altogether different. This is the framework of meaning of the memory of 9/11, the "War on Terror," and the wars in Iraq and Afghanistan. The reference point of the threat of terrorism is the center point of the suspicions and animosity of those who criticized the experiment.

The vast difference between these two points of view does not lie in the facts of the experiment but in their interpretation within their opposing frames of reference. That frame of reference contains underlying assumptions about the most fundamental matters, the nature of religion and its role in human life and society. And these hidden assumptions form the basis of the claims and attitudes of each side.

A contrast with the American approach to the hijab will clarify the point about the importance of considering the frame of reference in the study of religion. Often the United States and Europe are thought to share a common Western culture that is defined as "secular." Yet the American form of the doctrine of the "separation of church and state" is different from the clear-cut French view of secularism.

We find evidence of the different frames of reference in how the two societies have dealt with the issues of the Muslim "cover." In the United States, Kathleen M. Moore states that the right of religious freedom to wear the hijab is not as secure as many may think. Nevertheless, Moore's article shows that controversies over the hijab have not been settled by legislation. They have been handled by the action of the justice system and advocacy groups such as the American Civil Liberties Union (ACLU), the Becket Fund for Religious Liberty, the Council on American-Islamic Relations (CAIR), and various religious groups dedicated to religious freedom.[11]

The frame of reference of these disputes has been the United States Constitution as interpreted by landmark rulings of the Supreme Court on "separation of church and state" and religious freedom. Religious studies scholar Stephen Prothero observes that the courts have tried to balance the First Amendment's guarantee of the free exercise of religion with the amendment's "establishment clause" that mandates that the government must remain neutral without favoring any religion. The proponents of the hijab have set the issues within this framework: they are matters not only of religious duty but also of human rights.[12]

The debate has been waged in legal cases, especially those that allege religious discrimination. Moore refers to only a few cases about the question of wearing the "cover" in the public schools. She cites one case of a sixth grader who was suspended for wearing the hijab in Oklahoma. The intervention of the U.S. Justice Department secured her reinstatement. In another case, a twelve-year-old girl was banned from participating in a basketball tournament in Florida until CAIR negotiated an exemption to the NCAA rules. Another case had an ambiguous outcome.[13]

Rather than the classroom, the workplace has generated the most grievances from women who wear the "cover." In five recent years, the number of claims that Muslims brought to the U.S. Equal Employment Opportunity Commission (EEOC) doubled from 697 in 2004 to 1,490 in 2009. These cases had to do with work schedules and religious expression, as well as religious clothing. The EEOC mandates that employers modify their dress codes to provide reasonable accommodations for their employee's religious beliefs. These adjustments are required unless they would cause "undue hardship" such as a safety risk.[14]

In general, the U.S. government has taken the side of freedom in religious clothing. The face veil, however, has tested the limits of this tolerance. In the case of *Sultaana Lakiana Myke Freeman v. State of Florida*, a Florida appellate court upheld the ruling that a Muslim woman must take off her face veil for her photo identification on her driver's license. Otherwise, the photo would be of no use for identification and the allowance would be a threat to public safety.[15]

Prothero observes that American politicians have been reluctant to weigh in on the issues surrounding the "cover." In contrast, several European governments have attempted to deal with the question of the "cover" in its various types by legislation.[16]

In March 2004, the French Senate passed a law making it illegal for anyone to wear a headscarf or any other religious garb in public schools. Later legislation centered on another type of "cover," the burqa. In a technical sense, the word *hijab* simply means "cover."[17] (See the textbox on "Forms of Muslim 'Cover'" for a review of the types of "cover" worn in various Muslim societies.[18]) In April 2010, the French legislature prohibited any covering of the face in a public place, effectively banning the burqa as well.[19] The anti-burqa law stipulates that women wearing loose-fitting covering of the entire body and face veils will be fined 150 euros (about $215) and/or forced to take citizenship classes. Anyone who forces a women to wear a burqa can be fined 30,000 euros (about $43,000) and spend a year in prison.[20]

Forms of Muslim "Cover"

The word *hijab* in Arabic means "covering" or "veil." There are different forms of the cover that women wear to follow the command for modesty.

Hijab (common use): generally refers to the headscarf in many styles.

Khimar: a long cloth that extends to the waist, covering the hair, neck, and shoulders but still exposing the face.

Al-amira: a veil that has two pieces, the cap that fits the head and the scarf wrapped around it.

Shayla: a long scarf wrapped around the head and then pinned at the shoulders.

Abaya: a loose-fitting cloak that covers the entire body.

Chador: a cloak that covers the entire head and body.

Niqab: a veil for the face that leaves the eyes clear. Often used with an abaya.

Burqa: loose-fitting cover of the entire body and face with a long cloak and face veil, with only a mesh screen for the eyes.

However, France is not the only country that is concerned about the scarves and veils worn in the name of Islam. Countries including Australia, the Netherlands, Turkey, Germany, Egypt, Belgium, and Pakistan have been caught up in the debate about the wearing of the headscarf, according to the Harvard Pluralism Project report.[21]

In Germany, the German Federal Constitutional Court ruled that German states could pass laws to prohibit teachers in the schools from wearing the "cover." Eight of sixteen states have passed such laws.[22] (Five of the eight states with this prohibition allow exceptions for Christians, such as wearing a nun's habit.[23]) Moreover, the City of Berlin prohibits the wearing of all religious symbols in public, and the German state of Hesse became the first German state to ban the burqa.

In Belgium, 95 percent of schools, whether Flemish or French speaking, have adopted policies that forbid students to wear the "cover."[24] Like France, Belgium adopted a ban on the burqa in July 2011. The penalty was set at 137.5 euros and up to seven days in jail.[25] The governments of Italy[26] and the Netherlands also have taken steps to ban the veiling of the face. The legislatures of Spain have been divided on the issue.[27] On the other hand, protests against the ban have swept across Europe, including Germany and Austria.[28]

It might be understandable that the Europeans would cite security reasons for the prohibition of the loose-fitting clothing that hides the face. But the reasons that politicians offer for the prohibition of both face veils and headscarves go beyond reasons of preventing crime or terrorism. The rationale for the prohibitions reveals a frame of reference that is different from the framework of meaning that prevails in the United States even though it uses similar terms like "separation of church and state."

The ban on the hijab was proposed by a commission appointed by French president Jacques Chirac. The commission's task was to find ways to strengthen the secularism of French society in response to increasing religious diversity. At the time, Education Minister Francois Bayrou said that the scarf divided

Muslims from non-Muslims. The head covering, therefore, undermined the principle of the separation of church and state. In the same vein, the commission's reporter Remy Swartz said that French society upholds the rights of individuals, not groups. Wearing the veil violates the individual's rights. Furthermore, it promotes inequality between men and women.[29]

In 2003, when the hijab was banned in public schools, Nicolas Sarkozy, who would become the French president, said, "You shouldn't see in it a lack of respect for your religion. You must understand that secularism is our tradition, our choice."[30] Seven years later, President Sarkozy repeated the same themes when he said that the burqa was "not welcome on French soil." When he addressed the French Parliament, he added that the burqa was not a religious symbol. Instead, it was a sign of the women's subservience. Sarkozy stated, "We cannot accept, in our country, women imprisoned behind a mesh, cut off from society, deprived of all identity. That is not the French republic's idea of women's dignity."[31]

To understand the attitude of the French administration, we must understand the French view of *laïcité*, the clear-cut and absolute separation of religion and public life. This frame of reference holds that the public sphere must be entirely free of religion. This separation ensures that there is room for the religious freedom of individuals in the private sphere. When religions intrude in the public sphere, when they demand special accommodations, when they promote their sectarian agendas, they violate the neutral zone where individuals are free of the influence of religious institutions and persuasions.[32]

Sarkozy's remarks are a defense of the values of the secular state. In this view, religious symbols have no place in public life. Even wearing a scarf threatens the religious neutrality of the schools and other public institutions. When a religion imposes itself in the "free zone" of the public school, the government, or community, it divides people into believers and nonbelievers and members of a religion and members of other religions—or none at all. In civic life, all citizens, no matter their religious persuasion, are to be united in the "republic." Religions divide, but the "republic" embraces all in their dedication to the freedom of the individual and the common good.[33]

In this view, what might appear to be a restriction of human rights is the opposite. The elimination of religious symbols in public life frees *all citizens* to be religious or nonreligious in their own way without any pressure from others.

There is yet another idea woven into this web of meaning: one must have free choice in relationships as well as religion. Sarkozy assumes that the women wear the veil because of social coercion. Therefore, it is a sign of male domination. The burqa is especially objectionable because it diminishes a woman's dignity: she no longer can interact with others "face to face" but is a faceless voice behind a screen.

This discussion has shown that France's treatment of the Muslim "cover" is different from that of the United States because it is set in a different frame of reference. We have focused on France, but the same attitudes are voiced across the European continent. In France, 82 percent of the population supports the ban on face veils. The percentage of support is 71 percent in Germany, and 62 percent in Britain. In contrast, only 28 percent of the American population say they support banning the face veil.

Underlying these objections is the fear of the growing numbers of Muslim immigrants.[34] The percentage of Muslim immigrants in the European population is significantly higher than in the United States, where Muslims number 0.8 percent of the population, a percentage expected to grow to 1.7 percent by 2030. In contrast, in France 7.5 percent of the population is Muslim. In 2030, the percentage is projected to grow to 10.3 percent. In Belgium, the current percentage is 6 percent, but it is projected to grow to 10.2 percent by 2030. Besides these countries, Austria, Germany, the Netherlands, and Switzerland have Muslim percentages of over 5 percent. Almost 5 percent of the population of Sweden is Muslim, but the Muslim percent there will grow to 9.9 percent by 2030.[35]

A common complaint is that these newcomers refuse assimilation into the European society. In fact, research has shown that Muslims in the United States are more integrated into the larger society than in Europe.[36] Journalists Juliane von Mittelstaedt and Stefan Simon blame Muslims for refusing to fit into European culture: "Many believe that those who hide their faces are rejecting Western values along with integration and participation in the society in which they live. And, worst of all, those who hide their faces reject Europe's most precious birthright: Respect for the individual."[37] The appearance of Muslim women in their distinctive clothing, especially when they are faceless, evokes this deep-seated anxiety about a religious challenge to European secular culture.[38]

We have discussed the frames of reference of the American and European societies. But what about the framework of meaning of those who wear the "cover"? The director of an organization of Muslim women attorneys for human rights (KARAMAH), Raja Elhabti, claims that these fears are based on misunderstandings. Those who think that the "cover" is a sign of subjugation have not bothered to talk to those who wear them, she says. Hebah Ahmed of Albuquerque, New Mexico, states that she wears the niqab for religious reasons. She says that she covers her whole body, including her face and even her eyes, to be close to God. She also says it has a more practical reason. It liberates her from treatment as a sexual object. And it is a test of her faith. "The *niqab* is a constant reminder to do the right thing. It's God-consciousness in my face," she says. In the same article, Menahal Begawala of Irving, Texas, who also wears the niqab, states, "I suppose there is some part of me that wants to make a statement, 'I am a Muslim.'"[39]

These comments represent the view of many Muslim women who choose to wear the "cover." It has to do with the intimately personal matters of personal identity, gender and sexuality, and morality, as well as religion. All of these are fastened together in an intricate framework that is based on the deepest convictions of ultimate meaning. To understand these statements, we must understand the *frame of reference* in which they are set. The frame of reference is a complex network of ideas, attitudes, and traditions that provides a context for thought and perception. For the Muslim women, this framework of meaning is the web of ideas about how they are to live in the world. Among other things, this web of meaning concerns the Qur'an and its interpretation, gender roles, modesty, humility, religious duty, and devotion to God. Even among Muslims, the application of these ideas to the question of proper women's clothing in the modern world is still under intense discussion. Nevertheless, the Muslim frame of reference serves as the context in which we can make sense of the behavior and attitudes of Muslim women from their point of view.

These contrasting viewpoints about the "cover" of Muslim women shows how complex a seemingly simple issue such as wearing religious clothing can be. To understand the differing perspectives on religious clothing, this discussion has tried to show that we must consider their frames of reference. We may be quick to offer our own opinion, but our ideas would only come from our own frame of reference and its assumptions. The problem that religious studies faces is coming into focus: How can we make rational sense out of the issue of the Muslim "cover" when what we find are contending frames of reference that lead to opposing conclusions? And if we cannot make sense of the issue, what insight could the study of religion give to resolving it?

So Why Bother?

This discussion applied two of the principles of critical thinking to an issue of religion: identification of assumptions and consideration of frameworks of meaning. This expedition into critical thinking may seem to have made the topic more confusing than when we started. So why bother?

In today's global society, religious beliefs and practices are so intertwined with public life that we no longer have any choice. The hijab controversy shows how religion is tightly woven into the current issues of politics, education, society, and culture. Islamic studies scholar Mona Siddiqui explains that religion is changing the character of today's global conflicts.[40] Increasingly, religion is shaping the disagreements among peoples and societies.

In the Pew Forum proposal "Teaching about Religion in Public Schools," religious studies scholar Jon Butler notes that "the world is aflame with religion," yet American education has done a poor job of helping students grasp the nature and importance of religion. In Butler's view, the nation's schools can no longer neglect the study of religion. The Pew Forum proposal asserts that teaching religion as history is not enough. The majority of people in today's world build their lives on the foundation of religion. Religion continues to form their ideas of war and peace, good and evil, justice and truth, goodness and morality, and human nature and destiny.[41]

Of course, there are many reasons to study religion, as chapter 1 described. Nevertheless, perhaps the most direct benefit of religious studies is that the field can help us understand how religion is directing the lives of individuals, people, and societies in the twenty-first century. Most of the Earth's peoples hold that their religion is a total way of life that encompasses both the public *as well as* the private spheres of human life. Many religious believers in Western countries, as well as non-Western societies, are refusing to keep their faith locked up in the private domain. As a result, religion is taking center stage in the public drama of world events. Grasping the significance of the renewed role of religion in world affairs is the first step toward more informed and constructive responses to the current issues that involve religion.

Taking that step requires that we learn the frames of reference that people use to interpret and guide their actions. If we do not understand people according to these ways that they understand themselves and their world, misunderstandings are sure to arise. These misunderstandings result when people put the beliefs and behavior of other people into their own frameworks of meaning. Whether they are mistaken or not, people can only act on their understandings. Therefore, knowledge or ignorance of religion as well-informed understanding or mistaken opinion about religion has consequences for the way people get along with each other in our global society.

The field of religious studies has a vital contribution to make in this twenty-first century. It can interpret the religious dynamics of current events. It can provide us with tools for thinking about the claims of religion and for understanding the motivations of religious people. Most of all, it can help us avoid the misunderstandings that are at the root of many of the conflicts of this century.

Pitfalls of the Academic Study of Religion

If anything, critical thinking makes us aware of the limitations of our thought processes. The assumptions we hold within the frames of reference we accept can mislead us, especially if we use them to jump to conclusions. Learning requires openness to new information and ideas and, often, willingness to change our minds. Otherwise, we are not learning but only confirming what we already believe.

The American philosopher C. S. Peirce (1830–1914) proposed that thinking involves the tension between belief and doubt. To Peirce, beliefs are habits of thought. These habits make us comfortable and secure. Doubts, on the other hand, make us uneasy. Yet they provide the motivation for us to change our mind and develop new and better ways of thinking.[42]

On Doubt and Learning

"The irritation of doubt is the only immediate motive for the struggle to attain belief. . . . The sole object of inquiry is the settlement of opinion."

—C. S. Peirce

Peirce believed that the irritation of doubt is the most direct stimulus for learning.[43] He said, "The sole object of inquiry is the settlement of opinion." If we are fully satisfied with the answers we already have, we will not inquire about any other answers. But doubt prods us to seek more solid and stable opinions. In Peirce's mind, once we arrive at answers that satisfy us, we believe that we have solved the problem. Further investigation no longer interests us.[44]

The academic study of religion is an opportunity to reconsider one's habits of thinking about religion. The discipline of religious studies, therefore, asks its students to entertain some dissatisfaction with their current knowledge and opinions about religion. For some this will be more difficult than for others. However, the desire to learn more about religion does not mean betraying one's convictions. It does mean being open to new questions, to different points of view, and to different frames of meaning.

For example, what do we mean by the term *religion*? Notwithstanding Sarkozy's remark, the scarf and veil *are* religious symbols. The motivations of the women who wear them involve religious identity and duty. In fact, a key reason that the French want to ban the scarves and veils is that they are "religious." But what do we mean by the term?

Critical thinking does not accept an immediate answer even with such basic terms. As an academic discipline, religious studies takes time to explore, consider, propose, test, and then explore again. Its study begins, continues, and ends with open investigation, not predetermined positions.

Thus, an exercise in critical thinking is to test a typical understanding of religion with the case of the hijab. Many in Western societies hold that religion is fundamentally a private matter. In this view, religions are sets of private beliefs (about a "Higher Power"). Religious organizations are groups of like-minded people who hold the same personal opinions and who share them—but not in public.

What happens when this view of religion encounters women who insist on wearing a headscarf and even a burqa in public places? At least in the French view, a simple piece of clothing is a sign of confrontation with the social order. Wearing religious garb in public violates the ideal of a completely secular—that is, "nonreligious"—country. When combined with the apprehensions about immigration, security, and the association of Islam with terrorism, even the modest head "cover" can no longer be tolerated.

The secular view of religion also makes it impossible to understand the meaning of the clothing from the point of view of those who wear it. Why do the wearers insist on bringing what is assumed a private matter into the public sphere? Without considering the frame of reference of the wearer of the clothing, one can only speculate that she may be coerced, defiant, or just a fanatic. But these ideas only suggest that the wearer does not accept the majority view of religion.

Now we come to a clear view of the problem of studying religion. If critical thinking identifies assumptions and considers frames of reference to understand religion, how do they work? What are the mental operations that construct frames of reference and the assumptions that are built on them? Can we set them aside to learn something new?

A colleague of C. S. Peirce, the American philosopher William James (1842–1910), taught that whenever we encounter something new, we must fit it into what we already know. James argued that the first thing the intellect does with an unfamiliar object is to put it in a class with other things.[45] To learn anything, we have to do this. To learn, we have to sort things into categories. James called this basic process of learning *apperception*, a term that refers to the "act of taking things into our minds." For James, the way apperception works is the process of the *association of ideas*.[46]

James's view belongs to the *association theory of learning*. This theory proposes that we cannot define or describe anything except in terms of something else. We cannot explain the meaning of an idea without referring to other meanings of ideas. Thus, thought comes in clusters of ideas. One student would respond to every new idea that came up in a lecture, by saying, "That reminds me of . . ." She was conscious of the mental process of apperception. To achieve new knowledge, we must assimilate what is new in this way.

Take the example of the hijab. This chapter has shown that the frames of reference that lead to different reactions to the "cover" are clusters of ideas about religious freedom, religion and the state, or religious duty and identity. A frame of reference is an intricate network of associations of ideas connected to one another in a framework of meaning.

In this view, like beliefs, these associations of ideas are habits of thinking. According to James's theory, a "law of economy" governs the learning process. We encounter something new. We fit it into the categories of our minds. We put the new item where it will cause the *least disruption* to a previously constructed frame of meaning and its network of associations.

For example, James noted that children who have not seen snow before will call it "cold sugar." The Polynesians called the horses that Captain Cook had with him on his voyage of discovery "pigs." Perhaps some Americans might say that Muslim women who wear headscarves and veils are wearing "costumes." However, in American culture wearing costumes is associated with Halloween or theater. When we take the easy way of association, we think that wearing the Muslim clothing is a way of dressing up, perhaps for fun. Wearing this clothing is optional and occasional. Of course, this attitude fails to take the Muslim "cover" seriously.

As the examples show, we often make mistakes when we fit unfamiliar things into our usual patterns of thinking. Author Cheryl Benard claims that those who wear the "cover" in the United States are immigrants from rural areas, fundamentalists and traditionalists, and the elderly. They are also "young women who want to get attention and make a provocative statement in schools, colleges, or workplaces."[47] Notice the associations. Whoever wears the articles of "cover" for the head, body, and/or face does not know any better. If those who wear these articles are fundamentalists or traditionalists, they are obviously outside the norms and values of Western society. If the wearer is a young person, she is probably trying to get attention. These associations deny that wearing the "cover" might be an expression of the person's commitment to a sacred way of life.

These thoughts suggest that the task of studying religion in the twenty-first century requires disciplined thinking. It is not merely a matter of fitting observations and ideas into already constructed frames of meaning. Nor is it simply the task of adding to the pile of information of what we already know about religion. Critical study must find a way to break out of the webs of the familiar notions already formed in our minds. Otherwise, our past habits of associations within a predetermined frame of meaning will control our response to anything new. This investigation will turn out to be an exercise in "confirmation bias," the use of information to reinforce our own preconceptions.

On the other hand, we cannot simply start over and build a new framework of meaning with a new network of ideas. According to James's theory, we cannot think without making connections between thoughts and we cannot learn without classifying ideas. Our minds are already programmed with distinct mental structures, with language, with habits of thought, and with frameworks of interpretation. We have to start somewhere and so we need simultaneously to use the web of ideas that we have already acquired while reweaving the familiar ones.

James summarized the task of teaching and learning in a remarkably succinct way. He stated, "To break up bad associations or wrong ones, to build others in, to guide the associative tendencies into the most fruitful channels is the educator's chief task."[48] This statement also applies to studying and learning. It gives manageable shape to the problem of how to study religion in a fair, reasoned, and insightful way. In James's terms, the problem is to find an approach to study that would help us do two things at once. It would enable us to tear apart our limited associations of ideas and attitudes about religion. At the same time, it would help us rebuild new connections of information and ideas within more informed frameworks of meaning. The test of the solution to this problem would be whether it would help us overcome bias and gain insight into sacred ways that direct and give meaning to the lives of billions of people in today's world.

SURVEYING THE ALTERNATIVE APPROACHES: THE DEVELOPMENT OF RELIGIOUS STUDIES

Having set out the problem of the association of ideas that make up our frames of reference, we now move on to trace the foundations of the field of religious studies. As we do so, we will find the problem that the founders of the academic study of religion fit their ideas of the subject into preconceived networks of associations. We will find that the history of the field offers helpful approaches and rich resources for the study of religion, but none gives a fully satisfactory solution to the problem this chapter has laid out.

Defining the Subject Matter of Religious Studies: The Division of the Religious and the Secular

We have already suggested that the very idea of religion is part of a Western framework of meaning. Now we can use the seminal insight of historian of religions Jonathan Z. Smith to explore the origin and use of this term. Smith says that the modern use of the word *religion* began when Western Christendom broke up in the Protestant Reformation.[49] In chapter 1, this textbook introduced the Reformation as a time of conflict within Christianity sparked by the protest of Martin Luther against the Roman Catholic Church. The result of the Reformation was not just the wars between the Protestants and the Catholics. Another outcome was the division of Christianity in Europe into the Catholic Church and several different Protestant churches, each with its own leadership, theology, and practices, such as the Lutherans, Calvinists, and Anabaptists.

This fragmentation of Christianity into different organizations and ideologies posed a problem. What concept would encompass what all of these groups had in common? One could no longer say they were "catholic" or "universal" because the Protestants were separated from the Catholic Church. The answer was that they all were "religions" of different types.

At first, the term *religion* only applied to forms of Christianity. But when European explorers like Columbus, Cook, and Magellan "discovered" the new lands in America, Africa, Asia, and the Pacific Islands, they found that native peoples also had "sacred ways" that reminded them of certain ways of Christianity. Soon the term *religion* was used to categorize the beliefs of the native peoples and the rituals, prayers, and customs based on them.[50]

According to history and comparative literature scholar Tomoko Masuzawa, the modern sense of the term *religion* grew out of the recognition of differences among sacred ways.[51] *Religion* was a catchall term that put all the diverse ways into one category. In fact, many sacred traditions refused to use the word *religion* to describe themselves. They had the true faith and authentic way. Others were "religions."[52]

But what was "religion"? The standard for what was "religious" was Christianity because Christians set the terms for what was "religious." A "religion" had to have features that could be associated with Christianity.

Further clarity of what makes a religion came from a movement that came after the Reformation of the sixteenth century. This Enlightenment of Western society took place around the eighteenth century. The Enlightenment took its name from the goal that the light of human reason should replace the darkness of ignorant superstition, blind tradition, and arbitrary church authority of the medieval worldview. It fostered the development of science, not divine revelation, as a way to understand the natural world and improve the lives of people.

The Enlightenment sponsored new ideas of government such as democracy and human equality. Chapter 1 described one of the challenges: how to prevent the religious wars that had torn Europe and Great Britain apart.[53] The English philosopher John Locke (1632–1704) suggested that the solution was to separate the quarrelling faith groups from the power of government. He reasoned that when religions were stripped of political power, they would no longer have the means to disrupt the social order. This strategy amounted to a new idea of religion.

Locke developed this idea in his "Letter of Toleration" (1689). Locke wrote that churches are 'free societies.' He added, "A church, then I take to be a voluntary society of men, joining themselves together of their own accord in order to the public worshipping of God in such manner as they judge acceptable to Him, and effectual to the salvation of their souls."[54]

The language, of course, is Christian. However, the general idea is that religious organizations are dedicated to matters of the soul. Conversely, the state[55] is concerned with civil matters—that is, with everything else. The purpose of this idea was the *disestablishment* of religion, as religion was to be disengaged from public life, especially politics and government.

In this way of thinking, certain human enterprises are devoted to a distinct realm of human life called the "religious." Whatever is *not* in the domain of religion is covered under the concept of the *secular*, the "nonreligious." In this view, the secular and the religious define one another.[56] The individual's private belief, worship, and soul belong to the religious domain. Everything else belonged to the secular sphere.

Freedom of Religion and from Religion

The categories of the religious and the secular were useful to advance the cause of the Enlightenment. On the one hand, the secular was the place for govern-

ment, economics, science, literature, and the arts. As long as they were kept
in the secular realm, these aspects of public life could enjoy freedom from the
control of religious authority.

On the other hand, the sphere of religion was the place for religious organizations, leaders, and believers. As long as they stayed in this sphere, the different
religions could enjoy the freedom to believe as they chose. Society could tolerate
religion and religious organizations if they remained within their boundaries as
purely private matters apart from public life.

Emerging from the Enlightenment, this basic distinction between the religious and the secular was built into the Western consciousness. It enabled
Westerners to determine what is religious by distinguishing it from the secular.
Yet this very separation of religion from public life is now the issue of many of
the present controversies. As we have seen, it prompts the ban on the "cover"
of Muslim women. Laws against the Muslim "cover" are meant to guard the
fence between the two arenas of human life. To do this, the government removes religion from the public sphere to preserve the freedom of religion in
the private sphere.

The Secular and Religious Are Relative Terms

The secular and the religious define one another. What is religious is not secular but private,
personal, and spiritual. What is secular is what is not religious but concerns life in this world
and especially in human society.

In summary, the foundation of the Western idea of religion is the separation of the religious from the secular. This distinction provides the dominant
overarching categories that Westerners use to approach questions of religion. It
is written into the religious protections of the United States Constitution. In addition, the question of whether organizations, beliefs, or behaviors are religious
or secular is the central question of some important legal matters. These include
religious privileges such as tax exemption, conscientious objection to participating in war, requirements and funding of education, employee and other forms of
discrimination, display of symbols on public property, the right to refuse medical
treatment or social security, and many other issues.

Defining the Scope of Religion: It's about Belief

Once the sphere of religion had been distinguished from the secular sphere, the
study of religion could take another step. Scholars now had a basic classification
to use for defining religion. But how could scholars decide what would fit in the
category of religion?

The answer came from the associations of ideas from Christianity, particu-
larly Protestantism. The first of these ideas was that the foundation of religion is
belief. When the Enlightenment tried to find the universal characteristics of religion, they settled on the primary category of belief. Anthropologist Talal Asad
comments about the Enlightenment view: "The emphasis on belief meant that

henceforth religion could be conceived as a set of propositions to which believers gave assent and which, therefore, could be judged and compared between different religions and against natural science."[57]

For example, this principle would mean that in order to understand the hijab according to Muslim beliefs, we would have to explore the concepts of modesty, gender roles, sexuality, and the authority of the Qur'an.

The second and related association was the right of individual conscience. Locke, for example, asserted that belief was up to the individual. Religious belief could not be coerced. People would make up their own minds about their beliefs no matter what a government would do. This meant that tolerance was the wisest policy for dealing with religion unless believers began to challenge the state or break the civil law.[58] In this spirit, the Enlightenment took away all powers from religion except the rights of the individual to decide what to believe and to join with others who shared the same beliefs.[59]

As Westerners explored faraway lands, they used these associations as a frame of reference to study unfamiliar cultures that they encountered. In keeping with James's theory, they began to sort the cultures into categories. The first categories were beliefs and rituals based on them. The results of these comparisons were four loose groupings of religions:[60] Christianity and Judaism for sure; then, less certainly, "Mohammedism" (Islam); and finally, there was the catchall of "heathenism."[61]

Gradually clearer lines within these vague groupings were drawn. Scholars distinguished denominations and sects from one another according to their variations in beliefs. However, the different sets of beliefs could be lumped together because they were all personal opinions that could not be proven by observation or testing. In summary, the study of religion became an account of sets of truth claims that could be compared with one another.[62]

Enlightenment Approaches to Religion: Universal Religion and Essentialism

Enlightenment scholars did not stop at this point. They went a step further to define what "true belief" might be. Their standard for truth was reason. They especially relied on *empirical reason*, which makes conclusions based on evidence. If the evidence of empirical reason is what we can observe, measure, and confirm by experiment, then religion lacks adequate evidence. On this basis, many thinkers in the Enlightenment contended that most of the beliefs of religion were superstitions.

Some Enlightenment thinkers, however, did not want to abandon all religion. They intended to create a reasonable religion in keeping with the developing scientific mind-set. The ideas of these Enlightenment thinkers offer two more possibilities for how to study religion. First is the idea of a single universal religion. This religion would encompass the truths of all religions. The Enlightenment scholars reasoned that if the laws of nature were the same throughout the universe, the laws of religion also had to be the same everywhere. On this basis, Matthew Tindal (1657–1733) and others invented their ideal of *natural religion*.

Natural religion was a religion that did not exist anywhere on the planet. However, the inventors of this term thought that it *would* exist if "learned men" were free to build their religion on the foundation of reason. Unfortunately, religious institutions had strayed from this original, true religion.

Scholars now call the other possibility for the study of religion *essentialism*. The essence is the true nature of something. Essentialism reasons that everything can be sorted into classes of things according to their true nature. How can that be done? The basic nature of something is known by certain defining characteristics that distinguish it from all other things. That means that one can separate dogs and cats if one knows the basic characteristics that make a dog as opposed to what makes a cat. As one sorts dogs from cats, accidental features that are not essential characteristics of dogs should be disregarded. For example, dogs come in all sizes. Therefore, size does not make a dog. What makes a dog are the basic traits of "dogginess."

Essentialism applies this idea to knowledge. We know what something is if we know its essence—its defining characteristics. It is like having all-important X factors. Having the religion X factors qualifies a belief or practice as religious. Just as in sorting out dogs and cats, accidental traits should not confuse us. The idea is that religions are different in many features such as the content of their beliefs, the practices of their rituals, and the organization of their leadership. But all religions have the same basic X factors. If we understand these X factors, we understand religion.

The Prussian philosopher Immanuel Kant (1724–1804) is a clear representative of these two Enlightenment ideas of a universal religion and essentialism. Kant's view of religion came from his Enlightenment view of logic. For him, the principles of logical reasoning were supreme and universal. This means that truth claims, including those of religion, must be tested by logic. As a title of his book puts it, to be true, religion had to stay "within the boundaries of reason alone."[63]

In keeping with this principle, Kant reasoned that there could only be one true religion in the world. Moreover, that one religion would have to be universal in that it would be true in all places. This thought followed from the law of non-contradiction that two contradictory opinions cannot both be simultaneously correct.

But what was that one true, universal religion? To answer, Kant applied the idea of essentialism. He argued that the essence of religion is morality, since he thought that morality was the shared defining characteristic of all religions.

But what is morality? For Kant, morality was the performance of duty. This association of morality with duty meant two things. First, to be moral is to *will* to do one's duty. Second, like everything else, one's sense of duty must conform to the universal principles of logic. These thoughts led Kant to assert that religion teaches the universal and reasonable duties of human beings. These duties might be known in other ways, but the unique contribution of religion is that it presents these duties as commands of God.[64] Thus, religion is a highly effective way to promote morality.

We illustrate the way that the reasoning of Tindal and Kant works if we ask about religious clothing. How close is wearing the Muslim "cover" to the essence of religion? Are these behaviors just cultural customs, perhaps involving the oppression of women? Or do they meet the "X factor" test as genuinely religious? For Kant, the test was whether the believer strives to fulfill a moral duty based on a divine command.

For Saba Naeem, a professional pharmacist and mother in Great Britain, the headscarf is such a moral obligation. She says that wearing the hijab is "a religious duty, but also exists to preserve a woman's modesty. It means you are not just a sex symbol—you have something to offer other than just your looks."[65] Naeem's *intention* to obey a divine command passes Kant's test. From Kant's point of view, her behavior is religious.

The example of Kant demonstrates how the Enlightenment brought the concerns of humans down from heaven to earth. It changed the focus of learning from visions of supernatural to the knowledge of the natural world. In this spirit, the Enlightenment saw religion in terms of nature and even imagined a natural religion.

The field of religious studies has inherited this change of focus. Jonathan Z. Smith observes that scholars changed how they viewed the place of religious studies among the disciplines of higher education. From here on, the academic study of religion would not be a field of theology, the study of God, but of anthropology, the study of human beings. Accordingly, it would no longer look at human life from a supernatural point of view. It would study the natural history of human beings in this world.[66] As a result, scholars would investigate religion without relying on divine revelation or enlightened consciousness. They would use the same tools and rules of investigation that other academic fields of study use.

The Result of the Enlightenment: Three Ways to Study Religion

In summary, the Enlightenment set the direction for the study of religion as an academic discipline. In colleges and universities, religious scholars no longer had to argue about the supernatural basis or divine claims of religions. If religion was a human phenomenon, then the question of whether the contradictory beliefs of the world's religions were true could be set aside. Religious studies could teach about religion in a neutral, unbiased way.

Three Primary Ways to Study Religion

- The *theological* approach chooses one set of truth-claims—one religion. All beliefs and practices are studied and evaluated in terms of the presuppositions of that religion.
- The *religionist* approach looks at religion as a distinct dimension of human life. Religions provide various ways to fulfill genuine needs in a category all their own.
- The *naturalist approach* denies that there is a separate "religious dimension" of life and examines religion in terms of the social sciences.

As a result of this development, three primary ways to study religion emerged:

- The *theological* approach chooses one set of truth claims—one religion. All beliefs and practices are studied and evaluated in terms of the presuppositions of that religion.

- The *religionist* approach looks at religion as a distinct dimension of human life. Religions provide various ways to fulfill genuine needs in a category all their own.[67]
- The *naturalist approach* denies that there is a separate "religious dimension" of life and examines religion in terms of the social sciences.[68]

Of these, the field of religious studies would consider the theological approach too narrow and biased. As we have discussed, the academic study of religion does not accept the presuppositions of theology and its restrictions. Furthermore, it investigates the human origins and dynamics of religion rather than their supernatural origins and claims.

However, the field of religious studies embraces scholars who take either the religionist or the naturalist approaches. On the one hand, naturalism considers the beliefs, attitudes, and practices of religion as data to be understood in terms of the disciplines of the social sciences.[69] Naturalism treats religion as a topic of study. It is not a separate academic discipline, because it finds that religion works in ways that need not be categorized as "religious."[70] In the naturalist view, religions are best described in terms of psychological complexes, sociological functions, or "primitive sciences."[71]

Thus, the naturalists would assert that the social sciences can explain the practice of wearing religious clothing. They do not need to put these practices into a unique religious framework of meaning. For instance, the hijab and burqa can be analyzed in terms of the motives of personal identity, autonomy, and anonymity.

The religionists, on the other hand, consider that the beliefs, attitudes, and practices of religion are genuinely and irreducibly religious. Therefore, religion must be understood on its own terms. Religionists use the term *sui generis* to speak of the distinctive nature of religion. This term refers to religion having its own origins. It is not derived from something else such as social dynamics or human psychology. Thus, the purposes of religion are to get in touch with the realities of the spiritual world to fulfill religious needs. If these ideas about religion are correct, the field of religious studies must be a separate academic discipline in its own right. The distinctive dynamics of religion must be studied in themselves without reducing them to something else such as psychology or sociology.

According to the religionist way of studying religion, religious clothing can be understood without appealing to any other motivations than religious reasons. To interpret the Muslim "cover," religionists would investigate the beliefs of those who wear them. They would acknowledge that Muslim women hold that the origin of their beliefs is divine revelation. They would trace the association of the practice of the "cover" with the associations in the Muslim frame of reference. These associations might include the messengers of God, submission to the will of God, the equality of human persons, the differences of genders, and the values of virtue and modesty. In the religionist point of view, those most qualified to interpret the clothing in terms of this web of associations would be Muslims themselves.

In short, the field of religious studies advanced as a huge experiment in how to study religions. The ultimate goal was to free the study of religion from the web of associations of the divided religious groups, especially in Christianity.

In general, as the field developed, it followed the lead of the Enlightenment and tried to uncover the essence of religion. But the result was an assortment of methods, each of which still offers ideas and tools for studying religion in the twenty-first century.

Alternative Approaches: It's about the Gods (Max Mueller)

By the time Kant died in 1804, Western scholars had discovered, named, and catalogued the major world religions. It was now possible for religion to become a subject of academic exploration, study, and critique.

Virtually unknown today, the scholar who played a key role in the development of the scholarly methods of religious studies was Friedrich Max Mueller (1823–1900). Mueller's field of academic study was *philology*, the study of languages. He was an expert in the languages of Sanskrit, Arabic, and Persian. He pioneered the classification and study of Indo-European languages, the languages of India and Europe. As he did so, he worked to develop scientific methods of studying language.

Mueller believed that the languages must be studied in the context of their cultures. That led him to turn his attention to the core of culture, that is, religion. Mueller used the same way of thinking to understand religion as he used to understand language. He found that Sanskrit was the most ancient still-existing form of the Indo-European languages. Therefore, to study Sanskrit is to study the language that all Indo-European languages have in common. But Sanskrit is preserved because it is the language of the ancient Hindu scriptures, the *Vedas*. So to study the origins of religion, one must study the Vedas.

Mueller considered himself a geologist. As evidence of the ancient past is found in fossils embedded in the layers of the sediment, so Mueller believed that evidence of the thought of the ancestors of the human race was to be found in ancient languages. These languages are embedded in ancient texts.

Mueller thought he could work his way back through the layers of ancient texts to get to the bedrock of the primitive mind, the most ancient layer, primordial thinking. When Mueller applied this idea to the Hindu Vedas, he found that at the foundation of the Vedas was the belief in nature gods. He reasoned that these nature gods at the root of most ancient texts of the Indo-European languages represented the origin of religion.

The nature gods were personifications of the awe-inspiring forces of nature. Ancient human beings knew themselves to be frail and vulnerable before these tremendous powers. How could they possibly survive in the midst of them? In Mueller's understanding, this basic feeling of inadequacy, helplessness, and contingency is the underlying wellspring of religion.[72] Human beings feel inadequate before overwhelming forces that threaten their fortunes and their very lives.

Mueller believed that primitive humans developed the idea of god in an attempt to deal with this sense of human precariousness. They supposed that the powers that determine their lives are actually super persons. Like persons, these gods could hear and answer entreaties for help and protection. Through their prayers to the gods, believers felt they had some influence over what happens to them.

How did they invent the idea of deities, however? Mueller thought that the origin of these beliefs in the nature gods was a trick of language. The primitives had words that described the natural forces of the universe. But the study of ancient sacred texts revealed that ancient peoples turned these terms for the forces of nature into something else. They changed them into proper names for supernatural gods. For example, *luna* and *lucina* (Latin) referred to the moon we see in the sky. However, ancient peoples personified the moon as a goddess.[73] Her name became Luna or Lucina.[74]

In this way, Mueller found evidence for the starting point of religion from his analysis of words such as *deva* in the Vedas. In his analysis, Dyēus (*deva*) becomes, variously, *theos* (Latin), "Zeus" (Greek), "Jupiter" (the Roman "Ius Pater"), and "Dyauṣ Pitā (Sanskrit). It is the root of such English words as *deity*, *divine*, and *diva*. The root of the word means "to shine." It has to do with sky, light, and day. Therefore, in Mueller's thought, the luminaries of the sky become the "heavenly bodies" of the deities in a personified sense.

Naturalist Approaches: Spirits, Magic, and Deities (Tylor and Frazer)

Mueller's seminal work inspired the developing science of anthropology to set out on a long search for the origins of religion. The anthropologists believed that "primitive" societies preserved the beginning of human society. They looked to aboriginal sacred ways for clues to the roots of religion. Each theory tried to take a further step back toward the ancient origin of religion.

Three Tracks of the Naturalist Study of Religion

1. Anthropology
2. Sociology
3. Psychology

Mueller had proposed that religion began with the belief in nature gods. But one of the founders of anthropology, E. B. Tylor (1832–1917), was not satisfied. He asked where the idea of gods came from. Tylor answered that the source of religion is *animism*, the belief in spirits that inhabit the things of the material world. The belief in gods came later as the belief in spirits evolved into the idea of deities.

But where did the idea of spirits come from? Tylor answered that it came from the notion of an enduring spirit that is separate from the human body.[75] In turn, this idea came from the answer to the question of where people go when they dream or when they die. The solution to the problem of dreaming and death was that a spirit dwells in and animates the body. This spirit leaves the body in dreams as well as in death.

Once they had gotten this idea of a human spirit, primitive peoples applied it to animals and then to other living things and even natural features of the Earth. They also reasoned that spirits had to come from somewhere—a "spirit realm." This was a supernatural realm beyond the ordinary world.

At last, we come to the end of this way of thinking. Tylor believed that when people begin to give the spirits human characteristics, they invent gods. The spirits become individuals in their own right whether Zeus, Durga, Odin, Śiva, or Aphrodite. From there we arrive at a supreme, almighty, and single deity who rules over all and has no rivals—"God."

Another early anthropologist offered an influential theory of the beginning of religion. James Frazer (1854–1941) took a step back from Tylor. He asserted that magic came *before* animism just as animism came *before* nature gods. Magic is a way of controlling the natural forces on which humans depend for life. It depends on the idea of a "sympathy" or likeness of one thing or action to another. Both use that "sympathy" for purposes of dealing with natural forces. For example, a belief in the idea of imitative magic would be that if I run water through a sieve, it will cause the sky to rain.

According to Frazer, however, religion is different from these types of magic. Human beings arrived at religion when their magic did not work. Repeated failures to manipulate the forces of nature taught primitives that their magic was unreliable. Turning from impersonal forces, the prehistoric peoples reached out to superhuman beings. They imagined that these higher beings had power over the awesome natural forces that controlled them. Thus, they began to look to gods for security and comfort.

The thing about gods, though, is that if one wants their favors, one has to please them. Thus, prehistoric humans had to invent religion. For Frazer, religion has to do with appeasing the gods so that they will be good to you.[76] If the gods are satisfied with one's efforts, they will manipulate the forces of nature on one's behalf.

In Frazer's analysis, religion is profoundly different from the animism of its origin. The powers that are receptive to magic are impersonal and subject to the law of cause and effect. The gods that are receptive to prayer are personal and sensitive to human pleading.

Thinking the Same: Intellectualism and Psychic Unity

Scholars of religion now consider the findings of Tylor and Frazer out of date. But the lasting achievement of these two anthropologists was to lay the foundations for a method of studying religion that anthropologist Clifford Geertz (1926–2006) and others have advanced.

The *intellectualist school* assumes that the process of thinking that produced religion was not so different from the way we think today. We may consider the ideas of prehistoric humans to be far-fetched and even incomprehensible. To the intellectualist school, early humans used the same sort of reasoning that modern people do. For example, we make conclusions based on the evidence we find. The intellectualist school believes that early humans did the same. The only difference between ancient and modern human beings is the tools of thought that contemporary persons have to make conclusions from the data on hand.

For instance, an analysis of reasoning behind the notions of animism and magic shows that it works by the association of ideas. Tylor cites the illustration of the Zulu tribesman. If the tribesman wants to trade cows, he chews a stick of wood. This action will soften the heart of the other party to the trade. Obviously, the stick and the heart are two different things. However, the two are connected by the analogy of what one wants to happen to them.[77]

Tylor observed that this way of reasoning appears in cultures throughout the world.[78] Therefore, we should not make fun of the prehistoric societies for what seems to be "reckless reasoning from analogy." Most people do the same thing. In fact, for Tylor and other intellectualists, as well as William James, the association of ideas is the foundation of all thinking. The only advantage of contemporary people is that modern science puts more "checks on the mind's fancies."[79]

From the anthropology of Tylor and Frazer onward, the naturalist use of the social sciences built on these intellectualist ideas. Note that these sciences assume the *psychic unity* of the human race. This principle states that human beings reason in the same basic ways. Of course, we come up with different conclusions than ancient peoples. Nevertheless, the processes of thinking remain the same.

The principle of psychic unity is highly useful for the naturalistic study of religion for a number of reasons. First, it identifies similar patterns of thought and behavior among the bewildering variety of religions. Second, it explains why different cultures come up with these related patterns. Third, since they have common patterns of thinking, the notion of psychic unity enables us to compare these different religious ways. Fourth, the principle makes it possible for us to explain the dynamics of religion in different times and places.

Alternative Approaches: Totems and Society (Durkheim)

These thoughts lead to the important contribution of Émile Durkheim (1858–1917) and his sociological view of religion. Tylor and Frazer treated religion as a relic of past errors in thinking. In contrast, Durkheim held that religion must have some basis in reality. Otherwise, it would not continue to be the significant human institution that it is. This does not mean that Durkheim himself believed in gods, immortality, and special revelation. Like the anthropologists we have mentioned, he sought to find a foundation for religion by using scientific methods that did not appeal to supernatural sources for their truth.

As he set out to construct a viable theory of the origins of religion, Durkheim rejected the definitions of religion that use an imaginary time machine to go back to its starting point. Instead, Durkheim sought to identify the key elements of religion. His theory was that religion is built on these key elements. Thus, we can categorize Durkheim as an essentialist.

To prove this theory, he relied almost entirely on evidence from central Australia. It was not because the aborigines represented the oldest human society that Durkheim could find. It was because Durkheim believed that he had found among the aborigines the essential elements of religion in their simplest form.

Durkheim set a new direction in religious studies by changing the object of its research. Previous academicians had presumed that at its core religion was a matter of the belief of individuals. Durkheim believed that at its foundation religion was a matter of the unifying bonds of society.

In fact, to Durkheim, the most decisive factors in human life were social not personal. For him, human society comes before individuals in importance.

Individuals are born into societies that sustain them and shape them. Human life has social character. Thus, Durkheim's method of studying human beings was to study "social facts" within "social realities." *Social facts*, Durkheim thought, are the ways of acting that society imposes on its members.[80] They are the forces that bear down upon the individual, the values, morals, customs, and beliefs of society. A culture produces these collective ideals over time. They form a *social reality* that does not need any single individual to exist. Yet no individual can exist without it.

In this view, we must study human societies as total systems and not as a collection of parts that we can isolate from the whole. This means that we must understand religion as it functions within its social context. Therefore, Durkheim thought that Tylor and Frazer were mistaken when they selected different aspects of religion from different cultures to piece together their theories. In contrast, Durkheim insisted that the building blocks of religion are always located within a total social system. Different societies combine them in unique ways to make unique religions.

The Unifying Power of the Totem

In the aboriginal tribes in central Australia, Durkheim found the basic building block of all the elements of religion: the totem. In Australia, totems are symbolic representations of animals, plants, or forces of nature. These images give a sense of identity to the various social groups.[81] Totems, though, are not unique to Australia. Social organizations around the world have similar emblems. For example, the U.S. Congress designated the bald eagle as the national emblem of the nation in 1792. It is the center figure of the Great Seal of the United States. It appears on the dollar bill, on passports, military insignia, and many other places. Often, it is shown together with another totem, the American flag.

The *totem* is the most revered emblem of a society, a concrete representation of the group's life and solidarity.[82] Attacking the totem is the same thing as attacking the tribal group itself. The totem, therefore, represents the mysterious social bond that inspires the group members and calls out their utmost loyalty. For example, conservatives consider burning the flag in protest an act of desecration and disloyalty to the country. They have repeatedly tried to pass an amendment giving Congress the power to prohibit it.

Having discovered the significance of the totem, Durkheim had to explain why the totem is, in fact, the basis of religion. To do this, he observed that the members of a society feel its awesome power over their lives most keenly when they gather in ritual.

Think of ceremonies when the flag of the nation makes its entrance into a sports event or other assembly. No one just saunters in with the flag. A color guard escorts the flag into the meeting place with a great deal of ceremony. This "posting the colors" ritual unifies the people gathered in a sense of common allegiance. They may express this commitment as they sing or profess honor to their country, represented by the flag. In this way, the flag makes visible the invisible reality and power of the society it represents.[83]

This totem pole from Alaska shows the natural symbols important to its creator—salmon and an eagle.

Note that the members cannot treat the object or its name as commonplace. The symbol demands the highest respect. It is sacred. The totem is not just a piece of cloth, a bird, a bear, or a bug. It so closely represents that group's life, identity, unity, and survival that it cannot be separated from them.[84]

Here is the way Durkheim puts it: "The god of the clan, the totemic principle can, therefore, be nothing else than the clan itself, personified and represented to the imagination under the visible form of the animal or vegetable which serves as totem."[85] The totem symbolizes the power of group solidarity. It is made sacred through its inseparable association with that power. As a consequence, the totem reveals that the social order has powers like a deity. Society has all the authority, moral righteousness, inspiration, and right to demand ultimate sacrifice that any god would have. When we see the devotion that a group gives to its totem, we grasp the secret of the totem. The totem stands for the almighty power of the group over its members.

Durkheim rediscovered the fact that religion has been a highly effective way to unify a society and to make it "a single moral community."[86] But what about the role of religion in society today? Durkheim reached his conclusions about religion by studying relatively uncomplicated and isolated cultures. These societies could weave religion and culture together in one piece.

The social theory of Durkheim is more useful than the outdated theories of Mueller, Tylor, and Frazer, because it identifies a primary function of religion: unifying society. The Enlightenment ideal of tolerance was to ensure that there would be no official religious totems to unite modern people into one moral community, no religious rituals to bind them together, and no religious beliefs to serve as the foundation of public life. The result was a profound difference between premodern and modern approaches to religion. Now religion is no longer identical with the forces of social solidarity—quite the opposite.

Oh, Americans do have their national totems: the flag, the eagle, and the founding documents of America. The sociologists of religion Peter Berger and Thomas Luckman observed that these are symbols of a generic public religion. These leftovers from the past survive in the lap of modern secularism.[87] Nevertheless, to Berger and Luckman, these remaining totems only serve to remind us of the religions that have been displaced. Despite the emblems of the nation, religion in its full sense no longer serves as the core of culture and the foundation of the social order.

Durkheim himself predicted this outcome of modernism. He lived to see the implications of the weakening of the unifying role of religion in the Western world.[88]

However, the reassertion of religion into politics and world affairs may be an attempt to restore religion to its role of providing the foundation and focus for

The image on the front of a U.S. passport shows several American totems together—the eagle and the flag, and a motto of unity.

the unity of society. For example, the fundamentalist Christian attempt to set up the Ten Commandments on the walls of the courts and schools of the United States may be viewed as an attempt to reinstate a religious totem in America. This would make the Ten Commandments an emblem of America's return to her origins as a Christian nation.

Psychology: Religion and the Projections of the Psyche (Feuerbach, Marx, and Freud)

Durkheim was a social scientist who believed that the essence of religion was to be found in the social order. Now we turn to scholars who believed that the key was to be found in the psychic order. The developing science of psychology was the way to turn this key to open the secrets of religion.

Psychological Approaches: Knowing God Is Knowing Ourselves (Feuerbach)

The German humanist Ludwig Feuerbach (1804–1872) was one of the first to argue persuasively that the core of religion was in the fantasies of the mind. We have already noted that the Enlightenment shifted the study of religion from heavenly revelations to earthly knowledge based on empirical evidence. Like the study of other aspects of human life, the study of religion was the study of humans, not gods. The field of religious studies was not theology because it presumed to probe into the mind and ways of God. In Feuerbach's mind, the study of religion was anthropology, the study of humans and their cultures.

Feuerbach turned this shift into a personal agenda against religion. Bluntly, he said that he was out to "reduce theology to anthropology."[89] Moreover, he was determined to raise theology to the level of anthropology.[90] Thus, the starting point of his attack was the meaning of "God." Feuerbach said that modern people ought to understand that talking about God is just a way of talking about ourselves. "God" was the generic[91] sum of the highest and best qualities of human nature, our "essence."

Well, if that is true, what is religion? Religion is a way of celebrating the best of human beings. Religion reveals this inner, hidden essence to us. Religions are, in fact, sacred. It is not because of their beliefs regarding some external holiness. Religions are sacred because they are the ways in which humans came to know themselves as truly human. In this vein, he said, "Religion is the first form of self-consciousness."[92]

Some might object, of course, that God and humans are quite different since God is infinite, absolute, perfect, and almighty, while humans are not. Feuerbach would answer that those who raise this question do not realize what religion is doing to them. Feuerbach was dedicated to enlightening them.

Feuerbach explained that religion identifies the highest qualities of human beings. At our best, we are good, just, loving, and so on. However, religion does not give us credit for having these qualities. It gives these characteristics away—to God. It does so by the psychological mechanism of *projection*. Projectors cast an image on a screen. Psychological projection casts our feelings, attitudes, or traits from our mind to something or someone else. Thus, religion transforms the lofty ideals of humans into the perfect attributes of God.

Thus, Feuerbach's discovery of the secret essence of religion suggests a new reason to study religion. We should investigate religion to understand how it deceives the mind and damages the human spirit. If we did, we would realize that religion alienates us from our humanness by turning our most cherished ideals against us. God represents the perfection of human virtues such as love. Yet when we compare ourselves to God, we feel guilty for not living up to the divine ideal. Instead of motivating us to reach our human potential, religion makes us worry about pleasing God, who is only a mechanism of our own psychology.[93]

Religion Is Hazardous to the Worker (Marx)

The German philosopher and economist Karl Marx (1818–1883) inherited this idea of alienation from Feuerbach and pressed it even further. Both shared the idea that humans are strangers to themselves.[94] What does this mean? From what are we separated? We might think that everyone has a true and unique self. Our alienation is our failure to realize our unique potential as individuals. Feuerbach, however, thought our alienation was our failure to realize the humanness that we share with the human race as a whole. We are human because we share the qualities of love, justice, mercy, and reason that belong to us as a species.[95] Marx, as always, took the idea further. Our humanness does not consist of such inner qualities that he thinks are abstractions. Humanness consists of social relationships.[96]

Feuerbach believed that our sense of alienation comes from the mistakes of psychological projection. However, for Marx that is only a symptom of our problem. The foundation of society is not religion but economics. Thus, alienation is a problem of the practical relationship of workers to economic production in society. In Marx's view, humans are born to satisfy their needs, relate to their fellow humans, and fulfill themselves through productive work. However, industrial labor separates persons from the fruits of their work, from nature, and from the whole of humanity. Workers become cogs in a mechanical machine whose function is to fulfill the needs of others, not themselves.

Religion reinforces this status quo of alienation by turning the laborers' attention from Earth to heaven. The otherworldly comfort we seek in religion only diverts them from organizing ourselves about our real oppressors. Therefore, Marx made his often-quoted statement: "Religious suffering is, at one and the same time, the expression of real suffering and a protest against real suffering. Religion is the sigh of the oppressed creature, the heart of a heartless world, and the soul of soulless conditions. It is the opium of the people."[97]

Thus, for Marx, understanding religion and its origins is not enough. We should set our sights on the economic conditions of exploitation and alienation that produce religion. In summary, Marx represents those who connect religion with an unlikely set of associations, the web of economics. For Durkheim, religion serves to represent the social order. For Marx, religion serves to justify the economic order. Marx would say that wearing religious clothing is a sign of protest against the alienation and injustice of modern life. Yet it also shows that the wearers are suffering under the delusion of "illusory compensation" for their troubles.

Psychological Approaches: An Illusion with a Future (Freud)

Marx identified the economic causes of religion. Yet he seemed to agree with Feuerbach that religion itself is still a fault of mental processes. That takes us to Sigmund Freud (1836–1939), the founder of psychoanalysis. We can start by saying that Freud's imposing work is an example of naturalism. He believed that he could explain religion in terms of natural causes that do depend on extraordinary, supernatural knowledge. Freud also shared with Tylor, Frazer, Durkheim, Feuerbach, and Marx the evolutionary idea of the development of religion.

Freud, however, applied the past theories of religion to the human psyche. Freud constructed a bridge across the divide of the social and the psychological aspects of religion. The key idea was that the evolutionary stages of the development of religion in the human race were the same stages as the psychological development of the individual.[98]

Freud's Stages of the Development of Religion

Stage One: Animism and magic in religion and narcissism in psychology
Stage Two: The primal murder of the prehistoric father in religion and the Oedipus complex in psychology
Stage Three: Scientific thinking and psychological maturity to replace religion

—Celia Brickman

In her essay on primitiveness and psychoanalysis, psychotherapist Celia Brickman summarizes the stages of the development of religion and their corresponding stages in human development[99] (see the textbox "Freud's Stages of the Development of Religion").

In *Stage One*, psychological narcissism goes together with animism and magic. Narcissists have an exaggerated view of themselves, their capabilities, and their importance. Likewise, the believers in animism and magic had an overblown view of themselves. They thought that they could manipulate the forces of nature.

Stage Two requires a full explanation because it is the phase of the origin of religion itself. In Freud's psychology, the Oedipus complex refers to the unconscious sexual drives of the boy who competes with his father for his mother's affections. Freud applied this theory to the origin of religion. Freud speculated that the impulse of juvenile incest was at the beginning of religion.[100] In this way of thinking, religion began with the murder of the prehistoric father. The sons both loved the father and hated him because he was the rival to their mother's favors. In order to gain the father's power and sexual rights, the sons slew their father. Instead of producing the benefits that the sons sought, this heinous deed produced both guilt and longing. To handle these conflicting emotions, the sons replaced the ancient father with a totem. This ideal image eventually became God. He took on the familiar aspects of an all-powerful and immortal father figure.

Freud's theory may seem like just another myth to us.[101] Freud, though, insisted that it happened in fact! Freud believed that it was an "event of man's primal history."[102] At the same time, it was a parallel to the psychological growth of the individual.[103] Both religion and psychology merge in the unconscious operations of the psyche.

As the title of Freud's most famous work on religion, *The Future of an Illusion*, suggests, religion is founded on illusion. An illusion is not an outright error. At least no one can prove scientifically that it is in error.[104] Rather, religious beliefs have a unique character. We cannot prove that they are true. We only wish them to be true.

Freud had found the principle of wish fulfillment earlier in his *The Interpretation of Dreams* (1899). In this groundbreaking work, Freud showed that unconscious wishes come to the surface of consciousness in dreams. If so, then dreams are a window into the depths of our thoughts. Our waking minds may not want to acknowledge the impulses that lurk below the surface of our consciousness. However, these desires take form in our dreams. Psychology can unlock these secrets by the interpretation of these dreams.

When he studied religion, Freud found the same wishes that he had found in dream analysis. Like dreams, then, religious beliefs are shown to be wish fulfillment. In religion, the unconscious wish comes to conscious awareness as it is projected on a totem or full-fledged God.

Freud's idea of projection reminds us of Feuerbach. However, in Freud's system, the "father figure" (God) is not an ideal human type. He is an authoritarian autocrat who is as ready to punish as he is to protect. Is he a stern but benevolent father who will provide for our needs, as Freud suggests in *The Future of Illusion*? Or is he the rival who blocks us from fulfilling our most secret desires, as Freud proposes in the earlier work, *Totem and Taboo*? The answer is that he is both: our feelings toward our projection of the father figure are hopelessly ambivalent. Thus, ultimately in Freud's view, religion is a mental disorder, "the universal obsessional neurosis of humanity."[105]

In the end, for Freud religion is a disease that psychotherapy can help us get over. In Freud's final and third stage of development, psychological maturity and the scientific viewpoint go together. The end of religion is the same as the end of human development. Modern humans think scientifically. Their conclusions are based on empirical evidence. They give up magical pretensions and religious fantasies to live freely without such hang-ups.

Freud's theory of the origins of religion sounds fantastic. But he was the first to set foot on an unexplored territory of religion, the human psyche. Freud's pioneering work pointed toward the unexplored topic of the inner experience of religious people. It led away from the idea that religion is merely a set of beliefs that are either true or false. Instead, Freud showed that the study of religion must plumb the depths of the human spirit. The field of religious studies sweeps horizontally across the broad range of human societies. But since the time of Freud, it has also explored the vertical heights and depths of the individual's experience.

Evaluation of Alternative Approaches: The Critique of Essentialism

In general, the entire search for the roots of religion in human culture is a form of essentialism. Essentialism tended to reduce the complex dynamics of religion to a single set of characteristics. For example, Mueller suggested that religion comes from the mistaken belief that the forces of nature are gods. Tylor believed that the origin of religion was the notion of spirits. Frazer said no, it was magic. In each case, the religion is associated with one characteristic or one set of characteristics of a very complex topic.

The sociologist Durkheim identified the essential building blocks of religion in the totems of the aboriginal tribes of Australia. For him, the totem was a representation of the bonds of society, inseparable from the society itself. In a sense, to Durkheim, religion is no more and no less than society itself.

In psychology, Feuerbach explained all religion by the mechanism of psychic projection. Marx borrowed Feuerbach's idea but added that religion is a way for the elites of society to oppress the workers. Freud said that the basis of religion was a primal murder that he claimed was a historical fact.[106] Freud made ingenious associations between the "facts" of the primal murder and his theories of the unconscious and the Oedipus complex.

The groundbreaking work of these pioneers of the academic study of religion laid the foundations for today's religious studies. Yet with the problem of this chapter in mind, we can make one critique. In general, these founders of the study of religion reduced the complexity of religion to a simple key idea or cluster of ideas. In the terms of Clifford Geertz, this strategy tended to "thin" out the "thick" riches of religion. The religions of the world have to do with moral duty, nature gods, spirits, magic, the social order, projection, and psychological complexes. But they encompass much more than these topics. The search for the essence of religion in its origins or building blocks captured certain aspects of religion in the webs of meaning that the scholars wove for it. Yet, as the anticolonialists, feminists, and postmodernists have pointed out, the methods and aims of the scholars also distorted the religions that they studied and neglected significant features of them.

Evaluation of the Alternative Approaches: The Development of Religious Studies

This chapter has told the story of the development of religious studies from the Enlightenment to Freud. The field advanced as Europeans and North Americans tried to make sense of an ever-widening circle of cultures whose worldviews and ways of life were much different from their own.

The scholars could not help but apply their already existing ways of thinking to their new discoveries. The ideas of the Enlightenment and the hope to avoid religious conflict set the study in the direction of separating the religious from the secular. This path was a product of the strategy of containing religion to prevent religious wars. Furthermore, the focus on belief reflected the conflicts over the beliefs of Christianity.

The academic study of religion is now recognizing that the Western attitude to religion is unique. The scholars of the past tried to fit the religions of the world into their own networks of associations. In particular, religious studies developed with an unnoticed bias toward Western thinking. This bias became obvious as Western scholars finally noticed the assumptions behind their attitude toward what they saw as the opposite of Western ways, in the "East." This attitude was expressed in the broad movement called Orientalism.

This chapter's account of the history of modern religious studies began with Mueller's pioneering research into the language, literature, and religion of India. This excited fantastic interest in what was called the *Orient*. Nowadays we speak of the Orient as the "Far East," meaning (essentially) China, Korea, Japan, and Southeast Asia. At the time of the development of religious studies, the Orient included what we now call the "Middle East," the Indian Subcontinent, and the Far East. The terms are confusing. Overall, the Orient refers more to what Europeans and Americans thought were exotic ways of life than a certain geographical region. In cultural terms, the Orient refers to what is "Eastern" as opposed to what is "Western." The Western is the familiar culture of Europe and North America. The Eastern is what is unfamiliar, strange, and esoteric.

As Max Mueller and other Orientalists brought their reports of visits, translations of texts, and interpretations of Eastern thought back to Europe and America, Westerners were fascinated. The "Orient" captivated the attention of the "West" even more than reports of space exploration does today.

The high point of the Orientalist movement was the World's Parliament of Religion in Chicago in 1893. Part of the Chicago Columbia Exhibition, the meeting brought a greater variety of religious speakers together than had ever been assembled before. As a prime example of Orientalism, the Parliament excited interest in world religions and the study of religion. Yet, at the same time, the Parliament promoted a Western impression of these religions typical of Orientalism. The Chicago hosts betrayed their Christian background in the way they conducted the meeting. The stated goal of the conference was to advance the progress of civilization. This progress was to be founded on religion. But "religion" was about beliefs in God, immortal life, and the supernatural, ideas most friendly to Western Christianity. The Parliament sought to identify those beliefs that were "points of contact" with other religions.[107]

Highly publicized, the Parliament exposed ordinary Americans to Eastern religions. These included Hinduism, Buddhism, Zoroastrianism, Shinto, Daoism, Confucianism, and Islam.[108] However, the descriptions of those religions were "Westernized" to appeal to the American audience. The speakers came to Chicago seeking recognition that they were religions of equal stature with Western religions. Many of them went on national tours after the conference. The Japanese Buddhists, for example, used the conference to develop a Western form of Buddhism. They used the Parliament to test a way of presenting Buddhism to modern Westerners. After the conference, they took this version of Buddhism on the road in America. But they also took it back to Japan to promote a modern revival of Buddhism in their own land. In this process, Buddhism was reshaped as a universal and modern religion for all nations for the West as well as the East.[109]

The Faults and Fall of Orientalism: Edward Said

In its time, Orientalism broadened the study of religion. It is now out of favor in academic circles. Its popularity faded under the devastating critique of professor of comparative literature Edward Said (1935–2003). Said was educated in Cairo,

Princeton, and Harvard and became an activist for the Palestinian cause. His work, *Orientalism*, made a stunning critique of the Western bias toward the religions of the East.

Said asserted that Orientalism was a set of prejudiced ideas and attitudes about the East. He maintained that the presumptions of Western colonialism lurked below the surface of the Western "objective" interest in Eastern religions. According to Said, Orientalism constructed a framework of meanings around the idea of Asian cultures as the "Other." The West was advanced; the East was backward. The West was strong and purposeful; the East was weak and aimless. The West was rational; the East was irrational. Thus, the standard of evaluating the cultures of the East was Western culture. This meant that Western scholarship has dominated the study of Eastern religions in academics just as colonialism has dominated the East politically and economically.

Said purposely set out to challenge the Western academic study of religion while promoting the Palestinian cause. Not surprisingly, the academics of the day reacted vigorously. The eminent Oriental scholar Bernard Lewis complained that Said took a significant problem of scholarship and reduced it to "political polemics and personal abuse."[110] Others said that he went overboard and did not respect the conventions of scholarship. Most noted that Said selected the evidence that suited his political agenda.[111]

In America, however, Said's ideas swept over the academic world like a tidal wave. In their wake the new field of "postcolonial studies" appeared. The "postcolonial" movement charged that European and American scholars were tainted with the legacy of colonialism. Therefore, the only qualified persons to study the Eastern religions were representatives of those cultures. Soon the makeup of the academic departments of Middle Eastern and Asian studies changed to include professors representing Eastern viewpoints.[112]

The Male Bias: The Feminist Critique

The work of Said shows what can happen when we look at a field from a different perspective. Another important critique of the development of religious studies comes from feminism. Though the feminist movement has gone through a series of phases, in general, feminist studies has centered on the analysis of the inferior status of women and the theory of the roles and relationships of gender.[113] Currently, the field of feminist studies is expanding to become "gender studies." However, the field is still concentrated on overcoming the "traditional invisibility and marginalization" of women in education, society, and religious studies.[114]

Feminist studies asserts that women and their concerns have been overlooked in the study of religion.[115] The result has been that scholars of religious studies have looked at religion from a dominant male-oriented viewpoint. Concepts that seem to be neutral and theories that claim to be "objective," in fact, hide a male bias.[116]

For example, anthropologist Rosalind Shaw observes that some scholars have claimed that human beings are "naturally religious." They have used the term *homo religious* to refer to the supposedly religious human being.[117] What qualities make human beings "naturally religious"? Shaw alleges that those who use the term have in mind the general traits of "man." That is, they are referring to the traits of the male in contrast to the female. If this is true, then the scholarship that follows from this way of thinking is biased. Its generalizations come only from the religious experience of men. In summary, the field of feminist/gender studies asserts that the development of religious studies overlooked or misunderstood the variety of religious experiences and expressions of women as well as other marginal groups.

The Postmodern Critique: The Pretension of Objectivity

Postcolonial and feminist/gender studies are associated with a broader movement in academic circles loosely labeled *postmodernism*. Postmodernism is both a reaction to and an extension of modernism. Among other aspects of modern thinking from the Enlightenment, it responds to the assumptions of Western thinkers that scholars could attain objective and unbiased knowledge, especially through the methods of science. Recall the ideas of the "intellectualist school" and the "psychic unity" of the human race. The idea that human beings reason in the same way is useful to make comparisons and generalizations of peoples across time and place. Nevertheless, as we have seen, it makes primitive peoples into "junior scientists." In its view, these amateurs made mistakes primarily because they lacked sufficient data and suitable equipment for studying their world.

What happens when scholars presume to be objective and unbiased? They create everyone else in their own image. According to religious studies scholar Ursala King, here is a daunting critique of the background of religious studies. Using the insights of postmodernism, King states that scholars have assumed that their rational, impersonal, and male-oriented ways of thinking are universal standards that can be applied to all cultures. That assumption allows them to think that they are unbiased.[118]

King and postmodernists counter the claim of academic objectivity with what they call "the hermeneutics of suspicion."[119] This approach to scholarship subjects the methods and findings of modern fields of knowledge to critical scrutiny. In effect, postmodernism turns modernism and its critical thinking against itself. Using the methods of the French philosopher Jacques Derrida (1930–2004), they "deconstruct" the structures of thinking of modern scholarship. In this way, they tear down modern knowledge. The aim is to expose the foundations of what is thought to be true. For the postmodernists, the basis of modern thinking is not "objective truth" but power relationships. The postmodernists expose the way the Western mind-set legitimizes the domination of the white, male, upper class. They show how Western thought divides reality into "binary" dualisms such as "we/them, responsible/irresponsible, rational/irrational, legitimate/illegitimate, normal/abnormal."[120] When it puts everything into these categories, the Western mind assumes the superiority of the makers of these divisions. White, upper-class males construct these opposites and claim what belongs to the "good side" of the dualisms for themselves. Everyone and everything else is inferior.

The basis of the domination of men over women is the power to construct this binary reality. Postmodernism aims to challenge these habits of thought[121] and to promote a change of mind. This revolution in mind-set is the basis for the task of understanding and transforming the power relationships between men and women.[122]

The Critique of the Study of "Religion" from Within

Said's critique is a reminder that the very concept of "religion" originates in Western ways of thinking. We have seen how the term emerged from the differences within Christianity to its application to other cultures. Jonathan Z. Smith takes this thought further. He states that *religion* is a term that was invented by scholars for use in scholarly study.[123] For Smith, religion is the same as the concept of "culture" or "language." Like these, "religion" is a *heuristic* concept, a mental device that helps us think about something. People do not speak "language," but one of the languages of the world. In the same way, people do not believe or practice "religion" but follow the sacred ways of one of the religions of the world.

Smith adds that religion is a "generic concept" that sets a "disciplinary horizon" for study.[124] It is a catchall term that categorizes certain beliefs, attitudes, and behaviors while excluding others. Smith says that the "disciplined study of religion" cannot do without it. Yet it has its limitations. Therefore, Segal states that the question is not whether the concept of religion is useful or not. The question is this: "Does the data that we want to describe fit the category of religion or not?"[125]

With Smith and Segal's observations in mind, we can say that the concept of religion derived from the Western Enlightenment was the foundation of a broad Western framework of meaning concerning religions. Within its web of ideas were associations that dictated the way that religion should be studied. Misconceptions were unavoidable, and partial truths were inevitable. Based on Western ideas of religious truth, past scholars defined religion in terms of belief in assertions of truth. They took Christianity as the model and looked for similar kinds of beliefs in other religions.

Scholars went on to search for the universal essence of religion in its origin. In this effort, the basic idea of religion remained the same. However, the academicians discarded many of the associations with Christianity. They replaced the Christian theological frame of reference with the framework of the developing social sciences. Depending on their academic discipline, they found the origin and essence of religion in various places. The anthropologists found them in nature gods, spirits, and magic. The sociologist Durkheim found it in the totems that represent the overriding bonds of the social order. The psychologists found it in the psychological mechanisms of projection and complexes.

As the scholars developed their theories of religion, a movement developed that would open up the study of world religions to an audience outside the classroom. This was Orientalism. It constructed an ideal of Eastern religions as the esoteric opposite of the familiar Western religions.

As the field of religious studies developed, scholars became more aware of how to study religion without bias, the primary problem of this chapter. Cross-currents to the dominant Western trends alerted scholars to the hazards of fitting their observations about religions into preconceived webs of associations. Said and others who reacted against Orientalism revealed the Western bias of the study of Eastern religions. The feminists exposed the hidden assumptions that enforced the male domination of the field. The postmodernists challenged the pretense of objectivity of the religious studies. Finally, even scholars in the field took a critical view of the idea of "religion." They recognized that "religion" is not a thing that exists in and of itself. It is only a useful abstract concept for categorizing selected features of various religions. Therefore, critical thinkers use it cautiously.

Evaluation of Alternative Approaches: Political Challenges to Secularism

The greatest challenge to the Western idea of religion has not come from scholars, however. It has come from the unexpected worldwide increase in the visibility and influence of religion.

The Western concept of religion that evolved from the Enlightenment has had extraordinary influence. The separation of the secular from the religious is at the core of the Western framework of meaning. It establishes different forms of *secularism*, the commitment to the independence of public life from personal religion.

The Western view of separation of church and state has been useful for the promotion of religious peace and toleration. However, the course of events in the twenty-first century has proven that this ideal is a unique approach. It is not an inevitable outcome of unavoidable global trends.

European-American culture has assumed that it represents the future. It has believed that the rest of the world will catch up with its modern ways, including its division of the sacred and the secular. However, world affairs, such as the results of the "Arab Spring" of 2011, have proven that modernism and democracy are not necessarily tied to Western forms of secularism.[126] In fact, according to Peter Berger, in the twenty-first century, *secularism* only remains strong in Europe and Canada. In most other parts of the world, religion is gaining strength.[127]

Moreover, in many parts of the world direct resistance to the secularist view is growing.[128] Those who are disillusioned with what they consider the broken promises of secularism are reclaiming religion as the foundation of a new social identity.[129] In contrast to the Enlightenment idea of their separation, political power and religion are coming together in new ways. The religious clothing of Muslims, Sikhs, Jews, and other religious adherents are tests of what belongs on either side of the line between religion and public life. The women who wear the hijab or other articles of religious clothing insist on the right to wear religious symbols in the secular sphere. Those who object do so in part because they believe that religion is a private matter, and they do not want reminders of religion in the public space.

The issue of religious clothing is only one example of intense debate going on within the world religions. Since the turn of the century, we have witnessed worldwide efforts to restore religion to a public role like the one Durkheim describes. For example, the Protestant evangelicals are striving for greater influence on the politics and morality of America. Many are striving to restore America to their ideal of a "Christian nation" based on Protestant principles, morals, and values.

Similarly, Islamists who are dedicated to the revival of conservative Islam are promoting a return to Islamic law (*shari'ah*) in Muslim circles. The restored shari'ah would replace European principles of law as the basis of Muslim society. Christian fundamentalists are campaigning to reinstate the Ten Commandments as the foundation of American life. Hindu nationalists in such organizations as the Bharatiya Janata Party (BJP) are striving to redefine the modern, secular state of India. The nationalists are trying to reenvision the country as a "Hindu nation."

In the recent decades, this religious *fundamentalism* has exploded throughout the world. Religion scholar Gabriel A. Almond states that it has become one of the principal political forces in this century.[130]

In a comprehensive study, historian R. Scott Appleby and his colleagues found types of fundamentalism in many places and religions of the world. They concluded that all of these "fundamentalisms" are strongly reacting in various ways to the forces of secularism that displaces religion from its central role in society.[131]

Evaluation of Alternative Approaches: Concluding Summary

Therefore, religious studies has been a Western field of scholarship developed by Westerners. Secularism has been its major influence. (See the textbox "Presuppositions of Secularism about Religion" for a list of some of the presuppositions of the web of associations of secularism.)

Presuppositions of Secularism about Religion

- Religion is a separate sphere of human life that is private and subjective.
- Religions exist as separate entities (things) in isolation from other religions and cultures.
- Religious beliefs are personal opinions but religious organizations elevate them to unquestioned truths.
- Religious organizations are voluntary associations that their members have chosen to join.
- Religions are outdated and their influence will soon fade away throughout the world.

The global resurgence of religion has proven that these ideas are unique to Western society. They are the legacy of the Enlightenment. Throughout the world, even in Western society, movements are challenging these assumptions.

This textbook proposes that the changing status of religion at the turn of the century poses new challenges to the assumed understanding of religion. New issues have arisen such as the issue of the "cover" of Muslim women. These issues require methods of study that go beyond the assumptions of the Enlightenment and its assumed separation of religion from public life. The question is how we can study religion with fairness and insight without being caught in the web of these assumptions.

PROPOSING THE MOST PROMISING SOLUTION: STRATEGIES TO AVOID BIAS

This chapter has focused on the problem of finding a way to study religion with fairness and insight. We are looking for an approach that would interpret religion without limiting preconceptions. It would not fit the evidence into a preexisting network of associations. But it would attempt to understand the sacred ways of today's world within the context of their own frameworks of meaning.

> ### Three Alternative Ways of Avoiding Bias in the Study of Religion
>
> 1. Without any associations of ideas whatsoever
> 2. As a separate entity, asking the "insiders" of the beliefs to explain them to us
> 3. As its own thing, rejecting the associations of religion with anything else

This section will attempt to build an alternative method of studying religion that would escape bias. The proposed solution is simple: stop making the associations that prejudice the study of religion. How could this be done? The chapter will now lay out three basic ways to set aside the associations of ideas that distort the understanding of religion.

- We could study the phenomenon of religion without any associations of ideas, according to the Yogacara Buddhist School or the thought of Jiddu Krishnamurti.
- We could approach each religion as a separate entity, asking the "insiders" of the beliefs to explain them to us, as Wilfred Cantwell Smith exemplifies.
- We could approach religion as its own thing and reject the associations of religion with anything else, as the work Rudolf Otto demonstrates.

Direct Experience in Itself: No Associations Allowed (Yogacara Buddhism and J. Krishnamurti)

The Yogacara school of Buddhism (fourth to fifth centuries BCE) offers the first method of escaping the trap of predetermined associations. This "mind only" school of thought distinguishes immediate experience from the interpretations and conclusions that the mind makes from this experience. We perceive something with the senses. Immediately we use words, names, and concepts to put the "raw" stuff of the senses into sets of ideas. These sets of ideas are mental programs that society has given us. For instance, someone might observe a woman wearing a scarf. Her mind instantly interprets this data: She might think "woman-scarf-religion-Muslim-terrorism-male domination of women," and so on. If this were her way of thinking, her response to the woman wearing a scarf would be an immediate reaction to the bundle of ideas that it evokes. They would not be the original sense experience.[132]

In contrast, the author and philosopher Jiddu Krishnamurti (1895–1986) gained a worldwide audience for his teaching that we should stop labeling our experience. We should simply enjoy our immediate, unfiltered perceptions.

The notion that we can separate immediate experience from its interpretation suggests a way to study religion without being tangled in the webs of prior associations. This approach focuses on direct, instantaneous observation and rejects secondary thoughts about the primary data of the senses.

We see someone wearing a scarf. Then what? We do not allow the processes of thought to transform this simple, straightforward seeing into something else. We stick with our observations and do not name, categorize, evaluate, and make a conclusion about them. In this way, we set aside the mind's demand for interpretations, conclusions, and explanations such as "What is he thinking?" or "What is she doing?" We appreciate the sight of someone wearing the hijab or burqa in itself as its own thing. We do not try to interpret or explain this observation.

Each Religion in Itself: Only "Insider" Associations Allowed (Wilfred Cantwell Smith)

Those who study each religion within its own ways of thinking represent the second method of solving the problem of associations. Comparative religions scholar Wilfred Cantwell Smith (1916–2000) exemplifies this approach. He proposed that the only legitimate understanding of religion is from the viewpoint of the believer.[133] In this way of thinking, the believers of a religion are the "insiders," since they are "inside" the religious circle of faith and practice. Others who do not believe are "outsiders." To illustrate, those who do not know a foreign language have no idea of what people are saying in that language. In the same way, "outsiders" do not have a clue about what is going on "inside" the religious ways of others. As the understanding of unfamiliar foreign languages requires interpreters, so the understanding of unfamiliar sacred ways requires informants who can translate the ideas and experience of religious people to "outsiders."

However, Smith's ideas went further. Smith was one of the first to criticize the term *religion*. To him, religion was associated with the static and standardized ideologies that were at odds with each other in Europe. Instead, Smith insisted that religion was about individual faith. He thought that religions are only traditions that made the faith of individuals understandable to groups of believers.

It follows that only "insiders" are capable of understanding their religion and qualified to represent it as informants. These "insiders" of a religion should have control over how their religion is explained and interpreted. In fact, Smith made this notion an overarching principle of study: if the religious believers cannot accept a statement about their faith, then that statement is not valid.[134]

If we accept this principle, the only way to understand the distinctive apparel of religious people is to ask those who are wearing it. They are the "insiders" who know what the proper associations and meanings of their behavior are. "Outsiders," if they speak about the religion at all, can only repeat what they hear from informants. They must not develop their own independent explanations about the religion, especially those that insiders would find unacceptable. This approach would disallow terms with negative connotations like "primitive." Even statements that express appreciation for other faiths would not be valid.

Religion as a Topic in Itself: No Associations Outside of Religion Allowed (Phenomenology and Rudolf Otto)

The third way of overcoming preconceptions about religion is to isolate religion itself as a category from all other associations. This way is represented by the work of comparative religions scholar Rudolf Otto (1869–1937), who wrote the famous book, *The Idea of the Holy*.

Otto was a pioneer in the *phenomenology of religion*. Phenomenology studies religions as "phenomena" or observations that appear before our eyes. Its purpose was to counter what it considered the *reductionism* of other methods of study.[135] This chapter already mentioned the critique of essentialism: it reduces the complexity of religion to a single set of characteristics and so "thins out" the richness of religion to a rational explanation.

Phenomenology provided an alternative to the social science methods of studying religion that we have outlined. Developed by Edmund Husserl (1859–1938), phenomenology uses the method of bracketing interpretations. As a bracket ([. . .]) sets aside material in a sentence that is not directly relevant to its meaning, so the bracket in phenomenology sets aside any presuppositions, explanations, and evaluations of what is perceived. The task is simply to describe the phenomena according to the way it appears.

Otto himself had such experiences as we hear from his reports of his travels to North Africa, Egypt, Palestine, India, and the Far East. In Egypt, for example, the Sphinx of Giza in Egypt gave him the feeling of the "the unfathomable depth and mystery of existence," "in the evening silence of the sandy desert." In India, the three-headed image of the Hindu deity Śiva gave him a sense of the "grandeur" of the "mystery of the transcendent."[136]

However, it was in a dusty synagogue in Morocco that Otto experienced the most profound sense of the heart of religion. He happened to hear the chanting of the words "Holy, Holy, Holy" from a Jewish synagogue. He said that he felt these words to be "the most exalted words that have ever come from human lips . . . [words] from the depths of the soul, with a mighty shudder exciting and calling into play the mystery of the other world latent therein."[137]

One can only suggest what this experience is like. At this basic level, rational concepts cannot grasp the religious experience. It is "non-rational." Otto did not mean that religion is *irrational*. Religion is not nonsense. It has a logic of its own and that way of thinking can be studied by human reason. Nevertheless, the religious experience is much more than what logical reasoning can understand. Thus, previous scholars have been misguided when they have reduced it to human thought.[138] Nor is religious experience just whimsy, a fanciful subjective feeling. Rather the basic religious experience is an awareness that is different from rational knowing. It is an intuition, an inner knowing, that does not rely on the external senses or logical conclusions.

Since religion is based on subjective awareness of an unseen reality, how could anyone know or understand the religious experience of others? Otto's answer presumed that while individuals have their own religious experience, all religious experience is essentially the same. Negatively, Otto said that if his readers could not recall such "a deeply-felt religious experience," they would not be able to understand what he is saying.[139] Positively, Otto believed that if students have had religious experiences, they can learn about the religions of others. Students can appreciate the religious experiences of others by means of the shared feeling between themselves and those they are studying.[140]

Note that by their experience, religious people acquire knowledge of an actual reality, not something that their minds made up. Since religion gets in touch with a realm that is real, Otto said, religion is a unique form of human knowledge.[141] As a unique form of human knowing, religion is in a class by itself. It is *sui generis*, or unlike anything else. This means that religion goes by its own rules and that the study of religion has to develop its own methods.

To talk about religion as a distinct phenomenon of human life, Otto wanted a neutral term. This concept would not suggest the associations that would limit us to the preconceived ideas about it. Otto found what he was looking for in a Latin word that reminds us of animism. That word is *numen*, meaning "a spiritual force or influence often identified with a natural object, phenomenon, or place."[142] From *numen*, Otto coined the word *numinous* to refer to the strange and uncanny quality that is the wellspring of religious experience.

By using the term *numinous*, Otto struggled to capture the sense of an awesome, majestic, and overwhelming power that religions refer to as holy or sacred. An unforgettable attempt to visualize this power in modern film happens at the end of Steven Spielberg's *Raiders of the Lost Ark*. At the climax, the villains open the chest, the "source of unspeakable power" that everyone has been looking for. Inside, they expect to find the stone tablets of the Ten Commandments. All that remains is a fine dust. Suddenly, the invisible power once locked up in the ark stirs. Bursts of electricity burn out the lights and equipment. Everything goes dark except for the humming, smoking, brilliant light glowing inside the ark. Indy, the hero, warns the heroine, Marion, not to look at the light. The villains, however, see ghostly images of horror before their faces melt off, their heads are blown up, or lightning bolts pierce them through the heart.

Otto claims that religion concerns this awful reality that is alien to human beings. Thus, it is *holy* or *Wholly Other*. To encounter the holy directly is so shocking and unsettling that it fills one with overwhelming feelings. For example, when Otto heard the "Holy, Holy, Holy" chanted in the Moroccan synagogue, an unexpected "thrill of fear" overcame him. This combination of *dread and fascination* is the very core of the human response to the sacred. Otto claimed that it goes far beyond what humans ordinarily think or feel.

Religions arise as humans develop ways of giving proper respect to what is holy. In his review of the final scene from *Raiders of the Lost Ark*, Tim Dirks explains why the heroes Indy and Marion are not burned to cinders with the villains: "Only Indy and Marion survive the holocaust because of their humility and reverence for the awesome forces."[143] They respond in the proper way to the power of the sacred. With the same attitude, the diverse religions of the world are founded on the encounter with this same mysterious reality. Religious rituals, myths, and symbols express it. Religious doctrine defines it. And religious ways prescribe the proper way to approach it.

In summary, Otto believed that the encounter with the *numinous* was the most fundamental way that religion appears in human experience. With this view of the holy, Otto felt that he had escaped the web of Christianity that had dominated religious studies. Below the exterior of sectarian doctrines and rituals, he had discovered religion at its raw, unfiltered, and unmediated core. From this core, religious beliefs and practices emerged that express this universal religious sense.

EVALUATING THE MOST PROMISING SOLUTION: NO EASY WAY OUT

This chapter has suggested religious studies has a new role to play in the twenty-first century. The American Academy of Religion website refers to the context that makes this role necessary. In "Why Study Religion?" it explains,

> In our day and age, rumors of religion's demise seem very premature—and perhaps there's no grain of truth in them at all. Religion persists and is often on the rise, even as scientific and non-religious perspectives have become prominent. We still find religion everywhere, on television, in film, in popular music, in our towns and neighborhoods. We discover religion at the center of global issues and cultural conflict. We see religion in the lives of the people we know and love, and in ourselves, as we live out and wrestle with our own religious faith.[144]

If religion lies at the bottom of many of the current controversies of the global society, then the field of religious studies has a potential contribution to make to their resolution. The case of the "cover" of Muslim women shows how easy it is to react to the current issues and dynamics of religion with hasty judgments. These reactions only add to the controversies. Instead, issues like this call for an informed, reasoned, and insightful understanding of religion, religious diversity, and the growing role of religion in today's world. The field of religious studies offers information, tools, and methods to gain such an understanding.

Toward Informed and Insightful Interpretation of Religion in the Twenty-First Century

How can we study religion in a way that will achieve a more helpful understanding of religion and its dynamics in the twenty-first century? We have proposed that in order to understand anything new, we have to put it into some larger framework of meaning. Yet we must be careful about this process. William James suggested that our habits of thought depend on the store of ideas we have. Furthermore, our habits of behavior depend on the way we put these ideas into action. This chapter has confirmed his observation: unless the network of ideas in our minds changes, our reactions to events and circumstances will not change.

Suppose we are embroiled in a debate. We will stubbornly assert our point of view in the dispute unless we change our minds. What does it mean to change our minds? It means accepting new ideas and rearranging how these ideas fit together. The underlying challenge of the study of religion in the twenty-first century, therefore, is to find a way to promote a reconfiguration of our prior ideas about religion. To do this, we have proposed that we must deal with the preprogrammed networks of ideas that form our framework of meaning. This chapter has presented three promising strategies to do this. Now we ask, "How well would these proposals work?"

A Test Case: Teacher in Religious Clothing

The repeal of a law that prohibited teachers in the State of Oregon from wearing religious clothing would help us evaluate the strategies for unbiased study of religion given above. In 1923, the Oregon legislature passed a law forbidding public school teachers in the state from wearing religious garb in the classroom. Sympathizers to the Ku Klux Klan (KKK) proposed it as an anti-Catholic measure. Along with the prohibition of religious clothing, such as priests' collars and nuns' habits, the bill mandated that all students attend public schools. However, in 1925, the Supreme Court declared that Oregon could not make all students attend public school. But the statute against religious clothing remained.[145]

More than sixty years later, the Eugene, Oregon, school district fired Janet Cooper, a special education teacher, for wearing religious clothing. After Cooper became a Sikh, she showed up to teach in white clothes and a white turban. She refused the order to change her clothing, citing her First Amendment rights, and lost her job.[146]

Cooper's lawsuit went up to the Oregon Supreme Court in 1986. The court upheld the district's right to dismiss the teacher. Its reasons are worth noting. It held that the religious clothing in question would upset the "religious neutrality" of the classroom, neutrality that Oregon law intended to preserve. Likewise, the court said that wearing the Sikh clothing would represent an "unofficial endorsement" of the beliefs of that religion. Therefore, it would amount to favoring one religion over others. On the other hand, the court asserted that the ban on religious garb like the turban did not rule out religious belief, only the repeated expression of it.[147]

The Prohibition Repealed

In 2010, eighty-seven years after the legislation had been passed, a bill came forward in the Oregon legislature to repeal it. The proponents said that the bill would defend religious freedom. It was only fair because public school teachers had been allowed to wear crosses all along.

Opponents of the bill expressed concern that the permission would upset students, undermine parental rights to raise their children in a religion or no religion, and generate lawsuits. The American Civil Liberties Union (ACLU) joined the opposition. It warned that lifting that ban on religious clothing could "result in an inappropriate expansion of religious activity in our public schools." Oregon ACLU director David Fidanque worried that the bill could jeopardize the "religious neutrality" of the schools. He added that the permission would open the door to "Jesus T-shirts" and similar attempts to push religious beliefs in the classroom.[148] Former president of the Oregon ACLU Charles Hinkle warned that there might be an exodus of Christian students from the Oregon schools if Wiccans in "Witch clothes" were allowed to teach.[149]

Despite the opposition, the bill passed. When Governor Ted Kulongoski signed the bill, he appealed to the values of individual beliefs, religious diversity, and tolerance. But he also called for a state policy to ensure that the law was implemented fairly and uniformly.[150]

The Policy for School Districts

The policy that was issued a few months later defines religious clothing as religious dress "worn in accordance with a person's sincerely held religious beliefs." This clothing includes, but is not limited to, scarves, turbans, and other head coverings along with jewelry and emblems. The policy states that it is meant to implement the schools' legal requirements to include students of "all faiths or no faith" while "maintaining the religious neutrality of the educational environment." Therefore, religious garb is now allowed unless it would disturb "religious neutrality" or give the impression that the public schools were endorsing religion.[151]

The policy says that districts have the right to prohibit religious clothing if the wearer intends (or is likely to be perceived to intend) to indoctrinate or proselytize students or if the wearer suggests that the school endorses religion or the wearer's religion. The factors that would demonstrate intent or likely perception include the following:

- the size of the item
- the symbols or writing on the item
- religious statements that go beyond "a limited explanation of the religious significance or obligation associated with the wearing of the religious clothing"

Finally, the religious clothing must not disrupt the educational process, nor intimidate, harass, or coerce, or violate the rights of students, parents, or other employees of the district.[152]

Evaluation of the Case

It would seem that the policy settles the issue of religious clothing in Oregon schools. However, the study of religion might apply critical thinking to the process of the legislation and its implementation. When it does so, it notices strange anomalies in the case.

For one thing, the legislation and policy allows religious clothing unless it disrupts "religious neutrality." In this way, the government tried to balance the teachers' right of religious expression with the school's need to maintain a climate that is neutral to religion. However, less than fifteen years earlier, the Oregon Supreme Court suggested that this balance could not be achieved. The court said that wearing religious clothing was "incompatible" with a learning atmosphere that was neutral to religion.

Furthermore, the ACLU, an organization dedicated to preserving human rights, sided with the law that was left over from anti-Catholic bias in the 1920s.

Like the Oregon Supreme Court, its leaders treated wearing of religious clothing and symbols as a threat to the impartial environment of schools toward religion. They also conjured up scary scenarios of religious mayhem in the schools such as the appearance of "Jesus T-shirts" and "Witch clothes."

These anomalies reveal some hidden assumptions about religion. One presupposition is that religion is best excluded from public life, since it often tends to disrespect the freedom of the individual and impose itself on others. But if religion has to be visible in public life, religious clothing and other signs of religion must be treated as the exception to the norm. The idea is that religious expression in public life must be monitored and contained, lest it get out of hand and become a divisive and coercive force. According to the Oregon Supreme Court, this control of religious expression does not threaten belief. Presumably, one can believe without parading one's belief in public.

The ideal of "religious neutrality" in the public schools reminds us of the French *laïcité* form of secularism. This notion of the absolute separation between religion and public life, perhaps, is the frame of reference of those who worried about the legislation. It weaves together associations of religion with attempts to impose religion on others, disturbance of the public order, conflict, fanaticism, and narrow-mindedness.

However, the proponents of the bill assumed the right of freedom of religious expression. They wanted to reverse an outdated and prejudicial law. They also wanted teachers to enjoy the same rights of freedom to wear religious clothing that had been upheld for other workers. It seems that their attitude toward religion is the opposite of those who opposed the bill. Religion is not a threat. Americans may have differing religious persuasions, but we can all get along if we accept our differences.

The frame of reference here seems to have its center in religious tolerance. The Pew Forum notes that as America becomes increasingly diverse, for the most part, Americans are religiously tolerant. Typically, Americans tend to accept people of other faiths. They find they have to do this, because their family, friends, and neighbors now are taking a widening variety of religious paths. Within the emerging framework of American religious tolerance are associations of religious and cultural diversity, individual choice about how to live one's life, and a "live and let live" philosophy.[153]

The state policy for school districts framed to implement the law tried to balance these two frameworks of meaning about religion. It assumed that the matter was an administrative task requiring uniformity and fairness. Here, the frame of reference was the arena of state government and the political and civic interests it serves. Thus, the policy tried to manage and coordinate what seems like opposing goals and conflicting interest involved in the case.

Evaluating the "No Path" Approach

This case prepares us to evaluate the three strategies of addressing the problem of preconceived webs of associations. This first strategy was to avoid associations altogether, according to the teachings of Yogacara Buddhism or Krishnamurti. This method would focus on immediate experience and direct perception. But it would hardly work in the case given above. All parties to the political and judicial process of the legislation reacted to the issue of religious clothing based on their own network of associations. In fact, these associations were the driving force behind both the support and opposition to the bill. In this volatile situation, it would be impossible to get the people involved to abandon their webs of associations altogether.

According to James, the task of study is to unravel and then reweave the webs of associations so that we have a better understanding of what we are studying. The case, however, shows little concern about understanding the religions involved such as Sikhism (the turban), Islam (the hijab or burqa), and perhaps Judaism (the yarmulke or skullcap). The issue of the legislation was religious *behavior*, not the religion behind it. The policy definitions state that the motive for wearing the clothing must be "sincerely held religious belief." It does not even have to be the belief of a religious group. Thus, the Oregon policy about religious clothing is a generic one that applies to all claims of religious duty. The policy's assumption is that educators do not have to delve into the sense of duty that prompts the action as long as it is genuine.

The "no associations" strategy fits this approach. It suggests that we do not have to trouble ourselves with understanding the religions of others. Both the Oregon legislation and policy on wearing religious clothing and the "no associations" strategy assume that all people have their own personal experiences and their own reasons for believing or not believing. There is no reason to try to understand them.

However, this approach proves to be unsatisfactory. It puts all people in their own private spiritual bubble. The associations embedded in frames of reference may entangle us in bias, but these webs of meaning are the only way of breaking out of the private, spiritual bubble and knowing what the inner experience of others is like. We make sense of things by naming them, associating them with other things, and putting these associations into frames of reference. If we do not do this, raw experience is unintelligible. The challenge of religious studies is to think critically about these frameworks of meaning with the goal of gaining a more informed, reasonable, and fair understanding of religion. This would include a grasp of the reasons that some believers choose to wear religious clothing in the public sphere.

Evaluating the "Many Separate Paths" Approach

The second approach was to treat every religion as a separate thing in itself. In this strategy, each religion represents a distinct circle of meaning. Only those who stand within that circle truly understand it.

When we apply this strategy of "many separate paths" to the case above, we get a sudden realization. In the debates about the legislation, the issue was not why those who desired to wear religious clothing wanted to do so. The idea of religious obligation seemed to be taken for granted. If the legislators and governor had probed further into this question, they might have acquired a better understanding of the religious duty to wear special clothing.

The education policy of implementation, however, goes further into this possibly. It suggests that teachers may give an explanation of their sense of religious duty and the significance of the clothing. However, note that this statement is to be "limited" to the religious clothing. Surprisingly, in their concern to manage the behavior, the educators seem to have missed an educational opportunity. The strategy of "many separate paths" suggests that the interpretation of the religious clothing might lead to broader instruction about the religion of the wearer.

Presumably, the reason the wider teaching is prohibited is that it would favor one religion or that it would be too much of an influence on susceptible students. However, the United States Supreme Court has advised that teaching *about* religion is not prohibited in the United States but to be encouraged. Provided they accept this principle, wearers of religious clothing might offer valuable lessons about their religion to their pupils.

But the larger question about the "many separate paths approach" is whether the understanding of religion is limited to what "insiders" say about their own religions. Are those who wear its religious clothing the only ones qualified to say what the clothing means? Further, must religious studies accept everything that these informants say without question?

Jonathan Z. Smith points out that we tend to regard whatever we think is valuable as unique.[154] We do not like to think that our most precious possessions and we ourselves are just members of some larger categories of things. Yet Smith argues that if we do not put things into categories, we must deal with each thing by itself.[155] If we do not put the religions of the world into categories, their study would be impossible. To gain even a superficial understanding of the staggering number of religions in the world, we would have to study hundreds of distinct sets of ideas.

Fortunately, however, it is easy to find some common features of religion. We do not have to force religion in narrow categories. Studying one religion alone without making comparisons with others is unnecessary and impossible. Further, except in unusual circumstances, religions do not exist in isolation from one another. The history and development of religions involves the interaction of religions with one another. In this interchange, they influence one another. They are not as separate or distinct from one another, as the strategy of "many separate paths" suggests.

Moreover, religions do not come in pure forms. Most of them encompass a wide variety of types. Muslim women hold different opinions on the hijab and burqa. They wear this clothing in a wide variety of styles. The "cover" may be worn for modesty, but Turkey's Tekbir department store has turned the "cover" into high fashion. To understand the "cover," should we ask a clerk at the Tekbir store in Turkey, the wearer of a burqa in Pakistan, or the wearer of a simple headscarf in a classroom in Detroit?[156]

Furthermore, the implications of studying each religion by itself show that this method is impractical. The terms "insider" and "outsider" are relative terms. Whether one is an "insider" or not depends on the religion under consideration. One may be an "outsider" as a Jew but an "insider" as a Buddhist. But what kind of Buddhist? Because of the specific Buddhist tradition one follows, one may be a Buddhist but still be considered an "outsider." Thus, we can say that in most respects, everyone is an "outsider."[157]

The Oregon legislation and policy about religious clothing treat the believers as isolated individuals who have their own reasons for wearing religious garb. The strategy of "many separate paths" suggests that they could be considered "insiders" who could inform others about their religions. A critique of this strategy would admit that the comments of these informants would be valuable. However, their views about their religious beliefs and practices would give an incomplete view of their religion and religion in general. It would be one distinct perspective that would best be set in a wider context of understanding.

Evaluating the "Narrow Path" Approach

One strategy remains. This is the approach of phenomenology exemplified by Rudolf Otto. Phenomenology also seeks to avoid the problems of the predetermined association of ideas. It tries to bracket—that is, to set these prejudicial preconceptions aside. Then it can look at religion as a whole and distinct thing. When Otto used this method, he set religion apart from all human endeavors. It became a special category of human experience with its own interpretations and explanations.

When we apply Otto's method to the case above, we see more clearly that wearing religious clothing is a religious act. The legislation permits it. The policy tries to manage it. But in Otto's view, it has special meaning and makes unique claims because of its religious nature. In this sense, the concerns about the intrusion of the religious into the setting of "religious neutrality" are correct. Wearing religious garb in a public school is a public act that challenges the social order. It is not a neutral statement of the wearer's personal preference. It is no wonder that one-half of the German states prohibit schoolteachers from wearing religious clothing or symbols. Wearing religious clothing is a political act *because* it is a religious one. At minimum, wearing religious garb in public states that religion must be taken seriously in the secular sphere.

If religion deals with a "higher order" of reality that has its own ways and rules, one cannot settle the issue of religious clothing by simply putting it in the framework of toleration. The issue is more than the extent to which society should tolerate or accommodate religion in public places. In Otto's view, religion believes the reality that it knows is "more than" the ordinary world. Since it is transcendent, the realm the "holy" makes ultimate demands on human beings just as it gives an ultimate purpose to human life.

Otto expresses his sense of the demands and purposes of the "holy" within his own rich network of associations. James spoke of the "association of ideas." But Otto's associations are different. They can be called "associations of feelings." In Otto's mind, just as thinking about one idea leads to thinking about several other ideas, feeling one thing produces a number of other feelings.[158]

With this in mind, Otto built a set of associations centered in the feelings that the experience of the "holy" evokes. In Western Judaism and Christianity, for example, the feelings of dread that come from the encounter with the holy are mixed with the ideas of justice and righteousness. This combination of feelings and ideas engenders the concept of the wrath of God.[159] In the same way, the feelings of fascination that the encounter with the holy stirs up are mixed with the ideas of mercy and goodness. The combination produces the notion of the grace of God.[160]

We note that Otto did not see this web of the association of feelings as a problem. He saw it as the key to the understanding of religion. Thus, he did not solve the problem of how to avoid the trap of preconceived frameworks of meaning. In addition, despite his use of the method of phenomenology, Otto considered Christianity to be the most mature of the world's religions.[161] Thus, Otto's ideas of the development of the world's religions turned out to be quite similar to those of the European-centered scholars that we surveyed.

Otto believed that religion is its own domain because it refers to a "higher reality" that is "holy" or "other than" ordinary reality. To him, this meant that only those who have experienced that distinct reality could understand what he was talking about. Ironically, this notion would support the idea that Oregon educators need not try to understand the beliefs of those teachers who want to wear religious clothing in the classroom. If the schools are to stay neutral toward religion, they cannot assume an experience of a "higher reality," and they cannot expect their administrators to have that experience. Therefore, according to Otto's own understanding, they may not have a clue about the religious claims that are the foundation for the sense of duty to wear religious clothing. In the case of the Oregon schools, Otto's strategy, like the others, leads to a dead end. It does not promote the unbiased understanding of religion in the public school setting.

In summary, we must conclude that one of the most powerful attempts to solve the dilemma of bias in the study of religion failed.[162] An analogy with the computer will help explain. Otto's background had already installed the program of Protestant Christian theology in his mind. In order to defend religion against the developing social sciences, Otto clustered the evidence of religions around his notion of a mystical reality, a reality that was inaccessible to scientific investigation. The mysterious, ineffable *numinous* was already built into his mental program. It was an inherited Western framework of meaning. Thus, Otto added the experiences of his travels to the association of ideas he already had. Otto creatively placed his encounters with Eastern religions into the preconceived network of ideas of the Western framework of meaning.

Thus, the most promising solution for studying religion of this chapter seems to disappoint us. We might set our associations of ideas aside and concentrate exclusively on direct experience, each particular religion, or religion in general. However, each strategy fails to help us break free of the web of our own preconceived ideas and gain a fresh understanding of religion.

Today's Religious Situation: The Challenge to Western Assumptions about Religion

The review of the alternative approaches has not found a solution to the problem of this chapter. Yet at least it points out a pitfall in the search for an effective method of study. Treating religion as a separate, unique entity will not help the field of religious studies offer its insights on the dynamics of religion in today's world.

The controversy over the hijab is just one example of the religious dynamics of the twenty-first century. As the issues that this textbook will cover show, religion is no longer content to languish in a separate part of human experience. It has broken out of its private world and is playing an increasingly significant role in public affairs.

The field of religious studies is now facing the challenge of the renewed place of religion in this century. In the past, most scholars of religion accepted the Western view that religion was its own, unique realm of human experience. Some even felt that religion was a relic of the past. Many defined religion as if it were a substantial thing, existing in itself. Quite a few abstracted the central beliefs of religious people (Brahman, Allah, God, Tao, Nirvana, Ahura Mazda, etc.) into the special vocabulary of the numinous, the totem, the transcendental, and so on. Almost all treated religions as static, isolated, separate, and, for the most part, irrelevant to the course of human events. Nowadays, however, religion is breaking free of these dominating Western conceptions about it.

The academic study of religion has much work to do to keep up with the course of events. The vigor of the global religious resurgence is driving a wedge in the wall of separation between the religious and the secular. The case of the "cover" in Europe and America reveals cracks in the barrier between private religion and public life. Secularism is struggling to keep religion out of the public square. Likewise, modernism is striving to contain religions in their separate and private boxes. However, these efforts can no longer keep religion in check.

Furthermore, religious people across the globe have begun to speak in their own voice and on their own terms. If postcolonial studies have exposed the legacy of Western colonialism, various groups have found religion to be a handy tool against it. Muslim women are protesting against the ban of the hijab and burqa in secularist states from France to Turkey. Native Americans are taking measures to recover their own religious objects while demanding the right to pray without restriction or interference on their sacred lands. In the United States, South America, Europe, Africa, China, and the Far East, religious diversity is changing the religious landscape that was once dominated by one or two religions or by secularism.

To the surprise of the secularists, religion is showing its persistence and resilience. Contrary to the dominant Western outlook, today's religions, whether conservative or liberal, are proving that they are dynamic movements. They are not static sets of beliefs. The past study of religion founded on the Enlightenment mind-set has treated religions as objects for investigation. Now religions are pushing back as subjects against the objectifications and generalizations that attempted to tame them.

Religions are interacting with one another on the world stage. Unfortunately, this exchange is more in the marketplace than in the classroom, more in the circles of friends and families than in the academic forum, and more in the political arena than in the scholar's study. Yet the discussions going on in these surprising places show that religions are not insular worldviews. They are not strangers or mysteries to one another, as some have supposed. Most often in world history, religions have been in dialogue with one another through the transactions between their cultures, societies, and believers.

With all this going on, the field of religious studies has the task of changing some of the Western habits of thought that have shaped it. If religion is no longer a separate sphere of human experience, the field of religious studies can no longer think of itself as a separate academic discipline. Religious studies scholar Russell McCutcheon envisions scholars of religion as "public intellectuals" who apply critical thinking to the changing place of religion in global affairs. The increasing power and influence of religion calls for this new role. In McCutcheon's view, the field of religious studies must do more than it has in the past: describe, interpret, and defend religion. It must use its methods and tools to probe and question the ways that religion sanctions, empowers, and shapes the institutions and ways of life of contemporary societies.[163]

Emerging Questions in the Changing Religious Situation

The new state of religion in the world raises some questions that require some new thoughts about religion and its role in the world. We might ask how religion has become so pervasive in modern life when secularism had boxed it in a corner. More questions come to mind. What is the relationship of the resurgence of religion to secularism and to postcolonialism? Who can speak authentically and teach authoritatively about religion or any given religion? What are the rights of religious freedom? How can they be guaranteed in an age of religious diversity? How can the conflicts over religion be resolved? What is the relationship between religion and politics, economics, social structures, and cultural identity? How can we understand the inner spiritual life of religion and the trend toward spirituality? What is the relationship of an individual's participation in religion to social behavior, morality, health, class, and sense of identity?

Checks on Assumptions and Associations:
The Strategy of Multiple Perspectives

The list of questions continues to build. Scholars of religion are naturally interested in them. However, there is a pressing need for the public to gain some understanding of these questions and their answers. Preacher and theologian Peter Gomes (1942–2011) told the Harvard Divinity School, where he taught for many years, "It is urgent that . . . religious analysis be provided in a world where religions and their policies are front-page news in nearly every cultural climate, domestic or foreign. Never more than today have we needed every resource available to combat religious illiteracy."[164]

This chapter proposes that the field of religious studies is uniquely qualified to address the need for the education of the public about religion. It can provide an interpretation and critique of the increasing role of religion in public life. It can offer some helpful insights into the growing religious diversity of today's global society. Finally, it can teach the application of critical thinking to the claims, questions, and issues of religion so that hasty, uninformed, and erroneous conclusions can be avoided.

To achieve these things, scholars must widen the scope of their study to encompass all the arenas in which religion is appearing in today's world. For example, the issue of the Muslim "cover" involves much more than personal, inward religious feelings associated with ideas of the numinous. The range of issues in which religion is entangled includes politics, society, economics, education, institutions, and cultural identity as well as religious symbolism, ritual, belief, and affiliation.

To carry out its new role in public life as well as in the classroom, the field of religious studies faces the challenge involved in all learning. As William James advises, all who study religion academically must break apart their present network of ideas. Then they must construct new webs of knowledge in new frameworks of meaning. This is a continual but engaging problem for instructors as well as students.

This chapter has reviewed and evaluated a variety of approaches to religion with that challenge in mind. The failure to find a useable solution to the problem of the bias of webs of association leads to a conclusion. Perhaps no single approach to study will solve the dilemma of the limitations of thought in the study of religion. The solution to overcoming built-in bias may not be a single method. An effective approach to study may have to use many methods and a variety of perspectives.

Scholars in the field of religious studies are working on methods of checking their assumptions as they investigate religious topics. Their ongoing efforts include a critique of the development of the study of religion and an ongoing debate about the nature of religion. Many have concluded that no single method of study can encompass the wide scope of current issues of religion in this century. Therefore, they use the concept of *multiple perspectives* to describe the variety of disciplines that the field must use. These academic disciplines include anthropology, archeology, textual studies, psychology, sociology, philology, political science, business and economics, and theology. The advantage of this wide assortment of approaches to study is that viewing the subject through multiple lenses makes it possible for scholars to see it from different sides. Then, in addition, the findings of one discipline serve to check the findings of another.

A Learning Strategy for Religious Studies

1. Gain a "stock of ideas" to think about.
2. Pay attention to ideas that are especially disagreeable.
3. Think about the implications of the ideas for life in today's world.

(Adapted from *Talks to Teachers* by William James)

In his *Talks to Teachers*, William James suggests a program for helping students "think rightly."[165] He advises the following: First, supply the students with a "stock of ideas." Second, promote their "voluntary attention" as long as possible to ideas that they may find "unpalatable." Third, train students in patterns of action to implement these ideas.

This textbook will offer its readers the resources to engage in this process of learning as it introduces the fundamentals of the academic study of religion. It will present a selection of ideas, information, concepts, and perspectives as a starting point for the study of religion. These will give the reader a *store of information and ideas* to think about as he or she tries to understand religion in the twenty-first century. In addition, the book will attempt to *fix the reader's attention* on some unfamiliar ideas and perplexing controversies about religion. These will challenge the reader's viewpoints on religion. Moreover, to stimulate interest in further exploration, this text will probe for gaps, glitches, and contradictions in the typical thinking about religion in today's society. Finally, the book will not neglect *the implications* of what it presents. It will especially attempt to show the relevance of the information, ideas, and methods for the course of events in the twenty-first century.

This textbook invites its readers to join the ongoing academic deliberation about religion and its dynamics in the current world situation. Though this book is an introduction to the academic study of religion, the next chapters will engage readers in thinking about contemporary issues that matter to contemporary people. As it does so, it will cover many of the basic topics, theories, and methods of the field of religious studies. The goal will be to give the reader the intellectual tools to study religion in a fair, reasoned, and insightful way. In general, the book will engage its readers in the struggle that this chapter has introduced. It will strive to unravel preconceived networks of assumptions and to knit together new and wider webs of meaning for understanding religion in the twenty-first century.

KEY TERMS

Association theory of learning: the theory that to learn something new we must fit it into a web of ideas that already exists in our minds.

Assumption: a proposition that people take for granted to be true and on which they base their reasons for what they believe.

Empiricism: the ideology that claims that human knowledge comes through observation of the senses and is tested by experimentation.

The Enlightenment: the period of the 1700s (eighteenth century) in which the scientific method and human reason replaced religious authority as the standards of truth and knowledge.

Essentialism: the reasoning that everything in a class of things has the same defining characteristics.

Frames of reference: sets of ideas and attitudes into which we fit facts, information, and experiences and so understand their meaning.

Hijab: popularly, the headscarf Muslim women wear for modesty.

Laïcité: the French form of secularism that enforces a clear-cut and absolute separation of religion and public life.

Naturalism: the approach to the study of religion that treats religion as a purely human enterprise and that seeks human explanations for religious phenomena instead of appealing to supernatural causes.

Numinous: Rudolf Otto's term for the uncanny and unsettling presence and power of the sacred.

Oedipal conflict: the ambivalent feelings of a boy's sexual attraction to his mother and rivalry with his father.

Orientalism: the European approach to the study of the Middle East and Far East that treats them as strange, exotic, and captivating in their difference from the advanced and familiar Western world.

Phenomenology: the study of subjects as they appear without interpretations or explanations. In religion, the study of religious ways from the viewpoint of those who practice them without trying to explain them.

Postcolonialism: a loose set of ideas and theories associated with the aftermath and response to the imperialism of colonialism in lands once held by dominating colonial powers.

Postmodernism: a hard-to-define movement that is unified by its reaction to the modernist assumption of the objective certainty of scientific, rational, and universal knowledge.

Projection: in psychology, the mental mechanism by which humans attribute their feelings, attitudes, or traits onto something or someone else.

Psychic unity of the human race: the idea that all humans reason in the same basic ways, regardless of culture, time, or place.

Rationalism: the movement originating in the Enlightenment that identified logical reason as the sole source and means of human knowledge instead of either the senses or divine revelation.

Religionist (approaches): methods of studying religion that seek to understand religion according to the ways that religious adherents interpret and explain it.

The religious and the secular: in thesis secularization, two spheres of life that must be kept separate in order to avoid religious conflict and coercion.

Secularism: the commitment to the independence of life in society from religion. Secularists believe that knowledge, values, morality, as well as government have no need for religion. Religion is an unnecessary and potentially harmful element in public life.

Social facts: for Durkheim, the values, morals, customs, and beliefs that society imposes on its members with such force that they seem to be facts.

Theological study: methods of studying religion according to sets of truth claims held by religious believers.

Totem: for Durkheim, the most revered emblem of a society, a concrete representation of the group's life and solidarity.

Worldview: a total way of looking at reality and all that is in it given by one's culture.

Yogacara Buddhist School: a "mind only" school of thought that distinguishes immediate experience from the interpretations and conclusions that the mind creates from experience.

KEY QUESTIONS

1. Apperception (Theory of Learning by Association)
   a. William James said that it is not possible to learn anything without forming associations with the ideas that we already know. Can you think of something new that you learned without such an association? Explain why you can or cannot do this.
   b. Think of an example in which someone made a mistake by forming the wrong or limited associations such as calling snow "sugar." What was the reason for the mistake?
2. The French and American Views of Religion and the Secular
   a. What idea of religion did the French government have when it passed a law against wearing "conspicuous" religious symbols in government run schools?
   b. How is the America idea of religion (defined by the Supreme Court) and the secular different from the French view? How does the view affect policies about religious clothing in public schools?
3. The Religious and the Secular
   a. For John Locke and other Enlightenment thinkers, what problem about religion did the division between the religious and the secular solve?
   b. Explain why Locke advised the governments of his day that they did not have to bother with religion.
   c. What if religions refuse to be confined to the religious sphere? Would Locke's advice still hold?
4. Essentialism and the Enlightenment
   a. Explain why Kant's approach to religion is a form of essentialism.
5. Orientalism
   a. What role did F. Max Mueller play in the development of Orientalism?
   b. What role did Edward Said play in the loss of popularity of Orientalism?
6. The Naturalistic Study of Religion
   a. What is the difference between naturalistic and religionist approaches to the study of religion?
   b. What was F. Max Mueller's goal for the study of religion? How did this goal lead the study of religion down the path of naturalism?
7. Durkheim
   a. Why is religion a set of "social facts," according to Durkheim?
   b. What totems, if any, still serve to give social cohesion to the United States?
   c. Are these totems strong enough to unite the American society? Defend your answer.
8. Feuerbach and Marx
   a. Why did Feuerbach think that religion was harmful to human life?
   b. Why did Marx think that religion was harmful human life?
   c. Compare your answers. What ideas did Feuerbach and Marx share? What ideas were different?

9. Freud
    a. In Freud's view, how are religions like dreams? Why could he analyze religions in the same way he analyzed dreams?
    b. In Freud's view, what is the final state of human development and the development of religion? Describe what it means to "think scientifically."
10. "Outsider/Insider" Approaches
    a. Wilfred Cantwell Smith proposed that if insiders who practice a religion do not accept a statement about the religion, then that statement is not valid. Evaluate this principle.
    b. Are "insiders" necessarily more informed about their religion than "outsiders"? Explain.
11. Rudolf Otto and Phenomenology
    a. What is phenomenology, and how did Rudolf Otto use it to study religion?
    b. What are the basic human responses to the sacred according to Otto?
12. Challenges to Western Assumptions about Religion
    a. How is the global resurgence of religion challenging the Western ideas of religion and its separation of "church and state"?
    b. What new questions are being raised about the role of religion in human life in the twenty-first century?
    c. What methods of studying religion might be used to answer these questions?

❸

Would You Believe!
Religious Beliefs and Their Reasons

CHAPTER SUMMARY

1. Defining the Problem: Opinions without Sufficient Evidence

By definition, evidence from the senses cannot test religious beliefs. In the absence of the checks of empirical evidence from the senses, religious believers can believe in just about anything—and do. The religious diversity of today's global society makes it difficult to sort out and make sense of the bewildering variety of beliefs that people can choose. The task of religious studies is not to judge the truth of beliefs but to think critically about them. It is to make some rational sense of beliefs and their meaning for believers. Within the growing diversity of beliefs, the most popular idea is that religious beliefs are merely personal opinion. But that idea does not help us understand why opinions can be called "religious." The problem is to find a meaningful approach to understanding the nature of religious beliefs and why believers hold them.

2. Focusing the Problem: What Is the Nature of Religious Belief When People Are Free to Believe Anything?

Current surveys show that people in the United States continue to hold traditional Western beliefs in God, angels, heaven, hell, and the devil. A higher percentage of U.S. believers claim these beliefs than do those in Canada and Great Britain. However, research shows that there is a growing division between religious belief and religious membership. Many believers no longer choose to belong to religious organizations: they both believe and attend worship services "without belonging." Moreover, despite the teaching of established religious authorities, surprising percentages of Americans believe in paranormal beliefs not sanctioned by traditional religion.

Traditionally, religious institutions have defined and managed religious belief. The new trends present a challenge to scholars of religion. When religious belief is a matter of self-chosen opinion, then beliefs can include traditional religious teachings, paranormal phenomena, or even Santa Claus. If this is the case, why are some opinions considered worthy of being called "religious" and some not? Another way to put the question is whether the academic study of religions can tell the difference between traditional and paranormal beliefs.

3. Surveying the Alternative Approaches: The Justification of Religious Belief

In an attempt to understand the nature of religious belief this section will explore how believers justify their beliefs. At the extremes, fideism claims there is no need to justify one's belief. On the other hand, evidentialism claims that beliefs cannot be justified, because they lack sufficient evidence. Between these poles are the appeals to revelation or enlightenment, to authority, and to religious experience.

The evaluation of these approaches shows that the appeals satisfy those on the inside of the circle of faith who are disposed to believe. However, in a situation of religious diversity, "outsiders" ask why a particular message of revelation, insight of enlightenment, authority, or religious experience should be given more credibility than other foundations of belief, especially when they contradict one another. Granted, believers may claim their beliefs are self-justifying or that they rest on a higher authority. But what sense do they make to "outsiders"? These methods of justifying beliefs do not solve the problem of the nature of religious beliefs and how to make sense of them in the twenty-first century.

4. Proposing the Most Promising Solution: Beliefs and the Questions They Answer

Turning to the content of religious beliefs, this section will propose a method of interpreting the meaning of religious beliefs. It will assume that religious beliefs are answers to the most important and universal questions of human existence. That is, they are answers to "ultimate questions." Believers choose these beliefs not because they want to believe in fantasy, but because they address the situations that threaten their essential sense of the foundation, significance, and direction of their lives.

The suggested method gives a way of organizing the claims of religious beliefs and comparing them by means of the questions that they address. The chapter will show how the method works as it considers the questions of the origins and order of the universe, freedom and determinism, and suffering.

5. Evaluating the Most Promising Solution: Ways of Seeing and Ways of Life

The proposed method organizes beliefs into sets according to the questions they answer. But it still does not answer why believers should choose one set of answers over another, especially in an age where believers are freeing themselves from religious authority.

A test case asks whether one can predict whether believers in traditional beliefs will be more or less likely to believe in paranormal beliefs. It finds that one cannot tell the difference between the two sets on the basis of how believers justify their beliefs or the content of beliefs in themselves.

The proposed method gives a clue about the missing factor that can distinguish between personal opinions and religious beliefs. This section suggests that religious studies should focus on the meaning of beliefs to the lives of believers. This emphasis changes the common definition of religious belief. These beliefs would no longer be considered opinions lacking provable evidence. Instead, religious studies would think of beliefs as ways of thinking, perceiving, and knowing that change the lives of believers.

This insight offers a test that would distinguish religious beliefs from other notions: religious beliefs matter to the lives of believers. We can call a conviction "religious" when the believers treat it as a matter of ultimate significance so that it makes a profound difference in their lives. This test promises to help scholars of religion sort through the opinions and make sense of the diversity of beliefs in our global society.

DEFINING THE PROBLEM: OPINIONS WITHOUT SUFFICIENT EVIDENCE

Most of us distinguish beliefs from facts. Beliefs are opinions that we cannot prove. Facts are provable. Likewise, Western philosophy distinguishes uncertain belief from certain knowledge.[1] In this view, certain knowledge is based on sufficient evidence. Belief cannot be justified by reference to provable evidence.

The *Times* of London once asked some scientists to confess what they believed but could not prove. Cognitive neuroscientist Sarah-Jayne Blackmore said she believed in free will despite scientific evidence to the contrary. Fertility expert Lord Winston said he believed that religiosity is genetically determined in part. Neuroscientist and pharmacologist Susan Greenfield said she believed that "the good guy" would finally triumph. Former astronomer royal Sir Arnold Wolfendale said he believed but could not prove that God exists. Gerontologist Raymond Tallis said that he believed but could not prove that material things exist apart from his own perception of them. Sir John Krebs, principal of Jesus College, Oxford, said he believed that Mozart was a better composer than the less familiar composer Carl Stamitz. Furthermore, evolutionary biologist Armand Leroi claimed without proof that the first song that came from the lips of a human being was a yodel.[2]

The Immorality of Belief

"It Is wrong in all cases to believe on insufficient evidence."

—William K. Clifford

According to an often-quoted remark by William K. Clifford, all of these scientists are not merely mixed up, they are wrong. In his essay, "The Ethics of Belief," Clifford said, "It is wrong in all cases to believe on insufficient evidence."[3] He added that people might think that it is wrong to question what they take for granted. However, it is better to check out a truth claim than to risk accepting something that may be false.[4]

In daily life, we have to accept many truths that we cannot verify for ourselves. In these cases, we are wrong to believe something unless at least someone could conceivably make sure it was right.[5] For instance, whatever we do, we have to believe that nature is reliable and will not trick us. How could we get through the day unless we believed in a certain uniformity of the laws of nature? At an early age, we learn that if fire is hot and burns us, it will do so whenever we get too close to it. On the other hand, we learn that if ice cream tastes good the first time, it probably will not disappoint us the second or even twenty-third time. By such reasoning, we can conclude all sorts of things about the universe. If hydrogen produces certain readings on a spectrometer on Earth, then the same readings from the sun will indicate the presence of hydrogen there. Therefore, it cannot be wrong to believe in things that one has not experienced. It is only wrong to believe in things that reliable evidence could not possibly confirm.

When it comes to religious belief, however, it seems that all bets are off. How can religious beliefs appeal to reliable evidence? Whatever evidence religion would offer would fail the test of the evidence Clifford has in mind. Religious beliefs concern realities that transcend the senses, and states of consciousness that transcend the ordinary mind. So how could we possibly check them out by any ordinary perception, routine test, or conventional logic? For example, religious believers might suppose that miracles prove their faith. However, miracles violate the rule of the uniformity of nature. Miracles are arbitrary instances of divine intervention: they are unrepeatable, unreliable, and not subject to testing according to the laws of nature.

Religion can actually prosper because of the improvable nature of its claims. Since nothing can be proven, everything can be believed. Religious claims have distinctive status. They are received from revelation, inspiration, or enlightenment. Then they are handed down from one person to another in a chain that goes back to the gods or the ancient sages. This unique standing seems to authorize those who believe them to transgress the limits of human reason and common sense. As a result, religious belief can thrive without bothering to prove itself. As one might expect, religious beliefs multiply into a bewildering assortment of religious beliefs that are often contradictory, fantastic, and unfathomable.

The Definition of Belief

These initial thoughts suggest a problem for the academic study of belief. This problem comes to the surface when we attempt to define belief. In general, the definition of belief involves three interrelated terms: *belief, faith,* and *doubt.* In English, *belief* and *faith* are usually interchangeable words. However, in the sixteenth century, the Protestant Reformation began to distinguish belief and faith. Using the thought of Augustine, the Protestants taught that belief was an intellectual assent to revealed truth. In *belief,* the mind accepts religious truth claims without the support of empirical evidence from the senses. On the other hand, *faith* goes beyond mere assent. The Reformers defined *faith* as the personal trust in something or someone deemed worthy of trust. As absolute trust, faith calls for more emotional investment than intellectual agreement. Moreover, faith involves the will. As the Danish philosopher Søren Kierkegaard (1813–1855) emphasized, the believer must make a willful "leap of faith," a leap into what the unbeliever would call the "absurd."

These terms lead to questions about the relationship of belief and faith to knowledge and doubt. An overemphasis on the subjective side of faith would lead to the idea that faith has nothing to do with knowledge. Yet religions teach that faith is not such an empty container into which the believer can pour unrelated bits of nonsense. Even those religions that emphasize subjective faith teach faith *in* a Supreme Being, sacred reality, or higher consciousness.

If faith must involve commitment to a special kind of knowledge, then it must also entail doubt about it. Suppose Joe accepts a truth claim without a shred of doubt. He would no longer believe it. He would know it "for certain." However, the possibility of certain knowledge that eliminates doubt is practically impossible.[6] Religious believers must accept the risk that they may be wrong, misguided, or deluded. Therefore, though necessary, intellectual assent is not enough to make religious belief. One must have enough faith to be willing to invest in the truth or reality of what one believes.

Perhaps the Western theologian Anselm (1033–1103 CE) offered the most thought-provoking statement of the relationship of faith and knowledge as rational understanding. He said, "I believe that I may understand." Suppose I say the opposite, "I understand so that I may believe." If I say this, then religious belief is tied to what my rational mind can grasp. However, religious belief deals with the unseen and unknown. If I "believe in order to understand," then religious faith opens up the knowledge of things beyond what we know in ordinary thought.

This is a "different knowledge" than the ordinary knowledge that we can gain through the senses. If so, then it follows that we cannot use ordinary knowledge to make sense of it. The Western mind-set might answer that there is no need to go through the mental strain of doing so. After all, religious beliefs are only personal opinions. As long as we do not try to impose the personal opinions that we hold on someone else, we should be allowed to believe anything we want.

Yet the field of religious studies cannot be satisfied with this answer. Scholars of religion are interested in understanding what people believe and why they believe at all. On a deeper level, the field seeks to probe the nature of religious beliefs and why believers are justified in holding them. In this way, the academic study of religion sets out to think critically about belief to make some rational sense out of it. How can the discipline of religious studies give a reasonable account of such mind-numbing clutter? The problem is to find a meaningful approach to understanding the nature of religious belief, the beliefs religious people hold, and the reasons they do so.

FOCUSING THE PROBLEM: WHAT IS THE NATURE OF RELIGIOUS BELIEF WHEN PEOPLE ARE FREE TO BELIEVE ANYTHING?

We have shown in another chapter that Western scholarship has focused on religious beliefs, assuming that they are the foundation of religion. The Enlightenment set out to replace religious superstition with scientific knowledge. In spite of Enlightenment suspicion that religious beliefs were superstition, belief has survived, especially in America. Surveys show that Americans hold a surprising variety of religious beliefs. The percentages of those who hold such beliefs are high. They have remained remarkably stable even in the twenty-first century.

The Variety and Stability of American Beliefs

We can put the beliefs into three categories: (1) God, (2) traditional (Western) religious beliefs, and (3) paranormal and occult beliefs.

Table 3.1 shows a substantial percentage of Americans believe in God or a Universal Spirit. The trend, however, has declined somewhat from 98 percent in the 1950s and 1960s to 91 percent. This decline might continue, as 84 percent of young persons ages eighteen to twenty-nine say that they believe. Moreover, the number of those who say they disbelieve has grown from 1 percent in 1967 to 8 percent in 2011.[7] When given a choice, 12 percent of Americans will say they believe in a "Universal Spirit" rather than the concept of "God." Nevertheless, the numbers of Americans who profess belief in God or a "Higher Power" remain remarkably high.[8]

Table 3.1.   American Belief in God or a Universal Spirit

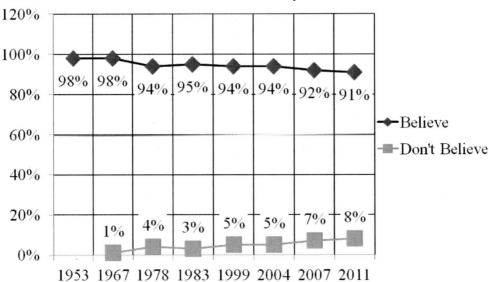

The Gallup surveys also found that Americans say that they hold many religious beliefs in other things besides God. Table 3.2 shows that two in three Americans believe in these spiritual realities.

Surprisingly, since 1994, American belief in the devil has gone up from 65 percent to 70 percent. Table 3.3 shows that increasing belief in the devil is a long-term trend.[9]

On the other hand, belief in angels in the United States has remained about the same at about three in four Americans. But belief in both heaven and hell has gone down. Surprisingly, these beliefs are not parallel because 12 percent more Americans believe in heaven than hell.[10]

People in the United States seem to be more inclined to affirm traditional Western beliefs than citizens of other North American and European countries. This is evident in the comparison of British and Canadian beliefs (see table 3.4).[11] In the United States, the percentage of beliefs in spiritual realities never drops below 70 percent. In Great Britain, the religious belief never rises above 52 percent. In Canada, it never rises above 71 percent. Excluding the belief in God, the *average* percentage of Americans who do not believe in these realities is 14 percent. In Great Britain, that average is 46 percent, almost half of the population. In Canada, it is 33 percent, one-third of the population.

The Shifting Sands of Religious Membership

Religious beliefs persist in America despite shifts in the involvement of Americans in religious organizations. In recent decades, a gap has appeared between religious beliefs and belonging to religious organizations. A Pew Forum survey found that nearly half of all Americans have left the religious affiliation of their childhood. Among those who were in the same religious group in which they

Table 3.2. American Belief in the Devil, Angels, Heaven, and Hell

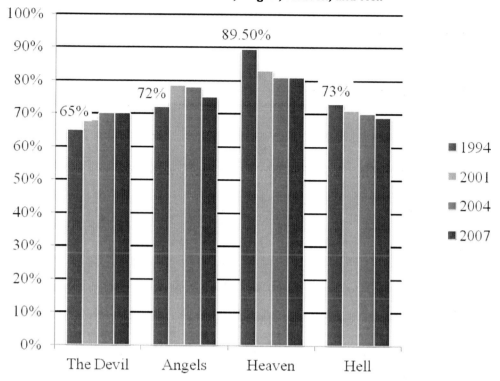

Table 3.3. Belief in the Devil Compared with Belief in Angels since 1957

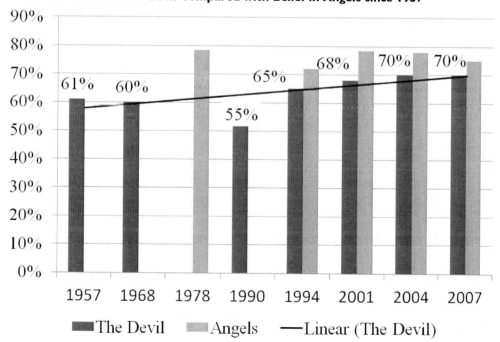

Table 3.4. Comparison of Beliefs: United States, Canada, and Great Britain

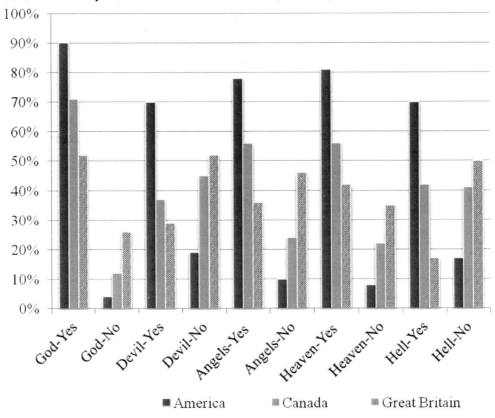

were raised, 16 percent had left the group but came back. In all, six in ten Americans have changed their religious membership at some time in their lives.[12]

Most of those who have switched are young Americans. If they are going to change membership, most Americans will do it before they reach the age of twenty-four. By the age of thirty-six, most have settled in to their current religious affiliation. Hardly any changed after they reached the age of fifty.[13]

We might expect that the membership declines and changes would mean that Americans are no longer showing up for religious services. Though attendance rates have fallen off from their record highs in the 1950s, religious attendance has not declined nearly as much as religious membership. Surveys consistently show that over 40 percent of Americans say that they have attended a religious service in the past week. These rates have remained stable since 1990.[14]

These statistics suggest that Americans are still attending religious services but more of them are attending as nonmembers. In fact, many Americans are attending the services of more than one religious group. Six in ten Americans who attend services once or twice a month attend services of different religious organizations: in fact, four in ten attend services of religions other than their own.[15] This practice shows that attendance can remain strong even though membership falls off.

Strangely, for the most part, the slump in religious membership has not affected the strength of American beliefs. Changes in religious beliefs are not the main reason for dropping out of religious membership. Less than half the unaffiliated said that they do not belong to religious organizations because they disagree with their religious teachings. Less than one in three said that the reason they left their former religious organization was that they realized that religion was based on superstition.[16] And, among the unaffiliated, only one in four say that they are atheists who deny the existence of God or agnostics who say humans cannot know if God exists.[17]

Believing and Attending but Not Belonging

We are finding that the downturn of American religious membership does not match the persistence of religious belief. Further exploration discovers the idea that belief can even be separated from belonging altogether. Grace Davie coined the phrase "believing without belonging" to explain why people in Great Britain claimed belief in God but did not attend worship services.[18] More and more, the phrase can be used for Americans.

There are two ways that surveys have defined religious belonging: one is formal membership and the other is religious identification. Since 1999, formal *membership* in American churches and synagogues has declined 9 percent.[19] Currently, 64 percent of the American population claims membership in a church or synagogue. (If other religions are taken into account, that percentage would increase but not significantly.) The numbers are higher when Americans are asked to name their religion—that is, their religious *identification*. In 1990, 8 percent of Americans answered that they were "atheist, agnostic, or no religion in particular."[20] Now, however, the percent of those who do not claim a religion has doubled to 16 percent. This is a growing phenomenon. One in four Americans ages eighteen to twenty-nine fit in this group, and it is now the fourth-largest religious group in America.

Recent polls also attest to the separation of belief from religious membership in this century. Despite the marked changes in membership and identification discussed above, beliefs have fallen only about 3 percent in the same period. In America, six in ten of those who have no religious membership say they are "certain" or "fairly certain" of the existence of God or a "Universal Spirit."[21] One in four say that they believe that the Bible is the "Word of God." One in five say they pray daily. In addition, only one in three of the unaffiliated say that they never attend religious services.[22]

Americans have found a way to describe this new notion of "believing without belonging." Many claim to be "spiritual but not religious." This new distinction associates "religion" with participation in religious institutions. The claim is that one can be religious in one's own way without organizational restrictions. That is, one can be "spiritual." The phrase carries a rejection of formal religious rituals, organizations, and teachings. Free of the dictates of formal authority, those who claim to be "spiritual but not religious" have open access to a world of religious resources for their "spiritual journey."

While the term was unheard of until the end of the last century, 30 percent of Americans now describe themselves as "spiritual but not religious."[23] Moreover, almost three in four young adults between the ages of eighteen and twenty-nine think of themselves in this way.

These findings show that beliefs have remained remarkably stable for several decades. The ties of religious membership have weakened, while attendance at worship services remains consistent. Beliefs in the paranormal, however, have grown significantly.

Beliefs Further Out

Further evidence that religious believing and belonging to religious organizations do not go together seems to come from surveys of the paranormal beliefs of Americans. One would assume that those who belong to and/or attend the services of religious organizations would follow their teachings. But that assumption presupposes that religious belief, attending, and belonging go together. However, we are finding that this is not the case. The astounding percentages of Americans who believe in paranormal phenomena seem to prove that Americans are so disposed to belief that they will affirm notions well beyond the teachings of the religious organizations they belong to or attend.

Note that eight in ten Americans identify themselves with some Christian tradition. Remember that, typically, Christianity rejects beliefs in the paranormal that lie outside its doctrine. Yet the Gallup polls show that three in four Americans believe in paranormal phenomena. Table 3.5 shows the wide range of American beliefs.[24] In this table, *mental telepathy* means communication by thoughts without the use of words. *Clairvoyance* refers to the ability to "see" into the past or future. *Astrology* refers to ways of knowing the course of events on Earth by the positions and movements of the stars. *Channeling* means spirit possession of the body.

Table 3.5.   American Beliefs in the Paranormal

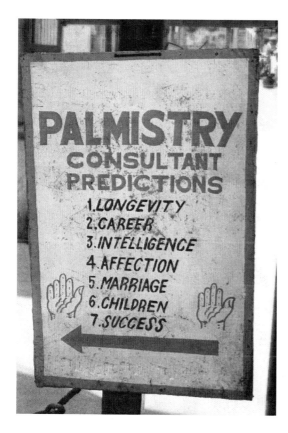

A sign for a palm reading shop. More than 25 percent of Americans believe in clairvoyance— the ability to see into the past or future.

By 2001, the percentages of Americans who believed in one or more of the paranormal notions increased noticeably over the previous decade.[25] Since then, the percentages have remained at the relatively high levels of the turn of the century. Almost six in ten Americans believe in at least two of the above phenomena. One in three believes in at least four of them.[26] Moreover, over one-half of American church members hold at least one of these beliefs.[27]

An analysis of these findings identifies a single, primary dynamic of American religious belief in the twenty-first century. The disconnection between religious beliefs and formal church membership is a growing trend. Increasingly, Americans find that they can attend religious services as well as hold religious beliefs without belonging to religious institutions. The principle of "spiritual not religious" expresses the rationale for the separation of what was connected only a few decades ago.

The Problem Stated

These findings give shape to the problem that the topic of beliefs has raised. We began with the question of how we make sense of the widening range of beliefs of America. To do this, we must understand the nature of religious belief itself. This question is tied to the topic of how believers justify their beliefs.

Clifford's maxim suggests that "when it come to belief, anything goes," since opinions cannot be proven by evidence. That would mean that the individual believer defines the nature of religious belief and how it is justified. The findings above seem to confirm this suspicion. When religious belief is tied to religious institutions, then these organizations define the nature and content of belief. The theology of each religious group gives an account of its beliefs just as it dictates what "true" belief is for its members. However, when individuals claim to choose religious beliefs and practices for themselves without the supervision of religious organizations, then it seems that all bets are off. This insight raises the question of how to make sense of this range of opinions. Why can items in this variety of opinions be called "religious"?

Another way of asking the questions is that the line between traditional religious beliefs (like God, the devil, angels, heaven and hell) and paranormal beliefs (like ESP, ghosts, and mental telepathy) is becoming blurred. Even many who belong to traditional Western religions are choosing beliefs from each category. What makes beliefs, whether traditional or paranormal, "religious" and, therefore, different from believing in leprechauns, Klingons, and Santa Claus?

It seems that the only answer to what makes belief "religious" is individual choice. The United States government refers to this idea when it appeals to "sincerely held belief." In this view, belief is merely personal preference. Yet the answer of personal preference begs the question of the reasons for believing. We might as well say that the choice of belief makes no rational sense. If so, then religious belief is a choice of assertions of nonsense.

Is there a way to tell the difference between religious beliefs and other opinions? Or do individuals arbitrarily choose to believe in heaven but not hell, ESP but not channeling, and angels and reincarnation? If we could answer this question, perhaps we could gain a more reasoned understanding of the nature of religious belief and why religious people believe the way they do.

SURVEYING THE ALTERNATIVE APPROACHES: THE JUSTIFICATION OF RELIGIOUS BELIEF

Two questions come together in the issue of how to tell the difference between traditional and paranormal beliefs. The first is how to make sense of the bewildering variety of religious beliefs in today's world. The second is the nature of religious beliefs. These come together in the question of why believers believe what they do. That is, how do they choose their religious beliefs from a range of options and justify their choices as religious? The field of religious studies does not answer these questions in terms of theology, since theology accepts the assumptions of particular religions. The discipline of religious studies does not hold or defend any particular set of truth claims. Its task is to think critically about the nature of these claims and why believers justify their choices of them.

Alternative Justifications of Religious Beliefs

1. Fideism (belief in belief)
2. Revelation from without
3. Enlightenment from within
4. Appeal to authority: the spiritual master or religious institution

Fideism: Belief in (Sincere) Belief

The first approach is to set aside the need for any justification at all. If asked why they believe what they do, many people of faith would answer that they "just believe" those things on the list that they believe.

In this option, called fideism, religious belief is self-justifying. In popular terms, this principle means that whether one is sincere is the only test of belief. In scholarly terms, the French mathematician and philosopher Blaise Pascal (1623–1662 CE) argued that true religious belief is beyond proof. Pascal stated that even *if* human philosophy could prove the existence of God by its logic or evidence, it would still not arrive at faith in the God revealed in the Bible. In the same vein, the Muslim philosopher and mystic al-Ghazali[28] (1058–1111 CE) taught that reason must give way to revelation whenever reason might come into conflict with the message of the prophets.

Fideism springs from the idea that there is a vast difference between the transcendent reality of the sacred and the human capacity to know it. For that reason, this way of justifying belief recognizes the limits of human reason. Yet, though fideism doubts the capabilities of human reason, it believes in the exceptional power of religious faith. Faith glimpses the mystery of the sacred, a mystery that the human mind cannot grasp. On this basis, religious belief tends to disparage the human intellect.[29] Those who refuse to justify their beliefs think that human reason cannot perceive the sacred. More than that, they believe that reliance on reason can block the sacred from view.

Few believers would own up to being irrational. They would only claim that belief goes *beyond* the rational. This claim asserts that it is reasonable, in fact, to believe in the limits of reason. Some who make this claim say that fideists do not object to reason. They oppose a certain form of modern reason, *evidentialism*, a topic discussed below.[30] Nevertheless, fideism answers the question of the nature of religious belief by asserting that they are arbitrary choices. Therefore, no rational account of these choices is necessary.

Appeal to Revelation or Enlightenment

Revelation from Without

Beyond fideism, there are several basic ways by which believers uphold the truth of their belief in the absence of the evidence of the physical senses. These ways are often used together. The first of these is the appeal to revelation or enlightenment.

In general, revelation is the disclosure of truths, commands, and realities from a transcendent source, a source that exists beyond the material world. If humans could use their own mental powers to gain this supernatural knowledge, they would not need revelation. The will and ways of the divine are so far beyond the physical world that they are hidden from the ordinary mind. Therefore, the revelation that bestows understanding of the divine is a gift that comes from the gods, a Higher Power, or other sacred source.[31]

A good example of the distinction between what humans can figure out and what must be revealed to them is found in Hinduism. In Hinduism, *smriti* is what is remembered from the traditions of human thought. It refers to what is learned. In contrast, *shruti* is what is revealed. It refers to what is heard *from* the divine. In the way of *shruti*, believers do not choose what to believe. The disclosure of the divine teaches them what is true.

The concept of revelation leads to other closely related topics. One of these topics is how the divine revelation is disclosed. Another is how the revelation is transmitted so that it becomes the foundation of the beliefs of the faithful.

Since revelation is a divine gift, it must be received. That reception comes to those who are chosen to receive it. But how? Hindus believe that the revelation of the cosmic and social order of the Sanatana Dharma was first whispered in the ears of the ancient sages. This thought provides a model for the sense of direct revelation. The truths of revelation literally come "from God's mouth to human ears."

The Amana Colonies in Iowa were founded on the principle of such divine transmission. The "Community of True Inspiration" believed that God had not ceased to speak directly to humans as he did in the biblical times. Just as God did in the Bible, God has continued to speak through *Werkzeug*, or "instruments." The last of these in the Colonies was Barbara Heiniman, who died in Amana, Iowa, in 1883. Likewise, the Islamic prophet Muhammad is claimed to be the last messenger of God because he heard the word of God directly.[32] The words that were dictated to him just "descended" on him.[33]

Traditional Muslims would say that the Qur'an is the divine message of Allah to human beings. No other explanation of how the message of God was received is necessary or appropriate. However, a *hadith*, or tradition based on a certified saying or deed of the Islamic prophet Muhammad, records what Muhammad said about his experience: "Sometimes it comes to me like the ringing of a bell and that is the hardest on me, then he departs from me and I retain in memory from him what he says; and sometimes the Angel comes to me in the likeness of a man and speaks to me and I retain in memory what he says."[34] In this case, the message was received in an ecstatic state.[35]

Here is a similar account of revelation from an interview with such an "instrument" in 1716:

> The Werkzeug or Prophet feels it first in his innermost being a gentle and pleasant glow which gradually becomes more intense and also fills the external body. Thereupon results an inflation of the nose, trembling of the whole body, often attended by kicking with hands and feet and shaking of the head. And in the centre of this internal fire the word of the Lord is born; and the Prophet is enabled

through the Bewergugen [the state of shaking of the body with inspiration] to pronounce the word of the Lord without fear or awe, as it was born in him at times syllable by syllable at times word by word, now slowly now rapidly so that the Werkzeug had no choice of his own but was used solely as a passive instrument in the hands of the Lord.[36]

In both accounts, the message is received in a mystical state. The message grabs hold of the messenger in an extraordinary state of consciousness.

Enlightenment from Within

Enlightenment is also a way that humans gain the "different knowledge" of belief. Like the knowledge of revelation, the knowledge of enlightenment is not available to the ordinary mind, the consciousness that is controlled by the senses. In the Japanese form of Buddhism known as Zen, enlightenment is called *satori*.[37] D. T. Suzuki teaches that in enlightenment (*satori*) one gains an "intuitive" insight into the nature of reality.[38] In order to gain this new perspective, one has to give up ordinary, logical ways of thinking, especially analysis.

In the Buddhist tradition, the Buddha found the extraordinary knowledge of enlightenment from within.

Suzuki applies the term "revelation" to this revolutionary viewpoint.[39] However, it is not revelation in the sense of a divine gift from above. Prince Siddhartha Gautama, who became the Buddha (the "Enlightened One"), needed no divine being to disclose the truths that are thought to rest in "empirical, experimental and experiential evidence."[40] In the same way, the experience of *satori* is a sudden sense of having "found the truth."[41] This realization of the truth comes in profound and thorough change of mind. It does not come from outside the mind but from within. It is a "self-revelation."[42]

As Zen demonstrates, the insight of enlightenment is realized in an extraordinary state of mind. Like revelation, the truth of enlightenment (*satori*) overcomes those who receive it.[43] Thus, like the experience of revelation, the transcendent knowledge of enlightenment is received in an extraordinary experience.

The approach of certifying belief by referring to revelation or enlightenment does what fideism cannot do. It establishes what religious belief is. Divine revelation or enlightenment sets the standard for genuine religious belief. In this case, terms such as "traditional" or "paranormal" would not apply. The revelation or enlightenment would set its own terms for what makes belief "religious."

Appeal to Authority

A closely related approach is the appeal to *authority*. The claim that the revelation or enlightenment is given or realized in a special state of mind gives it special weight over those who accept it. This quality of exceptional insight gives the message compelling power to influence the thoughts and lives of those who believe in it.

The authority of belief rests on the claim of some transcendent revelation, wisdom, or consciousness. This special insight is then handed down by tradition from its unquestioned source. Believers often do not pursue matters beyond the claims of authority, since to question authority is ultimately to question the revelation or enlightened insight.

How does a person, scripture, or organization gain such power to dictate the belief of others even through many generations? Religious revelations or enlightened insights are not passed along from one person or group to another as if they were rocks or potatoes. To be convincing, the revelation or insight must touch something in the hearer's own mind and heart.

Heaven's Gate was a "cyber cult" that believed that the world was about to end. The only way to survive the coming disaster was to find an exit from the planet. When the Hale-Bopp comet appeared, the leader convinced the group that a UFO was following the comet. It would pick up the souls of those who exited the Earth and would transport them to another level of existence far above the human life they now lived. In March 1997, as the Hale-Bopp comet passed by, the leader of the cult and thirty-eight members committed suicide and indeed left this world.

What made them do it? The members of the cult had a need to believe, and the message of the founders[44] spoke to that need. Religious studies professor Irving Hexham and anthropologist Karla Poewe speculated that the message of Heaven's Gate touched the longing for something more than the mundane and uncertain life on Earth.[45] If so, the cult's message touched this yearning, even though it was a curious mixture of notions of the end of the world, UFOs, *Star Trek*, extraterrestrial visitation, computer technology, and New Age spirituality.

Thus, hearers of the message of revelation or enlightened insight will accept it if it meets their need to believe. This means that those who receive a message of revelation or enlightenment must hear it in terms of their particular felt needs. To be grasped by the message, they must connect it with these needs. If they can do that, they will invest in the message and give it special authority.

However, the message comes through a messenger. The messenger cannot pass along the message as if it were an inert stone. The messenger must first adapt the message so that its hearers can grasp it. Then the messenger must ensure that the hearers "get it right." Thus, the messenger must shape the message if the community is to receive it as exceptional truth. Conversely, the message must also shape the response if the community is to receive the truth. The messenger is the link between the message and the hearer. For the hearers to believe the message, they must also invest the messenger with unique authority. Thus, religious "founders" such as Moses, Jesus, Muhammad, the Buddha, and Guru Nanek have a distinctive relationship to the truth of the religion.

Yet what about those who transmit the message after the founders? These representatives of belief must also be invested with uncommon authority. This can take two forms: the personal master-disciple relationship or institutional authorization of spiritual specialists within organizations.

The Authority of the Spiritual Master

The first form of the special authority of teachers of belief is the relationship between the spiritual master and his disciples. The master in Hinduism is the *guru*; in Buddhism, the Zen *roshi* or Tibetan *lama*; in Hasidic Judaism, the *tsaddiq*; in Russian Orthodoxy, the *starets*; and in Sufism, the *shaykh*.[46] All of these spiritual guides must have reached the highest level of spirituality. They also must be capable of leading others to that realization by word and example. Yet, to be effective, spiritual masters depend on the total commitment of their disciples to the path they advise. In the Maitri Upanishad, the disciple says to his guru, "In this world I am like a frog in a dry well. O Saint, thou art my way, thou art my way!"[47] In a state of trust, disciples must surrender themselves to the discipline of their masters. This personal relationship takes precedence over the written scriptures or hierarchy. Still, the authority of the masters only goes as far as their disciples' recognition of it. Thus, it is said that in Hinduism the disciple makes the master.[48]

The Authority of the Religious Institution

The second type of authority is the institutional form. As religions develop, they devise ways of investing chosen and trained experts with authority that sets them apart from the community. The authorization to proclaim and teach is given through such rites. For example, Jewish candidates receive vigorous training in all aspects of Jewish law and history before being ordained as rabbis.

Christian priests, pastors, and ministers also typically receive seminary training before ordination. In Catholic and Orthodox Christian circles, only those ordained as bishops have the authority to ordain priests and deacons. In the Protestant Presbyterian churches, the "presbytery" of elders ordains others to the office of teaching. Other Protestant churches confer authority by rites of ordination conducted by clergy and/or layperson. Typically, rites of ordination involve the "laying on of hands," a way of conferring the transcendent, spiritual gifts of the Holy Spirit for ministry.

Islam, on the other hand, has no ordained clergy. However, it does have specially trained religious leaders who belong to the *ulamā*—that is, the body of scholars and teachers of Islam who have studied at recognized schools.[49] These trained leaders receive appointments to lead the community in prayer, to preach, and to minister to the local Muslim community.

Provisions for authorizing teachers of the faith are found even in religions that focus on the master-disciple relationship. In Hinduism, teaching traditions (*sampradāyas*) pass on the teaching authority from one guru to the next.[50] In Zen Buddhism, only a roshi may certify the rigorous training and attainment of suc-

A rabbi studies the Torah. Jewish rabbis receive many years of training before they are ordained with the authority to teach.

cessive Zen masters. The goal is to pass the "mind of the master" to the pupil.[51] Experiences of enlightenment not given in this way are suspect. The realization of genuine enlightenment requires the master's guidance. When a Zen master authenticates a pupil's enlightenment, the newly enlightened person is thought to join a line of teaching of the dharma that goes back to the Buddha himself.[52]

Institutional authorization typically develops into a religious hierarchy. Those who belong to it form a selected group with special responsibilities and privileges. Their role is to preserve the transmission of the revelation or insight. For example, the "teaching authority" of the Roman Catholic Church is called the *Magisterium*. It consists of the bishops with the pope as the head. The role of this church agency is to guard the truth on which the life of the church and the faith of its members depend. To carry out this duty, the Magisterium has the power to prescribe the faith and morals of the church. The "Extraordinary Magisterium" refers to the pronouncements of the pope alone or pope along with his bishops, as in a General Council. These are considered infallible—that is, free from error. The "Ordinary Magisterium" refers to teachings of lesser standing made by the pope or by the bishops. Though they do not have the same guarantee of trustworthiness as infallible teaching, they still define the faith and morals of the church, and Catholics are expected to follow them.

If the religious leaders in their hierarchies lose the trust of their flocks or do not meet their needs, some will invest themselves in someone or something else. In the competitive religious marketplace of America, religious entrepreneurs are ready to snatch up these dissatisfied believers into their own enterprises. Many of these are self-appointed. They authorize themselves to be purveyors of religious truth. As their groups mature, they will also find ways to develop a set of experts to pass along the "true faith" of the developing institution.

Our investigation has found that a definite structure of the reception, transmission, interpretation, and teaching of belief forms and shapes the followers of a religion into a believing community. On the other hand, the believing community possesses the teachings of belief as its own. Within the believing community, beliefs have unique meaning and power to inspire, guide, and motivate members of the body of faith.

When authority is the standard for religious belief, then it determines the nature, content, and justification of belief. In fact, the religious authority of Western traditions has made the distinction between traditional beliefs that it endorses and paranormal beliefs that it puts down.

Appeal to Experience

A closely linked way of defining and justifying belief is experience. We have already discussed the way that the founders of religions typically base their teaching on the experience of revelation or enlightenment. The authority of these founders derives from the testimony of their personal experience and their community's acceptance of it as especially meaningful. In this way, religions are based on the experience of their founders.

Yet we have observed that if the teachings of a prophet or master are to grasp the commitment of its hearers, they must touch something in the hearers' own inner life. The experience of the original revelation or enlightenment acts like a contagion. When others have what they regard as the same experience, the founder's authority is confirmed.

This textbook will explore the rich topic of religious experience in another chapter. In this chapter, we are interested in how believers use experience to justify their beliefs. We begin with the observation that human individuals learn how to determine what truths are reliable from their culture. In general, Western societies generally hold that the following are reliable:

1. Immediate experience (such as the fact that one has a headache)
2. The self-evident (mathematics and logic)
3. Empirical evidence from the senses (perceptions that can be tested)

Religious experience is neither self-evident nor based on empirical evidence. Rather, the appeal to experience to justify belief is an appeal to immediate experience, the first type listed above.

A forceful defense of their claim comes from the philosopher John Hick. Hick states that in daily life, it is rational to presume that there is a world outside our minds that we must deal with. In fact, it is irrational to deny there is such an external world.[53]

Hick applies this principle to religious experience. He argues that "it is rational for people to believe what their experience leads them to believe." If they have an experience of God, then they cannot help but believe in the existence of God and the truths that go along with this belief. Hick further affirms that founders of religions like Moses, Jesus, Muhammad, the Buddha, Guru Nanek, and many others had religious experiences that came with such intensity and force that it would have been irrational of them *not* to believe in the truths that came to them.[54]

However, Hick observes the modern people do not live in past centuries. For people in the twenty-first century, is it rational to accept the beliefs of centuries ago? For example, it may have been reasonable for people in the past to believe in demon possession, but can we justify this belief today?[55]

Hick's answer is that it is rational for modern people to hold beliefs that are founded on someone else's experience as long as those beliefs fit their own experience and beliefs.[56] Therefore, rational persons in the twenty-first century will be open to the religious beliefs of the past.

However, what about the religious experience of ordinary believers in the present? Hick says that believers are entitled to trust their own experiences.[57] Yet, in view of aberrations like Heaven's Gate and Jonestown, he qualifies his endorsement of the appeal to experience. The religious experience must fit into other beliefs that one holds. It must not contradict one's general knowledge of the world. And it must have a powerful effect on one's life.[58]

Hick asserts that typically the experiences of people today do not come with the force and intensity of the founders of religions of the past. Moreover, the experience of the founders is primary. Most often, the religious experiences of people today are shaped by the religions that are founded on the experience of the past founders such as Moses, Jesus, Muhammad, the Buddha, Guru Nanek, and others. Therefore, the appeal to experience to justify belief does not usually stand alone. The religious experience of the follower confirms the truth of the teachings of the founder of a religion. Conversely, the experience of the founder authorizes the religious experience of the follower.[59] Therefore, in general, the religious experience of believers is not separate from the religious authority that is based on the exceptional religious experience of the founders of religions.

Thus, established religious authorities are not opposed to the religious experiences of their followers as long as these experiences confirm the authorized beliefs. But what about experiences that lead people to paranormal and other beliefs that are not authorized by established religious authority? The term "paranormal" implies that the beliefs go against the normal and cultural ideas of reality. Those who believe them, therefore, no longer accept the frames of reference of their society. Since they accept different webs of associations, their thinking goes against the mainstream. Thus, they move toward a privatized spirituality.[60] This is especially true when established religious authorities disapprove these experiences.[61]

The appeal to experience explains that people choose their beliefs based on their religious experience. This approach leads to the question of the origin of religious experiences and their relationship to established religions and unauthorized ways of believing. This book will explore such questions in a later chapter.

The Counter Appeal: Lack of Evidence

This discussion of the alternatives to the justification of belief began with fideism. It now ends with its opposite. Fideism refuses to give any justification at all for belief. *Evidentialism* says that beliefs could not be justified even if one tried.

Evidentialism holds that the only justification for one's beliefs is sufficient evidence. (Recall Clifford's statement at the beginning of this chapter: it is wrong to believe anything without sufficient evidence.) In this view, beliefs must have warrants. That is, they must have reasons why they are proper knowledge and not mere fantasy.[62]

This principle leads to a further question: what sort of evidence is "sufficient"? The answer is that the evidence must be "certain."[63] But what is certain? Evidentialism will accept what is self-evident, whether from logic, memory, or introspection. Apart from these, only provable observations or conclusions from sense perception qualify as sure foundations of beliefs.[64] This principle rules out all supposed supernatural or super-conscious phenomena as untestable, unreliable, and uncertain.[65]

From the perspective of evidentialism, the British philosopher Anthony Flew (1923–2010) made a famous case against religious beliefs in his "Parable of the Gardener." To begin with, Flew assumed that religious beliefs are proposed statements of fact. The assertion "There is a God" is a statement like "It is raining." If so, then the statement is a *univocal* statement. That means it has only one meaning: it must be taken literally as a "matter of fact."

On this basis, Flew reasoned that religious statements must be subject to verification. That is, they must be confirmed by sufficient evidence. One can verify the statement "It is raining" by going outside to prove it is true.

What about the belief in God? The problem with religious beliefs, Flew observed, is that believers cannot produce any observable evidence to verify them. On the contrary, he says, believers typically will not accept any evidence that might discount their beliefs.

With that in mind, Flew told the story of explorers who stumbled upon a garden of flowers along with weeds in a clearing of a forest. One of them insisted that there must be a gardener who tended the garden. The other denied it. The two devised ingenious traps to find out the truth. No gardener was ever spotted or caught. But the first explorer continued to believe. He claimed that the gardener was invisible. We cannot expect to catch him. The second asked, "What is the difference between an invisible gardener whose existence cannot be proven and no gardener at all?"[66]

Flew's devastating argument against univocal beliefs reminds us of positivists like A. J. Ayer (1910–1989). The positivists held that an assertion must be capable of proof by verification, or it is meaningless.[67] If one says something is true, others must be able to test it to see if that claim is right. If the statement cannot be tested, then it is not only false but the statement also makes no rational sense.

Which of These Statements Is Meaningful?

Suppose a child says that a monster is hiding under her bed. The parent looks but finds no monster. "No," the child says, "the monster hides whenever someone looks for it." Which of the child's assertions is a meaningful statement if by "meaningful" we mean provable?

In the textbox above, the first statement seems to be testable. The parent can investigate the underside of the bed. So the child's first statement is meaningful. However, the child's second assertion is not testable. The positivists would say that it is neither a true nor a false statement. It is simply meaningless.

The positivist principle has been discredited,[68] but the principle of falsification grew from its soil. According to Flew, if one claims that something is the case, then one is also claiming what is not the case. If nothing counts against an assertion of what is the case, then nothing can count for it. The statement is neither a true nor a false assertion. It is not an assertion of a truth at all.

Therefore, according to the falsification principle, religious statements only pretend to be statements of truths like "It is raining."[69] That is, if I assert there is a gardener that tends a garden, but I can produce no verifiable evidence that the gardener exists . . . moreover, if I believe that the gardener exists no matter what . . . I might as well say that the garden is tended by an invisible but industrious piece of Provolone cheese.[70] Since both traditional religious and paranormal beliefs can offer no evidence to support them, they are both nonsense. Religious studies need not bother trying to make sense of them.

Evaluation of Alternative Approaches

We have outlined some representative approaches of scholars to religious beliefs. How well do they help us understand what beliefs are to those who believe them? We will find that these theories still put us in the stands as spectators of games that go by rules that we do not fully understand. Moreover, they do not solve the problem of our test case.

Evaluation of Fideism

As a way of justifying religious belief, fideism would not distinguish between beliefs, whether they are considered traditional, paranormal, or otherwise. In this view, the standard for evaluating beliefs is not the content of the belief. It is whether it is "sincerely held." This norm would approve a vast amount of opinions without distinction.

Fideism seems to take religious studies to a dead end. It might be called "non-rational" in that it claims a higher ground of human knowledge than reason. However, to common standards of reasoning, fideism seems irrational. If believers refuse to give any reason for their beliefs, then the study of religion has no way of making sense of these beliefs or giving a reasonable account for them.

It may be reasonable to believe in truths that go "beyond human reason." In this weaker sense of fideism, religious belief is not opposed to human reason. Belief speaks about mysteries beyond ordinary human comprehension. This view assumes that the human mind is not a completely reliable and capable instrument. Something more than the ordinary mind is required to grasp religious realities than ordinary reason or perception.

However, this weaker sense does not answer the question. It asserts that religious belief has to do with mysteries beyond ordinary human comprehension. Once again, the field of religious studies is at a loss. Fideism gives no reason that would account for belief in these mysteries other than its own belief. Moreover, if faith goes beyond reason, reason will not help us understand why believers should believe in angels but not ghosts. Even if, in general, it is not against reason to believe in religious claims, it does not follow that it is reasonable to select certain beliefs and not others.

Evaluation of Appeal to Revelation/Enlightenment and Authority

We can take the appeals for revelation/enlightenment and the appeal to authority together. We have seen that the authority of the founders of religions is based on the special insight of revelation or enlightenment received in an extraordinary state of mind. However profound, this transcendent experience has no bearing on anyone else's beliefs unless others receive it as especially authoritative. The believing community that receives the teaching of revelation or enlightenment is the key. Without the believing community, the experience of the potential founder of a religion would be just a matter of personal experience. The "will to believe" of a circle of believers is necessary if the religious experience of the founder is to become a viable religious tradition.

We have seen that religious authority that is ultimately based on revelation or enlightenment defines the content of religious belief. But such authority also defines the nature of belief and how believers justify what they believe. Thus, religious authority decides what to authorize and therefore puts in the categories of traditional belief, paranormal opinion, or other classifications.

However, these insights raise the question of the limits of religious authority. Religious leaders like South African human rights activist and Anglican bishop Desmond Tutu or the peace activist, poet, and Buddhist master Thích Nhất Hạnh may gain considerable respect outside their communities of faith. Yet their authority to prescribe religious belief extends only as far as the boundaries of the circle of their followers. Religious authority has unmatched power to justify belief within the believing community. Yet that authority has no power outside the community except that it represents the beliefs of the followers.

The point is that the authority to justify belief only works within the "insiders" of the religion. The appeal to authority may be so powerful to "insiders," but it is of little help to "outsiders." From the view of religious authority, if scholars of religious studies want to make sense of the beliefs that religious authority defends, it will have to take the word of "insiders" for it. We see this clearly in the case of the distinction between traditional and paranormal beliefs. "Insiders" of established religious authorities make this distinction and contemporary society just accepts it.

Evaluation of the Appeal to Experience

Another chapter of this textbook will delve into the problems and possibilities of religious experience. This evaluation will deal with the problem of how believers can use personal experience to justify their beliefs by the appeal to experience. The difficulty with the appeal to experience to justify belief is similar to the difficulty of appealing to authority. If immediate personal experience is grounds for belief, it is hard for anyone else to understand it.

William Alston notes that the appeal to experience is a circular argument. How do we know that our sense perceptions are reliable? The only way is to check one set of sense perceptions with another set. It is like trying to check out the accuracy of a clock. The only way is to compare its time is to compare it with another clock. To tell time, we have to assume that the clocks that are checked by other clocks are right. To get along in society, we have to assume that if our perceptions are validated by other perceptions, they must be reliable.[71]

Likewise, how do we know that our religious experiences are so true that they can be the basis of our beliefs? We have to check them out against other experiences. We may appeal to religious authorities. But we have already found that their authority is based ultimately on the experience of others, going back to the founders of the religion. No objective source lying outside of human experience is available to humans. Therefore, no independent source is on hand to check human belief.[72]

So then how can believers rely on religious experience to justify belief? Surprisingly, the answer is a matter of tradition—that is, of social convention. Alston states, "There is no appeal beyond the practices we find firmly established, psychologically and socially."[73] In other words, Alston maintains that we can rely on those belief-forming practices that do not contradict one another and that fit our worldview. Religious experience, therefore, is reliable insofar as it is "socially established."[74]

These thoughts suggest that the only reason for the difference between traditional and paranormal beliefs is social convention. Social standards define the nature and justification of religious belief. Angels and demons have social endorsement. Ghosts and aliens from outer space do not.

But what logical basis does a society have in choosing one set of beliefs over another? Until recently, what religious authorities call paranormal beliefs have not enjoyed the status of religious beliefs. Now that the authority of established religious organizations is weakening, the two sets are beginning to compete with one another on equal terms. In this new situation, believers cannot reasonably appeal to experience to make their choice between the two. Believers in the paranormal have contradictory experiences just as they hold different opinions. The appeal to revelation or enlightenment and authority does not solve the problem of how to make sense of the choices that believers are making about beliefs.

Evaluation of the Evidentialist Approach

As we see in Flew's parable, the principle of sufficient evidence makes justifying religious belief extremely difficult. Perhaps it makes the task too difficult. Some scholars say that if religious belief must achieve undeniable certainty, then the standards for proof are impossibly high. Even philosophical assertions cannot reach the high standard of absolute certainty that evidentialism unfairly sets for religious belief.[75]

Moreover, the demand for certainty based on evidence seems to offer a false dilemma. For example, Clifford and Flew would say that if one cannot provide an unassailable proof of God's existence, then one does not really believe in God in the full sense. Therefore, without sufficient evidence, one's belief is unreliable, unreasonable, and unethical. But religious belief includes the dynamic of doubt. Though some believers would not be as candid, many would admit that belief is based on probabilities. Apart from those who cling to fideism, believers often oscillate between moods of confident belief and uneasy doubt.[76]

In a wider sense, if belief attained the degree of certainty demanded by the arguments for God, then it would not be religious belief in the way we use the word. Religious beliefs are based on faith, not factual evidence. When one gains factual evidence, one has ordinary knowledge, not religious belief.[77]

Another argument against evidentialism is that its demands for strict rationalism seem to force religions to do the impossible: to prove the infinite from the finite.[78] If human reason could prove faith, it would rest uneasily on shaky ground since its basis would be the limited human mind.

A final argument is that evidentialism is based on a premise that does not apply to itself. What is the evidence for the belief that all beliefs that are not founded on sufficient evidence are wrong? Unless evidence for this proposition is forthcoming, by its own standard, it is wrong.[79] Thus, postmodernism has moved beyond this unachievable standard of proof.

In summary, evidentialism has no contribution to the solution to the problem of finding a rationale for distinguishing paranormal from traditional religious beliefs. Like fideism, it is a dead-end to religious studies. When it writes off all beliefs, it has nothing more to say about them.

Summary of Discoveries

We have reviewed some major strategies for the justification of religious belief hoping to discover an answer to the question of how to make sense of beliefs in the twenty-first century. We have seen that in the past, religious belief was tied to belonging to and attending the services of traditional religious institutions. Scholars could understand belief in the terms that various religions and their denominations presented them.

But now in the twenty-first century, the task of finding a rational understanding of religious belief has grown more difficult. We have reviewed the wide range of beliefs in the United States and described how traditional and paranormal beliefs have become overlapping categories.

In this emerging religious situation, beliefs no longer are contained within religious institutions governed by religious hierarchies. Contemporary Americans favor self-directed spirituality and self-chosen beliefs. Many prefer to pick their personal beliefs from a cafeteria of different religious traditions. As a result, the actual beliefs of today's Americans range over a number of social variables. The key to belief has shifted from social conditions to individual choices.[80]

Prevailing academic discussions of belief are struggling to catch up with the changing ideas and attitudes of people in the twenty-first century about beliefs. Personal and subjective interests have replaced the formal and objective discussions of theological truth and philosophical verification. Contemporary persons want exposure to a variety of religious beliefs and practices and ways to experience them. The emerging attitude is that belief is merely a matter of personal preference that belongs solely to the individual. With this in mind, many demand the right of personal preference. The challenge of religious studies is to find a way to make sense of these choices to gain an adequate understanding of them. If religious belief is an individual choice and not social obligation, then why do people choose to believe? If they do choose, how can we give a rational account of these choices? And on what basis can we call these choices "religious"?

PROPOSING THE MOST PROMISING SOLUTION: BELIEFS AND THE QUESTIONS THEY ANSWER

The alternative approaches above centered on the question of why believers hold their religious beliefs. Now this section turns to the question of the content of beliefs in the hope of finding a way to understand religious belief in this century.

What do believers mean by "God" and "demons" on the one hand and "haunted houses" and "aliens from outer space" on the other? This section proposes that we might make sense of religious beliefs if we study what they mean to the believers. In this vein, this section suggests that believers best justify their beliefs by appealing to the meaning that their faith has to their lives. Likewise, this section suggests that the topic of meaning might solve the problem of finding a reasonable distinction between traditional religious and paranormal beliefs.

We could address the question of the meaning of religious beliefs by studying the content of the beliefs of major religious traditions one after the other. This would be the approach of a textbook on world religions. However, a critical thinking approach to beliefs would ask a more fundamental question: How does the meaning of beliefs to their believers help us understand what counts for religious belief? This is the approach of this textbook.

We have asked several questions, including those about the nature and justification of religious belief. This section will propose that most promising solution to the problem is that religious belief concerns the most fundamental questions of human life. Further, believers choose these beliefs because they seem to answer these questions. Another way of approaching the question is to search for the difference between traditional religious and paranormal beliefs. The difference that this proposal suggests is that religious beliefs make the most profound difference in the lives of those who hold them.

Faith and Ultimate Concern

The German-American theologian Paul Tillich (1886–1965) spoke of the search for answers to the most crucial questions of human life when he defined faith as "the state of being ultimately concerned."[81] In Tillich's view, belief is the assent to religious truth claims. But faith is more than belief. According to Tillich, faith has to do with what "concerns us ultimately." In faith, we are grasped by something that calls us to something more than physical survival.[82] In faith, our total personality is caught up in the relationship to what is most important in human life. This "most important" is what we depend on for our very existence and what we look to for the meaning of our lives.

What then are beliefs? Beliefs are not arbitrary declarations of truths that we must accept at face value. Further, they do not merely point to some inscrutable mysteries that have no definite character. Faith has cognitive content.[83] It must be ultimate trust in *something*. Religious beliefs express this content of religious faith.

What is ultimate must be greater than our reason. This means that faith always involves risk. We can choose to put faith in something that is not worthy of being an ultimate concern. If this is the case and our chosen ultimate concern fails us, then the foundation for the meaning of our lives collapses.[84]

Question and Answer in the Method of Correlation

The growing awareness of the diversity of beliefs in the twenty-first century puts the question of belief in a new framework. How are beliefs to be understood when they make such opposing truth claims? Tillich's "Method of Correlation" gives an answer. It offers a way of comparing the different beliefs of world religions fairly and reasonably.

This method treats religious beliefs as symbolic answers to questions of our ultimate concern. Tillich states its basic assumption: "Man [*sic*] is the question that he asks about himself." That is, at the deepest level, human life involves questions that have to do with the very existence and meaning of life. It is human to ask questions of our existence. Moreover, to be human means living with the supposed answers to these questions. Religions address the deepest longing of existence by giving answers from revealed or enlightened insight to the most pressing questions of life.[85]

Seven Categories of Ultimate Questions

1. The nature of "Ultimate Reality"
2. The origin and order of the universe
3. Human bondage and liberation or salvation
4. The origin and nature of suffering and evil
5. The nature of what is morally good, right, and just
6. Human freedom and determinism
7. The end of the cosmos and human life

Tillich's method suggests a way of making sense of religious beliefs. It is to categorize and compare them according to the basic existential questions that they attempt to answer. For example, beliefs can be grouped and compared according to the several major questions of human life. (See textbox "Seven Categories of Ultimate Questions" for a list.)

The questions involved in these topics are universal and ultimate concerns of life. They are universal because they apply to all human beings everywhere. They are ultimate because they are the final and basic questions of all human beings. They are also universal and ultimate because they are the most serious concerns of all of human life. Without answers to these questions, human life loses its sense of meaning.

Universal and ultimate questions have to be asked by all people everywhere and be about the most basic matters of our lives. Therefore, these questions come out of our human "condition." All human beings cannot help but ask these questions because they are human.

Testing the Most Promising Solution:
The Origin and Order of the Universe

Ultimate questions are universal but human beings become aware of them in different ways in their different cultures. Einstein's response to the findings of quantum physics is an example of how the question of the origin and order the universe comes up for contemporary people.

When quantum physics began to disclose an unsettling randomness at the innermost core of the atom, Albert Einstein saw the implications of this seeming basic chaos perhaps more than anyone. In 1926, Einstein wrote to Max Born, who was working out the theory, and admitted that the methods of quantum mechanics were indeed useful, but he protested that the new physics "hardly brings us close to the secrets of the Ancient One." "I am convinced," he said, "he [God] does not play dice."[86] Einstein could not bring himself to contemplate a universe where there is no rational order, a basic structure of reality that the human mind can apprehend.

Even when relying only on its own logic, the mind seems inclined to posit a reality larger than itself. We seek a "ground" or "foundation" of our rationality. The highest capacity of the human being lies in the gift of our reason. Yet if the world is unreasonable—if the universe is grounded in chaos—then what is the use of this gift?

We know that the human mind tends to project rational order on its perceptions. Yet if that rational order is simply a function of our own consciousness, then the very rationality that allows us to think about this question rests on the most insecure and ultimately unreliable basis. If human life is thus just a game of roulette, then there is ultimately no standard of truth, right, or goodness. If the universe is just a big lottery, reason serves no other purpose than making us very clever and cunning creatures.

As it was for Einstein, it is hard for us to believe that there is no universal, transcendent "Reason" behind the universe, a reason that our minds can know. It seems natural for us to believe that somehow this "Reason" operates by the rules that our minds know as logic. As we begin to ask ourselves what this universal and transcendent foundation of the universe could be, we start to ask the question of origin and order of the universe. We try to use our reason to search for some transcendent source.

We may or may not accept the "big bang" theory of astrophysics or the evolutionary theory of Darwin. Whatever our relationship to these theories, we cannot help but search for some guiding hand, some reasonable direction, or some principle of coherence that ties our experience together into a meaningful whole. It may be too much to expect this source to be provable, but we can ask about the probability that it lies before, behind, and beneath the processes of nature.

Do we have a need for such a hypothesis? Note that this is a question of the ultimate meaningfulness of our existence. It is not a scientific question. Nor is it a philosophical way to prove or disprove the existence of God. The question is whether reality is ordered in such a way that it can be understood as rational and meaningful. In his seminar on Sigmund Freud and C. S. Lewis, "The Question of God," Armand Nicholai states:

> As we look at the world around us, we make one of two basic assumptions: either we view the universe as an accident and our existence on this planet a matter of chance, or we assume some intelligence beyond the universe who not only gives the universe design and order, but also gives life meaning and purpose. How we live our lives, how we end our lives, what we perceive, how we interpret what we perceive, are all formed and influenced consciously or unconsciously by one of these two basic assumptions.[87]

In the same vein, Langdon Gilkey (1919–2004) stated that philosophy depends on the principle of coherence, an assumption of logical and orderly relationships.[88] God is a symbol for the "ground" of this principle and not an instance of it. Thus, whatever the foundation of a logical order to the universe is called, our sense of order and meaning depends on it.[89] Religion seeks to know and experience what that "ground" is.

To engage in this search, humans must use capacities that include but that go beyond reason. William James called the divine basis of reality the "Something More" because it is much greater than the physical universe. In *The Varieties of Religious Experience*, James explored the many ways that humans use to get in touch with this "Something More." Why can human beings attain a knowledge of it? James says that the "Something More" that is the divine source of reality and the highest part of human persons share the same quality.[90] This quality that can rise above the limits of the physical universe is more than human reason. It is an intuitive sense that answers the question of the "ground" of reality.

Thus, the question of the origin and order of the universe emerges from the human need to believe in a source of order in the universe. We can call this need an ultimate concern. Without such a sense of order to life, we would have a feeling of drowning in a swirling sea of chaos, a maelstrom of existence without reason and without meaning.

The Steps of the Proposed Method

Now that we have presented the question side of Tillich's method of question and answer, we can fill in the rest of the method. The task is to draw out the mutual relationship between the existential questions as we have described it and the answers found in the symbolic content of belief.

Steps in the Proposed Method of Studying Beliefs

1. Identification of the topic or belief
2. Conversion of the topic or belief into a question
3. Description of how that question arises in human life
4. Discussion of different answers to that question—in several different sets of beliefs
5. Comparison and evaluation of the answers as to how they answer the question

Our proposal, therefore, involves the steps that are outlined in the textbox titled "Steps in the Proposed Method of Studying Beliefs." Remember that beliefs are answers to the deepest questions of human life. The proposed method uses critical thinking to analyze, compare, and interpret them.

The first thing we have to do in our proposed method of study is to turn a topic or belief into an ultimate question. Take, for example, the Hindu belief that the universe was created out of the primal sacrifice of a giant reality, the *Puru-sha*. The parts of the giant became the parts of the universe and human society. How these body parts were arranged became the cosmic and social order.

Instead of dismissing this story from the ancient Hindu text of the Rig Veda or delving into its symbolic meaning, we turn the story into a question: What is the origin of the universe and the way it is ordered? Then we explore how it and other sets of beliefs answer that question.

Studying beliefs in this way will have certain advantages over simply describing different belief systems or analyzing their claims. This method helps us categorize the different beliefs of various religions according to the questions they answer. It then enables us to compare and contrast beliefs within those sets. Finally, it helps us evaluate the "adequacy" of the answers of belief to the ultimate questions that everyone asks.

Testing the Proposed Method: Freedom and Destiny

The best way to test this method is to put it into practice to see what results it yields. Within the orbit of one's daily affairs, everyone seems to have choices and responsibility for those choices. The daily routine offers some alternatives. We may not like the options we have. We may feel under pressure, but we still seem to be able to choose.

The boundaries of society, however, seem to set certain parameters for our choices. The struggle for human rights continues into this century. These rights are set within the frame of reference of the struggle for freedom. In this web of associations, freedom means that society can no longer set limits for our choices based on race, ethnicity, social class, and background. If the struggle succeeds, all people will have the right to make personal choices in housing, employment, education, health care, and our way of life.

It may be the struggle for human rights is succeeding and the scope and number of human choices in our society are increasing. However, it is interesting that when American society talks about the wonderful choices it offers, it mentions things on the surface of life. We have choices of value meals in fast-food restaurants, of cable or satellite TV, cell phone plans, and, perhaps, medical treatments. All these choices presume a certain amount of wealth. For many who are unemployed or working without supplemental benefits like health care insurance, their options, in fact, may be more and more restricted.

Nevertheless, even if one has the resources that are required for "freedom of choice," we are limited in our decisions. Language, knowledge, mental capability, and psychological temperament are not the only things that hold us back. Our nature as physical creatures is limiting. Humans are finite beings. We live lives that are contained within that finitude.

Yet though we are bound to our physical existence, we can imagine that we are free from these limitations. What, after all, is freedom of choice? What is freedom from limitation of choice? Is Bill Gates truly free—even with his billions? Reflection on this question leads to a religious search for more options than this physical universe seems to give us. Thus, we ask the question of how to attain a true and lasting freedom that is not bound to such restrictions as health, social standing, mental ability, education, and personal strengths or weaknesses.

The advertising slogan that ranks eighteenth among the last century's best is the U.S. Army's "Be all that you can be!" Devised by the N.W. Ayer & Son advertising agency, the slogan asserts that we are here on Earth to fulfill our hidden potential of greatness and significance.

Despite the attraction of that ad, something in us yearns for even more than it promises. We seek unlimited possibilities. The question of ultimate freedom emerges from our hope to "Be *more* than we can be." Limitations of any sort seem to threaten the sense of greatness and significance of our lives. As we have noted, we seem to have a calling to achieve or relate to a "Something More" than this life offers. If we fail to arrive at that "Something More," our lives seem unfulfilled.

Many live as if the accumulation of material riches, power, popularity, and reputation were an answer to this question. Of course, this striving is bound to fail. Ultimately, we will have no choice, and all our choices will be for nothing. To the religious, one can only be free if one is connected with the infinite, for only the infinite is free of limitation.

Eastern Views of Freedom as Liberation

These thoughts naturally lead to what we might call Eastern views of freedom. In these views, human beings do have choices. But these choices do not equal freedom. According to the law of karma, one is, in fact, bound by one's choices. Choices of thought and action have natural consequences leading to more thoughts and actions. Thus, one is tied to the wheel of *samsara*, the karma-driven, endless cycles of birth, life, death, and rebirth.

Eastern views seek liberation from the most basic realities of our worldly existence. For instance, in Hinduism, liberation may be achieved when one real-izes union with the Absolute (Brahman). The answer to freedom from limitation is clear. It is found in one's inner Self and the realization that this Self has the same eternal, pure, perfect—and free—nature as the Absolute (Brahman).

On the other hand, Buddhism seeks freedom from suffering by the realization of a level of consciousness that transcends the illusions of the Self. Limitations come from the illusion of a permanent, substantial Self. The egoistic desires of the Self tie it to the endless, circular chain of karma. The answer of Mahayana Buddhism is difficult but clear. One must realize the higher consciousness. In that "pure consciousness," the burning flame of desire is extinguished. Eventu-ally, even the lamp of the illusion of "Self" vanishes.

Another way to put Eastern views of freedom is to say that freedom is the ability to live according to one's nature. When one lives according to the under-standing of the "way one truly is," one experiences no constraints, no limita-tions, and no restrictions. In Hinduism, one's true nature is the "Self" that has the same eternal nature as the Absolute (Brahman). In Buddhism, one's true nature is the "Buddha-Nature," the "luminous mind" of mental clarity that is realized in enlightenment.

The Focus of Western Views: Freedom as a Matter of Choice

On the other hand, the essential category of Western thought about freedom is the will. Most Westerners insist that human beings should have the right to make personal choices of their religion. Most suppose that humans have free will to accept or reject the freedom that salvation gives, no matter what version of salvation is offered.

For the Western traditions of Judaism, Christianity, and Islam, the Creator made humans "in the image of God." An important and necessary feature of this image that constitutes human nature is the will. The power of agency gives humans the capacity to make choices and, therefore, to carry out plans. In this sense, then, the Creator's superior will gives a certain amount of freedom to human nature. Within the parameters of that Divine will, humans have choice. The most important choice is the ability to choose freely for or against God and His will.

The Muslim view of human freedom illustrates this point well. Note that if human beings understand the Divine will of God correctly, they have the capacity to submit to God and obey his commandments. God is the All-Merciful because he has given humankind the clear revelation of His will and intentions for humans through the prophets. This disclosure is summed up and made universal by the Islamic prophet Muhammad.

How is obedience to the divine will freedom? It is important to note that in Islam the definition of freedom is expanded and perhaps changed. Freedom is not the ability to do anything one chooses. In fact, often what people willfully choose makes them less free, since they are bound to their choices.

Muslims believe that humans have choices. They will be accountable for those choices at the Judgment. Yet Muslims also believe in destiny. What happens is written in the book. Muslims believe that while God knows past, present, and future, that does not mean He makes individuals do what they do. The calling of human beings is to come to know and live in harmony with the divine will. In Islam, one achieves freedom by perfect obedience to the good will of God who is the Creator.

Christians, in contrast, have divided opinions on the question along the lines of the poles of freedom and determinism. Of course, even the strictest Calvinist who believes in the determinism of predestination would allow that human beings are responsible for their everyday decisions. However, the founder of Western theology, Augustine (354–430 CE), set two directions in Western thought that undermine the assumption of human freedom when it comes to their ultimate destiny.

The first is the idea of predestination. The combination of beliefs in the perfection and omniscient (all-seeing) nature of God form the basis of this idea. When we put the perfection and all-seeing nature of God together, we reach the conclusion that the destiny of each individual is predetermined. If God knows everything, then God must have perfect knowledge of the future. If God has perfect knowledge of the future, then human beings cannot help but do what God already knew that they would do in his divine foresight.

The second and corresponding idea is Augustine's teaching of original sin. Augustine taught that the disobedience of Adam and Eve had so corrupted human nature that the human will was turned against the Creator. Augustine constructed this theory of human nature in opposition to the heretic Pelagius (354–c. 440 CE), who proposed the optimistic view that humans can choose for or against their salvation. Against the Pelagian view, Augustine countered that human beings must absolutely depend on the saving grace of Jesus Christ if they are to be saved.

Augustine's view that salvation was predetermined put these two ideas together. Humans do not deserve salvation because they are sinners through and through. However, in his mercy, God has decided to save some from punishment. Since he has perfect foresight, he already knows who these "elect" are as well as those who are destined for damnation. By this theology, Augustine introduced a marked pessimism about human freedom into Western thought.

Protestantism emerged when first Martin Luther, and then John Calvin and others, asserted a different interpretation of this Augustinian view against the sacramental system of the medieval Catholic Church. The medieval Catholic Church taught that God has set up the means for human persons to become worthy of salvation. It was up to humans to use them. The Protestants believed that only "by grace" could humans ever hope to be saved. In this Protestant view, salvation was entirely God's choice. It was not the choice of a human being.

While Luther agreed with Augustine's doctrine of predestination, it was John Calvin who carried the thought all the way. In Calvin's theology, God has predestined some of the human race for heaven and some for hell. Only "the elect" whom God has chosen will go to heaven.

Even at the risk of denying human freedom, the Reformers felt they were accomplishing several things through these theological moves. First, they were defending the absolute necessity of the crucifixion of Jesus Christ for the payment of sin. Second, they were maintaining God's sovereignty over every human being and human institution, including the church. Third, they were reassuring the troubled conscience that was seeking some way of earning God's favor.

The work of John Calvin, especially, was so fixed on the human lack of ultimate freedom that it was bound to be resisted. Many turned against the predestination theory of Calvinism with the rise of Arminianism. Jacobus Arminius (1560–1609) was a Dutch theologian who reasserted human choice over Calvinism. Arminius did not deny that the human will is corrupted by original sin. Yet when it comes to salvation, he taught that God offers sinful human beings a free choice. When evangelical Protestants call on everyone "to make a decision for Christ," they confirm that in their circles, Arminius has won the argument. People are free to accept or reject the Gospel, and in believing in the Gospel we have freedom from sin.

Both the Roman Catholic Church[91] and the Protestant Arminians agree that humans have freedom of choice in the matter of salvation. The difference between the Protestant Arminians and the Catholics may not be so much the affirmation of human freedom as the means by which humans choose the salvation that God offers. For example, does one receive salvation by a decisive emotional acceptance of Jesus Christ as Savior, an evangelical Protestant way? Or is it through the faithful use of the sacraments of the church that are conduits of the grace of Christ, the Catholic way?

Eastern Orthodox Christianity has another view that does not go back to Augustine's doctrine of original sin. Both Catholic and Protestants build their ideas on Augustine's teaching that human nature is fundamentally corrupted with the *guilt* of the primal sin. In this view, all human beings share in the rebellion of Adam and Eve against their Creator. However, Orthodox Christianity rejects the idea that one person's guilt can be transferred or inherited. Sin remains a personal act and inherited guilt is impossible.[92]

In the Orthodox view, the "ancestral sin" of Adam and Eve corrupted human nature not with guilt but with mortality. The problem of salvation therefore shifts from the emphasis on the escape from punishment for the original sin of Adam and Eve to overcoming human mortality. According to Orthodoxy, death casts a shadow on the human race. It leads humans into the sinful passions of greed, lust, and pride as they try to satisfy their desires before death overtakes them.[93]

Orthodox Christians hold that Jesus Christ overcame the curse of death by his death and resurrection. In so doing he put human beings back on the track of fulfilling the purpose for which they were created: eternal life in communion with God. To achieve this purpose, humans must align their will with the divine will. Instead of dwelling on the helplessness of humans, Eastern Orthodoxy affirms the idea of *synergy* of divine-human cooperation. The idea is that the saving grace of God acts in and through human efforts.[94]

Orthodox Christians do not speculate about the foreknowledge of God. It is sufficient to believe that God does not violate the freedom of humans made in the image of God. The fulfillment of freedom is found in the realization of a never-ending and always growing communion with God.

A comparison of Eastern and Western views reveals that an important difference is on the matter of choice. Eastern views would tend to say that humans have choices of thought and action. Karma holds us responsible for those choices. However, in an ultimate sense those choices enslave us. They attach us to the endless cycle of birth and rebirth. Freedom is found in the liberation from karma.

Though the majority of Western views stress freedom of choice, Calvinism denies that humans have a choice when it comes to their destiny. With other Protestants, they affirm that salvation is only "by grace." To Calvinists, the doctrine of grace means that humans can do nothing that will affect their salvation. Not even the will and its decisions have anything to do with it. Through His foreknowledge, God has already decided the destiny of all human beings, as we have described above.

Today's Western Christians tend to reject these views of grace and predestination and uphold human choice. In Islam, humans must choose submission to the will of God. In Protestantism, humans exercise choice in accepting or rejecting the Gospel. In Catholicism, humans exercise choice in receiving the spiritual graces to grow in holiness and attain salvation in Christ.

Eastern Orthodox Christians believe that freedom, though limited and often misdirected, is one of the divine gifts that make us human. Like certain Eastern religions, Eastern Orthodoxy believes that the passions of desire are limitations to true freedom. The overcoming of the passions is the way to the realization of the gift of human freedom "in the image of God."

In summary, the concentration on the limits of freedom of choice dictates much of the discussion in Western circles, especially those influenced by the Protestant Christian ideas of human nature and predestination. Nevertheless, along with other religions Christianity asserts the responsibility of humans for their choices in life. Yet, in non-Western religions, freedom is more than choice. In fact, there is freedom even without choice.

Evaluation of the Answers to the Question of Freedom and Destiny

How can we evaluate these answers to the quest for human freedom? If human life is determined, then whatever we do in this life loses its ultimate significance. We are left to wrest whatever contentment we can wherever the currents of life take us. However, contentment is not freedom. It is resignation. On the opposite extreme, freedom and choice are not identical. Choices can enslave us, and we can become slaves to choice. Self-determination defined in terms of choice, therefore, is not an adequate answer to the question.

Zen Buddhist training involves long, highly disciplined sessions of *zazen* in which they sit in meditation for long periods of time. However, the end is *kensho*, in which a glimpse of enlightenment bursts in the consciousness like Fourth of July fireworks. Those who realize this state exhibit a sudden rush of wild spontaneity, a giddy creativity, and a sense of unlimited release. All obstructions are removed. They can live freely with no obstacle before them and no hindrance holding them back.

Perhaps this experience provides the standard to evaluate views of freedom. In these terms, freedom means that one is not bound by anything, not even one's choices. When we achieve this state, we have reached *self-transcendence*, the end of our quest for freedom. However, self-transcendence does not entail freedom from external forces. Self-transcendence is not an infinite cafeteria of alluring options. It is liberation of the inner spirit, a freedom in which each moment has ultimate significance.

These thoughts bring us back to the beginning of the consideration of human freedom and destiny. The statements of belief presume the questions that they answer. This discussion suggests that the question prescribes the answer. How the question is framed is, therefore, extremely important. If we assume that freedom is a matter of choices, then the search for freedom of choice sets the limit of what we will find.

Testing the Proposed Method: Suffering

The question of suffering is a good example of the importance of how the question is framed.

What are we asking when we consider the dilemma of suffering? The question has three different levels:

1. The universal condition of all human beings
2. The experience of mental/emotional distress
3. The question of why a merciful God would allow innocent and massive suffering

Suffering as the Universal Condition of Human Life

Buddhism poses the question of the causes of suffering with a view toward overcoming it. In Buddhism, the term *dukka* (suffering) refers to the whole human condition. Dukka is the sense of dissatisfaction (unsatisfactoriness) that pervades all of life.[95] Even pleasure is tinged with it.

The dharma of Buddhism teaches the way of overcoming suffering as dukka. The basis of the way of liberation from suffering is the Four Noble Truths.

1. Life is suffering.
2. The origin of suffering is desires.
3. If desires cease, suffering ceases.
4. There is a way to attain the cessation of desire. It is the Eightfold Path.

According to the Four Noble Truths, the cause of suffering is *tanhā*, usually translated as "desire." A better word would be "craving." If we trace the ways that "craving" causes frustration, we find the mental states of greed, aversion, and delusion. The mind is controlled by greed that stirs a hunger for pleasure, possessions, power, and prestige. It is enslaved by aversion that breeds anger, hatred, and resentment and by the delusions of fantasies, images, and pretensions that darken our minds.[96] These basic mental states then branch out into all sorts of secondary and unhappy feelings.

However, according to Buddhism, below the basic mental states is ignorance. Ignorance is not a lack of knowledge of the world as it appears to the ordinary mind. Ignorance is the lack of insight into the true nature of things.[97] It is the way humans fool themselves about the basic condition of their lives and the state of their minds.

Suffering as the Experience of Mental/Emotional Distress

Outside of the circle of Buddhism, most would not think of the problem of suffering in such broad terms. In common terms, suffering refers to distress caused by such emotional states as grief, unhappiness, and anxiety. As personal injury lawyers can attest, there is a difference between pain and suffering.[98] Pain primarily refers to the discomfort of physical sensation. Suffering refers to mental and emotional anguish. Pain can cause suffering. Yet suffering can exist without physical pain. However, emotional suffering can cause the physical symptoms of pain.

Defined in this way, mental and emotional anguish is a problem of human existence. It seems natural to wonder why human beings must suffer, and some more than others. Rabbi Jack Bemporad observes that religions address suffering as a problem in two ways. First, they try to put it into a larger context of the way things are in reality. This is the question of the meaning of suffering. Second, they offer ways to overcome or transcend suffering. This is the question of how humans can rise above suffering.[99]

These questions differ from the broader Buddhist approach in that they seem to presume that ordinary life is, or should be, more than suffering. The answer may be a different outlook on suffering and one's existence. The causes of suffering are defined as something different than delusions of the mind. Therefore, suffering is more than illusion.

The Problem of Theodicy

In general, the problem of suffering is the question of why humans must suffer. A narrower version of this problem is called *theodicy*. This way of putting the question of suffering presupposes Western theistic ideas of God. The Western monotheism of Judaism, Christianity, and Islam views God as almighty. Yet these three faiths also view God as merciful. The problem of theodicy arises in the face of innocent and massive suffering. Theodicy asks about the justice of suffering that seems out of proportion to anything that the sufferers deserve. In short, how could a merciful God allow innocent or massive suffering?

Of course, the answer could be to drop one of the presuppositions—or both. God may not be mighty enough to prevent suffering. Or God may not be merciful enough to want to prevent suffering. Or God, as defined, may not exist. Most Western believers are stuck with the question because they do not want to take any of these options.

Answers to the Question of Suffering

In general, theories of suffering can be put into categories. (See textbox "Theories of the Answer to Suffering" for a list.)

Theories of the Answer to Suffering

- Retribution Theories (Suffering is deserved.)
- Reward Theories (Suffering is overcome in greater good.)
- Training and Testing Theories (Suffering builds or tests human character.)
- Dualistic Theories (Suffering is involved in the struggle between good and evil.)
- Self-Chosen Theories (Suffering is accepted for spiritual goals.)
- Divine Sovereignty (God only knows the reason for suffering.)

Retribution theories may be broken into two kinds. The first is the Eastern view of *karma*. Karma is simply the inventible working of "action." One can never escape karma because every action has a consequent action. Therefore, suffering is the result of previous action and one gets what one's action "deserves." The second is the religious view of punishment. In this case, suffering is the result of divine punishment. The difference between these two theories is that the one needs an agent of punishment, a "judge," and the other does not.

Reward theories also can be broken into two kinds. The first is that there will be compensation in heaven if one endures suffering well here on Earth. The second is that the same kind of reward will be given on Earth.

Training and testing theories assert that suffering is good for us. It builds character. Suffering therefore helps us grow in virtue. It strengthens our character by testing us. Without the challenge of suffering, we would not reach maturity as human beings.

Dualistic theories assume that there are two different realities or forces in the world. In this view, the world is a battleground between the forces of good and evil. Whether or not we know the origin of evil, our suffering shows that we are caught in this struggle. A version of this theory is that suffering is the result of a world in which humans have free will. As we have seen, in Western viewpoints, free will means choice. Some choices will result in suffering. However, if harmful choices were restricted, freedom of choice would be restricted. Therefore, for freedom to exist, the potential for evil must exist.

The *self-chosen* approach is that suffering is accepted for higher goals. Religious believers may purposely seek suffering in order to prove or strengthen their devotion to God or the sacred world. Others may dedicate their suffering for the good of others.

Most of these theories stumble over the question of innocent and disproportional suffering. A tragic case is a boy who was shot randomly as his aunt dropped him off at the door of his school. It is possible but hard to imagine what would explain, justify, or compensate for such senseless violence against the innocent. This is not to mention human agonies throughout the world: genocide, war, hunger and poverty, disease, and natural disasters.

For this reason, some accept the *divine sovereignty* theory. The biblical book of Job teaches that the only answer to suffering is surrender to the mystery of God. For those who have not wrestled with the issue of suffering, this may seem to be a too-easy resignation. For believers who are undergoing severe distress without explanation, however, it may be the most honest answer.

Evaluation of the Theories of Suffering

This brief review of theories of suffering shows that the ultimate questions may be framed in different ways. The questions and answers have a mutual relationship in which one influences the other. While a religion may tend toward one of these theories, most major religions combine a number of them. However, all religions offer beliefs that answer the universal and ultimate questions like freedom and determinism or suffering. As we have seen in the case of freedom and destiny, religions use specific sets of ideas and attitudes to answer these questions. However, a given religion will not only set out the answers to these questions in a specific way, it will also define the question in its own way.

EVALUATING THE MOST PROMISING SOLUTION: WAYS OF SEEING AND WAYS OF LIFE

We have shown how the proposed method takes us down a path of analysis and comparison of beliefs. By following this way of thinking, we can gain some insight into the human condition and into the beliefs that attempt to address it. It may be that the path we have followed crosses the boundary from religious studies into theology. In fact, Tillich proposed his "Method of Correlation" as a form of apologetic theology. However, this method need not assume the truth of any of the viewpoints it analyzes. It can compare the multiple viewpoints of different religions in its framework without favoring any of them.

A Test Case to Evaluate the Most Promising Solution

This chapter has tried to solve the problem raised by the changing religious situation. Contemporary attitudes toward belief are moving away from the doctrines of religious institutions to personal self-chosen opinions. This attitude demands choices among a widening variety of possibilities for belief. The problem is how to make sense of religious beliefs in this new religious climate. That means understanding the nature of religious belief as distinct from other beliefs.

We can focus this problem with the question of the difference between traditional and paranormal beliefs. In the new situation where many Americans no longer accept established religious authority, why do they choose from one category or the other or both?

Research into this question provides a test case for the proposed "most promising solution" given above. The initial question is why believers choose beliefs from traditional, paranormal, or both categories. Political science professor Tom Rice observed that for twenty-five years scholars have tried to identify the types of persons who would subscribe to these sets of beliefs. Most have held the *deprivation theory*. This explanation is that people who are poor use religion to cope with their physical and psychological hardships. From the research, Rice found that this theory works for traditional beliefs. However, the likelihood that individuals will hold paranormal beliefs depends on the *type* of belief, not the income or educational level. For example, those with less education are more likely to believe in ghosts, astrology, and reincarnation. Yet those with more education are more likely to believe in telepathy, ESP, and déjà vu.[100]

To focus the inquiry into the differences between traditional and paranormal beliefs, Rice asked about their relationship. The distinction itself seems arbitrary since it comes from the theology of Western monotheism. This way of categorizing belief officially sanctions beliefs in God, heaven, hell, and the devil. But it rejects fortune telling, magic, witchcraft, and conjuring the spirits of the dead. Why do some accept this distinction and others ignore it? Why do many people today accept truth claims from both lists?

Who Are Likely to Entertain Paranormal Beliefs?

Option A: Those who hold supernatural (traditional) beliefs will be more likely to hold paranormal beliefs.

Option B: Those who hold supernatural (traditional) beliefs will be less likely to hold paranormal beliefs.

To answer, Rice asked if it is possible to predict who will choose paranormal beliefs. Researchers have found that predictions based on culture, social status, and educational level do not hold up when it comes to the belief in the paranormal. There are two remaining live options: either those who hold supernatural (traditional) beliefs will be more likely to hold paranormal beliefs or they will be less likely to hold those beliefs. (See textbox "Who Are Likely to Entertain Paranormal Beliefs?" for a list of the options.[101])

Option A supposes the paranormal beliefs are but a short step from traditional beliefs. Traditional believers learn that beliefs cannot be proven. Their background makes them more susceptible to the claims of paranormal beliefs. Consequently, the factor that determines the conclusion that there is no difference between the two sets of belief is credulity, the willingness to believe.

Option B assumes that the teaching of established religious authorities will make believers less likely to add paranormal beliefs. These believers will understand the difference between the two sets and/or obey the doctrines of religious authorities. In this case, the determining factor would be compliance, the deference to authority.

Rice found that research has failed to prove either of these options is correct.[102] The research is contradictory. Some scholars have presented data to support Option A. Some have presented data to support Option B.

This outcome suggests that there is something missing in our understanding of belief. We cannot tell the difference between the two by the way believers justify their choices according to the analysis above. And we cannot tell the difference by the content of religious belief. The content of the teachings of religious authorities on paranormal beliefs is clear. But many believers choose to disregard it.

Evaluation of the Proposed Method

The proposal of the "most promising solution" deals with content. The method compares different answers to the ultimate questions it frames. Once again, the question arises about why people choose one set of answers to a fundamental question of life over another set. Previous answers would say that the deciding factor is belonging to a religion or religious group that holds that opinion. However, outside the religious traditions, as many are, how do people decide? The method advises the comparison of the answer with the question. However, that is a matter of individual judgment. In this respect, the method does not solve the problem of this chapter.

The proposed method has one other flaw. Its process of thinking turns beliefs into abstractions that ordinary reason can grasp. However, to turn living beliefs into dead ideas is like killing a living body to study it as a corpse. As a corpse, the body can be pinned down, dissected, categorized, compared, and analyzed. However, the living body is much more than a corpse.

Aspects of Belief Often Overlooked

We have found that we cannot make sense of contemporary choices of religious belief by the way believers justify them or by content. We have to look at some other factor to explain those choices.

Tillich's method gives a clue to what that missing factor is. His idea of faith as ultimate concern asserts that for believers, belief truly matters. Believers do not treat their beliefs as abstractions to be analyzed, criticized, and evaluated. They regard them as indispensable truths on which they build their lives.

This insight leads to a concluding solution to this chapter. Religious studies might reach a better understanding of belief if it investigated two essential aspects of the living beliefs of religious adherents. First, beliefs are ways of knowing. Second, these ways of knowing direct the lives of those who follow them. If these points are true, beliefs are not merely opinions that lack sufficient evidence. Opinions are notions, sentiments, and judgments based on personal viewpoints. Opinions are limited to points of view that are changeable and arguable. Hardly anyone would die for a personal opinion. On the other hand, to this day, believers are giving up their lives for their beliefs. They are doing this because they hold that their beliefs are true ways of knowing the most important things of human life.

Because beliefs are thought to be opinions without evidence, beliefs are often accused of being unreasonable imagination. Against the charge that religious belief is simply sophisticated fantasy, Alvin Plantinga says that Christianity would deny that it is irrational. If so, Christianity would either have to be mistaken or misdirected. However, Christianity holds that when people come to faith, they come to right understanding. In this view, religious faith is a kind of knowledge.[103]

This view of belief is not unique to Christianity. One of the elements of the Buddhist Eightfold Path is "right understanding." Buddhists understand suffering and all of life in the light of the dharma. Other religions have a similar principle. In the light of belief, believers understand everything else.

Ludwig Wittgenstein (1888–1952) had the same idea. According to the rules of historical or scientific evidence, religion is unreasonable. Yet religious beliefs have their own reasons.[104] Suppose one person affirms belief in the Last Judgment. Another person says he does not believe this. If the believer and nonbeliever both are referring to an actual event at the end of time, then they are arguing about the same thing. Who is right? Presumably, if we could take a time machine and "time travel" to the end of the world, we could find out whether the belief in the Last Judgment is warranted.

However, according to Wittgenstein, believing in the Last Judgment means a lot more than a prediction of the end of time. Presumably, one could believe in the likelihood of such a catastrophic end of the world without being a religious believer. Conversely, one could admit that it is impossible to produce empirical evidence to back up one's belief in such an event. Yet that admission would not make one a nonbeliever. Religious believers insist that they know the truth of the Last Judgment. They claim to know it "by faith," not according to empirical reasoning.

What is the difference between accepting the probability of the end of the world and believing in the Last Judgment? The answer that Wittgenstein gives is that believers are willing to set aside the question of evidence and stake their lives on that claim.[105] The belief in the Last Judgment gives believers "guidance for life." In fact, they embrace this belief so tightly that it regulates and controls their whole lives.[106]

Concluding Summary: The Difference between Traditional and Paranormal Beliefs

In summary, the question is not whether we can test the probability of a future event in history such as the Last Judgment. The question is whether we can understand the Last Judgment the way religious believers do. Wittgenstein's point is that the religious believer in the Last Judgment and the disbeliever think in different ways. In the mind of the unbeliever, the lack of evidence for the Last Judgment settles the issue. In the mind of the believer, the kind of evidence that the unbeliever demands is irrelevant.[107]

In this view, to study belief is to study different ways of thinking.[108] These different ways of thinking give believers a different picture, or way of looking at the world—a religious outlook.[109]

Flew's debating partner R. M. Hare (1919–2002) made this point in his response to Flew's parable. Hare said that religious beliefs are not matter-of-fact assertions at all. They are basic perspectives that he calls *bliks*.[110] Hare coined the word *bliks* to say that religious statements are ways of looking at the world, not truth statements. Thus, religious beliefs do not provide descriptions and explanations of the way things are. Religious beliefs are ways of seeing.

By the inner sight of religious faith, humans know what is real, what is true, and what is good. By the insight of religious belief, humans gain a sense of the meaning of life and a way to understand how to live on this Earth. In summary, the world of the religious believer is not merely a physical world known by the senses. It is a world whose web of meanings is woven out of the associations of religious beliefs. Everything that is known fits within this frame of reference, and daily life is built on its foundation.

The Key to Evaluating Religious Beliefs

Do the beliefs change the way one thinks and transform the way one lives?

Thus, the religious outlook changes the way one thinks and the way one lives. Religious believing is more than affirming a set of ideas. Believing changes human beings. It not only alters the way they think but also transforms the way they live. By believing, human persons accept the challenge of "living out a new vision of the world."[111]

To make reasonable sense of religious beliefs, we cannot study them as they are in themselves. We certainly cannot study them as abstractions. In order to make sense of religious beliefs, we must study them in their contexts where they are guides for total ways of life. Studies that abstract beliefs out of their contexts fail to consider the part these beliefs play in the believers' lives. For example, a Gallup poll found that just about half of American men believe that aliens from space have visited Earth.[112] The polls also showed that four in ten American women believe it as well. However, is the belief in extraterrestrial life a casual opinion or a significant religious belief? The answer would depend on whether the belief has an effect on the way of life of those who hold it. To understand and evaluate this paranormal belief, we would have to put it into context of how those who hold this opinion live their lives.

The academic test of the difference between traditional religious and paranormal beliefs, therefore, does not lie in fideism, revelation and enlightenment, religious authority, or experience. It lies in the nature of the belief itself. Does the belief in haunted houses, ESP, clairvoyance, or aliens from outer space make an ultimate difference in the lives of believers? Alternatively, does the belief in angels and demons make an ultimate difference in the lives of believers? Theology would evaluate the content of these beliefs. This proposal suggests that the difference is proven when religious belief transforms the lives of those embrace it.

In the twenty-first century, understanding religious beliefs is becoming increasingly urgent. To get along in our world, we need a basic awareness of the religious beliefs of our neighbors, whether they live next door or on the other side of the world. With understanding comes toleration and even cooperation. Without understanding, we are prone to harbor mistaken and biased suspicions about the religious faiths of others. Many Western scholars tend to treat religious beliefs as abstractions, unjustified opinions, or even as immoral errors of judgment. These approaches do not help us to appreciate the role that sincere religious belief plays in the lives of the majority of the world's peoples. The field of religious studies has a significant role in promoting the understanding of religious belief necessary for us to achieve peace and harmony among religious groups. This chapter shows that an initial step is to realize the crucial relationships between religious beliefs, ways of looking at the world, matters of ultimate concern, and the ways of life of believers.

KEY TERMS

Arminianism: the reaction to Calvinism in Protestantism championed by Jacobus Arminius that reasserted that humans have a choice of whether to accept the Gospel and be saved from damnation or not.

Belief: the acceptance of a truth claim that is not verifiable by evidence of the senses or inferences from such evidence.

Bliks: a word coined by R. M. Hare suggesting that religious statements are basic ways of looking at the world, not truth statements.

Dualism: the belief that reality is divided into two basic categories that exist side by side; in theories of suffering the idea of a basic, cosmic struggle between the forces of good and evil.

Evidentialism: the idea that sufficient evidence is the only warrant (justification) for belief (see foundationalism).

Faith: a trust or confidence in something or someone that one deems worthy of such an attitude.

Fideism: the rejection of any outside tests of belief other than belief itself.

Four Noble Truths: the summary of the teachings of Buddhism concerning the universal human condition of suffering and how it is overcome.

Freedom and determinism: the philosophical problem of the relationship of free will to ideas of a determined outcome of the course of world events or of an individual's life.

Karma: in Hinduism and Buddhism the law of consequent action: every action produces a subsequent and corresponding action.

Method of Correlation: a systematic method designed by the theologian Paul Tillich that analyzes and explains beliefs in terms of the ultimate questions that they answer.

Original sin: the Western doctrine based on the teaching of Augustine that the fall of Adam and Eve into sin corrupted human nature. The guilt as well as consequences of that fall are passed down genetically to each person in the human race.

Paranormal beliefs: beliefs in realities and phenomena that are not sanctioned by traditional and official doctrines.

Predestination: the idea of the Protestant reformer John Calvin and others that whether human persons are to be saved or damned is already determined by the will and foreknowledge of God.

Protestantism: a form of Christianity originating from the Reformation of the sixteenth century that mounted a lasting protest against the failings of the Roman Catholic Church; a wide variety of beliefs, practices, and denominations that arose from the Reformation churches.

Religious experience: the justification of belief by the inner feelings, sensations, and apprehensions of the personal, inner life.

Retribution: the payment one deserves; in theories of suffering the idea that suffering is deserved.

Samsara: in Hinduism and Buddhism the karma-driven endless cycle of birth, life, death, and rebirth.

Satori: the experience of enlightenment in Zen Buddhism, a deep and personal realization of the nature of reality in the overcoming of illusion.

Theodicy: the puzzle of suffering that arises from the twin beliefs of the almighty power and mercy of God: How can a merciful God allow innocent and disproportional suffering?

Ultimate concern: a phrase coined by the theologian Paul Tillich that refers to the most serious matters of human existence. In Tillich's view, religious faith deals with matters of ultimate concern.

Ultimate questions: the most profound questions that arise from the "human condition" that every human person faces. These are universal and fundamental, but religious beliefs answer them in different ways.

Univocal statements: statements that have a single meaning that is expressed on the surface level of the grammar and vocabulary of the statement.

KEY QUESTIONS

1. Statement by Clifford and Evidentialism
   a. Why is the statement of William K. Clifford about insufficient evidence an expression of evidentialism?
   b. What kind of evidence does evidentialism accept to establish truth?
   c. Evaluate Flew's argument against religious beliefs made in the "Parable of the Gardener." Is it convincing? Defend your answer.

2. Surveys of Religious Beliefs
   a. What do polls of religious beliefs contribute to the study of beliefs? What are their limitations?
   b. How do the religious beliefs in the United States compare with those in Canada and Great Britain?
3. Believing and Attending without Belonging
   a. Americans are breaking away from the authority of religious institutions to find their own self-chosen beliefs. Why is this change a challenge to the past understanding of the nature of religious beliefs?
   b. How do the changing attitudes toward religious beliefs encourage beliefs in the paranormal?
4. Fideism
   a. How does fideism justify religious beliefs?
   b. If the standard for religious belief is that it is "sincerely held belief," how would someone tell whether a believer is sincere or not?
5. Revelation and Enlightenment
   a. As sources of belief, what do revelation and enlightenment have in common?
   b. What are the differences between them?
6. Religious Authority
   a. On what basis do founders of religions claim special authority?
   b. Why is a "believing community" that accepts the revelation or enlightenment of the founder necessary for the founding of a religion?
7. The Question and Answer: The Method of Correlation
   a. How does the method of treating beliefs as answers to ultimate questions help scholars compare beliefs?
   b. Here is a list of questions. Which ones are universal and ultimate questions?
      (i)   What did you have for breakfast?
      (ii) Why is there so much undeserved suffering in the world (the question of suffering/evil)?
      (iii) Will I have a satisfying career?
      (iv) Do human beings really have a choice about the outcome of their lives and their fate (the question of destiny)?
      (v)   Is there a rational order to the universe (the question of the origin and order to the universe)?
8. Answers to Ultimate Questions
   a. Freedom and Determinism: If one had the choice of everything one wanted on Earth, would one be free? (Choose a religious perspective and give your answer from its point of view.)
   b. Suffering: choose a case of innocent and/or disproportionate suffering from current events. Use that case as a test of one of the theories of suffering presented in this chapter.

9. The Difference That Beliefs Make
    a. This chapter proposed that the standard for deciding whether an opin-
    ion is a religious belief is that it makes a difference in the lives of
    believers. How would that standard help scholars tell the difference
    between religious and paranormal beliefs?
    b. How has this chapter changed your mind or added to what you think
    about belief?

4

The Right to Sacred Things
Symbol, Myth, and Ritual

CHAPTER SUMMARY

1. Discovering the Problem: Old Bones Create New Controversy

By the federal law of the Native American Graves Protection and Repatriation Act (NAGPRA), museums and educational institutions must return bones and artifacts taken from the graves of native peoples if the tribes claim them as their heritage. Among these are "funerary objects"—that is, objects buried with the human bodies and other "sacred objects."

For years, museums and schools have collected, studied, and displayed the funerary and other sacred objects as well as the human remains objects. They have claimed them for scientific and educational purposes. However, because native peoples view these artifacts as sacred, they have successfully pressed the federal government for the right to repossess them.

Over twenty years have passed since its passage, but the federal law and its implementation are still involved in controversy. Native peoples throughout the world continue to insist on their right to possess their cultural and religious heritages. They treat the objects from graves as sacred. Many scientists and educators express concerns about the loss of these irreplaceable sources of knowledge from the past because the law forces them to relinquish the objects that they need for study. They treat the objects from graves as scientific evidence. Opposing ideas regarding the nature of the objects raise a problem for religious studies: how to understand the claim that the items are sacred objects from an academic point of view.

2. Focusing the Problem: Museums Change Their Ways

As we reflect on the continuing "antiquities wars," a problem takes more definite shape. What is meant when an object is said to be "sacred"? What is included in the term "sacred," and how do we distinguish between sacred objects and artifacts that are not sacred? What or who could authenticate the claim that an object is sacred?

Of course, we could simply accept the word of native peoples at face value. Yet that would not give scholars an understanding of their point of view. Without that understanding, we might still give equal or more weight to the counterclaim that the objects are necessary for study and teaching.

The contested items under NAGPRA represent a challenge to the field of religious studies to contribute an understanding of what religious people mean when they say that an object is "sacred." This is a fundamental question. A grasp of what is meant by the sacredness of a religious object is the primary step to understanding what a religious object means to believers. These thoughts focus the problem. The task is to find a way of interpreting sacred objects in academic terms comprehensible to scientists and educators.

3. Surveying the Alternative Approaches: Investigating Symbol, Myth, and Ritual

This chapter will divide the alternatives for solving the problem of how to understand the religious claim that objects are sacred into three approaches: we can treat the artifacts as religious symbols; we can study their origin and meaning in myth; and we can interpret them according to their role in ritual. But this simply divides the same problem three ways. This chapter will present alternative theories of the nature and role of symbols, of myths, and of rituals.

Symbols have exceptional power to represent and present meanings beyond themselves, a power that leads to controversy about their use. Myths are stories that speak of deeper truths for a society, but they also ignite controversy. How can modern people interpret them? Do they apply to reality as a whole, the tribal societies that believe in them, or perhaps human psychology? In each case, the "insiders" to the religion (the believers) know what the symbols and myths mean. However, when outsiders (such as scientists and educators) attempt to understand them, they necessarily take them out of the context of that belief. The problem of how to understand the sacredness of religious objects and their meaning to religious believers remains.

4. Proposing the Most Promising Solution: The Ritual Context within a Social Setting

This chapter will propose that the most productive way to understand the sacred objects under question in the NAGPRA program is to study them within their ritual contexts. According to the theory of this chapter, in the ritual context, symbol, myth, and ritual come together. Rituals initiate their participants into transcendent worlds and alternative realities. Their purpose is to transform the participants and then return them to ordinary society with a new social status and a new spiritual state.

In ritual, symbolic objects attain special, sacred power as they present and represent meanings beyond their normal use. This chapter proposes that the sacred objects in question are best understood in the context of the specific rituals in which they are used. By studying their ritual context, "outsiders" might grasp the meaning of the disputed objects as the native people understand them. This approach would help museums and schools who hold collections of the sacred objects in question to appreciate the viewpoint of the native peoples and why they demand the return of their religious items.

5. Evaluating the Most Promising Solution: Dispute over a Hawaiian Object

This chapter ends with a test case of the proposal that religious symbols and myths can best be understood within their ritual context. The ritual setting gives the objects their sacredness. Thus, scholars can interpret the sacred objects in question by studying their use in ritual.

A controversy over a Hawaiian spear rest will test this theory. A museum in Rhode Island refused the claim of a native Hawaiian group to the artifact because it said it was a functional object to hold fishing spears, and, perhaps, an "art object." It was not a sacred object. The native Hawaiians made a convincing case when they changed the context of the hearing from a courtroom atmosphere to a scene of ritual performance. In the ritual context, the artifact could be viewed in terms of its sacred use in the Native Hawaiian religion. The chapter ends with the observation that the NAGPRA legislation has far-reaching implications for the academic study of religion. It discourages scholars from reducing religious believers to objects for study and sacred artifacts to scientific evidence. It emphasizes that academic study should pay close attention to the details of particular cases instead of fitting evidence into broad general categories. Finally, it urges collaboration between native peoples and scholars to advance the knowledge of human history and the sacred ways of native peoples.

DISCOVERING THE PROBLEM: OLD BONES CREATE NEW CONTROVERSY

A road crew uncovered twenty-seven skeletons near Iowa City in 1976 when they were relocating a pioneer cemetery. Twenty-six were immediately reburied in another cemetery. The Iowa State Archeologist Marshall McKusick sent the last set of bones to Iowa City for study. The bones that were returned to the earth were Caucasian. The bones sent to the lab were the remains of a Native American woman.

When Maria Pearson (Running Moccasins) heard what had happened, she complained to the Iowa governor about discrimination. The lack of response prompted her to start an intense grassroots campaign. In 1982, the protest resulted in the first state law to require the return of Native American burial remains and objects to their communities.[1]

The movement did not stop with Iowa state law. Riding the tide of human rights struggles, a widening protest against the desecration of graves, human bodies, sacred sites, and ceremonial objects resulted in the Native American Graves Protection and Repatriation Act (NAGPRA) of 1990. Among other protective measures, Congress mandated that all museums that had received federal funds provide an inventory of human remains, funeral artifacts, sacred objects, and items of cultural heritage. Native American and Hawaiian communities were to be notified so that they could reclaim the remains of their dead and their sacred objects.

NAGPRA turned out to be a monumental piece of civil rights legislation. It was acclaimed as a breakthrough in the campaign for human rights.[2] It also stirred similar movements of indigenous peoples in Australia, Great Britain, Canada, and other parts of the world.[3]

The promise of the recovery of their heritage accelerated Native Americans' drive for self-determination and tribal sovereignty. Conversely, the possibility of the repossession of artifacts changed the procedures of museum exhibits and academic departments across the globe. Museum curators no longer were certain about what their institutions owned. Archeologists and anthropologists had to renegotiate their relationship with the descendants of the peoples they studied.

In the United States, the task of drawing up the inventory of remains and objects has been daunting. In 1990, the Congressional Budget Office estimated that museums and other institutions were keeping the remains of between 100,000 and 200,000 indigenous persons and 10–15 million associated objects in their collections.[4] After over twenty years, the forty-fourth meeting of the NAGPRA Review Committee heard that 601 museums and 386 federal agencies had submitted inventories of their collections.[5] (See the textbox "NAGPRA Objects Inventoried" for the incredible numbers of items that the museums and agencies had inventoried and submitted for review.[6])

NAGPRA Objects Inventoried

- 41,278 human remains from identified indigenous groups
- 1,019,890 associated articles (objects found with human remains)
- 148,782 unassociated funerary objects (items that probably came from graves)
- 4,321 sacred objects (ceremonial objects needed for the ongoing practice of traditional religions)
- 962 objects of cultural patrimony (items that have ongoing cultural importance)
- 1,217 objects that could be classified as sacred and as objects of cultural patrimony

As far-reaching as the legislation was, both the tribes and institutions have been frustrated with the progress of the program. The tribes have complained about the slowness of the process. The museums have raised questions about the rules. Both sides have reported that they are confused about the definitions and overlapping responsibilities of the program.[7]

The Controversy: Who Owns These Bones?

Predictably, the program has stirred controversy from the beginning. The headline of a *Washington Post* article announced, "Museum Collections Shrink as Tribes Reclaim Artifacts." The *Post* article referred to an empty museum case at the Milwaukee Public Museum where Iroquois ceremonial masks used to be kept. It threatened more vacant spaces in museum displays if Native Americans could remove any article that they claimed belonged to them. The article suggested that the Native Americans may not know what to do with the items and that the best place for them might be the museum.[8]

Cultural historian Samuel J. Redman responded that the numbers of objects returned has been much less than projected. They represent only a small percentage of museum holdings.[9] Moreover, he said that the required relationships between museums and native tribes could be beneficial to both. However, he insisted that some culturally sensitive items *should* be removed because the reasons for their display were insensitive or racist.[10]

Redman's comment suggests that the controversy is more than a conflict about property rights. The concern is why the remains and artifacts were collected and displayed in the first place. At its root, the controversy has to do with conflicting assumptions about the nature of these items. The opposing ideas of the nature of the objects raise a problem for religious studies: from an academic perspective, how to understand the claim that the items are sacred objects.

FOCUSING THE PROBLEM: MUSEUMS CHANGE THEIR WAYS

Dead bodies evoke a certain reverence. It is understandable that native peoples would object when the public is allowed to gawk at the bones of their ancestors. However, the issues involved are broader than respect for the dead. That reverence is tied to the critical notion of the sacred. This is seen most clearly in the changes that museums have made in their practices.

Even before NAGPRA, the International Council of Museums' Code of Ethics (1986) required that museums care for the items in their collections according to professional standards. They were advised to handle the items in ways "consistent with the interests and beliefs" of their communities of origin. However, now the NAGPRA program demanded a change in consciousness. It compelled museums to adjust their guidelines to a new awareness of indigenous sensitivities.[11]

Before the NAGPRA legislation, anthropologists had practically abandoned the term "sacred" because it was too variable and vague. Accordingly, Native American human remains were treated as scientific specimens, and sacred objects were regarded as cultural artifacts. Now, however, museums have begun to treat the items according to the sensitivities of Native Americans.[12]

Changes of the Treatment of Objects and the Limits on Access

The NAGPRA program raised concerns that this would undermine the research and educational missions of the museums and schools that hold the collections. The obvious problem is the limitation of access to the items for research or educational purposes. Various strategies are being implemented to deal with these fears.

Of course, some of the items have been lost to scholars and museum patrons because the tribes have repossessed them and buried them. Some have simply stored them away. Short of keeping the items from public view, tribes can often use the items in ceremonies or display them in their own tribal museums.

If the native peoples do not reclaim the artifacts, some museums have developed policies for their special treatment. They might display or store the objects separately. They also might ask visitors to perform purification rituals before or after viewing them.

The Smithsonian Institution demonstrates some of the most far-reaching methods of respectful treatment.[13] At the Smithsonian National Museum of Natural History, for instance, a Cheyenne Sun Dance priest conducted a ceremony to calm the spiritual energy remaining in a ceremonial buffalo skull because "it was still alive with power."[14] The skull was then removed from public view and placed in a lodge specifically designed for it.

The museum has also set aside a ventilated space for the ritual burning of tobacco, sage, or sweet grass for the spiritual cleansing of sacred objects. Moreover, a Buddha statue that was stored on a bottom shelf was moved to the top shelf to show respect to the "Enlightened One" of Buddhism. The pig bones in an exhibit of Moro items from the Philippines were also removed because the Muslims of the Philippines believe that pigs are unclean.[15]

One measure that is sure to offend some museum visitors is restricted access to certain types of persons, ages, or genders. For example, to comply with the stipulations of the Jemez Pueblo of New Mexico, the National Museum of Natural History deftly solved the problem of limiting access to some sensitive items by storing the selected items in drawers. In addition, one drawer reads, "Caution Jemez visitors: The Jemez people feel that only men over the age of eighteen should look at objects in this drawer."[16]

Concerns of the Scientists and Educators

The limitation of access, whether by reburial or other methods, provoked strenuous and persistent objections. Two decades after the legislation was adopted, the Department of Interior stipulated that items that could not be traced to any specific tribe had to be reported to *all* tribes that might have a claim to them. The president of the American Association of Museums, W. Ford Bell, complained that the ruling would disrupt the developing cooperative relationship between the museums and the tribes. It would also put an impossible burden on museums to contact an indefinite number of tribes and to decide who deserved the items in question.[17] A group of forty-one scientists warned of the irrecoverable loss of a source of knowledge to science. They said that the ruling would decimate the collections of museums. It would rob science of the potential to discover new knowledge from the evidence as new scientific technologies were developed.[18] Other scientists joined in sounding the alarm.[19] These protests showed that the controversy was far from being resolved years after it began.

After twenty years, only about one-quarter[20] to one-third[21] of the human remains have been returned. Moreover, the Government Accounting Office reported that even key federal agencies had failed to "comply fully" with the legislation.[22] However, Deputy Director Peggy O'Dell stated that the National Park Service had not yet identified the barriers to the return of human remains to the tribes.[23]

The response to the program reveals the fundamental difference between scientific and Native American circles. Before NAGPRA, the museums, archeologists, and anthropologists assumed the right to tell the story of the "prehistory" of North America. Many scholars and museums still claim this right. Paleoanthropologist Geoffrey Clark asserts that human remains and associated objects belong to the universal heritage of the human race. He charges that the tribes have no scientific basis for the claim that they represent prehistoric peoples that existed before about five hundred years ago. Even if they did, they are not the only ones who can tell the story of "prehistory."

But Clark goes further. He believes that only science can achieve a provable and, therefore, accurate understanding of ancient peoples and that NAGPRA has obstructed scientific investigation and undermined scientific knowledge.[24] Others have charged that NAGPRA is an affront to Enlightenment values[25] and that it gives mysticism priority over science.[26] These comments express the widely held assumption that scientific study and education have a priority right to the objects.

The Demand for Respect for Indigenous Sacred Ways

Some scholars as well as indigenous leaders, however, have challenged the privileged status of science for the understanding of native peoples and prehistory. They believe that the disagreement between the supporters of NAGPRA and its opponents is a cultural conflict. In such a clash, the views of science and the perspectives of Native Americans are two different ways of knowing.[27] Both worldviews are equally valid and there is no way of judging which is right.[28]

While the frames of reference of scientists and Native Americans may both be worthwhile, that does not mean that they have equal status in the modern world. The supporters of NAGPRA charge that anthropological studies and archeological exhibits have promoted colonialism and racism. They allege that the collection of human remains and artifacts was based on the prejudice that native peoples are leftovers from the distant past. Thus, these indigenous cultures were simplistic, stagnant, and bound for extinction.[29] American museums and schools had the right to save as much of the remnants of the life of ancient peoples as possible. From this viewpoint, trading in the bones of the ancestors continues the oppression of living native peoples.

Many scholars admit that past scholarship has been condescending and unsympathetic to the peoples they have studied. For example, the founder of American ethnography, Samuel G. Morton, collected skulls from around the world to develop his theory that the size of the skulls of indigenous peoples was related to their lack of intelligence and brutality.[30] Scholars like Morton presumed to scientifically explain the origin and identity of indigenous peoples. As they did so, they took part in constructing the repressive power structures of colonialism.

Native American activists have reacted strongly against the idea that Western science should establish their cultural identity and history. In one dispute with archeology, attorney Marla Big Boy stated, "We don't need science to tell us who we are or where our people came from."[31] Her point was that the Native Americans do not need the tools and methods of archeology or anthropology to discover their identity. In this Native American view, the customs, rituals, and ways of Native Americans extend the past into the present. Thus, "the past lives in the present."[32] The evidence for their knowledge of their ancestors is embedded in their way of life.

The Problem of What Makes Something "Sacred"

This chapter has shown that the seemingly simple question of the ownership of artifacts from ancient graves opens up a tangle of deeper issues. These matters of disagreement include cultural identity, political power, sources of knowledge, views of history, scientific methods and evidence, cultural traditions, and religious beliefs. Often, what is at stake is the question of who has the proper authority to decide the issues: the NAGPRA program, the institutions, the tribes, the courts, the legislature, the organized groups representing native interests, or public opinion.

Some might naively suggest that the solution to the problem is that the parties simply respect each other and their different points of view. Yet toleration of divergent opinions is not the same as understanding. Toleration is a thin covering over disagreements that will surely surface again when vital interests are at stake. The search for understanding investigates disagreements to see if there is some way that the disputing parties can reach an agreement. It probes into divergent ideas and experience to arrive at some meaning that can be shared among the differing points of view.

Does the field of religious studies have a role to play in the search for understanding beyond toleration? Do scholars of religion have anything to add to the ongoing discussion of the issues that NAGPRA and the tribal rights movement raise? It may be too much to ask that the study of religion resolve the conflict or mediate between the opposing sides. However, it can provide ways of interpreting the religious aspects of the dispute, it can promote an understanding of the religious aspects of the controversy, and it can offer some insight into the issues that have surfaced. It can also use critical thinking to detect the assumptions below the conflict and the frames of reference in which these presuppositions are embedded.

Museum experts Dominique Ponnau and Pierre Fortin have identified a place where religious studies could begin to make their contribution to the situation. They assert that the idea of the sacred is the point where cultures meet.[33] Taking this seminal idea as a clue, this chapter is built on the idea that *the sacred is the critical term*. This chapter will take for granted the duty of respect for the dead. To explore the topic of symbol, myth, and ritual, it will focus on the issue of sacred objects.

The problem of this chapter now comes into focus. A critical thinking approach to the issues of the Native American artifacts stops to reflect on a fundamental question: What *are* "sacred objects"? The NAGPRA law defines "sacred objects" as those that are "needed by traditional Native American religious leaders for the practice of traditional Native American religions by their present day adherents."[34] This definition leads in the right direction but requires elaboration and explanation. What is meant by "traditional"? What is meant by "religion" and "religious"? What qualifies as a "traditional religion"?

Probing the Definition of the Sacred Object

The basic question is deceptively simple: What makes an object "sacred"? However, the answer may not be so easy. John Moses, a Canadian natural history researcher, states that sacred objects are artifacts that have been "made holy or sacrosanct by virtue of their religious or ceremonial associations."[35] Note that Moses assets that the associations with the religious or ceremonial is what makes the artifact "holy" or "sacrosanct." In the web of meaning that Moses spins into this definition, the words "sacred," "holy," "sacrosanct," and "religious" are synonymous. Simply put, an article is sacred by being treated as sacred.

Moses goes on to say that sacred objects must have a role in *spiritual focus and empowerment*.[36] The object has to have a *continuing*, spiritual function. An exploration of this idea of an ongoing, living function of a sacred object will help us focus the problem of what makes an object sacred.

Here are two examples of sacred objects to consider. One of the objects is a four-faced statuette of a deity holding a scimitar with his foot on a goat. This figure may represent Marduk, who is treading on Tiamut, the sea monster that represents chaos, or a version of this myth.[37] The statuette at the Oriental Institute Museum of the University of Chicago comes from the "Old Babylonian" period of about 1700 BCE and represents an ancient religion of Babylon. This religion and its mythology do not seem to be live options for anyone living today.

The other artifacts are Buddhist art objects. In 2008, the Rubin Museum in New York City displayed sculptures from Bhutan, the country that lies midway

A drawing of the Babylonian deity Marduk standing on a sea monster. A statuette that may represent such a deity who is victorious over the powers of chaos is on display at the University of Chicago. It has four faces.

between Nepal, China, and Bangladesh.[38] These were art treasures with gold and turquoise inlays, horn trumpets, and intricate paintings. The Bhutan Buddhists revere these figures of *lamas* (holy persons) and *buddhas* (enlightened persons) because they embody the spirits of the holy men that they represent.[39]

Which could be considered "holy and sacrosanct"? The statuette of Marduk? Or the statues and paintings of the lamas and buddhas? Both? Neither? On what basis would one decide?

A discussion of these questions would illustrate how Moses's definition glosses over the questions involved. Once an artifact has become "holy and sacrosanct," does it preserve these associations? For how long? Moreover, do the objects give "spiritual focus and empowerment" to everyone who views them? Or only to believers?

It might help to know that no one attends to the statuette of Marduk in the Oriental Institute Museum. However, a delegation of five monks accompanied the Buddhist artifacts from Bhutan. The monks were there to perform frequent rituals and prayers to appease the deities portrayed and to secure their protection.

This example suggests a reason why the implementation of the NAGPRA legislation has been difficult. It shows two different approaches to preserving and displaying cultural-religious artifacts. The Marduk statue is housed in a museum dedicated to the academic study of the Near East. It is treated as an educational exhibit and an impressive piece of historical evidence. The Oriental Institute states that its mission is to "integrate archaeological, textual, and art historical

This masked dancer from the Buddhist country of Bhutan is an example of the sacred art displayed at the Rubin Museum in New York City. The exhibit featured priceless statues of the Buddha, paintings, and other objects. Ritual dances performed by Buddhist monks were shown on four screens. Monks accompanied the exhibit to ensure the blessings of the sacred.

data" to understanding the ancient civilizations of the Near East.[40] The items are not considered sacred and no special handling is required.

On the other hand, the escort of the Buddhist monks with the Buddhist sculpture emphasizes that they are sacred objects. Note that the monks served as an escort for the sacred items in order to "pacify" the deities that the statues portrayed. The monks were also to ensure the "protection" of the sacred powers in the items.

The treatment of the Buddhist statues exemplifies the idea that the preservation of sacred objects is more than a matter of collecting, studying, and displaying them. The Buddhists believed that the statues had continuing spiritual powers. We have seen in the Buddhist example that these powers could be either beneficial or harmful to humans. It depends on their treatment. From the point of view of the native peoples as well as the Buddhists, the sacred objects cannot fulfill their proper role of spiritual empowerment without the proper respect and care.[41]

The comparison of the treatment of the two objects illustrates the difference in the frames of reference of the scientific and Native American views of the artifacts. Both are dedicated to the protection of the objects. But the rationale and methods of this protection are based on two different worldviews.

This chapter proposes that the field of religious studies might help bridge the divide between the two sides of the disagreement. Students of religion might use the tools of critical thinking to probe the assumptions and associations of each way of thinking. The critical concept of the sacred would be the focus of this effort. Religious studies might contribute an understanding of what religious people mean when they say that an object is "sacred." This is a fundamental question. A grasp of what is meant by the sacredness of a religious object is the primary step to understanding what a religious object means to believers. These thoughts focus the problem. The task is to find a way of interpreting sacred objects in academic terms comprehensible to the scientists and educators.

SURVEYING THE ALTERNATIVE APPROACHES: INVESTIGATING SYMBOL, MYTH, AND RITUAL

Three broad areas in the field of religious studies offer possibilities for solving the problem of understanding what is meant by sacred artifacts. These are the areas of sacred symbols, myth, and ritual.

Alternative Approaches: Focus on Sacred Symbols

The first approach views sacred objects like the Buddhist statues or the indigenous artifacts as religious symbols. Although it is often taught, the derivation of the word "symbol" is not the "throwing together" of two distinct ideas. True, in broad terms a symbol is something tangible that takes the place of a thought that is otherwise intangible. Yet the origin of the word is the idea that the tangible objects disclose some hidden mystery.[42]

The Variety of Symbols

In the twentieth century, the exploration of the nature and function of religious symbols captured the attention of most religious scholars. Scholars focused on symbols because they believed that religions speak in the language of symbols.[43] In this view, to understand a religion, one must understand its symbols. If this is true, then studying world religions is an overwhelming task. Each religion has its own language of symbols. All languages have an underlying basic grammar that they share. Even so, religious symbols share some common characteristics that make learning the languages of symbols easier.

The Definition and Characteristics of Symbols

The countless variety of symbols makes them fascinating and difficult. (See the textbox "Types of Religious Symbols" for a sample list.) The unique nature of symbols makes them more difficult to understand than they may seem. But that is not the only reason why "outsiders" find symbols hard to comprehend.

Types of Religious Symbols

The countless variety of religious symbols makes them both fascinating and difficult. Here are a few selected types:

- Sound: the three-syllable AUM of Hinduism
- Objects: the Native American sacred pipe
- Foods: the matzah or unleavened bread of the Jewish Passover
- Elements of nature: the water of Christian baptism
- Hand gestures: the mudras of Buddhism and Hinduism
- Articles of clothing: the clerical collar of Catholic clergy
- Weapons: the ceremonial dagger (*kirpan*) worn by Sikhs
- Styles of hair: the dreadlocks of the Rastafarians
- A piece of cord or thread: the *kusti* or sacred thread of Zoroastrianism
- Verses in a holy book: the calligraphy of Islam
- Shapes: the form of the Buddhist stupa housing relics of the Buddha masters
- Geometrical figures or designs: the yin/yang symbol of Daoism

The initial question is, usually, what does the symbol represent? Whenever "outsiders" to a religion encounter an unfamiliar religious symbol, their first question is likely to be similar: What does it represent? Consider the following example. Zoroastrians wear the sacred thread (*kusti*). The cord is tied three times around the waist as a badge of their faith. It reminds them of the ethic of good thoughts, good words, and good deeds. Periodically throughout the day, wearers of the kusti untie and tie the thread again while they recite ancient prayers for protection. According to Mrs. Pervin J. Mistry, the cord is woven of 144 threads of fine wool.[44] These are twisted into seventy-two threads and passed around the loom seventy-two times. Then they are divided into six strands of twelve threads. (See the textbox "What the Zoroastrian Sacred Thread Represents" for a brief explanation of what the numbers involved represent.)

What the Zoroastrian Sacred Thread Represents

- 144 threads of fine wool = (1 + 4 + 4 = 9) immortality
- 72 threads and passes around the loom = 72 names of Ahura Mazda (the Wise One)
- 72 beats per minutes = the average number of heartbeats of human beings, the unity of the human race
- 72 years = number of years for the sun to pass one degree along the zodiac; the astronomical cycles of the universe

The attempt to explain the significance of the numbers of the sacred thread illustrates the complications involved in the question of what a religious symbol represents. It also raises the question: What are we asking when we ask what a sacred symbol stands for? Most likely, "outsiders" will suppose that the symbol must have a direct, one-to-one relationship to what it represents.|According to this point of view, there are symbols on the one hand and abstract thoughts on the other. The symbol is a reminder of the connection between the two.

In this way of thinking, the outsider gets an answer that the seventy-two threads of the kusti stand for seventy-two names, seventy-two beats per minute, or seventy-two years. However, what meaning do the seventy-two names, seventy-two beats per minute, or seventy-two years have? What is their significance?

The answer given above is that the seventy-two names represent ideas about the *deity (Ahura Mazda)*; the seventy-two beats per minute represent ideas about *nature*; and the seventy-two years represent ideas about the *zodiac*. Again, the explanation sounds logical, but what understandings do "outsiders" receive from it?

In the twentieth century, scholars of religion took a "linguistic turn" away from this typical one-to-one approach to symbols. They accepted the thought of philosophers such as the American philosopher C. S. Peirce (1839–1914). Peirce said that we do not have objects on the one hand and meanings on the other. We have symbols everywhere. Peirce was asserting that we do not live in a world where objects are separate from thoughts. We live in a world of meanings where objects and thoughts are inseparably joined. Tangible objects have intangible meaning.[45] The number 72 and the sacred cord go together to make the symbol. The meaning of the sacred cord is, in fact, tied up in the practice of wearing it.

Imagine if the Olympic committee decided to eliminate all ceremonies for awarding metals. There would be no cheers as the athletes mounted the platform, no national anthems, no flags rising in the background, no medals decked around the necks, no triumphant salutes to the admiring crowds. What then would winning mean? The athletes still would have won their events and performances, yet what would their achievement signify? What would the Olympics be without the medals? The medals and what they stand for are one and the same.

Beginning Insights into Symbols: C. S. Peirce

To analyze how symbols express meaning, we turn to the work of the philosopher C. S. Peirce, who founded the academic discipline of *semiotics* to answer this question.[46] Signs stand for whatever they represent. In Peirce's analysis signs are pointers that indicate something beyond themselves. For example, the stop sign points to the place where drivers are supposed to stop their vehicles. The stop sign does not make a vehicle stop. It designates where to stop. A sign consists of a pointer—that is, a *signifier*—and something that the signifier represents, the *signified*. Again, in Peirce's view, the signifier points to what is signified.

Three Interrelated Aspects of Signs

1. Signifier: a word, image, action, or other item that stands for something else
2. Signified: the concept that the signifier represents
3. Meaning: the association of signifier and signified *made by the interpreter*

But that is not all that is needed for meaning. Imagine that someone had never seen a stop sign. Would he or she know what it meant? This realization shows that signs need someone who knows their meaning. When the interpreter grasps the relationship between the sign (signifier) and what it signifies (the signified), then the purpose of the sign is achieved.

For Peirce, symbols are special types of signs.[47] Their meaning is given by the social custom, their accepted use in a community.[48] For example, the German government recently proposed that the European Union prohibit the symbol of the swastika throughout Europe. It hastily reversed its proposal when Hindus in the EU protested. The Hindus said that it was an ancient symbol signifying good fortune. The symbol is found on many Hindu and Buddhist temples and carries the meaning, "May goodness prevail!"[49] The Hindus charged that those who wanted to ban the symbol were grossly misinterpreting it.

Obviously the swastika can mean two different things: Nazi hatred or Hindu good will. Therefore, the third factor of symbols, the interpreter, is crucial. What the swastika means depends on the interpreter. Likewise, to understand the symbolic significance of Native American sacred objects, we must ask what they refer to. More importantly, we must also ask *to whom* they have such a reference. These thoughts bring us back to the problem of how to discern the meaning that religious believers find in sacred objects.

What Symbols Represent and What They Mean

We have found that to understand the meaning of a symbol, we must ask what it is, what it represents, and who makes the connection between the two. Consider the lotus as a religious symbol. The lotus is a water plant. It emerges from the mud, but its flower represents purity and creativity. These characteristics make the lotus a key symbol in Hinduism and Buddhism.

In Hinduism, the lotus is the seat on which the deities sit. Moreover, it also stands for the dwelling place of the subtle Self (*atman*) in the heart. On the other hand, in Buddhism, the lotus is one of the "Eight Auspicious Symbols." The Buddha sits on a lotus blossom. Buddhists explain that the lotus represents the purity and clarity of enlightenment. Enlightenment blossoms from the mud of worldly experience on the stem of the practice of the disciplines of Buddhism.

The explanations about the lotus and what it stands for in Hinduism and Buddhism may inspire interest. However, they barely scratch the surface of how Hindus and Buddhists might understand them. The more we think critically about it, the more we find that a simple explanation begs the deeper questions. The Hindu symbolic meaning raises questions about the nature of the deities (gods) and what is meant by the "Self," which sits enthroned in the heart. The Buddhist symbolic meaning of the lotus raises questions about the nature of enlightenment and what is meant by its illumination in purity and clarity.

An explanation of what the symbol represents, therefore, will not give "outsiders" an adequate understand of their meaning. The reaction of then-mayor Rudolph Giuliani to a controversial painting of the Virgin Mary illustrates the point. At the turn of the century, New York City Mayor Rudolph Giuliani threatened to cut off funding to the Brooklyn Museum of Art. The museum was displaying the work of British artist Chris Ofili. In one of the pieces, Ofili used elephant dung to portray the Virgin Mary. The mayor joined New York Archbishop John Cardinal O'Connor in complaining about "Catholic-bashing" and the desecration of a beloved Catholic symbol.

Why were the mayor and archbishop upset with a work of art? From within the circle of meaning of Catholicism they perceived the item as a desecration of the cherished sentiments of Roman Catholic Christians to the Virgin Mary as the "Mother of God" and "Queen of Heaven." For them, the symbol of the Virgin Mary meant something *more than* the explanation of what she *represents*. This case shows that sacred symbols evoke feelings. To understand their meanings requires that one pay attention to the underlying connotations beneath the surface of what they represent.

Thus, to apply this insight on symbols to the problem of the nature of sacred objects, Native Americans and scientists might agree on what the sacred objects represent. However, this does not mean that they would necessarily agree on their meaning. To gain an understanding of why the objects are considered sacred, the outsiders to the religion would have to know the deeper feelings that the objects evoke.

The Presentational Nature of Symbols

What accounts for the intensity of the feelings underlying the symbols? To explain, we can refer to the American philosopher Suzanne Langer (1895–1985). She contrasted two types of language: the *discursive* and the *presentational*. According to this distinction, ordinary language is discursive.[50] It consists of a linear series of ideas, one idea following after the other as if in a line. Discursive language is useful for dealing with facts and abstract ideas. However, Langer argued that when it comes to human emotions and intuitions another type of language is needed.[51] Langer used the term *presentational language* to describe the "nondiscursive" quality of religious and artistic symbols. This type of communication *presents* our inner life with its sensations, emotions, imaginations, and intuitions. These deep realities of the soul are otherwise invisible to others.[52]

Langer promoted the idea that religious symbols are similar to music, art, and poetry. Like the arts, symbolic language communicates what cannot be said otherwise. One cannot pin down the deep meaning of symbols to a single, discursive, and linear statement. In that sense, their meaning is *ambivalent* or uncertain.

In summary, symbols are the language of religion because they have the unique capability of expressing deep layers of meaning and visualizing intangible levels of human experience. In this view, religious symbols are doorways into another "world," a deeper dimension of reality that cannot be expressed in descriptive words. The poet and philosopher Samuel Taylor Coleridge (1772–1834) said that symbols are "translucent."[53] As the light of a lamp filters through a sheer linen lampshade, so the light of the "Eternal" shines through the "temporal" symbol. And as this light of the meaning shines upon believers, they are immersed and transformed in its glow.

The Interpretation of Multivocal Symbols

So far this chapter has described the characteristics of sacred symbols. How do they work? As we have seen, C. S. Peirce asserted that the meaning of symbols is arbitrary. The symbol represents what it does only because its believers have learned to respond in this way by some habit or rule.[54] For example, the swastika is only a geometric figure. One has to learn how to interpret it and respond to it.

Coleridge and the Protestant theologian Paul Tillich (1886–1965) would disagree with Peirce when it comes to religious symbols. To them, religious symbols powerfully involve the believer in the reality of what they represent. Thus, in believers' perception and experience, the symbols are intimately and inseparably connected to their meaning.[55]

The masks of Papua New Guinea furnish an example of how the symbol might "partake" of the reality it depicts. The Papua New Guinea Museum displays dancing masks of the Sulka people who dwell on an island off the mainland. Men of the tribe secretly construct these masks and destroy them after their use. They take pains to prevent women and children from realizing that they are made by human beings. Thus, the masks that anthropologists bring back to museums have to be carefully treated. After permission is granted, the masks have to be whisked away under the cover of darkness. When they are displayed, the museum has to be sure that no Sulka woman or child will ever see them.[56]

The reason that the masks are restricted is that the masks *are* spirits. They do not merely *represent* spirits. That is, the mask and the spirit it represents are one and the same. There is a complete identification of one with the other. Seeing the mask outside its use in ceremony would confuse the women and children. They would think that the mask is separate from the spirit it represents. Likewise, the indigenous tribes who are reclaiming the sacred objects of their ancestors would be insulted to hear that they had simply made up the meaning of their cherished symbols. These symbols present the sacred reality of what they represent to the believers.

The Sacramental Interpretation of Symbols

Christians take two basic approaches to the meaning of symbols. One approach is the *sacramental*. In the beliefs of the Roman Catholics, Eastern Orthodox, and some Protestants, the physical elements of the ritual (such as water, oil, or bread and wine) become in actuality what they represent. To explain the concept of "sacrament," the Western church father and theologian Augustine (354–430 CE) said, "Sacraments are a visible sign of an invisible grace." Thus, the physical elements convey the actual or "real presence" and power of the sacred reality. The sign and the "grace"—that is, the sanctifying gift of the ritual's spiritual presence, power, and blessing—are identical. This view corresponds with the ideas of Coleridge and Tillich above.

Alternatively, other Protestant Christians take various approaches to the basic rites of Christianity. These stances fall along a continuum from the full sacramental approach described above to its opposite. A common idea in Protestantism is that the elements of Christian rituals represent the sacred presence or event in *remembrance*, but not in actuality. The physical elements of the ritual, therefore, call to mind the sacred meaning but do not convey the presence or power of it. This view corresponds to the view of Peirce explained above.

The Iconoclastic Interpretation of Symbols: Several Religions

The Protestant view of sacraments as "remembrance" is an example of how many religions attempt to moderate the power of symbols. Certainly, some sacred ways revel in symbols and do not try to control them. Hindu temples present a mind-boggling array of images that seem excessive until one realizes that the symbols are united in a grand cosmic vision.[57] However, many religions or movements are wary of the power of symbols.

In general, Western monotheism has a special sensitivity to pictorial representations of the divine. This hesitation comes from prohibition of the Hebrew Bible against *graven images* (Deuteronomy 5:8, King James Version). "Graven images" are representations, most often carved of wood or stone, that are worshipped as deities. Western monotheistic traditions call such images "idols." These are "false gods" because there is only one true, invisible God. To worship something else is to make something else more important than the one Creator and Ruler of the universe.

In contrast, Hinduism does not have such sensitivity about representations of deities and uses the term "idol" to refer to its sacred images. On the other hand, because of the commandment against graven images, mainstream Jewish, Christian, and Muslim traditions have refrained from making pictures of God Almighty. In Judaism, even the sacred name of the Almighty is not to be uttered aloud in the original language of the faith, Hebrew.

To what extent other pictorial representations are permissible has provoked lasting controversies in the Western monotheistic religions. For example, in the eighth and ninth centuries, bitter conflicts over the use of icons in worship and prayer tore apart the Byzantine Empire, the eastern half of the Roman Empire. The iconoclasts ("icon-smashers") gave their name to the impulse to destroy all holy pictures of Jesus Christ, the Virgin Mary, and the saints. In 787 CE, a conference of bishops from throughout the empire[58] restored the traditional use of icons.

The use of visual representations of Jesus Christ, the Virgin Mary, and the saints provide a way to categorize different forms of Christianity. Roman Catholics allow three-dimensional statues of all of these. Eastern Orthodox Christians limit images to icons that are two-dimensional representations. Most Protestant Christians will allow pictures of Jesus Christ, the Virgin Mary, and the apostles, but they do not give them special reverence as Catholic and Orthodox Christians do. Finally, some Protestants will not use pictorial representations at all, especially in their places of worship.

For the most part, Islam has substituted geometric symbols and calligraphy for pictorial images. However, the ban on pictures is not found in the Muslim holy book, the Qur'an, as some suppose. The Qur'an does not forbid even pictures of the Islamic prophet Muhammad. The prohibition comes from *hadith*—that is, the certified traditions of the Islamic prophet Muhammad's words and deeds. The interpretation of hadith has fostered a strong iconoclastic tendency in Islam.[59]

Calligraphy is a revered art form in Islam that enhances the meaning of the sacred message.

Foremost among the Muslim iconoclasts was Muhammad ibn 'Abd al-Wahhab (1703–1792). In the eighteenth century, Wahhab initiated a puritan reform against the corruption of Islamic society in the Arabian Peninsula. In his work on the oneness of God, Wahhab cited the traditions of hadith to teach that those who make images of any living thing with a soul will burn in hell. Images are an affront to God because they imitate His singular role as Creator.[60] This approach returned to the conservative idea of religious symbolism and surfaced in the recent protests against the images of the Islamic prophet Muhammad.

In the twenty-first century, iconoclasm has continued to be a major factor in global affairs. In 2001, the Taliban Islamic militants in Afghanistan blew up two ancient statues of the Buddha that had been hewn in a cliff 1,500 years ago. The Bamiyan images were 120 and 180 feet tall, the tallest images of the standing Buddha. The United Nations had designated the statues as part of the World Heritage. Nevertheless, the Taliban, who are promoters of strict Islamic law (shari'ah), said they were the "gods of the infidels."[61]

In 2005, a Danish newspaper published several provocative caricatures of the Islamic prophet Muhammad. The editor said that he wanted to test the limits of what he thought was the media's self-imposed censorship. The test resulted in the eruption of the Muslim world with demonstrations, riots, burning of embassies, and the desecration of flags.

Three years late, Wikipedia received over 80,000 protests against its posting of medieval pictures of the Islamic prophet.[62] In response to the outcry, the Wikipedia FAQ page defended its "neutral approach." It asserted that the prohibition against images, even of the Islamic prophet Muhammad, was not universal. It referred to Persian and Ottoman paintings from the thirteenth through sixteenth centuries.

Although often associated with Western monotheism, the negative stance toward images is also found in Eastern religions. In Buddhism, the popular adage "If you meet the Buddha on the road, kill him!"expresses the typical iconoclastic sentiment. This startling slogan expresses the mistrust in symbols because they conceal as much as they reveal.[63] Thus, in Zen Buddhism seekers of enlightenment are not only to "kill the Buddha," they are also to trash Buddha images, slap their Buddhist masters, refuse to follow what they have learned, and generally reject doctrine, tradition, and authority.[64] From this point of view, symbols can obscure the truth and stand in the way of the knowledge of reality.[65] If so, then the symbol needs to be eliminated.

Evaluation of the Symbolic Approach to the Interpretation of Sacred Objects

This chapter investigates what makes certain objects sacred and worthy of special treatment. One option is to treat the object as sacred because it is a religious symbol. So far, we have discovered various points of view about the relationship of the symbol to what it symbolizes. How close is this relationship? This question is the key to the critical analysis of symbols. Behind it is the crucial problem of religious language, the puzzle of how something in the ordinary world can mediate a meaning beyond itself.

We can apply this key question to the discussion of the case of the NAGPRA program and sacred objects. We can ask if the symbolic objects found in graves are intrinsically and inseparably bound to the reality of what they mediate. Alternatively, as symbols of sacred power, do the objects retain that power? In addition, does a sacred object continue to be sacred when it is housed in a museum, school collection, or art gallery?

> ### Attitudes toward Religious Symbols
>
> - Symbols are irreplaceable.
> - Symbols do not have permanent meaning.
> - Symbols are useful up to a point.
> - Symbols are obstacles and must be discarded.

Symbols Are Irreplaceable

The answers to these questions uncover some divergent approaches to sacred symbolism. There are several options. In the first place, many believe that the physical symbol is so closely attached to its spiritual meaning that what happens to the symbol happens to what it represents. If one dishonors the flag, one dishonors the country. If one honors the flag, one honors the country. To insult a representation of the Islamic prophet Muhammad or the Virgin Mary is to insult a holy person.

In this view, an object dug up from a grave retains its holiness. Therefore, disrespect or careless treatment of the sacred object amounts to desecration. Note that the Cheyenne holy men claimed that the buffalo skull in the National Museum of National History is still alive with sacred power.[66] A special ceremony put the powers to rest, and a special box preserves that condition. Presumably then, the spiritual powers of the symbolic object still remained.

Symbolic Meaning Is Not Permanent

On the other hand, in the processes of modernization, symbols also lose power as their meanings shift. In the *Inferno*, the medieval poet Dante pictured hell as a place of the horrors of just retribution. A recent Pew Forum poll shows a steep drop in the belief that the eternal punishment of hell awaits those who "live bad lives." In seven years, the believers in Dante's idea of hell dropped 12 percent. Now 59 percent of Americans say they believe in hell while 74 percent believe in heaven.[67]

One explanation for this trend is that Americans might be changing their minds about other religions.[68] It may be that Americans do not want to consign their friends and neighbors to hell, even if they are of different religions. Their view of religious tolerance leads them to believe that there is no unbelief but only different beliefs.[69] Nevertheless, the power of the symbol of hell to evoke the terror of damnation seems to be weakening among many Americans.

If symbolic objects can lose their significance and if their meaning can change, then it may be that the sacred status of objects is not as fixed as we supposed. This prompts us to ask: how do objects gain their sacred power in the first place? Natural features like mountains, waterfalls, and canyons may have a built-in sacred power. However, typically, objects may be made for sacred purposes but they do not have symbolic power until it is ritually invoked into them. In Thailand, for instance, the construction of a mask of the *khon* dance requires prayers and purifications for the mask and the dancers.[70] Finally, the "Opening the Eyes" ceremony invokes spiritual power into it and the mask comes alive as a sacred object.

Once the item has become sacred, in most cases that sacredness remains for an indefinite period. The masks used in Thai classical dance are reverently stored. Some are over one hundred years old.[71] Native Americans keep the sacred pipe and other sacred artifacts in a holy bundle that no one except the keeper of the bundle may handle. Other Native American objects, such as those used in the Sun Dance, may be left to "return to the earth." In other cultures, objects used in sacred rituals may be burned. In India, idols are immersed in a body of water and abandoned. In New Delhi, the custom has caused so much pollution of the Yamuna River that authorities are promoting the use of a recycling pit instead.[72]

Symbols Are Useful Up to a Point

Another approach is that symbols are necessary to identify sacred realities but only for beginners. Once the believer grasps the meaning, the symbol is no longer useful. Recall Peirce's view that symbols are signs that point to meanings that social custom accepts. This meaning is not obvious, though "insiders" to the community understand it. In this view, religious symbols point to a reality beyond the senses. They point the way into that reality. But when we arrive at that reality and experience it, then it is an obstacle to further progress.[73] It is like a boat that we have used to get to the other side of a river. Unless we want to go back across the river, we have to abandon the vessel and go forward without it.

Symbols Must Be Discarded

We have seen that some believers hold that we do not realize the meaning of symbols until we go beyond them. This leads to the last option. In this negative view, symbols are a corrupting force in religion. They actually block the way to what they represent. The believer must set aside symbols in order to attain the proper understanding or experience of something the symbol hides or deforms. Christian Protestants, for example, may throw out all images, icons, visual symbols, and even sacraments to clear a direct pathway to a "personal relationship" with Jesus Christ.

The New Age guru Eckhart Tolle advises the complete disassociation of the symbol from its meaning. Tolle observes, "The word 'honey' isn't honey." One has to taste honey to know what it is. After one has tasted honey, one is free of the word "honey." This way of thinking teaches that we must get beyond the delusion of symbols in order to realize the truth of the present moment.[74]

Summary of the Evaluation of Symbolic Approaches

In summary, as we have seen, symbols have an essential role in religion because of their tremendous power to represent meanings beyond themselves and to make what they represent present to believers.

However, we have found that even if "outsiders" are told what the symbols represent, they still do not know what they mean. We have shown that to comprehend a religious symbol, one must grasp the relationship between the symbol and what it represents. Then meaning is achieved. However, we have noted that this meaning is a matter of social convention—that is, of culture. For those who are not immersed in the cultural context of the symbol, the relationship between the symbol and what it stands for may seem quite arbitrary. For those in the culture, the relationship is taken for granted. These "insiders" know the associations that are woven into the symbol and the feelings and attitudes that the symbol calls to mind. Moreover, religious symbols point to an intangible reality beyond the senses. For some, the symbol mediates that reality; for others, it simply suggests that reality; for still others, it hides that reality. Believers may hold that symbols are highways to the truth or detours into falsehood.

From the modern viewpoint, the objects of Native American graves and ancient cultures are works of art or are scientific specimens. If the schools and museums could be convinced that they are religious symbols, what would be achieved? The concept of religious symbols involves assumptions, associations, and frames of reference that the scientists and educators may not be prepared to accept. But could these "outsiders" accurately understand the symbols if they set aside the question of the existence of spiritual realities? Could they grasp the meaning of the symbols if they disregarded the question of the complex relationship between the symbols and the spiritual realities they represent? In view of our discussion, we would reply that the understanding of religious symbols has to rely on the interpretation of "insiders." Only the "insiders" know the meaning of their religious symbol as their social group interprets them. Yet the symbols point to an intangible and indefinable reality that cannot be described in words. The Native Americans would find it impossible to explain the meaning of the objects without referring to this supernatural reality, a reality that the scientists and experts deny. Both sides can agree that the Native Americans view the artifacts as religious symbols. But that simple fact does not solve the problem of how the academic study of religion can explain *why* they are considered sacred objects.

Alternative Approaches: Focus on Mythology

These insights lead us to another area of study. Scholars might treat the objects in question in terms of the mythology in which they are embedded. Myths are complexes of symbols ordered in story form. Thus, one possibility for solving our problem of the nature of sacred objects is to study the myths of native peoples. This approach would assume that the myths of native peoples are the contexts in which the objects in question have sacred meaning. This train of thought, in fact, is in keeping with the traditions of native peoples. They often teach what a sacred object is by telling a story of its origin and original use.

The Definition and Characteristics of Myth

Historian of religion Mircea Eliade taught that the basic type of myth was the *myth of origins*. In the most fundamental sense, myths are sacred stories that tell of a time of beginnings. In this time, the way things are in the world was established. Conversely, myths tell of a time of endings that will destroy the way things are now.[75]

Myth, therefore, divulges the secrets of the primal time when the foundations of reality were laid or will be torn down. In other words, myth tells how something that exists now came into being through the deeds of supernatural beings. What was created may be the whole of reality or only a fragment of reality, such as an island, a species of plant, a specific human behavior, or an institution of society.[76]

For example, the Lakota tell the story of the appearance of the Buffalo Calf Woman. She showed herself to two hunters before the people knew the ways of the sacred pipe. One hunter had lustful thoughts about this sacred being. He was turned to dust. The other showed proper reverence, and she offered him the sacred bundle containing the sacred pipe. She told him to gather the people together. She gave them instructions about the use of the sacred pipe and the seven major rites of the people. Then she turned into a red buffalo. The red buffalo rolled over on the ground and became a white buffalo. The white buffalo rolled over and turned into a black buffalo. Finally, the buffalo bowed to the four cardinal directions and disappeared over the hill.[77]

Embedded in this story, we find the basic characteristics of Eliade's concept of myth. The narrative happens in the *primordial time of origins* when the Buffalo Calf Woman taught the people how to walk the Earth in a sacred manner and to pray with the sacred pipe *for and with everything*.[78] It is an event of the appearance of a *supernatural being*, the Buffalo Calf Woman, who is said to be *wakan*, or holy. It tells how a *reality came into existence*. This is the reality of a "human behavior"—not only the use of the sacred pipe but the sacred way of life that is centered in it. This is, then, a time of beginnings when the foundations of our present reality, "our world," were laid.

Myth brings its hearers into its narrative world with a captivating charm. However, this imaginative appeal leads moderns to associate it with fable, legend, fantasy, and fabrication—not factual reality. A recent book titled *When Prophecy Never Fails: Myth and Reality in a Flying-Saucer Group*[79] illustrates the standard use of the term. An Oglala Sioux, Ed McGaa, reflects this same sense when he states, "Indian people feel that it is very poor manners to refer to the Buffalo Calf Woman's appearances as myth or superstition."[80]

While they have tried to be respectful, for the most part, scholars of religion have confirmed the popular opinion about myth. Myth has been interpreted in terms of primitive science, dreams and the unconscious, and mystical timelessness. All of these approaches assume that myth is incompatible with the physical and objective world known to modern science.

The Rationalist Interpretation of Myth

For two centuries, in general religious scholars have tried to decide what modern people can make of mythology. Scholars have assumed that modern people cannot believe the view of the world that myths portray on the surface level. Worlds cannot be created out of cosmic eggs. The universe does not consist of the butchered body parts of a giant. The good Earth did not materialize from gobs of mud that a huge duck has dredged up from a primal swamp. Native Americans have to come from somewhere, a location that DNA evidence can determine.

Ways of Interpreting Mythology

1. Rationalist: myths explain the primal origins and operations of the universe and society.
2. Romantic: myths are explorations of an original sacred reality above and beyond the ordinary universe.
3. Psychological (an outgrowth of the Romantic interpretation): myths are manifestations of the inner dynamics of the human psyche.

After noting the difference between the mythic and modern worldviews, scholars have divided into two camps: the *rationalists* and the *romantics*. Early scholars of myth, E. B. Tylor and James Frazer, took the rationalist approach. They led the study of mythology down the *intellectualist* path of assuming that the purpose of mythology is explanation. For example, in Frazer's view, the central fertility myth of the dying and rising of a god-king explained the cycle of the seasons. As the god was sacrificed and died, winter came and vegetation died. When the god revived, spring and vegetation came to life again. Frazer found this mythic structure in the myths of Osiris (Egyptian), Adonis (Greek), Dionysus (Greek), Attis (Phrygian), and Marduk (Babylonian), as well as many others. In this view, primitive peoples thought the same way as modern people. The problem was that they thought incorrectly. Therefore, to Frazer, mythology is a rational but mistaken view of the universe.

In the rationalist view, such explanations, however, provided more than information. They had practical implications for the people's survival. The "dying and rising" myth became a matter of life and death for the Babylonians each year. They chose a condemned prisoner to replace the king in the ritual enactment of the cycle of fertility. For five days, the convict sat on the throne in the place of the king, issued royal decrees, and slept with the king's concubines. Then he was summarily executed, and the king resumed his reign with renewed strength. This and other rehearsals of the myth of the cycles of the dying and rising god-king ensured the fruitfulness of the earth and the vitality of the king.[81]

From the perspective of the twenty-first century, the views of Tylor and Frazer about mythology might seem almost as quaint as the myths they tried to explain. The romantic approach has taken over.

The Romantic Interpretation of Myth: Eliade

The Greek philosophers led the way into a modern solution to the interpretation of myth that may be broadly classified as romantic. In this view, myth is relevant to today's world because it has two levels of meaning. It represents two types of reality.

Mircea Eliade and others have founded their study of myth on this two-tier approach. In *The Sacred and the Profane*, Eliade warned against the error of assuming that primitive humans thought of the natural world in the same way that moderns do. To the mythic mind-set, a sacred stone is not just a stone and a sacred tree is not really a tree. To the mythic mind-set, stones and trees are *hierophanies*. That is, they are manifestations of invisible and mysterious spiritual power. The features of the natural world thus become sacred symbols that contain a greater reality than the physical world of appearances.[82]

In this mind-set, the world and its natural features are the result of an eruption of sacred power. As molten lava erupts from beneath the surface of the Earth, so reality was formed from an overflow of sacred reality from beneath the surface of physical reality.[83]

Myths tell the human story of these upsurges of sacred reality that formed the world. Religious festivals dramatize these myths. As they reenact the myths of origins, the celebrations take the present world "back" to that transcendent reality from which it came. By this reconnection to the primal time, the world is renewed. To Eliade, therefore, the festival must be held, the story must be remembered. The original eruption must be repeated. When people forget the original primal event, they lose the creative and life-giving power of connection with the sacred.[84]

Underneath Eliade's description of the mythic mind is a note of nostalgia. He seemed to yearn for the lost sense of the sacred. He regretted that moderns have discarded mythology, ceased to celebrate the mythic festivals, and cut themselves off from sacred power. For Eliade, myth and its opposite, the profane, are two ways of seeing the world and living in it. Having chosen the profane mode of being, modern people are no longer in touch with the sacred sources of spiritual vitality and meaning.[85]

Eliade suggested that there was only one chance for moderns to recover the lost sense of the sacred. He stated that for most moderns "religion and mythology have been 'eclipsed' in the darkness of their unconscious."[86] Therefore, the only way forward is psychology. To understand the meaning of symbolic objects in terms of myth, modern people cannot look to native peoples for their interpretations. They must look to the psychologists.

Carl Jung on Myth

One psychologist who found the meaning of myth at the level of the psyche was Carl Jung. For Jung, as for Eliade, myths and symbols tap into another reality. Eliade taught that only premodern people could know this reality. However, Jung tried to show that modern people also could know the same transcendent reality. To defend this idea he appealed to the concept of the psychic unity of the human race. For Jung, ancient and modern people are bound together but not by ways of thinking about the external, physical world. They are bound together by a common psychology. Jung believed that modern people could discover this psychic unity in the hidden reaches of the psyche.[87]

Like Eliade, Jung believed that moderns are unique. Modernism has developed *directed thinking.* This way of thinking follows a disciplined line of reasoning using words, concepts, and abstractions. While modern people are especially adept at linear thought patterns, they still engage in the opposite –*non-directed thinking.* This way of thinking mixes images, impressions, and feelings in a nonlinear way.[88]

Jung claimed that modern people still used "non-directed thinking" especially in dreams. In his theory, the images of dreams give form to the nonlinear, universal *archetypes*. Archetypes are clusters of psychic energy. They serve as the templates for the images that appear in dreams. For Jung, they are universal structures of the mind inherited from the collective experience of the human race. Among these are the *anima* (the feminine, especially active in the male); the *animus* (the masculine, especially active in the female); the wise old man; the witch; the shadow; and the earth-mother. Examples of archetypes that structure these energies are the self, the circle, and the four quadrants (of the self).

Jung maintained that the same archetypes that take shape in dreams are the universal structures of myths. For example, myths involve the same figures of the anima and animus. For Jung, mythology lived on in dreams, and the principles of interpretation that applied to dreams applied to myths.[89]

Joseph Campbell on Myth

Among the most successful adapters of the psychological approach was mythologist Joseph Campbell (1904–1987). Through the TV series *The Power of Myth*, Campbell popularized a new appreciation of mythology to a vast American audience. "Mythology," Campbell said, "is the secret opening through which the inexhaustible energies of the cosmos pour into cultural manifestations."[90] Like Jung, he believed that psychology was the only way to recover the "power of myth." Reading myth literally, factually, and historically prevents us from getting down to the psychological level. To get to that level, we cannot look to religion. We must look to the mystics who through the ages concentrated on direct and inner experience of the sacred.[91]

In his book *The Hero with a Thousand Faces*, Campbell mixed myths from across the globe into a fascinating tale of the psychological journey of the hero. That journey involved the three stages of the hero's separation from the ordinary world, his initiation into another world, and his return to ordinary life as master of both the ordinary and sacred worlds.

In Campbell's theory, myths dress in different costumes, but all mythology clothes the same *mono-myth*, the super-myth. In Campbell's own soaring prose, "A hero ventures forth from the world of common day into a region of supernatural wonder: fabulous forces are there encountered and a decisive victory is won: the hero comes back from the mysterious adventure with the power to bestow boon on his fellowman." This journey is really a trip into the depths of the psyche. Accordingly, the function of myth is to divulge the secrets of how to negotiate its hazards successfully so as to become a triumphant hero.[92]

Campbell's blending of Freud and Jung with aspects of Hinduism and Buddhism in the maxim "Follow your bliss!" earned him a preeminent role in the human potential movement. His theories became a foundation of the self-help category of book publishing. Lasting through several decades, Campbell's main message declares that modern humans have gotten control of the Earth, the plants, and the animals. Now the last frontier is the human psyche. The last mystery is "man himself," "the inexhaustible and multifariously wonderful divine existence that is the life in all of us."[93] The recovery of mythology will teach us how to realize this mystery. We will not achieve that recovery through science or through religion. The only way is through psychology.

Thus, modern "outsiders" can appreciate the sacred objects of the native peoples as mementos of an ancient worldview. They can take a romantic attitude toward the native peoples and their ways. In this nostalgic view, the objects might be useful for moderns to get in touch with the symbolic world of their psyches. However, that treatment is far from the understanding that native peoples have of their sacred objects. They believe that these objects belong to them and their sacred ways, not to Westerners who want to use them to explore their psyches.

Evaluation of the Mythological Approaches

The Traditional versus the Modern Mind

We have explored rationalist and romantic methods of studying mythology. They both propose strategies that are alternatives to the way traditional societies treat myths and their objects. These strategies are designed to be acceptable to the Western children of the Enlightenment.

The German philosopher Ernst Cassirer (1874–1945) proposed a distinction that will explain the difference between the traditional view and the Western "modern mind-set." The difference in ways of thinking lies in the question of levels of meaning or even levels of reality.

Cassirer called the traditional view the *mythical consciousness*. This form of awareness does not separate the natural from the spiritual. This way of thinking recalls the sacramental view of Coleridge and Tillich described above. In the sacramental understanding, the symbol is a vehicle of the spiritual reality. The symbol is not separate from that reality. Likewise, in the mystical consciousness, the symbol and its meaning exist on the same level. They are one and the same.

For example, consider the description of the Hindu god of fire Agni: "In everyone's heart and hearth; he [Agni] is the vital spark of life, and lives in all living things; he is the fire which digests food, as well as the fire which consumes the offerings to the gods. He is the fire of the sun, in the lightning bolt, and in the smoke column which holds up the heavens."[94] In this example, fire does not *signify* sacred power. It *is* sacred power. The various forms of fire *are* the god. They do not just "symbolize" the god.[95]

This way of thinking is quite different from the Western, modern way of looking at symbol and myth. Cassirer called the modern thought patterns *theoretical knowledge*. In this approach, the symbol of fire and the meaning it expresses are separate. Therefore, the Western mind wants to know what the fire "signifies" as something different from itself. This idea that the symbol is separate from what it represents reminds us of Peirce's view.

In summary, the knowledge of "mythical consciousness" is immediate, direct, and concrete. The sacred object and the story of myth *are* their meanings. No explanation or interpretation is necessary. However, knowing in terms of theoretical knowledge is divided into signs and what they signify. With the advent of *theoretical consciousness*, Western thought began to treat symbols as representations, generalizations, and abstractions. And it began to look upon myths as fables.

Cassirer's distinction shows that for most modern thinkers, the gulf between these two kinds of knowing remains. Once Western culture crossed over into this theoretical knowledge, there was no turning back.[96] This led them to devise different attitudes toward myth and away from understanding the way native peoples view their sacred objects.

Evaluation of the Mythological Approaches: Myth Is a Choice against Science

Though the rationalists see some benefit in studying the worldviews of religious people, they treat mythology as an outdated way of thinking. In the end, religion and its mythology have to be abandoned in favor of science. Since science deals with facts that can be verified and theories that can be tested, it wins the contest of certainty. In this approach, therefore, the academic departments and museums involved can be sympathetic to the concerns of religions, but they will put priority on scientific research because of its modern benefits and applications. Ultimately, rationalists like Tylor and Frazer give those who want to understand mythology a choice. We must either accept the truths of mythology at face value or dismiss myth as an outdated explanation of the world.

Eliade and others who take the romantic approach to myth are well aware of the mental divide that separates modern people from the mythic societies. At first glance, they may seem to fit into the rationalist type. However, Eliade and his school of thought do not believe that mythology sets out to explain the world around us. Rather, myth brings us back to the primal time of origins on which the world and society are founded. Because they refer to the reality beyond time, the truths of myth are timeless: ordinary time and history have no real significance. Therefore, the essence of both myth and religion are "ahistorical," though the forms they take are historically conditioned. Myth and religion transport people into the timeless, an "ahistorical" reality beyond the world of time.[97]

However, for modern Westerners, this view does not get much further than the rationalist view. Phenomenologists like Eliade admit that modern people cannot understand myth in the way it presents itself unless they are able to enter into its eternal reality. Yet this is the very thing that the modern mind-set cannot do because of its "dis-enchanted" view of the world. Once again, the choice is between myth and science.

Evaluation of Mythological Approaches: Myth Should Be Reinterpreted

However, we have seen that Eliade identifies one path that seems to remain open to modern thinking, the psychological. Represented by Jung and Campbell, this approach tries to save mythology from the outright rejection of modern science. Robert Segal notes that these scholars did not directly confront science. They adapted mythology to science instead. Since myth can no longer be read literally or as an explanation of the material world, the common strategy has been to take refuge in the unconscious. Practically speaking, this strategy turns mythology into a means of self-realization.[98] We use mythology to probe the ways of the unconscious mind. Myth brings to the conscious mind the ways of the unconscious so that it no longer controls us and how we perceive the world.

So far, we have investigated the topics of religious symbols and mythology. We have found, though, that the understanding that we have gained is incomplete. We still have not found a way to interpret mythology that would be meaningful to the modern mind-set and yet satisfactory to the native peoples.

The three choices that this discussion has identified are as follows: (1) to treat these claims as mistaken and an obstacle to science; (2) to treat these claims as otherworldly and irrelevant to human life in history; or (3) to treat these claims narcissistically as mirrors of the psyche. None of these options offers the understanding of the objects under question in the NAGPRA program that we seek. None provides a rationale for why native peoples should repossess items because they are sacred objects.

The first choice would lead to the conclusion that the museum directors, scientists, and educators should prevail in their attempt to keep and use these objects as a source of scientific knowledge. The second choice would conclude that the indigenous claims are unimportant and that the objects' use for science and education should have priority. The third choice would admit that the Native Americans are claiming the objects for their own self-understanding. But again, that understanding does not necessarily uphold the rights of the Native Americans. From the viewpoint of Jung and Campbell, the artifacts would be useful for uncovering the psychological dynamics of *all* humans. The museum directors, scientists, and educators could claim that artifacts from past centuries are part of the whole human heritage and that indigenous peoples have no special claim to them.

Alternative Approaches: Focus on Ritual

The NAGPRA legislation and typical museum guidelines refer to "ceremonial objects" and objects that have been part of the death rites of an indigenous culture. In these definitions, the objects have their significance in ritual. This chapter has left the discussion of this part of the definition until now. We will find that it sets out a promising direction for the solution to the problem of the academic interpretation of sacred objects. The study of ritual will complete the survey of the options for how religious studies might interpret the sacred objects.

In the first part of the twentieth century, a group of scholars stressed the importance of ritual for ancient societies and their myths and texts. These Cambridge Ritualists argued that ritual and mythology are inseparably tied together. Further, they maintained that ritual involves both symbols and myths. These insights suggested that ritual might be a key to understanding symbols and myths.[99]

Ritual is often defined as symbolic action that takes place in ceremonies. When we apply this definition to religion, we can say that religious rituals are sacred ceremonies with religious symbolism. This definition begs the questions of what the terms *symbolic* and *religious* mean, but those are the questions that we are asking.

Types of Rituals

Rituals so saturate and shape human life that almost everything is ritualized, from the way we get up in the morning to how we turn in for the night. Not surprisingly, there are innumerable ways of classifying rituals. Each way draws out a feature of the riches of ritual. One way of classifying them is by their setting, such as the community, workplace, home, or personal life. Another way to classify them is by function. Rituals can celebrate births, solemnize marriages, or conduct funerals. They can also attempt to control the weather, to ensure the food supply, secure protection, gain healing, attain forgiveness, or even to attain salvation.[100] Yet another way is to categorize them into negative and positive patterns. The negative draws and maintains the boundaries between the sacred and the profane realities. By contrast, the positive brings the participants into a unity of the sacred and profane.

The Definition and Characteristics of Ritual

Ritual scholar Evan Zuesse defines rituals as "those conscious and voluntary, repetitious and stylized symbolic bodily actions that are centered on cosmic structures and/or sacred presences."[101] This definition identifies the essential characteristics of ritual. These are given in the textbox titled "Characteristics of Ritual."

Characteristics of Ritual

- Repetitious and styled actions
- Focused on sacred presences
- Concerns cosmic structures of reality

First, it emphasizes that ritual primarily consists of actions, not words. Words and even scriptures may provide content or accompany and interpret the ritual action, and yet without action there is no ritual.

In the Zoroastrian religion, there are five times of daily prayer. Each time, the believers wash their face, hands, and feet. Then they untie the sacred cord (*kusti*) that encircles their waist and stretch out their hands in prayer. They pray to Ahura Mazda ("The Wise Lord" and Creator) and renounce Angra Mainyu (the evil spirit) as they flick the end of the cord. Then they wrap the cord three times around their waist and tie it again.[102]

Second, the actions are also *repetitious*. Not only are they repeated each time the ritual is performed, but often actions are repeated in the same enactment of a ritual. The untying and tying of the sacred cord takes a short time but repeating it is a constant reminder of faith throughout the day.[103] Repetition drives home the meaning of the ritual.

Third, the definition adds that these repetitive actions are *stylized*. Repetitions give the ritual actions a familiar structure. As this structure is repeated, it becomes a pattern of action that engages the participants and gives a characteristic form to the ritual.

Fourth, the definition observes that religious rituals are "centered on cosmic structures and/or sacred presences." The repeated prayers call to mind the *sacred presences* of both the Creator and the "evil spirit."

Finally, ritual supposes that *cosmic structures* of reality give order to the universe. Thus, ritual upholds the basic construction of the universe. Typically, these structures of reality include the divisions between the sacred and profane and between good and evil. Other divisions that rituals sustain are the pure and impure and even male and female.[104]

Opposite to the rituals that reinforce the cosmic structures of division are those that bridge the distinctions. These rituals include *transition rituals* such as initiation rites, marriages, and funerals. They bring the participants into a different "order of reality." For example, in some cultures a funeral rite will escort a deceased person across the division between living persons and the ancestors.[105] Rituals are thus centered on the cosmic structures that join human persons together with sacred presences or powers in the same sacred space and time.

The Distinctions in the Relationship of Myth to Ritual

The association of ritual with myth and symbols is obvious. Still, modern scholars have vigorously debated the precise relationship of ritual to myth and symbol. The question has been whether myth or ritual came first. This may seem to us to be a "chicken and egg" conundrum. Nevertheless, the argument has significant implications for the understanding of the topic of ritual.

Bible scholar and encyclopedia editor William Robertson Smith (1846–1894) incited a prolonged squabble among scholars when he insisted that *ritual* comes before myth. Smith charged that modern scholarship was trying to stuff myth and ritual into the framework of Western thinking. They assumed that religion was founded on belief and that belief is expressed in logical ways.[106] These Western scholars tried to discern the logic of the meaning of symbol and myth.

Smith countered that the basis of primitive religion was not rational belief. It was ritual. Without ritual, the display of the sacred symbol or the telling of the myth did not achieve the results.[107] In other words, one can possess the sacred thread of Zoroastrianism; one can know its origins, and be able to explain its meaning; but these do not have the same spiritual power as the repeated action of untying and tying five times a day.

Classical scholar Jane Ellen Harrison (1840–1928) offered the most powerful argument in support of the priority of ritual. She argued strenuously that ritual was *expressive*. To Harrison, ritual enabled its participants to relive the experience of such primary activities as the hunt or the battle. The reenactment expressed the feelings of the members about the event. In doing so, it reinforced the feeling of belonging to the clan.[108] In contrast, myth only played a secondary role in the expressing of the group's emotions.

The storm of the debate that W. R. Smith started has subsided. Yet Harrison and her fellow Cambridge Ritualists made a lasting impact on religious studies because they insisted that the premodern societies do not think in modern ways. Recall Cassirer's distinction between premodern mythical consciousness and modern theoretical consciousness. Moderns think in terms of concepts that are generalizations and abstractions. Thus the modern tendency was to reduce symbols and myths into general statements of what is believed to be true.

But Harrison showed that ancient people thought of myths as "things spoken" and rituals as "things done." The "things spoken" (the myths) of the tribe are in support of "things done" (the rituals). The most important thing is what needs to be done. For example, before a hunt or battle, the things that need *doing* are to build the unity of the group in a common feeling and to invoke the sacred powers to ensure success.[109] The task at hand is not to remind the groups of their beliefs about hunts and wars. It is to make its outcome favorable.

The Interpretation of Ritual According to Its Own Logic: Evans-Pritchard

The argument about the priority of ritual cleared the way for twentieth-century treatments of the subject. Much of the research on ritual depends on the groundbreaking work of the anthropologist E. E. Evans-Pritchard (1902–1973). In general, one of Evans-Pritchard's most important contributions to religious studies was that he undercut the prejudice against the thinking of prehistoric peoples.

Prior to Evans-Pritchard, the dominant bias was in the widely held distinction between two modes of thinking: *mythos* and *logos*. *Mythos*, the Greek word from which we get the word *myth*, denotes the way of thinking that appeals to supernatural realities to preserve, order, and give meaning to human life. *Logos*, the Greek word from which we get the word *logical*, stands for the rational, practical, and scientific. Logos looks to natural causes for explanations to what happens in this world. In these terms, the opposite of logos is the irrational, impractical, and unscientific. Therefore, if we look at myth from the point of view of logos thinking, it is merely fantasy and falsehood.

According to this distinction, either myth is fantasy or it is logos thinking gone wrong, since it makes fundamental mistakes in its attempt to make logical sense of the world. Evans-Pritchard's study of the Azande of Sudan, Africa, represents a lasting challenge to this distinction. It counters the view that mythical thinking and its rituals are essentially "irrational."

Many consider his groundbreaking book *Witchcraft, Oracles, and Magic among the Azande* (1937) the most significant work in anthropology of the twentieth century.[110] In this book, Evans-Pritchard asserted that we should take the ways of the Azande on their own terms. If we would do so, we would find that they are, in fact, proficient in empirical and practical reasoning. That is, in their own way they are skilled at logos thinking.

Evans-Pritchard's insistence that the Azande are skilled in practical reasoning might be a surprise. Modern Westerners easily find flaws in their way of thinking, since their society is permeated with witchcraft. However, Evans-Pritchard noted that the Azande show impressive ingenuity in the way they explain the failures of their magical system. They also show remarkable inventiveness in the tests of magic that are built into the system. Yet, of course, their reasoning is contained within the limits of their system. But within those limits it is quite sensible.[111]

For the Azande, witchcraft is the practical way to fix blame for catastrophes, illnesses, crop failures, adultery, and even quarrels. To assign fault, the Azande people use *divination*, the art of discovering hidden knowledge of the past, present, or future through magic. Feeding poison to a chicken while repeating the name of an accused person is the most frequent ritual technique. If the chicken dies, the person is guilty. There is even a procedure for appealing to the chief's court.[112]

While practices like this might be considered bizarre, Evans-Pritchard showed that the Azande form of magic has its own system of logic. He found that magic and its symbols were part of an integrated ritual complex that included oracles, divinization, and witchcraft.[113] In turn, this ritual complex was an integral part of a larger context of the whole social structure of the group. Thus, magic was woven into the fabric of ordinary life, and no one thought witchcraft was extraordinary.[114]

Evans-Pritchard explained that the ritual system was sensible within the Azande worldview because it was necessary to counteract the magical powers of other people.[115] In the Azande society, magic provided a system of redress of grievances, promoted proper behavior, and validated the authority of the chief and his court. Every time magic was practiced the system was confirmed.

For example, suppose you would consult an oracle about traveling. If you are advised that travel is unsafe, you would probably stay home. Now suppose that nothing happens to you while at home. In that case, you would consider the oracle's word to be verified. Obeying the oracle and staying home was an effective way to stay out of trouble. Suppose, however, that things just did not work out. What if you stayed at home and had an accident? The Azande acknowledge that discrepancies and inconsistencies can happen. However, the tribe never allows these failures to undermine the whole ritual system. Rather, the Azande regard them as malfunctions. Perhaps the magical ritual was incorrectly performed. Perhaps its magic was applied in the wrong way. In any case, complicated reasoning is used to maintain the system.[116]

The groundbreaking work of Evans-Pritchard led to a more contemporary view of ritual and how it might be studied. First, the symbols, myths, and rituals have meaning within a whole *ritual system* of interlocking parts. The analysis of these parts should recognize their role within the system. Second, careful study of the evidence should correct the theory. In this way, Evans-Pritchard offered a model for exacting fieldwork and detailed study of cultures that has become standard in the twenty-first century.

If we would take this model as an approach to sacred objects, we would make an exhaustive study of the cultures of the native peoples involved. We would study the whole ritual system of the tribe and how that system fits into the whole social context. Then, within that overarching cultural context, we would analyze the logic of the use of the sacred objects. We would expect that this logic would be far different from the logic of Western Enlightenment reasoning.

The Interpretation of Ritual According to Place: J. Z. Smith

Another scholar who criticizes the presuppositions of modern religious scholars is Jonathan Z. Smith. Smith suggests that the study of ritual has been sidetracked by the Protestant view of ritual as "vain repetition." In Zuesse's definition, we found repetition to be an essential characteristic of ritual. However, those who put the highest value on sincere belief, words and actions that are repeated in ritual lose their significance. This view warns that ritual can easily become empty of meaning. It often accompanies the iconoclast view that images lead believers into false worship and erroneous doctrines.

Smith counters that those who reject ritual because it is repetitious miss the purpose of ritual. Far from being "vain repetition," ritual is a way of paying attention. In ritual, everything that is ordinary becomes significant—that is, sacred. Ritual takes profane things, people, and places and puts them into the transcendent context of the holy.[117] As it does so, it elevates the awareness of the sacredness of these things.

In Smith's view, the sacred realm is not a place that believers find and then honor because it is holy. Rather, ritual constructs the sacred space in which ordinary things and activities are transformed. The supernatural world that ritual creates is a perfect world where everything is carefully controlled. It is like a carefully constructed stage. Ritual sets the ordinary aspects of daily life on this stage where they are part of a supernatural drama. Thus, ritual presents the things of everyday life the way they ought to be, not the way they are.[118] The purpose of ritual is to overcome the imperfections of ordinary life by their transformation in the perfect world.[119]

For example, Smith refers to the "Bear Festivals" of the Arctic regions. In this ritual, a bear cub is adopted. For a few years, the native group gives the cub much attention and affection. Then, at the time of the festival, it is paraded through the village in a playful way. After that, it is ritually tied down, addressed with formal ceremony, and killed. At the conclusion of the festival, the members of the tribe eat the bear meat. They pray that the bear's soul will bring a report to the spirit world about how well it was treated.[120]

Smith says that this ritual enacts the *perfect* bear hunt. In the "wild," bears and people do not act in this elegantly predictable way. However, the perfect bear hunt shows the hunters what the ideal hunt should be. In doing so, it teaches the ultimate significance of the hunt.[121]

In summary, Smith's theory suggests that ritual creates a supernatural context in which ordinary objects *become* sacred. If we applied Smith's theory to the problem of understanding the sacred objects of native peoples, we would study how ritual creates an alternative and sacred reality to the modern world. Then we would study how that setting changes the meaning of sacred objects.

Evaluation of the Ritual Approach to the Understanding of Sacred Objects

Life in the twenty-first century is filled with ritual. For instance, one cannot imagine a sports contest without it. Consider the Super Bowl. The entire event is ritualized from the pregame homage to past football heroes, the coin toss, the introduction of the players as superhuman, the singing of the National Anthem, the play-by-play dramatization of the game, the handshake of the coaches, and the award ceremony, to the postgame interviews with the players. All these rituals elevate the game to a higher level than the ordinary. They give the game a significance it would not have without them.

Some would call the rituals of the Super Bowl "religious." In the week before her halftime performance at the Super Bowl in 2012, pop singer, songwriter, and actress Madonna told CNN newscaster Anderson Cooper that she was nervous about appearing in the middle of what she considered the most important American religious celebration. She said, "The Super Bowl is kind of like the holy of holies in America. I'm going to come in halfway through the church experience and I'm going to have to deliver a sermon that's going to have to be very impactful."[122]

In the same vein, commentators have compared the Super Bowl to the religious festivals of the past. The Super Bowl combines sports with politics, religion, and myth as well as business, the arts, and the media. In the same way, the ancient Olympic games, the Roman gladiatorial contests, and Mayan ball games combined sports with these same aspects of society.

The origins of sport are in religion. Sport has its cathedrals, saints, "gods" or superstars, true believers, symbols, pilgrimages, ruling authorities, special (holy) days, and other features that are similar to facets of religion. But *are* sports "religions"? Commentators have often noted the religious aspects of sport. Indeed sports can fulfill some of the functions of religion in an individual's life. But, as Michael Novak observes, that does not make sports "religions" in the sense that organized religions such as Methodism are "religious."[123]

Tim Delaney and Tim Madigan express the common Western understandings of the difference between "sport" and "religion." They say bluntly, "Sports are real and religion is spiritual." They assert that the believers in "sport" believe in their teams. But the game is a reality that is observable and tangible. However, believers in "religion" have to believe in a reality that is unseen and intangible. Sports strive to achieve material goals in the everyday world. Religions have spiritual goals that transcend the concerns of "this world." The rituals of sport aim at these tangible outcomes. The rituals of religion are processes that sweep a person up into a different reality: the ritual of eating a hot dog is far different from the ritual of participating in the Catholic Mass.[124]

In their distinction between "sport" and "religion," Delaney and Madigan assume a fundamental notion of Western ideas of religion and ritual. This presupposition is not merely the gap between the ordinary and the spiritual world. It is the priority of the ordinary, tangible world over the ethereal, spiritual realm.

This supposition is in the background of the theories of ritual that we have reviewed. Religious ritual applies to ancient or "primitive" peoples. In contrast, modern humans have graduated from it and now participate in only "secular" rituals like sports. Thus, Eliade's idea of myth as something "lost" in the modern world also applies to ritual.

Since the theories of ritual discussed above approach religious ritual in this way, they do not solve the problem posed in this chapter. They do not help us understand why religious ritual is necessary to modern people in the twenty-first century. If religious ritual is outdated in today's world, then modern people cannot understand why native peoples living in the twenty-first century should need the objects of the NAGPRA program in question for their religious rituals.

Evaluation of the Idea That Sacred Ritual Is Emotional, Not Logical

Note, for example, that Jane Ellen Harrison and other Cambridge Ritualists did not reject the basic division between logos and mythos in Western thought. They nimbly jumped from the logical and practical sense of logos to the enchanted mythos side of the divide. Harrison believed in a "religious and mystical spirit." This spirit is aware of things that cannot be grasped by logos thinking. The expression of this spirit must be "felt and lived" rather than intellectually analyzed.[125]

However, when it came to rational logos thought, Harrison, in fact, shared the evolutionary views of Tylor. To her rational side, religious dogma was false. In an essay on the influence of Darwinism on the study of religion, she stated that religion was "based on the delusions of a noncritical intellect" and an "over-confident will."[126]

Harrison was referring to a way of thinking that treats religions as "primitive" and its rituals as "savage." Those who think in this way might eloquently lecture about the sacred objects from the graves of the ancestors of indigenous people just as Harrison shared her artistic appreciation of Greek vases. Yet, for her, both indigenous sacred objects and Greek vases belong in museums, not in the practice of a living faith.

It turns out that Harrison's scholarship set religious ritual apart from the ordinary life of modern society. In the spirit of romanticism, the method of the Cambridge Ritualists might allow some "primitive" peoples to have their delusions. However, it would not explain why native peoples in today's society need specific objects for sacred rituals. The "religious and mystical spirit," after all, could be expressed in other ways. Furthermore, new objects could be made to replace the items of the past.

Evaluation of the Idea That Sacred Ritual Has Its Own Logic

Evans-Pritchard was careful to respect the rituals that he studied. He was, indeed, eager to state that these rituals had their own logic. Evans-Pritchard tried his best to get inside the primitive mind as he set out to describe the way their magical thinking works. He shared some insight regarding how the Azande people persist in their magical ways despite the contradictions that appear obvious to us.

Evans-Pritchard's insights help us to see that modern people often use the same type of rationalizations that he found among the Azande. However, the most respected anthropologist of the twentieth century still held that there is a significant difference between modern people and the Azande. Unlike the Azande, modern people are capable of grasping the misleading dynamics of rationalization. They can understand the flaw in the reasoning that a prayer did not "work" because it was not said correctly.

Moreover, when Evans-Pritchard said that the Azande have their own practical logic, that did not mean that others, especially modern people, can comprehend it. He criticized Tylor and others like him for presuming that they could imagine what was going on in the minds of primitive peoples. This criticism proves that Evans-Pritchard understood the separation between sacred ritual in traditional societies and in modern life.

Notwithstanding the profound insights of Evans-Pritchard on the study of human culture, it is questionable whether "outsiders" in the modern world could understand Native Americans' claims on sacred objects. In the Evans-Pritchard view, indigenous peoples have "their own" logic. This observation has circled back to the problem that we must simply accept what Native American informants tell us about their sacred ways. We have not found a bridge between the worldviews of the native peoples and the scientists and educators. The return of the objects would be a token of the toleration of modern people who appreciate the rights of other worldviews.

Evaluation of the Idea That Sacred Ritual Has It Own Place

Evans-Pritchard believed that sacred ritual has its own logic. J. Z. Smith believes that sacred ritual has its own place. Yet Smith's view of ritual is similar to the other views that we have cited. It emphasizes the difference between ritual and ordinary life. However, in Smith's view, the difference is not in mythical thinking. According to Smith, ritual creates the difference from ordinary reality by constructing an ideal place. This is a place where the processes of ordinary life can be perfectly performed.

Smith's theory offers a valuable insight about the role of place in Native American ritual. It helps us understand why dislocation from ancestral lands is a religious tragedy for Native Americans. It also helps us see why unrestricted access to sacred sites is a priority for Native Americans. However, Steve Weitzman notes that Smith's conception of ritual makes it a "self-insulated system."[127] In Smith's theory, there is no interaction between the world of ordinary experience and the ideal world of ritual, even in traditional societies. Smith argues that the separation between "ritual and reality" is at the heart of the purpose of ritual and that the participants in ritual are well aware of it. So then, we might ask, what prevents us from concluding that Native Americans want the ritual objects in order to conduct their own ceremonial activities that have no bearing on life in the twenty-first century?

The Problem with Western Categories of Interpretation

Thus we have not found a satisfactory solution to the problem of how to understand what native peoples mean when they claim that an object is sacred. In general, the alternative approaches tend to suggest that what native peoples mean by the concept of sacredness is not understandable to persons in the twenty-first century.

As we review these tendencies, one can detect an underlying assumption of Western secularism that segregates religion from public life. According to this mind-set, if religious symbols, myths, and rituals have any relevance in modern society, they have meaning in some privatized world of the psyche. Otherwise, they are lost features of a premodern and irrecoverable past. They are the remnants of the religious past kept barely alive by societies that have not yet caught up with the present world.

Critical thinking might take one more step backward in its analysis of the problem. It might ask about the frame of reference that contains the assumption of the division between the religious and the secular. Anthropologist Peter Jones proposes an answer as he reflects on the often tense relationship between anthropology and Native Americans.

Jones asserts that Western thinking separates everything into two opposing parts—that is, dualities. For example, it divides the subject matter of this chapter into such *binaries* as premodern and modern, logos and mythos, scientific and primitive, science and religion, Western and indigenous, theoretical knowledge and mythic consciousness, discursive and presentational, rational logic and ritual logic, and sacred place and ordinary place. Jones notes that binaries like these gloss over the rich complexities of life by forcing everything into opposing categories.[128]

He goes on to show that such dualistic categories are useful only to the extent that one buys into the binary system.[129] For instance, the category "indigenous" is only true if there is the opposite "non-indigenous" or "Western." This division removes all the indigenous peoples from anything that is "Western." The mistake that this dualism makes is obvious. The history and life of most indigenous peoples are closely intertwined with Western cultures.

Issues surrounding the sacred objects of native peoples challenge religious studies to reconsider the Western thinking on which it has been based. As we are finding in this chapter, it seems impossible to solve many of the problems of understanding religion in the twenty-first century if we are bound to past habits of thought.

PROPOSING THE MOST PROMISING SOLUTION: THE RITUAL CONTEXT WITHIN A SOCIAL SETTING

This chapter now proposes that the field of religious studies has a pivotal role in interpreting religious symbols, myths, and rituals in the midst of the issues of religion in the twenty-first century. We have reviewed selected approaches to the study of symbol, myth, and ritual. This review leads to a two-part principle about their interpretation. First, the interpretation of symbol, myth, and ritual should respect the meanings that religious believers give to their sacred ways and objects. Second, "outsiders" to the religion should be able to understand this interpretation. The optimal goal is that perhaps scholars of religion might even suggest a common ground for the mediation of conflicts concerning the funerary and ceremonial objects.

How, then, can religious studies interpret religious symbols, myths, and rituals with fairness and insight in the midst of the controversies of this century? The next part of this chapter will present the "proposed solution" in two steps. First, it will suggest that the *social setting* in which we find symbols, myths and rituals is the overall context in which they have meaning. Second, it will propose that the study of a *ritual* is the best place to begin to investigate the meaning of the symbols and myths embedded in it.

The Social Context of Sacred Objects

When we want to know the meaning of a word or phrase, we can look it up in the dictionary. But what about utterances like "Heavens!"? We only know the meaning of such phrases by their specific context. Perhaps the interpretation and explanation of the claim that an object is a religious symbol, that a myth has religious significance, and that a ritual is a sacred rite depends upon its social context.

The philosopher Ludwig Wittgenstein (1889–1951) proposed that the meaning of a word is its use in language. If so, then the *use* of a word or object in its setting *is* its meaning. A religious object might have one set of meanings in a religious setting such as a lodge, temple, mosque, or shrine. It would acquire other meanings when placed in a museum, and it would attract still other meanings when placed in a grave or when "found" centuries later.

For example, the Cheyenne holy men pacified the spiritual energy of the buffalo skull in the Museum of Natural History. Then they advised that the symbol be put back into its appropriate context. Consequently, a unique box in the shape of a Sun Dance Lodge was prepared for it.[130] This box not only preserves the artifact, it also provides a ritual and social context in which the buffalo skull can be understood as a sacred object.

This investigation leads to an emphasis on the social contexts in which religious symbols, myths, and rituals have understandable meaning. Perhaps if we could understand their context, we would not have to fit them into our own preconceived mental framework. Nor would we have to take the native informant's word for what they mean. We could understand them within their own frame of reference. This approach leads to the promising task of studying the contexts of sacred items and practices in a way that enables scholars to more accurately interpret them.

Building the Solution: Avoiding Generalities

The modern Western disengagement of religion from public life coupled with the appeal of psychological theories of religion may mislead us into thinking that religious symbols and myths are primarily private matters. In other words, the context of their meaning is private and lies in the psyche, subjective experience, or individual opinion. If so, then we must take one of two paths: the general or the particular. Both are dead ends.

We might follow the path of those who interpret the religious objects under dispute as *instances* of universal archetypes, deep structures, or ritual patterns. This method would fit the meaning of distinctive objects into generalities that all human beings are thought to share. In this case we would ignore the particularity of the object and its meaning for the group that owns it. However, this way of looking at the meaning of religious symbols, myths, and rituals fails when it comes to matters of their specific nature and location. If the symbols, myths, or rituals under question are just expressions of universals, why insist that these specific objects be returned? In terms of this chapter's problem of how to understand the objects of native peoples, why should the ownership of a specific sacred object be such a pressing concern?

For example, the Northwest Indian Cemetery Protective Association appealed to the courts to stop the U.S. Forest Service from constructing a paved road though federal land in the Six Rivers National Forest in California. The Native Americans claimed that the road would disturb the effectiveness of sacred rituals historically conducted in the area.

The court dismissed the Native Americans' claim that the road would "doom" their religion. Furthermore, the court stated that it was impossible for it to settle disputes between competing beliefs in a pluralistic society. In other words, the court acknowledged that the Native Americans *believed* that the site was necessary to their rituals. However, this was merely an arbitrary claim of private opinion that existed alongside other opinions. It was not a deciding factor in the case.[131]

The Supreme Court's ruling is a good example of the problem with trying to find common universal meaning across many different cultures. Such generalizations overlook the specific meaning of actual sacred places and objects. If the artifacts involved in the NAGPRA legislation are only miscellaneous instances of universal meanings, then one object is as good as another. For example, the Bishop Ford Museum in Hawaii promises Native Hawaiians access to the "items of antiquity" in its collection. However, it says that the preservation of native religious practices does not need the use of these "rare and priceless items." Objects like them can always be "newly made." This comment dismisses the particular sacred nature of the objects under dispute.

On the other hand, how can "outsiders" grasp the meaning of the staggering variety of specific symbols, myths, and rituals? Unless they have a broader framework of interpretation, they will only have a collection of items that are supposed to be sacred. They will have to accept whatever the "insiders" say about the specific items. The Supreme Court regarded the claim of the Native Americans to perform specific sacred rituals on the specific lands at face value. The court called it a *sincerely held belief*.[132] However, the court had no way of understanding why the Native Americans held this belief. It could only say that beliefs were matters of privately held opinion.

Building the Proposed Solution: Meaning in the Social Context

In an attempt to solve these challenges, anthropologist Clifford Geertz (1926–2006) set the direction for the study of the social context in which sacred objects can be best understood. His method treats cultures as *symbolic systems* that interpret the world in distinctive ways. Using this approach, the scholar must "read" a culture as a literary critic would read a text. In short, the anthropologist is an interpreter of cultures.

In keeping with his method, Geertz did not attempt to identify the origins or to explain the causes of religion. As the chapter's proposed solution suggests, he interpreted religions in their cultural context. What is this context? If cultures are symbolic systems, then so are religions. In contrast to other aspects of the cultural web, these sacred symbols concern the most basic understandings of reality. That is, the religious symbolic system presents cultural patterns that are "models *of*" and "models *for*" the reality of the collective group.[133] Embedded in myths and actualized in rituals, symbols describe the "world" in which the group and its members dwell. They explain how everything is ordered, harmonized, and unified to make a whole.

For example, among the Navajo, sand paintings are used for healing. The paintings are models *of* a world of healthy people and models *for* ways of healing.[134] Spiritual experts carefully construct the painting as a depiction of the proper balance and harmony of the world. Once the sand painting is completed, its spiritual power is brought to life when pollen and corn meal are sprinkled over it. The sick person is then set down in the painting.[135] He or she now sits in the center of the healing energies of the perfectly ordered sacred world.

The sand painting and its ritual are obviously more than representations of what the Navajo think or feel about the natural world. The ritual is an actual "healing event." It is not merely "symbolic" in the Western sense of an arbitrary connection between the symbol and what it signifies. The ritual *makes* the worldview of the Navajo happen as it restores the "order, balance, and beauty" of the perfect universe. In the restored world the person is healed.[136]

Geertz's approach suggests that to understand the sacred objects under dispute we should see them as parts of the cultural system in which they have meaning. How did Geertz advise scholars to understand the meaning of the symbolic objects within that system? To avoid separating cultural analysis from the specifics of everyday life, Geertz advised scholars to observe the actual behavior of the people in detail.[137] In keeping with this advice, Geertz's work demonstrated what he calls a *thick description* of culture. A "thin" description will skim off selected details of cultural life, perhaps in order to provide data and examples for uncluttered generalizations. A "thick description," on the other hand, records the way life is actually lived with all its contradictions and inconsistencies.

To apply Geertz's theory to the question of the sacred objects of native peoples, we would study how these objects fit into the total symbolic system of the culture. The investigation would give a "thick description" of the use of the sacred objects in the day-to-day affairs of the society.

Geertz's theory of an interpretive approach to culture is an impressive step toward a possible solution to the problem that the NAGPRA controversies raise. However, it has limitations in its application to the challenges that the field of religious studies faces in this century. As the work of Evans-Pritchard among the Azande shows, it would take years to comprehend the innumerable details of a total culture.

Is there a more manageable context of symbols, myths, and rituals that would give scholars a better start in the task of interpreting them? This chapter's proposal suggests that there is. The obvious but often overlooked[138] context in which symbols and myths play a clear role is ritual. The most promising solution to the problem of this chapter is that ritual might be the key to the meaning of symbols and myth. In this view, scholars might focus on the *use* of the contested objects in ritual as a more productive approach to studying them.

Building the Solution: The Ritual Context

The cultural anthropologist Victor Turner (1920–1983) is noted for developing methods of studying symbols in the context of ritual. Like Geertz, Turner treated culture as a symbolic system and believed that scholars should carefully observe the details of rituals. They should not rely on the account of the believing informants about the ceremonies. The details provide understandings that add to the reports of informants regarding the meaning of the symbols and myths involved.

For example, when Turner studied the African puberty rites of the Ndembu people in Zambia, the informants extolled the power of the puberty ritual to unify the people in the surrounding villages. However, Turner noticed that on the last day the girl's mother prepared a dish of cassava and beans for everyone. The guests then competed to be the first to grab the serving spoon and eat from the dish. The informant told Turner that the girl would be married to a man from the village of whoever gets the spoon. The girl's mother added that she hoped that someone from her own village would get the spoon. To Turner, this suggested a sense of hidden rivalry among the villages. However, that was a meaning that the native informants did not offer.[139]

Thus, Turner believed that scholars should study rituals while they were being performed. They should not rely on reports about the rituals or transcripts of what is said and done in them. Only observations on the scene give researchers a full sense of the dynamics of the ritual.[140]

The Ritual State of Liminality

Turner's research on the rites of passage of the Ndembu people of Africa naturally led to his conclusion that rituals are central phases of larger social processes. By means of rituals, societies deal with changes in lives of individuals, the group, and the environment. Many of these processes involve changes of social status, and even changes in state of being.

In rites of passage, initiates are often secluded from society and made to undergo various trials until they reemerge from their ordeals with a new position in society. From his observations of such initiation rites, Turner developed his seminal category of *liminality*.

According to the theory of liminality, the initiates go through three phases of social process. (See the textbox "Turner's Idea of the Liminal Process of Ritual" for a summary.) The first is the phase of *separation* from ordinary society, and the last is the *reintegration* of the return to society. In the middle of these two phases is the critical *liminal* state, a state of "in-between." This may be the time between childhood and adulthood. Alternatively, it may be the time between existence in this world and one's afterlife as an ancestor.

Turner's Idea of the Liminal Process of Ritual

1. Separation from ordinary life and society
2. Engagement in the liminal ("in-between") stage of transformation from one state of being and role in society to another
3. Return to society as a transformed person

According to Turner, rituals thrust their participants into the liminal state in order to transform them. Entering into this state is like returning to the womb. From this womb the initiates are reborn as a new person. By this rebirth they acquire a new inner character as well as a new outward status.

In their "in-between" status, the initiates experience what Turner calls *communitas*. The ordinary state is a state of social order. The social order provides structure to one's life that makes it predictable, regular, and normal. However, in the liminal state, this familiar social order is overturned. The standard norms no longer apply. The everyday structure of society yields to *anti-structure*.

Once stripped of their former identities and social status in the situation of "anti-structure," the initiates are open and vulnerable to the authority of the gods and the elders. They can receive without question the secret wisdom of the tribe and the folklore of the clan. Moreover, they can form new bonds with their fellow initiates. Finally, the ritual can give them their new identity and new status in the society.

Turner notes that the liminal state is a crucial feature of religion. For example, it is the time of the Mardi Gras before the disciplines of Lent. It is the time of the playful throwing of colored powders and dyes during the Hindu festival of Holi. It is the joyful occasion of splashing water on loved ones at the Thai Buddhist New Year festival of Songkran. It is the new clothes and joyous feasting of the Muslim Eid ul-Fitr festival after the fasting during the month of Ramadan. It is the night of "Trick-or-Treat" on Halloween before the somber observance the next morning of All Saints commemorating all the saints who have died.

The clothing that Muslims wear in Mecca during the pilgrimage to Mecca, called the hajj, is a good example of a sacred object that signifies the liminal state. The hajj is one of the "Five Pillars" of Islam. It is a five- or six-day ritual at the central shrine of Islam. Muslims who have the means to do so are obligated to go on this pilgrimage to the city of Mecca in Saudi Arabia at least once in their lifetime.

The *pre*-liminal" state of the hajj consists of the journey to Mecca. This is the period of preparation in which the concerns of the ordinary world are left behind. Before coming into the *haram*, or holy site, itself, Muslims say prayers, shave, trim their nails, and put on the *ihram*, a white garment. For men, the ihram consists of two pieces of white cloth. It is the only clothing to be worn. The dress code for women is more flexible, but they must wear modest clothing, often a long white gown. Their face and hands, however, must be uncovered. Once the Muslims don the ihram, they are in a special state of holiness. Such things as sexual activity, killing animals, eating meat (except the meat from the sacrifice), fighting, making oaths, using perfume or deodorants, wearing shoes instead of sandals, shaving, and trimming one's nails are prohibited.

Wearing the ihram signifies purity, humility, and equality. All normal distinctions between people such as nationality, class, race, and social status are obliterated. Everyone is now in the "in-between" state where they are open to the sacred power and meaning of the rituals of the hajj. This state lasts for the ritual acts in Mecca until the ritual sacrifice of an animal. After that ritual is complete, the Muslim men shave or trim their heads. The women cut a fingertip length of hair. After that, they enter into the *post*-liminal" state. They shower and dress in everyday clothes. The pilgrimage is completed with the circumambulation seven times around the sacred, central shrine of the Ka'ba, and other optional rites.

Though the ritual has ended, it has a lasting effect. The time of liminality permanently transforms the character of the pilgrims. The successful completion of the ritual also gives pilgrims a new status within the ordinary structures of society. For example, those who return from the hajj are given the honorary title

Hajji (men) or Hajja (women). Many take their ihram home with them to be used for their burial shroud.

This time of liminality is profoundly real. It is not simply symbolic and ceremonial in the sense of many rituals in America such as graduations. In these rites, the graduates simply cross a stage to get the appearance of a diploma. They get the real diploma when they pay their fees. The initiates of religious rituals often endure some very real ordeals. Tattooing, circumcision, shaving of the head and body, scarification, removal of teeth, going without sleep, exposure to the elements, beatings, and humiliations are other examples of the raw reality of the liminal state.

Symbols in the Context of Ritual

Having reviewed Turner's views on the ritual context, we note that the NAGPRA legislation applies to funerary and ceremonial objects. Thus, the objects in question have come from a ritual context because they have been part of burials or have been dedicated for use in indigenous ceremonies. If we follow Turner's way of interpreting their meaning, we might better understand their symbolic place in the rituals involved.

Turner recognized that symbols are *multi-vocal*. Literally, they speak in many voices. This means that symbols express a wide range of meanings. How does one know what meanings are correct? Within the range of possible meanings, a symbol will have a more definite meaning in the ritual context in which it is used.

In Turner's use of terms, some symbols are *instrumental*. They appear in only one ritual and have a particular meaning in that ritual. Other symbols are *dominant* because they appear in different rituals and have different meanings depending on the rituals in which they are used. Dominant symbols possess the widest variety of meanings. Each ritual that uses the dominant symbol engages some of these meanings but not all of them.[141]

An example of a dominant symbol is the Eastern Orthodox Christian ritual treatment of the cross. Orthodox Christians have several feasts involving the cross, the central symbol of Christianity. Christendom commemorates the crucifixion of Jesus Christ on the Friday before Easter (*Pascha*). For Eastern Orthodox Christians, this day is like the Western "Good Friday," the most solemn day of the church year. On this day, the cross signifies the event of the crucifixion of Jesus Christ as the pivotal event of divine redemption.

Yet Catholic and Eastern Orthodox Christians also commemorate another day that focuses on the cross, the feast of the "Exaltation of the Cross" in September. This day recalls the finding of the "true cross" in Jerusalem in 326 CE. According to this feast, the original cross was found under a temple that the Emperor Hadrian erected to Venus at the site of the crucifixion. On this feast day a cross is decorated with flowers and placed on a stand for the faithful to venerate. Unlike Good Friday, the mood of this day is one of joy and triumph.

Eastern Orthodox Christians have another day of focus on the cross that is patterned after the "Exaltation of the Cross." This is a Sunday in the middle of the Lenten time of fasting and repentance. Once again, the cross is placed ceremonially in the middle of the church. This time it signifies the call to follow the way of the cross. Thus, on this day, the cross symbolizes self-denial, discipline, and the overcoming of the passions.

As a dominant symbol, the cross has undertones as a sign of sacrifice and redemption that carry across each of these ritual observances. However, we should note that each ritual engages different and additional meanings as well as meanings that are only understood in the context of the various rituals.

Myths in the Context of Ritual

In Turner's thought, the ritual context determines the meaning of visual symbols and symbolic actions. However, rituals also involve words in the form of myths and belief statements. Like Smith and Harrison, Turner rejected the conventional idea that myth is the mother of ritual. He believed that ritual engenders myth.[142] Therefore, he maintained that scholars should study mythology in terms of its role in ritual.

The most obvious place of mythology in ritual is its recitation, in full or in part, within the sacred rites. For instance, Bon Tibetan marriage ceremonies recite the myth of the primordial marriage, the union of a man with a goddess. The couple is given ritual objects representing the gifts that the gods gave the first couple. Then the couple joins the priest in singing the story of the first couple.

Recitations like these are found in most religions. In the Jewish Passover, the recitation is the story of Israel's liberation from slavery in Egypt. In the Hindu Appearance Day, it is the story of the Appearance of the Hindu Lord Sri Krishna. In the Muslim Lailat al Miraj, it is the twofold narrative of the Islamic prophet Muhammad's journey to Jerusalem and then into the heights of heaven. In the Christian Christmas, it is the narrative of the birth of Jesus Christ. In each case, there is a formal telling of the story. This telling is, in a sense, the official version of the story and it may be accompanied by commentary that gives an authoritative interpretation.

Statues or paintings that depict the characters of myths also exemplify the role of mythology in ritual. The images may be housed in temples or homes. At times they may be ritually displayed in festivals that reenact the myth of the celebration. For example, in India, towns and villages bring out the images of their deities from their holy places and parade them in the streets. These exuberant festivals make the sacred and transforming power of the deities available to all.

In the sacred city of Puri, India, three wooden chariots carry the images of Lord Jagannatha, his brother Blabhadra, and his sister Suhadra in a breathtaking ritual. Lord Jagannatha's chariot towers forty-five feet in height. It has sixteen wheels, each more than seven feet in diameter. It takes four thousand people to pull it. There are numerous legends that tell of the origins of the festival. Each one should be understood in the light of the ritual theme of the "chariot journey" of the deity. Such ritual processions of images are liminal times when communities unite in worshipping the deities or join in prayers for divine favor or forgiveness.

Building the Proposed Solution: Ritual in the Social Setting

Though Turner is best known for promoting the idea of liminality, his theory also emphasizes the role of ritual within ordinary public life. In Turner's thinking, ritual does not present an ideal of the way things should be in ordinary life. Ritual itself has an *anti-structure* that seems to be the opposite of the patterns of ordinary public life. Yet the *anti-structure* is closely related to the structure. Sacred ritual is set within and has an essential role in living experience.

Thus, in his fieldwork, Turner found that he could not study rituals apart from the larger social processes in which they were embedded. In secular societies the rituals of religious institutions are most often separated from public life. However, before the disestablishment of religion, religious rituals were part of the social order.

The feasts of Christianity usually marked the calendar and the cycle of the seasons. For example, in Great Britain and Ireland, the Feast of St. Michael the Archangel on September 29 (Michaelmas Day) was the day of the completion of the harvest. It was also the day of the beginning of the academic year. Furthermore, it was the day to pay debts, to hire servants, and to elect officials. On this day, the custom in the United Kingdom was to eat a well-fattened goose to ensure prosperity in the coming year. It is clear that Michaelmas Day combined social affairs with religious observances.

Western scholarship has often reflected the secularism that separates religious ritual from the everyday public processes of society. Typically, it has assumed that religion has no relevance to public life. Yet that separation was never complete. Some ties between ritual and society remain. They are evident, for instance, in the American Christmas holiday that combines both religious and social activities. Furthermore, religious organizations and their rituals were seldom insulated from the larger context. They still have been subject to the larger trends in society.

Religious ritual continues to change with the society. One need only to consider the impact of immigrant Hispanics on the American Catholic Church. The Catholic weekly *America* reported that Hispanics are bringing a new sense of worship to American Catholicism. Many Hispanics expect lively worship that might even include "speaking in tongues," "faith healing," "evangelism," and a literal interpretation of the Bible. When they do not find vital worship in the Catholic Mass, some are joining evangelical and Pentecostal groups that specialize in dynamic, "charismatic" worship.[143]

Yet such social processes are historical and ever changing. Thus, as the society impacts the ritual context, the meaning of the symbols and myths within that context will also evolve in a dynamic tension between continuity of tradition and change brought about by responsiveness to society.

For example, the Catholic celebration of Our Lady of Guadalupe involves a procession of an image of the Virgin Mary, who appeared to the Mexican peasant Juan Diego in 1531, leaving her image on his cloak. Among other meanings, this appearance signified divine approval for the planting of Catholicism among the native population in the New World. In time, the image of Our Lady of Guadalupe became a symbol of Mexican identity.

According to the Catholic News Service in 2007, the Los Angeles procession had the theme of "Mother without Borders."[144] The theme was part of a call to action for immigration reform from the California Catholic Conference of Bishops. Cardinal Roger M. Mahoney, archbishop of Los Angeles, stated that the Virgin of Guadalupe is a symbol for all the marginalized. He explained that she unites all who are striving for justice, peace, compassion, and dignity, especially for the immigrants who are being kept on the fringes of society by a broken immigration system.[145]

The social processes that have resulted in the recent immigration of thousands of Hispanics to the United States provided the larger context of the procession. The "Mother without Borders" theme of the procession pointed to a contemporary meaning of the processional that linked the marginalized status of immigrant Hispanics with the peasant status of Juan Diego who received the original revelation of the Virgin. The American context of cultural diversity added another contemporary meaning: the Virgin of Guadalupe was a symbol uniting all Catholics "across borders." It did not merely apply to Mexicans.

We see in this example how the interpretation of religious symbols and mythology should take into account the meanings that emerge from changes in the social context.

Our Lady of Guadalupe depicts the Virgin Mary, who appeared to a Mexican peasant during the sixteenth century.

> **A Proposal for the Study of Sacred Objects**
>
> - *Interpretative purpose*: respecting the unique forms of sacred symbols, myths, and rituals
> - *Social setting*: concentrating on shared meanings in public life
> - *Contextual meaning*: investigating how meaning arises in the context of the actual use of symbols, myths, and rituals
> - *Ritual context*: interpreting the symbols, myths, and rituals in the context of their function in contemporary rituals

The Proposed Solution: Principles of the Suggested Approach

In summary, the work of Clifford Geertz and Victor Turner suggest a practical way of interpreting symbols, myths, and rituals in the midst of issues such as those that NAGPRA has raised. This method is to investigate the dynamic role of specific symbols and myths *within* their ritual contexts. Once we understand the meaning of a symbol or myth in this way, we can investigate the role that the ritual has in its social setting. The following principles would elaborate on this method and identify principles that help us test this approach:

- *Interpretative purpose*: The study of symbols, myths, and rituals would respect their unique and particular forms. Scholars would examine them as they appear in current use in this century without explaining or evaluating them in terms of universal structures, general frameworks, dualistic (binary) categories, or all-encompassing systems.
- *Social setting*: The study would avoid speculating about private or esoteric meanings that are matters of inner experience. It would concentrate on meanings that are shared in public life.
- *Contextual meaning*: The study would understand that the meaning of symbols, myths, and rituals changes with time and circumstances. Meaning arises in the context of the actual use of symbol, myth, and ritual in human life. The study would take into account changes in the social context.
- *Ritual context*: The study would avoid isolating the assessment of symbols, myths, or rituals in abstract philosophical discussions. It would use the study of actual rituals of contemporary societies as the key to understanding the shared meaning of symbols and myths.

Such a solution appears to be in keeping with the spirit and provisions of the NAGPRA. Recall the NAGPRA definition of sacred objects: "Specific ceremonial objects which are needed by traditional Native American religious leaders for the practice of traditional Native American religions by their present day adherents."[146] This definition suggests that if the objects are "ceremonial," then they might be studied in terms of the ceremonies in which they are used. Furthermore, the definition refers to the current practice of these ceremonies. This ritual context might answer the question of why these objects have the sacred significance that they have. This may seem to be an obvious point, but it is easily overlooked in the quarrels over ownership of the objects. This chapter proposes that the most promising solution to the question of the nature of the sacred objects rests here. By appreciating that ritual context, "insiders" and "outsiders" alike might come to closer agreements about the items and their return to the native peoples.

The objection to the return of ceremonial objects has already surfaced. Why not ask the indigenous peoples to make new ceremonial objects? This chapter shows that religious symbols have an integral relationship to things in the sacred world that they represent. Moreover, mythology tells the story of the sacred primal time of the ancestors. Furthermore, ritual puts its participants into an "in-between" space in which they encounter the sacred realities that transform them. Symbol, myth, and ritual come together in this liminal space and time in which the sacred objects are used. Within the ritual, the sacred objects are thus physical and spiritual connections to the ancestors, spirits, and powers in the sacred world. When the sacred objects of the past are taken away, this sense of physical connection is lost.

Whether they are museum directors, scientists, educators, or scholars of religion, "outsiders," will not grasp this sense of the sacred objects if they reduce them to mere abstractions. To get a feeling for the sacred object, scholars would do better if they investigated the specific rituals in which the sacred object is used. The best way to get a sense of the sacredness of the objects would be actual exposure to these rituals so that the objects could be observed in their ritual context.

In summary, as the NAGPRA definition suggests, the key to understanding the sacred objects is their use in the ritual context. This chapter proposes that the field of religious studies might offer this approach as an effective method for studying and preserving sacred artifacts.

EVALUATING THE MOST PROMISING SOLUTION: DISPUTE OVER A HAWAIIAN OBJECT

The case of the dispute over a Hawaiian artifact between a museum and a group of Native Hawaiians offers a convenient test for the proposed theory. Anthropologist Greg Johnson suggests the importance and usefulness of this case in his article "Ancestors before Us: Manifestations of Tradition in a Hawaiian Dispute."[147] The artifact under dispute was a human-like image with a blue head about two feet tall. It had inlaid mother-of-pearl eyes and was standing in a crouched position with a protruding chin and chest and an upraised left hand. The image had obvious features of a rack that was mounted on a canoe.

At the beginning of the case, the Roger Williams Museum of Providence, Rhode Island, had possession of the artifact. The institution claimed that it was a utilitarian item, most likely a spear rest. Yet the item was noteworthy as a charming and playful art object from the period of the eighteenth or nineteenth century.

When the museum moved to sell the item, a group of Native Hawaiians entered the picture. This native group demanded the item's return under the NAGPRA legislation. They identified the object as a *ki'i lā'au* (wooden image). This idol was an image of a war god, an ancestral deity or *'aumakua* that individuals and families looked to for strength and guidance.

The museum rejected the claim of the Native Hawaiians, and the dispute came before the NAGPRA Review Committee in November of 1996[148] and again in March 1997.[149]

The Confrontation at the NAGPRA Hearings

Imagine the scene at the NAGPRA hearings. On the one side were the museum and a parade of experts. These included a curator for the Pacific Collection at the Smithsonian Institution, a professor and curator emeritus of the Department of Anthropology at the University of Pennsylvania, an artist and canoe builder, and a professor emeritus at the University of Hawaii who was the founder of the Council for Hawaiian Elders under the Office of Hawaiian Affairs.

On the other side were members of a Native Hawaiian group, named *Hui Mālama I Nā Kupuna 'O Hawai'i Nei*, together with the Office of Hawaiian Affairs. Their witnesses included a land and natural resources officer with the Office of Hawaiian Affairs, a counsel to the Native American Historic Preservation Council, a trustee of the Office of Hawaiian Affairs, and leaders of the *Hui Mālama* organization.

Although the Native Hawaiians alleged that the object was from a grave and an item of cultural patrimony (cultural heritage), these claims were hard to prove. The primary question had to do with the nature of the artifact. Was it a delightful art object from the past or was it a sacred object filled with symbolic meaning?

For a variety of reasons, the museum's experts argued that the object was secular and not religious. It was a utilitarian object. Most likely, it was a rest for spears that were used for the ordinary task of fishing, not warfare.[150] It was also an art object because its charm, playfulness, and forceful carving and decoration were not typical of recognized religious objects.[151] Yet *even if* ancient people had once used it for religious purposes, the museum argued that their religion was no longer formally practiced.[152]

The museum further argued that the Native Hawaiians admitted ancestral power had to be called into the item. Therefore, it was not inherently sacred. The ancestral spiritual power could just as well be called into another object.[153] In summary, the spear rest was not necessary for the practice of any of today's religions.

The Native Hawaiians claimed that the figure was a *ki'i 'aumakua*, a receptacle for an ancestral deity.[154] The symbolic meaning of the image was that it housed a deity. This divine being would hold and guard the spears of a warrior of high standing. In battle it would guide them to their target.[155] The Hawaiians insisted that *'aumakua* practice continues in our time and that it would be unthinkable to sell or trade such a sacred object.[156] They described the rituals by which the spiritual power of the *'aumakua* were to be called into the image and explained that a "residual power" remains after the *'aumakua* leaves the object.[157]

Analysis of the Case Using the Principles of the Proposed Solution

Both sides presented powerful and plausible arguments. The challenge of religious studies is to offer some insight into the dispute, especially concerning the conflicting claims surrounding the artifact. We are testing the proposed principles for study to determine if they might provide some insight that "outsiders" to the religion as well as "insiders" might find balanced and helpful.

Interpretive Purpose

First, the proposed solution lays out an *interpretive purpose* that would not try to explain or evaluate the artifact in terms of abstract universals and generalities. It would respect its unique character. Museum advocate William Davenport suggested a contrary approach: "My feeling is—is what the Board . . . needs to consider, is what is the relative weight, in fact, going to be between available, existing, scholarly literature, categories, typologies versus what documentation and data might be provided by the members of the Hawaiian organizations and Native American groups overall."[158] This statement represented the conventional Western academic view of the purpose of the hearings. The decision on ownership rested on whether the artifact would fit into the categories of scholarship. Of course, the experts said that the spear rest did not fit their classification of the sacred. They challenged the Native Hawaiians to provide documentation and data to prove otherwise.

In light of the proposed interpretive principle, we can see that the museum's experts did not acknowledge that the item could be viewed in different ways. In fact, their perspective on the item was twofold. The museum was a museum of natural history, not an art gallery. As a museum of natural history, was it looking at the item as a specimen of the field? If it was simply a utilitarian item, why would it be worth the $200,000 to $250,000 price tag the museum set on it? On the other hand, was it an art object? What artistic standards would make it a highly valuable art object worth a quarter of a million dollars?

The arguments of the museum came down to their use of Western binary categories—what Johnson called "Western dichotomization." The experts asserted that the item was utilitarian, physical, and playful. Therefore, it could not be religious. As Johnson notes, this analysis falls into the dualism of the categories of sacred versus profane. In the analysis of the museum, the sacred is what is ceremonial, spiritual, and serious. The profane is what is useful, physical, and, perhaps, playful. According to these standards, the knife used for the ritual sacrifice of animals should not be considered "religious" because it is a utilitarian instrument. Moreover, sacramental elements such as water, bread, or oil would not be sacred because they are physical. Conversely, many Buddha statues would not be considered sacred because they are playful.[159]

As Johnson notes, the Native Hawaiians presented a different interpretation of the artifact. Had they accepted the challenge to find "documentation and data" to fit into the "categories and typologies" of their opponents, they would have lost the argument. However, as we will see, they offered an alternative interpretation to the scientific scholarship of the museum's experts.

Social Setting

This chapter's proposed solution suggests that the interpretation of sacred objects is to be found in the *social setting*, not personal interpretations or categories of universals. Of course, the object has personal meanings. In fact, Mr. Kunani Nihipale, the leader of the *Hui Mālama* group, introduced his personal *'aumakua* to the hearing as an "image of how he sees his ancestors."[160] Yet this approach is not convincing. An individual might give a powerful personal meaning to an object. However, others might derive other meanings from it. American courts generally refuse to judge between personal religious meanings.

On the other hand, perhaps the object has universal symbolic meaning as Jung and Campbell describe it. If the meaning applies to everyone as an archetype, then everyone has a right to own the item. Once again, there is no definitive way of deciding who gets the object. For the court to decide the case, the argument has to be about the social meaning of the object relative to the community that claims the right to possess it.

Contextual Meaning

Johnson's analysis shows that the museum's experts treated the object as if its meaning were located only in the past.[161] This meaning could only be discovered by the scientific investigation. However, this chapter proposes a *contextual social meaning* of symbols, myths, and rituals that is not fixed but fluid. The Native Americans claimed that the *'aumakua* religion is still in practice and that the object has past, present, and future meanings.[162] The object was "needed to renew old ceremonies"[163] and to bring "spiritual healing, well-being, and success" to those who seeking the object for present-day use.[164]

These claims show that the background of the dispute was the current global resurgence of indigenous ways. This movement seeks to *restore* the indigenous sacred ways because the processes of Western oppression have suppressed and stolen them. Within this contextual meaning, the conflict over the object was viewed as a struggle for cultural identity together with religious freedom. Here is the way Office of Hawaiian Affairs representative Linda Kawai'Ono Delaney put it:

> The disruptions and destructions of those years [from European contact to the current time] left the people dispossessed and dispirited. Now, we stand to reclaim and return to our rightful stewardship; our bones, our ancestors, our Gods, the lands, and the self-determination of the Hawaiian people.[165]

What was at stake was the authority of interpretation. Who had the right to tell the story of the meaning of the object, the anthropological experts who assumed superior weight on the basis of scientific study or the Native Hawaiians who claimed to be the heirs of the ways of their ancestors? The hearings thus elevated the importance of the object. On the one hand, the spear rest became a piece of crucial scientific evidence for the museum's view of the past. On the other, it became a tangible connection to the suppressed way of life of the Native Hawaiians. A ruling in favor of the museum would endorse the social processes of conventional anthropological and archeological study. A ruling in favor of the Native Hawaiians would sanction the social processes of the reestablishment of their heritage. In addition, it would give legitimacy to the *Hui Mālama* group as leaders in the restoration movement.

Ritual Context

We have described how the museum presented its case, but what about the Native Hawaiians? The strategic action of the group showed that the *ritual context* is a key to the interpretation of symbols such as the spear rest.

As long as the context was a court hearing, then the museum's superior expertise gave it the upper hand. However, at the second hearing (according to Johnson, who was an eyewitness to the proceedings), the *Hui Mālama* group surprised everyone. They started chanting prayers in Hawaiian. As they offered these petitions, they were no longer speaking to the officials at the hearing. They were addressing the higher authority of their *'aumakua* deities. This ritual action demonstrated the claim that the object had symbolic religious meaning more powerfully than any verbal argument. And its meaning was for people in the present, not merely in the past.[166]

In the *first hearing*, the Native Hawaiians had referred to rituals that invoked the ancestral spirits into the symbolic object and into the war spears it would hold. They told how attaching the artifact to the war canoe made the whole vessel spiritually powerful. Now, in the *second hearing*, the native people constructed a ritual context. In this religious setting they could go on to describe the consecration ceremonies that prepared the chiefs for battle. They could explain how the figure was a conduit of the deity to blind the enemy with its eyes and to empower the spears it held.[167]

When the Native Hawaiians addressed the group, they alluded to the mythic story of their settlement of the Hawaiian Islands. They told the story of the building of a civilization that covered the largest geographical area in the world. Their narrative continued with the European contact and destruction of that civilization and the recent recovery of their heritage. Then they prayed again that the ancestors would forgive their faults and give them "life in the true Hawaiian sense."[168]

The interpretation of the object as a sacred symbol was convincing because the Native Hawaiians were asking for bravery, strength, and guidance from the same ancestral spirits that the object symbolized. The hearing and the current disputes over the ownership of their land and inheritance were the new battles of the people. Now they needed the object because it could connect them with their ancestors who had fought many past battles. In this present fight, it would give them ancient, spiritual power.[169]

The ritual context powerfully showed that the artifact was not a dead specimen of the past. In fact, it was a living image. To the Native Hawaiians, it represented the restoration of their relationship to the gods and ancestors of their past and the renewal of the ancient, sacred ways of their heritage. In this way, the ritual demonstrated the meaning of the symbolic object in a more powerful way than any explanation could do.

The Surprising Outcome of the Case

The narratives differ on the details of the outcome of the case. Johnson states that both review committees ruled in the Native Hawaiians' favor on the basis that the item was a sacred object.[170] A summary of the museum version of the story says that the first review committee did recommend that the museum return the object to the Native Hawaiians. However, it said that the second review committee did not have sufficient evidence to determine the right of possession. But it added that the committee suggested that the museum consider whether it had a moral duty to return the object.[171] The review committee minutes of the second meeting state that the committee did not have sufficient evidence to make a recommendation on repatriation. However, the record states "that the Committee recommends that the City of Providence return the item to Hui Mālama and the Office of Hawaiian Affairs."[172]

Despite the recommendation of the review committee, the museum refused to surrender the object. The City of Providence sued NAGPRA, the Native Hawaiians, and others involved in court for attempted unlawful seizure of property without fair compensation. However, before the case went to court, the parties settled the lawsuit out of court. The Office of Hawaiian Affairs donated $125,000 to the museum, and the museum surrendered the object on August 27, 1998.

Jennifer Hope Antes, the anthropologist on staff, had the duty to turn the item over to the Native Hawaiians. She said that she had no choice. She reported that she did not stay to witness the ensuing native celebration in rituals, chanting, and photographs. She simply walked away.[173]

Antes commented that the case fanned the flames of the movement of tribal sovereignty. On the other hand, it gave museum directors clues about how to contend with NAGPRA in its gray areas. She concluded that museums are on the front lines of the debates about science and knowledge and called the dispute a practical "confrontation of religion and science."[174]

The case has applied the principles of the proposed solution to the way the Native Hawaiians defended their view of religious symbols. Their example seems to promise that this chapter's proposal about interpreting sacred objects might prove to be useful to scholars. The ritual context promises to help religious studies gain deeper insight into the way indigenous people perceive their symbolic objects.

More Than One Ritual and Ritual Context

Would that interpretation be acceptable to everyone, however? Probably not. For example, the museum and its experts remained unconvinced and continued to press their suit. Ritual can be a useful context for the interpretation of symbol and myth. However, remember that this ritual context is set within larger social processes. These social processes influence both the ritual and the interpretation of it. In this case, the competing educational, economic, and sociocultural interests of the parties to the dispute propelled the conflict forward. In other words, the social setting was political. It was a social matrix of power relationships, not merely a setting of religious devotion and scientific investigation.

The application of the principles of contextual interpretation of the spear rest controversy suggests that the NAGPRA hearing is itself a ritual context. Likewise, the enforcement procedures of the NAGPRA legislation are social processes. We have found that the meaning of symbolic objects is not fixed but changes in such social contexts. Therefore, in the dynamics of the NAGPRA issues and transactions, we are witnessing the ongoing development of sacred meaning. As present-day rituals use symbols and myths, they are constructing and shaping their sacred meaning for the changing social context of the twenty-first century.

Lessons Learned about the Treatment of Religious People as Well as Sacred Objects

This chapter has offered a proposal for how the field of religious studies could contribute to the ongoing topic of the ownership of the past. However, the NAGPRA program has already contributed to the study for religion. It has set an irreversible and practical direction for religious studies and its related disciplines. Because of it, like the anthropologists and archeologists, scholars of religious studies have had to engage with the subjects of their studies on more equal and collegial terms. Before the turn of the century, the scholars of religion could generally treat the religious people they studied as objects, whether they were indigenous peoples or Eastern societies. Now members of these indigenous and Eastern cultures are demanding their place at the head of the table of the discussion about their sacred ways. The increasing participation of representatives of "non-Western" ways is already having an effect on the direction of religious studies.

These observations lead to a final comment. To expand on a thought of Geertz, interpretation is empty unless it deals with what actually happens to people in their lived experience. The field of religious studies has untapped potential to play a significant role in the issues of religion in the twenty-first century. However, to play that role, it will have to leave the sanctuary of universals, generalities, and transcendent truths. It will have to deal with the complex, contradictory, and downright messy conditions of real people in real time. In short, it will be compelled to interpret religion as it is lived in this century, not as it is imagined to be in an idealized past or in the hidden recesses of the psyche.

Conclusion: From Universal Abstractions to Concrete Settings of Human Life

The study of symbol, myth, and ritual has been at the core of religious studies. This study involves a daunting range of academic disciplines: philosophy, semiotics, psychology, sociology, archeology, folklore, anthropology, theology, and the humanities (especially art, music, and dance). Because it involves the profound questions of human language, belief, meaning, and truth, such study will continue to be on the cutting edge of religious studies. Yet because it demands a multidisciplinary approach, it will be at the forefront of many other academic disciplines for decades to come.

In describing the swing of the pendulum away from universals to the concrete particularities of human life, this chapter was not meant to discount theory in the study of religion. The study of religion should include the general theory of what religion is and how it should be approached. On the other hand, a current trend in religious studies emphasizes that its theories should be based on the complex data of how religion is lived in our time. The twenty-first century promises to provide many opportunities for religious scholars to devise new theories of symbol, myth, and ritual on the basis of detailed evidence. It will also give scholars the chance to test these theories by applying them to a growing set of real issues, issues such as those associated with the NAGPRA legislation.

KEY TERMS

Cambridge Ritualists: members of a movement centered in Cambridge, England, that argued that ritual takes priority over symbols and myths and that ritual is the key to understanding them.

Discursive language: according to Suzanne Langer, the communication of ideas in a serial, linear fashion (one after the other).

Expressive view of ritual: the view that myth is neither educational nor practical. It is expressive. It helps its participants relive and release the emotions of such primary activities as the hunt or the battle.

Hajj: the Muslim pilgrimage to Mecca that is an example of Turner's ritual theory of liminality.

Iconoclasm: the practice of destroying symbolic representations (such as icons) because they are seen as "idols." The iconoclasts believe that symbolic representations are material things that are worshipped as if they were the ultimate spiritual reality—that is, God.

"Insider": term for believers who understand the religion from within its worldview and way of life.

Liminality: in the theory of Victor Turner, the quality of ritual that refers to the "in-between" state of the ritual participants where the ritual can transform them.

Multivocal: the quality of symbols that refers to their multiple levels of meaning.

Mythic consciousness: according to Cassirer, the awareness in which there is no separation of the symbol from what it stands for. Symbols cannot be explained; their meaning is built in.

Myths: complexes of symbols ordered in story form.

Myths of origin: narratives that tell a sacred history of how certain realities came to be.

Native American Graves Protection and Repatriation Act (NAGPRA): federal legislation of 1990 that mandates that all museums and schools that receive federal funding provide an inventory of human remains, funeral artifacts, sacred objects, and items of cultural heritage. Native American and Hawaiian communities are to be notified so that they can choose to reclaim these objects.

"Outsider": term for a person who studies a religion from outside its worldview and way of life.

Presentational language: according to Suzanne Langer, the communication of dynamics of our inner life that are not given in linear, discursive fashion.

Primordial time of origins: the mythic time when the foundations of the realities of our world were laid.

Psychological interpretation of myth: a way of interpreting myth by relating it to the inner working of the psyche (e.g., Carl Jung and Joseph Campbell).

Ritual system: according to Evans-Pritchard, the complex of interlocking parts of ritual that form the context for understanding the symbols, myths, and actions of rituals.

Rituals: symbolic actions connected with ideas of the cosmic order and/or supernatural beings.

Romantic interpretation of myth: the approach to myth that assumes that myth represents a separate reality apart from the ordinary reality of the senses.

Sacramental: the quality of certain religious symbols that refers to their ritual function of becoming what they represent so that they convey that spiritual reality to believers in a tangible way.

Symbol: according to C. S. Peirce, a sign that conveys abstract meaning by means of the association or convention of the interpreter (e.g., a swastika).

Theoretical knowledge: according to Cassirer, the knowledge that assumes that symbols represent "something else." To understand the meaning of a symbol is to understand the underlying idea that it represents. (Note: In this sense, the important and constant thing is the meaning. The less important and variable things are the symbols that represent it.)

KEY QUESTIONS

1. The Dispute over the NAGPRA Legislation
    a. This chapter observes that museums, anthropology departments, and Native Americans understand the nature of the items disputed in the NAGPRA program in differing ways. Contrast these ways of viewing and treating the objects.
    b. Explain why museums and anthropology departments claim priority over these items.
    c. Explain why native peoples claim priority over these items.
2. Symbols
    a. Explain why "outsiders" do not understand what religious symbols mean to believers even if the "outsiders" know what the symbols represent.
    b. Contrast the "sacramental" idea of symbols held by Catholic, Eastern Orthodox, and some Protestant Christians with the "in remembrance" theory of Christian rituals.
    c. Give an example of "iconoclasm" and explain why it arises in Western monotheism.

3. Myth
   a. Contrast the rationalist theory of myth with the romantic theory.
   b. Many scholars hold that modern people cannot understand myth the way that ancient peoples did. Describe how Carl Jung, Joseph Campbell, and others who advocated the psychological interpretation of myth applied myth to modern people.
4. Ritual: Liminality
   a. How does the clothing of the Hajj exemplify Turner's state of liminality?
   b. List the stages of ritual according to Turner and then analyze a ritual such as the Hajj, a marriage service, or a graduation exercise according to these stages.
5. Ritual
   a. Is the magic of the Azande people that Evans-Pritchard studies "practical"? In what sense? Is it logical? In what sense?
   b. Is the Super Bowl a religious event? Give reasons for your answer.
   c. In modern society, to what extent is religious ritual separated from public life? How does this situation affect the common understandings of religious ritual and the sacred objects of native peoples?
6. The Ritual Context
   a. What is the most important feature of ritual: what is said or what is done?
   b. What does your answer imply about how scholars should understand symbol and ritual?
   c. What argument does this chapter give for the assertion that religious symbols and myth are best understood in their ritual context? What are the strengths and weaknesses of this argument?
7. The Test Case of the Hawaiian Spear Rest
   a. Contrast the views of Providence's museum and the Native Hawaiians' view of the spear rest under dispute.
   b. What different frames of reference did these perspectives represent?
   c. Explain how the Native Hawaiians set the question of the object into a ritual context and why this was a way of arguing their case.
   d. Which side had the best argument? Defend your answer.

5

Inside the Religious Brain
New Research into Religious Experience

CHAPTER SUMMARY

1. Discovering the Problem: Finding Religion in the Brain

The neuroscience of religion is using scientific technology to peer into the working of the brain during states of meditation and prayer. The results are changing the way that the study of religion is viewing religious experience and even religion.

The neuroscience of religious states of mind rests on the foundation of studies of what scholars have called "religious experience." In religious studies, religious experience refers to the inner awareness and/or feelings of religious believers when they are in touch with a transcending and invisible power, presence, or state of mind. The emerging findings of the neuroscience of religion might lead to revisions of past theories of the nature of that experience. They also open up the possibilities of new answers to the question of why human beings throughout the world report such experiences.

2. Focusing the Problem: The Current Challenges to Past Studies

Scholarship since William James's study *The Varieties of Religious Experience* treats religious experience as unusual, extraordinary, and even abnormal. Scholars have focused on mysticism and found the defining characteristics of religious experience in its altered state of consciousness. However, sociological surveys and mounting results of the neuroscience of religion provide evidence that religious experience is common in human societies and that it is not merely the product of certain abnormalities in the brain. The religious experiences of people throughout the world can be classified into five different levels. Therefore, the inner experience of religion is widespread and has certain universal characteristics. But the actual content of what is experienced is quite diverse. The focused problem is how to account for the origins of religious experiences, its widespread scope in the human population, and its vast diversity expressed in different religions and cultures.

3. Surveying the Alternative Approaches: Essentialist and Contextualist Theories

Scholars have proposed a range of alternative theories of religious experience. The *essentialists* identify the defining characteristics of religious experiences across cultures. They tend to treat religious experience as extraordinary, even a strange form of consciousness. Taken together, their view is that religious experience originates in perceptions of an unseen, supernatural level of reality, whether they are true or not. Alternatively, they arise in the recovery of the original and pure consciousness that realizes the unity of all things instead of their divisions.

Essentialist approaches include Maslow's "peak experiences," Eastern thought, the "perennial philosophy," and evolutionary biology.

The *contextualists* appeal to culture to account for the diversity of religious experience in human life. They tend to treat religious experience as common and pervasive because cultures promote their own versions of it. Contextualists suggest that religion is a product of culture. The contextualist approaches include the constructivism of Katz and Proudfoot and feminist perspectives.

The evaluation of these theories concludes that each has strengths in accounting for either the universal aspects of religious experience or the diverse forms of these experiences. But none of these theories account for both taken together.

4. Proposing the Most Promising Solution: A Three-Point Program

A comprehensive theory of religious experience that would account for how common it is in its characteristics and yet how diverse it is in content has yet to be developed. This theory is built on three major points from current research: (a) the *plasticity* of the brain as a living organ whose structures and processes change throughout life as they are exercised; (b) the *emergent* character of culture and its role in shaping the actual structure and operations of the brain; and (c) the *interaction of brain, mind, and culture* that produces religious experience. The "mind" that the interaction of culture and brain produce is more than the "brain." In short, the emergent character of culture that works "top-down" on the brain accounts for how physical processes that can be observed produce experiences that are nonphysical. Moreover, the "hardwiring" of the brain accounts for the common features of religious experience. The interaction of culture and the brain in the "programming" of the "mind" produces the diverse content of religious experience.

5. Evaluating the Most Promising Solution: Prayers, Nursery Rhymes, and a Test Case

A test case confirms the proposal of the emergent character of culture and the interaction of brain, mind, and culture to produce religious experience. However, the test case does not deal with the plasticity of the brain because the scans were done only once. The assessment of the solution depends on further study of the question of the relationship of "mind" and "brain." Academic study, however, is not likely to answer the question of whether religious experience is purely subjective and mental or whether it has some basis in a reality outside the brain, as "critical realism" holds.

DISCOVERING THE PROBLEM: FINDING RELIGION IN THE BRAIN

To learn about religion, where do we look for help? Most would not think of looking to science to give them any understanding of religion. Until now, the modern mind has assumed that science cannot know or prove anything about the supernatural. Now many scientists are claiming that they have located the sacred in the one place that has been overlooked, the human brain. Prying into its deep secrets, researchers have caught the brain in the very act of experiencing the supernatural. The techniques and theories have varied. However, the conclusion has been the same. The reason for the prevalence of religion in all cultures is that religion is "hardwired" into the brain.

This new quest for the holy in the brain came to international attention in 2004 when *Time* magazine published a cover story, "Is God in Our Genes?" The *Time* article publicized a popular book by molecular biologist Dean Hamer titled

"The God Gene." According to *Time* magazine, Hamer had found the gene that is directly related to religious feelings.[1] This supposed discovery was the result of tests of a gene that regulates the flow of chemicals involved in emotions such as joy, sadness, and anxiety. Those subjects of the study who had a specific type of this gene scored higher on tests that measure spirituality. Hamer concluded that spirituality is based on a "genetic and biochemical mechanism" that for the most part is inherited.[2]

Other scientists soon joined Hamer in the "God quest." Since then, researchers have used advancements in medical technology to unlock the secrets of religion. They have tried to find the relationship between the genetic makeup of human persons and their religious habits, attitudes, and interests. They have compared identical twins for religious feelings, attendance, and affiliation. They have hooked up Catholic Franciscan nuns and Protestant Pentecostals to Single Photon Emission Computer Tomography (SPECT) imaging cameras. They have put Buddhist monks on electroencephalograph (EEG) machines. They have even subjected the atheist Richard Dawkins to electromagnetic charges designed to stimulate religious feelings.

A New Way to Do Religious Studies: The Neuroscience of Religion

The research underway is associated with a wider movement in religious studies called the neuroscience of religion. The study of the role of the brain in religion began when religious scholars applied the new field of *cognitive science* to religion. To cognitive science, the mind is like an advanced computer that receives and processes information. Cognitive science uses a wide variety of academic disciplines to understand human intelligence by scientifically studying the operations of this complex computer-like system of the brain.[3] Unlike the standard approaches, the research does not stop with a description of religious beliefs and practices.[4] It asks how the human mind works when it engages in them. The fundamental idea of cognitive science is that everything we experience and everything we do is the product of chemical and electromagnetic activity in the brain.[5]

When applied to religion, this basic assumption means that when human beings believe in or experience sacred things, they are using the brain in complex ways. Religion, therefore, is founded on specialized structures and complicated processes in the brain.[6] This realization has led to a new field of research that this chapter will call the *neuroscience of religion*. Its goal is to develop theories and models of this mental machinery of religion that researchers can test scientifically.[7]

Triggering the Religious Response

Much of the cognitive science of religion takes advantage of the latest technology in the field of neuroscience, the study of the brain and nervous system. The most significant advances have come since 1980 with the development of functional imaging methods. These methods give us a living picture of what is going on in the brains of normal persons as they respond to stimuli or perform an action.

They show the blood flow that delivers the necessary oxygen and glucose for the various parts and systems of the brain to do its work.[8] The primary technology includes Functional Magnetic Resonance Imaging (fMRI), Positron Emission Tomography (PET), and Single Photon Emission Computer Tomography (SPECT).

However, even before the development of brain imaging, Vilayanur S. Ramachandran had done pioneer work in the field. Scientists already knew that persons with certain forms of *temporal lobe epilepsy* (TLE) have an unusually strong interest in religion. This obsession is often a result of epileptic seizures that generate religious visions, feelings of intense communion with God, and/ or a sense of the deep meaning of the cosmos. To test this association between religion and epilepsy, Ramachandran wired a group of his persons suffering from TLE to a lie-detector machine.[9] He then showed them provocative words and images. Some of these were sexual; some were violent; some were religious; and some were neutral. Typically, we would expect that sexual or violent words would stimulate the most intense response. They did for members of the control groups. However, Ramachandran found that his TLE patients scored the highest interest in religious words and pictures.[10]

Ramachandran devised the theory that this strange finding was evidence that the brain has special circuitry for religion in the temporal lobe. He thought that most likely these religiously sensitive brain circuits are overactive in epileptic seizures. Stimulation of these areas in surgery produced similar results and supported his theory.[11]

Following this lead, Michael Persinger devised a way to simulate the experience of TLE persons. He designed a helmet that stimulates the *temporal* and *parietal lobes* with a weak magnetic field. Persinger found that when the right temporal lobe is stimulated with magnetic fields, up to 80 percent of the subjects are aware of an invisible "presence" with them in the room. Persinger thinks that this experience is the model for the impression of spirits, ghosts, aliens, and perhaps God.[12]

Persinger explains that this prototype of religious experience involves two parts of the brain buried in the temporal lobe: the *hippocampus* and the *amygdala.* The hippocampus is a center for picturing images. When it is stimulated, the person may experience memories or fantasies.[13] The amygdala controls emotions such as pain and pleasure. When it is roughly stimulated, the person experiences fear and anxiety. When it is more gently stimulated, the person experiences deeply meaningful experiences such as out-of-body sensations or unity with the cosmos.[14] These two brain parts are located near other parts of the temporal and frontal lobes. Therefore, they are associated with the sense of "self" created by those nearby upper portions of the brain.[15]

According to Persinger, these mechanisms give all humans the capacity for religious experience. However, everyone will have a different degree of this religious sensitivity in the temporal lobe. And cultural factors as well as the setting will shape human experience into distinctive forms. In whatever way believers understand their experience, though, it is the result of a brief, focused electrical incident in the brain.[16] Like Ramachandran, Persinger believes he can replicate this event in his lab.

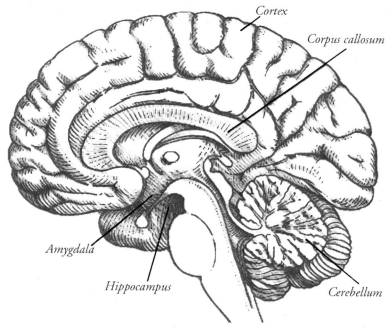

Cortex

Corpus callosum

Amygdala

Hippocampus

Cerebellum

Brain research shows activity during religious experiences in the temporal lobe, hippocampus, and amygdala.

Revelations of the SPECT Brain Scanner

Perhaps the best-known researcher is Andrew Newberg. Newberg used the SPECT brain scanner to peer into the brain while believers were praying or meditating. He started his experiments with Buddhist monks. When the monks signaled that they had reached a state of meditation, Newberg injected a radioactive tracer into an intravenous (IV) line in their arms. Then he scanned their brains to measure blood flow in the brain. By this method, he could tell which parts of the brain were active.[17]

Newberg found increased activity on a place on the frontal lobe just above the eyes. He called it the "attention area." This area plays a central role in focusing, planning, performing tasks, language, memory, and processing religious beliefs. This result was not surprising, since the monks were focusing their minds in alert attention.[18]

However, he was surprised to find that activity in another area of the brain decreased at the same time. Newberg called the area that was less active the "orientation area." It is the area of the parietal lobes. This part of the brain is necessary for a sense of oneself as a separate being located in a particular place. When their parietal lobes are not functioning, humans have the sense of suspension beyond space and time. They lose the sense of self-awareness. They feel connected to everything, as they might feel when they make love or exercise vigorously.[19]

Newberg called the state that happens when the parietal lobes shut down "Absolute Unitary Being (AUB)." He speculates that many religious people hope

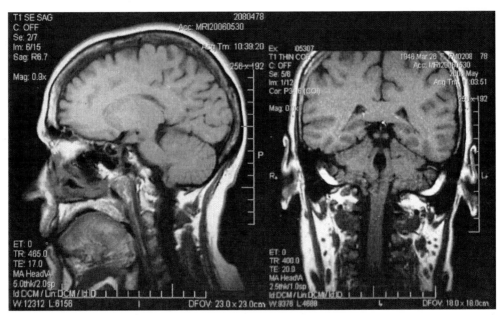

MRI scans like those shown here, along with other types of brain imaging, can show which parts of the brain are active during different types of activity, such as meditating or praying.

to achieve this experience in meditation and prayer. Some think of it as "union with God." Others describe it as a *Pure Consciousness*, a state of mind without any sense of separation from the world around us.

Next, Newberg studied three Franciscan nuns while they were practicing "centering prayer."[20] "Centering prayer" uses the meditation technique of repeating a sacred word, brief prayer, or verse from a sacred scripture. Newberg found that the Catholic nuns showed the same increase in the "attention areas" and decrease in the "orientation areas" that he found in the Buddhist monks. This meant that, like the Buddhist monks, the nuns were increasing their mental attentiveness while decreasing their orientation in space and time.[21] However, he was surprised to find increased activity in another part of the parietal lobes. This was a part of the brain associated with language. Newberg speculated that this region was active because the practice of "centering prayer" is verbal. The Buddhists did not need this part of the brain because their form of meditation was visual, not verbal.[22]

Then Newberg turned to Pentecostal Christians who "speak in tongues." "Speaking in tongues" (*glossalalia*) is the spiritual practice of uttering syllables that sound like human speech but are unintelligible to the speaker. They also make no sense to everyone else except to those who have the special gift of interpreting them. Pentecostals believe that this speech is a sign that one is under the influence of the Holy Spirit.[23]

This time the brain scans were different. Instead of an increase in the "attention area" that would signal that the subject's attention was focused, there was a decrease. Newberg thought that the decrease in the frontal lobe might give one a sense that someone else was in control of his or her mind and actions. Pentecostals, indeed, purposely relinquish their own normal thought processes. In their view, they are letting the Holy Spirit take over. Thus, the brain imaging and the state of awareness that the Pentecostals report seem to agree.[24]

In all cases, Newberg gained one more important finding. He discovered that meditation and prayer are linked to an increase in the activity of the *thalamus* located on top of the brain stem. The thalamus relays information from all the senses except smell to the brain. It also manages the motor control of our bodies and regulates patterns of sleep and wakefulness. However, most importantly for Newberg, it creates a sense of reality. Thus, increased activity of the thalamus seems to make the experience of the person vividly real. In fact, many who have experiences like those of the monks, nuns, or Pentecostals say that they seem more real than ordinary experience.

Protests and Prospects: The Response to the Latest Findings

Neurotheologians like Hamer, Ramachandran, Persinger, and Newberg have captured unusual public attention. One reason for the consternation in the media was the reckless headlines. The headings of books and articles hinted that the researches had found "The God Gene," "The God Spot," "The God Module" or the divinely installed religious hardwiring in the human brain. Popularizers even wrote books such as *The "God" Part of the Brain*.[25]

Criticisms of these overinflated claims prompted researches like Ramachandran to qualify their statements. Nevertheless, the findings still stir controversy, especially over what they imply about religion. For example, Ramachandran has speculated that the religious equipment of the brain has been placed there to ensure order in society.[26] Persinger has said that religious experience is merely a "side effect of our bicameral brain's feverish activities."[27] Newberg has stated that we could not know a "higher reality" like God, even if such a reality exists, unless the brain were constructed the way it is.[28]

Some dismiss this research, and others think it has far-reaching effects. Columnist David Brooks of the *New York Times* says that neuroscience and genetics are revolutionary because they are changing the way people see the world. As a subset of this science, the cognitive science of religion is also changing the way people view religion.[29]

According to Brooks, until the findings of cognitive science, people in the modern world had the basic choice of either believing in God or denying his existence. Therefore, the most fundamental argument was over the existence of God. For those who believed that God exists, religion was a matter of receiving and following the revelation of God. However, for those who believed that God is the product of the imagination, religion was a way of uniting and controlling society or offering psychological benefits to individuals.[30]

Now, however, today's neuroscience has changed the way we think about religion. The new research suggests that the brain has hardware that predisposes humans to experience spiritual moments. At these times, they are aware of another dimension of reality, a transcendent world beyond the limits of the physical world.[31]

According to Brooks, the cognitive study of religion redefines the issues that religion raises for the modern mind. The debate is no longer about gods, spirits, or ancestors and their existence, benefits, or control. Now "God" can best be conceived in terms of what human persons experience at those transcendent moments. Brooks believes that as the focus of religion shifts to inner experience, the challenge of atheism to religious belief will become no more than a sideshow.[32]

This new research does not simply challenge today's basic assumptions about religion. It also brings up new questions for the study of religion. On the one hand, it challenges the simplistic notion that divine revelation is simple and direct and that the brains of believers do not filter the message in the process of receiving it. On the other hand, the new science challenges the notion that religions are arbitrary inventions to control people, maintain the social order, or give them psychological comfort.

The brain science research disproves the notion that religion merely comes from wishful thinking. The studies confirm that the structures and activities of the brain are associated with the awareness of a kind of reality beyond the physical world. The findings shift the field of the study of religion to the investigation of these structures and activities. How do they work? What regions of the brain account for different types of experience? What are the lasting effects of religious practice on the brain? Why do certain processes in the brain make us think that there is more to reality than what our senses perceive?

These are promising questions for further research. Yet a critical thinking approach to religious studies steps back to ask some fundamental questions. What are the underlying assumptions of the emerging field?

Scholars like Ramachandran have claimed to be neutral in their scientific research. He has said that scientists cannot prove or disprove whether God speaks to epileptics during their seizures on empirical grounds. Nevertheless, when Ramachandran speculates on the implications of his research, he reduces religion to the function of establishing order in society. Michael Persinger says he does not intend to put down anyone's religious or mystical experience. He wants to detect the parts and patterns of the brain that produce the sense of invisible presences from aliens to gods.[33] Yet outside the laboratory, he speculates that religion is an "artifact" of the brain. The brain manufactures this "cognitive virus" as a pacifier to sooth the anxiety of death.[34]

Andrew Newberg also says that the question of whether the brain creates God or God creates the brain is a highly complex problem. Most often people approach that question with their own biases. But when he considers the implications of his research, Newberg proposes the development of "neurotheology." This endeavor would apply neuroscience to the questions of religious belief. Unlike Persinger, Newberg is open to the *possibility* of the existence of God. Neuroscience shows that the brain is equipped to conceive of a "Higher Power" in certain ways, whether God exists or not. For example, we can only think of a Creator or "First Cause" because our brains can think in terms of cause and effect. Newberg asserts that his "neurotheology" can use neuroscience to evaluate the cause-effect idea of the Creator and "all other ways of understanding God." This evaluation will clarify what human beings can know about reality.[35]

It is clear from these examples that each of these researchers puts his research findings into a preconceived frame of reference. The comments about the neutrality of science restrict the research to the method of naturalism that we discussed in chapter 2. Naturalism would only allow explanations for religious experience that appeal to dynamics within the material universe. It would rule out speculation about the existence or nonexistence of realities beyond the natural, physical world. But by definition religious experience concerns the awareness of supernatural realities or extraordinary states of consciousness. However, despite Newberg's openness, naturalism does not believe what the subjects of this research say they experience, whether it is God, AUB, or some other "higher" power or consciousness. Naturalism makes a judgment for the reality of brain activities but against the reality of what these processes are said to produce.[36]

These thoughts lead to the basic question of what the neuroscientists assume they are studying. If the answer is "religious experience," then a critical thinker would ask what it is. "Religious experience" is a vague term that the neuroscientists apply to a wide assortment of practices. For Newberg, it covers Buddhist meditation, Catholic prayer, and Pentecostal "speaking in tongues." For Persinger, it covers a sense of an invisible "presence." For Ramachandran, it covers an intense interest in religion stemming from episodes of intense sensations of communion with God and oneness with the universe.

Why do all of these qualify as religious experience? Matthew Ratcliffe notes that religions and religious experiences differ in fundamental ways. It is not clear what these experiences have in common, especially if we only look at the brain activity of individuals. Ratcliffe claims that the cognitive science of religion lacks a clearly defined subject matter.[37] In other words, neuroscientists are unclear about what constitutes a religious experience. Their models tend to be persons who are skilled in religious and/or meditative practices who can indicate when they have reached a "religious" or "meditative" state.

Why can we apply the term "religious" to this diverse collection of states of mind? We might reply that when experiences focus on a religious object, then they are religious. For example, we might say that religious experience involves the awareness of God. Yet, like religious experience, "God" is a broad term, and furthermore, some who claim religious or spiritual experience do not believe in any "God."

We might also claim that religious experience is a certain type of awareness. Then, however, we have to distinguish that experience from others. Yet we have already seen that brain science research encompasses a widening range of types of awareness as researchers apply the technology to different religious practices. For example, the Buddhist experience is remarkably calm and detached while the Pentecostal experience is highly vigorous and emotional. How can these moments be the same kind of awareness?

These reflections lead to the observation that the neuroscience of religion is not a new, independent field of research. It rests on a rich tradition that staked out the territory of the field of religious experience ahead of it. Before the technology of neuroscience was developed scholars such as William James had already explored the terrain of the inner life of believers. They constructed a rich assortment of descriptive words, ideas, and approaches that are summed up in the concept of "religious experience."

The scholars of the past who laid the foundation for the study of religious experience defined it in terms of profound inner states of mind. The essential characteristic of these mental states was the awareness of a transcendent, supernatural reality, or superior level of consciousness. Neuroscience has accepted these assumptions and associations. What is new is that neuroscientists have applied medical technology to the brains of people that past scholarship has already selected to be worthy of study.

The neuroscience of religion is intriguing. But the reports of the findings of this new field that we have reviewed seem to beg the question of how science can deal with religious claims of supernatural realities or super-conscious states of mind. Can the study of religion set aside the question of the existence of what religious people believe in, realize, and/or experience? If it does, religious people might say that whatever it discovers about how religion works, it misses the point about what religion means.

In summary, the new neuroscience of religion presents a challenge to our common ideas about religion. It represents the contemporary shift in thinking from concentration on abstract beliefs in debatable realities to personal experiences that elevate the human spirit beyond its normal limits. Neuroscience has begun to show that these experiences are grounded in physical and observable processes in the human brain. People do not make them up. They are not wishes or abstractions. However, what neuroscience gives with one hand, it is prone to take away with the other. Yes, it confirms the experiences that make God, enlightened consciousness, cosmic unity, or spiritual presences real to us. Nonetheless, it tends to reduce these experiences to the activity of certain regions and processes of the brain. And this seems to suggest that the actual experience of the person is not real despite the way it feels.

A puzzle is beginning to take shape. The question is how the brain activities seen on the brain scans and their corresponding religious experiences relate, a variation of the problem of the relationship of brain and mind. Granted that science can describe and, perhaps, even stimulate the brain processes that are associated with religious states of mind. But how do these processes "add up" to the experience? One could attach someone who is attending a Madonna concert to some functional imaging technology such as an fMRI, PET, or SPECT scanner. But the images on the screen would not begin to describe the experience of the music.

Moreover, suppose we put several people on the same imaging technology. The screens may register approximately the same brain activity. But will the subjects have the same experience? Their descriptions of the experience will vary with the personal history and cultural background that they bring to the experience. Why will they do so, since they are the product of the same brain functions?

To solve this puzzle, we will have to give it a focus that is more definite. To do this, we will explore the theories of religious scholars about the nature and characteristics of religious experience. We will also investigate who is qualified to have such experiences. Finally, we will also look into the amazing diversity of experiences and how scholars have categorized them.

This chapter will explore various options for answering these questions.

FOCUSING THE PROBLEM: THE CURRENT CHALLENGES TO PAST STUDIES

The Narrow Sense of Religious Experience: William James and Mysticism

The neuroscience of religion has raised some intriguing questions about religion. It assumes that all awareness depends on the operations of the brain. If religious experience is a term for certain kinds of awareness, then certain structures and operations of the brain bring that consciousness to us. The emerging neuroscience of religion has begun to identify these structures and operations.

However, the preceding discussion has proposed that this line of thinking depends on the idea that there is something called "religious experience." This section will briefly give some background on the development of the term. In this way, it will shape the problem into a manageable form.

We will start with the American philosopher William James because James laid out the basic terms for studying religious experience. James set the direction for study in his classic work *The Varieties of Religious Experience*. This single volume gave birth to the modern psychology of religion by defending the experience of believers against their modernist critics.

The story of the book gives insight into its lasting importance. James traveled from America to Europe on July 15, 1899, to write and deliver the prestigious Gifford Lectures. These were scheduled for the spring of 1900.[38] However, James had a heart condition and was exhausted, causing a postponement, although it was not only his health that held James back, but also the academic challenge. James admitted as much in his first lecture. He observed that scholarship usually flowed from Europe to America. However, now the situation was reversed. Europeans were going to hear from an American. Furthermore, James knew he was talking to a skeptical audience. The finest scholars of the times had rejected religion. James worried that the skeptical Europeans would view him as "an eccentric product of Protestantism," a representative of outdated, superstitious thinking.

After a year's delay, James was finally able to present his first lectures in May 1901 and to finish them in 1902. Carefully and cautiously, James upheld the significance of religious experience before the foremost scholars of the age.

James was an American, yet he adopted the method of a European, the German theologian Friedrich Schleiermacher (1768–1834). Like Schleiermacher, James hoped to mount a credible academic defense of religion against the skepticism and scientism of the modern mind. In the Enlightenment, philosophical doubt replaced the certainty of religious faith. The provable experiments of science replaced the unprovable speculations of religious belief. To the modern scholars, religion was uncertain, unscientific, and untenable. So then how could anyone believe in it?

Schleiermacher became the father of liberal Protestantism when he invented an ingenious way of saving religion from its Enlightenment despisers. To protect religion from modern skepticism, Schleiermacher found a refuge for religious faith. This haven was the one place thought safe from the need for scientific proof: it was the inner, subjective life of the individual.

This was a clever move that became the basis for contemporary liberal theology. Yet what kind of inner experience would qualify as religious? Schleiermacher settled on the most eccentric type, the mystical. Mystical experience is the mysterious sense of direct and immediate knowledge of extraordinary beings, realities, powers, or forms of consciousness beyond those that can be known by our senses. This kind of experience was surely something beyond any philosophical doubt or scientific questioning.

Using the same approach, James laid out the definition of religion and religious experience in terms of the individual. James stated, "Religion . . . shall mean for us the feelings, acts, and experiences of individual men [sic] in their solitude, so far as they apprehend themselves to stand in relation to whatever they may consider the divine."[39] Note the word "solitude." This word indicates that religion concerns the private, inward, and deeply personal aspect of human life. Religious experience happens in the inner self in that "solitude."

James not only used Schleiermacher's approach to theology, he also selected mysticism as the model for religious experience. As the title of his book announced, he set out to explore the *varieties* of religious experience. Therefore, James spoke about prayer, confession of sins, and rituals of sacrifice. However, he only seemed to cover these topics to round out his book. James's real interest was in the dramatic. Only the extraordinary was worthy of his attention. Many might call the common feelings of inspiration, joy, guidance, or awe "religious." Yet James thought they were only secondhand imitations of the profound awareness of direct contact with the supernatural. Thus, he summarized, "personal religious experience has its root and centre in mystical states of consciousness."[40]

The Characteristics of Mystical Experience According to James

James's view that mysticism is the heart of religious experience set the direction for the scholarship that followed. From here on, religious scholars would regard mystical awareness as the *standard* religious experience. Yet what did James mean by "mystical"? The characteristics of the mystical experience do not just define mysticism. They also set the standard for all religious experiences. (See the textbox "James's Characteristics of the Mystical Experience" for the key qualities that identify a mystical experience and their definitions.)

James's Characteristics of the Mystical Experience

- *Ineffable* (inexpressible): like powerful feelings, the experience cannot be put into words.
- *Noetic* (giving inner knowledge): the experience fills the subject with profound and deep insight into realities not known to the ordinary mind.
- *Transient* (short-lived): the experience itself and the memory of it are temporary, but the effects may be long term.
- *Passive* (received): the experience does not happen because the person wills it, but it is like a gift given to the subject.

In the mystical experience, we enter *temporarily* into a sacred, supernatural, and awesome realm of reality. We *passively* receive an incredible *noetic*, inner knowledge of this reality that is *inexpressible*. James considered these the essential defining marks of mysticism.[41]

Here is a short example of such an experience from James's book:

> "I know," writes Mr. Trine, "an officer on our police force who has told me that many times when off duty, and on his way home in the evening, there comes to him such a vivid and vital realization of his oneness with the Infinite Power, and this Spirit of Invisible Peace so takes hold of and fills him, that it seems as if his feet could hardly keep to the pavement, so buoyant and so exhilarated does he become by reason of the inflowing tide."[42]

The word *ineffable* describes the overflowing feelings of the police officer. This term means that the feelings are so profound that they cannot be put into words. Yet the knowledge that the police officer receives in his mystical moments is also *noetic* in that it brings him deep insight. This insight, however, is ineffable or inexpressible. Moreover, in keeping with James's categories, the officer reports that they are not feelings that come from him. They are *passive* because they come to him. However, these feelings of "Infinite Power" and "Invisible Peace" seem to be *transient*. They are short-lived but repeated as they happen on his walks home from work.

Mystical Experience Defines Religion

For both James and Schleiermacher, mysticism was even more than the core of religious experience. It was the origin of religion. James asserted that religions begin with the direct, unmediated experience of their founders. Siddhartha Gautama, Muhammad, and Jesus of Nazareth based their teachings on their personal and immediate experience of the sacred reality. After them, the religious organizations of their followers turned these raw, original experiences into secondhand dogmas, rituals, and hierarchies.

In James's mind, the founders of the world's religions were spiritual geniuses. They were exceptional and eccentric. They were subject to obsessions and fixations. They saw visions, heard voices, fell into trances, and were carried away into behavior that borders on the pathological. To the founders, religion was an "acute fever."[43] Conversely, the religion of ordinary believers is but a "dull habit."[44] Religion begins with the wild, spiritual excesses of its founders. However, after the founders, other, less inspired bureaucrats tame the unearthly experience of the religious eccentric. Brought down to Earth, the fiery zeal of the founders is lost in conventional, static, stale, and uninteresting religious organizations.

Again, these ideas amplify Schleiermacher's thought. As the father of Protestant liberalism put it, "Dogmas are not, properly speaking, part of religion: rather it is that they are derived from it. Religion is the miracle of direct relationship with the infinite; and dogmas are the reflection of this miracle."[45]

Thus, under the influence of Schleiermacher, James, and, eventually, Rudolf Otto, the inner subjectivity of religious experience stole the show from dogmatic belief. Mysticism was now on center stage in religious studies. The spotlight was on the spiritual geniuses who have a direct encounter with a separate, otherworldly reality. For decades, the study of religious experience as a topic of religious studies would rest on this revolutionary development. Scholars would assume that religious experience is extraordinary, strange, and rarified.

Types of Mystical Experience

It would seem that concentrating on one type of religious experience might make religious experience easy to study. However, mysticism is a difficult concept, and it comes in an amazing variety of forms. The British philosopher W. T. Stace tried to clear up some of the confusion in his seminal work *Mysticism and Philosophy*.[46] As William James had argued that the essence of religious experience was mysticism, Stace, in turn, contended that mysticism had a common core.

Two Types and Three Forms of Mysticism

- Extrovertive Mysticism
  - *Theistic mysticism*: believers are united to God.
  - *Nature mysticism*: believers are united with the totality of nature.
- Introvertive Mysticism
  - *Non-theistic mysticism*: believers achieve unity in their minds without divided thoughts—everything comes together as one.

Stace went on to identify three types of mysticism depending on what the believer is united with: *theistic, nature,* and *non-theistic.* (See the textbox "Two Types and Three Forms of Mysticism.") In all three cases, mystics feel a wonderful sense of elation because they no longer feel separate and alone. They know that they have a deep connection with a perfect and lasting reality. Here is one expression from a twenty-year-old male:

> I remember getting up and looking at my closet and it was very blissful, standing was very blissful, walking around was very blissful. I remember going downstairs and sitting on the couch and meditating again, and this time I heard another voice repeating "All is One." "All is One." And I remember a very distinct feeling that there was something or someone watching over me, I felt a presence of something that I can't put my finger on. I felt like I was one with everything—that I wasn't separate from it.[47]

Recall that James calls such an experience *noetic.* The experience gives a special way of knowing. However, as we see in the example, the knowledge is not something that would appear on an exam. It is a deep sense of an underlying, pervasive oneness without division. The man in the example realized, "All is One." That seems like plain nonsense or psychobabble. However, in the mystical state, all things in your mind come together as One.

If all mysticism shares the common sense of unity, how do we get the three different types? Stace proposed that there were two types of senses of oneness:

extrovertive and *introvertive* mysticism. The extrovertive type includes all experiences in which there is something to which the mystic is united. Extrovertive mystics can think of this *something* as God or Nature. For example, the term *God* stands for the creator and source of all reality. To theistic mystics, all things are united in God, their divine source. Consequently, when one is united with God, one is united with all that God has created. On the other hand, *Nature* stands for all the things of the universe. In the Nature form of extrovertive mysticism, the mystic feels the invisible bond that ties all things of the creation together.

In contrast, in the introvertive type, the sense of oneness is so profound that the mystic no longer can distinguish between what is "outside the mind" and what is "inside." In fact, in this experience, there are no separate, discrete thoughts, whether outside or inside. All that remains is *Pure Consciousness*—that is, an alert awareness without separate, specific perceptions or thoughts.

Like William James, Stace viewed mysticism as a strange way of thinking. Ordinary language must have a division between the subject of a sentence and its object. Likewise, ordinary thought depends on the distinction between the thinker who is the subject and the object of thought. However, according to Stace, in the mystical state of knowing, there is no split between subject (the knower) and object (what is known). No wonder James says that the mystical experience is ineffable—that is, inexpressible. With their built-in divisions, ordinary words and thoughts cannot capture it.

This idea of mysticism sets the mystical way of knowing apart from all other kinds of knowledge. The knowledge of ordinary things comes through the senses. However, mystics know extraordinary things through direct and immediate intuition. In the normal ways of knowing, everyone assumes that they are the subjects who perceive the things around them as objects. However, mystics get the sense of an underlying unity in which reality is no longer divided into the categories of subject and object. Thus, we can say that mysticism is not irrational but "non-rational."[48]

The Implications of the Focus on Mysticism

The fixation on mysticism as the prime altered state of consciousness had significant implications as the study of religious experience advanced. In summary, following the lead of the pioneers of the psychology of religion, scholars assumed that religion was based on religious experience. The mystical experience was the prototype of religious experience. In addition, mystical experience was an extraordinary, even abnormal mental state.

Rudolf Otto, the author of *Mysticism East and West*, drew out the implications of these assumptions in more detail. For Otto, the foundation of religion was the indescribable mystery of the holy. He maintained that this mystery was so uncanny that nothing could compare with it. It is in a class by itself—that is, it is *sui generis*. Consequently, it can only be understood by its own terms.[49]

Others like James did not go so far. However, from Schleiermacher on, scholars criticized those who tried to reduce religion to the categories of the ordinary mind. They insisted that science could not observe, measure, or understand it.

In fact, they claimed that only insiders who have deep religious experience could understand it.[50] "Outsiders" who had no sensitivity to inner spiritual experience need not try. Though they may be uneducated and unintelligent, those who experience religion knew more about it than the most erudite scholars.[51] Thus, religious experience itself provided its own unique terms for its study. Even if we tried to explain religious experiences using other, ordinary terms, we were bound to fail. Indeed, according to the tradition of Schleiermacher, James, and Otto, whether an experience should be called "mystical" or not depended on the one who experiences it.[52]

In the tradition of Schleiermacher, James, and Otto, what qualifies as religious experience is an awareness of oneness with God, nature, and/or the cosmos that overcomes the separations of ordinary perceptions and consciousness. By definition, this experience is both extraordinary and filled with overwhelming power and profound insight.[53]

Yet who is qualified to have such an experience? According to this scholarly tradition, all human beings have a capacity for mystical experience. However, James set the focus of study when he purposefully selected religious geniuses for study. He said that to learn any science we must go to the experts. It is true that all humans "have the germ of mysticism."[54] However, in the religiously gifted, the germ of mysticism breaks out in an acute fever. Ordinary believers are bound by tradition and habit, but the religious have the original experience that others must imitate. James admits that religious experience is broad and can be categorized in a series or continuum. At times, he starts with mundane, commonplace examples. However, those who have more dramatic and unusually powerful experiences set the criteria for evaluating all others.

In other words, to the scholars who laid the conceptual foundations for the study of religion, most of the human population is not talented in the ways of the spirit as the religious geniuses are. It is the difference between the audience and the musical composer. The audience is responsive to the music. However, the composers have reached a higher stage of musical expertise. They are qualified to have the original experience of music and to set the musical standards for the rest.

Religious Experience as Ordinary and Common

The history of the study of religious experience seems to answer our questions of the nature of religious experience. Within the tradition of Schleiermacher, James, and Stace, religious experience refers to inner and subjective mental states. It appears in different times and places but only to the religiously gifted. It can be recognized by the descriptions that characterize it as an indescribable, temporary, passive, and extraordinary kind of knowing that is filled with extraordinary power and insight.

Now we turn to another option for understanding the nature of religious experience. The scholars that we have mentioned define it narrowly. Using the defining characteristics set by James and others, they have sifted through various reports of experiences that are associated with religion. They have sorted out those inner states that are unique and unusual. However, what if we broaden the scope of what is called religious experience beyond these narrow boundaries?

New evidence in religious research challenges the answers to the questions of what qualifies as a religious experience and who is qualified to have such a state of awareness. These findings come from the social sciences as well as the neuroscience of religion.

Studies of the General Population

James relied on the experience of exceptional individuals for his study. However, what happens if the scope of the investigation is widened? Research shows that significant portions of the general population report that they have had moving experiences that they call "religious." Since 1969, the Alister Hardy Religious Experience Research Centre now located at the University of Wales, Lampeter, has recorded anecdotes of the spiritual experiences of ordinary people. The center keeps an archive of experiences that the writers define as "religious."[55] Another source is "The Mystical Experience Registry." It collects and stores hundreds of unedited reports of what people claim are mystical experiences.[56]

In the same vein, the National Opinion Research Center (NORC) found that four in ten Americans say that they have had a religious or spiritual experience that has changed their life.[57] Moreover, over half of the population reports that they feel something that we would typically regard as religious or spiritual on a daily basis. Table 5.1 shows the percentages of those who said they have such

Table 5.1. Religious Experiences Many Times a Day, Every Day, or Most Days

Experience	Percentage
Feel the presence of God	62%
Never feel the presence of God	13%
Feel inner peace and harmony	65%
Never feel inner peace and harmony	7%
Am touched by the beauty of creation	73%
Never touched by the beauty of creation	6%
Feel a "connection to all life"	62%
Never feel a "connection to all life"	8%
Feel an uplifting joy in worship	65%
Never feel an uplifting joy in worship	15%
Feel guided by God in daily life	58%
Never feel guided by God in daily life	16%
Feel God's love directly	63%
Never feel God's love directly	15%
Feel God's love through others	88%
Never feel God's love through others	13%
Want to get closer to God	63%
Never want to get closer to God	11%

feelings daily or most days. The lower numbers are the percentages of those who never have such feelings.[58] These self-reported responses are from an American population in which almost 30 percent consider themselves *very* spiritual and another 40 percent consider themselves *moderately* spiritual.[59]

Americans are most likely to think of religious experience in the theistic terms of belief in God. Amazingly, almost one in nine Americans is comfortable with saying that they feel God's love through others. This is a higher percentage than those who feel a deep sense of peace or who are touched by the beauty of creation. Over six in ten Americans also say that they feel God's presence and feel God's love directly. That means that the feeling is not secondhand but an immediate, personal, and inner sense.

But is religious experience merely learned attitudes and behavior from the American culture? What about other cultures? Recently, the Alister Hardy Centre joined the Ian Ramsey Centre for Science and Religion at Oxford in a study of religious experience in China. Supported by the John Templeton Association and with the assistance of scholars from seven Chinese universities, the project completed survey interviews of 3,196 people. The results showing how the Chinese subjects defined themselves were what we might expect: 8.7 percent said that they were "religious"; 4.4 percent said they were Buddhist; and 2.8 percent said they were Christian.[60]

However, when a survey asked about their inner spiritual life, the results of the Religious Experience Research Center (RERC) were amazing (see table 5.2). In a society governed by an officially atheist party, less than one in ten described themselves as "religious."[61] Yet well over one-half reported what could be called a sense of a spiritual power. Four in ten referred to what could be considered religious purposes in life. Almost one in three respondents said they find comfort or strength through prayer or worship.

With the exception of a contact with a power that cannot be explained or controlled, the respondents spoke in typical religious terms. Almost one in five

Table 5.2.   Chinese Inner Life

An image of the Buddha in Beijing. Almost one in three of Chinese reported praying to the Buddha and almost one in five reported the influence of the Buddha in their lives.

reported the influence of the Buddha or a *bodhisattva* (an enlightened being who is dedicated to the enlightenment of others). Furthermore, four in ten use religious language to speak of the goal of life. This may be glorifying God, the Lord of Heaven (a traditional term for the divine overlord of the universe), the Buddha, or ancestors.

In this society, religious experience is still present. Especially notable are the percentages of those who feel the influence of a mysterious power of the Buddha or *bodhisattva* (18 percent) and those who find comfort or strength through prayer or worship (27 percent). If we use a question that corresponds to the Gallup polls, we can make a comparison between the Chinese subjects of study and Americans. The Gallup organization asked, "Have you ever been aware of, or influenced by, a presence or a power—whether you call it God or not—which is different from your everyday self?" In 1990, 54 percent of the American respondents said "yes," and in 2001, 70 percent said "yes."[62] In China, the percentage who answered "yes" to a similar question was 56.7 percent.

The Wide Varieties of Religious Experience

Many of the reports of religious experiences happen on a daily basis and do not seem unusual. Yet others are extraordinary. The following groupings show that range of religious experiences:

Class 1: Everyday experiences of a sense of supernatural presence, inspiration and guidance, feelings of joy and peace, and/or senses of awe, appreciation, harmony, and peace.

Class 2: Dreams and visions when one perceives otherwise hidden sacred realities, including visions of the spirits, appearances of holy persons, and revelations of the future and end of the universe.

Class 3: Ecstasies that take one out of oneself and into an altered state of vitality, insight, and joyfulness, including out-of-body experiences, trances, euphoric states of union with God, glossalalia (speaking in tongues under the influence of the Spirit), spirit possessions, and conversion experiences.

Class 4: Enlightenments that give a sense of piercing through illusion to a higher level of consciousness achieved by ascetic, spiritual discipline, study of holy texts, following a guru, and, above all, meditation.

Class 5: Mystical experiences in which one directly knows a unity with a "higher reality" and/or the whole cosmos.

Religions and spiritual ways might specialize in one or more of these. However, the major world religions include all of them.

Classes of Religious Experience in Brief

Class 1: Everyday experiences
Class 2: Dreams, visions, sense of "presences"
Class 3: Ecstasies and out-of-body experiences
Class 4: Enlightenments
Class 5: Mystical experiences of oneness

Religious Experience Classified as Altered States of Consciousness

As it is commonly used, "religious experience" is a very broad term. Scholars often use the concept of *altered states of consciousness* (ASC) to refer more specifically to the states of awareness involved in religious experience. Generally, we think of consciousness as our normal awareness while we are awake. However, the human mind is capable of many other states from dreaming to euphoria.[63] Most of us have seen the EEG (electroencephalography) squiggles on a chart that trace someone's brain waves. The EEG identifies different types of these waves: *beta waves* of wakefulness, *alpha waves* of states of relaxation and receptiveness, and *theta waves* of the first stage of sleep or deep meditation. Both alpha and theta waves produce states of mind that can be considered different forms of consciousness. These mental conditions are "altered" in the sense that they are different from the rational state of reasoning, planning, and problem solving that Westerners consider the norm of ordinary consciousness. Therefore, some would call them "non-rational."

Classification of Religious Experiences Being Discussed

Class 1: Everyday experiences
Frequent experiences of the presence of God, peace and harmony, beauty, joy, etc. (Surveys)

Class 2: Dreams, visions, sense of "presences"
The sense of a "mysterious presence" induced with electromagnetic stimulation (Persinger)

Class 3: Ecstasies and out-of-body experiences
The intense religious feelings of the persons with epilepsy (Ramachandran)
The aim of the prayerful state of mind of the Franciscan nuns (Newberg)
The aim of the ecstatic states of the Pentecostals (Newberg)

Class 4: Enlightenments
The aim of the meditative states of mind of the Buddhists (Newberg)

Class 5: Mystical experiences of oneness
Experiences of unity with God (James and Stace)
Experiences of unity with Nature (James and Stace)
Experiences of the unity of all things (James and Stace)

The textbox titled "Classification of Religious Experiences Being Discussed" contains an analysis of the types of religious experiences that we are discussing. Those experiences below Class 1 (experiences of everyday life) involve "altered states of consciousness." Beginning with Class 2 (visions, dreams, and sense of "presences"), the experiences involve ways of perceiving and thinking that are different from ordinary.[64] The further down the chart of classes of experience, the less the subject is in touch with the physical world. Thus, the subject's awareness has an increasingly unusual and "altered" quality.

Altered states of consciousness can be involuntary like dreams. On the other hand, the voluntary use of chemicals, hypnosis, or intoxicants can produce them. In between these two extremes, religious practices of meditation, fasting, vigils, dancing, whirling, ordeals, and chanting can also bring on different mental states. In fact, most religions use at least some of these practices for this purpose.

To summarize, in the popular use, the term embraces a wide assortment of types. The polls show that many people claim to have religious experiences in their everyday lives. In addition to paranormal experiences, there are different types of altered states of consciousness that are included in the common concept.

However, we will now see that in religious studies the term has a more technical and limited meaning. In the development of the modern study of religion, "religious experience" came to refer to the inner subjective awareness of individual persons. It especially concerned private episodes that individual persons thought especially spiritual.

The Challenge of Empirical Research

In summary, Schleiermacher, James, Otto, and Stace drew the modern approach to religion back into the safety of subjective experience.[65] By showing that the basis of religion was a direct, personal, and inner experience, they defended religious faith against its modern critics. In doing so, the three captains of religious thought led the study of religion into a defensive position where the truth and reality of religion was safe from Kant's skepticism and the need for scientific proof. In this refuge, the innermost sanctuary was mystical experience.

However, the retreat into the privacy of the inner consciousness set religious experience apart from life in society. It suggested that only a gifted few were capable of the best and most genuine type of religious experience. Furthermore, it held that only those who had an insider's view of mystical experiences could understand them.

We have found that a significant percentage of the population reports experiences that they think are religious or spiritual. Moreover, a review of different types of religious experience suggests some reconsideration of the legacy that the founding psychologists of religion left us. Do they really account for the evidence?

For one thing, surveys like the Gallup polls consistently find that 25–50 percent of Americans and British believe that they have had mystical experiences. Within that range, the number depends on the wording of the question. For those who actively participate in religious activities, the rate of mysticism is usually between 70 and 80 percent. In fact, some religions expect all their members to have the same experience as their saints and leaders.[66]

Ralph Hood developed a more precise instrument than the popular surveys based on Stace's "extrovertive" and "introvertive" types of mysticism. His findings match and refine the results of other tests of mystical experiences.[67] Together with many other studies, Hood's work shows that mystical experiences are not rare or unique. In fact, they are widespread across cultures. For instance, the "M scale" showed a remarkable similarity of mystical experience between American students, Shi'a Muslims in Iran, and Lutheran Protestants in Finland.[68]

The "M scale" identifies mystical experiences regardless of the culture in which they are found. Such experiences are not limited to cultures where religion dominates. This means that those who are not committed to a religious belief system or organization still have mystical experiences. Hood reports that sometimes these will use the religious language they know because they cannot find other ways to express themselves. At other times, they will try to use nonreligious language.[69] Nevertheless, whether they use religious language or not, the subjects report the same core sense of union. Hood believes that these results suggest that mystical experience is not bound by religious interpretations.

Two other findings also challenge the idea of past scholarship that mysticism is rare and abnormal. First, Hood found that the mystical experiences of vast numbers of people throughout the world is the same kind of experience as that of the mystics that James, Otto, and others praised. The difference is only in the intensity of the experience. Second, Hood's research indicates that mystical states are not necessarily signs of mental disease or severe emotional disturbance. The "M scale" could not predict neuroticism, psychosomatic sensitivity, or psychosis. Both psychologically healthy and unhealthy persons have similar rates of reports of mystical experience.[70]

The Challenge of Neuroscience

As David Brooks has suggested, brain science presents the latest challenge to the typical conceptions of religious experience. The researchers have found the tools to probe into the real-time operation of the brain. Using the developing technologies, they have invaded the private inner sanctuary of the mind where the experience of the mystical had once been secured. To those who believe that religion should be protected from the skepticism of modern philosophy and science, the new biopsychological methods of study feel like a violation of their private world. To others, it might offer a possibility of new cooperation between science and religion.

Together with empirical research, the findings of neuroscience call for religious scholars in the twenty-first century to reconsider past theories and their assumptions. As we have observed, the study of religious experience began as a defense against skepticism and scientism. As James wrote in his classic work at the beginning of the twentieth century, modern scholars had concluded that religion was an outdated way of thinking. If religion had survived in modern times, it was an anachronism. Those who had religious faith had relapsed into the primitive superstitions of savages. Furthermore, religious experience, especially in its extreme forms, was abnormal, even pathological.[71]

As James countered these prejudices, he set a trend that continued through the work of Stace, Otto, and later religious scholars. They accepted the limiting notion that mysticism was the standard model of religious experiences. They concluded that religious experience in its fullest sense could be found in all human societies, and yet it was rare, unique, and even abnormal. (See the textbox "Summary of Past Studies of Religious Experience" for a list of its characteristics as described by the scholars.)

Summary of Past Studies of Religious Experience

1. It is personal and subjective.
2. Its standard model is mysticism that elevates the awareness to a blissful state beyond words.
3. In its standard form it is given to only a few talented persons.
4. In its standard form it is unusual, if not abnormal.
5. In its standard form it can be isolated from the interpretation of the experience.
6. In its standard form it can be separated from its context in cultures, religious organizations, and worldviews.

In contrast, this section of the chapter has shown that the current research has found that religious experience is not rare just as it is not abnormal. It is widely distributed in nearly all cultures. It is common to one-third to one-half of the populations of contemporary human societies. In addition, religious experience seems built into the human brain. It is grounded in physical structures and processes in the brain that neuroscientists can now observe.

In summary, the results of current surveys of social science and the research of neuroscience show us a somewhat different picture of religious experience than past scholarship. We can summarize with three main points that do not seem to fit together. Religious experience (1) *originates* in the human brain, (2) is *widespread* throughout the human population, and (3) is *diverse* in its actual appearance in human societies. (See the textbox "Key Ideas of Current Research on Religious Experience" for a summary of these findings.)

Key Ideas of Current Research on Religious Experience

1) Religious experience *originates* in the human brain.
   a) It is associated with parts and processes of the brain.
   b) It does not happen without these brain structures.
   c) It is felt as a different level of knowledge of consciousness than the ordinary.
2) Religious experience is *widespread* throughout the human population.
   a) It is felt and reported as "religious" in many different context and cultures.
   b) It is found in a wide variety of human societies.
   c) It is common among human individuals in different societies.
3) Religious experience is *diverse* in its actual appearance in human societies.
   a) It is described and interpreted differently.
   b) It is conditioned by culture.
   c) It is varied in type.
   d) It is focused on different objects of belief or modes of consciousness.

After reviewing the history and development of the term "religious experience," we can now formulate the problem of this chapter in terms of three challenges that current research poses to religious studies. The first challenge is how to account for religious experiences that are qualitatively different from normal consciousness. The current research shows that such transcendent experiences are the product of physical processes in the brain. But it seems odd that physical processes could yield such spiritual results. This is the question of the origins of religious experience.

The second challenge is how to account for the fact that these experiences are so widespread throughout the human population. We might hold that the experiences are the result of malfunctions or abnormalities of the brain. But it seems strange that more than a significant proportion of human persons report some degree of religious experience. This is the question of the scope of religious experience.

The third challenge is how to account for the fact that the types of religious experience and ways that people describe them are astonishingly diverse. We might believe that the experiences have the same origin in the brain and the same basic characteristics. But it seems odd that the descriptions of these experiences should vary so much. This is the question of the diversity of religious experience.

SURVEYING THE ALTERNATIVE APPROACHES: ESSENTIALIST AND CONTEXTUALIST THEORIES

The last section arrived at a basic problem of understanding religious experience in terms of three questions about the origins, scope, and diversity of religious experience. This chapter will divide the alternative approaches into two categories along the lines of a long-standing debate between religious scholars. On one side are the *essentialists* who dominated the study of religious experience until the middle of the twentieth century. On the other side are the *contextualists* who countered the essentialists in the last part of the past century. The debate between these two approaches has given shape to the challenges that the current study of religious experience faces.

Essentialism is the philosophy that each thing has a built-in set of properties. These characteristics make the thing what it is, and they distinguish it from all other things. As we have seen, William James set out the essential characteristics of mysticism. Because he convinced scholars that mysticism is the most developed form of religious experience, these characteristics became the norm for defining religious experience. Accordingly, scholars like Huxley thought that they could find these characteristics wherever they looked in all religious experiences throughout the world. To Huxley and other essentialists, religious experience is the same throughout the world.

What about the differences in the accounts of religious experience? According to essentialism, the differences in the reports of religious experiences come when those who have them try to put them into words. The actual, raw experience without the words that interpret it is the real thing.

For example, dying people may have near death experiences (NDE) of visions of being dead and being brought back to life again. These people often report that they have died and that they were floating above their body. They often report feeling that they are moving through a tunnel toward a bright light. Moreover, they often report seeing their deceased relatives or a "being of light." Who is this "being of light"? For some, it is merely a holy person. In Christian cultures, it is often God or Jesus. In Buddhist cultures, it may be the Buddha. In Hindu cultures, it may be a Hindu god. Michael Grasso states that "the being" is a universal element of near-death experiences. However, what "the being" means depends on the person's cultural and personal background.[72]

Conversely, the *contextualists* complain that the essentialists have reduced the mystical experience to unreal abstractions. Contextualism is the philosophy that nothing can be known or understood "in itself" but only in the situation in which it appears. Those who hold this view contend that we cannot separate the interpretation of our experiences from the experiences themselves. The experiences of persons are the product of their culture. Of course, their culture teaches us how to interpret their experiences. However, it does more. Their culture provides the images, impressions, and ideas out of which their religious experiences are made.[73] If patients report seeing Jesus, Buddha, or Allah, then the religious scholar should not presume to say that they experienced something else.

Here is a sample experience:

> One evening I sat on my sofa listening to music. All of a sudden, I seemed to be transported into a dream, though I was not asleep at the time. I seemed to be transported into the Paradise of God, and there, I was a "watcher" looking about at the beauty of nature in that place. I saw three beings in long white robes ascend a hill, and as they reached the top, they turned and faced towards me. They began singing, as if praising God. All of a sudden, I was brought close to the face of the

one standing in the middle and knowledge came into me that it was "myself" in Paradise. At that moment, God's Love seemed to fill every cell of my being. I had always heard that He Loved me. However, I had never felt it before. I began to weep, and the dream left me. At that moment, I decided within myself . . . Love this vast, this . . . required a response from me. And I determined that no matter what the sacrifice to myself—I would give my life, my all to my Creator that Loved me.[74]

The report uses culture terms such as "Paradise of God," "watcher," "God," "He," and "God's Love." This vocabulary is inseparable from the feelings of the experience. Without this vocabulary, there is no experience. With it, the experience evokes a sense of awe and provokes an impassioned response. The experience and its interpretation are the same thing.

Each of the two sets of approaches has its drawbacks. In general, the essentialist approach can explain the similarities among mystical experience but not the differences. These differences are in not only the type of experience but also the basic terms of the experience. Alternatively, the contextualists readily explain the differences in religious experiences. However, their approach falters when it tries to account for the similarities among them. Some examples will illustrate and give some clues for a possible solution to the problem.

Essentialist Approaches: Focus on the Universal

Peak Experiences: Maslow

First, we will review a Western psychological theory. The psychologist Abraham Maslow proposed that religious experiences were psychological states of mind. He called them "peak experiences." What is a peak experience? These are times when everything comes together in a sense of harmony, creativity, joy, and vitality. No, these times do not just happen in commercials. These are the most satisfying moments of human life. Human beings reach their purpose in life when this kind of exuberant fulfillment happens to them. One of the most common ways to achieve it is religious or mystical experience.

According to Maslow, "peak experiences" are at the top of a "hierarchy of needs." Once their needs for physical necessities, security, and self-esteem are met, individuals can move on to the top level of life. They can now actualize their human potential. Peak experiences help them do so. They make the higher values like truth, wholeness, contentment, and creativity real to us. They are the most fulfilling experiences that humans can have. They are so powerful that they are life changing.

Life-changing peak experiences have the identifying characteristics that James listed for mystical experience.[75] However, Maslow identified a number of other characteristics that appear in James's discussion of mysticism. Consider the following experience from the Alister Hardy Institute:

I was sitting one evening, listening to a Brahms symphony. My eyes were closed, and I must have been completely relaxed for I became aware of a feeling of "expansion." I seemed to be beyond the boundary of my physical self. Then an intense feeling of "light" and "love" uplifted and enfolded me. It was so wonderful and gave me such an emotional release that tears streamed down my cheeks. For several days, I seemed to bathe in its glow and when it subsided, I was free from my fears. I didn't feel happy about the world situation. However, I seemed to see it from a different angle. So with my personal sorrow. I can truly say that it changed my life and the subsequent years have brought no dimming of the experience.[76]

Like the experience of others, this person's awareness went beyond the boundaries of "self" into a typical kind of selfless state. In this condition, the person looked at the world's problems from a different angle. She no longer judged them in terms of her narrow ego self-interests but was open to the world as it is without evaluation. Her feelings expanded so that she was uplifted and "enfolded." Maslow speaks of this expansion as a sense of "timelessness" and "spacelessness."[77]

When Maslow described peak experiences like the one above, he revealed his personal values. In the peak experience, one accepts the way things are without compartmentalizing, comparing, or complaining. Everything in the world has a place and is in place and everything fits together in a marvelous whole. Clearly, what Maslow called the "core religious experience"[78] has the same characteristics as the mystical experience that we have already described. In fact, to Maslow, mysticism was just one type of peak experience.

By categorizing "core religious experience" under "peak experience," Maslow tried to account for the similarities and differences of religious experience. Like Stace, Maslow agreed that as a form of peak experience, all mystical experiences have a common fundamental nature. Moreover, like James, Maslow believed that the intense, personal experiences of the founders of the major world religions were but versions of the same mystical experience that modern people still have.[79] Therefore, at their basis all religions are the same.[80]

So if peak and mystical experiences have the same core, why do the *different* religious interpretations arise? To Maslow, Moses, Jesus, and Muhammad were "lonely persons." Their revelations came in their solitude. The "organizers" and "legalists" later shaped the original message to appeal to the masses. They are to blame for the differences in religions. Beverage companies have found a way to bottle the natural, flowing waters of the ecosystem. In the same way, the legalists found a way to dispense the raw, mystical spirituality of the founders. They put it in bottles of dogmas, rituals, buildings, and institutions.[81]

In summary, Maslow proposed that religious experience was a form of the optimal psychological states he called "peak experiences." They come when other physical and psychological needs are met. The result is a state of well-being, harmony, and creativity. Maslow held that this state has common characteristics. However, those who realize this state describe it according to their personal history, background, disposition, and culture. This means that they are "religious" if the subject chooses to conceive of the experience in the way that religious leaders teach.

Eastern Thought: The Yoga of Patañjali

The idea of a common core to mystical experience is not only found in the West. The teachings of the Yoga master *Patañjali* (second century BCE) represent an Eastern approach that has its own psychology.

As we see in James's *Varieties of Religious Experience*, Western thought tends to think that mystical experience is extraordinary and thus abnormal. Eastern approaches to consciousness reverse this way of thinking. In Patañjali's system, *ordinary* thinking is not normal. What is wrong with our ordinary thinking? Though useful to our survival, everyday thinking is uneasy and unfulfilled. Our restless minds are always chasing after one thing and then another. It is hard for that frenzied mind to even imagine a state in which it is perfectly serene, perfectly still. However, in Patañjali's Yoga, the peak experience and highest form of consciousness is complete peacefulness called "Pure Consciousness."[82]

To understand, consider why the human mind is so restless. Whenever people try to quiet their mind, they realize how it darts from one thought to another. It is like a little goldfinch that flits from one branch to the next. Attempts to catch it just make it more skittish.

Patañjali taught that by degrees, the mind (*citta*) drifts from its pure and peaceful state to the striving of the ego, and then to the slavery to material things. How does it happen? The mind is like a super transformer toy that keeps changing from one thing to the other. These mental changes start with the basic, tranquil mind. Out of this mind, the egoistic self develops with its sense of "I," "me," and "mine." From the ego, the intellect (*buddhi*) develops. By using the intellect, the mind now distinguishes one thing from another. Once the mind begins to sort out one thing from another, it naturally wants some things and does not want others. Thus, the desiring function of the mind is born. Once aroused, desire drives us to act to fulfill it. In this way, the mind is changed from its original peaceful state to a restless condition. The mind ceaselessly pursues one thing after another while it flees from one concern after another. The beautiful and serene mind has been transformed into an agitated monster.[83]

According to Patañjali, to regain peacefulness of mind, humans must get control of their mental powers. This requires a steady and persistent will. They have to be on guard against the ways that the ego mind yanks them around: the charms of the senses, the craving of the ego,[84] and conflicts with others. They must develop habits of calmness and self-control and eventually learn to quiet the restless fluctuations of the mind.[85]

Only when the mind is detached and serene is it capable of the next step: meditation. The mind has to recover sufficient control to become "one-pointed" in an intense focus. Then it can engage in *samadhi*—that is, the concentration of the mind. In this state, the mind can progress through the levels of concentration from the ordinary separateness of things to the unity of Pure Consciousness, a state of mind that knows no separation between things.[86]

The process of meditation starts with the contemplation of external objects such as pebbles on a beach. At first, we see distinct things, a pile of stones. Then we progress to mental images, and we create a picture of rocks in our mind. From there, we grasp the concept of rocks, and then we come to know the essence of "rocks." From there, we realize the unity of rocks with all things in a fundamental oneness of reality. In this way, each stage of perception comes closer to the unified mind of Pure Consciousness.[87]

By degrees through the stages of samadhi, the mind recovers its original state. One finally comes to the point where the mind is fully aware, but it does not compare, evaluate, judge, or discriminate between one thing and another.[88]

This seeing into the deepest reality of all that exists is the highest state of mental processes. It is a much different way of knowing than ordinary perception, which is based on the senses. In fact, a Yoga master says that it "transcends the mind."[89] According to the ancient Hindu philosophical text, the Māṇḍūkya Upanishad, those who practice meditation reach a stage of consciousness where there is no knowledge whether of the inner or external reality. Yet there is no ignorance either. This is a stage of neither perceiving nor not perceiving. It is an indescribable state of mind that perceives only itself.[90] In James's terms, the experience is both ineffable and noetic.

Even then, the samadhi practice is not complete. The division between the realization of wisdom and the one who realizes it still lingers.[91] When there is not the slightest hint of an "I" that has attained a different state, then there is perfect samadhi. No more seeds of the division remain to sprout and grow into distinctions between one thing and another. The consciousness stands alone, freed from its bondage to the ever-changing mental processes (citta).[92] This is the final state without further transformation. It is pure, clear, serene, and stable awareness without disturbance.[93]

Buddhism has a similar structure of thinking and helps us understand the original source of consciousness. It has to do with the root of consciousness. Neuroscientists might say that consciousness originates in the brain. In contrast, Buddhism distinguishes between mental activity (javana) and the root or "ground" (bhavaṅga) of that activity.[94] Mental process like sense perception, thought, memory, imagination, and desire arise as branches from the tree of the subtle ground of the mind. In contrast to the assumption of the neuroscientists, they do not originate in the brain but in consciousness.

The Tibetan Buddhist Great Perfection School further elaborates that this "ground" has two forms. The first is the root of an individual's mental activity. By meditation, one can quiet the mental activities sufficiently to "see into" this "ground" of mental activity. The result is that one can see how the "ground" of the mind works to produce thoughts and perceptions. Whether the mind looks outward or inward, all that appears is like the mist rising up from a lake at sunrise. The mind is like the lake. Its thoughts and perceptions are like the mist that rises from the lake. Appearances emerge temporarily from the void of the absolute, perfect, and undivided unity of the original mind. Yet they soon fall back into that void, the stillness of the mind.[95] In enlightenment, those who meditate achieve an awareness of the lake itself. No thoughts or perceptions emerge from this lake or return to it. The lake is perfectly still and perfectly pure.

However, this condition of bliss and mental clarity is only a temporary realization of the individual mind. The next level of meditation reaches the absolute ground of all awareness, the primordial consciousness (jñāna). In this state of awareness, no words or discrete thoughts divide reality into separate things. Thus, the distinctions between self and other, mind and matter, subject and object no longer apply. All that is left is an overriding sense of total and unlimited unity.[96]

We have described Eastern thought by the twin metaphors of drifting away and then returning or of rising up and then falling back. In each case, ideas and appearances come out of the source of Pure Consciousness. When the practitioners reach the level of the source, then they attain peace of mind, overcoming of struggle, and release from suffering.

In summary in the teachings of Patañjali and the Buddhist Great Perfection School, "religious experiences" are experiences of the illumination of consciousness. In the realization of Pure Consciousness, the mind returns to its original, peaceful, and unified state. It has retraced the process by which the consciousness has drifted by degrees from the development of the ego to the divisions of separate things and from there to the slavery of desire. While Maslow laid out a hierarchy of needs that aimed at the goal of an experience of unity, these Eastern philosophies outlined a hierarchy of consciousness aimed at the same goal of unity.[97]

If this is the case, "religious experiences" of illumination arise because they are the restoration of the original, universal state of the human mind in Pure Consciousness. They are similar because the consciousness and its operations are the same throughout the human race. Therefore, the goal of clarity and unity of mind is possible for all persons, and all who engage in the arduous practice of meditation can realize it. From this point of view, differences such as the differences of cultural forms and divisions in religions are obstacles to the oneness of enlightenment and must be set aside.

Huxley: The Perennial Philosophy

Eastern thought gave some Westerners a new perspective from which to reconsider the mysticism of both Eastern and Western religions. One of the most prominent of these Westerners, Aldous Huxley, was the pioneer of an influential approach that he called *The Perennial Philosophy*. In a book by the same name, Huxley integrated the reports of both Eastern and Western mystics. The book was a masterful demonstration of how a "common core" of ideas keeps appearing across the divisions of time, place, and culture.

Four Principles of the Perennial Philosophy

1. Everything comes from and depends on a hidden "divine Reality."
2. The divine Reality is not anything physical. It exists on a different level than the physical world.
3. Inside of us, we have an invisible "soul," or "higher consciousness," that can connect with this divine Reality.
4. The goal of human life should be to come to "know" this divine Reality.

What is that common core? Huxley says it comes down to four principles (listed in the textbox "Four Principles of the Perennial Philosophy"[98]). The section on Eastern thought concentrated on introvertive mysticism. The following section will explain the four points of the Perennial Philosophy according to the extrovertive type.

Extrovertive mysticism discerns that a single source invisibly binds everything together. The existence of this hidden "divine Reality" is the foundation of the beliefs of the Perennial Philosophy. In theistic traditions, that source and bond of all things is God the Creator of the world.[99] In other traditions, that foundation of reality may not be personal.

The mystical idea of this divine source is not merely a remote "First Cause." Rather, the "ground" of reality is like the relation of a flame to the rays it shines into a room. The beams of the candlelight depend on the flame, not the reverse. Yet the rays of light are united in the flame. It is in this sense that theistic mystics believe that all reality depends on an invisible "divine Reality."[100]

The philosophy's second point supposes that if the source of the universe existed on the same level as physical things, it would not be the ultimate source of reality. Among the religions of the world, we encounter a baffling variety of names for the origin and source of reality. Some of these names are deities, the gods. Others are impersonal titles for the nameless source such as the *Tao* of Taoism. The Perennial Philosophy explains that these names are but human and limited concepts of the mystery that exists on another level of reality than the physical.[101]

This leads to another essential point to understand about theistic mysticism. How can the unknowable source of reality be known? The Perennial Philosophy says that all forms of mysticism give the same answer. This is the third article of belief of the Perennial Philosophy: all humans have a built-in means to connect with this divine Reality.

The basic idea that applies to the third point of the Perennial principles is "like knows like." This concept of likeness is the key to the conclusion that all mystical experience has a common core. It is so crucial that Huxley begins his description of the Perennial Philosophy with its most radical version. This way of speaking about the knowledge of the divine source of Reality is the oft-repeated phrase from the Upanishads,[102] *tat twam asi.* ("That art Thou!")[103]

The sage Nikhilananda (1895–1973) refers to the teachings of Advaita Vedānta Hinduism to explain this key insight. He states that meditation on the nature of Brahman and Ātman leads to the astonishing realization that they are identical. Brahman (the "That" of the famous phrase) and Ātman (the "Thou" of the phrase) are one and the same. Therefore, to find the Ātman (the "Thou") in oneself is to find the Pure Consciousness of the Brahman (the "That") and so achieve liberation from the limitations, illusions, and sufferings of the ordinary mind.

In the case of Nikhilananda's teaching from the Upanishads, the "soul" that can connect with the Brahman, the absolute source and principle of all existence is the Ātman. In Christianity, human beings are "made in the image of God." Unlike the Hindu Advaita teaching, Christianity does not claim that this divine image within human beings is identical with God. However, human persons "made in the image" are created to reflect the divine Reality of its Creator.

According to the Eastern Orthodox Church father John of Damascus (676–749 CE), the "*nous* is the 'eye of the soul.'" This nous is the organ of spiritual discernment that has the capacity for direct, inner knowledge of God. As disease can darken the physical eye, so the passions that crave worldly pleasures can darken this spiritual eye. However, when the nous is purified of the vices like pride, anger, greed, and lust, the light of God illumines the eye of the soul, and one sees the spiritual vision of God.[104]

How, then, can the nous be purified? The mystics must close the doors of their physical senses and turn their attention inward. By meditative prayer, they must put thoughts, impressions, and sensations out of their mind and concentrate with watchful attention on God in stillness (*hesychia*). This stillness of the mind makes the soul receptive to the inner purifying work of the divine Reality in the soul. Thus, the purification of the soul is the work of the divine Reality within. It is an action of God's grace. The active energies of divine grace bring the believer to the vision of God, the perfecting of the image of God, and finally union with God.[105]

This union is so complete that Eastern Christianity speaks of "deification" in which human beings realize their divine "likeness" to God. Then the "image of God" in human beings perfectly reflects the divine Light of God, and human beings fulfill their ultimate purpose.[106]

Similar concepts of the inner faculty for the mystical knowledge of God can be found in Sufi Islam. In Sufi thought, the *qalb* (spiritual heart) is like the nous of Eastern Christianity. It is the instrument of spiritual wisdom and understanding. When it is spiritually illumined, the heart knows God. However, like the nous, the qalb can be so corrupted by the world of the senses that it no longer reflects the light of God. Like a dirty mirror, the qalb must be cleansed of the impurities of the lower self such as "ignorance, pride, envy, uncharitableness, etc." Then, when the marks of the "worldly impressions" have been erased from the heart, as the Sufi poet Rumi (1207–1273 CE) says, "He becomes . . . the mirror of the reflections of the Unseen." Then the qalb will grasp the "knowledge of the Prophet," the understanding of the divine mind. Then the mystic will achieve *fanā*—that is, the annihilation of the ego with its limited and divided attributes or traits—to take on the divine attributes of God.[107]

The third principle of the Perennial Philosophy seems to apply to Christianity and Islam as well as Hinduism. However, Christianity and Islam believe that the likeness to God can be pushed too far. In general, the monotheists draw an absolute line between the one Creator and the many created things of the universe. Despite the boundary between the Creator and creation, the monotheistic religions believe that the Creator is intimately involved in the creation. The Creator is present everywhere in the creation as the source and foundation of reality. Therefore, to connect to God is to get in touch with the inner bond that upholds the universe and ties all things together.

Perennial Philosophy would point out that in mysticism this unity of the universe can be experienced directly without appeal to the name of a deity. Whether the mystic takes the indirect path to the experience of mystical union through devotion to a deity or the direct path of the oneness of all things, the goal is the same. This goal is Huxley's fourth principle, the knowledge of the divine source of Reality.

In summary, Huxley and the Perennialists claim that wherever it is found, mysticism supposes two universal, reoccurring ideas: (a) the existence of an intangible divine Reality, and (b) the capacity of human persons to know this Reality. This idea is the center of what we might call the "mystical frame of reference." Within this framework of meaning, religious experience is founded on the nature of reality and the nature of human persons. Thus, the Perennialists summarize the fundamental thought of all mysticism. All things in the universe have a common bond in a common, transcendent source. And all human beings have a capacity for mystical experiences because by nature they have a soul that is capable of knowing and uniting with the infinite divine Reality.

The Perennialists find evidence for this "mystical frame of reference" in the core of the common characteristics of mysticism throughout the world. However, how do they explain the vast differences in the way that experience is described? To the Perennialists, the differences in how mysticism is conceived are cultural. They appear when humans try to put the experience of spiritual things into ideas that the ordinary mind can grasp. Thus the diversity of the world's religions and their interpretations of religious experience are superficial. Below the varied expressions of religion is the experience of union with the divine Reality that is ineffable and so cannot be put into words.

Boyer and Others: Evolutionary Biology

Evolutionary theory offers yet another way to uncover the common basis of religion. Evolutionary biologists like Pascal Boyer have developed scientific answers to the problem of how to explain why religious experience is universal in human cultures and yet there are so many different conceptions of it.[108] Their theory starts with the premise that they share with the neuroscience of religion: religious experience is the product of the brain. Regardless of culture, humans share the same basic structures and operations of the brain.[109] Therefore, it is not surprising that it exists in nearly all human cultures.

Evolutionary theorists tend to accept the idea that the brain has different systems. Each of these *modules* has its own way of operating in specific *domains*—that is, areas of mental activity. We might think of modules as information-processing units. These systems evolved as problem-solving mechanisms, not as instruments of abstract thinking. For example, using built-in mechanisms, infants develop the ability to recognize faces a few days after birth.[110] The theory reasons that some systems of the brain give humans the capacity for religion. Human cultures developed religious beliefs and behaviors as they exploited this mental ability.

Beyond these basic assumptions, evolutionary theory divides into two camps. It disagrees about whether religions are products or by-products of the evolutionary processes of natural selection. One side asserts that religious beliefs and behaviors utilize brain modules that are specifically dedicated to religion. These systems evolved as *direct products* of the challenge of survival and reproduction. One argument for this claim is that societies with more elaborate rituals than others achieve a greater amount of cooperation. Cooperation is essential for group survival. When the group survives, then its members survive and reproduce. Therefore, groups with elaborate rituals are more likely to flourish and so religion will take hold in the human population.[111]

But how does this process work? To answer, the theorists must appeal to the controversial notion of *group selection*. According to evolutionary theory, the process works by the selection of traits that survive through the generations of a species. An example of individual selection is the evolution of the giraffe. We can imagine that giraffes with long necks were healthier and lived longer than giraffes with short necks. Over time, as they reproduced with other giraffes with long necks, the process of natural selection established this trait in the whole population of the species.

But *group selection* is different. The evolving traits of religion are definitely good for the group. However, they may well come at a high cost to individual members of the group. For example, sacrificing oneself for the good of the group is not beneficial to the self-denying individual. Nevertheless, it is highly advantageous for the group. When a group has members that sacrifice themselves for the common good, these altruistic members do not survive, but the group goes on. And because of group survival the disposition for sacrifice is passed along.

The other and more widely held side of the evolutionary theory debates believes the brain has no special modular systems that are dedicated to religion. The use of these modules for religion is an *indirect* result of evolution. In this view, religious thinking is a by-product of otherwise normal brain functions. The ordinary operations of the brain are already there. However, religious thinking uses them like a parasite.[112] In the view of Boyer and others, religious beliefs are counterintuitive. They twist ordinary categories of thinking into contortions.[113] Thinking that is properly grounded in the senses would not suppose that humans can exist without bodies. It would not believe that deceased relatives come back from the dead. Moreover, there is no reason to believe that invisible beings watch every move that human persons make. And furthermore, humans cannot be filled with supernatural power. Yet in the distorted thinking of religion, all these ideas are considered plausible.

If they are counterintuitive and unusual ways of thinking, how did religious beliefs develop? A favorite example of the by-product theory is how humans came up with the notion of "supernatural agents"—or, in common language, "gods." Evolutionary theorists explain that belief in gods comes from the overuse of an important tool for survival.[114] This mechanism is the *agency detection system* (ADS). Through the ADS brain module, we have the ability to distinguish agents from objects. Using the ADS system, humans can tell the difference between agents who make choices about what to do and objects that cannot. In addition, this ability enables humans to guess what these agents might decide.

Mental programming like this is quite useful out in the bush. Imagine a group picking berries. Someone sees a sudden movement. Immediately, her ADS system activates, and she cries, "Bear!" The group runs. Nine times out of ten, it will be a false alarm. However, the tenth time, the device may save the lives of everyone in the group.[115] Thus, what Barrett calls a "hyperactive agency detection device" is a useful adaptation for survival. The good thing about it is that it helps humans survive. The bad thing is that it enables the mind to imagine the presence of spirits, the dead, ancestors, or gods that do not exist.

The construction of the concept of "god," however, requires one more step. Humans have ADS mental equipment that makes them prone to believe in the presence of other beings, even those that are invisible to them. To get gods, they must simply combine this idea of agency with other brain modules, the systems that produce the idea of cause and effect. These brain systems are so strong that they compel people to seek causal explanations for almost everything that happens to them. For example, planes that crash for unknown reasons immediately suggest terrorism. Assassinations of revered leaders give rise to conspiracy theories. Lacking other reasons, people can always blame invisible gods.[116] If disaster or disease overtakes them, they are disposed to attribute the cause as well as its cure to a deity.

In summary, evolutionary theory is convinced that all religion, not just mystical experience, is a function of brain systems. Religion arises as either a product or by-product of the modules of the brain. Religious experience is distributed throughout the human population because the brain has the capacity for it, and it is useful to the individual and the group. Religion is like language. The mechanisms for language are built into the brain. Human cultures use this equipment to develop different languages. In the same way, humans develop religion. Of course, the actual religious beliefs, rituals, and other ways of achieving group cooperation will be different in different societies because they are functions of society.

Constructivist Approaches

Contextualism

So far, the options for understanding religion that we have introduced can be classified as *essentialist*. From the groundbreaking work of William James at the beginning of the twentieth century on, these approaches were dominant in religious studies. However, in the latter part of the twentieth century, the philosopher Stephen Katz and others[117] launched a countermovement to the essentialist camp. Despite its critics, this alternative to essentialism has gained prominence in religious studies.[118]

Katz calls the method against essentialism "contextual" because it seeks to recover the key role of context in religious experience.[119] Contextualism is an approach to knowledge that presupposes that all human actions happen in their cultural situation and cannot be understood except in that setting. From this standpoint, the goal of essentialism is impossible. Believers do not have a mystical experience and then find a way to understand, report, and explain it. But the experience and the understanding happen simultaneously, each one affecting the other.[120]

The initial principle of the theory is very succinct: direct and immediate experiences are impossible. All experience comes through learned, cultural ways of knowing. These ways channel, filter, and shape our thoughts and perceptions.[121]

Religious studies scholar Robert K. C. Forman notes that this principle is hardly news to most contemporary scholarship. Most current scholars accept it as a matter of course.[122] However, note that this maxim runs headlong against the basic characteristics of mysticism that this chapter has outlined. In James's terms, mystical experience is ineffable and noetic. It cannot express what it knows in words. But words are given in human language and used in culture. Thus, mystical experience knows a level of reality beyond these cultural forms.

For example, the Pure Consciousness of Hindu Yoga and Buddhist enlightenment has no specific content. It is a sense of complete unity in which there are no separate thoughts. Since this awareness is "beyond" ordinary thinking, no thoughts can bring it to us. It is completely unmediated. But this is not the only example. This chapter has outlined many forms of the idea that the standard of religious experience is mysticism and that in this view, mysticism is the direct, immediate experience of the supernatural or super-consciousness.

Moreover, the theory of the cultural conditioning of experience rejects the whole program of essentialism. Essentialism attempts to identify and isolate the fundamental characteristics of religious experience beneath its cultural forms and specific religious expressions.

Constructivist scholars make their argument in direct contrast to this once dominant idea. In their view, the term "religious" is not merely a label stuck onto an experience. It is an inseparable part of the experience itself. Wayne Proudfoot notes that what makes a religious experience is that the subject considers it "religious."[123] Katz goes so far as to say that the religious and cultural background of the subjects of religious experience has a causal relationship with these experiences. The culture teaches its members to anticipate and expect the experience. It coaches its members in methods meant to induce the experience according to these expectations. It then ensures that the subjects find the meaning of their experience accordingly.[124]

For example, a long list of beliefs about God, the soul, the covenant, and the Torah influences the experience of Jewish mystics. Jewish mystics do not abandon the unique heritage of their religion when they seek religious experience. An intricate network of concepts, rituals, images, and practices called *Kabala* are woven together in their worldview. This web of religious beliefs and practices determines the kind of experience the Jewish mystics seek.[125] The cultural context plays an active role before and during the experience. It is not added later as an afterthought.

We have discovered the problem of how to account for the universal presence and yet widespread diversity of religious experience. How does contextualism address it? The program of contextualism is dedicated to the notion that all mystical experiences are *not* essentially the same. In Katz's words, contextualism represents a "plea for the recognition of differences" among religious experiences. Katz and his colleagues complain that the essentialists ignore these differences. The essentialists may think that they can find the common core of mystical experience. However, to do so they ignore the different, actual reports of mystics and reduce the rich variety of religious experience to their own simplistic notion. If anyone disagrees, the essentialists will say that they do not understand the nature of the experience.[126]

In summary, contextualism proposes that the origin of religious experience lies in the different cultures and their religions in which it appears. This approach denies that the subjects of religious experience are seeking the same thing. Even if the mystics seek an underlying "unity" of reality, their goals differ from one another. Hasidic Jews dedicate themselves to the supreme goal of *devekut*, or "cleaving" to God. Through the cleaving of devoting themselves to God in everything, the Hasidic mystics reach an ecstatic state.[127]

Hasidic Jews practice meditation to purify the soul from attachments to the material universe. But they do so that their soul can be freed to make the ascent toward the total state of clinging to God. On the other hand, Buddhists meditate to do away with the very soul ("Self" or Ātman) that the Hasidic mystics hope to unite with God. Buddhists seek to cut off all attachments, even the ultimate attachment of the soul's union with the divine. In Katz's view, Nirvana is the "absence of all relation, all personality, all love, all feeling, all individuality, all identity," in a state of perfect peace and serenity.[128]

The point of sketching these goals is to show how different they are. They have different starting points in their contexts. To extract the goal from this context is to misunderstand it. For instance, the Jewish goal starts with the problem of finding blessedness in relationship to God. The Buddhist goal starts with the problem of the cause of suffering and the liberation from the karma-run wheel of birth, life, death, and rebirth. God, the focus of Judaism, is not even a factor in Buddhism.

The contextualists admit, of course, that religious experience is found throughout the human race. Their point is that it is never found in "pure" form that is not conditioned by culture. Just how far that conditioning goes depends on whether the theory asserts that culture "shapes" religious experience (a "soft constructionist" approach) or that religious experience is a "necessary consequence" of cultural, linguistic, social, and theological factors.[129] Nevertheless, the contextualists take the fact of religious and mystical experience for granted.

Feminism

Contextualism denies that we can get down to a common core that all religious experiences have in common. It holds that like all experiences, religious experiences are diverse because human cultures are diverse. The contexts of unique cultures evoke, shape, and interpret the religious experiences of their members.

An important field of religious studies explores a set of contexts that shape the human experience of religion. This is feminism, an area of scholarship that is allied with contextualism. Feminism accepts the principle that culture constructs the world of human beings and their beliefs, morals, ways of life, relationships, roles, and practices. Yet it adds to this insight that men are the ones who do this social constructing of reality and that they do it to their own advantage. Within the frame of reference of feminism, male domination, therefore, is the distinctive characteristic of the religious experience of women.

At the foundation of feminism is this understanding of *patriarchy*.[130] This term describes social orders in which men have power and control over women and children. It is the fundamental concept that lies beneath the feminist goal of liberation from the oppressive structures of the male-oriented society.

Feminists use the fundamental category of gender relationships for analyzing human societies and religions. From this point of view, they show how religion gives legitimacy to the power structures of patriarchal societies. In male-oriented communities, religions define and enforce the domination of men over women. Yet even though most societies since the Bronze Age can be described as patriarchal,[131] not all patriarchal societies are the same. Likewise, not all patriarchal societies have similar religious beliefs and practices.[132]

These insights put the feminists on the side of the contextualist approach to religious experience. Since the social context shapes all experiences, patriarchy molds the religious experiences of all the members of patriarchal societies. To the extent that this is true, women, as well as men, will experience the sacred reality in the patriarchal terms given by their male-oriented society.[133]

From the feminist point of view, the theories of religious experience that have dominated religious studies conceal the bias of patriarchy. For example, Rudolf Otto maintained that the fundamental categories of religion are the *sacred* and the *profane*. To Otto, the mystical experience was an encounter with the sacred conceived as God, the "Wholly Other." As an awesome, transcendent reality, God was thought to be the very opposite of the profane—the natural, material, and finite world.

In keeping with his Lutheran background, Otto associated the sacred with the "spirit,"[134] and he thought of the profane as "flesh." Religious studies scholar Melissa Raphael-Levine admits that Otto presented the "flesh" as worldly, not feminine. Yet Raphael-Levine notes that the word "flesh" connotes "sexuality and finitude." "Flesh," therefore, conceals a hidden prejudice, because sexuality and finitude are associated with women. As typical interpretations of the story of Adam and Eve suggest, from the beginning, women have represented the "temptations of the flesh." The implication of the seemingly benign dualism of "spirit" and "flesh" is that women and their experiences are not merely profane. They are contrary to the sacred. Thus, the Western mystical way demands an overcoming of the "lusts of the flesh" that the daughters of Eve represent.[135]

We have taken the first step in understanding the feminist critique of the theories of religious experience. We have shown how patriarchal cultures shape the religious experiences of women as well as men. The next step is to recognize that the position of women *in* culture shapes their religious experience in unique ways. The cultural forms that impinge on religious experience may be the same for both men and women. Yet the feminists assert that women will experience these cultural forces differently, and their personal religious experience will vary from that of men.[136]

For example, according to Otto, the experience of the sacred will give the mystic a sense of being a "creature" before "the Holy" Creator. Raphael-Levine says that women will have an enhanced sense of this "creature-feeling." Women are not only creatures of God. In the worldview of Western patriarchy, women are also creatures of men, since Eve came from Adam's rib. Moreover, they are creatures of the male, cultural image of the feminine. In contrast to men, women in male-dominated societies will feel this sense of being a lowly, earthly creature three times over.[137]

Yet another step is to understand that a third set of factors shapes the religious experience of women. The essentialists ignore the fact that gender issues are always crucial factors in culture, religion, and personal experience. When we take gender into account, we realize that women have a more profound sense of the body, its natural rhythms, and the biological and social roles that have to do with their sexuality.[138] In contrast to men, women will bring their sense of the body to their religious experience.

As the work of Otto illustrates, men tend to focus on the transcendence of the sacred. To the masculine mind, "the Holy" is infinitely distant and qualitatively different from the material creation. This means that men will tend to emphasize that the sacred exists outside of the created world. In contrast, feminists describe women's experience as one of immanence. They will naturally think of the sacred as close to the earth. To them, the sacred is found within the material universe. In this view, the divine reality is known "in and through" finite things. The body is not a barrier to religious experience but the means of attaining it.[139]

Like contextualism, feminism undermines the once dominant approach to religious experience centered on mysticism. The feminists' critique charges that essentialism reflects the patriarchal bias of its male promoters. Their male prejudice establishes the norms for religion experience. Indeed, their definitions dictate what counts for a true religious experience and what does not. These norms discount the religious experiences of women. They even suggest that these experiences are false.[140]

In summary, feminism tends to focus on the origin of religious experience of women in patriarchal societies, not religious experience in general. Male domination in these societies reaches to the foundation of beliefs, values, and ways of life on which society is based. Therefore, to a large extent, male control has shaped the religious experience of women.

At the same time, the feminists maintain that another origin of women's religious experience is their own physical, psychological, and spiritual experience as women. Their sense of the female body and its functions is perhaps the greatest influence that makes the religious experience of women different from men.

The feminists' positive focus on life in the body leads them to support the idea of a variety of religious experiences. If religious experience is an experience within the female body, then it will be profoundly personal, intimate, and creative. With this emphasis, feminists naturally reject the reduction of religious experience to a disembodied, esoteric awareness that male scholars have made of mysticism.

Thus, like contextualism, feminism values religious differences. Nevertheless, in contrast, feminism suggests that the religious experiences of humans in all cultures share a common character. It asserts that gender relationships form their primary makeup. Furthermore, since patriarchy is present in nearly all cultures, it maintains that gender inequality has a major impact on almost all religious experiences.

Evaluating the Alternative Approaches

We have reviewed a wide variety of theories of religious experience. How well do they meet the challenges of accounting for the origin, universal scope, and wide diversity of religious experience?

Evaluation of Maslow's Theory

Maslow's theory is a good example of a positive psychological approach to religious experience. His key concept is that religion is a type of peak experience that comes when other human physical, psychological, and social needs are met.

Maslow's theory addresses the question of why peak experiences are found throughout the human race. Since this state inspires personal creativity and the fulfillment of the individuals' potential, it suggests why these experiences are so diverse. But these high points of human life are not necessarily "religious." This leads to the question of why people report and interpret some experiences as "religious." Other than cultural conditioning, why should they think this way at all? Maslow said that psychology could fully explain even the profound experiences of religious founders such as Moses, Jesus, and Muhammad. However, that is not how they or other religious people regarded these experiences. Maslow's thoroughly naturalistic explanation ignored the religious descriptions and interpretations that believers gave of their experience. It fails to answer why religion emerges in human psychology.

Evaluation of Eastern Approaches

Eastern theories believe that the Pure Consciousness is the original and primary state of mind for all human beings. Thus, within the frame of reference of their view of consciousness, they can account for the experiences of "religious experiences" of illumination. They are the restoration of the original, universal state of the human mind in Pure Consciousness.

These theories also seem to address the question of why such experiences are found across cultures. Indeed, Eastern theories promote a state of mind that transcends the languages and cultural forms that separate humanity and even the divisions in reality. Thus, they would tend to reject the distinctions among the religions and to deny that there are significant differences in religious experiences.

However, Eastern approaches are not as universal as they often claim to be. In fact, they aim at one class of experience among the many types that we have listed—"Class 4: Enlightenments." The other forms of religious experience are thought to be only preliminary, partial, or misleading.[141]

Moreover, the Eastern mystical experience is supposedly open to everyone. Yet, in practice, it is limited to those who invest in training for it. In fact, this training has very specific cultural forms, and it takes the utmost effort and discipline to achieve its goals. For example, Zen Buddhists teach that the experience of enlightenment (*satori*) cannot be put into words. However, language still plays a role in the "cultural shaping" of the experience. In fact, the notion of the inexpressible (ineffable) is a major concept of Eastern cultures. Religion professor Dale S. Wright points out that it forms the experience that cannot be put into words.[142]

Zen training is extremely rigorous and involves long periods of sitting in meditation. Through the rigors of training in skills, beliefs, customs and language, the adept becomes capable of the experience of the unity of Pure Consciousness.[143] However, Zen practice is permeated with Eastern cultural forms such as the practice of sitting in meditation, the focus of mediation on word puzzles (*koans*), the role of the Zen master, and the marathon sessions of group meditation. Thus, the experience is clearly culturally conditioned. Eastern theories, therefore, are more specific to their cultures than their appearance suggests. They do not adequately account for the wide variety of religious experience that we find in the religions of the world.

Evaluation of the Perennial Philosophy

The Perennialists offer a compelling account of why the religious experience of mysticism exists throughout the world. They identify a universal core of characteristics of mysticism and painstakingly show examples of these traits in mystical thought and experience scattered throughout world history.

According to the principles that the Perennialists abstract from the core characteristics of mysticism, religious experience gives humans a glimpse into the nature of reality and its source in a divine Reality. At the same time, the cumulative weight of countless mystical experiences over the centuries confirms this vision of the nature of things.

The genius of the Perennialists is that they are able to fit the mystical experience of both East and West into the "mystical frame of reference" that they claim to have identified. But they select one type of experience as the standard for all religious experience. If the Perennialists would have their way, all religious believers would practice meditation. As Huxley puts it, "The life of contemplation is the proper and normal development of the 'interior life.'"[144]

What if one does not have the personality or opportunity for contemplation, a life devoted to prayer and meditation? Huxley has no answer except to speculate on a second chance in one's next reincarnation. Apart from that, Huxley can only emphasize the importance of meditation practice.[145] Thus, the Perennial universalism turns out to be another form of exclusivism. It does not appreciate the wide range of types of religious experiences that spiritual people report. It recognizes that some people are more disposed to mystical experience than others. However, it can only advise those less inclined to the spiritual to try their best.

Then again, the problem is not just that mysticism is the sole standard for real religious experience. In order for a religious experience to fit the Perennial Philosophy's ideal, it must be interpreted in a particular way. As Huston Smith admits, the Perennial Philosophy has its own concepts and language.[146] Religious believers interpret their experiences according to their own cultural traditions. Many would not recognize their sacred ways in the descriptions of the Perennial Philosophy and some would not agree with the description if they did. In conclusion, the Perennial Philosophy offers religious studies more than an objective description of religious experience. It selects its evidence primarily from the literary texts of the world's mystics. Then it prescribes what the experiences of the world's religious believers should be.

Evaluation of Evolutionary Theory

As the scientific study of religion advances, evolutionary theory is rising in popularity among scholars of religion. The evolutionists ask the right question when they propose ideas about why religions appear throughout the world. However, their answers are deeply divided.

Evolutionary theory is primarily a rationalistic account of the origins of religious *belief*. It does not focus on experience and the commitment that goes with it. Thus, Ilkka Pyysiainen notes that Boyer fails to take into account the important role of emotions in belief and experience. Humans do not believe in gods simply because they calculate that they are useful. Humans put their trust in gods and not in Mickey Mouse and Donald Duck not merely because they believe that one kind of being is real and the other is not. Their belief also involves an emotional commitment to the gods. Consequently, religious experiences have incomparable emotional weight. It is this emotive power that makes them life changing, not their rational utility.[147]

The by-product theory assumes that religion is a matter of ordinary brain systems gone wrong. Religions are the same because people everywhere have the same mental equipment that is subject to the same mistakes. This evolutionary view is convincing because it seems to offer a simple explanation for theistic beliefs across human cultures. It is easy to conceive of gods as "supernatural agents" detected by hyperactive agency detection devices.

In contrast to such a simple notion, gods are no mere "presences" or abstract "agents." They have an astounding variety of personalities. How did human societies get from "detecting presences" to full-blown notions of gods? The answer requires more than the appeal to natural selection. This line of reasoning suggests a hidden weakness in evolutionary theories: they do not help us understand the evolution of diverse religions and different types of religious beliefs.

Evolutionary theory gives the false notion that when we explain its origins we understand religion. This is a form of the *genetic fallacy*. It is like saying that we can understand all we need to know about today's cars by describing the Model T.

Evaluation of Contextualism

The arguments about the importance of context to experience have convinced many of today's scholars.[148] Though controversial, contextualism represents a formidable challenge to the dominance of the essentialist position since the latter part of the twentieth century. It is an appealing theory to today's scholars because it agrees with the notions of postmodernism. It supports the program of religious pluralism. And it resonates with feminist scholars.

Contextualism concentrates on the particular and therefore does not have much to say about why religious experience is scattered throughout human history and cultures. Unless we are willing to make some generalities about religious experience, we might as well suppose that religion just pops up everywhere by "spontaneous generation."

A critical thinking approach to study would step back to consider the assumptions of the theory. Contextualism is founded on the principle that there is no awareness that is not culturally conditioned. Forman charges that Katz does not prove this fundamental presupposition but merely gives miscellaneous examples of it.[149]

Besides this objection, there is another flaw in contextualism. If we do not accept Katz's dogmatic principle, it *is* possible to conceive of times of being aware without words. Human beings have these moments frequently. For example, we have moments when one train of thought interrupts another, and we are "at a loss for words."[150]

Recall that James said that the mystical experience is ineffable and noetic. What is happening when mystics have the sensation of knowing that cannot be put into words? The answer is that their mental processes have blocked language from their awareness. This practice is widespread. Religious traditions throughout the world have devised methods of setting language aside through such ways as fasting, chanting, dancing, and meditating.[151]

Therefore, we have reason to question the founding principle of contextualism. Religious experiences are found throughout the world. But are they similar enough to be classified together? If they are not, then the only thing that they have in common is that their subjects call them "religious." However, the vast amount of study on religious experience that this chapter has reviewed shows that scholars can study religious experiences as one general category of human life.[152]

In summary, we can appreciate contextualism for its rejection of methods that do not appreciate the differences among religious experiences and reduce them to general abstractions. However, the empirical findings of neuroscience along with social surveys bear out the essentialist claim that there are profound similarities among religious experiences. Religious experiences share some common features across the varied contexts of cultures. We cannot explain these comparisons without making some overarching generalities that go beyond the specifics of each case.

Evaluation of Feminist Approaches

Like contextualism, feminism emphasizes that religious scholars should understand religious experiences in their contexts. Therefore, it proposes that male domination not only shapes but also controls the religious experience of women in the vast majority of human cultures. In this sense, the religious experience of women originates in their position in society. On a more basic level, it is an experience in the female body in its physical, psychological, and spiritual aspects.

A major problem with its approach to religious experience is that it takes both sides of the essentialist-constructivist divide. In agreement with the contextualists, the feminists maintain that different cultural contexts result in different religious experience. The study of women's experience must necessarily focus on the particular and unique life stories of women in distinct settings.

Yet that anti-essentialist program may go too far. The philosopher Alison Stone notes that some feminists have concluded that there are *no* common features across cultures that would unite women as a class. This would be a consistent anti-essentialist stance, but it undermines the basis for the collective political action of women.[153] It also would make it difficult to answer our basic question of what qualifies as a religious experience.

Stone reports that some feminists are rethinking the stance of essentialism. To simplify the discussion, we can refer to two types of essentialism: biological and social. Early feminists had rejected the idea that the category of the female body was a universal and essential feature of the experience of women. The feminists downplayed that idea because of the way men used it to justify their oppression. Now most feminists recognize that though female biology is the same across cultures, the very ideas of the "woman" and "body" are culturally conditioned.[154]

While retreating from *biological essentialism*, some feminists have entertained a *social essentialism*. This approach holds that patriarchy is found almost everywhere in the world. Therefore, regardless of time and place, gender determines nearly all religious experience.[155] The factors of the unequal roles in society, the compulsory role of nurturer, and the treatment as a sexual object affect everything, including religion.[156]

Yet even social essentialism has its critics. Some would say that any definition of a common core of women's experience across cultures does the same thing as the patriarchal position. It privileges a certain type of women's experience among the diversity of experience in the world. Feminists are left with the hope to promote the unity of women throughout the world as an oppressed class and the realization that essentialist claims to establish that unity will prove to be untrue.[157] Even the forms of their oppression in patriarchy are different.

In summary, feminism offers a necessary body of knowledge, theory, and criticism to the study of religious experience. Further study may clarify the issues raised to give a more comprehensive response to the challenges of understanding religious experience.

Summary: Evaluation of Alternatives

This chapter is seeking a way to understand the origins, scope, and diversity of religious experience. It is interested in setting the direction of a comprehensive theory of religious experience. It does not seek a scientific explanation but a rational way of integrating all available evidence into an organized framework of ideas. The work of James and Huxley are models for such a theory. They bring together a vast assortment of reports, examples, and observations into a convincing and comprehensive body of knowledge.

The key to such a theory is how well it integrates all aspects and factors of the subject matter into a larger whole. In this case, the theory would address all three of the challenges that combine to pose the problem of understanding religious experience.

We have found that the alternative approaches deal with one or more of these challenges well but not all of them. Maslow's theory of "peak experiences" gives a psychological explanation for why these experiences are found throughout the human race. But he ignores the questions of why many people call these high points of life "religious" and how that idea comes up in human life. The Eastern philosophies have a profound theory of the origins of the "religious experience" of illumination but do not recognize that their ideas and methods are not as universal as the goal of their practice. The Perennial Philosophy excels in identifying common and universal characteristics of mystical experience. Nevertheless, it does so at the cost of discounting the diversity of religious experience. Evolutionary theory has a limited view of religion in terms of gods and supernatural presences. It does not seem to appreciate the diversity of religious beliefs and experiences throughout the world.

The above approaches are adept at constructing generalities that apply to all religions. But their categories and abstractions fail to fully appreciate the diversity of religious experiences throughout the world. However, the *contextualists* champion the diversity of religious experiences to the near exclusion of all other questions, especially the universal characteristics of these experiences that other scholars have found. The *feminists* have raised the forgotten questions of the religious experience of women, especially in terms of male oppression. But they do not agree to what extent the experience of women in patriarchal societies has common, universal characteristics.

In addition, neuroscience is providing a new source of evidence. The findings of the new cognitive science of religion offer a test of others' theories. An adequate theory will be able to integrate these findings in its body of knowledge.

PROPOSING THE MOST PROMISING SOLUTION: A THREE-POINT PROGRAM OF STUDY

This chapter is searching for a theory that would adequately account for the origin of religious experience as well as the universality and diversity of religious experience. To do this, we have considered a number of sample approaches divided into two groups: the essentialists and the contextualists. Each of these theories has certain advantages. None can account for the origins of religious experiences, their common characteristics, and their diverse forms.

The proposed theory will make use of two sources: the past study of religious experience and the recent findings of the neuroscience of religion and the social sciences. As we indicated, the tradition of scholarship is significant because it marked out the territory of "religious experience," the basic terms that would name its features, and the basic methods of exploring its terrain. The neuroscience of religion and studies of social science depend on the work of these scholars. However, just as modern maps correct as well as add more detail to the maps of past explorers, the current research modifies the discoveries of past investigations. The combination of past and contemporary research will help us propose a more satisfactory and comprehensive theory.

Neuroscience Prompts a Reconsideration of Past Studies

Before we build the proposed solution to the problem of this chapter, we might review the ways that the recent findings of neuroscience call for a reconsideration of the some of the key ideas of the former study of religious experience.

The first idea is that subjective experience is entirely private, since the inner, psychic life of the individual is inaccessible to others. Now, however, the neuroscience of religion has enabled researchers to peek into the once unseen domain of subjective experience. Its methods have enabled researchers to study what was once thought off limits to scientific observation and investigation. This chapter has already established that identifiable sets of networks, circuits, and neurotransmitters are associated with religious belief and practice.[158]

A second idea that neuroscience prompts us to reexamine has to do with the religious experiences of individuals. Scholars have assumed that personal religious experiences are isolated not only from the experiences of others but also from other kinds of experiences. That is, they are *sui generis*, which means that they are in a class by themselves. However, the neuroscience of religion has found that the brain does not have distinct compartments for religious experience. There is no unique "God Spot" to be found in the brain of religious people, because the brain uses the same parts and pathways for religious belief and experience as it uses for other functions.

A study of Danish Lutherans at prayer confirms this finding.[159] The subjects of this study were young Lutheran men in Denmark who thought of prayer as a personal conversation with God. The brain scans of these men showed that when they were praying, the areas of the brain dealing with intersubjective relationships were especially active. The active regions were the same ones that the brain uses when someone is in conversation with others or when someone is negotiating the "give-and-take" in a mutual relationship. These parts of the brain include the junction between the *temporal-parietal and parietal lobes* and the *precuneus*. These structures help us look at ourselves from the viewpoint of others and to empathize with them.[160] This study showed that for these men "praying to God is an inter-subjective experience comparable to 'normal' interpersonal interactions."[161]

Another test confirmed this finding. Instead of praying spontaneous prayers, the men were asked to pray the Lord's Prayer (the "Our Father"). This practice involves recitation, not conversation. The scans registered a difference from times when the men were engaging in extemporaneous conversations with God and the ritual recitation of the formal prayer. Then the men were asked to make wishes to Santa Claus. The results showed that the men were using a different set of brain operations to make wishes to Santa Claus than they used for prayers.[162]

The third idea is that religious experience involves altered states of consciousness. The notion that the awareness is "altered" seems to imply that it is rare, abnormal, or even artificially induced. For example, some speculated that the sensation of the supernatural is a result of the malfunction of the right temporal lobe.

The study of the Danish Lutherans showed that these ideas are too simplistic. By all accounts, the men had normal brain functions. Moreover, the images of their brains showed that they were using the normal pathways of conversation in their personal prayers to God.[163]

A final idea that is up for reexamination is the separation of the religious experience from its interpretation. Past scholars have used this idea to propose that religious experiences have common, universal characteristics. The interpretation, though, uses cultural forms, and that accounts for the diversity of religious experiences. But cognitive research is finding that the brain works as a whole and that functions of the brain integrate multiple systems. The brain scans of the Danish Lutherans are associated with brain processes that are used to address personal beings, not fictional characters like Santa Claus. The men's belief that the object of their prayers is real and personal cannot be separated from their experience of praying. So they naturally think of their entire experience as religious.

On the other hand, Newberg claims to have identified the brain patterns that are associated with Absolute Unitary Being (AUB), a sense of an all-embracing unity beyond the division between subject and object. This is the mystical experience that is realized in the absence of words or images and, therefore, interpretation.

If we consider both prayers to God and AUB to be religious experiences, we have no reason to choose one over the other. AUB is a type of mystical experience, but not a common characteristic of all religious experience. We must find the defining qualities of religious experience in other factors.

The findings of neuroscience, the results of surveys of ordinary people, and the analysis of the theories given in the alternative solutions section indicate a need for a more adequate and comprehensive theory, as we have suggested. In general, the problem with past theories is their attitude toward the reports of those who have had the experiences. Past scholarship as well as the neuroscience research has relied on these self-reports because they are firsthand evidence of the experience. On the other hand, even though researchers have had to depend on these accounts, they have not trusted them. Some scholars have sought explanations of the experiences other than the believers' accounts of their supernatural or super-conscious source. Others have made generalizations about the reports that believers would not understand or agree with.

Now the situation has changed. Neuroscience has shown the remarkable match between the reports of the subjects of religious experience and glimpses into the activity of their brains during the experience. For example, neuroscience has found distinctive patterns of the parts and processes of the brain that are associated with various religious states. The brain scans of Lutherans who are engaging in conversation with God look much different from the scans of Buddhists who are engaging in mindfulness meditation. The reports that the Lutherans and Buddhists give of their experience match this difference.

In short, neuroscience suggests that we can trust the reports of the subjects of religious experience who are tested in the science lab. This gives us some reason to trust the reports of those who are not wired to technology. The neuroscience of religion continues to broaden its research to other types of religious experiences. We can anticipate that further research into more types of religious experience will find a correlation between the descriptions of these experiences and the processes of the brain. This conclusion would encourage us to take a second look at the rich storehouse of accounts of religious experiences in different times and cultures.

Setting the Direction of a Promising Comprehensive Theory

Having cleared the way, we can go on to build a more promising theory of religious experience that would solve the problem of how to account for its origins, scope, and diversity. This theory would take all the evidence available into account, including the growing body of data from neuroscience and social surveys. It would add these sources of data to the literature of the mystics as well as the anecdotes of religious experiences. In addition, it would explain the broad range of types of religious experience without singling out one as the model for any others. Finally, the theory would integrate the multiple factors involved in religious experience.

Building Blocks for a Proposed Theory of Religious Experience

1. The plasticity of the brain
2. The emergent character of culture
3. The interaction of brain, mind, and culture to produce religious experience

The proposed theory is built on three major points from current research (listed in the textbox "Building Blocks for a Proposed Theory of Religious Experience").

The Plasticity of the Brain

The first insight is the "plasticity" of the brain. The common idea is that brain capacity grows rapidly during childhood and then remains static until it decays in old age. Moreover, the human brain has stayed the same throughout the ages. But current brain science has confirmed that the brain remains pliable and can change throughout life in response to stimuli. Studies have confirmed that this finding also applies to religious experience. For example, one study compared Buddhists who practiced a form of concentrated awareness called *insight meditation* with a control group. The brain scans of the Buddhists showed increased thickness in the prefrontal cortex, especially in the right hemisphere.[164] This area is associated with attention. Interestingly, the most dramatic increases were in older persons who usually have a thinning of the cortex.[165]

But meditation is not the only activity that changes the brain. Other research has shown that patterns, rhythms, and repetition of ritual also alter brain structure and processes.[166] Of course, religions have already known about the effects of repeated behavior. They have relied on meditation, ritual, ascetic disciplines, and group processes to train and nurture believers in religious experiences. As we have seen in the theories of Patañjali, Huxley, and even William James, the training involves more than objective descriptions of the mystical state. They prescribe what believers are to experience.

Surveys and studies of ordinary people have shown that religious experience is not merely a capability of a few gifted individuals. The findings of neuroscience suggest that the systems of the brain make it capable of religious experience. It may be that the brain is predisposed to it. However, religious experience is not predetermined. Humans cultivate this trait in various ways and to various degrees.

The Emergent Character of Culture

Why do all people have this trait in the first place? We have described the views that religion is only a product of the malfunction of brain systems. If so, then religions are coaching people in mental disorders. But this chapter has shown that religious experience is so common and widespread that, in general, it cannot be viewed as abnormal. To counter the notion that religious experience is merely the result of faulty brain chemistry, some scholars propose that consciousness is an *emergent* characteristic. If so, as a form of awareness religious experience is a form of that emergent trait.

The *theory of emergence* holds that there are different levels to reality. For example, we can go downward through these levels from mind to brain, from brain to brain cells (neurons and *glial* cells), and from cells to atoms and from atoms to electrons, etc. As we go downward, each level represents a simpler system. As we go upward, each level represents a more complex system.

According to the analysis of emergence theory, each system on its level has four main characteristics. First, the whole consists of parts. The whole depends on these parts and their interactive relationships. A motorcycle, for example, does not exist without its parts. In addition, there is no motorcycle unless its parts are arranged in a certain way. Second, the whole is greater than its parts. One can list and describe all the parts of a motorcycle. However, one still has not described what a motorcycle is. The third characteristic is that the whole has an impact on other things as a whole. This means that relative to other things, the system can be said to be real. It is an entity. All the parts of the motorcycle work together as a whole to zoom down the road. We do not say, "There goes a bunch of metal parts going down the road." We say, "There goes a motorcycle!" as if it were a whole and complete thing. Fourth, this whole called a "motorcycle" functions according to higher rules of operation. Assembling all the parts of a motorcycle into a whole does not guarantee that it will run. The parts of the motorcycle engine have to be almost perfectly in tune according to the principles of internal combustion for it to start.[167]

Now we have the concepts needed to understand why the "mind" is more than brain chemistry. The emergence theory recognizes that the mind depends on the physical level just as a whole depends on its parts. However, in human beings the brain has a complexity that attains another level of reality. The brain is transformed into mind, creating something new, an emergent entity.[168] This mind can be considered a reality since it has agency.[169] It makes choices and acts on these choices. It is conditioned but not determined by its parts.

Further, the "strong" emergence theory asserts that the mind has a causal effect on other things at its level and the levels below it.[170] A familiar experiment gives its subjects a small electric shock on their back. Depending on what they have been told to expect, the subjects of the experiment experience the stimulus as either heat or cold. In this example, there is no direct causal link "bottom up" from the stimulus to the feelings. Yet the stimulus is necessary for the sensation. The sensation is not simply reducible to its stimulus since the stimulus could be many different things. The experimenter could say it was a heat tolerance experiment or even leave a tube of burn ointment on the table. The expectation that the subject will feel heat works "top down" to make the brain believe what it is sensing is indeed heat.[171]

The "top-down" force of the mind governs most of what we experience in society. For example, the mind conceives of the concept of a motorcycle. This concept shapes behavior as the concept goes from idea to the draft of its construction, and then to the fabrication of its parts, and finally to their assembly. Further, the concept has a powerful effect on the behavior of its owner. It engenders habits of thinking, of relating to others, of valuing, and of forming a personal identity. As Durkheim would say, the concept of motorcycle is at the center of a cluster of ideas, attitudes, and behaviors that have the status of "social fact." Moreover, this set of ideas has an impact on mental functions. One has to learn to drive a motorcycle—that is, to train the brain to processes that become "second nature."[172]

This suggests a possible explanation of how cultural context has an essential impact on the experience of the brain and how the expectation of religious experience can shape it. According to Terrence Deacon and Ursula Goodenough, three emergent factors cooperate to make us uniquely human: brain, symbolic language, and culture.[173] Each of these acts on the others. The key, however, is language. Language is a remarkable adaptation that only one species of animal on Earth has perfected. We cannot explain human language by simply describing the anatomy of the brain any more than we can explain a motorcycle by listing its parts. It is an *emergent phenomenon.*

The essential point is that language has a top-down effect on the brain. In Deacon's account of the development of language, this defining feature of human beings started with simple symbol systems. These systems, however, had an impact on brain development. That impact made the development of symbolic communication easier. Thus, over the generations, the interaction of the brain and the emerging mind produced a brain three times as large as might be expected. More than that, it caused a "radical re-engineering of the whole brain."[174]

The result is a human brain that is capable of highly complex symbol systems—that is, human languages. But languages come in multiple forms. For example, this textbook is written in just one of the hundreds of human languages. English has certain rules of grammar that make it a distinctive language. These rules are based on its "deep structure," the way the English language works. However, the "deep structure" of English shares common fundamental principles with other human languages. The brain has built-in systems for learning and applying these principles.

As human languages developed over time, human cultures developed as webs of values and meaning embedded in language. These *symbolic cultures* had the "top-down" force of shaping the consciousness of those who lived in them. Concepts that combine ideas and images like "motorcycle," "money," and "marriage" became the "facts" of the ways of thinking and living in society. Babies born into these cultures already had the brain aptitude for language. The symbolic culture activates and shapes it. Thus, human language is universal but human languages are amazingly diverse.

The Interaction of Brain, Mind, and Culture

How do these ideas apply to religious experience? The understandings of the development of language and culture lead to the affirmation of the contextualists' emphasis on the cultural influences on religious experience. Religion is a part of culture. In fact, it provides the core of the cultural symbolic world. Like language, religion has a basic "deep structure" hidden from view. This underlying foundation consists of the operating principles that religious teachings, rituals, morals, and collective identity follow. Like language, religion is universal in human life because the human brain has a built-in capacity to understand and use the "deep structure" of religion.

Our proposed solution suggests that the theories of essentialism are probes into the universal "deep structure" of religion. The common characteristics of experience that essentialism identifies (the qualities of "peak experiences," the core beliefs of mysticism, the mental processes of the Eastern philosophies, and the supernatural agents of "agency detection systems") may be attempts to put the underlying principles of religion into general concepts.

But just as languages activate and shape this capacity, so the cultural forms of religion activate and shape the religious experience. Religion and its experience are found throughout human societies because of the inherent capacity of the brain. Religions and religious experiences are so diverse because of the variety of cultures that use this faculty.

The theories of the contextualists and feminists remind scholars that "religious experience" is an abstract idea that does not appear in life. The theories that emphasize the cultural context insist that religious studies should not deal in generalities that are removed from the way religious experience actually appears in particular human societies.

How does the emergence theory address the question of the origin of religious experience? In its view, religious experience is not a new level of reality that surpasses the mind. As consciousness depends on the working of the brain, so religious experience depends on the operations of the brain.[175] But as the mind is more than the processes of the brain, so religious experience is more than brain chemistry.[176] The theory of emergence offers an alternative to the evolutionary biologists' explanation of how religion developed. This option does not deny the physical basis of religious experience in the brain. But it also does not reduce what believers consider "spiritual" into its physical building blocks.

The evolutionary theory proposes that religious experience is built from the bottom up, from brain systems such as "agency detection." Our proposal suggests that religious experience is a product of the interaction of brain and mind that is shaped by culture. It is both a "bottom-up" and "top-down" process.

Normally we would think that the emergence would go from the bottom up, each level providing the parts for the greater complexity of the next level. For example, the rhythms of ritual can produce changes in the brain. The Sufi "whirling dervishes" wear white skirts that represent their burial shroud. In the Sema ritual, the Sufi mystics spin on one foot in a dance that is meant to bring them to a state of harmony with the universe in the love and praise of God. The music of the dance uses fast rhythms to aid the dancers. Neuroscience suggests that the rapid beat of the music stimulates the "arousal system" to the point of being overwhelmed. The brain reacts by shifting to a quiescent state, and the subject feels a deep sense of serenity and harmony.[177] Newberg and d'Aquili call this a "bottom-up" method because the brain produces mental effects going from the lower structures of the brain to the higher structures.[178]

On the other hand, the music and dancing of the Sufi ritual are cultural forms. The theory of interaction suggests that the culture provides the distinctive triggers of the Sufi music, dance, and physical behavior. The brain responds

Sufi whirling dervishes spin in a ritual dance that is meant to bring them into a state of harmony with the universe in union with God.

with the activation of processes that bring mystical awareness. In the same way, religions provide countless ways of triggering the systems of the brain to bring on numerous types of religious experience. Moreover, the culture provides the models for that experience. Saints, heroes, ancestors, gurus, shamans, masters, and monks and nuns are just a sample of the cultural forms that provide images of what to expect in the experience. These cultural forms provide guidance and motivation to believers even in mystical or enlightenment traditions that seek experiences that transcend words and interpretations.

Neuroscience has shown the practice of meditation and prayer makes lasting changes in the brain structure, such as the thickening of the neocortex. It is likely that religious practices that cannot be studied in the laboratory give shape and structure to the brain. These ways of practicing religion train believers' minds and increase their ability to enter into religious experience. In religious experience, then, the universal capacity of the brain, the training of the brain in the formation of "mind," and the particular cultural form of a religion come together in the inner experience of the individual.

We have tried to find a promising direction for the further study of religious experience. In summary, the review and evaluation of theories of religious experience has found that it is a highly complex mental event. It is a form of consciousness that depends on the physical structures and operations of the brain. Yet it is more than mere brain chemistry. Consciousness emerges from the complex interaction of the brain, language, and the "symbolic world" of culture. As a form of consciousness, religious experience arises from the same basic dynamics. Moreover, these three factors relate to each other in a number of ways. This explains why there are so many types and why it appears differently in each culture. Yet the interactions of the three involve common elements in the brain and a common, hidden, and built-in structure of mental processes. This explains the origins of religious experience, why religious experience appears throughout the world with identifiable core characteristics, and why its forms are so diverse in the human population.

EVALUATING THE MOST PROMISING SOLUTION: PRAYERS, NURSERY RHYMES, AND A TEST CASE

Our discussion has proven how complicated the topic of religious experience is. The twenty-first century presents religious studies with exciting challenges to understand the latest evidence about religious experience coming from the laboratory and the field. We have shown that scholars have used various approaches for research in the past. The most promising direction to advance the research would be to find a more compressive theory. This theory would account for the origins of religious experience in the brain, mind, and culture. It would achieve an understanding of the complexity and diversity of religious experience. At the same time, it would identify what religious experiences have in common.

A Test Case: Prayers and Nursery Rhymes

A test case indicates that this proposal might have merit. Psychologist Nina P. Azari and her colleagues used a PET scan to study the brain activity of twelve German subjects in three different states: religious, happy, and neutral. One-half identified themselves as religious and the other half did not. The religious subjects were teachers in a private evangelical secondary school. Each related that they had had a conversion experience and that they read the Bible literally. The nonreligious were students at the University of Dusseldorf in the natural sciences. The subjects did not differ in visual imagination, verbal ability, personality, and life satisfaction.[179]

To trigger the religious state, the subjects recited Psalm 23, a biblical text of comfort in the trust in God as a shepherd. To produce the happy state, the subjects recited a German nursery rhyme. To reach a neutral state, the subjects just rested. Before the scans, the researchers tested and interviewed the subjects. And the subjects rated themselves about how well they had achieved the religious or happy state after the test.[180]

The results showed a difference between the religious and nonreligious in all three conditions. All of the self-identified religious subjects reported that they had reached the religious state. But none of the nonreligious subjects achieved it, though they said that they achieved the happy state.

These results showed that brain scans can identify the religious state in distinction from the happy and "at rest" states in the religious subjects. In this state, but not in the others, the most significant region among several areas of the brain involved was the *right dorsolateral prefrontal cortex*. Along with the *left temporal parietal junction*, this area is associated with the ability to take the perspective of another person and to respond and cooperate with others. It also plays a role in beliefs and in making inferences as well as managing thought and memory.[181]

The study confirmed the conclusions of earlier studies that besides the frontal areas, the parietal brain structures were also involved. These structures are associated with the ability to acquire and process information and knowledge. Azari et al. concluded that the experience is the result of complex, cognitive processes in the brain that are associated with the central factors of thoughts and beliefs.[182]

Evaluation of the Proposed Solution Using the Test Case

How does our proposal measure up to this test? The evangelical subjects had learned a specific form of religious experience. Like the Danish Lutherans, they were proficient in what they believed to be personal conversation with God. The research did not study the changes to the brain that this practice might have produced. Thus, it did not give empirical evidence of the *plasticity* of the brain. Both groups were able to recite the psalm. Moreover, presumably the nonreligious had the same brain systems as the religious. It was reported that the subjects were indifferent to religion.[183] They either chose not to use these systems to "converse" with God or did not develop them. Is "talking with God" a learned ability that changes the brain? Further research on evangelicals might test subjects before their conversion and at intervals after it. But the research did not go that far.

The experience of the evangelical subjects was a well-integrated whole. Like the Danish Lutherans, the experience of praying could not be separated from their believing in God. Azari states that the focus of the experience is on relationship. It is not merely an acceptance of a truth claim. It is a distinct knowledge of a *relationship with* a supernatural agent. This concept is what makes the experience "religious." It is a cultural force of evangelical Protestantism that works "top down" to direct and shape the operation of the brain.[184]

The test results disprove one "bottom-up" theory. This is the theory of Ramachandran and others that religion is a state of arousal before cognitive thought. As explained above, the malfunction of the temporal lobe and associated limbic structures cause an intense, emotional interest in religion and produce religious experiences. But as we have seen, the evangelical's religious experience of relationship is cognitive and founded on thought and belief, not raw emotions.[185] The test confirms the proposal of religious experience as an emergent phenomenon.

This is not to say that the religious experience of the evangelicals was purely an abstract idea. The experience was an *interaction* between the structures of the brain acting "bottom up" and the mental structure of the concept of *relationship with* a supernatural being acting "top down." The recitation of the psalm activated the physical systems of the brain. But these systems were already culturally programmed to induce a sense of a give-and-take conversation with God. Thus, the test confirms the proposed assertion of the interaction of brain, mind, and culture.[186]

Inside or Outside the Mind?

Some might be disappointed that the proposed solution has not referred to the "object" of religious experience such as a god, higher power, or spirit. However, we have sought a theory that would account for all types of religious experience within the discipline of religious studies and not theology. We have described religious experience of the relationship to or unity with divine beings. But we have also studied religious experiences that have a sense of transcendent oneness or consciousness without referring to supernatural agents. Therefore, we have tried to avoid a judgment on the question of whether the objects of belief and experience exist outside the human mind. Such an opinion would favor one type of experience over the others.

Is this escape clause warranted? According to philosophy of religion professor Wayne Proudfoot, it is not. He asserts that undergirding all religious experience is a conception of what is true and real. This sense of reality is given as special noetic knowledge in the experience. The sense of extraordinary knowledge is so powerful that the subject cannot help but believe it to be true. Thus, to the believer, the experience and its truth are self-justifying and need no further proof. Moreover, to a believer, those who realize such compelling truth in their personal experience will believe that it holds for others as well as for themselves.

But if others are to accept these claims, they will either have to trust the one who makes them or find some standard of judgment that would confirm or deny them.[187] This raises the question of whether scholars can believe the truth claims of those who have had religious experiences. Of course, theology would give an answer to this question. But if we moved to theological considerations, we would leave the field of religious studies, because theology accepts the presuppositions of the religion it represents. Other than the standards of a specific religion, we would have no standard of judging whether they were true or not.

Critical Realism as a Matter of Faith

If we cannot base religious studies on a specific theology, can we assume that *all* religious experiences point to a higher reality or consciousness? Prominent advocates of this theory of *critical realism* are world religions professor Huston Smith and philosopher John Hick. Critical realism agrees with Immanuel Kant that we cannot know anything directly. On the one hand, all knowledge is filtered through the human brain as fallible and limited. On the other hand, as realists, Hick and others hold that there are realities that are independent of our own minds. Our minds are not entirely deceived. There are "things out there" for us to know in our imperfect way. Hick states, "There are realities external to us. However, we are never aware of them as they are in themselves but always as they appear to us with our own particular cognitive machinery and conceptual resources."[188]

The critical realism of Hick and Smith is an attractive option. However, its beliefs are different from the beliefs of the religions that they embrace. Often, they are the opposite. For example, practically every religion teaches beliefs that contradict the ideas of other religions. Yet the critical realists gloss over these differences. For example, they maintain that despite their variety, all religions are true manifestations of the "Real," the "Ultimate," and the "Transcendent." This is a truth claim that is more a matter of faith than evidence.

Conclusion: As Far as Religious Studies Can Go

At a conference on religion and science, National Public Radio (NPR) religion correspondent Barbara Bradley Hagerty gave an answer to the question of the reality of the object of religious experience. She said the answer depends on two ideas of the brain.[189] Is it a CD player or a radio?

A CD player is a closed system. If we compare the brain to a CD player, we would suppose that if certain pathways in the brain would be destroyed, God and religious experience would disappear. However, she proposed that the brain might be like a radio. Radio waves exist outside the radios that receive them. It does not matter whether the radios are turned on or off and how high or low the volume is set. But humans would not know of the existence of radio waves without some kind of radio or receiver. Radios need to be tuned in to the radio waves to detect them. Even then, they can be tuned to different frequencies.

Expanding on this metaphor, the brain is equipped to sense the "waves" of supernatural realities or super-conscious insights. Whatever lies on the supernatural level exists whether the brain knows it or not. Yet human beings do not know these things without the receiving structures of the brain. Moreover, the fact that the brain picks up different kinds of religious sensations does not mean that the brain is making up whatever it wants to think. The brain tunes in to the already existing radio waves and puts them in a form the human ear can hear. Furthermore, the brain receives different aspects of the sacred, just as radios tune in to different wave frequencies.

By her metaphor of a radio, Hagerty raises an intriguing option that is a form of critical realism. Nevertheless, whether the brain is a CD or radio and whether critical realism is true are questions that go beyond the scope of religious studies. It must be left for other disciplines. Hagerty said that science cannot prove which view of the brain is correct because it cannot prove or disprove God.[190]

Even evolutionary science is incapable of answering the question. For example, evolutionary psychologists think that their concept of the hyperactive agency detection device disproves God. However, suppose that the human brain does have this device. It would not prove that there are no supernatural agents to detect. Believers in supernatural agents may respond that humans were created so that they could become aware of their Creator.

At the same conference, Hagerty speculated about a divine reality and said that the next question for the "science of spirituality" is the question of whether consciousness exists without the brain. Hagerty's remarks bear out David Brooks's prediction: the focus of interest in the study of religion has shifted from the endless debates about the existence of God to the nature of inner spiritual experience. The trend is clear. People in our century will demand freedom to explore different ways of spiritual experience. It is possible that many will look to neuroscience and not traditional religion to explain and confirm their spiritual journeys. The discipline of religious studies has an impressive foundation in the investigation of religious experience. But if it is to understand and interpret the shifting attitudes toward religion in the twenty-first century, it will have to reconsider the conclusions of the past. It will have to adjust its theories of religion to the new evidence from neuroscience, the surveys of social science, and the personal reports of contemporary people, as this chapter has tried to do.

KEY TERMS

Absolute Unitary Being (AUB): Andrew Newberg's term for the experience of being suspended beyond space in a state of "egolessness" and union with everything.

Agency detection: a term that evolutionary biologists use to explain why religious people often sense an invisible presence.

Altered states of consciousness: the term for mental states that are different from the ordinary, rational states.

Contextualism: the philosophy that nothing can be known or understood "in itself" but only in the situation in which it appears. In the study of religious experience, the theory that the cultural interpretation of religious experience cannot be separated from it.

Critical realism: the philosophy that assumes that we cannot know anything directly. All knowledge is filtered through the human brain. Yet it also assumes that there are "realities" outside the mind that we know indirectly and imperfectly through our mental structures.

Emergence theory: the theory that the mind is different from the brain because it is a complex but whole system (of systems) that depends on its parts and yet exists as a distinct entity.

Essentialism: the philosophy that each thing has a built-in set of properties that make the thing what it is and distinguish it from all other things. In the study of religious experience, it describes theories that posit a "common core" of defining characteristics of religious experience.

Extrovertive mysticism: according to W. T. Stace, the basic type of mysticism that retains a sense of the distinction between what the mystic is united to and the mystic.

Feminism: a broad set of movements that concern justice for women. These movements regard gender as a major category of analyzing human life and the gender politics of male domination over women as the major dynamic of society.

Hierarchy of needs: according to Maslow, the series of levels of human needs that are fulfilled in succession until one reaches the highest state of human fulfillment, the peak experience.

Ineffable: according to William James, the characteristic of religious experience that describes how the experience is so awesome that it cannot be put into words.

Introvertive mysticism: according to W. T. Stace, the basic type of mysticism in which there is no sense of division or distinction, whether within the mind or without it. All is one.

Modular theory: a disputed theory that the brain has different systems (modules), each of which has its own way of operating in specific areas of mental activity. Evolutionary biologists use this theory to explain how religious experience is a product of evolution.

Mysticism: the practice of the direct experience of transcendent realities not accessible to the senses.

Neuroscience of religion: the field of research that applies scientific and technological methods of studying the brain to investigate religion and religious experience.

Noetic: according to William James, a characteristic of religious experience that fills the subject with profound and deep insight into realities not accessible to the senses.

Patriarchy: various forms of ordering society in which men have power and control over women and children.

Peak experiences: according to Maslow, the highest sense of human fulfillment that is attained once other needs are met.

Perennial Philosophy: a term that Aldous Huxley invented to speak of the "common core" of universal concepts of the connection of the "soul" or "higher consciousness" with a transcendent Reality. It is "perennial" because it arises in vastly different cultural contexts.

Plasticity of the brain: the research finding that the brain is pliable and moldable even after the assumed period of formation in early childhood.

Pure Consciousness: according to the Yoga Master Patañjali, the state in which there is no longer any divisions or distinctions in awareness. The mind is completely unified in a state without separate thoughts.

Temporal lobe epilepsy (TLE): a disorder of the brain in which there are seizures in the temporal lobe. This lobe plays a key role in perception. In some persons the TLE condition is associated with interest, even obsession, with religion.

KEY QUESTIONS

1. Mysticism
   a. Describe the characteristics of mysticism according to religious scholarship.
   b. Is the study of mysticism adequate for our understanding of religious experience? Explain your answer, citing the research evidence from religious surveys.
2. Surveys of Religious Experience
   a. How do the surveys of religious experience challenge the attitude of William James and other past scholars about the value of the religious experiences of ordinary people?
   b. List three types of religious experience and give an example of each.
3. Neuroscience of Religion
   a. Some have suggested that the recent brain research indicates that religious experience is "merely brain chemistry." Do you agree? Defend your answer.

     b. Explain how the technology of brain imaging shows the structures and processes of the brain when a person is involved in a religious or meditative experience.

     c. Explain why brain research depends on the self-reports of the subjects of the experiment as well as the brain imaging technology.

4. Plasticity of the Brain and Spiritual Development

     a. Explain what is meant by the "plasticity of the brain."

     b. According to the theory of the "plasticity of the brain," what effect do habits of prayer and meditation have on the brain?

5. Emergent Character of Culture and the Interaction of Brain, Mind, and Culture

     a. Explain what is meant by the "emergent" character of culture.

     b. In the example of the test study of Germans who recited a psalm and a nursery rhyme, explain the roles of the brain and of culture in their religious experience of personal "conversation" with God.

6. Critical Realism and the Results of the Chapter

     a. Explain why Hagerty's analogy of the radio that receives radio waves expresses the ideas of critical realism.

     b. Evaluate evolutionary biology's ideas of the origin of religion from the point of view of critical realism. Then, conversely, evaluate the theory that critical realism gives of the origin of religion from the point of view of evolutionary biology. What premise of critical realism does evolutionary biology reject?

6

Trouble in the Global Village

Violence in the Name of Religion

CHAPTER SUMMARY

1. Discovering the Problem: Strange Actions and Odd Alliances

Religious tensions and violence have grown so much that Christian and Muslim leaders are joining in efforts to solve them. Likewise, a noted atheist has proposed that religious education might make religious violence less likely. Both strategies against religious violence assume that the problem is the lack of understanding of religion. Nonetheless, despite the typical teachings of love and peace, religion has been involved in violence in various ways throughout history. In the twenty-first century, religious aggression has become even more troublesome.

2. Focusing the Problem: The Complexities of Religious Violence

Religious violence is a complex topic. Scholars classify it into different types and motivations. This section will outline the categories of analysis and give examples. The rise of religious violence since the last of the twentieth century was a surprise to most scholars. They had assumed the secularization thesis. They assumed that secularization had worked and that religion would no longer incite social and political conflict. When that supposition turned out to be incorrect, the field of religious studies scrambled to devise theories that would explain this sudden reappearance of religiously driven violence. The problem of this chapter is to sort through these approaches to religious violence to find a valid and useful theory that would understand its nature and causes.

3. Surveying the Alternative Approaches: What Does Violence Have to Do with Religion?

This section will divide the alternatives for solving the problem of religious violence into categories that religions are naturally violent, sometimes violent, or violent if false. Within these categories, the sections will present the selected views of atheism, political theory, psychology, sociology global studies, and religious studies.

The evaluation of these theories finds significant flaws in all of them. The theories tend to focus on single factors that cannot account for all the dynamics of the problem. The review of the theories leads to the conclusion that religion in itself does not produce violence. Religion becomes a sponsor of violence under certain conditions.

4. Proposing the Most Promising Solution: A Multiple Conditions Approach

Thoroughgoing studies of the Carnegie Commission and R. Scott Appleby have identified five sets of conditions for the involvement of religion in violence: sociological, psychological, educational, political, and religious. According to this theory, religion serves as a catalyst for violence when multiple conditions for violence are present. The role of religious leaders is crucial. They can lead their followers to respond peacefully or violently to the conditions of grievance.

5. *Evaluating the Most Promising Solution: Empirical and Practical Tests*
   Jonathan J. Fox's analysis of the empirical data offers an independent confirmation of the five-conditions theory. The application of theory to the peacemaking work also supports the theory. The five factors can be identified in the situation of the Pakistani *madrasas* (schools based on the Qur'an). These peacemakers are encouraging religious leaders to promote the peaceful resolution of their grievances, not violence. The section ends with reflections on the relationship of theory to its practical application in religious studies.

DISCOVERING THE PROBLEM: STRANGE ACTIONS AND ODD ALLIANCES

Perhaps the most troubling thing about religion in the twenty-first century is the rise of religious conflict. Strange things are happening nowadays in response to the worldwide threat of violence in the name of religion.

For example, a number of Muslim clerics met in Rome with Pope Benedict XVI and other Catholic leaders in November 2008 for three days. The aim was to relieve growing tensions between Christians and Muslims. In a concluding joint statement, the conference concluded that Catholics and Muslims alike have a calling to "promote love and harmony among believers" and to renounce any "oppression, aggressive violence, and terrorism, especially what is committed in the name of religion."[1]

Tensions Bring Religious Leaders Together

The meeting marked an astonishing turn of events. Just two years earlier, the new pope had infuriated the Muslim world. In a scholarly lecture against modern secularism, Pope Benedict had quoted a Byzantine emperor of the fourteenth century. The quote said that the Islamic prophet Muhammad had only brought forced conversions, holy war, and inhumanity to the world. The pope was trying to say that reason, not hostility, should inform religious faith. However, that thought was lost in the negative remark about the founder of Islam. Instantly, the obscure comment unleashed furious worldwide protest, including the fire bombings of a church in Iraq and five churches in the West Bank and Palestine.[2] The pontiff was even burned in effigy in India.[3]

Alarmed, the pope quickly said he was "deeply sorry" and that the quotation did not express his own views.[4] But within a month, 138 Islamic scholars from across the Muslim world published an open letter pointing out the speech's misunderstandings of Islam. The official website for the scholars claimed that it was the first time in recent history that Muslim clerics had issued a common message on the truth of Islam.[5]

A year later, a broader statement expanded the "Open Letter" to the pope. The Muslim clerics sent the groundbreaking document to Catholic, Protestant, and Orthodox Christian leaders. Titled "A Common Word between Us and You," it asserted that the world's future depends on peace between Christianity and Islam, since the believers of these two religions include over one-half of the world's population. Further, the letter stated that the harmony between the two faiths could be founded on the common ethic of love.[6]

This document prompted the November 2008 meeting with the pope at the Vatican. In turn, the conference with the pope led to the establishment of a Catholic-Muslim forum. In the months that followed, many religious scholars praised the letter as a step toward easing the tensions between Christians and Muslims. In the same spirit, Protestant and Eastern Orthodox Christian leaders also responded favorably to the Muslim initiative. Over 300 Protestant leaders signed a "Christian Response" to its results.[7] Also responding positively were the Russian Orthodox patriarch of Moscow, the Church of England's archbishop of Canterbury, and the two chief rabbis of the State of Israel.[8]

According to Giorgio Bernardelli, the letter "created an unprecedented echo" in the West and Muslim countries.[9] Bernardelli added that the letter is still a "reference point" for Christian-Muslim conversations. After inspiring numerous events, it was the basis of the United Nations' declaration of an annual "World Interfaith Harmony Week." The UN resolution affirms that the common values of "people of good will" far exceed their differences.[10]

One could never have predicted that a single negative remark of a Catholic pope about Islam would eventually lead to such positive results. In summary, the global climate of religious conflict forced the leaders of the two largest world religions to draw back from their traditional differences. The furious response to the pope's comment showed that relations had gotten out of hand. The key leaders of both religions acted swiftly to prevent the escalation of historic animosities into open hostilities.

Tensions and Violence Remain

In spite of years of meetings, however, the relations between Christians and Muslims remain tense, if not volatile. The "Common Word" website posted an article from *Christianity Today* that asked whether relations had improved since 9/11. The answer was that relations between the West and Muslim societies had not improved. One church leader said that the tensions had become worse. Despite the positive development of interfaith, peacemaking programs, fear of Muslims had grown in America. In addition, persecutions of Christians in several Muslim countries had occurred.[11] At a conference to establish Muslim-Christian peacemaking teams, Jordanian Prince Ghazi bin Muhammad bin Talal also noted the friction between Christians and Muslims in an astounding list of places of hostility.[12]

If we think critically about this situation, we note a contradiction between the statements of the religious leaders about peace and the actions of their followers. The joint declaration of the original meeting between the Muslims and

Pope Benedict said that Muslims and Christians are to be "instruments of love and harmony." It urged believers to renounce aggression and uphold justice. It referred to the common morality of the "love of God and neighbor."[13]

Nevertheless, we might ask: If love is the moral basis of both religions, as the statement declares, why are the warnings against hatred, revenge, and violence necessary? Why must religions that teach "love and harmony" emphatically renounce "any oppression, aggressive violence, and terrorism . . . especially in the name of religion"?[14] It would seem that all believers of these religions would understand that.

The answer lies within the traditions of each religion. Both of them have histories that include religious warfare. Both religions cling to doctrines of justified violence. Both have principles regarding the conduct of war. The Christian and Muslim proclamations of peace, therefore, do not rule out the possibility of violence. The Muslim "Open Letter," for example, says that *jihad* is the "struggle in the way of God" and that it "takes many forms including the use of force."[15] Similarly, Christianity's tradition of "just war" goes back to the founder of Western theology, Augustine. Each religion also must admit that religious violence is in its history. Thus, the leaders of the two largest world religions have reason to warn their followers against taking up arms against each other.

The process that brought many leaders of Western monotheism together produced some strange but welcome results. However, the academic study of religion must ask about the unspoken assumptions about religion and violence lying below the public statements of religious officials. The pronouncements of the Muslim and Christian leaders seem to assume that misunderstanding is the cause of religious aggression. If believers would only grasp the central moral teachings of their religion, they would abandon any thought of violence. They would do so especially if they knew that their potential enemies also share the same ethic. However, that notion overlooks the teaching of the legitimate use of force that both religions share. At times, misunderstanding is not the cause of violence. Genuine threats and grievances provoke it. Therefore, the invocation of "love and harmony" does not always banish religious violence from these religions.

The fact is that religious violence has been an aspect of religion in the past. And it is a persistent aspect of religion in the present. We can laud the efforts of enlightened religious leaders. Nevertheless, we have to ask about the underlying causes and complex dynamics of violence among Christianity, Islam, and all religions. Is violence so entangled with religion that religion cannot exist without it? Or is violence just a choice that is either unavoidable or misguided?

Religious Violence Prompts an Atheist to Promote Public Religious Education

The alliance of Muslims and Christian leaders might be surprising. Even more astonishing is the proposal of the atheist philosopher Daniel Dennett. In a book written in 1995, Dennett spoke harshly against parents who teach their children that the Earth is flat and that Darwin was wrong. Dennett insisted that religion has no place in modern society except in museums. The future of the Earth depended on teaching children not to pay any attention to religion.[16]

Ten years later, Dennett decided that merely criticizing religion would not break its spell. Likewise, merely teaching more science would not get rid of religion. Dennett concluded that children should be inoculated against religion's absolute and fanatical claims. So he surprised everyone with the suggestion that all school children should be exposed to the teachings of all major world religions. That's right. He launched a campaign to promote compulsory education about religion in schools.

Dennett proposes that all students, from kindergarten to twelfth grade, should be required to learn about the major religions of the world. Even parents who homeschool their children would be required to teach the basic "facts" of religions—their beliefs, customs, rituals, texts, prohibitions, morals, and so forth. And no, Dennett does not care about the attitude of teachers regarding the subject of religion. He states that as long as the teachers do not try to close the minds of students or keep them from asking questions, they may teach whatever doctrines they want.[17] Any religious beliefs? Even teachings against Darwin? Dennett says that he does not care if teachers call the curriculum "garbage, the work of Satan, and a miserable political compromise rammed down our throats." The students will be tested on it and poor test results will put the school's credentials into jeopardy.[18]

It seems that Dennett has changed his mind. Now he wants American students to have *more* knowledge about religion, not less. Bring it on! But if Dennett believes that religion is outdated, erroneous, and dangerous, why should he want students to be exposed to it? We might assume that any atheist would want to ban the teaching of religion in the public schools along with school prayer. What is Dennett up to?

The answer is that Dennett is concerned about the subject of this chapter: religious violence. Deterring religious conflict seems to be more important to him than promoting the truth of Darwinism. Like the Muslim and Christian leaders in the case above, he is alarmed by the raging fires of religious violence sweeping across the globe. He states that sometimes, though not often, religions go berserk with group hysteria. He asks, "What if these fanatics get their hands on modern weapons of mass destruction?"[19]

These concerns lead Dennett to plead for a renewed study of religion in today's world. He states that scholars of religion should teach how religion works. More than that, scholars should investigate why some religious people turn to violence and some do not. Dennett even admits that there are fair-minded believers in all religions. He wants to join other believers and nonbelievers in examining "the moral quandaries of the world [like religious violence] on a rational basis."[20]

Dennett's call for the study of religion puts him in strange company. Religious leaders might easily endorse Dennett's program in its broad outline. At least they might applaud his intentions. Like Dennett, the Muslim and Christian leaders who are now talking about "A Common Word" seek to disarm religious fanaticism. Anxiety about religious violence has brought the two largest religions of the world together to seek ways of understanding and cooperation. Incredibly, it seems to have united these same believers and a prominent atheist in a common interest in acquainting children with religion. But like the Muslim and Christian leaders, Dennett also makes some assumptions about religion and violence. To him, religion is an irrational and improvable belief in the supernatural. Most belief is foolish but benign. However, some forms become "toxic" when they excuse suicide bombings and other violent acts that otherwise would be considered atrocities.[21] Moreover, Dennett believes that religious beliefs spread like viruses. As children can be vaccinated against measles, so they can be vaccinated against religion, especially its "toxic" forms.

Despite his negative attitude toward religion, the assumptions of Dennett's program are not far from those of the Muslim-Christian interfaith effort. Like the religious leaders, Dennett distinguishes between types of religion that are acceptable and forms of religion that are malignant. Like the religious leaders, he believes that education about world religions as well as toleration are the keys to the prevention of violence. Unlike the religious leaders, of course, Dennett does not believe that any religion is true.

Both the religious leaders and Dennett are primarily interested in developing programs for the prevention of religious violence. These programs are based on theories about the nature, causes, and effective remedies for religious violence. The main idea of the religious leaders is that teaching the basic moral values that religions share will promote mutual understanding and prevent religious violence. Dennett's chief idea is that teaching about other religions will widen the viewpoints of students with the same result.

But what if these theories are mistaken or incomplete? If the underlying theory is flawed, the methods of prevention based on it will be ineffective.

FOCUSING THE PROBLEM:
THE COMPLEXITIES OF RELIGIOUS VIOLENCE

Religions clothe themselves in the garments of peace and goodwill. Yet with few exceptions, religions are not so innocent of aggression. Most have had illicit affairs with the gods of war. Yet, even if religious institutions have not drawn the sword themselves, they have found ingenious ways of excusing those who do. Nowadays, the observation of the philosopher Duane Cady does not shock anyone: "It is difficult, perhaps impossible, to find a major global conflict where religion has no crucial part among the unions and divisions in contention."[22]

Most people want immediate solutions to violence. But the instinct of the academic study of religion is to probe into the question of why religion is implicated in violence. Therefore, this chapter proposes that once we know the nature and causes of religious violence, we will be able to deal with it.

Three Levels of Religious Violence

The starting place is to understand the nature of violence. We can identify three broad levels of such violence: personal and domestic, group and society, and nation-state and international.[23] (See the textbox "Three Levels of Violence.")

Three Levels of Violence

1. Personal and domestic: the mental and physical harm that members of a household inflict on women and others
2. Group and society: the persecution, discrimination, and segregation of one group in society against another, usually not for political goals
3. Nation-state and international: violence involving nationalism that often has political as well as religious goals

This chapter will deal primarily with the second and third types as social and national violence is the common emphasis in the twenty-first century, the wars in Iraq and Afghanistan, and the war on terror. The key to understanding these types and the role of religion in them is the matter of "legitimacy." Violence can get social approval for religious as well as political reasons. Likewise, both political powers and religions can disapprove violence.

Legitimate and Illegitimate Violence

In *Holy Terrors*, historian of religions Bruce Lincoln uses the concepts of legitimate and illegitimate violence to analyze religious conflict. On that basis, Lincoln divides religions into "Religions of the Status Quo, Religions of Resistance, and Religions of Revolution."[24] (See the textbox "Types of Religious Conflict.")

Types of Religious Conflict

Type of Religion	Group & Society	Nation-State & International
Religions of the Status Quo		Religious war Religiously sanctioned war
Religions of Resistance	Majority oppression of a minority Minority against another minority	
Religions of Revolution		Ethnic-religious rebellion against the government

Religions of the status quo are religious authorities that uphold the power and privileges of the ruling class of a society. In this type, a dominant class controls the government. The government gives privileges to a favored religion. In return, the favored religion gives sacred legitimacy to the government and its exclusive right to use deadly force.

Religions of the status quo may become entangled in two forms of religious conflict that can be categorized as "nation-state and international violence." In each case, the dominant class will consider the conflict legitimate. The ruling class of a society may engage in *religious hostilities* with a rival religion. For example, Catholicism was the "religion of the status quo" of the dominant class in medieval Europe. It waged the Crusades against what it considered a rival religion, Islam. Alternatively, the dominant class may simply use religion to endorse a war of the *nation against another nation*, basically for secular purposes.[25]

For example, in World War II the United States fought against the nation-states of Germany, Italy, and Japan. America did so with the full backing of the "religions of the status quo" at that time—Judaism, Protestantism, and Catholicism. Note that in this case, the American society considered the warfare "legitimate."

On the other hand, *religions of resistance* inevitably arise when governments do not have the support of their citizens. This type has its origins in the alienation of certain groups from the government and society. Often, they will demonstrate their alienation by refusing to accept the ideology of the established religion. These alienated powerless groups may be involved in violence in two ways.

First, they may be the victims of violence from the ruling class. A dominant ethnic/religious group may oppress a minority group without *direct* government involvement. Technically, this would represent illegitimate violence. However, the government and the religion of the status quo may ignore it or passively condone it.

For instance, from 1880 to 1930 white supremacist groups like the Ku Klux Klan were responsible for the lynching of over 5,000 African Americans. Mary Talbert and other African American women in the NAACP led the fight for legislation to end these racist atrocities. The protest raised national awareness, but it did not result in government action. From 1901 to 1920, the United States Congress repeatedly refused to adopt bills that would penalize state, county, and local governments for failing to prevent the lynchings of African Americans. Federal inaction amounted to tacit government permission for this "group and society" violence.

Second, an ethnic/religious group with a religious ideology that has no political power may target another group that does not have power either. In this case, the ruling class considers the violence to be illegitimate.

Take, for example, the terrorism of "The Order," a white-supremacist group in Idaho. This group was responsible for a crime spree that climaxed in the murder of Denver radio host Alan Berg in 1984.[26] It is part of the larger anti-Semitic Christian Identity Movement. An estimated 50,000 members in the United States are involved in this faction. It believes that the final battle of Armageddon will be a race war.[27] The movement does not engage in national or international violence because it has little political power or influence. Instead, its hatred is directed against minority groups that also have little political clout. We can classify its aggression as "group and society violence."

Religions of revolution occur when religions of resistance break out of their defensive stance toward the government. Lincoln observes that the alienated groups will revolt against the established order under certain conditions. One condition is that groups must suffer extreme oppression. Another is that they must question the legitimacy of the government. If such conditions are met, the group will become aggressive. It will marshal recruits and resources for violent attacks on the government.

This type of violence is typically *ethnic* because it involves a cultural group whose members claim a distinctive identity. It is typically *religious* in the sense that a particular religion defines the group's cultural identity. It is *political* because it has aims to create or defend goals of national sovereignty.[28] Inevitably, the majority group will label this type of violence "terrorism."

An example of the violence of "religions of revolution" was the failed effort of the separatist Hindu Tamil Tigers against the Buddhist majority government of Sri Lanka. Another example is the uprising of Muslims in the Philippines against a government dominated by Roman Catholics. According to the Center for International Development and Conflict Management, in the 1950s Christians began migrating into Moro tribal areas of the southern Philippines.[29] The new settlers were Catholic and represented the favored majority in the Philippines. The local residents, the Moros, were a collection of southern tribes with a Muslim culture. When the Catholic Christians began moving into the territory of the Moros, conflicts arose about the use of land and resources. Then violence erupted as Christians and Muslims organized armed defense groups.

If that was as far as it went, we could categorize the Moro uprising as "group and society" violence. However, as the hostility increased, the conflict became political. The Moros took the next step when they formed the Muslim (Mindanao) Independence Movement (MIM). From this organization, two revolutionary groups arose, the Moro National Liberation Front (MNLF) and the breakaway Moro Islamic Liberation Front (MILF). The cause became a "religion of revolution," and the violence became permeated with political nationalistic goals.

Terrorism

The distinction between legitimate and illegitimate raises the question of terrorism, a concept that implies violence that the majority of society deems repulsive. "Terrorism" comes from the Latin *terrere*, meaning "to cause to tremble." The term first referred to "an assault on the civil order" during the "Reign of Terror" of the French Revolution.[30]

The word stirs up emotions because its popular use refers to heinous attacks on noncombatants meant to intimidate the civilian population. However, if we look at the term "terrorism" objectively, we find that it refers to violence that is unlawful in the eyes of established governments. Terrorists commit acts of desperation as a means of grasping power or influence.[31] "Religions of resistance" that are deprived of voting or other political rights may turn to terrorism. In doing so, they become "religions of revolution." Such groups are likely to engage in the "guerilla" tactics of "asymmetric" warfare that offset their relative weakness. To their supporters, they are revolutionaries.

In summary, religious violence is more complex than the common use of the word "terrorism" suggests. The challenge of religious scholars is to develop the approaches and tools that would give an informed and insightful interpretation of violence in its various forms.

The Challenge: Finding a Viable Theory

Since the last part of the twentieth century, the field of religious studies has tried to make sense of the complex conditions and causes of violence that we have outlined. At the outset, the majority of scholars had to change their minds. Most had assumed the *secularization thesis*—that the process of secularization had almost succeeded in banishing religion from the political realm. Because it had been stripped of any connection with military as well as political power, religion could no longer stir up trouble.

Of course, the scholars of religious studies still were concerned about religion. But other teachers and researchers in the fields simply wrote religion off. The field of international relations believed that the time when religion could cause wars was over. Likewise, sociologists believed that modern leaders could now construct societies on rational and scientific foundations without considering religion. All academic disciplines looked for causes of war and violence in economic and military as well as political factors, not religion.[32]

Then, unexpectedly, the world turned upside down. Scholars had to make sense of the prominent role that religion had assumed in national and world politics. Scholars worked hard to devise theories to explain the disturbing re-emergence of bloody conflicts involving religion. Was it religion itself—or at least unrefined religion—that had not been tamed by modernism? Was it certain religions? Was a perversion of religion to blame?

The critical problem was to find a theory that would explain the seeming rise of religious violence. Since the turn of the century, many have proposed such theories. The problem of this chapter is to find a theory that would support a strategy for reining in the many types of religious violence. We are seeking a general theory of the nature and causes of religious violence that would be both valid and useful for addressing it.

SURVEYING THE ALTERNATIVE APPROACHES: WHAT DOES VIOLENCE HAVE TO DO WITH RELIGION?

One approach to the theories of religious violence is to categorize them according to different topics of study. Sociologist Charles Selengut presents such a list in *Sacred Fury*:[33]

- *Scriptural*: conflict as it is inspired or justified by sacred scriptures
- *Psychological*: conflict as it fulfills psychological drives
- *Civilizational*: conflict between broad cultural groups
- *Apocalyptic*: conflict driven by otherworldly goals against evil and for salvation and eternal reward
- *Sacred Suffering*: beliefs in martyrdom and self-sacrifice that has religious ends

This chapter will consider the validity and usefulness of the theories as well as review them. To do this, we will need a simple format. We want to address the question, "Why do religions get involved in violence?" The theories that we will study are divided by their fundamental presuppositions (see the textbox "Presuppositions of Theories of Religious Violence").

Presuppositions of Theories of Religious Violence

- All religions are violent by nature.
- Some religions are inherently violent, while others are not.
- Only false religions are violent.
- Religions go bad under certain conditions and in combination with certain other nonreligious factors.

Religions Are Violent by Nature

The survey of the types and evidence of religious aggression might lead us to believe that religious violence is neither incidental nor exceptional. There must be something wrong with religion that even meetings between the pope and Islamic world leaders cannot fix. Religion must somehow be inherently violent.

The Argument from History: Dawkins and Harris

Richard Dawkins and Sam Harris are theorists who argue that the historical evidence is clear enough. History proves that religion is not only irrational but also intrinsically violent. As Dawkins begins his book *The God Delusion*, he asks his readers to picture a world with no religion. He asserts that a world without religion would be a world without the atrocities that he selects from world history: wars, persecutions, suicide bombings, witch-hunts, scandals, financial scams, oppression of women, and so forth.[34] By reminding his readers of the horrors that religion has committed, Dawkins suggests that the world would be a more peaceful place without it.

In the same vein, Sam Harris claims in *The End of Faith* that religion caused "millions of deaths in the last ten years." He asserts that religion is now, and always has been, a source of violence because "religions are *intrinsically* hostile to one another."[35]

Dawkins and Harris make graphic references to genocide; suicide bombing that kills innocent civilians; rioting, raping and pillaging; blood feuds; slavery; prejudice; racism and anti-Semitism; persecution; execution for blasphemy or apostasy; crusades and holy wars; abuse of women; sexual abuse of children; and many other horrible things that have been done in the name of religion. They argue that these atrocities are sufficient proof of the built-in malice of religion.

For both writers, the "bad faith" of religion makes religion dangerous. Dawkins claims that this threat is even more serious because of the possibility that religious fanatics could get their hands on weapons of mass destruction. Harris goes on to say that today's global society must get rid of religion because "billions of our neighbors" believe in the lethal combination of martyrdom and the catastrophic end of the world. These beliefs might prompt them to acquire and use chemical or nuclear weapons.[36]

Why Is Religion Naturally Aggressive?

For Dawkins, absolutism, fundamentalism, and "strong religious faith" go together. Absolutism believes in truths and morals without evidence or logic. Its opinions are unqualified certainties. Fundamentalism is a form of absolutism because it believes in the literal truths of the Bible without exception. Moreover, "strong faith" is another type of absolutism because it holds to its beliefs without doubt or wavering.[37]

What is wrong with absolutism? Absolutist claims divide human beings against one another. Because of religious hostility, believers end up killing one another. The irony is that they murder each other in the name of an absolutist God that cannot be proven and does not exist.[38]

Harris believes that the West made religion a private matter because it recognized that religion was a threat to society. Nevertheless, he thinks that this strategy of secularization is impossible. Religious beliefs, he says, lead to violence because they are principles of action. When believers inevitably put these beliefs into action, they affect others.

Why Religious Moderates Are Still to Blame

Many believers would object to the charges of Dawkins and Harris against religion. They would insist that they are neither fanatical nor intolerant. They say that they are not involved in violence, and therefore not all religions are intrinsically violent.

A common objection to the charge that religious people hold absolute and intolerant beliefs is that not all believers have such extreme views. The response of the "new atheists" to this fact makes clear the reason why they think that all religions pose a threat to the world. According to Dawkins, even though they may condemn religious violence, religious moderates still set the climate for religious extremism. They remain responsible for religious aggression because they teach children to accept the certainties of religious belief.[39] This uncritical attitude makes their children susceptible to absolutist claims. Instead of teaching children to accept such dangerous nonsense, Dawkins wishes that we would teach our children to think for themselves. Then demagogues and hucksters who want to march them off to war could not influence them.

Harris presses the charge against religious moderates even further. He says that moderation in religion is a myth. Moderates are not true believers because they mix ancient and silly religious beliefs with more educated modern ones. They are "failed fundamentalists" because they do not live up to the literal "letter of the texts" of the scriptures. They use the scriptures selectively and thus inconsistently. The implication is that the moderates do not "really believe." Their moderation comes from other modern cultural factors and not their religion. Harris assumes that he knows their religion better than they do. So the moderates are responsible for religious violence because they are tolerant of those who "*really* believe" in the unreasonable teachings of religion, which he believes obviously incite bloodshed.[40]

Dawkins sums up the argument of both theorists by asserting that suicide bombers believe that they owe God their highest devotion and that God will reward them in Paradise for absolute dedication. Killing others even by the most atrocious deeds is simply a way to put this belief into action. Where did they get this idea of absolute religious commitment? Dawkins alleges it was from their kind, gentle, and moderate schoolteachers.[41] Thus, moderate religious teachers unwittingly infect their children with ideas that lead to aggression.

Why Is Religion So Widespread When It Is So Harmful to Human Life?

If religion is so harmful to human life, why is it so widespread? A clue is the contention that moderates contaminate youngsters with a "mental virus." Somebody gets an idea of a spirit or a god and it appeals to others. So, like viruses, religious beliefs spread by reproduction. Dawkins uses genetic theory as an analogy. As genes copy themselves through countless generations, so there are units of "cultural replication" that are self-reproducing.[42]

Dawkins calls these units *memes*. Memes reproduce as humans pass them around from one person to the other through a process of imitation. Memes can be skills like constructing paper airplanes or they can be sophisticated beliefs. Like human genes, memes exist in a pool or set of competing units. The measure of success of each unit is not whether it gives humans any worthwhile advantage. The measure of success is whether the meme gets reproduced. In the meme pool some units excel at replication because they have a certain psychological appeal in themselves. For example, the belief in immortality satisfies wishful thinking. Other units persist because they fit together with other memes in a complex of memes.[43] For example, beliefs about escaping the relentless wheel of karma (the law of cause and effect) fit into the Hindu beliefs in reincarnation.

We note that Dawkins recognizes that his theory is only an analogy.[44] But he states that it is a useful comparison for explaining the origins of religion and its intrinsic association with violence. It supports the idea that religion is irrational and that those who advocate religious ideas are irrational. Moreover, it explains religious violence by proposing that religion is a violent contagion that infects the human race.

The Argument from Psychology

French anthropologist and literary critic René Girard offers us another major theory that explains why violence is intrinsic to religion. For Girard, religion is the heart of culture. But within that heart, something is hidden. Religion insists that it is good and makes people good. Indeed, Girard believes that. Nevertheless, violence lurks within its supposed goodness.

Dawkins and Harris believe that religion causes the problem of religious aggression. Girard believes that it represents the *solution* to human violence. However, the foundation of that solution is a dreadful secret, a secret that religion keeps even from itself.

To disclose what religion will not admit, Girard begins with some basic human emotions: jealousy, covetousness, resentment, and revenge. Girard agrees with the world's religions that human beings are driven by desire. But Girard points out that humans learn *what* to desire from one another. Human beings are inveterate imitators. Therefore, when we see that others want something, we want it too.

Human Conflict as Rivalry

Girard names this human disposition to imitate others *mimesis*. Mimesis, in fact, is the source of civilization, because people learn from one another primarily by imitation. For example, children learn most of what they need to know to be integrated into society by the magic of mimicry.[45] Thus, imitation builds society.

On the other hand, imitation tears down society. It is the mechanism of conflict through what Girard calls *mimetic rivalry*. Competition with others arises because we learn from one another what is valuable. This means that we instinctively want what others have. And we will fight to get it like two children fighting over a toy in a sandbox. (See the textbox "A Scenario of Mimetic Conflict.") Unchecked, this mimetic rivalry is bound to end in acts of aggression. Since humans are so prone to imitate each other, downward spirals of mimetic (imitative) violence will inevitably ensue.[46]

> ### A Scenario of Mimetic Conflict
>
> Watch two small children in the sandbox with an assortment of toys. Suzy randomly chooses a toy truck to play with. Betsy now sees what Suzy has. Instantly, the truck becomes the most precious toy in the sandbox. Betsy is now obsessed with getting the toy; Suzy is now focused on making sure that Betsy does not get it. They start to fight over the truck. Pretty soon, the bad feelings of the fight take over. The truck is forgotten. Now each child merely wants to get back at the other. The conflict escalates to become a veritable sandbox battle.

Girard observes that what is true of personal relationships holds for social groups and whole societies. The power of imitation is so strong that competition between a few people will attract other contestants until the rivalry spreads like a contagion to the whole group.[47]

So far, we have conflict driven by the basic human emotions of desire, jealousy, covetousness, resentment, and revenge. Imitation turns into competition and competition spreads so that it takes over whole societies and cultures. At this stage, we have violence, but it is not yet religious.

To explain the source of religious aggression, Girard observes that the conflict over the object spirals to another level. The contestants no longer fight each other just to win the object. Each fights to conquer the other. Revenge takes the place of envy. Resentment takes the place of jealousy. The rivals begin to mirror one another's animosity to each other. The imitators become "doubles" of each other as they mutually thwart one another.[48]

For example, suppose that two workers have a petty disagreement that grows into a major conflict. They become entangled in mutual animosity. Each one does his best to get back at the other. As doubles, they mirror each other's aggression.

The Scapegoat and the End of Rivalry

If conflict gets to the point of resentment and revenge, a simple resolve to forgive and forget will probably not resolve it. According to Girard's psychological theory, a *catharsis* or purgation of the deep and contradictory emotions is necessary. This is especially true if the rivalry has spread to the whole work crew. Most likely, if the hostility is deep enough, this will happen. The members of the group will take sides, and the tension will be multiplied.

In Girard's theory, the *scapegoat* provides a surprising way of resolving the escalating antagonism. At a critical point, the conflict gets out of hand. Now both sides reflect the rancor of each other. All have forgotten why they are fighting. Now winning is everything.

In the case of the two rival workers, suppose that one of the work crew has stood aloof, not wanting to get involved. Then it happens that someone notices that he has not taken part in the dispute. The group turns on this unhappy bystander because he is different from them. Both sides begin to taunt him. Soon everyone begins to blame him for the group dysfunction. Alienated from everyone in the group, the crewmember quits. The work group is surprised but relieved. For the moment, it believes that the cause of its troubles has been eliminated.

The conflict of the workers exemplifies Girard's theory that at a critical point of mimetic crisis, the cycle of violence turns from division to group solidarity. The means of this astonishing transformation is the scapegoat. The scapegoat becomes a convenient lightning rod for the anger that the members of the group have built up against one another. Why the group picks a particular individual as a scapegoat does not really matter. The victim just needs to be different, helpless, blamable, and available. Driven by unconscious feelings, the warring parties unite to gang up on this hapless victim. The infuriated throng heaps the full force of its fury on the victim. The victim suffers horribly. But his death brings the catharsis of cleansing of the bad feelings of hostility. The wrath of the crowd is satisfied. Its hostility is exhausted. Former enemies experience a rare moment of harmony and peace.

So far, this theory does not seem to involve religion. In Girard's view, religion arises on the "day after" the dreadful event of the persecution and murder. As time goes on, the participants are bound to look at what happened with awe. The momentary end of the otherwise endless cycle of violence will seem miraculous. In this new light, the scapegoat who has borne the blame for the ills of the people will acquire a sacred status as a god. The group will begin to think that this horrendous murder was a lawful sacrifice. Thus, the foundation of religion is laid.

Girard proposes that as long as the participants are ignorant of the secret psychology of the scapegoat process, the peaceful effects of the violence will be short-lived. Soon mimetic rivalry will infect the society again. When conflict reappears, the divided community will have to find new victims to replace the original victim. This repetition will restore the initial, miraculous peace.[49]

The first murder may have been a senseless crime of mob violence. Over time, as the group reenacts the original event, the horror will become a dramatic ritual. A myth will recount the original killing. A ritual of sacrifice will reenact it. The myth and ritual will cleanse the whole community of its aggression. In due course, the newly formed sacrificial cult of sacrifice will substitute animals or precious objects for human victims. This process will give birth to a system of sacrifices with myths, rituals, priests, and sacred objects—that is, a religion.

Violence and Human Culture

For Girard, the religion of sacrifice is also the foundation of culture. This foundation involves four different factors: mimesis (imitation), mimetic rivalry (imitative competition), scapegoat mechanism (projection of hostility on a victim), and the sacrificial system of religion (the organized religion).

Girard's Religious Foundation of Culture

1. Mimesis (imitation)
2. Mimetic rivalry (imitative competition)
3. The scapegoat mechanism (projection of hostility on a victim)
4. The sacrificial system of religion (the organized religion)

Mimesis (imitation) builds up and transmits culture. Conversely, the competition of mimetic rivalry destroys what culture builds up. The scapegoat mechanism temporarily solves the problem. It replaces the cycle of destructive violence with a new creative cycle of sacrificial rites. As it does so, it reestablishes the social order, and that renewal allows the culture to flourish in peace.[50] Violence is, therefore, not only intrinsic to religion, but religious violence is also necessary for human culture.

In Girard's theory, the founding myths of cultures are versions of Freud's notion of a primal murder. In this case, this murder is interpreted as a sacrifice. For example, in the Hindu sacred scripture the *Rig Veda*, the universe is the result of a primeval sacrifice. The body of the "Purusha," the primal cosmic being, is sacrificed and dismembered. Its body parts are set in the heavens and Earth as the elements of the universe. Likewise, the body parts become the castes of the Hindu society. In other words, the process of this ritual sacrifice, dismemberment, and disposition of the body parts gives order to the universe and to society.

The Exposure of the Secret and the End of the Ritual Scapegoat

According to Girard's theory, myths and rituals of sacrifice gloss over the dark secret of the necessary role of violence at the very foundation of religion and culture. In fact, they hide the awful truth of the origin of religion.[51]

But according to Girard there has been a turning point in the religions of the human race. The mystery of religious aggression has been unveiled. From his Catholic Christian perspective, Girard maintains that the Bible discloses a growing insight into the hidden nature of the scapegoat mechanism and the Creator's rejection of it. Beginning with Cain, who goes on from murdering his brother to found a city,[52] the Bible tells one story after another of the violence at the bottom of religion and culture.

Girard points out, however, that the biblical narratives change the perspective. Whether the story is about Cain's brother Abel or the slaves of the pharaoh in Egypt, it is told from the viewpoint of the victims. From this viewpoint, the stories lead to a climax. According to Girard, the narratives ultimately conclude with the revelation of the awful secret of ritual sacrifice. At length, a sacrifice exposes the true nature of religious ritual. This unveiling of the mystery at the core of religion is the crucifixion of Jesus. Girard observes that he dies as a scapegoat, yet he is clearly innocent. The obvious innocence of this victim shows that the ritualized legitimacy of the sacrifice is a sham. The ritual displacement of hostility on hapless victims is nothing but ritual killing.

At last, we have arrived at the solution to religious violence. The human race knows that ritual sacrifice was the religious solution to social violence. Now the exposure of the scapegoating at the heart of religion brings an end of this awful practice. The appropriate response to scapegoating, sacred sacrifice, and all religious aggression is to renounce the use of violence to solve violence.

Isn't Religion to Blame?

If Christianity has taken religion to the point of renouncing all violence, then how does Girard explain the dreadful record of religious violence in history since the death of Jesus up to today?

If the crucifixion of Jesus was the end of sacred violence, then the Crusades prove that much of Christianity did not get the point. In fact, Charles Bellinger notes that a primary reason for the Crusades was to stop the infighting within Christian Europe. The solution to the mimetic rivalry of Christians was to refocus the hostility on the Turks. The Turks thus fit the role of scapegoat in a massive and bloody religious ritual known as a "Crusade."[53]

Yet Girard persists in believing that the secret of the violent nature of ritual sacrifice is out. Obviously, the scapegoat mechanism still works in today's world. Above all, the Holocaust has horrified the world with the unspeakable evils of scapegoating. However, in Girard's view, the scapegoat phenomenon has been taken out of the context of religious ritual—for the most part. Because it is desacralized, it is easier to see its dynamics.[54]

But there is a downside to the new insight into religious violence and the end of ritual sacrifice. Scapegoating still continues, but it now takes new disguises that hide its horrors from the realization of what is being done.[55] If so, we can expect that nowadays groups that thrive on scapegoating will have to spin even more elaborate justifications of it.

Without the outlet of ritualized violence, Girard's theory predicts that mimetic rivalry also is bound to intensify. Girard believes that in the twenty-first century, mimetic rivalry is happening on a worldwide scale through the competition of global capitalism. In his view, economic competition is bound to produce violence because some will win and many others will lose. For example,

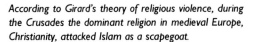

According to Girard's theory of religious violence, during the Crusades the dominant religion in medieval Europe, Christianity, attacked Islam as a scapegoat.

within Muslim societies, organized resistance has arisen among those who feel themselves the victims of Westernization and losers in global capitalism. In this new conflict, the "West" and "Islam" are "doubles" who are locked in recipro-cal conflict. According to Girard, the conflict is not merely about the differences between religions or between religion and secularism. It is about the contest of rivals whose methods and values mirror each other.[56]

Dawkins and Harris base their theories on the historical record of religious violence. Girard bases his theory on the psychology of competitive rivalry. An-other approach starts with the concept of social identity. These theories suggest that religion is the necessary foundation for group identity in society, culture, and civilization. The logic of these theories is that identity requires a sense that my group is different from yours. This sense of difference obviously divides people. These divisions can easily lead to conflict. According to the social iden-tity approach, many religions manage their tension with outsiders without overt aggression. Some, however, cross the line into violence.

Religion Necessarily Involves Conflict but Not Violence: Wellman and Tokuno

Comparative religion scholar James Wellman and East Asian scholar Kyoko Tokuno observe that group identity and solidarity depend on definite boundaries between the group members and outsiders. Nothing does a better job of draw-ing those lines than religion. It is often the core of the social identity of groups. Religions are, therefore, innately divisive.[57]

Moreover, the divisions inevitably produce tension with those on the other side of the borders. This tension is not just natural—it is also good for groups.

Opposition unifies the group's members in a common cause. Thus, according to Wellman and Tokuno, groups thrive on religion just as religions feed on conflict. Without external conflict, the borders of the group may become so blurred that the group will lose its unique identity. Or the members may fight one another, creating new boundaries that subdivide the group.[58]

In this theory, religion functions as an incredibly powerful engine for group identity. Here is how it works to produce violence. In ritual, myth, and story, religions make truth claims that define what is true, genuine, normal, and moral. At the same time, these claims teach that beliefs that do not conform to these standards are false, unreal, inauthentic, abnormal, and immoral. Naturally, these distinctions between "us" and "them" produce powerful emotions. They prepare the insiders to defend the group against the "Other" at all costs. Thus, the zeal for the defense of the faith leads to violence.[59]

But religions also supply the fuel that powers this engine. Religions convince believers that they represent an authority that goes beyond any other. Consequently, religion is not subject to any higher ethic. It defines what is moral. Thus, religion has the unique capacity to legitimize attitudes and mobilize behavior that otherwise would be questioned.[60] This makes religion an incredibly dangerous force in human affairs.

A good example of Wellman and Tokuno's group identity theory is the case of ethnic/religious turmoil in the Punjab in India in the 1980s. The religion of the majority of the population of the rich Punjab region is Sikhism. Sikhism represents the fifth-largest world religion and has its own distinctive scriptures, culture, and identity. The Sikhs have had a long and complicated relationship with Hinduism and Islam.

Religious violence in the Punjab region flared up in the late twentieth century. The hostilities started when Sant Jarnail Singh Bhindranwale led a movement against smoking, drinking, prostitution, drugs, and vulgarity in the movies. This was a religious revival to defend the Sikh way of life against the incursion of the unholy modernism of Western culture. According to Sikh scholar Pritam Singh, the movement drifted toward violence in stages as it fought against moral impurity, heresy, and Hindus until it reached the stage of joining the political forces seeking Sikh autonomy.[61]

As Wellman and Tokuno suggest, the issues involved were matters of ethnic identity. The group felt it must defend its borders against the intrusion of the "Other" at all costs. The creeping immorality of such actions as smoking and cutting the hair and beard threatened its moral boundaries from without. Heresy threatened its core beliefs from within. The Hindus' claim that Sikhism was just another form of Hinduism threatened to tear down its boundaries altogether. Violence committed by both sides escalated this sense of mortal danger. According to Singh, in the midst of the turmoil, Bhindranwale began to teach that violence would achieve "victory," not political moderation.

The violence reached a climax when Bhindranwale and a few hundred supporters retreated to the Sikhs' most holy shrine, the Golden Temple at Amritsar. The Indian government dispatched seven army divisions to attack this sacred center of Sikhism. In the gunfight, Bhindranwale and more than 5,000 people were killed.

This example also shows how religion has the ultimate power to make violence legitimate. It might seem that Bhindranwale's approval of violence was

The Golden Temple in Amritsar, India, is a holy Sikh shrine that was attacked by the Indian Army during a 1984 religious conflict.

contradictory to Sikh beliefs. The founder of Sikhism, Guru Nanuk (1469–1539), taught peace and instructed the original believers to make friends of their enemies. To justify the contrary teaching, Bhindranwale proclaimed that the "Hindu imperialists" were trying to destroy the Sikhs.[62] To meet this challenge, Bhindranwale appealed to another thread of the Sikh tradition. Guru Gobind (1666–1708) taught the concept of righteous war (*dharma yuddha*). This idea was that fighting is acceptable as a last resort. Bhindranwale had only to convince the believers that the present threat demanded this "last resort."

Bhindranwale's movement believed that their religious group identity was at stake. They had to maintain that identity against the Hindu majority of India as well as Western culture. In Wellman and Tokuno's theory, this distinctive identity did not necessarily have to lead to violence. But the example illustrates how the course of events can lead to the escalation of tension into bloodshed.

Religion in the "Clash of Civilizations"

We can recognize similar views in the well-known "Clash of Civilizations" theory of Samuel Huntington (1927–2008). Huntington proposed that the nature of worldwide conflict changed after the Cold War. Global conflict plagued the twentieth century, but the hostilities were between coalitions of nation-states. Huntington predicted that in the twenty-first century, however, global conflict would erupt between broad "civilizations." By a "civilization," Huntington meant the largest subdivision of the human race, a distinct but major culture. Members of civilizations identify themselves by their language, history, customs, and institutions, but principally by their religion.[63]

Huntington identified about eight or nine such civilizations; a list of these can be found in the textbox "Huntington's Civilizations." In addition, the textbox shows *cleft countries* that exist on "fault lines" between civilizations. Also listed are *torn countries* whose leaders want to move the nation from its historical background to another civilization. Huntington acknowledges *Buddhist civilization* as well, but he felt that its forms overlapped other civilizations.[64]

Huntington's Civilizations

Civilizations

- *Western civilization*: North America, Australia/New Zealand, and Europe
- *Latin America*: Central America, South America, and Cuba
- *The Orthodox world*: regions of the former Soviet Union (but not Central Asia and the Baltic states), some of the former Yugoslavia, Croatia, Bulgaria, Cyprus, Greece, and Romania
- *The Eastern world*: Buddhist regions of Bhutan, Cambodia, Laos, Mongolia, Myanmar, Sri Lanka, and Thailand
- *Hindu civilization*: Mauritius, Nepal, and the Indians scattered throughout Asia
- *The Muslim world*: Greater Middle East (excluding Armenia, Cyprus, Ethiopia, Georgia, Greece, Israel, Kazakhstan, Malta, Sudan, and Turkey), northern West Africa, Albania, Bangladesh, Brunei, Comoros, Indonesia, Malaysia, and Maldives
- *The "Sinic" ("Confucian") civilization*: North and South Korea, Taiwan, Vietnam, and the Chinese population spread out in Southeast Asia
- *Japanese*: Japan
- *Sub-Saharan Africa*: Southern Africa, Middle Africa (excluding Chad), East Africa (excluding the Horn of Africa, Comoros, Kenya, Mauritius, and Tanzania), Cape Verde, Côte d'Ivoire, Ghana, Liberia, and Sierra Leone

Countries between Civilizations

- *Cleft countries* (exist on "fault lines" between civilizations): China, between the "Sinic" ("Confucian"), Turkic, and Tibetan Buddhist groupings; India (between the Hindu and Muslim civilizations); the Philippians and Indonesia (between Muslim and Christian civilizations); Sri Lanka (between Hindu and Buddhist civilizations); and Sudan and Tanzania (between Muslim and Christian civilizations)
- *Torn countries* (nations whose leaders want to move it from its historical civilization to another): Russia, torn between the Western civilization and the Orthodox world; Turkey, torn between the Western civilization of its secular aspirations and the Muslim world; Mexico, torn between Latin and North America; and Australia, torn between identification with the west or with Asia
- *Buddhist overlapping civilizations*: (Theravada Buddhism) Sri Lanka, Burma (Myanmar), Thailand, Laos, and Cambodia; (Mahayana Buddhism) Tibet, Mongolia, and Bhutan

---

Religion is at the core of Huntington's civilizations because it defines their opposing worldviews. For Girard, societies fight because of mimetic rivalry over what both parties regard as valuable. For Huntington, civilizations fight because their worldviews are different. Societies that see everything differently will clash upon contact with each other. Religion is to blame because it provides the foundation for this differing of worldviews.[65]

Thus, according to Huntington, the partnership of civilization and religion is the first step in understanding violence in the twenty-first century. The next step is to grasp the importance of globalization. The greatest factor of the twenty-first century is that the world has become a global society. Take the following example, a case that would be unbelievable just a few decades ago. An employee who lives in Cincinnati, Ohio, works for an international company headquartered in Brussels, Belgium. Her desk was made in Jiangsu Province in China. She wears shoes manufactured in Ho Chi Minh City, Vietnam, for a company that is centered in Herzogenaurach, Bavaria, Germany. She uses a computer assembled in Penang, Malaysia, while she talks on a cell phone designed in Espoo, Finland, though it was manufactured in India.

Though we seldom think about it, this scenario is normal in this time of globalization. Because the world has become a global village, different cultures and their religions are now in unavoidable contact with each other. They have to interact whether they like each other or not—and most likely they will not. Moreover, one civilization is pushing this seemingly irresistible process. As the Western civilization promotes its own values, attitudes, and interests, it is bound to incite resistance from other civilizations. It will face opposition especially from those who do not believe that Western progress is benefiting them.[66]

The process of globalization has broken down age-old social identities. The scenario above shows that the boundaries of tribe and nation are no longer relevant to today's economic and political realities. As Wellman and Tokuno have also pointed out, religion has a unique capacity to draw boundaries between people. Thus, religion alone remains as a viable foundation of identity over the mass global society. Because it can fill the vacuum left by the loss of national group identity, a wave of fundamentalism has surged within almost all world religions. Fundamentalist groups offer their believers a restored social identity with secure boundaries. And they give traditional believers a way of standing up against the secularizing forces of modern society. In Huntington's view, these fundamentalist religions provide the solid core to the "civilizations" that are opposed to Western (secular) influence.[67]

But does the natural antagonism between civilizations *necessarily* lead to violence? More specifically, does the growing opposition of religious fundamentalists to Westernization *necessarily* mean that they will take up arms? Huntington believed that religious violence is not inevitable but predictable. He states, "Differences do not necessarily mean conflict, and conflict does not necessarily mean violence."[68] Some other factor is necessary besides religion to cause violence.

Only Some Religions Are Violent

Joining the Battle between Good and Evil: Juergensmeyer

Almost a decade before September 11, 2001, religious studies scholar Mark Juergensmeyer examined Christian, Jewish, Muslim, Sikh, and Buddhist incidents of religious violence. His book *Terror in the Mind of God* is a groundbreaking cross-cultural study of religious terrorism. For Juergensmeyer, the combination of religion with the political ambitions of nationalism is especially explosive. He distinguishes between three types of this lethal mixture of religion and nationalism: (1) ethnic, (2) ideological, and (3) the combination of the two, "ethno-ideological religious."[69]

The term *ethnic religious nationalism* is comparable to Tokuno and Wellman's "group identity conflict" and Bruce Lincoln's "religions of revolution." Ethnic religious nationalism is founded on religion, since religion defines the identity of the ethnic group. As the group fights for independence, however, it uses its religion for political purposes. For example, Muslims in Chechnya are fighting to break free of the government of Russia. And in the former Yugoslavia, three ethnic/religious groups, the Orthodox Serbs, the Catholic Croats, and the Muslim Bosnians, have fought one another to establish their own political states.[70]

The *ideological* form of violence is the subject of Juergensmeyer's book. This type does the opposite of ethnic religious nationalism. Religious nationalism makes religion political. Ideological nationalism makes politics religious. The religion provides the ideological goals. These goals direct the political actions of the group. The revolution against the Shah of Iran in 1979 is a good example. Religious principles and aspirations motivated this revolt and led to the establishment of the Iranian Islamic Republic.[71]

Ethno-ideological religious nationalism lies in the middle between the two poles of religions. It is a mixture of the two forms.

How can we distinguish between these types? We can do so by defining the group's enemy. Ethnic religious nationalism fights against the forces that are oppressing the group. But ideological nationalism is against everyone who does not share its belief system. Ethno-ideological religious nationalism fights against both.

"Cosmic War" and Religious Terrorism

Of these types, Juergensmeyer believes that ideological religious nationalism is perhaps the hardest for Westerners to understand. For one thing, this way of thinking deliberately sets itself against Western ideas and values. Ideological religious nationalism believes that secular nationalism has failed it. Its fatal flaw is the separation of politics and religion. These must be reunited in a proper mutual relationship. Political means can truly succeed if they have religious ends. And religious ends can only be fulfilled by political means.

For example, the Temple Mount Faithful Movement believes that the Jewish Temple must be rebuilt on the Temple Mount in Jerusalem.[72] There is one problem: the site is now where the Muslim Al-Aqsa Mosque, the third holiest shrine in Islam, now stands. The political act of tearing down the mosque and building the temple must happen before the religion's hope for the coming of the Messiah will be fulfilled. Yet the Jewish people must unite in this religious hope if there is any chance that this reconstruction will happen.

According to Juergensmeyer, this type of "ideological religious nationalism" has started another Cold War. It appeared without warning after the fall of Soviet Communism but now represents the major challenge to the secularized West. To

Juergensmeyer, secular and religious nationalism are emerging as the new global rivals. Both claim to establish social order over social disorder. But the way they do this is entirely different. Religious nationalists believe that a secular social order marginalizes religion. This disenfranchisement of religion is a grave concern because religion is the foundation of society and morals. To them, a religious social order puts political authority in its proper place.[73]

"Ideological religious nationalism" appears in different religions. However, Juergensmeyer found that a common idea motivates all its followers. This is the conviction that the true believers are chosen recruits for an impending "cosmic war." The deadly battle on the horizon will pit absolute goodness and truth against total evil and falsehood. As this war of the universe approaches, every human being on Earth must choose which side to join.

The belief in "cosmic war" has exceptional explanatory and motivating power. It transforms the circumstances of seemingly arbitrary suffering into the battlefields of meaningful combat. It transforms human opponents into superhuman devils. It transforms sickening atrocities into moral actions. It transforms suicidal bombings into heroic sacrifices. Most of all, it transforms the despair of apparent defeat into the hope of eventual victory.[74] In short, the ideology of the sacred religious war gives ultimate meaning and eternal significance to a mundane human struggle.

Juergensmeyer believes that this provocative concept is the key to religious violence. Only *some* religions are bound to be violent. Not even those religions that mix religion and politics are *necessarily* violent. But the religions that believe in a final sacred struggle are most likely to be violent. Thus, religion itself is not to blame for violence. Rather, the fault is in the religious conception of an ultimate cosmic battle between good and evil.[75]

Examples of "Cosmic War"

The idea of a *cosmic war* explains why religions that usually represent peace and mercy turn to uncommonly atrocious acts of aggression. In times of crisis, religions may turn to the cosmic war ideology. And they may use it to justify a violent response to this distressing time. In fact, some religious leaders will create a sense of a dreadful threat in order to stir believers to action.[76]

For example, the Buddhist Aum Shinrikyo terrorist group in Japan began as a "new religious movement." A yoga student who called himself Shoko Asahara founded the cult in 1987. Combining elements of Hinduism, Tibetan Buddhism, and Christianity with the occult teachings of Nostradamus, it offered a program of steps toward higher consciousness. The Japanese government gave the group official religious status in 1989, and the cult grew in popularity and profits. The group was so successful that in 1990 Asahara and two dozen of his followers ran for seats in the Japanese Diet (parliament).

The defeat of all the candidates for office signaled the beginning of a downward spiral for the sect. The sense of failure added to the growing opposition from anticult groups, which pushed the group toward aggression.[77] Appealing to the cosmic war idea, Asahara published prophecies of a worldwide cataclysm. He called it "Armageddon," the Christian term for the final devastating battle at the end-times. Asahara taught that World War III would start with the war between the United States and Japan. Japan would be laid to waste, but the elite—that is, Asahara's followers—would survive.

The feeling that the cult was a victim of assaults and hostility heightened the sense of crisis. In a speech on April 27, 1994, Asahara charged that he and his group had been victims of poison gas attacks wherever they went since 1988. "The hour of my death has already been foretold," he said. Two months later, on June 27, the Aum Shinrikyo group attacked five trains on the Tokyo subway with poison sarin gas. The coordinated operation killed twelve, seriously injured fifty-four, and sickened between 900 and 5,000 others.[78]

Why should rational people believe in such a sense of impending doom? Frightful scenarios are ways to explain otherwise seemingly random and meaningless events. Believers typically are distressed about the course of world events and feel helpless in the face of them. This feeling of powerlessness is both deep and personal. It can be summed up in the feeling of "humiliation."

An example of the motivation of humiliation is Osama bin Laden's response to the treatment of the Saudi Arabian government. Bin Laden returned to Saudi Arabia in 1990 flush with his victories in Afghanistan. He asked for a meeting with the Saudi Arabian defense minister, Prince Sultan bin Abdelaziz al-Saud. He was prepared to offer a defense force of 100,000 men to replace the "indignity" of the presence of American troops on Arabian soil.[79] The defense minister was cold to the offer. He referred to Sadam Hussein's recent invasion of Kuwait: "There are no caves in Kuwait. You cannot fight them from the mountains and caves. What will you do when they lob missiles at you with chemical and biological weapons?"[80] Bin Laden replied, "We will fight them with faith."[81]

The prince declined bin Laden's proposal. Rebuffed, bin Laden began to challenge the legitimacy of the Saudi government, since it was allowing the indignity of the "infidel" to occupy the land of the holiest sites in Islam.[82]

The origins of the Aum Shinrikyo terrorist group and bin Laden's al-Qaeda suggest that the theory of cosmic war arises from a cycle of humiliating relations with the larger culture. It is a downward spiral of confrontation and rejection.[83] Thus, shame and hopelessness inflame the ideology of "cosmic war." The notion of such a universal conflagration appeals to those who believe that they are powerless to defend their identity and integrity without divine and supernatural help. The ultimate crisis calls for the most radical action, a battle against the world.

Cosmic War by Another Name: Apocalypticism

If the idea of "cosmic war" is the key factor that motivates and justifies religious terrorism, what religions harbor this notion? To answer, we must introduce the concept of *apocalypticism*. This term refers to the belief in the catastrophic end of the world as we have seen. In this way of thinking, the final battle between the forces of good and evil is about to happen. In this imminent war, human society and the whole cosmos will be destroyed. The word *apocalypse* comes from the belief that the secrets of the course of events at the end of time have been revealed to a chosen elect. The crucial message of this revelation is that those believers who remain faithful in the midst of the struggles of the "end-time" will be saved and enjoy eternal life in a new age.

This religious ideology is an outgrowth of the tradition of the Jewish prophets. It is the framework of the belief within Judaism and Christianity of the coming of the "Messiah," or "Anointed One." This "Chosen One" is the divinely appointed agent who will restore the greatness of the reign of King David at the beginning of a new age.

In Christianity, Jesus of Nazareth is considered to be the Messiah. His return to Earth in the "Second Coming" will be the climax of world history. The present world will be destroyed in a final confrontation between the forces of God and Satan. Then Jesus the Christ (the Messiah) will rule over an eternal kingdom.

However, the structure of this worldview is not only found in Christianity. In Islam, it appears as the ultimate hope of both Sunni and Shi'ite believers. This hope is centered in the coming and rule of the *Mahadi*, the Muslim messianic figure.[84]

Hindus and Buddhists believe in vast cycles of time with inevitable creation and destruction. Thus, both Eastern religions have beliefs in the end of the world that have apocalyptic aspects. The chief difference lies in the cyclical nature of time. Unlike Western monotheistic worldviews, the cyclical Eastern views do not believe in an absolute end of time.[85] Nevertheless, medieval Chinese Buddhism contained a form of apocalypticism. This "medieval Chinese Buddhist apocalypticism" foretold the end of the present era.[86] In its view, in the present time, the *dharma*—that is, the enlightened teachings, of the Buddha—was thriving. However, at the end of history, the understanding of the *dharma* would fade away into moral decay and the universe would come to an end.

In its complete sense, apocalypticism belongs to the three great traditions of Western monotheism. Therefore, although Juergensmeyer refers to Eastern religions, the principal ideologies of cosmic war are versions of the apocalypticism of Western ideologies. Yet note that even in the Western monotheist traditions, apocalypticism is not inherently violent.[87] The apocalyptic worldview is the religious foundation for much violent terrorism in the name of religion. But in the majority of cases it takes a nonviolent form.

Calling All Moderates—Others Need Not Apply: Diana Eck

As we have seen, Juergensmeyer puts the responsibility for current religious violence on ideological nationalism. Diana Eck teaches another way of approaching religious aggression. The director of Harvard's Pluralism Project, Eck is a well-known advocate of interfaith cooperation among religions. She maintains that increasing immigration in the last part of the twentieth century has resulted in a "new religious America." The country has graduated from its Christian upbringing. It is now the home of a much wider diversity of religions than we realize.[88]

The heart of Eck's program is her typology of religion. Her widely accepted categories divide religions into *exclusivist*, *inclusivist*, and *pluralist* types.[89] (See the textbox "Eck's Types of Religion" for how these types relate to other religions and how likely they are to promote or discourage religious violence.) When we put together Eck's theories with the research of Robert Wuthnow, we can say that approximately one in three Americans is an exclusivist who believes that no other religions are true but Christianity. One in four Americans is an inclusivist who believes that Christianity has the truth but other religions have at least some of the truth. Wuthnow's research does not apply to Eck's term "pluralist."[90]

Eck's Types of Religion

Type of Religion	Response to Diversity	Relationship to Violence
Exclusivist	Intolerant	Leads to conflict
Inclusive	Tolerant	Allows for conflict
Pluralist	Accepting	Prevents conflict

A 2008 Pew Forum survey confirmed Wuthnow's results. For example, it found that one in three Americans hold that only their religion leads to eternal life. This compares almost exactly to Wuthnow's findings. Significantly, the Pew study found that the number of exclusivists grew by 11 percent in six years.[91]

The exclusivists are Eck's chief concern because she associates their belief with intolerance. For her, intolerance, in turn, is the parent of prejudice, hatred, and violence. In Eck's mind, religions that claim to have a monopoly are associated with the traits of inflexibility, competitiveness, tribalism, and extremism. Like Wellman and Tokuno, she claims that they cling to their religious, cultural, and/or national identity. And this predisposes them to engage in violence or to endorse it.[92]

Eck's typology of religion constructs a frame of reference that supports her program of preventing religious violence. Eck observes that globalization has brought people and religions closer together. Contact among religions is now unavoidable. But will contact lead to conflict or cooperation? According to Eck, globalization presents a clear choice between two poles. At one end of the spectrum is dialogue and cooperation. These will increase mutual understanding and wipe out intolerance. At the other end is "the new tribalism and religious extremism"[93] that causes religious violence.

But Eck's idea of "pluralism" goes beyond toleration of other religions. She thinks toleration is an easy "live and let live" attitude that does not engage in meaningful relationships with other religions. In place of toleration, Eck advocates "pluralism." Pluralism acknowledges many paths of faith and multiple understandings of truth. Inclusivism still favors one religion over the others. Pluralism puts all religions on the same level. From this viewpoint, only pluralism will foster the attitude that will prevent religious violence. It will foster peace among religions because it will teach believers of all faiths to accept one another in spite of their differences and to live in peace with one another.

Only False Religions Are Violent

A closely related theory to the idea that only *some* religions are disposed to violence is the notion that violence is the sign of a *false religion*. This popular way of thinking divides the religions we approve from those we dislike.

For example, British Prime Minister Tony Blair said that the "authentic voices" of religion should be heard above the shouts of religious extremism. According to Blair, the "overwhelming majority" of Muslims want to play their role as loyal citizens, and they represent "genuine Islam." Blair said, "The voices of extremism are no more representative of Islam than the use, in times gone by, of torture—to force conversion to Christianity—represents the true teaching of Christ." Using a now familiar metaphor, Blair charged that the fanatics had "hijacked" the peaceful religion of Islam.[94] Meeting together in the "Religions for Peace World Assembly," eight hundred religious leaders came together in Japan to oppose the same "hijacking" of religion.[95]

The theory that only "false" religions are violent assumes that one can tell the difference between true and false religions based on the evidence of religious aggression.

Karen Armstrong, for example, claims that fundamentalists in Judaism, Christianity, and Islam believe that secular society is trying to destroy their religion. With this feeling, some choose to ignore the passages in their scriptures that have to do with compassion and select those that have to do with aggression. In doing so, she says, they "distort the tradition." Armstrong will not accept this justification for violence; even if a religion feels threatened, it becomes "inauthentic" if it is involved in violence.[96]

Evaluation of the Alternative Approaches to a Theory of Religious Violence

The theories that we have reviewed consider whether violence is built in to the nature of all religion, some religion, or just "false religion." We began with the idea that religion is intrinsically violent and ended with the idea that "true" religion cannot be violent. Which of these theories is right? Theories help us understand the otherwise unmanageable torrent of information that engulfs us. But they also guide the thoughts about what should be done about that information. Therefore, we need to ask some critical questions about them. For instance, we might first ask, does the theory give a reasonable and convincing argument? Second, does the theory help us discover and account for what is really the case? Third, is the theory useful for dealing with religious aggression because it accurately describes its causes?

Dawkins and Harris: Is the Attack on All Religions Fair?

Dawkins and Harris provide a formidable amount of historical evidence to prove that religion is violent by nature. They are right in what is wrong with religion. Nevertheless, for them, whatever good is to be found in religion turns out to be bad as well. For example, in Dawkins's view, moderates who favor peace are still responsible for religious violence because they encourage unquestioning faith.[97] All religious belief makes people susceptible to the manipulation of fanatics. Likewise, in Harris's mind, religions are immoral because they promote war. However, if religions renounce war and promote pacifism, they are also immoral. Pacifism leaves people defenseless against evil.[98]

Both Dawkins and Harris lay out some questionable arguments. Dawkins's book is a study in selective evidence. He piles up a mound of evidence that connects religion to violence, but dismisses heaps of contrary evidence that link religion with peace. Moreover, H. Allen Orr notes that when Dawkins compares the record of atheism with religion, he compares the *theory* of atheism with the actual *practice* of religion.[99] Thus, Dawkins will not admit that atheism can be anything but benign. For instance, he admits that Stalin was an atheist. Then he dodges the conclusion that atheism can be a source of violence. He states that Stalin did not commit his atrocities in the "name of atheism."[100] In other words, religion can do no right and atheism can do no wrong.

In contrast, Harris admits that sometimes religious people do the right things. For example, he refers to "innumerable instances" when European Christians sheltered Jews from the death camps in the Holocaust.[101] We can agree with Harris that these acts were not "innumerable enough." But the point is that at least some religious people do good for religious reasons.

Dawkins and Harris are entertaining and persuasive writers. Yet both argue in broad generalities that require closer analysis. We might ask, for instance, whether these generalities gloss over important details about this chapter's topic. For example, Dawkins states that believers become suicide bombers because they believe what their religions have taught them.[102]

However, a critical approach to religious studies would question Dawkins's evidence. For example, political scientist Robert Pape researched 315 terrorist incidents from 1980 to 2003. He found that religion is often an ingredient in such bombings, but it is not the only one. It is not a "sufficient cause" of suicidal terrorism. Moreover, these suicide massacres were not for religious ends. The purpose was to rid the terrorists' homeland from foreign military occupation. He states that terrorists use religion for recruiting and other operations. Nevertheless, it is "rarely the root cause" of suicide bombings.[103]

Dawkins's book is unsatisfying because he does not help us think through the evidence that he does give for religious violence. We would expect the head of a Humanist Society to praise Dawkins's work. Instead, the humanist Fred March complains that Dawkins fails to probe the reasons that religion is toxic. Moreover, he assumes that all religions have the same ideology.[104] March concludes that Dawkins's approach will stir up many religious people against him. It will not help anyone find a cure for the toxic effects of religion that Dawkins describes.[105]

For his part, Harris claims that religion is violent because it is irrational.[106] Take a close look at these statements and one will find that Harris assumes a causal connection between unjustified belief and unjustifiable violence. It is true that religious people tend to believe improbable things. It is also true that religious people sometimes commit acts of violence. However, what is the *necessary* cause and effect in the relationship between the unfounded belief and the violence? Many religious believers accept many things that have no proof, and yet they do not wage war in the name of their beliefs. Some ardent religious believers are even pacifists. Millions, as Harris admits, intentionally act as peacemakers because of their faith.

Concluding Evaluation of Dawkins and Harris: An Emerging Question

Of the new atheists we have studied, Dawkins comes closest to claiming that religion and violence are inseparable. The others admit that some religions, sometimes, are not violent. Harris recognizes that the religious faith of millions of religious people inspires them to acts of self-sacrifice for others.[107] Likewise, Daniel Dennett acknowledges that religion inspires many to do great things for justice and education.[108] Yet for other believers religion is poisonous.

A set of questions begins to take shape in this review of the theories of the "new atheists." If some religious people shun aggression and do good while others yield to violence, what makes the difference? If religion causes violence but does not do so in all circumstances, then what situations activate it? If religion is prone to violence, then what turns potential aggression into actual assault? If some religions are "toxic" and others are "nontoxic," then what ingredients go into the witch's brew of poisoned belief?

So far, there are two possible answers to the emerging set of questions. One answer is that the good that religions do in the present will be revealed as evil in the end. Consider Mother Teresa's work among the poor in India or Thích Nhất Hạnh's teaching of compassion. Their actions appear to be constructive. However, both promote unquestioning faith. Therefore, in the view of Dawkins and Harris, the seeds of their apparent goodness will at last reap the harvest of violence. Yet that answer seems harsh. How can the denunciation of all religious deeds no matter what good they do be justified?

The alternative answer is that some religions are more reasonable than others. Perhaps those religions that are more reasonable are less violent. If so, then reason seems to have an influence on religion. How can one sort out the reasonable and less violent religions from the others? In addition, can a religion be reasonable in some circumstances and not in others?

Girard: The "End" of Ritual Violence?

Like Dawkins and Harris, Girard offers a comprehensive theory that seems impossible to prove or disprove by empirical observation. Instead of factual evidence, it relies on Girard's astute insight into world literature, mythology, and scripture. In fact, Girard states that the test of his theory will be how well it fits a wide cross-section of rituals and myths from different times and places.[109]

Certainly, Girard's insights into the dynamics of desire, social rivalry, scapegoating, and sacrifice give much to ponder. His work is stimulating and troubling. From his vast knowledge of world literature and history, he makes expansive claims. The case he makes is compelling in its insight into human nature. However, critical thinkers would question the evidence he uses to support his proposal.[110] For all his learning, Girard mixes myth and history so that it is hard to know how to interpret statements such as the claim that the crucifixion of Jesus of Nazareth was the "end" of ritual sacrifice. Is it a fact of history or a theological statement?

At the center of Girard's theory is the claim that the secret of the scapegoat is now out in the open for all humanity. This exposure has happened, however, only within a specific religious tradition. Girard states that the Jewish Bible begins to uncover the secret. The innocence of Jesus at his crucifixion in Christianity finally fully uncovers it. Girard asserts this crucifixion is the end of "violent and archaic myths."[111] This seems to be a theological statement, not a conclusion of the impartial study of religion.

Girard claims that the ritual violence of sacrifice has "ended" with the disclosure of the secret of the scapegoat. In his view, religious ritual sacrifice has been "demystified." This means that it has lost its sacred power because its mystery has been unveiled. Because ritual sacrifice no longer has a role in modern life, Girard claims that it cannot perform its function.

It is true that we are witnessing mimetic violence on a worldwide scale.[112] But this increase is not the result of the abolition of rituals of scapegoating in modern times. The Holocaust can be considered ritual violence against a people who were murdered as scapegoats. In addition, unknown numbers of African Americans, homosexuals, immigrants—whoever was considered "Other"—were victims of the ritual violence of scapegoating throughout the last century. Moreover, many atrocities in the twenty-first century have had a ritual quality. For instance, the world has seen the sickening spectacle of the ritualized beheadings of the journalist Daniel Pearl and the private citizen Nick Berg. These atrocities were staged as ritual spectacles of bloodshed comparable to the ritual sacrifices of the past. If the mystery of the scapegoat was disclosed 2,000 years ago, why did it continue throughout history and persist even in the twenty-first century?[113]

Thus, it seems that we cannot say that the world has come to the "end" of ritualized sacrificial violence—not if we mean the historical "end." The religious rituals of "sacrifice" may not be so visible, and modern people may not see sacrifice as a religious institution[114] (though some religions still practice animal sacrifice), but ritualized scapegoating persists, and this plague seems to represent a significant share of religious violence in today's world.

Still, the sacrifices of scapegoating do not account for all violence in today's world, not even all religious violence.[115] Our analysis of the types of religious violence bears this out. For a solution to our problem, we must go on to other theories.

Wellman and Tokuno: Why Aren't All Religions Violent?

Unless we read them carefully, we might get the impression that Wellman and Tokuno agree with Dawkins and Harris. Like them, Wellman and Tokuno state that religion is inherently divisive and dangerous. Religion inevitably produces "conflict and tension" between the "insiders" and the "outsiders" of a faith.

However, the two researchers clarify that religious "tension" does not *necessarily* result in overt aggression.[116] They state that religions generate conflict but not always violence and that not many religions, new or old, nourish violent goals.[117] This raises the question of why most religions remain peaceful when they naturally define themselves against other groups. If religions must defend their identity at all costs, why do most religions restrain themselves from armed hostility? Given what the two researchers say about how groups define themselves against the "Other," it is remarkable that *all* religions are *not* engaged in open warfare.

As Wellman and Tokuno suggest, the relationship of religions to those who are outside the group is not necessarily antagonistic. Hospitality to the stranger (the "Other") is also a theme in world religions. The two researchers claim that religions thrive on tension with outsiders. But this theory does not explain why religions should teach, if not practice, welcome to the outsider.

Like Dawkins and Harris, Wellman and Tokuno seem to discount the influence of moderation in today's religions. Moderates, in fact, represent the majority of religious believers in today's world. But Wellman and Tokuno tend to overlook them. Instead, to make their case they take their examples from the extremist streams of the traditions. These rare instances of the radical fringe include the Jonestown mass suicide; the Branch Davidian gunfight with the Bureau of Alcohol, Tobacco and Firearms; and the Buddhist Aum Shinrikyo sarin gas attack on the Tokyo subway.[118] These examples slant their case toward the minority of the world's religions. This is obvious when the researchers dwell on the Aum Shinrikyo sect. It gives the false impression that this tiny group represents the mainstream of Buddhism.[119]

Wellman and Tokuno exemplify the approach that *some* religions are violent, *sometimes*. This assertion leads to the question of what makes religions cross the line from their natural rivalry with each other to open aggression. To answer, we will find that conflicts of group identity have distinctive causes other than religion that can be identified.[120]

Huntington: Description or Self-Fulfilling Prophecy?

Like Dawkins and Harris, Samuel Huntington seems to warn that violence is built into religion since religion is at the heart of civilizations and their "clashes." But critical thinking would find that Huntington's theory has a frame of reference from a previous era. Huntington's thought fits neatly into the past Cold War ideology, the dualistic division of the world into spheres of good and evil.[121] The plot of conspiracy against freedom and the American dream is the same as it was in the Cold War. But now the actors are different.

Upon reflection, one can see that Huntington treats his civilizations as unified, homogenous, and separate wholes. They are like chess pieces on the board of global politics. Huntington arranges them on the chessboard of his own design. Then he predicts how they will act according to his own playbook. Yet, as Edward Said observes, what Huntington calls civilizations, such as the Muslim sphere, are complex clusters that are intertwined with other cultures and religions.[122]

There is also a more troubling undercurrent in Huntington's work. It is hard to tell whether he is describing a situation or prescribing a course of action. An article in the *Journal of Peace Research* notes that Huntington's theory is such a powerful idea that it has the potential to do more than analyze events.[123] If the world's leaders acted as if it were true, it could also shape events and so become a self-fulfilling prophecy.[124] It might create the very conflict it claims to describe.[125]

Huntington himself suggested that his "clash of civilizations" did not necessarily mean global warfare. He believed that religious violence is not inevitable. It is only predictable. He stated, "Differences do not necessarily mean conflict, and conflict does not necessarily mean violence."[126] Therefore, the question is the same as we raised about Wellman and Tokuno's theory: Granted that the center of the civilizations are religions, but what provokes a civilization to move from differences, to conflict, and then to violence?

Juergensmeyer: What Is the Difference between Secular and Religious Nationalism?

Juergensmeyer's approach to religious violence believes in the power of ideologies. Much of the evidence for his *Terror in the Mind of God* came from his interviews of prominent leaders of terrorist groups. He believed the religious justifications of these leaders and found a common basis for religious aggression in their rationalizations.

The book graphically describes how the cosmic war mind-set sanctions and motivates appalling acts of terrorism. It also shows how the assumptions of cosmic war shape the acts of violence. According to the argument of the book, terrorist atrocities are performances played to the public audience that dramatize the worldview of the actors. They enact the cosmic drama and the roles of martyrs and heroes on the side of God against the devil.

Juergensmeyer's exploration of apocalypticism followed his previous study that, like Huntington's thesis, recycled the assumptions of the Cold War. We have shown that Huntington believed that the structure of seven or eight competing civilizations had replaced the dual framework of the Cold War. On the other hand, Juergensmeyer's book *A New Cold War?* asserts that only *two* competing ideologies shape the new world order: religious and secular nationalism.

Both of Juergensmeyer's studies are convincing. But critical thinking raises a question that gets at the limitations of his focus on ideology. What is the difference between these two ways of thinking?[127] The author suggests that unlike secular violence, religious aggression comes from symbolic and absolute beliefs. These convictions have ultimate significance above the limits of time and place in this world.[128] The apocalypticism that Juergensmeyer blames for religious violence in *Terror in the Mind of God* fits that description perfectly. Nevertheless, Juergensmeyer admits that secular warfare has the identical characteristics. Warfare places the differences between societies on the absolute scale of life or death. War is a struggle for the annihilation of an enemy that represents a threat to one's beliefs, identity, and way of life. Accordingly, the symbolic images of the confrontation magnify it into a larger-than-life contest between forces of pure good and unmitigated evil. War allows no hesitation, no uncertainty, and no willingness to compromise. It elevates the present time into a critical age that determines the future.

If this description of war is correct, then the concept of "cosmic war" cannot be used to distinguish between secular and religious violence. Cosmic war seems to be unique in its conception of a special, transcendent destiny. However, secular war asks its soldiers to sacrifice for its own version of a higher destiny.[129] Both secular and religious nationalism make ultimate claims: each asks people to kill and be killed for an ultimate cause.

We must look elsewhere for an answer to why religious people turn to violent aggression. Juergensmeyer himself points to a potential way of answering this question. He states that "religion is not innocent. But it does not ordinarily lead to violence. That happens only with the coalescence of a peculiar set of circumstances—political, social, and ideological—when religion becomes fused with violent expressions of social aspirations, personal pride, and movements for political change."[130] The deciding factors that tempt believers to resort to open hostilities are likely to be found in the "set of circumstances," not the ideology. This insight points to a potential answer to the question of why some, but not all, religions become violent.

Eck: Preaching to the Choir?

In the popular mind, the blame for religious violence rests on fanatical, absolute, irrational, fundamentalist, divisive, or scapegoating belief systems. This view believes that the vast majority of ordinary religious people are peaceful. Only a small percentage of religious believers are extremists, and these give religion a bad name. The rest are moderate and harmless. Dawkins and Harris too easily dismiss the moderates as unwitting sponsors of violence. Other theories tend to overlook them. However, Diana Eck represents the view that the moderates have a positive role in the solution to religious violence.

Eck's Pluralism Project has contributed to current religious studies by documenting the ever-widening diversity of religions in the United States. The project shows how globalization and immigration have scattered world religions across the face of America. Hardly anyone would disagree with her cause of replacing prejudice with mutual goodwill among the expanding variety of religions in the nation.

Eck's typology is so popular that it dominates religious studies. It serves as the prevailing model for categorizing religions in terms of their likelihood for violence.[131] Yet there is a hidden problem with her disapproval of exclusivists who believe that only one religion has a special claim to the truth. Surprisingly, world religions professor Huston Smith[132] raises this objection. He recalls that Eck refused to participate in an "ecumenical dialogue" sponsored by Rev. Sun Y. Moon of the Unification Church. He commented that her work reveals a "shadow side" when it disparages those who disagree with its philosophy as "intolerant, exclusive, narrow-minded, dogmatic, and jealously possessive of their God."[133] Smith questioned whether it is wise to impugn the morality of those who are unwilling to participate in the interfaith dialogues that she recommends.

Religious studies professor Russell McCutcheon adds that one would think that the exclusivists would be the very people that Eck would want to engage in conversation.[134] According to her theory, the exclusivists are most likely to turn prejudice into hate and hate into violence. Yet to come to the table of religious pluralism, they would have to accept its premises and give up their exclusivism. Eck's idealistic program of religious pluralism turns out to be a fellowship of the like-minded. We see in Eck's stance toward exclusivism that the pluralists also construct their own boundaries between "us" and "them," the very thing they say they are against.

Moreover, Eck's reasoning against exclusivism is questionable. Exclusivism may generate prejudice; nevertheless, it is not a sufficient condition of violence.[135] Most exclusivists, including one in three Americans, do not go to the extreme of engaging in religious violence. Something must happen for believers to turn into extremists who take up arms in the name of their faith. On the other hand, exclusivism can support the opposite of violence. Religious pacifists are often absolutely certain of their beliefs in the immorality of participating in war. Joel Kaminsky observes that both Osama bin Laden and Mother Teresa could be considered religious "fanatics."[136] Again, critical reflection about Eck's types of religion finds that religious violence stems from more than absolute, exclusive religious belief.

Only "False Religions" Are Violent (and They Aren't Us)

The claim that only false religions are violent is a form of essentialism. A "true" religion must have one necessary characteristic: peacefulness. According to this logic, any religion that would be involved in violence would be "false."[137] Yet it is hard to find a religion that does not have a history of association with violence. If that principle were correct, only a few pacifist religions would be considered "true."

In reality, the difference between "true" and "false" religion is a matter of subjective judgment, not objective fact. Those who insist that they are peaceful and therefore "true" tend to gloss over the legacy of their own religions. For example, Hinduism's beloved scripture, the Bhagavad-Gita, is set on a battlefield. The hero is actually encouraged to enter into the fray of combat. The Jewish scriptures likewise contain the history of bitter conflict over the Holy Land. To apply the sole qualifying criterion of peacefulness to the foundations of these religions would be to say that their historical basis is false.

Most religions would insist that they are "peaceful," though they have ways of justifying violence. We have already mentioned the Christian "just war" principles. Likewise, we referred to the Muslim tradition of justified and defensive warfare, the "lesser jihad." In many cases, religions have waged war and sanctioned violence based on such standards. Wellman and Tokuno correctly point out that religions claim ultimate authority to legitimize violence. In fact, they go on to develop some principles for the use and limits of violence. Therefore, a critical approach to the question of religious violence would say that identifying religions as "peaceful," and therefore "true," represents shallow and uninformed thinking. The question remains: Under what conditions do religions cross the line and engage in or approve of violence?

PROPOSING THE MOST PROMISING SOLUTION: A MULTIPLE CONDITIONS APPROACH

We have presented and analyzed a wide range of theories about why religion is often associated with violence. These theories view religious aggression from the perspectives of their authors. (See the textbox "Theories of Religious Violence and Their Viewpoints" for a chart of these approaches.) They represent the wide variety of viewpoints and the theories that scholars have offered in recent times.

Theories of Religious Violence and Their Viewpoints

Type of Theory	Perspective	Theory Reviewed
All Religions Are Violent	Atheism	Dawkins, Harris, and Dennett
	Psychology and Literary Studies	Girard
Some Religions Are Violent	Religious Studies	Wellman and Tokuno
	Political Science	Huntington
	Sociology and Global Studies	Juergensmeyer
	Comparative Religions	Eck
Only False Religions Are Violent	Naïve or Promotional	Tony Blair and many religious leaders

The topic of religious violence is so critical to the world's future that it deserves careful study from many points of view. This chapter is searching for a comprehensive theory that would offer an understanding of the nature and causes of religious violence. The hope is to find a theory to guide effective efforts to curb it and even prevent it.

This review has found problems with the notion that *all* religions are inherently violent on the one hand, and the protest that only *false* religions are violent on the other. Moreover, single factors like ritual sacrifice, ethnic identity, ideologies of "cosmic war," or exclusive, absolutist beliefs also fail to explain why some religions remain peaceful and others embrace violence. As we applied critical thinking to these theories, a reoccurring observation surfaced. Our analysis of these theories suggests that religions cause or sanction violence *under certain conditions*.

If this is true, the task of building a theory of religious violence must identify these conditions. Only then will we have a reliable basis to decide what to do about religious aggression. These preliminary thoughts about a solution to our problem are in line with the report of the Carnegie Commission on Preventing Deadly Conflict. That study found that religion does not cause violence in most cases. Rather, the Carnegie Commission observed that the "interplay" of social, economic, and political conditions provides the opportunity for aggressive leaders to stir up violence.[138] According to the Carnegie report, successful strategies of prevention will address these underlying conditions.

Building the Most Promising Solution: The Types and Conditions of Religious Violence

In *The Ambivalence of the Sacred*, researcher R. Scott Appleby recognizes that extremism is not sufficient to provoke religious leaders and their followers to violence. Instead, Appleby lists a set of external factors that make the choice of violence more likely (shown in the textbox "Appleby's External Conditions for Potential Religious Violence").[139]

Appleby's External Conditions for Potential Religious Violence

1. Weak or unresponsive political institutions
2. Poor or structurally unjust economy
3. Religious discrimination
4. A sense of a broken social contract and demand for justice

In themselves, none of these conditions will inevitably spark religious aggression. Appleby asserts that the religious leadership is the key to whether these conditions will flame up in violence. Violence erupts when religious leaders decide to exploit the conditions of discontent that Appleby lists. Typically, these skillful militants will not perform the violence themselves. They will recruit sympathizers and incite them to acts of protest, revenge, and hate.[140]

In Appleby's view, religious leaders have a choice. Either they can persuade believers to act on their grievances against society or they can promote peaceful responses to the volatile situation of dissatisfaction. Thus, religious leaders have the power to steer their followers toward violence *or* peace.[141]

A positive example comes from Nigeria.[142] Imam Muhammad Ashafa, a Muslim preacher, and Pastor James Wuye, a minister of the Evangelical Christian Church, were both leaders of militant religious youth movements in Nigeria. However, as they matured, both realized that their faith taught peace, not aggression. Turning from engagement in warfare to involvement in peacemaking, the two founded the Interfaith Mediation Center. Through the center, they were able to turn many youth in Nigeria and West Africa away from hostility toward peaceful lives. Moreover, they were mediators in the ethnic-religious conflict in Zagon-Kataf, Nigeria. Their story is told on film, and they are now global speakers for religious peacemaking.[143]

What conditions influence the rise, development, and decisions of religious leaders like these for or against violence? Appleby claims that the leaders' status in the society makes the difference.[144] Do the clerics have (relative) independence from the state? What relations do they have with other religious groups? Are the leaders free to recruit members, gather resources, and cultivate their following? The answer to these questions will determine the stance that the leaders take toward the social order.

What about the religious believers who are the potential soldiers in religious warfare? What factors will incline believers to follow religious agitators? What will entice ordinary believers into cycles of violence? The critical factor here is religious education in the home and religious institutions.[145]

To predict whether ordinary religious believers are likely to follow extremist militants, we must investigate the group's teaching about their identity, their past, and their attitude to outsiders. These teachings determine how the group will respond to the challenges it faces. When the group is under duress, they will be the most important factor in whether the group members answer the call to violence.[146]

Summary of the Most Promising Solution

Appleby's work makes a significant contribution to the understanding of religious violence. It has the added advantage of suggesting some practical steps toward the prevention of that violence. Thus, his results show the promise of looking for multiple conditions and factors of religious violence instead of a single, essential cause. With this in mind, we can categorize the conditions of religious violence according to major spheres of human life. (See the textbox "Categories of the Conditions of Religious Violence.") By charting the situations of potential religious violence according to these primary areas of life, we get a more comprehensive picture of its multiple sources.

Categories of the Conditions of Religious Violence

Category	Description	Theory of Violence
Sociological	the social setting of a group's perceived threat or violation	Wellman and Tokuno, Appleby, Fox
Psychological	the psychological dynamics of competition and grievance	Girard
Political	the political aim of nationalism and an activist religious leadership	Huntington, Fox
Educational	the trained receptivity of the religious group to violence	Dawkins, Harris, Dennett, Appleby
Religious	the religious ideology of sacred struggle	Juergensmeyer

The chart also shows that the theories that we have studied deal with aspects of the conditions for religious violence. For the most part, we can blend these theories with Appleby's list of "external factors" of religious violence to get a clearer picture of the circumstances that promote religious aggression. For example, under the *sociological* category, we can add the threat to group identity from Wellman and Tokuno to Appleby's sense of "religious discrimination" and "demand for justice." Moreover, the *psychological* category of "competition and grievance" enlarges Girard's theory, though it still includes *mimetic rivalry* and persecution. These factors suggest the psychological effect of Appleby's "sense of a religious discrimination," an "unjust economy," and "demand for justice."

The *political* category of Huntington's "clash of civilizations," however, does not match Appleby's political dynamics. But under the political category we can add the aim of "nationalism" from the analysis of Bruce Lincoln and the "activist religious leadership" from Appleby's list.

The *educational* category of the training of believers to be receptive to violence and the *religious* grouping of the ideology of the sacred struggle go together. These remind us of the theories of Dawkins, Harris, Dennett, and Eck about the disposition of religious believers to violence. It also clarifies that the apocalyptic ideology of Juergensmeyer is a "religious ideology of sacred struggle." It likewise makes students more susceptible to militants who aim to incite violence.

In short, these five categories of conditions incorporate the theories of violence that we have found so far. We have found that none of the theories is sufficient to account for the rise of religious violence. Now, we can understand the reason for their failure: each only deals with one aspect of the problem. Our proposed solution suggests that the field of religious studies might construct an all-encompassing understanding of the conditions for religious violence if it combined all of them into a single, comprehensive approach, a *multiple conditions theory*.

These conclusions prompt us to reframe the question of religious violence. The question is not whether religions cause violence. It is not what type of religion causes violence. The question is the role that religion plays in violence. We have found that religion can justify, intensify, ritualize, incite, and directly engage in violence. It also has the power to give conflict an ultimate and sacred meaning. However, it is rarely the exclusive and sufficient cause of violence. The most comprehensive interpretation of religious violence would look at the interlocking dynamics of these five conditions in two phases. First, what combination of conditions turns religious groups to violence? Second, how does religion interrelate with these factors?

EVALUATING THE MOST PROMISING SOLUTION: EMPIRICAL AND PRACTICAL TESTS

How would we test this proposal? One way would be a comparison of theories. For example, we have found the emerging theme of multiple factors from our review and analysis of representative approaches. Comparisons can give us different perspectives on the topic. However, the theorists do not agree. Even if they did, that would not validate their viewpoints.

Testing the Multiple Conditions Theory: The Use of Empirical Data

One way to test the theory of multiple causes of religious violence is to compare it to empirical data. Does independent evidence bear out the theory? Impressive studies that speculate about causes of religious violence are now easy to find. Some are based on painstaking research into historical and current examples and cases. However, it is hard to find comprehensive empirical data.[147] Especially needed is information that is unmixed with theoretical perspectives.

One source of reliable information is the work of Jonathan Fox, who has gleaned observations from three sources of empirical data. These "datasets" are the Minorities at Risk (MAR) dataset, which studies minority groups that are responding to discrimination with political action; the State Failure (SF) dataset, which studies wars between ethnic groups, revolutionary wars, and wars involving genocide; and the Religion and State (RAS) dataset, which studies government involvement in religion, especially endorsements of religion, restrictions, regulations, and discrimination. (See the textbox "Datasets on Religion and Violence" for a graphic description of these collections of evidence.)

Datasets on Religion and Violence

Dataset	Years	Description	Sponsor
Minorities at Risk (MAR)	1945–2004	Groups responding to discrimination with political action	Center for International Development and Conflict Management: University of Maryland
State Failure (SF) dataset	1955–2007	Ethnic wars between groups, revolutionary wars, and wars involving genocide	Political Instability Task Force, School of Public Policy: George Mason University
Religion and State	1990–2002	Government involvement in religion: state endorsements, restrictions, regulations, discrimination, legislation	Religion and State Project: Bar Ilan University, Ramat Gan, Israel

Political scientist Jonathan Fox used various methods to categorize and analyze the evidence from the raw data. He studied the relative weight of key threads that are woven together into the fabric of violent conflict. These included ethnic identity, minority discrimination, and aspirations of rebelling social groups for their own independent nation-states.

Findings from Empirical Databases on Religious Violence

The results of Fox's study give us some highly useful quantitative data to balance the qualitative theories of other studies. Most people have the impression that religious violence has increased so much that it is the principal cause of conflict in the world. Further, some would have us believe that religious conflict is between different religions or even "civilizations." Many have concluded that religions fill people with prejudice and hate. Moreover, they even promise eternal rewards for those who act on this sacred animosity.

Key Points of Fox's Empirical Research on Religious Violence

1. Religious violence has increased since 1980.
2. By *itself* religion is not a major factor in ethnic conflict.
3. Religion is one of a multiple set of factors that engender violence.
4. The primary cause of ethnic violence is the struggle for a separate, independent nation-state.
5. Religion increases the chances that an ethnic group that aspires to independence will resort to violent revolution.
6. Some religions are more involved in religious violence than others.
7. Most incidents of religious violence are between groups within the same religion.

If we accept these ideas, Fox's findings might surprise us. Fox confirms that incidents of religious violence have risen in recent times. However, that increase started twenty-five years ago, long before the public became aware of it. The proportion of religious conflicts to nonreligious conflicts began to change in the late 1970s with such events as the 1979 revolution in Iran. By 1991 and 1992, religious conflicts had become as frequent as nonreligious conflicts. But in 2002, the number of nonreligious conflicts began to drop while religious conflicts continued to rise. Thus, mostly unnoticed, the increase of religious violence started before the turn of the century and September 11, 2001.[148]

Fox found that a number of factors play a role in "ethnic/religious" conflicts. These include political discrimination, economic discrimination, cultural discrimination, repression, an expressed desire by a minority for autonomy, political demonstrations, and rebellion.[149] Other external factors include international support for the group and whether the conflict spills across national borders.[150]

But Fox discovered that religion *in itself* does not play a significant role in ethnic conflict. Religion only intensifies the hostility. The key cause of ethnic warfare is nationalism. When ethnic groups aspire to separate from the existing government and become their own independent nation-states, violence is likely. In Bruce Lincoln's terms, the religion of an alienated group will remain a "religion of resistance" until it advances to nationalistic goals. Then it becomes a "religion of revolution." Fox found that this has been happening with greater frequency from at least 1995.[151]

Furthermore, while the determining factor is nationalism, religion seems to play a role as a catalyst for violence in volatile situations of ethnic tension. We should not forget that religion plays a significant part in shaping group identity and defining differences in human society. These differences often lead to discrimination against the minority group and discrimination can lead to grievances that spark unrest. Fox has found that religion increases the likelihood that an ethnic group with aspirations of national self-determination will violently rebel. In fact, the chances are much more likely if the group seeking independence has a store of religious grievances.[152] If religious grievances are low and religion is seen as unimportant, there will be less protest. If religious grievances are high and religion is seen as important, there will be more protest. But the protest of religious grievance will turn from protest to revolt if there are aspirations for group self-determination.[153] Fox found that since 1980, religion has intensified the violence of conflicts involving the struggle for independence by a factor of 67 percent.

But Fox found another way that religion contributes to armed hostility. In the post–Cold War period, nation-states often get involved in the ethnic/religious violence of other countries to support the beleaguered minorities of the same religion as the intervening government. Fox states that this type of violence is increasing and is especially true of conflicts involving Muslim states.[154]

If religion plays a catalytic role in ethnic violence, does it matter what type of religion it is? Is conflict more likely among different religions? Fox found no significant difference in either the incidence or intensity of ethnic conflict if the parties are of *different* religions.[155] In fact, he found that the majority of ethnic conflicts are *intra*-religious. They are between members of the *same* religion.

Empirical Research and the Evaluation of the Proposed Comprehensive Theory

In summary, Fox's research confirms the multiple conditions theory of our "most promising solution." Fox's list of external factors that set the stage for the involvement of religion in violence can be compared to Appleby's list as well as the categories of conditions of religious violence. This comparison is found in the textbox "Comparison of Conditions for Violence." This chart shows that we can fit Appleby's specific conditions into the types of political, economic, and cultural discrimination that Fox lists. We can also group them under the major spheres of human life, our "categories of conditions." Fox's factors and our chart show that the proposal missed one area of life, the economic sphere. This omission suggests that the theories the chapter reviewed largely overlook this important source of the dissatisfactions that lead to violence.

Comparison of Conditions for Violence

Appleby	Fox	Categories of Conditions
Weak or unresponsive political institutions	Political discrimination	Political
	Repression	Sociological
Poor or structurally unjust economy	Economic discrimination	
Religious discrimination	Cultural discrimination	Religious Psychological Sociological
A sense of a broken social contract and demand for justice	Political demonstrations	Political Sociological Psychological
	Desire for autonomy (an independent nation)	Political
	Rebellion	Political Educational

Appleby makes a major contribution to the proposal when he points out that the religious leadership is the deciding factor of the potential of religious violence. Fox adds that the key to ethnic violence lies in the aspiration of a group for independence from a government that is discriminating against or repressing it. We might conclude that the militant religious leadership exploits the religious and cultural grievances of a minority group and the hope of national independence to incite violent revolt.

The analysis of Appleby and Fox shows that neither absolutist beliefs nor exclusivist religious group identity is enough to cause religious violence. Religious extremists use dogmatism and exclusivism to stir up violence. But the research of Appleby and Fox shows that their ability to do so depends on underlying conditions of grievance and discrimination. This means that if religion were eliminated from situations of conflict, the likelihood and intensity of violence would be reduced somewhat. However, the political, economic, and social factors that lead to violent conflict would still be present.[156]

This chapter's proposed solution to the problem of religious violence offers the insight that these underlying factors involve the major spheres of human life. An adequate theory must be comprehensive enough to grasp how these conditions in their totality set the stage for violence. The role of religion is to ignite and fan the flames of these conditions. But the role of religious leadership is to light the match that causes the explosion. The proposed theory would reason that if we can identify the volatile circumstances that have the potential to flare up into violence, then the focus of addressing religious violence must be on the deciding factor of religious leadership.

Testing the Multiple Conditions Theory by Its Application

Our analysis leads to the question of how scholars could test the proposed theory. This chapter proposes that the ultimate test of theories of religious violence is their usefulness in moderating or preventing it. This means that we must apply the proposed approaches to concrete situations that are likely to result in violence.

With that insight, we turn from the questions of theory to the challenges of practice. Practical application of theory cannot be done in the classroom, office, or laboratory. It has to be carried out in the field. The application of theory "on the ground" is especially important in the case of religious violence because of what we have found about religious aggression. We have suggested that religion is one factor of a complex set of causes of violence. Each situation, therefore, will have its own combination of these variables and dynamics of how these factors relate.

This chapter presented a multiple-factor theory inspired by Appleby as a guide for solving the problem of the relationship of religion and violence. The theory suggests that to prevent religious violence, we must identify the places where it is likely to occur. Then we should work with the local religious leadership. The religious leaders are the ones who can persuade their followers to address these conditions in a peaceful and nonviolent way.

Appleby himself points to methods of peacekeeping that respect the distinctive situations of actual and potential conflict.[157] Concerned peacekeepers are trying out modes of peacemaking within and across religious traditions. In situations where the conditions for religious violence are identified, they are trying to reach local religious leaders in the hopes of persuading them to steer their communities away from hostility and toward the peaceful settlement of their grievances.

One such peacemaker is Marc Gopin. He believes that his work at the George Mason University's Center on Religion, Diplomacy, and Conflict is opening up a new field of study.[158] Rabbi Gopin has led peacemaking workshops in Ireland, Israel, India, Switzerland, Italy, and the United States. His method is to combine the serious theoretical study of particular religious traditions with the practice of conflict resolution in local settings. His center lists work in Israel and Palestine, Syria, Uzbekistan, Afghanistan, Morocco, and Liberia.

Gopin believes that much of Western peacemaking has failed because governments and schools have ignored the role of religion in current conflict. The resurgence of religion has so intimidated these secular institutions of education, government, the military, and foreign policy that they have ignored what they cannot handle. The rabbi calls for governments and schools to take courage and come to terms with the rising influence of religion in today's global society.

That does not mean digging up the theological doctrines of "just war." These historic approaches offer only two options, "war" or "peace." They do not account for current dynamics in their unique circumstances. Instead, Gopin advocates a focus on the concrete realities and conditions of conflict and the role of religion in its context.[159]

A Test Case: An Educational Project to Prevent Religious Violence

An example of Gopin's approach is the work of Douglas Johnston, who heads the International Center for Religion and Diplomacy (ICRD).[160] Johnston's center has worked with hundreds of *madrasas*, the schools in Muslim societies whose curriculum is based on the Qur'an.[161]

The thousands of madrasas in Pakistan are Islamic religious schools but in the West they carry the suspicion that they are the first level of training for terrorists. The education they offer is centered on the Qur'an learned by rote memorization in Arabic. Since the students only know their native language of Urdu, it is alleged that the students do not understand what they are memorizing. The charge is that this makes the students susceptible to militants who twist the meaning of the Qur'an to their agendas.[162]

Muslim parents send their sons to these schools not only because they offer free education with room and board but also because they want their children to learn the principles of their religion. The institution began in Baghdad in the eleventh century as a school of higher learning for Muslim clerics. The movement spread throughout the Muslim world until modern times. In the 1970s the restoration of the institution became part of the "Muslim revival." Many believe that in the 1980s the United States and Middle Eastern states supported the madrasas in Afghanistan and Pakistan as a training ground for the *mujahideen*, the Muslim fighters against the Soviets. Numerous Taliban ("Students") leaders were former mujahideen that were recruited from the madrasas. Whatever their origin, madrasas represent a traditional education in Islam that is associated with the rejection of Western materialism and immorality.[163]

When the Pakistani government learned that four terrorists who attacked the London subway system in 2005 had attended a madrasa in Pakistan, it demanded that the Qur'anic schools be registered with the government. It has registered over 13,000. Concerned about the threat of the madrasas, the United States government has also spent millions on basic education programs in Pakistan and some Arab nations.[164]

According to this description of their religious conservatism, the madrasas do not seem to be a good setting for peacemaking. But recall Appleby's insight that religious leaders are the key to deciding whether alienated religious believers will turn to religious violence.

The International Center for Religion and Diplomacy (ICRD) has stepped into the situation to work with the educators who head the schools and decide on their curricula. Johnston says that the center presents the program as a "reform effort," not something imposed on them from the West. He notes that the heritage of Islam includes the arts and sciences as well as religious toleration. On the basis of the Muslim religion, the ICRD project helps the educators of the madrasas to broaden their curriculum. This includes teaching the meaning of the Arabic of the Qur'an instead of merely memorizing the holy book. The aim is to help the students in the Qur'anic schools understand their world as well as their religion. Ultimately, it is hoped that the students will gain the skills and attitudes necessary to resist the call of extremists to violence.[165]

Johnston reports that 2,700 religious leaders from more than 1,600 madrasas have been involved in the program. The project offers workshops that teach Muslim educators how to expand their course of studies. The conferences promote a broader curriculum that includes the physical and social sciences together with an emphasis on religious tolerance and human rights, especially the rights of women. But the workshops make their recommendations without challenging the core of the beliefs on which the madrasas are founded. Johnston says that he gets constant feedback of the changes of attitudes of the religious leaders and that the program has earned the respect of the United States State Department, Central Intelligence Agency, and Department of Defense.[166]

To appraise the multiple-factor theory in this practical way, we can analyze a report of a panel from the ICRD center. This panel assessed the ICRD center's

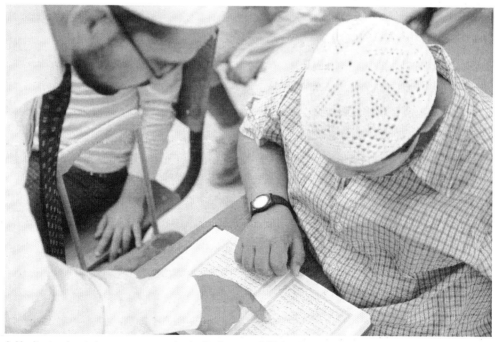

A Muslim teacher points out a passage in the Qur'an to a child. In Muslim madrasas, the core of the curriculum is the recitation of the Qur'an from memory.

work with the Pakistani madrasas. The test is whether we can identify the proposal's five categories of conditions for potential religious violence.

In terms of *sociology*, the report notes that the social condition in which the madrasas exist involves a sense of threat. This sense that the group identity is at risk is based on the experience of British colonialism. It also stems from how the madrasas view the United States. In the past, the United States treated the schools as training grounds for "freedom fighters" against the Soviets. Now they believe that America labels them and all Muslims as "terrorists." Thus, the schools operate in a social climate that demands the defense of their Muslim beliefs, values, and way of life.[167]

Touching the area of *psychology*, the report says that the rigid, old-fashioned methods of teaching developed in opposition to colonialism. This comment suggests the larger *psychology* that the traditional Muslim society tends to distrust Western "outsiders" and to recall the perceived abuses of Western powers in colonial times. The mind-set of the society surrounding the madrasas most likely harbors resentments and suspicions about the West. It is easy to think that the Americans have just taken the place of the former colonialists.[168]

Religiously, the report notes that those who send their children to the schools are devout Muslims who want their children to grow up in their religious heritage. The report notes that the educators will resist anything that they believe will lead to secularization. This suggests that the schools are dedicated to a traditional, absolutist, and exclusivist view of the faith.[169]

Politically, the report says that many Muslims in their traditional society tend to feel the religious extremists like bin Laden understand their needs and aspirations better than the government. They do not feel that the government speaks for them or acts on their behalf. Moreover, the schools are not funded by the government but rather by religious charity. This suggests that the schools have the potential to stand for the aspirations of the people against the government.[170]

Educationally, the schools focus almost entirely on the rote memorization of the Qur'an in Arabic, a language the children do not understand. This raises the fear that those who have attended will be vulnerable to the militants who will instruct them in their version of what the Muslim holy book means. The stories of terrorists that have attended these Islamic religious schools seem to confirm this fear.[171]

This brief overview shows that the five sets of conditions for religious terrorism exist in this situation. The analysis does not include the economic conditions. But the report notes that many of the students come from poor families who take advantage of the free education, room, and board. The economic circumstances of this situation could easily turn into a sense of grievance against those in power.[172]

The categories of the proposed theory help us think critically about the dynamics of the case. We find that the situation of the madrasas meets the conditions that signal a potential for violence in all the spheres of life. Therefore, the analysis verifies that the danger that the situation will breed terrorism is real.

We note that religion is a factor in this situation but even its absolutism, exclusivism, and ideology do not guarantee violence. The report notes that the parents are not sending their sons to these schools to make them terrorists. They want them to get a foundation in their religion. Nevertheless, we can see the role that religion plays in establishing the context for potential violence. Moreover, it is possible that the program's focus on religious leaders could use the religious ideology of the sacred struggle to incite violence in this specific setting.

Our critical reflection on this case reaches the conclusion that the threat of religious violence in this situation is real. We have also found that religion has a significant role in relationship to the other factors. Thus, we can see how the educators hold the key to the future, even if they themselves do not directly promote violence.

Taking into account all the factors, we can understand why the work of the ICRD concentrates on religious education. Education is the way that religious leaders will guide their followers either toward violence or away from it. Therefore, the project is working carefully with the Muslim educators who are also the religious leaders. Focusing on them should have an indirect but positive impact on the chances for peace. If the program can convince them that their educational programs should include science, social studies, religious tolerance, and critical thinking, then the students may not be as open to the preaching of religious aggression. The goal is not to take away the religious devotion of the society. It is to direct it to peaceful ends.

The appraisal of the ICRD project suggests that the five-conditions approach would be useful for addressing the problem of religious violence. This proposed method would give researchers a more thorough understanding of religious violence than a single factor method. It would also give peacemakers a method of addressing the multiple factors that make religions likely to be violent.

Conclusion: The Important Role of Religious Studies in Addressing Religious Violence

The study of the puzzle of religious violence shows the importance of religious studies for the twenty-first century. This chapter has shown how scholars of religion are meeting the challenge of interpreting the dynamics of religious violence in today's world.

Our review has demonstrated the important role of theory in academic study. Theory directs and shapes the search for the understanding of religion in today's world. Sound theories are the best basis for efforts to deal with the dynamics of religion such as religious violence. Whatever we do to address the problem will be as valuable as the theories that it implements.

In the coming century, the worldwide forces of globalization and tribalism, modernism and antimodernism, nationalism and internationalism, secularism and the resurgence of religion will continue to ignite the fires of religious aggression. We can predict that interreligious hostilities will continue between religions. It will occur less frequently between what Huntington called civilizations. However, if trends continue, conflict between groups that share the same major world religion will be even more common. Thus, in the future, our global society will probably have to deal with religious violence between and within religions. We may have to contend with hostilities between religious antimodernism and Western secularism. The most dangerous combination, however, will be the explosive combination of nationalism, religion, and ethnic identity. Tragically, the field of religious studies will have more than enough cases to look at.

Insights for Further Study

This study of a contemporary issue of religion has produced several insights about how the field of religious studies might go about the work of interpreting religious violence. First, one's prior viewpoint often hides, distorts, and limits one's understanding of what is the case. In addition, a single viewpoint is probably incomplete. A critical thinking approach to religious studies casts a broad net to capture as much information, ideas, and approaches to study as it can. It considers a wide range of studies from careful works that are full of details and polemical works that jolt us into new thinking. Yet scholars in the field of religion should develop the critical ability to recognize the difference between one kind of work and another.

Tips for Studying Current Issues in Religious Studies

1. Begin with an open mind and review as many studies and viewpoints as possible.
2. Use multiple academic disciples to view the topic.
3. Test theories by the usefulness of their practical application.
4. Find empirical evidence to build and check theories.

Second, if the proposal of this chapter is correct, then the use of multiple disciplines of study is essential for scholars to interpret such phenomena as religious violence. Since there are sociological, psychological, political, and educational as well as religious aspects of religious violence, religious studies will have to use these disciplines to understand it. A variety of viewpoints also helps scholars avoid bias and achieve a more informed and comprehensive understanding of their topic.

Third, religious aggression is much too important to be left to the theorists. Religious violence hurts real people in real circumstances. Theory is necessary for us to understand the dynamics of religious violence. We must have useful theories to have any chance of successfully dealing with it. However, this chapter suggests that scholars must critically evaluate, test, and apply their theories to find out if they are workable. The theories that we have reviewed are significant attempts to deal with a crucial human problem. This chapter's investigation points to the need for more work on how these theories apply to the prediction and prevention of religious violence.

Fourth, this study has shown the value of testing theories with empirical data. The theories that we have summarized represent different levels of evidence. Some are almost purely conceptual. Others represent insights gleaned from the painstaking research of a wide range of cases of religious violence. Theories help us make sense of religious phenomena. But comparing theories with actual statistical evidence helps us correct and refine them. As we begin the new century, religious studies seems to have a sufficient supply of theories and qualitative research about violence in the name of religion. However, more quantitative data and analysis of the role of religion in violence is needed.[173] As the study of religious violence advances, it will require the use and development of reliable databases such as the ones that Jonathan Fox uses.

Finally, this study has naturally concentrated on the association of religion and violence, not peace. However, we have found that religion can be the deciding factor for peace as well as war. It is unrealistic to think that scouring religion from the face of the Earth could solve religious violence for all times. In Appleby's terms, religion has "ambivalence."[174] The major world religions contain teachings that can be interpreted in various ways—some helpful and some harmful. Thus, religious aggression is not inevitable. It depends on the choices of human beings. Religion can be used for destructive purposes. However, with wise insight and skillful means, it can be also be used for good. Religious studies might develop a comparable body of literature on how religion fosters peace to the massive studies that treat how religion engenders war.[175]

Concluding Summary: The Better the Theory, the Better the Understanding, the Better the Application

We started this chapter with a report of strange actions and surprising alliances. Nevertheless, these are just some examples of the current worldwide efforts to quench the fires of religious aggression.

This chapter suggests that we should be careful about the assumptions we make about the nature and causes of religion-inspired hostility. The challenge of religious violence is so crucial to the future in the twenty-first century that we need to consider these presuppositions thoughtfully. Here is where the field of religious studies has a critical role. Scholars of religion have developed a rich store of theories about the association of religion and violence. The discussion and evaluation of these theories can inform the way people of the twenty-first century think about violence. A critical thinking approach to these proposals can prevent misguided attempts to deal with it. It can also help scholars develop a more workable theory on which peacemakers might base their efforts to prevent it or stop it. Continued development, refinement, and testing of proposed theories are critical to finding ways to address one of the most critical problems of the twenty-first century.

KEY TERMS

Apocalypticism: the belief in the catastrophic end of the world by means of a final confrontation between the forces of good and evil.

Clash of civilizations: the theory of Samuel Huntington that after the Cold War global hostility will erupt between broad "civilizations" instead of nation-states or empires. There are eight or nine of these civilizations.

Cosmic war: the final conflict between the forces of good and evil that believers believe will result in the destruction of the universe followed by the creation of a new order of reality.

Datasets: a grouping of information arranged in a table of statistics.

Exclusivist religions: religions that believe that they alone have the whole truth.

Group and society religious violence: hostilities that involve social groups without the factor of nationalism. This type of violence includes persecution, discrimination, and segregation of minority groups.

Inclusivist religions: religions that believe that they have the truth but others may have at least partial truths.

Intrinsic: built in to something's basic nature.

Memes: in the use of Richard Dawkins, the cultural units that are passed along from one person to another in a society by imitation.

Mimesis: in René Girard's theory, the process of imitation that builds up and transmits culture.

Mimetic rivalry: in René Girard's theory, the destructive hostility that begins when two subgroups compete with one another and ends with each trying to wipe the other out.

The "Other": in the theory of Wellman and Tokuno, the alien group that lies outside the boundaries of an ethnic group or society. The ethnic group or society defines itself in contrast to what is considered foreign.

Pacifism: ideology that rejects violent conflict in all circumstances as a matter of religion and/or individual conscience.

Pluralist religions: religions that recognize that no religion has a claim on the universal truth.

"Religions of resistance": according to Bruce Lincoln, ideologies of dissident groups that are alienated from the government and society and choose to insulate themselves rather than rebel actively.

"Religions of revolution": according to Bruce Lincoln, ideologies of dissident groups that choose to break out of their defensive isolation and engage in armed rebellion against the government and society.

"Religions of the status quo": according to Bruce Lincoln, ideologies that uphold the power and privileges of the ruling class.

Religious war: a war fought in the name of religion against an opposing religion or ideology.

The scapegoat mechanism: the process of displacement of hostility of mimetic rivalry from the antagonists to a convenient victim. It unites the warring parties in a common release of hostility that results in the sacrificial death of the scapegoat.

KEY QUESTIONS

1. The Talks between Christian and Muslim Leaders
   a. In the view of Sam Harris and Richard Dawkins, are the meetings between the Catholic pope and other Christian leaders likely to help the cause of world peace? Explain.
   b. In the view of Diana Eck, are the meetings between the Catholic pope and other Christian leaders likely to help the cause of world peace? Explain.

2. The Theory of René Girard
   a. Apply the theory of René Girard to the Jews in Nazi Germany. How did the "scapegoat mechanism" apply to them?
   b. Using the theory of René Girard, explain why religious violence continues in the modern world.
3. Group Identity as a Source of Violence (Wellman and Tokuno)
   a. Do ethnic and religious groups have to define themselves in contrast to an "Other"? Defend your answer.
   b. Does group identity always lead to violence? Defend your answer and give an example.
4. Apocalypticism
   a. Explain why apocalypticism ("cosmic war ideology") leads to religious violence such as suicide bombings in the theory of Mark Juergensmeyer.
   b. Does apocalypticism necessarily lead to violence? If not, what factors must be added to this ideology for it to incite violence?
5. Empirical Research (Jonathan Fox)
   a. According to Jonathan Fox, what are the factors that play a role in "ethnic/religious" rebellion?
   b. According to Fox, what role does religion play in violence?
   c. Explain how datasets of empirical evidence can help religious studies develop theories of religious violence.
6. Multiple Conditions Theory
   a. What are the factors ("external conditions") that R. Scott Appleby states make religious violence likely?
   b. What role does religion play in igniting violence in contexts where these factors exist?
7. Testing the Multiple Conditions Theory
   a. In the test case of Johnston's work with Muslim madrasas, why does education play a key role in the prevention and treatment of religious violence?
   b. Give an example of how peacemakers are using religion as a way to solve and not promote violence.

7

Making It After All
The Future of Religion

CHAPTER SUMMARY

1. Discovering the Problem: The Secularization Thesis Revisited

In the middle of the twentieth century, most scholars agreed with the "secularization thesis." As societies become more modern, religion would lose its power in society and its influence over individuals. The secularization thesis held that modern societies were based on rationality and therefore no longer subject to religious superstition. Besides that, the theory held that modern societies are divided into different sectors: the educational, economic, political, and cultural spheres. The theory assumed that forces of rationalism and differentiation would expel religion from public life and eliminate its role as a guiding and unifying force in society.

At the turn of the century, many scholars began to change their mind about this thesis. Even as religions became engaged in global conflicts, they grew in influence. Moreover, in many parts of the world outside of Europe and Canada, the majority of the population persists in their religious beliefs and behaviors. Now that scholars seriously question the theory, the field of religious studies is searching for its replacement, a comprehensive theory that could safely predict the future of religion.

2. Focusing the Problem: Evidence for a "Resurgence of Religion"?

Most blame the "resurgence of religion" for the fall of the secularization thesis. We might ask whether there is evidence for such a *resurgence of religion*. The exploration of this question will help us focus on the problem of the chapter.

If the "resurgence of religion" means that religion has a greater influence on world and national affairs in the twenty-first century, then the term needs no more confirmation. If religions consist of members, what about the number of believers? A review of the demographic predicts that the *rate* of growth of the Christian, Muslim, Hindu, and "nonreligious" world populations will exceed the rate of growth of the world's population. Other religions and viewpoints may increase in raw numbers but will lag behind the rate of global population growth. Thus the numerical "resurgence of religion" is taking place among some but not all religions.

Some scholars assert a modification of the secularization thesis. They say that religion loses its influence on society and individuals as the quality of life rises. They point to the high numbers of unbelievers (atheists, agnostics, and nonreligious persons) in highly developed countries. To test this idea, this section categorizes countries using the United Nations

Human Development Index (HDI) and compares these lists with the list of countries with high and low rates of unbelief. While the correlation between quality of life and unbelief holds for Europe, the analysis finds that some countries that are relatively high on the HDI index also have low rates of unbelievers. Therefore, the HDI index alone cannot predict whether a country will have high or low rates of unbelievers.

The problem with the secularization thesis is that it no longer can explain the complex dynamics of religion in today's global society. Moreover, it can no longer predict the future of religion with any certainty. The problem of this chapter is to find a viable theory to replace the secularization thesis.

3. Surveying the Alternative Approaches: Four Theories of Prediction

This chapter will explore four options for a new theory that would forecast the future of religion: (1) the projection of population (demographic) trends; (2) the revision of the secularization thesis; (3) the effects of immigration of human populations in today's global society; and (4) the likely religious responses to the overall trends of globalization. In all cases, the predictions cannot take into account unforeseen forces, especially the choices of human persons, religious leaders, and religious organizations.

4. Proposing the Most Promising Solution: The Rational Choice Theory

The evaluation of the alternative theories for predicting the future of religion gives us a clue for a more useful solution. Using an economic model, the *rational choice theory* supposes that human persons make choices based on what they consider their best interests, whether right or wrong. Applied to religion, this theory suggests that human beings will continue to make religious choices that they believe will benefit them. The demand for religion is constant, since religion offers answers to the most enduring and momentous questions of human life. However, the supply of religious answers to the questions will vary with the available religious organizations and leadership. As they try to find religious ways that will satisfy their demand, people in the future will make choices that suit them. Thus, the future of religion is secure, but what kinds of religion will exist in the future is and will be a question. It depends on the choices that persons will make.

5. Evaluating the Most Promising Solution: A Test of Two Catholic Settings

The rational choice theory (RCT) is a viable option to the secularization thesis. Researchers can test its formula that religions thrive in settings of religious diversity and competition. This formula passes tests such as Stark's research into Catholic parishes where Catholics are in the majority compared with parishes where Catholics are in the minority. However, researchers disagree whether the RCT formula holds in places like Great Britain. Moreover, some scholars doubt whether the theory is useful in predicting the future of religion instead of merely explaining its past. The chapter concludes that the future of religion in the twenty-first century is still an open question. The ending suggests that human persons are agents who make choices. Individuals, organizations, and societies are not passive victims to the forces of globalization in the twenty-first century. They will make choices that will determine the course of history and the future role of religion in the world.

DISCOVERING THE PROBLEM:
THE SECULARIZATION THESIS REVISITED

Since the Enlightenment, many traditional religious believers have tried to defend their faith against the relentless forces of secularization in the modern world. Now the secularists are rallying to defend themselves against religion. In 2007, a private research group dedicated to upholding the secular society hosted a conference in Lower Manhattan across from the ruins of the World Trade Center. The sponsor, the Center for Inquiry, called the meeting "The Secular Society and Its Enemies." The publicity for the event sounded an urgent alarm, stating, "Religious fervor in the United States and abroad remains at an all-time high."[1]

If anything showed that secularism is losing its grip on world affairs, it was the anxious tone of the meeting. The stated purpose of the event was to organize the guardians of secularism against the perceived dangers of religion, the religious threats to science, politics, education, and the judicial system. In summary, the conference worried about the "ominous threat of de-secularization."[2] The message was that secularists must get together to arrest the religious resurgence that this textbook has documented.

The Secularization Thesis Defined

The secularization thesis is the theory that the processes of modernism that separate religion from government and other functions of society will inevitably lead to the decline of religious influence over society, groups, and individuals.

Secularists, it seems, feel betrayed. For decades in the last century, the *secularization thesis* was the model for predicting the future of religion in the modern world. This theory held that the forces of modernization would inevitably lead to the decline of religion and its influence on the people of our planet. However, events and movements at the turn of the century show that secularization is not as certain or as predestined as the secularists imagined it to be.

This theory was so dominant we could call it a *paradigm*, a mental framework of rules and procedures about how a subject is to be studied.[3] As a paradigm, the thesis set the standards of the problems for investigation, theories, methods, and instrument of research into religion.[4] But it also offered a compelling set of projections about the diminishing role of religion in modern society.[5] Thus, this ruling model of study was useful for the description of the dynamics of religion in modern times. Yet the theory did something more than simply describe changes in the role of religion in the world. It described a process, the process of *secularization*. It mixed description with prediction.

We can trace the theory to the French philosopher and father of sociology, Auguste Compte (1798–1847). Compte proposed that history has advanced through stages. The human race has gone through the successive forms of animism, polytheism, and monotheism. Now we have reached the last stage, when we can solve the world's problems with science, not superstition.

The eminent sociologist Max Weber (1864–1920) built the secularization thesis on Compte's ideas of social evolution. Weber asserted that the three characteristics of the modern world were *rationalization, intellectualization,* and *disenchantment* of the world. The first two defining factors of modernism had to do with the shift from the dependence of supernatural revelation to the reliance on human reason. These two changes in the mind-set of modern people had resulted in the third characteristic. Disenchantment had broken the spell of religious mystery and exorcized the supernatural powers from modern public life. Now modern people relied on their intellects to master the forces of the universe. As various fields of knowledge developed apart from religion, religion lost the credibility of its belief. It was backed into the corner of the private and inner experience—the "mystical life." In this subjective realm, people could believe what they liked.[6] Alongside Compte and Weber, other founders of sociology such as Émile Durkheim (1857–1917) and Karl Marx (1864–1920), together with the psychologist Sigmund Freud (1836–1939), fostered this same theory.

Generations of scholars accepted the idea that the process of secularization would finally wipe religion out of the minds of modern people altogether. For academic study, the secularization thesis was not merely a forecast of the demise of religion in public society. It was not merely about the loss of power of religious authority over other institutions of society. It not only advocated the separation of church and state but also stated that when religion lost its hold on institutions, it would also lose its power over individuals. For most people, the rational thinking of science would replace personal and subjective faith.[7]

In this vein, before he changed his mind, the eminent sociologist Peter Berger referred to the "secularization of consciousness." In Berger's thought, the decline in the influence of religion in public life, the decay of religious institutions, and the downfall of faith would reinforce one another. As a result, the modern mindset would be thoroughly secular without any lingering thought of religion.[8]

A skyscraper towers over a church. Generations of scholars have predicted that secular life would grow and religion diminish, but research shows that not to be the case.

The Fall of the Secularization Thesis

In the final decade of the last century, though, the challenges to the theory increased. The thesis claimed that modernism would lead inevitably to a downturn in religious interest, influence, and impact. But a sufficient amount of evidence is available to conclude that this prediction has failed. Noting the changes in today's global society, the renowned German sociologist Jürgen Habermas openly expressed doubts about the thesis. He asserted that current events and issues throughout the world had undermined the idea that religion is irrelevant to modern life.[9] In America, the noted sociologist of religion Peter Berger admitted that what he and other sociologists had written about religion was a mistake. They thought that the processes of modernization and secularization went hand in hand. But in the twenty-first century, he observed, most of the world is religious, not secular.[10]

Berger and Habermas agree that the only place where the secularization thesis still holds true is Europe. However, the worldwide trends are against the continued expansion of secularism. Europeans can no longer assume that the world will follow its lead of displacing religion. Yet even in Europe, religion is growing in influence and visibility. In this century, Europeans face the challenge of sizeable and growing populations of immigrants who have carried their religions with them into the European secular society. Suddenly, Europeans who have dismissed religion for themselves have to engage with religious believers in their own communities.

Sociologist R. Stephen Warner states that it is an "open secret" that the secularization thesis does not work because it has failed to produce convincing results.[11] The thesis cannot explain the persistence of religion in America and other parts of the world, not to mention the worldwide upswing in religious fervor in the twenty-first century. At least it cannot do this in its original form. Sociologist Rodney Stark states, "After three centuries of utterly failed prophecies and misinterpretations of both present and past, it seems time to carry the doctrine to the graveyard of failed theories."[12] Now the secularists who once were confident that the process was unstoppable are organizing to defend it.

If Warner and Stark are right, the obvious question for the academic study of religion is whether it can devise a revised theory or an alternative hypothesis that would replace it. The secularization thesis had the advantage of being a comprehensive hypothesis that would apply to evidence from throughout the world. Scholars could use it to explain religious trends and make predictions about the role of religion in today's world. Some still believe that it is helpful. Bryan R. Wilson (1926–2004) said that the theory may be incomplete but it is the best theory we have.[13] This statement hardly gives scholars confidence in the theory. Instead, it lays down a challenge for religious studies to find a better one.

FOCUSING THE PROBLEM:
EVIDENCE FOR A "RESURGENCE OF RELIGION"?

The secularization thesis had such a hold on the study of religion that the announcement of its demise is unsettling to the field of religious studies. Before we search for alternatives, we might ask whether the announcement is, in fact, premature. Most scholars point to a "religious resurgence" to explain the downfall of the thesis. For example, sociologist Martin Riesebrodt blames the demise of the theory on the global revival of religion. He states that few scholars were prepared for the upsurge of religion as a "public force" and "power shaper" of religious believers.[14]

Counterevidence to the Secularization Thesis?

1. The increasing visibility of religion in national and global affairs
2. The increasing role of religion in politics, international relationships, and moral issues
3. A *resurgence of religion* that claims that religion has a place in public as well as private life

---

Riesebrodt suggests that the rising influence of religion on the affairs of society and the lives of individuals destroyed the thesis. The issues that this book discusses corroborate the increasing role of religion in the world. Such influence is qualitative. Is there measurable evidence that would undercut the secularization thesis?

A Resurgence of Religion?

Several sources of demographic data on the status of religion in the twenty-first century are available. One source for the world's population and projections is the "Population Estimates and Projections" section of the United Nations Department of Economic and Social Affairs.[15] Among other demographic data, the UN resource has statistics and projections on population, fertility rates, mortality rates, and migration.

Another source is the Central Intelligence Agency's *World Factbook*.[16] This resource has statistics for the major world religions. It has a listing of countries and the percentages of the major religions of each nation.

The last resource is the *World Christian Database*. According to Barney Warf and Peter Vincent, the World Christian Database (WCD) is "arguably the most accurate, reliable, and widely used source in existence."[17] Even its critics like Phil Zuckerman and Gregory Scott Paul use it, but with their own corrections.[18]

Table 7.1 presents a summary of the available demographic data. This pie graph illustrates the relative sizes of major world religions from the *CIA Factbook* for 2011. This chart shows that almost seven of ten humans on Earth belong to three religions: Christianity (33.35 percent), Islam (22.43 percent), and Hinduism (13.78 percent)[19]

After the three largest religions, the chart shows that almost one in ten persons is classified as *nonreligious* (agnostic or those who do not specify a religion). Note that the class of nonreligious differs from the class of atheist. Atheists only represent 2.04 percent of the world's population.

The *CIA World Factbook* chart groups 11.7 percent of the global population under "other religions." The WCD database for 2005 breaks down the same category into some surprising divisions:[20] "Chinese Universists" (6.3

Table 7.1.   Percentages of Major Religions—World Populations 2011

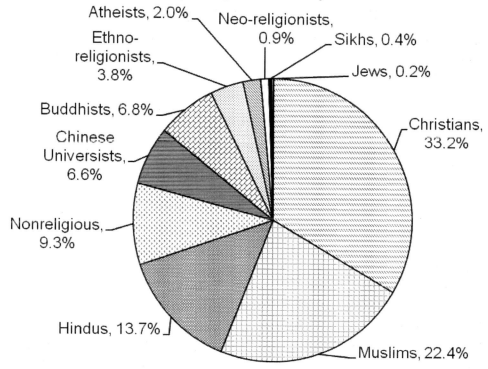

percent); Ethno-religious" (tribal) (4 percent), Sikhs (.4 percent), and Jews (.2 percent). (See the chart "Detail on Other Religions" for their relative sizes.) Chinese Universists are Chinese who practice a folk religion that mixes the philosophies of Taoism, Buddhism, and Confucianism with ancestor worship, spiritism, animism, divination, shamanism, and other esoteric beliefs. Ethno-religious includes the tribal religions that are spread throughout the world. The New Religions (neoreligionist) are religions that have modern origins and lie outside the scope of traditional religions.

Do such statistics show a current and future resurgence of religion, the downfall of secularization? When all religions are added, the *CIA World Factbook* shows that less than 12 percent of the Earth's population can be categorized as atheist or nonreligious.[21] Despite the forces of modernity, almost nine in ten human beings belong to an identifiable religion. The "big three" religions of Christianity, Islam, and Hinduism enjoyed spectacular growth in the twentieth century. In 1900 barely one-half of the world's population belonged to one of the "big three" religions. At the beginning of the twenty-first century, more than two-thirds belonged to these groups,[22] and by 2025, the figure will increase even more.[23]

Or Does the Secularization Thesis Still Hold?

Researcher and author Gregory Paul and sociologist Phil Zuckerman represent the observers who disagree that religion is gaining strength in this century. They

Table 7.2.   Detail on Other Religions—Relative Sizes

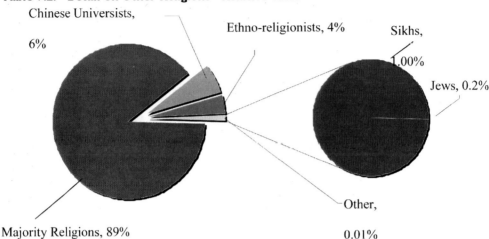

Chinese Universists, 6%

Ethno-religionists, 4%

Sikhs, 1.00%

Jews, 0.2%

Majority Religions, 89%

Other, 0.01%

refer to charts from the *World Christian Encyclopedia* to claim that Christianity is "edging downward"[24] and that Hinduism "shows no significant increase." They recognize that Islam is projected to grow from one-eighth to a projected one-quarter of the human population by 2050. However, they say that most Muslims live in undemocratic societies and are poor and uneducated. Therefore, the Muslim expansion does not count, since it is occurring in places where the forces of modernization are not working.[25]

Paul and Zuckerman go on to quote the WCE to say the that number of non-religious has skyrocketed from 3.2 million in 1900 to 697 million in 1970, and on to 918 million in 2000. Moreover, they state that WCE overestimates Christianity. Further, they refer to a WCE statement that many of the "nonreligious" are probably the descendents of Christians but are still counted as Christians.[26] They conclude that the nonreligious probably soared past the billion mark already, and the three great faiths total 64 percent at most.[27]

When we analyze their claims, we find that the writers agree with the WCE that two in three humans on Earth belong to one of the "big three" religions. They offer no empirical evidence for their statement of "probabilities" and "overestimates." Then, in addition, they do not consistently distinguish between the atheist and the nonreligious (agnostics). Analysis that is more careful would note that these are two separate groups, as we see in the WCD statistics.

The writers also overlook contrary evidence to their claim. For example, the writers refer to the WCE's observation of the "massive defections from Christianity" due to secularism in Europe and materialism in America,[28] but they fail to take into account that these losses are offset by gains in the Third World. The Pew Forum reports that in sub-Saharan Africa, the number of Christians has grown seventy times larger since 1900. The number of Muslims has grown twenty times larger.[29] Moreover, their view of Muslims ignores the wealth and education of Muslims in the oil-rich Middle Eastern states where expressed unbelief is at very low levels.

Yet despite these flaws, we should not dismiss what Zuckerman and Paul point out. The atheist and nonreligious categories increased significantly in the twentieth century. This increase seemed to support the secularization thesis. On the other hand, the statistics of a worldwide rise in religion are definite enough to force most scholars to reconsider their prediction of the modern decline of religion. Most now accept that the term "religious resurgence" applies to today's world.

If we look carefully at the data, we still see scattered indications that the secularization process may be at work. According to WCD figures, a number of countries have high rates of atheists and nonreligious. Among these are Russia, China, North Korea, Germany, Sweden, Kazakhstan, Cuba, New Zealand, and Uruguay. However, South Asia, Muslim societies across the globe, a large part of Africa, the United States, Ireland, Central America, and South America have significantly lower percentages of those not identified with a religion.[30]

Analysis: The Difference among Nations

Paul and Zuckerman claim that the difference between these two groups of countries is the "result of social, political, and especially, economic conditions." This argument modifies the secularization thesis. It originally stated that modernization will inevitably lead to secularization. But the writers refer to the claim of political scientists Ronald Inglehart and Pippa Norris that the deciding factor is the level of personal and social security. In this view, the healthiest and wealthiest countries have the highest percentages of atheists and nonbelievers.

However, is the argument correct? To answer, we might use the Human Development Index (HDI) to see if there is some correlation between a prosperous quality of life and high rates of atheists and the nonreligious.[31] The United Nations Human Development Program formulated this scale to measure the opportunities for quality of human life in countries throughout the world. It combines the factors of life expectancy, education, and standard of living. Zuckerman refers to this index when he states that of the top twenty-five nations only Ireland does not have a significant percentage of "organic atheists." On the other hand, he says that of the bottom fifty nations, none had significant percentages of nonbelievers.[32]

See table 7.3 for a list of selected countries according to the HDI divisions of "Very High," "High," "Medium," and "Low" numbers of the HDI.[33] Using Zuckerman's figures for unbelievers, the table categorizes selected countries under these divisions according to whether they have high or low percentages of atheists and nonreligious people.[34] For example, the column on the far left lists countries with a "Very High" HDI number that have significant percentages of atheists and nonreligious. The next column is shaded and lists countries with a "Very High" HDI number that have relatively low percentages of atheists and nonreligious.

This chart demonstrates Zuckerman's point that many of the most highly developed countries have relatively high percentages of atheists and nonreligious. As we go across the chart from "Very High" to "High," "Medium," and then "Low HDI" countries, we find fewer atheists and nonreligious people. On the "Low HDI" column, we find almost none.

Table 7.3. Standard of Living and Percent of Atheists and Nonreligious (Selected Countries)

Very High HDI	Very High HDI	High HDI	High HDI	Medium HDI	Medium HDI	Low HDI	Low HDI
High % Atheist/ Nonreligious	*Low % Atheist/ Nonreligious*	*High % Atheist/ Nonreligious*	*Low % Atheist/ Nonreligious*	*High % Atheist/ Nonreligious*	*Low % Atheist/ Nonreligious*	*High % Atheist/ Nonreligious*	*Low % Atheist/ Nonreligious*
1. Norway	4. United States	48. Uruguay	57. Mexico	101. China	103. Thailand	North Korea (not indexed)	143. Kenya
2. Australia	7. Ireland	51. Cuba	56. Saudi Arabia		95. Jordan		152. Tanzania
3. Netherlands	30. United Arab Emirates	68. Kazakhstan	61. Malaysia		123. Philippines		156. Nigeria
5. New Zealand	31. Cyprus		63. Kuwait		124. Indonesia		164. Zambia
9. Germany	37. Qatar		73. Venezuela		129. Nicaragua		166. Rwanda
20. France	39. Poland		84. Brazil		134. India		169. Sudan
	44. Chile		88. Iran		139. Cambodia		181. Afghanistan
			92. Turkey				186. Niger

However, contrary to Zuckerman, some countries with *low percentages* of atheists and nonreligious also score very high on the HDI index. For example, among the forty-seven "Very High HDI" countries are the United States, Ireland, Poland, and Chile. Also listed are the oil-rich Middle Eastern countries of the United Arab Emirates and Qatar. Zuckerman fails to note these countries because he does not go far enough down the list of what the 2004 United Nations report called "High HDI" countries.[35]

Moreover, in the "High HDI" group of forty-six countries, we find an assortment of countries that have low percentages of atheists and nonreligious like Mexico, Venezuela, Saudi Arabia, Kuwait, Iran, Malaysia, Brazil, and Turkey. In the "Medium HDI" group of forty-six countries, we find many Asian countries such as Thailand, Cambodia, and India as well as the Pacific island nations of the Philippines and Indonesia.

In the "Low HDI" category (thirty-seven countries), almost all nations have low percentages of atheists and nonreligious people. The countries include the African countries of Kenya, Tanzania, Nigeria, and Niger along with Afghanistan.

For the purpose of illustration, table 7.4 depicts the relationship between the HDI standard of living index and percentage of atheists and nonreligious of

Table 7.4.   Quality of Life and Percent Nonbelievers Illustrated

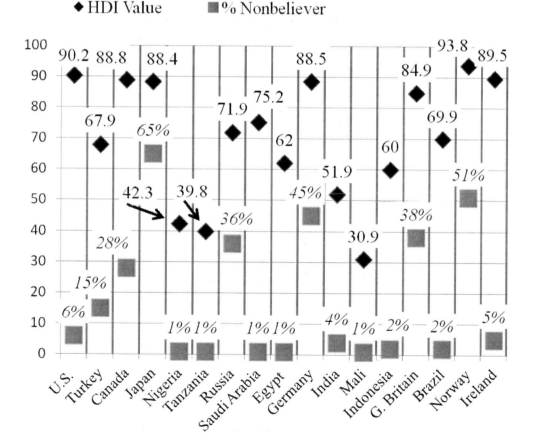

selected countries. The diamond shapes indicate the HDI value—that is, the relative quality of life. For example, the score found above the United States is 90.2 points. However, Tanzania scores 39.8 points. The square shapes indicate the relative percentages of atheists and those who do not believe in God or a Higher Power, according to Zuckerman.[36] The number above the square box represents the percentage of atheists and nonreligious of the country.

This chart shows that areas in northern Europe (excluding Ireland), Russia, and Japan whose quality of life is relatively high *also* have relatively high percentages of nonbelievers. On the other hand, those countries that have relatively low standards of living *also* have relatively low percentages of unbelievers. In fact, the numerous countries that are listed as 1 percent have less than 1 percent according to Zuckerman.[37] However, the chart shows exceptions to this rule: the United States, Turkey, Saudi Arabia, Brazil, and Ireland enjoy relatively high standards of living, with an index of about 70 or above. However, no more than 6 percent of the populations can be counted as unbelievers.

This analysis shows that Paul and Zuckerman are overeager to prove their point about the relationship of religious belief to poverty. In their view, educational, economic, and social inequalities explain all religious belief. Their assumption is that desperate people cling to religion for security. They forget to mention the oil-rich Middle Eastern countries that have very low percentages of unbelievers. Moreover, they ignore countries like Ireland and Brazil.

The two champions of unbelief explain the high rates of religious belief of second and third world nations along with the United States as a result of "comparatively primitive" conditions, especially the gap between the rich and the poor. Thus, their reasoning for America's relatively low number of unbelievers is that American society is divided into the vast, insecure lower class that is religious and the secure, elite upper class that is not.[38] This is a subjective judgment that is arguable.

Ruut Veenhoven has indexed data from the World Database of Happiness that surveys citizens of over 150 countries. He has taken the score of the level of happiness of each country and adjusted it for inequalities of happiness among its citizens. The result is an "inequality-adjusted" number. For example, Denmark and Costa Rica have the highest average scores of over 8 (out of 10) points, with an adjusted level of overall satisfaction of 73 points. The United States has an average score of 7.5 points, with an adjusted overall level of satisfaction of 63 points.[39]

Table 7.5 shows the average score of selected countries according to Veenhoven's calculations. The diamond shapes at the bottom of the chart show these figures. The table also shows the score adjusted for inequality, the relative gap between the happiness scores of the rich and those of the poor. The square shapes represent this score.

According to Veenhoven's calculations, Ireland has an adjusted happiness index score of 65, the United States has an adjusted score of 63, and Brazil has an adjusted score of 61. These countries all have relatively low percentages of unbelievers. In contrast both Germany and Great Britain have lower scores, but they have relatively high percentages of unbelievers. Saudi Arabia compares to Japan in terms of adjusted score and average scores. But Saudi Arabia has one of the lowest percentages of unbelievers, and Japan has the highest. These results

Table 7.5.   Happiness Index Adjusted for Inequality

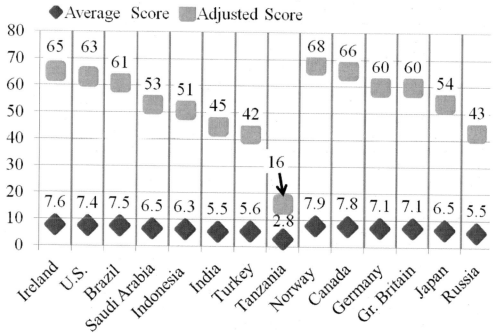

show that other factors besides the insecurity that comes from a gap between rich and poor influence the religiosity of a country.

Several flaws weaken Zuckerman's argument even more. He typically gives wide ranges of percentages of atheists, agnostics, and "nonbelievers in God." For example, Zuckerman estimates that the percentage of unbelievers in Norway, the nation with the highest quality of life, ranges between 31 percent and 72 percent. In Canada, the nation with the sixth-highest standard of living, the estimate ranges from 19 percent to 30 percent. The average gap between the high and low estimates of the percentage of population for countries with the highest quality of life is 20 percent. This imprecision undercuts the usefulness of the statistics.

Moreover, Zuckerman overinflates the importance of the percentages of unbelievers. Outside six European countries, Vietnam, Japan, and South Korea, the highest percentage of his ranges of unbelievers never goes above 50 percent. He lists the United States with an estimated range of from 3–9 percent of unbelievers on the list of the top fifty countries with "nonbelievers in God." America is one of nine countries on his list that, in Zuckerman's most generous estimate, has about 9 percent unbelievers. These wide estimates hardly represent convincing support for his argument.

Overall, the evidence fails to give conclusive proof that the quality of life measured by life expectancy, education, and standard of living is necessarily tied to low levels of religious belief.

By the HDI standard *alone*, we cannot predict whether the countries in the "Very High," "High," or "Medium" HDI index categories will have high or low percentages of those who reject religion. It is probable that countries with a high HDI index will have a relatively high number of unbelievers. But there are too many exceptions to make it a rule.

It Is Hard to Be a Secular Country

Even if the general principle is true, this does not mean that the secularization thesis holds for the future of religion in the twenty-first century. Surprisingly, Zuckerman admits that religion may be growing and atheism may be declining in this century. He notes the high birthrates in the religious countries in contrast with low birthrates in countries with high rates of unbelief.[40] Thus, Zuckerman does not rule out the possibility of a "resurgence of religion" based on birthrates in developing countries.

If political and economic factors define the secularization process, then it may only work in countries that have the right qualifications of education, prosperity, democracy, and the fair distribution of wealth. Living in these conditions may be an impossible dream for most of the world's population. Most of the peoples of the world may be too impoverished and insecure to attain to the heights of unbelief.

Therefore, even if we could prove the supposed link between a secure and prosperous quality of life and religion, the analysis of Paul and Zuckerman casts doubt on the capacity of the secularization thesis to predict the future. In fact, they state that economics may determine the future of religion instead of choice or even the fertility rates of believers.[41] Having dealt with the objections of Paul and Zuckerman, we can go on with the task we set out to accomplish. The puzzle for religious studies is to formulate a theory that would do a better job of describing the emerging role of religion in the twenty-first century.

The Search for an Alternative Theory

The above analysis confirms the conclusion of the majority of sociologists. The secularization thesis is no longer viable, at least on a global scale. Without doubt, it describes the situation in Europe and Canada. But we must still investigate the question of what impact the forces of the modern world will have on religion in this century.

The crucial reason for the downfall of the secularization thesis is that it did not predict the present situation. The statistics above show that religion has prevailed despite the dynamics of modernization. Moreover, without doubt, religion has come to play a visible, vigorous, and vital role in current national and world events.

The secularization thesis shaped the research of generations of scholars. It controlled how they understood the data on religion, how they analyzed it, and what conclusions they made from it. But the evidence summarized above seems to have outstripped the theory. We cannot use it for understanding or analyzing religion, and it is not helpful for forecasting its future.

This discussion has focused the problem of this chapter. The challenge is to find an alternative theory to the secularization thesis. This theory might be called a new "explanatory paradigm"—that is, a model that would interpret and explain what is happening in the contemporary world. The test of this theory would be whether scholars could use it to make reasonable forecasts of the future of religion.

SURVEYING THE ALTERNATIVE APPROACHES: FOUR THEORIES OF PREDICTION

The future of religion is a broad topic, and scholars of religion have approached it in various ways. This chapter will explore a sample of four of these approaches (described in the textbox "Alternative Ways of Predicting the Future of Religion").

Alternative Ways of Predicting the Future of Religion

1. Estimates of the growth of religions based on population trends
2. Revision of the secularization thesis centering on the division of society into separate social institutions and the loss of religious authority
3. Effects of globalization on human populations: massive migration of populations (immigration) and urbanization
4. Responses to globalization: self-chosen identity, defense of certainty, promotion of religion

Preliminary Remarks on Prediction

Most of us are captive to the power of predictions. We rely on weather, traffic, and stock market forecasts to make daily decisions. We trust job market projections to plot a direction for our education. To decide what to make and sell, businesses rely on predictions. Consumers want to know what the latest thing is and when they can get it. Governments are struggling to respond to predictions of global warming, nuclear threats, terrorism, and swings in economic conditions. Politicians depend on the polls, voter profiles, and election projections. In whatever media we get our news, we want to know what will happen more than what has happened.

Scientific experimentation centers on prediction. A hypothesis is tested by the prediction of results. For example, based on his general theory of relativity Einstein said that starlight bends as it passes by the sun on the way to Earth. This effect of the sun's gravitational field could be precisely measured. The theory of general relativity predicts that this measurement would be half again as large as the numbers that Newton's laws of physics would predict. Sir Arthur Stanley Eddington (1882–1944) proved Einstein's prediction correct during a solar eclipse on May 29, 1919. His measurements of light as it passed by the sun caused a media sensation and made Einstein an instant celebrity.

However, predictions do not always pan out. At the turn of the century, the Y2K bug was supposed to shut down the world's computer networks. And at the beginning of 2008, economists were expecting a "sluggish" year. Economists predicted that the S&P Index would grow but only in single digits.[42] Meanwhile, they trusted the "Fed" to keep interest rates low in order to save the economy. Early in the year, Lehman Brothers issued a report predicting 1.8 percent growth in the GDP. The report said that the economy "may bend but not break" in the coming year.[43] A few months later, on September 10, 2008, Lehman Brothers declared bankruptcy. The federal government refused to bail the company out in the midst of a devastating recession.

Nevertheless, such failures have not dampened the world's enthusiasm for predictions. Here are some predictions about religion from several years of *The Futurist* magazine:

1. In China, growth in capitalism may kindle growth in religion. Christianity is the fastest growing religion there.
2. In the Middle East, religious interest may decline. Popular support for religious governments is fading.
3. In the United States, organized religion has less appeal. Church attendance is falling off despite an increase in the population.
4. Terrorist incidents increase and become more deadly. Jihadists will gain political as well as social power and will probably obtain nuclear weapons in the next ten years.
5. Religious tolerance will gradually increase. The competition among religious faiths will be offset by global communication and interaction among the world's peoples.[44]

In general, these predictions seem to be safe. All of them project current conditions into the future. They speak in terms of generalities and not precise statistics. And they have indefinite time frames.

A critical thinking approach to these claims would ask "what are they worth?" Notice that the predictions stated above seem to mean something. However, they speak in generalities. To say that something will "increase" while something else will have "less appeal" does not give testable measures to answer questions like: How much? When? Why? The only specific in the predictions from *The Futurist* magazine is that the jihadists will gain a nuclear weapon within ten years. So how and when would they be proven true?

Predictions are based on trends. They identify factors that are changing. Then they extend these current changes into the future. The accuracy of these forecasts depends on a variety of dynamics of the change. These include the strength, direction, and rate of change. Moreover, their reliability depends on a correct understanding of the conditions in which the process of change would happen.

Predicting the Future of Religion by Population Trends

The discussion above leads to the idea that we could use population statistics like those that we have already presented to project the future of religion. Stated succinctly, this theory is that religions consist of believers and that trends in the number of believers forecast the future of religion.

Factors to Consider When Using Population Trends for Predictions

1. The size of the group
2. The period of growth or decline
3. The measurement in percentages or raw numbers
4. The rate of growth or decline (gains versus losses)
5. Comparisons with other groups
6. Comparisons with the population growth or decline

Often, religions refer to gains in members to claim that they are the "fastest-growing religion." A critical thinking approach to religion, though, would disregard these unsupported assertions. The textbox "Factors to Consider When Using Population Trends for Predictions" suggests that claims of a group doubling or tripling in membership are meaningless unless other factors are considered. A small group may have exponential growth, perhaps even doubling and tripling in size in a few years. Yet its relative size and the importance of its growth would be minimal. In addition, we must ask how the gains in membership are calculated and how the rate of increase compares to the overall growth of the population. Then we must ask about the religions used for comparison since there are thousands of religions and yet a specific religion is supposed to have the *fastest* increase of all of them.[45]

Though we cannot identify the "fastest growing" religion, we can give some growth rates for selected religions. We can do this without comparing them to all religions. Most religions grew numerically since the beginning of the century. However, in spite of numerical increases, we cannot say that a religion is growing significantly unless it keeps up with the escalating growth of the world's population. This is not easy. Since 1960, the global population has more than doubled. The United Nations population unit has estimated when the world population will reach the next billion (see table 7.6).[46]

The Key to Prediction: Growth Rates

Table 7.7 shows the rise of the growth rate from 1950 to estimates in 2050.[47] In the demographic approach, this rate of growth is the foundation of forecasts of religion. According to the United Nations Population Division, the rate of growth of the world's population was 1.21 percent per year from 2000 to 2005.[48] The following major world religions showed growth rates from 2000 to 2005 that exceeded this global rate of growth: Islam at 1.84 percent per year; Sikhism at 1.62 percent per year; Jainism at 1.57 percent per year; Hinduism at 1.54 percent per year; and Christianity at 1.38 percent per year.[49]

Not all religions will grow at these rates, however. Buddhism increased in numbers but fell just short of the world's growth rate by 0.2 percent. Also, Judaism's growth failed to reach to the world average by 0.3 percent. Of the prominent world religions, Shinto is the only one that decreased in actual numbers. It declined by just over 1 percent.[50] The categories of atheism and the nonreligious

Table 7.6.   Growth of the World Population in Billions

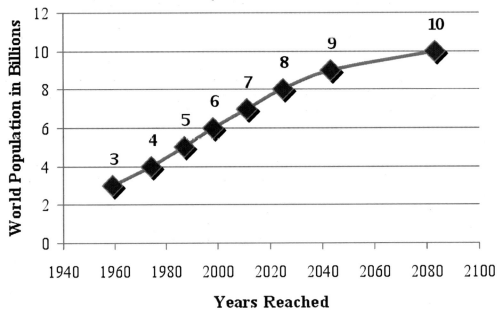

Table 7.7.   World Population Growth Rates

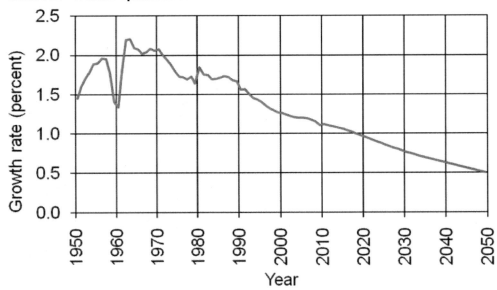

also failed to keep up with the world growth rate, although they grew in some parts of the world.[51]

Researchers calculate projections of the future of world religions based on expected rates of growth or decline. The first task is to establish a baseline. Statistician David B. Barrett (1927–2011) directed the World Christian Database (WCD) until his death when Global Christianity scholar Todd Johnson assumed that role. The WCD has gathered a staggering amount of data from 1982 onward not only for Christianity but also for world religions. It was developed for the substantial two-volume *World Christian Encyclopedia* (WCE) for the years 1990–2000 and again for 2000–2005.[52]

The WCE researchers started with the WCD statistics. They then calculated the expected gains to the religions from births minus deaths using United Nations growth rates and other sources. They adjusted these figures of growth rates by the calculations of the rates of expected gains by conversion and losses by attrition. Finally, they adjusted the figures by the projected influence of migration in and out of the countries where the religions were located.[53]

Table 7.8 displays some sample results.[54] Of the selected religions on this chart, Islam and Christianity are expected to increase in their share of the world's population. Other categories, such as Buddhism, atheism, and the nonreligious, will decline in terms of the percentage of the global population.

Is the secularization thesis right in its prediction that religion will inevitably decline? Or is there a "resurgence of religion" that will sweep the world's religions to new levels? The answer depends on the religions and regions that we select. If

Table 7.8.   Changes in the Share of the World's Population to 2100

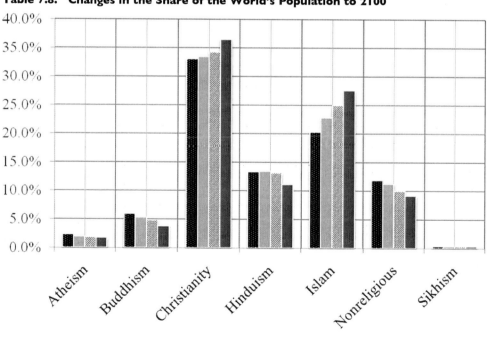

■ 2005   ■ 2025   ▒ 2050   ■ 2100

Muslims praying in Jakarta, Indonesia. The World Population Data Sheet estimates that the growth of Islam will exceed the growth of other major religions between 2005 and 2025.

by resurgence of religion, we mean growth in numbers, then we have established that the increase must be beyond the growth of the burgeoning world population.

For example, the World Population Data Sheet estimates that from 2005 to 2025, the world population will grow by 20 percent.[55] Johnson projects that in those twenty years, Islam will grow by 33 percent, Hinduism by 22 percent, and Christianity by 21 percent. On the other hand, from 2005 to 2025 Sikhism will increase by 15 percent. Buddhism will grow by 12 percent, Judaism will grow by 6 percent, and ethno-religions (tribal religions) will grow by 4 percent. These increases will not keep up with the 20 percent growth of the world population. Moreover, the researchers estimate that atheism will shrink by 14 percent, far below the growth of the global population.[56]

The changes that this chart displays will make a significant difference in the future of religion. Among the major world religions, Johnson projects that Islam will probably claim an increasing share of the world's population. By 2050, Islam will grow by 70 percent. This will mean that Muslims will increase from 20 percent to almost 28 percent of the world population. Hindus will increase by 52 percent by 2050 and so exceed the world's growth rate of 46 percent in the same period.[57] If Johnson's estimates are correct, Christianity will remain the largest world religion. But it will fall behind the world's population growth by increasing only 42 percent by 2050.[58]

Johnson projects that by 2050 Sikhism will just keep up with the world population growth. Buddhism, tribal religions, and Judaism will fall significantly behind the global growth of the human population. Surprisingly, Johnson predicts that atheism will increase only by 12 percent and the nonreligious by 16 percent, at least 30 points below the growth of the human race.[59]

Two Alternative Futures

Johnson's estimates are based on current trends. But what if the dynamics of religion change? If we can anticipate the changing conditions, we can adjust our predictions. For example, what would happen if Islam experienced a surge in numbers even above its present high growth rate? On the other hand, what if the numbers of nonreligious grew significantly beyond their present rates?

Johnson answers with calculations of three selected contingencies. For the purposes of this chapter, we will only give examples of two of these possibilities. Moreover, this chapter will only show samples of what would happen to the "big three" religions and the nonreligious under these conditions.

Johnson shows that if there were an upsurge of Islam, it might grow past Christianity by 2200. Suppose that the number of Muslims in the world grew from over 20 percent of the population in 2000 to 38 percent in 2200. Johnson estimates that then Christianity would decrease from 33 percent of the population to 31 percent. Hinduism would decrease from over 13 percent to fewer than 7 percent. The percent of nonreligious would go down slightly from 12 percent to just over 10 percent.

However, what would happen if the numbers of nonreligious would swell? Suppose the number of nonreligious rose from about 12 percent in 2000 to over 33 percent in 2200. In that case, it would surpass both Christianity and Islam. The numbers of Christians would decline to 25 percent of the human population. The numbers of Muslims would decrease to 18 percent of the world. And the number of Hindus would decline to 8.5 percent.

Johnson's projections help us imagine what the future of religion would be under selected conditions. They assume that the growth of one religious perspective would be relative to the others. Both scenarios that we have reviewed are conceivable. Which is most likely? That is an open question.

Predicting the Future by Reviving the Neosecularization Thesis

The statistics and dynamics described above seem to have dealt a fatal blow to the secularization thesis. Yet a set of scholars has worked hard to resuscitate it. The result is the *neosecularization* thesis. This approach claims to present the genuine theory instead of the sweeping notion of religious decline. As it does so, it revises and refines the secularization thesis. Stated succinctly, the neosecularization thesis describes the process of secularization, but it refrains from making overgeneralizations about the likely outcome of this process.

The Neosecularization Thesis

The thesis of secularization only describes the modern process that divides society into separate units or institutions. Secularization does not predict the future of religion because societies can respond to it in different ways.

The neosecularization thesis backs off what its supporters now call the naïve theory of the original approach. Most important, the scholars who seek to recover the secularization thesis say that the foundation of the modern society is *social differentiation*. Social differentiation refers to the way modernity breaks up the once unified social system into independent units or institutions.[60] These separate components of society include government, education, economics, agriculture, literature, the arts, and medicine as well as religion.

When the society divides into these separate subsystems, religious institutions no longer include and integrate the functions of society.[61] Religions no longer have a central and predominant role in the social order. Religion is only one aspect of society, and religious institutions represent only one set of interests among many.

As a result, in this view, religious belief and participation in religious organizations does not necessarily decline. Instead, social differentiation narrows the scope of religious authority.[62] Neosecularists emphasize that secularization purposely cuts off the grasping arms of religion. Intentional social differentiation prevents religion from seizing and misusing its power over people. According to Chaves, the authority structures of religion lose power on three levels:[63]

1. On the social level, religious elites no longer control social institutions.
2. On the level of religious organizations, religions no longer have control over resources in the religious sphere.
3. On the individual level, religious authorities can no longer control the actions of individuals such as marriage, family, intimacy, and conception.[64]

What happens when religion loses its central role on these three levels? In contrast to the classic secularization thesis, the neosecularist thesis states that they cannot predict how religions and social systems will respond when the social system is broken up.[65] They can reestablish the role of religion in the culture in different ways. In this way, the neosecularists manage to save the thesis, but give up the approach's ability to say anything about the future of religion.

Predicting the Future by Studying the Effects of Globalization

The neosecularists avoid making predictions about the future of religion because of the variety of possible responses to the loss of religious authority. However, another way of making predictions about religion is to anticipate the likely responses of the world's religions to the forces that are shaping the world's future. Stated succinctly, this theory states that the future of religion depends on the impact of the primary driving force of the twenty-first century: *globalization.*

Like all general concepts, globalization is hard to define. It refers to a complex constellation of economic, political, scientific, educational, communication, and cultural relationships that are creating a worldwide community. In general, globalization refers to processes that remove barriers between territories and nations and promote free interchange among the world's people.[66]

Perhaps the most powerful forces of globalization are *global capitalism* and worldwide technological communications. Global capitalism makes the whole world a free market where goods, services, and ideas can be traded without obstacles. Technology makes this worldwide trade possible.

Globalization has produced one of the most important dynamics that will change religion in the future, the shift in the world's population. The last section mentioned this factor, human migration. Scholars have called the mass displacement and migration of people the "third wave of globalization."[67] The first wave refers to the free movement of goods and services across borders. The second wave refers to the unimpeded transfer of money from and to anywhere in the world. The third wave refers to vast numbers of people who are leaving their homeland to seek economic opportunities or security elsewhere.

According to the United Nations "Population Newsletter," in 2000 the number of international migrants was 178 million or 2.9 percent of the world's population.[68] In 2010, according to UN estimates, the percentage of immigrants rose to 214 million people or 3.1 percent of the global population.[69] As the text-box "Countries with the Highest Number of Immigrants" shows, most migrants have moved to developed countries.[70]

Countries with the Highest Number of Immigrants

- United States: 43 million
- Russian Federation: 12 million
- Germany: 11 million
- Saudi Arabia: 7 million
- Canada: 7 million
- France: 7 million

In America, during the last decade of the twentieth century, only one in ten workers was foreign born. In 2004, one in seven workers was born outside the United States. Twelve percent of the American population is now foreign born. And one-quarter of Americans under eighteen years of age are immigrants or children of immigrants.[71]

Trends in the United States

This profound rearrangement of the world human population is bringing predictable changes in religion. In her book *A New Religious America: How a "Christian Country" Has Become the World's Most Religiously Diverse Nation,*[72] Diana Eck takes pride in the growing diversity that immigration is bringing to America. She was perhaps overly enthusiastic. She thought Americans should notice the multiplication of non-Christian religions in the country. However, the Pew Landscape study[73] shows that these groups represent a small minority of the American population. Moreover, though immigration has added to the diversity of religions in the United States, most of the immigrants are Christian. Of those who immigrated during 2000 to 2007, almost 60 percent were from Latin America,[74] and 93 percent of them identify with Christianity. Only 6 percent do not claim any religion, and only 0.5 percent identify with another religion.[75]

Based on their overwhelming numbers, we can predict that Latinos will have a profound effect on the Catholic Church in the future. Now one-third of Catholics in America are Hispanic.[76] Moreover, one-half of Catholics under thirty years of age are Latinos. By 2050, the percentage of Hispanic youth in the Catholic Church in the United States will be over 60 percent.[77]

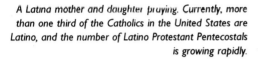

A Latina mother and daughter praying. Currently, more than one third of the Catholics in the United States are Latino, and the number of Latino Protestant Pentecostals is growing rapidly.

In general, surveys show that Latinos are attracted to forms of religion that offer direct, personal experiences of the sacred. Of the Hispanics born in the United States, 37 percent claim to be "born again." Of those born elsewhere, 40 percent claim have had a "born-again" experience that is associated with Protestant evangelicalism.[78]

But even more amazing is that over one in two Hispanics claim to have received the supernatural gifts of the Spirit, a claim that is associated with Protestant Pentecostalism.[79] The Pew Forum says that these "charismatic" believers represent Renewalist Christianity, a form of religion that experiences the miraculous spiritual power of the Holy Spirit in worship and daily life.[80] This interest in experiential spirituality rather than doctrine may lead the American Catholic Church to emphasize the personal and spirit-filled aspects of religion.

Hispanics also tend to cluster in ethnic-oriented religious groups. Two-thirds attend Spanish services with Hispanic leadership and fellow members. These numbers include American-born Latinos as well as those coming from Latin America. Thus, Hispanic religion offers a lasting identity to those who engage in it.

Because of the global trend of immigration, Latinos are changing the character of the American Catholic Church. Alternatively, the American religious situation is also changing the Hispanics. An article in the *National Catholic Reporter* chides the Catholic Church for failing to understand that America offers an abundance of religious choices. The article claimed that the Catholic Church is losing 600,000 immigrants a year because it is failing to help Hispanics deal with the challenges of building a life in America.[81]

Given the influence of Protestantism in America, it is not surprising that numbers of Latinos take advantage of the choices of their new homeland and become Protestant.[82] Less than one in six Latinos is Protestant in the first generation of residence in this country. By the third generation, it is more than one in three. The Pew Forum study found that the process of assimilation was at work in these conversions. Among those whose primary language was English, 26 percent had changed their practice of religion. Of those who were bilingual, 20 percent had changed. On the other hand, of those whose primary language was Spanish, only 14 percent had changed.[83] We can assume that becoming proficient in English increases one's exposure to the processes of assimilation. This Pew study seemed to confirm this assumption when it found that 28 percent of Hispanics had abandoned religion altogether. Overall, these new nonreligious Latinos are college graduates who claim English as their primary language.[84]

Secular Trends in Great Britain

The dynamics that we have described hardly suggest that secularism will make religion irrelevant for the United States. If the American Catholic Church was weakening, certainly the influx of Latino Catholics has strengthened it.

But what about Europe? Secularization theorists say that Europe proves that the secularization thesis still holds. But is Europe as secular as the thesis predicts? Perhaps the best way to approach this question is to explore the contrast between America where the secularization thesis does not seem to hold and other places where it seems to work. A ready comparison is the contrast between America and Great Britain that scholars have already explored in depth.[85]

A study by David Voas and Rodney Ling on the British Social Attitudes Survey found that in 2008 one in two Britons identified with Christianity.[86] In 2009, the percent plummeted even further to 43 percent.[87] In contrast, the Gallup poll for 2007 found that 82 percent of Americans identify themselves as Christian, though Voas lists the percentage as 76 percent. Moreover, Voas also published a study that only 12 percent of the British say that they belong to a church.[88]

Behind these facts lie some deeper attitudes. Table 7.9 shows that while three in four Americans think of themselves as "very religious" or "somewhat religious," only one in three of the British feel the same way.[89] But an even smaller proportion of Britons think of religions as "very important." Only 17 percent rank it highly, as opposed to 60 percent of Americans.

These attitudes are revealed in worship patterns. A generous figure is that 17 percent of the British say that they attended worship last weekend in contrast to at least 37 percent of Americans.[90] Other studies put the figure of British weekly attendance at 10 percent. In fact, two in three say that they never attend church. The Gallup polls said that in the same year 16 percent of Americans said that they never attend religious services.[91] But they may have no reason to attend worship. One in three Britons said that they do not believe in God or are unsure about God. In contrast, Voas and Ling state that 8 percent of Americans express the same doubt.[92]

Table 7.9. Comparison of Religiosity: Great Britain and the United States

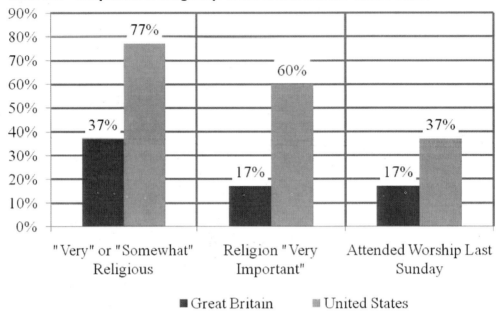

Secular Trends in Europe

Turning to the European mainland, one in five Europeans say that God plays an important role in their lives[93] compared with almost two in three Americans.[94] In Sweden, 2 percent of the population regularly attends worship, though about 81 percent of the population holds membership in the Church of Sweden. Moreover, the church conducts about 90 percent of the funerals and about 60 percent of the marriages in Sweden. Remarkably, the Church of Sweden baptizes almost 70 percent of Swedish infants. About 40 percent of these go through the Lutheran rite of confirmation in adolescence.[95]

This selection of figures appears to support the consensus that indeed America and Europe live in two different spiritual universes. Many Europeans still identify with Christianity and look to the church for ceremonial functions. Yet religious belief and participation has declined in Great Britain and Europe more than in America.

The Challenge to European Secularism

Now in the twenty-first century, European secularization faces a critical test. Numbers of immigrants are arriving in Great Britain and the continent. In the countries of the European Union, the migration resulted in a net gain over of 1.8 million people from immigration in 2005 alone. Amazingly, this figure represented 85 percent of Europe's population growth in that year.[96]

It is difficult to get exact figures, but all agree that the fastest-growing minority in Europe comes from Muslim countries. In 2008, there were five million Muslims in France, three million in Germany, and two million in the UK. In the entire EU, the number is about sixteen million, about 3 percent of the popula-

The Central Mosque in London holds five thousand worshippers. One half of the Muslims in England live in London. The rapid growth of the Muslim population in Great Britain and Europe has caused tensions. But population projections do not support the exaggerated fears that Muslims will eventually take over Europe.

tion.[97] However, Muslims may be more visible because they tend be clustered in larger metropolitan areas. In 2003, one of every two Muslims in the United Kingdom lived in London, or 8.46 percent.[98]

Projections of high Muslim birth rates together with very low European birth rates have led to sensationalized predictions of a Muslim "population time bomb." According to Jonathan Laurence, at least one in five persons living in Europe will be Muslim by 2050. Wild rumors are circulating that by the middle of this century, Muslims could outnumber non-Muslims in France and, perhaps, all of Europe.[99] Even the eminent Middle Eastern scholar Bernard Lewis predicted that Europe would become Muslim by the end of the twenty-first century, if not sooner.[100]

A Pew Global Attitudes study underscored the growing concern about changing attitudes in Europe toward Muslims. Tension is rising in Germany, the Netherlands, Spain, and Poland, where the Pew survey found that less than half of the populations have favorable attitudes toward them. Not all share the prejudices, however. In contrast to the hostile feelings of some, 64 percent of the citizens of France and 72 percent of the citizens of the Great Britain expressed favorable views of Muslims.[101]

Many Europeans hope that the Muslims will be integrated into their societies. However, a Pew Forum report notes the feeling that the processes of assimilation are not working.[102] Some want to take drastic measures. In 2009, the Swiss voted to ban the construction of minarets that broadcast the call to prayer from mosques.[103] In 2010, the government of Belgium banned the burqa and France and the Netherlands soon followed. Furthermore, political pressure is building in the Netherlands and other places to limit or ban immigration from Muslim countries. The Pew report says that recent developments are troubling. It asserts that the Europeans have yet to come to terms with the racial and identity issues that Muslim immigration has raised.[104]

Of course, the "strong" secularization thesis would hold that the European's anxiety is unfounded. The processes of religious decline are already established in Europe and it is only a matter of time until they overtake the Muslim religions as they have Christianity. However, European Muslims are not deserting their faith as the secularization thesis predicts. In fact, the trend is going in reverse. A Pew study found that 80 percent of Muslims in London say they frequently attend mosque. Though they represent around 3 percent of the population, more Muslims in Great Britain are attending mosque with regularity than Christians are attending Christian churches. In fact, in reversal of secularization the second and third generations are adopting visible Muslim practices that their immigrant parents used to hide or abandon.[105]

Noting these trends, some scholars predict that the European secular society will soon face a challenge. They project that Europe might become the setting for the kind of religious conflict that it has not seen since the French Revolution. Sociologist Jan Rath states that the "social collision is becoming inevitable."[106] Several outcomes might result from the interface of the two groups that seem to be going in opposite directions. One is that the vitality of Muslims will spark a revival of European Christianity. That might further complicate the situation and return Europe to religious battles. On the other hand, many believe that a "moderate Islam" can accept democracy and toleration and become part of a new, more pluralistic Europe. Finally, some think that it will become a kind of "Eurarbia" where the Judeo-Christian background would disappear.[107]

However, we should not overlook one additional factor. All predictions depend on the fertility rates among Muslims compared to the low rates among non-Muslims in Europe. The fertility rates among Muslim women are higher than that of the Europeans. This disparity is the result of secularization. In competition with traditional religion, secularization works to its own disadvantage because it brings cultural changes that lower the birth rate. On the other hand, traditional religion promotes large families. Traditional religion results in birth rates of about five or six children per woman. Secularization results in fertility rates of about 1.2 children per woman. If traditional religion has its way, then the European Muslim population will continue to grow relative to the secular Europeans. It will do so even without ongoing new immigration. The result may be that Europe will no longer be a thoroughly secular society in the future.[108]

However, a critical thinking approach to this question would ask about the evidence for this speculation. Indeed, fertility rates among Muslims are higher than the rates of Europeans. But studies show that they are dropping in Muslim lands and in places of immigration. In the former West Germany, for example, female Muslim immigrants from Turkey had twice as many children as their German-native counterparts. However, from 1970 to 1996, the gap decreased so that Muslim women had only one child more on average than the secular Germans.[109]

Table 7.10. Muslim Growth and Fertility in Europe to 2030

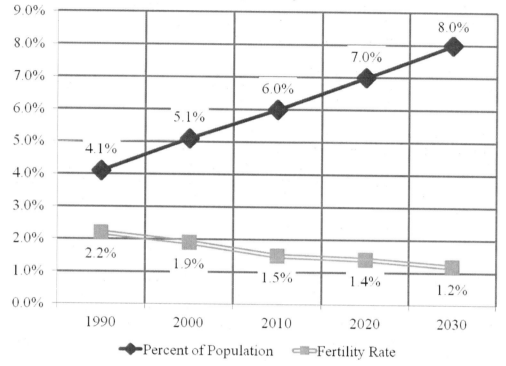

The Pew Forum projects that the fertility rates of European Muslims will drop. In fact, by 2030, they will reach the 1.2 children per woman rate of secular society (see table 7.10). However, the study also projects growth in the Muslim population as the fertility rates go down over time. Another source of growth will be the result of immigration, though it is also declining. Because of these two factors, in twenty years, the Pew researchers project that 8 percent of the European population will be Muslim. Though France, Austria, and Sweden will reach a Muslim population of 9 to 10 percent, these percentages are far from the exaggerated claims that Muslims will inundate European society.[110]

Responses to Globalization

The challenge of this chapter is to find an overall theory that would help us project a probable future for religion in the twenty-first century. We have focused on a major factor of globalization and its effects on American religion and on European secular society. This is the inescapable dynamic of immigration. Though we have found that the secularization thesis seems to work in Europe, we find that even there immigration is posing a formidable challenge to it. Meanwhile, however, another process of modernization is at work, the downward trend of fertility rates. This factor must be added to the conditions that scholars must consider in developing a theory that would predict the future of religion.

Now this chapter moves on to another set of alternatives for a replacement of the secularization thesis. So far, our approach has suggested that the process of globalization is an unyielding force that is carrying the world along. Our discussion has not considered the ways that groups and individuals may respond to a dynamic such as globalization. Stated succinctly, this strategy for developing a viable theory of religion supposes that religions and religious believers will not be passive victims of the dynamics that will shape the future. They will respond in foreseeable ways.

Responses to Globalization: Adaptation to the Urban Setting

A good example of the way religions will respond to the conditions of the twenty-first century is the effect of the migration of populations: *urbanization*. The United Nations Population Fund reports that in 2008, over half of the world's population, some 3.3 billion people, lived in cities. By 2030, the world will have to support 5 billion city dwellers, 81 percent of the planet's people. According to a United Nations study, this stunning growth will have the greatest bearing of any factor on human development in the twenty-first century.[111]

How will this trend affect religion and its role in the world? In his United Nations Population Fund report, George Martine observes that one of the most visible trends in global urbanization is the rise of religion.[112] This surprising shift toward religion in the cities is, in fact, the opposite of what the secularization thesis expected would happen.

Martine emphasizes that the resurgence of religion across the globe is an urban phenomenon. But Martine also asserts that the revivals of various religions in the cities do not merely preserve the old, largely rural traditions. They renew the historic, traditional religions as they adapt to the new urban circumstances of their members.[113]

Some of these adaptations are so innovative that they can be called "new religions." However, most of all, the urban scene is nurturing fresh variations of the old religions. Among the most vigorous adaptations are radical Islam in the Arab Middle East, Pentecostal Christianity in Latin America and parts of Africa, and the cult of Shivaji, a devout Hindu king and hero of Indian independence, in parts of India.

Together with immigration, urbanization promotes a rich diversity of religious options. Urban dwellers can choose their own sacred path. The direction they take may range from the disengagement from society of New Age religions to the intense social engagement of political activism. Cities offer a setting of ideas and experiences that is so rich in its diversity and vitality that it is bewildering to newcomers. Yet out of this mix of challenge and change, believers fashion amazingly creative ways to respond faithfully to their new environment. In summary, urbanization is affecting the future of religion as religious believers adapt to the urban setting, inventing new religions and reinventing traditional sacred ways. An alternative theory to the secularization thesis might be built on the study of the growing urban context of religion.

Response to Globalization: Voluntary Religious Organization

Peter Berger points to another possible response to globalization, the assertion of a self-chosen religious identity. His thoughts suggest that we might be able to build a theory of the future of religion on the possibility that greater numbers of people throughout the world will take the opportunity of religious diversity to define themselves according to the choice of religion.

In Berger's view, globalization has not resulted in secularism. It has fostered global religious pluralism—that is, worldwide religious diversity. Today's un-impeded flow of communication, finances, trade, and people has brought the religions of the world to everyone's doorstep.[114] No one can avoid the awareness of other faiths and their competing claims to truth.

This rather rude awakening to the incredible variety of religious beliefs in the global society changes what people think of religion.[115] People recognize that other people hold beliefs that seem just as valid as their own. This realization undermines the absolute authority of their belief system. It is difficult to explain why one's beliefs should be superior to everyone else's opinions. Unless one pur-posely rejects the implications of this new awareness, one's own beliefs become relative to the others.[116] Religious practices become matters of individual prefer-ence. Religious obligations become matters of personal choice. Religions become voluntary organizations. And belonging to religious groups becomes optional.[117]

When we consider these changes, we realize that religious diversity is just the latest form of modernity. The new global forces of modern life undercut the certainties that believers had once taken for granted.[118] In the new context of the global society, the external separation of religion from other institutions of pub-lic life is not the crucial factor that undermines religious authority. It is under-mined from within the religion itself. In the new setting of religious pluralism, religious leaders can no longer assume the power of their organizational status. They must establish their authority by persuasion.[119]

Many feel that the splintering of religious authority is liberating. The ac-cident of their birth no longer defines their spirituality. And the boundaries of their religious background no longer determine their faith. They can use pieces of various religions to customize their own. Doing this is as simple as joining in the latest social media or downloading the latest video clip.

Newly invented technologies are rapidly fragmenting the mass media and shattering one of the last sources of unquestioned authority. Now people can customize their own sources of communication, information, and ideas to their taste. Thus, in Berger's mind, modernity comes down to choices.[120] New technol-ogies are multiplying these choices and individuals are in the habit of expecting them even in religion. And why not, since they are all relative anyway?

The dynamics of contemporary media have profound implications for all world religions. If globalization changes the way that individuals relate to religion, glo-balization changes the way that religions relate to society and other religions. To attract and keep their members, religions have to compete with each another. As they do so, they have to respond nimbly and effectively to the latest trends and the needs of their members without compromising their sacred traditions.

As they respond to the global marketplace, religions will naturally offer the choices that contemporary persons expect. The Pew Forum's Religious Landscape Study notes that Americans are taking advantage of the opportunity for choice of religious affiliations. It found that 44 percent of Americans had left the faith of their childhood to belong to another religious group, often in the same broad religious faith, such as "Protestant." Those who leave the religious community of their youth often do not immediately join another. The "unaffiliated" has become the fastest growing religious grouping in America.[121] But this category of the uninvolved is also the most changeable class of Americans. For many, it is merely a way station on the way from one faith community to another.[122]

The instability of religious membership in the United States itself supports the theory that scholars can find the secrets of the future of religion in the responses that religious leaders and believers make to the swirling diversity of the global religious situation. With this alternative to forecasting the future of religion, researchers can study the trends of how creativity can be balanced with solidity, choices can be balanced with commitment, and innovation can be balanced with tradition—and above all, how the appreciation of religious diversity can strengthen and not dilute religious faith.

Responses to Globalization: Self-Chosen Religious Identity

One might conclude from the Pew survey and analysis that the choices of Americans about religious belonging are superficial and changeable. This idea would agree with the secularist notion that religion is unrelated to life in society and is only a matter of personal choice. However, globalization may stimulate a deeper sense of religion, and this religious fever may be a deciding factor in the future of religion. This stronger commitment to religion goes beyond choice of religious affiliation to the choice of personal identity.

How Globalization Undermines Individual Identity

- Immigration and urbanization displace individuals from the communities and histories that gave them identity.
- Consumerism treats all persons as individual consumers in a vast global market of goods.
- The mass society disregards national, ethnic, and family identities.

As we see in Martine's report on urbanization, globalism raises the question of personal identity. The textbox "How Globalization Undermines Individual Identity" lists three factors of the global society that make this problem acute.

In general, the processes of modernization supersede the traditional sources of identity in tribe, language, and heritage. The last stage in this process, nationalism, replaces them. Now even the nation-state has been surpassed. The international forces of globalization, especially the transnational corporation, have undermined it. In this massive process, the consequences for the individual go unnoticed. But they are critical. As the nation-state diminishes, it loses its power to provide a meaningful identity for its citizens.[123]

Feeling disinherited, people in the global mass society look to local associations to replace their national identity.[124] We have already noted that this process is found in the growth of new forms of religion among displaced persons who are flocking to the cities. We also see it in the distinctive form of Christianity that Hispanics are developing in America.

Religion is the one factor that most powerfully unites these new local associations of identity. In fact, the self-chosen identity of these groups is often intentionally religious since the participants view religion as an alternative to the faults of globalization.

A significant case in point is found in the plight of the Muslim immigrants in Europe and especially their children and grandchildren. Who are they? They no longer can claim the national identity of Turkey, Senegal, or Pakistan. They may speak a European language perfectly, yet the native Europeans will deny that they are really German, Dutch, or Spanish.[125]

So where can they acquire a personal identity? Many find it in their religion. To these reawakened believers, their religion will mean much more than it did in their homeland. Their native religion will give them an identity on which to base their lives. The secular, global society may make them feel alienated. Their shared faith will give them a solid sense of personal power and worth.

This phenomenon reveals a seeming contradiction. The global society throws people of all cultural backgrounds into a vast, mass society. In this society, the individual is faceless and nameless. In response, the members of the mass society often turn to value the personal.[126] They seek associations where they have a face and a name. These associations give them a sense of personal uniqueness in the midst of the "lonely crowd." Often, when they find such a special identity, they feel the need to assert it in public. One way to do so is to dress in special religious clothing like the hijab. Wearing their religion is a way of standing up against the relentless, impersonal forces of globalization and claiming one's own personal power.

For these revitalized believers, programs of assimilation into the larger society will not work. In fact, those who have recovered their faith in a self-chosen identity will view programs of integration as intolerant and racist.[127] Ironically, when believers reclaim their religious identity, their alienation from the larger society is not relieved but reinforced. In places such as Europe, this response to globalization may be a driving force for the ongoing resurgence of religion and a source of conflict in society.

Response to Globalization: Clinging to Religious Certainty

These observations about the growth of self-chosen religious identity raise another possibility. The key to the future of religion might be what is popularly called religious *fundamentalism*. Fundamentalism is so visible in today's world, that we might think that it is the key to the future of religion. This powerful dynamic of today's world stems from the pursuit of religious certainty.

We have shown how globalism and the awareness of religious diversity undermine religious authority. Many have responded positively to the modern shaking of the foundations of faith. They have used the weakening of traditional religious authority as an opportunity to reform religion and to correct its abuses of sexism, racism, exclusivism, and superstition.[128]

However, others are not so ready to respond to the loss of authority in such a positive way. Their negative response leads to the assertion of religious certainty in fundamentalism. To explain, theologian Edward Farley asks students of religious studies to step back to consider it from the point of view of the fundamentalists. To use his word, it is like being immersed in a huge, churning body of water.[129]

How do believers feel when they are thrown in to the sea of secularism? Farley compares their feelings to what the Jews must have felt in their exile in Babylon.[130] The Exile took the Jews away from their land and its way of life. The institutions of temple, priesthood, and kingship that had supported their religious faith were gone. To sustain their religious faith, they had to develop new institutions and a new way of life. Moreover, they had to do it in a setting that was hostile to their beliefs.

In this view, the origin of fundamentalism is in feelings of religious alienation brought on by secularism. According to the researchers of the Fundamentalism Project, fundamentalism is the reaction of "beleaguered believers" to pressures to be absorbed into an irreligious culture.[131] Since they are unwilling to accept the removal of religion from its central and all-important place in life, fervent believers are bound to feel estranged from the secular society.

In this sense, fundamentalism is a contemporary response to modernism founded on a deep sense of alienation. Because they feel threatened, believers will naturally try to shore up the bulwarks of their faith. To preserve their own distinctive identity, they will resort to the foundational beliefs and practices of their religion.[132]

Farley observes that struggling believers will cling to those things that have brought them the experience of the sacred. As if they were drowning, they will grab onto whatever will reassure them of their belief. They will grasp their beliefs so tightly that whatever confirms their faith will become an end in itself.[133] It may be sacred scripture, religious organization, religious leadership, or all of these. In any case, the anxious believers will desperately hold on to the guarantor of their belief against the threat of a disbelieving world. As they do this, their sense of religion will change. To be religious will be to uphold the authority of the sacred against any threat to its truth or legitimacy.

Strictly speaking, fundamentalism refers to the Protestant movement that began at the turn of the twentieth century. This movement laid out a handful of the basic principles of Christianity, the "fundamentals." Certain Protestant traditionalists were upset with the compromises that modern Protestant liberalism had made to adapt to the modern, scientific worldview. These conservatives identified the Christian principles that could not be changed at any cost. Fundamentalism was the program that defended these core Christian doctrines.

However, in the twenty-first century, many use the term broadly to refer to resistance to the forces of globalism, secularism, and pluralism. Some speak of the religious movements that resist modernism as *fundamentalisms*. This term suggests that there are many varieties of religious struggle for certainty against the corrosive forces of secularization.

Response to Globalization: Muslim "Fundamentalism" (Salafism)

An important example of the search for religious certainty against the loss of religious authority is Islamic Salafism. This movement began in the nineteenth century when traditional Muslims became concerned about the progress and expansion of the Western nations. Worried that the West was outstripping the "Muslim world," they looked for a revival of Islam. According to the Salafists, to respond to the developing challenge of Western culture, Muslims must return to the ancient ways of the faith. Therefore, they insisted that the Qur'an and Sunna (the traditions of the sayings and deeds of Muhammad and his companions) were the only and sufficient authority for Muslim faith and practice. Qur'an and Sunna represented God's guidance for life until the Judgment Day. They were to be read literally and followed faithfully. They need no explanations or interpretations.[134]

From these origins, the movement of Salafism, the way of the forbearers, continues to this day. One of its basic principles is jihad. The original Salafi fundamentalism of the nineteenth century defined jihad as the struggle against those who will not accept the sovereignty of God and follow the teachings of the Qur'an. This contest was not only against the infidels, the unbelieving non-Muslims, but also against Muslims who were denying the sovereignty of God. How did the fundamentalist know whether leaders or citizens were rejecting the authority of God? The deciding factor was whether they keep the strict tenets of shari'ah—that is, Islamic law. Now the restoration of shari'ah is the center of the Salafist program against Western modernism.[135]

This principle of jihad motivates and shapes the active confrontation with the global, secular society in the twenty-first century. In the Salafist view, globalization, modernism, colonialism, and secularism all go together. In concert, these threaten the very roots of Islam and its way of life. The response of Salafism to this global menace is to return to the certainty of traditionalism. The way to do this is what Peter Berger calls *reconquista*.[136] This word comes from the Spanish and refers to the Christian struggle to recapture the territory of Spain from the Muslim Moors. In the same way, the fundamentalists are dedicated to taking back the social and political power that religion has lost in modern times.

This goal to regain the lost territory of religion and the authority of shari'ah demands contemporary forms of jihad. It may involve political and educational action. It may even involve militant action in what may be called *Salafi jihadism*. This militant form of today's Salafism believes that the Islamic principle of jihad involves a real, active, and continual battle against the secular world.[137]

Scholars might study this hope of recapturing the authority of religion in the global society as a determining factor for the future of religion. But Salafism represents only one of two forms of reclaiming the central role of religion in the secular society. The strategy of founding a subculture that is separate from secular society represents another way that traditionalists can resist globalization.[138] In this model, traditional religious groups attempt to hang on to the authority of religion without engaging in active battle with them. The nonviolent stance means that they must take defensive measures against the influence of secularism and the encroachments of globalism. These protective methods might involve the emphasis on distinctive beliefs and practices, a separate educational system, a different language, unique customs, and, most likely restraints on social interaction like restrictions on marriages. In the United States, the Amish have had success in preserving an antimodern subculture. Pentecostalism demonstrates another way that believers can form a subculture against the secular society. In this case, distinctive religious practices bind the faithful together and strengthen them against the onslaughts of the larger society.

Response to Globalization: Use of Global Technology

So far, we have the impression that global society undermines religion because it is inherently secular. With this in mind, many believe that religion is traditional and naturally averse to change. Moreover, many think that fervent religious belief is reactionary. However, political scientist Stephen Vertigans and sociologist Philip W. Sutton state that we will not understand Muslim fundamentalists if we only think of them as backward and destructive. These scholars propose that to understand today's Islamist Muslims, we must set aside our Euro-American biases. We must realize that the Islamists are not fighting globalization so much as using it to advance their religion. The Muslim activists seek to direct the dynamics of the global society toward their vision of worldwide unity. In this sense, they are not reactive but proactive. Their goal is not merely to defend their beliefs against secular ideas. They are using the mechanisms of the global society to unite humankind in a worldwide *ummah*, a unified community of believers in the one true God. Thus, the Islamists movements are inventing a new, alternative form of globalization. This form of the global society would be based on a universal religion, not a worldwide economic system.[139] For them, success would not destroy but reorder the global society around the religious principles of Islam.

The theory of Vertigans and Sutton suggests that contemporary religion can exploit globalization for its own ends. Far from inevitably destroying religion, many aspects of globalization foster religion.[140] In the global society, religions are no longer contained within their traditional geographic and ethnic boundaries. The global media make them capable of reaching untold numbers of people everywhere in the world. Population shifts enable them to plant new religious communities wherever their people go. The very separation of religion from traditional social systems frees them to concentrate on specifically religious interests and goals.

So many religions have now "gone global" that sociologists Robert Wuthnow and Stephen Offutt state that religion must now be seen and studied as a "transnational phenomenon."[141] Wuthnow and Offutt show how closely today's religious believers are linked together with others throughout the world. The connections include contact through immigrants, exchange of religious workers, transmission of money, participation in religious and humanitarian products, and worldwide distribution of religious literature, education materials, and training manuals. Understanding these dynamics would be the basis of an alternative theory that the future of religion depends on the skillful use of the conditions of globalization to promote religion throughout the world.

Response to Globalization: Global Christianity

One of the most striking examples of the globalization of religion is the extraordinary growth of the world's largest religion, Christianity, in places where it has been transplanted. For centuries, Western Christianity and European culture were inseparably linked. But in recent years, Christianity has grown rapidly outside of Europe while it declined sharply in Europe. As a result, some observers are saying that Christianity is becoming a "Third World religion." Perhaps that is an overstatement. An editorial in the British journal *Studies in World Christianity* states that Christianity will be able to call itself a "Third World religion" when adopts a "Third World" view of reality.[142] However, the new type of Christianity appears in a wide variety of forms and backgrounds. It is really a set of local expressions of the faith adapted to specific contexts. Yes, it is flourishing in the "Third World," the developing lands outside of Europe and America. But it is also spreading in European and American territory. It is returning to the places of its roots and revitalizing Christianity in the places of its historic development.

Nevertheless, observers can speak of a North-South divide of Christendom. According to Humanities professor Philip Jenkins, Euro-American Christians represent the "Northern world." Others in Africa, Asia, and Latin America represent the "Global South." Both groups of Christians read the same Bible. But they are apt to find different things in it. Jenkins observes that most "Northern-world Christians" discount views of miracles, exorcisms, and spiritual warfare. Conversely, "Southern-world" Christianity is a "healing religion par excellence."[143] The growing Christianity in the Third World believes that the devil is real and evil is an objective fact. With this worldview, "Southern-world" Christianity is more conservative in its teaching, stricter in its morality, and more traditional in its organization.

If trends continue, the future belongs to this "Southern-world" version of Christianity. In 1900, 10 million Africans were Christian, about 9 percent of the African population. In 2005 411 million Africans were Christians, 46 percent of the African population. Table 7.11 shows the rapid rise of Christianity in Africa and the projections for future growth to 2050.[144] The chart also displays the percentage that Africans represent of *all* Christians. Already one in five Christians is African. It will be almost one in three in 2050. By 2025, over two out of three Christians will live in Africa, Asia, and Latin America. Almost one in three will live in Europe and America.[145] By 2025, three in four Catholics will live in Africa, Latin America, or Asia.[146]

These trends can be summed up by locating the geographical center of Christianity. In 200 CE, it was on one of the Greek islands. In 1000 CE, it was in Istanbul. In 1700, it was in northern Italy. In 1900, it was in the middle of Spain. In 1970, it was on the coast of Morocco. In 2000, the center slipped southeast to Mali. Finally, in 2100, the map locates the center of Christianity farther south in Nigeria.[147]

Christianity has been a worldwide religion. Now we can say that it is a globalized faith. Professor of Global Christianity Todd Johnson observes that in the last century, Christianity's major concern has been how to respond to secularism. However, in the twenty-first century, Christianity faces new challenges. In an age

Table 7.11. Growth of African Christianity—Numbers and Percentages

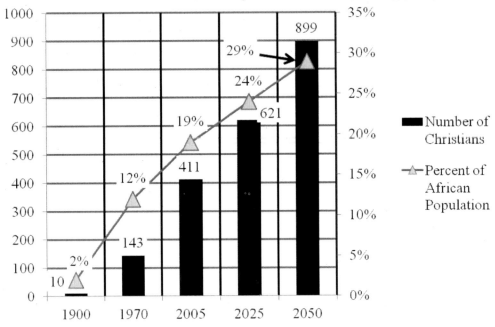

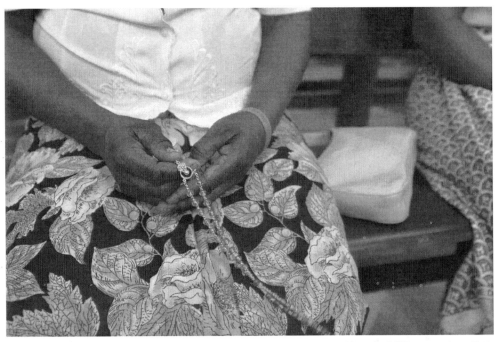

An African woman prays with a rosary. One in five Christians worldwide lives in Africa. By 2050, one in three Christians will live in Africa.

of global pluralism, many observers say that Christianity should pay more attention to religious diversity.[148] The potential clash between Christianity and Islam in Africa—especially Nigeria, Ivory Coast and Uganda—is cause for concern.[149] But the most difficult, as well as creative, dynamics will probably be within the broad family of Christianity. The tension between the historic "Northern" and emerging "Southern" styles of faith and practice is just beginning to surface.[150]

In summary, globalization is the overarching condition of today's religions. Religions and religious believers live in today's global society and must respond to it. One approach is to take a stand against the forces of globalization as we see in the assertion of self-chosen religious identities and the varieties of fundamentalism. Another approach is to select and use the technologies and social structures of globalization for the promotion of religion. In any case, religions are responding to the forces of globalization in complex and diverse ways. To make projections about the future of religion based on these varied responses is an interesting but challenging task.

Evaluation of Alternative Approaches to the Future

We have reviewed four approaches to predicting the future of religion. Would any of these represent a theory that might take the place of the secularization thesis? That depends on the evaluation that follows.

Evaluation of the Projection of Demographic Trends

The analysis above reports that three religions seem to be surpassing the rest. Two of these, Hinduism and Christianity, are keeping up with the world's population explosion. One, Islam, is doing even better. On the other hand, some traditional religions like Judaism, Buddhism, and Shinto are falling behind the world population increase. Except, perhaps, for Baha'i, the figures show no significant impact of the newer religions, sometimes called "new religious movements." According to this analysis of data and trends, religion is not declining overall but the numbers of adherents to the religions is changing. While some religions are keeping up with the growth of the human population, others are falling behind. In addition, over the century, the numbers of the atheists and nonreligious have increased, but the research does not predict that these groups will grow significantly in the future.

Will these projected trends continue? We have shown some examples of projections even as far out as 2200. How can we evaluate these predictions? To begin with, we might ask whether the statistics are reliable. Since the statistics of this chapter rely so much on the World Christian Database statistics, the WCD figures deserve closer inspection. Note that the WCD presents its numbers as empirical data. However, note that evangelical Protestants have compiled them to support worldwide Christian missionary efforts. Reviewers like Glenn Masuchika have found the *World Christian Encyclopedia* that presents the WCD statistics to be confusing and suspect.[151] Historian Mark Noll admits that the WCE presents an overwhelming amount of information compiled by hundreds of researchers. But he endorses the monumental effort of the project.[152]

Sociologist Becky Hsu and her associates studied the correlations of five data-sets: World Christian Database (WCD), World Values Survey, Pew Global Assessment Project, CIA *World Factbook*, and the U.S. Department of State. The most comprehensive of these, the WCD, correlates highly with the other four datasets, except in the category of nonreligious.[153] Still, Hsu's group prefers the WCD for the nonreligious, and it states that the WCD has the most detailed information for the most countries.[154] In general, the discipline of religious studies can accept the information presented.

Next, we might evaluate the method of the predictions. Todd Johnson, the current editor of the WCD, states that the method of prediction is to keep on collecting data. As information comes in, the task is to integrate it into the developing database. Then the researchers must relate the bits of information to one another. Finally, they must revise their predictions according to the results.[155] Thus, the project constantly tracks the changes taking place and revises its estimates.

However, the changing conditions produce changes in the projections. This chapter has already presented two different alternative futures projected from two different sets of conditions. Johnson explains that the method of the projections given in the section "Two Alternative Futures" is in three stages:[156]

- *Stage One* takes United Nations projections of population growth as a base and then adjusts by birth and death rates
- *Stage Two*
  - *Step 1* adjusts the findings of Stage One by revising the birth and death rates of specific religious communities within an area
  - *Step 2* adjusts the result of Step 1 according to rates of converts and defectors
  - *Step 3* adjusts for known and anticipated immigration trends
- *Stage Three*
  - Calculates a Muslim resurgence by estimating percentage gains of Muslims by region and taking these gains away from the other religions in the region
  - Calculates a nonreligious resurgence by taking percentages away from Christianity and Islam

An analysis of these methods helps us see that the soundness of predictions depends on the baseline starting point. The projections above rely on the accuracy of the census takers of the 6.5 billion people of the world. These include the United Nations demographers and the World Christian Database.

If we accept the accuracy of the baseline, then what about the projections? Of course, the further we go into the future, the more we venture into uncertainty. Moreover, the more steps we take, the more they become speculative. Rates of conversion and defection of religious groups are variable and hard to count. Likewise, immigration trends depend on circumstances that may not be foreseen. Moreover, if the estimates for immigration and conversion in Stage Two are only approximate, the estimates in Stage Three are only arbitrary guesses.

This leads to the crucial question: on what basis did Barrett and Johnson estimate the variables for the Muslim surge or growth in nonreligious? Johnson admits that they simply added or subtracted 10 percent to the baseline for the year 2100 and another 10 percent to that figure for year 2200![157]

The estimates that Johnson presents seem like measurable statistics. They show up in exact percentage and even raw numbers on his charts. Yet the numbers he offers are only raw guesstimates of what might happen. For example, the percentages of the Muslim surge represent expected births minus deaths adjusted by rough estimates of the gains and losses of the religions. These projections depend on estimates of the net rates of change of births minus deaths. In addition, they rely on estimates of the net rates of change of the conversions and defections. But a critical assessment of the calculations notes that Johnson arrives at the final projections merely by multiplying the numbers times ten.

Scholars would make estimates that are more accurate if they would identify the conditions that will affect several key factors: (1) the birth and death rates; (2) conversions and defections; and (3) the migration of religious believers. Yet this would only be a beginning step to foreseeing the future. The theory that we can use population statistics to predict the future of religion stumbles over the uncertain conditions that will affect the rates of change.

Evaluation of the Neosecularization Thesis

If we are to find an approach that will help us forecast its future, neosecularization theory seems to be the least helpful. The neosecularists revise the theory to answer the objections to it. They define secularization as the division of society into separate institutions. This allows them to answer the charge that in many modern societies, rationality and science have not wiped out religious belief.[158] The focus is on the decline of religious authority. This means that they can ignore the fact that in many modern societies, significant numbers of believers still practice their religion. They deny that the theory makes predictions. Therefore, they do not have to admit that the thesis was wrong.

In summary, sociologist Rick Phillips states that instead of a thesis, the neosecularists offer a definition. In other words, the original secularization thesis predicted that modern people would become less religious when social systems were freed from religious control. In contrast, the neosecularization approach simply describes the modern, secular society. It refrains from predicting anything. Therefore, it no longer is a working hypothesis of what will happen under the conditions of the modern mind-set.[159]

Neosecularists admit that social differentiation alone cannot be used to predict the future. Societies will respond to the division of the traditional social order in different ways. France is a highly differentiated society. Under the theory of *laïcité*, religious institutions and religious behavior are isolated from public society. The line between religion and the public functions of politics, government, and economics is clear-cut. In contrast to France, the United States continues to debate the relationship between religion and public life. Americans are divided about the proper role of religion in politics, social services, education, and social ethics.

Americans also tend to disagree with the secularization thesis that religion is "out of date." Almost six in ten Americans believe that religion can solve most of the world's problems. Only one in three believes that religion is "old-fashioned."[160]

It is obvious that America is not France. In the United States, even if secularization is reduced to the definition of the neosecularists, Americans still have a divided mind. About one half of the American population agrees that religion should be separated from other social institutions like government and education. About one half do not. The neosecularization thesis fails because it cannot predict which side will win. Is the approach of the neosecularists useful? If all it does is to describe the separation of social systems in society, Rodney Stark asks, "What is there to argue about?"[161]

Evaluation of the Focus on Worldwide Migration of Human Populations

When it reviewed the alternative approaches to looking ahead to the future, this chapter presented a considerable amount of statistics and trends. It did so because it is easiest and safest to extend the known dynamics of the present into uncertain conditions of the future. But how do we know, for example, that population shifts will continue at the same pace? How do we know that fertility rates will remain more or less constant? Human behavior is changeable. How do we know that the actions of people in this century will not suddenly reverse?

Obviously, we are speaking in probabilities. Probabilities represent the relative certainty of possibilities. The more stable the conditions, the more reasonable the predictions. The trends of urbanization and immigration seem to be constant enough for making forecasts about the future concentrations of human populations. Yet life in the global society is extremely complex. It is almost impossible to gain the breadth of knowledge necessary to factor in all the conditions that will result in the mass migrations of people. For example, the Pew Hispanic Center reported that immigration from Mexico had declined from 1,026,000 in 2006–2007 to 636,000 in 2008–2009, largely because of a drop in unauthorized immigration.[162] Among the factors was the recession of the first decade of the century.

Moreover, we cannot predict what seem to be random events or sudden reverses in the course of events. For example, we might accept the forecasts of global warming. But how will global warming affect the shifts in the human population? And how will it affect religion? The answers are unclear.

Moreover, our review of the situation in America and Europe shows that the situation involves choices of groups and individuals. The immigrants live between two forces: assimilation into their new society and preservation of their former identity. The future of religion depends on the relative strength of these forces and how the immigrants will respond to them. As we see in the issue of the Muslim burqa, each society and immigrant group will deal with these dynamics in a unique way.

Evaluation of Responses to Globalization

It is hard to make reasonable predictions about the external factors that will affect religion in the future like immigration. It is even harder to forecast the way religions and religious believers will respond to the dynamics within the religious sphere. We have explored the theory that the future of religion will depend on the human responses to the dynamics of the contemporary global society. However, the movements described above under the alternative of "responses to globalization" are broad and ambiguous. The future of these movements depends on external circumstances such as migration patterns and internal factors such as leadership. Human responses are variable, as the Pew U.S. Religious Landscape Survey shows.[163] To achieve satisfactory results from this theory, scholars would have to identify the likely options that religions and believers would have before them. These options would vary according to the local situation. Then the scholars would have to determine the most likely options that the religions and believers would choose in these settings.

In summary, the theories that we have reviewed take into account a limited number of conditions that will influence the future state of religion. Therefore, their forecasts are limited.

Our review has established that the key force for change in the twenty-first century is globalization. As the latest form of modernization, globalization promotes religious diversity, and religious diversity both undermines traditional religious authority and offers choices for self-chosen faith and personal identity. Religions will adapt to the development of the global society in a number of ways. Some religions will embrace the processes of globalization and some will resist them. But many religions will use the technology and communication systems of the new world order to promote their organizations and agendas. As they respond to the dynamics of worldwide social change, religions will also change in perceptible and imperceptible ways. (See the textbox "Conditions That Have a Bearing on the Future of Religion" for more detailed results of our analysis.)

Conditions That Have a Bearing on the Future of Religion

- The processes of globalization are all-pervasive and inescapable.
- Globalization is a latest development of the forces of modernism.
- Secularization affects society by breaking up the social structures that were once united in religion. This is the essence of secularization.
- The result of globalization is religious diversity.
- Religious diversity has the negative effect of undermining religious authority but the positive effect of offering choices of religious belonging and identity.
- Secularism has produced counterforces of fundamentalism, which seeks to recover the certainty of faith and the authority of religion over all aspects of life that the forces of secularization have undermined.
- In response to the forces of globalization, religion can be transformed into a means of asserting a self-chosen identity and even gaining political power.
- Religions adapt in various ways to the forces of globalization including the use of technology for promotion, recruitment, and the development of global networks.

Here our discussion of selected alternative theories of predicting the future of religion ends. In summary, we have found that we cannot predict with certainty how persons, religious groups, and religions will respond to the processes of globalization in the twenty-first century. Our study suggests that individuals will be free to make choices about religion that were not available before. It also suggests that those who feel the loss of a sense of identity in the global mass society may look to religion to recover and defend a personal identity. Further, it suggests that some believers will strive to recover the all-pervasive authority that religion once had in society. On the other hand, other believers may form subcultures against the social order because they feel that it is no longer centered in religion. The question remains: On what basis will they make the choices that will determine the future of religion?

PROPOSING THE MOST PROMISING SOLUTION: THE RATIONAL CHOICE THEORY

The last theory of this chapter attempts to answer the question of the basis of human choices in religion. Called *rational choice* or, alternatively, *supply-side theory*, this approach is the most comprehensive rival to the secularization thesis. In a global society that prides itself on offering choices, it is not surprising that scholars would come up with a theory centered on choice. This theory of choice addresses the questions of the persistence, change, and expansion of religion in the global society that this chapter has raised.

This theory asserts that the secularization thesis was based on false premises. The thesis supposed that religious authority would decline when the functions of society had been divided into separate institutions. Social differentiation would take away religion's controlling and unifying role in society.

Moreover, the secularization thesis also supposed that as modern persons became more rational, they would lose their personal interest in religion. They would no longer have reason to believe.

Rodney Stark and economist Laurence Iannaccone counter that the secularization thesis had the wrong focus.[164] In terms of their market theory, the thesis concentrated on the religious organizations that were providing the goods and services of religion. It neglected to consider the consumers of these religious benefits. Because of this, the approach supposed that if the traditional religious institutions would lose their authority in society, religion would decrease. Most important, Stark and Iannaccone charged that the secularization thesis concentrates on the demand side of religion.[165] The thesis supposes that the demand for religion is limited. It holds that the supply of religious benefits may be constant even in a secularized society, but the people will not want it.

Stark counters that the secularization thesis failed to recognize the basic function of religion. In Stark's view, religion's fundamental purpose is not to unify society. The function of religion is to address the most important and enduring concerns of human life. These concerns are universal. Therefore, the *demand* for religion is constant. It is the *supply* of religion that is changeable.[166]

The Supply Side Theory Illustrated

Take laundry soap. Economic boom or bust, people still have to wash their clothes. Therefore, soap is a "staple," a product that has a constant demand. For staples, the supply will vary but the demand will not change. This is what the rational choice theorists claim about religion.

Now, given the constant demand for soap, how is the Stupendous Soap Company going to sell its soap? If the supply is low, no problem. But if the competition is strong, the company must do something. It will have to adjust price, advertising, features, or packaging to get a market share of the demand that still persists. The Standard & Poors financial research firm observes that in recessions people do not stop buying soap. They purchase products with private labels or store brands that are cheaper and less flashy.[167] The demand is constant. Changes happen on the side of supply such as modifications to the product, the price, or the packaging.

Now what if people suddenly stop buying the Stupendous Soap? People would be foolish to say that they are no longer interested in cleaning their clothes. They may be taking their clothes to the cleaners. Maybe they are making their own soap in the backyard. More likely, they have just chosen another brand.

Using this analogy, rational choice theory says that if people are not coming to church, it is not because they have suddenly lost their appetite for religiosity. They are making other choices. They may have switched churches or even religions. They may have started a "house church" in their home. They may be gaining inspiration from the mass media or the Internet. They may have found another way to "do religion" and have called it "spirituality."

As a theory about human choice, this theory goes on to assume that people, whether religious or nonreligious, are "rational actors."[168] This does not mean that people are sitting down with a calculator when they make choices about religion. It means that they are agents who make what they believe to be reasonable choices among available options.

How do people make these sensible choices? The same way they make choices of soap. Their choices are based on weighing the benefits of a choice over its costs. The fact that people evaluate their options in religion in this way leads to the fundamental assumption that the choices people will make are predictable. The needs and interests that humans use to evaluate the net gain of their choices are constant. They do not vary from person to person or over time. Further, society consists of communities of rational actors. Individuals make choices based on their calculations of self-interest. These choices direct the course of society. Likewise, choices propel the dynamics of religion in society.[169]

It is easy to see how rational choice theory might apply to buying soap. Potential customers of the new brand of Stupendous Soap might weigh the costs against the promised benefits. These costs would include not only price but also the risk of trying something new, and the loss of satisfaction with the present product. Then again, believers do not usually see religion as a commodity. And even if they do, the benefits are not tangible, instant, or measurable.

To answer these objections, Stark and sociologist Roger Finke observe that as rational agents, people make choices within the limits of the options available and the information at hand. Realizing that we cannot have everything we want immediately, we will accept promises of later benefits.[170] Religions offer scarce and infinitely precious commodities. For example, they offer the benefits of life after death, permanent release from suffering, and ultimate fulfillment. But even the best religion cannot hand these eternal realities to us in the present.

Instead, religions offer *compensators* that are promissory notes for payments in the future. These compensators are substitutes for tangible rewards. People accept them on faith that in the future they can cash them in for benefits that they cannot gain in this life.

Recall the chapter on belief. Religions are human organizations whose business is providing compensators for the deepest questions of life.[171] Religions uniquely supply these IOUs because they trade in the supernatural. Only the supernatural is capable of providing satisfying answers to the ultimate questions of life, and religions promise that believers will eventually receive these answers as they reach the level of the supernatural.

For example, in Stark and Bainbridge's thinking, the primary and most pressing human desire is for immortality. It is highly desirable to live forever. The demand for eternal life is universal and constant. Yet our finite existence cannot offer us the infinite life of eternity. Humans must look to an eternal reality beyond the flux and flow of the material universe to satisfy their demand for immortality.[172] In the view of rational choice theory, religions will endure because they offer socially acceptable means to get in touch with this eternal reality. Religions that offer believable promises of immortality will prosper. However, if a religion fails to focus on this human need, the demand for this highest of all goods will be as strong as ever. It is just that people will look elsewhere to fulfill it.

What's more, on the market model, those who want goods and services must pay for them. With that in mind, the rational choice theory supposes that religions are businesses that exact a variety of costs for the compensators of eternal rewards.[173] Above all, the cost of everlasting life is faith in the conception of the supernatural and its promises. Beyond that, each religion also requires a unique set of attitudes, behaviors, and relationships based on the foundation of its distinctive beliefs. On the spiritual level, these religious ways are structured interactions with the supernatural reality in terms of worship, prayer, morality, and works of compassion. On the material level, these costs include time for religious activities and money for the support of the religion.

The pricing of these religious obligations is critical. Religious compensators can be offered at too high a price or sold too cheaply.[174] If the social and personal costs of belonging to sects and cults are high, most will not join. However, for those who are willing to pay it, the high price increases the value of the group's promised rewards. For members of sects and cults, one of the greatest costs is the tension with the mainstream of society. Yet this tension increases the distinctive group identity and commitment to the group. On the other hand, groups with low costs will tolerate more "free riders" and enjoy more favor in society. Yet they are likely to lack group solitary, individual commitment, and the involvement of many members.

Rational choice theory assumes human religiosity is a constant demand. Humans will always seek answers to life's deepest questions. This age-old quest ensures that the demand for compensators will remain high. People realize that the fulfillment of their ultimate concerns is not immediately or directly attainable. Thus, the future of the religious organizations that offer these compensators is open. To summarize, rational choice theory applies supply-side economics to religion. The supply of religious goods will vary. The options and alternatives that are available to individuals to satisfy the universal need for religious benefits will change.

How Rational Choice Theory Explains the Dynamics of Religious Belonging

Rational choice theory explains the rise and decline of religion in a different way from the secularization thesis. It states that in general when a single religion has a monopoly on the supply of religious goods, then interest in religion will fade. The need for religion will still be there, but the dominating religion will be relatively less interested in or capable of fulfilling it.[175] The result will be a lack of vitality in the religion and its institutions. According to this idea, the problem in Europe is not the forces of secularization. It is the history of state-sponsored, monopolistic religions.

In contrast, competition among religions raises interest. Religions are more focused on supplying the religious needs of people because of the rivalry with their competitors. This fact explains why religion in America is noticeably stronger than in Europe.[176] It also explains much of the revival of religion in the "Third World." For example, in Latin America, Pentecostalism has become a competitor to Catholicism. Catholic studies professor R. Andrew Chestnut describes Latin America as a new religious economy that has no place for the lazy religious organizations of religious monopolies. In typical rational choice theory terms, he observes how Latin American religious groups "develop an attractive product" and skillfully market it to eager consumers.[177]

We have searched for a theory that might serve as a replacement for the secularization thesis. It would be an explanatory paradigm or model for explaining and interpreting the dynamics of religion in the twenty-first century. Rational choice theory seems to be a viable candidate. It holds that the demand for religion is constant. This explains the persistence of religion. It also asserts that the ways that religious organizations serve the demand on the "supply side" vary. This explains the variety of religious organizations in the world. Further, it holds that involvement in religious organizations depends on how well they meet the demands of the religious consumers. This explains the marked shifts in religious participation of this century. Finally, the theory holds that a vibrant marketplace of competition will motivate religious firms to strive to meet the demands of the religious consumer. This explains the alleged "religious resurgence" that is happening as globalization produces worldwide religious pluralism.

The rational choice theory explains the dynamics of religion in the twenty-first century, but it also makes predictions about the future of religion. Stark and Iannaccone have stated a succinct formula that the theory can use to forecast the future of religion: When religions compete in a diverse setting, people will be more involved in religion, but when one or two religions have a monopoly on the religious marketplace, people will be less involved in religion.[178] According to this formula, religious pluralism may undermine the authority of the religious establishment. Yet religious diversity may also encourage adaptation and innovation in religion to meet the demand of religious consumers in terms of their perceived needs. The result is the vitality of religion and vigor of religious institutions.

EVALUATING THE MOST PROMISING SOLUTION:
A TEST OF TWO CATHOLIC SETTINGS

The predictions of the rational choice theory are specific enough that they can be tested. For example, Stark tested the accuracy of the theory in a study of Catholics in the United States. To begin, he formulated the hypothesis that Catholics in locations of religious pluralism would show greater *commitment* and churches would show greater *innovation.*

Stark set out to test this hypothesis by comparing dioceses in the East where the percent of the Catholic population is high to the South where the percent of the Catholic population is low.[179] For example, he compared the activities of the Catholic churches in Boston where 54 percent of the population is Catholic to those in Knoxville, Tennessee, where the Catholic population is 2.6 percent.

After choosing the locations of his research, Stark determined his measurements. To measure innovation, he calculated the numbers of deacons, nuns, and laypersons who were performing functions usually reserved for priests. To measure commitment, he totaled the number of the ordination of priests, the number of seminarians, and the rate of adult baptisms (conversions) per 100,000. In each case, he found a strong negative correlation between the percent of Catholics in the population of the diocese and the rates of innovation and commitment.[180] This confirmed that settings of market competition increased both innovation to serve the needs of the consumers and the level of commitment to the compensators that Catholicism offered. Stark claims that over eleven of such studies in America and Europe confirmed the theory. Only one did not, and the results could not be corroborated.[181]

Stark refers to experiments like the study of Catholics in America to assert that the rational choice theory does a better job of predicting the future of religion than the outdated secularization thesis. But what about the decline of religion in Europe since the Middle Ages? Rational choice theorists address the objection in several ways. First, they challenge the benchmark. They claim that the widely held view that the Middle Ages was especially religious is mistaken. Stark and Iannaccone cite numerous studies to show that the masses of people in England and Europe had very poor rates of worship attendance. Moreover, the masses had little knowledge of religion, and their Christianity and piety was laced with magic and animism.[182]

Second, the theorists refer to their key formula. Until the Reformation, a religious monopoly dominated Europe. After that, most of Europe was divided into Catholic and Protestant monopolies. The supply-side theory holds that such monopolies dampen participation in religious organizations.[183]

Finally, it may be true that secularism destroyed the sacred character of European culture. But to the supply-side theorists, this banishment of the supernatural from society did not mean that religious demand declined. The objection to the rational choice theory assumes that the doctrine and the ceremonies of an official religion make a society sacred.[184] But in the view of the theory, dogma and ritual are not the same as religiosity. A summary of studies and polls in the United Kingdom showed that two of three citizens believe in God, but only one in four believes in a personal God. Moreover, two of three persons say they pray.

Even four in ten of those who never attend worship say they pray. Six in ten say they would be concerned if their local church or chapel were closed.[185] Stark and Iannaccone interpret such findings as signs of the constant demand for spirituality and the potential demand for organized religion.[186]

In summary, the advantages of the rational choice theory over the other theories we have studied is that it is comprehensive and that it explains the past and current dynamics of religion. More important, it sets out the conditions that will affect the future of religion. Based on these conditions, researchers can test their predictions with empirical studies.

Criticisms of the Rational Choice Theory

The rational choice theory has enjoyed so much popularity among scholars that it has been called "the new paradigm." Naturally, its status has provoked much criticism. The first of these objections is that it is difficult to define what rational choice would be in religion. In religion, individuals do make choices to gain expected rewards. But that insight does not have much meaning. If people make choices for what they consider to be good for them, any choice might be considered rational.[187]

A second criticism is that though the theory seems to explain the European situation, on closer examination, the theory does not account for its complexities. The rational choice theory proposes that religious diversity enhances competition. In turn, competition makes religions more responsive and that makes them more successful. However, this theory does not seem to work in many places. Some scholars observe that Great Britain has the greatest diversity of religion among the major European nations. Yet interest in religion in the United Kingdom has declined just as it has in Scandinavia and in the Netherlands. In the United States, religious diversity does not necessarily increase religious participation.[188] These are only a few examples of numerous cases where the evidence does not seem to confirm the rational choice theory.

A third critique of the theory is that its terms need further clarification and study.[189] What is a "religious monopoly"? How do we measure "religious vitality" or "participation"? How do we measure "religious diversity"? And if there is a relationship between vitality and diversity, what are the variables involved? These questions suggest that the analysis of the rational choice theory could be refined with more precise terms.

Sociologist Frank J. Lechner voices the last and most important criticism. He asserts that the rational choice theory does not really do what we hoped a comprehensive theory of religion would do. It claims to both explain the evidence and make future projections; however, most of its adherents' studies do not look forward but look backward.[190] They reflect on present or past cases and explain why the actors behaved "rationally" in their circumstances. Perhaps this is the best that the theory can do. How individuals make choices is complex. What individuals choose also varies over time and from person to person. The Pew "Faith in Flux" study shows how unpredictable people in the twenty-first century are when it comes to religion.[191] The significant changes that are happening to contemporary religion suggest that rational choice theory may be able to predict some general trends, but it cannot make accurate, detailed forecasts, because it cannot foresee how individuals will weigh the costs and benefits of religion ahead of time.[192]

Rational choice theory is a powerful idea that appeals to the present mind-set of global capitalism. As far as explaining some dynamics of religion in the global society, it is an alternative to the secularization thesis. Yet the theory requires further developing and testing if it is to become a reliable way to make predictions about the future. Further research is needed to clarify its terms and give measurable evidence for its claims. Moreover, it faces the challenges of objections to its assumptions, methods, and results.

Conclusion: The Resilience of Religion, the Adaptability of Religions

The theories for foretelling the future of religions in our global society outlined above come down to five basic methods: (1) predictions based on the current trends of population; (2) the neosecularization thesis; (3) the analysis of the effects of immigration; (4) the projection of potential responses to the forces of globalization; and (5) rational choice theory. As we conclude this chapter, we might ask how these methods treat religion. Though religious studies must treat religion in an academic way, there is a problem to this approach.

In order to understand religion, scholars in religious studies make generalizations that should be based on evidence. Yet, especially in this chapter, the theories seem far away from the "lived experience" of the religious believers. In order to make the generalizations of this chapter, we have *reified* religion. That is, we have treated religion as if it were a thing. The abstraction of religion enables scholars to study the present and anticipate the future of religion. However, this chapter has talked about religion as if it were an existing and specific entity. That is, this study has objectified the religions of the world. Instead of looking at religions as ways of life of human persons, we have treated them in several abstract ways. The chapter has looked at them as collections of numbers, organizations that carry out certain functions, institutions that have more or less authority, or as the total of individual decisions.

Reflection on our attempt to find a reliable way to forecast the future of religion might give some insight into religious studies. The lesson is to be on guard against the tempting academic attitude toward the sacred beliefs and practices of the world's peoples. We should beware of treating them as if they were things, more acted upon than acting.

For example, the secularization thesis seems to be more than a description of the processes of modernism. It seems to be a prescription of the inevitable. Strangely, the secularists who champion freedom seem to be the most invested in this unnoticed determinism. In the middle of the twentieth century, some academics were so convinced of the secularization thesis that they advised the surrender of religious beliefs. But the believers did not give up. Now religious belief is advancing, and secularism is on the defensive.

For over a century, the question of how to deal with secularity has stirred much of the ferment in religion. The liberals as well as the fundamentalists have actively wrestled with issues of secularism. For example, this chapter suggested that Muslim fundamentalists are not passive reactionaries. They are attempting to shape the forces of globalization according to their vision for humanity. Christian and Hindu fundamentalists are trying to do the same. On the other hand, liberals also are grappling with the issues of their adaptation to the secular mind-set.

This chapter has shown that in the twenty-first century, another challenge has arisen for both conservatives and liberals. Because of globalization, religions can no longer isolate themselves from one another. Our global society has produced a rich religious diversity as a new setting for religions and their believers. This chapter has shown how this diversity tends to undermine the authority of religious leaders.

On the other hand, the discussion has suggested that globalization may be the unappreciated driver of a "resurgence" of those religions that can meet its challenges. Rational choice theory predicts that increasing competition among religions will strengthen religion in the future. Yet it is not the only theory that suggests that globalization will have a positive impact on religion. We have shown that this century's extensive human migration and urbanization could provide the settings that might foster the growth of religions. Moreover, global technologies could provide the tools for vigorous and creative ways of promoting religion. Most of all, interchange of religions and believers could enliven and enrich the faith and practice of those religions that are open to it.

This is not to suggest that the future of religion will be entirely positive. Past and present trends suggest that relationships between religions and factions within religions will involve tensions and conflict. As we saw in the chapter on religious violence, the nature and extent of that discord depends on local conditions and the leaders in these specific settings.

Predictions based on trends also tend to assume that religions and religious believers are conditioned. For example, to make statistical projections, scholars must assume that given the conditions of secularization, globalization, urbanization, immigration, and fertility rates, people will act in certain ways. This presumes that since people act in certain ways now, they will act in the same ways in the future. We might call this assumption "statistical determinism."

Likewise, persons, societies, and cultures respond to changing conditions in different ways. We cannot reliably predict these by studying trends. For example, Muslims in Europe are not only the object of the forces of the European secular societies. They are active participants in a situation with an undetermined outcome. How Muslims interact with the native Europeans is an open question. The interaction of Muslims, Christians, Jews, and other religious people, together with the secularists in Europe, will shape the future of the continent. In summary, religions are organic and responsive to changing circumstances.

It is true that the rational choice theory treats human beings as agents. Nevertheless, it limits choices to individuals. In the view of the rational choice theorists, religions are simply aggregates, the sums of individual choices. Cultural anthropologist Andrew Buckser notes that the theory assumes that human desires are fixed.[193] Religions address these felt human needs to varying degrees of success.

The problem with this attitude is that it disregards the role of religions in shaping those needs. For example, Buckser notes that Calvinist Protestants and

Catholic Franciscan monks have opposite attitudes toward material possessions. Religious beliefs shape these attitudes. Likewise, religious belief determines the conception of immortality. This conception of life beyond death defines the compensators that believers will seek.[194]

Throughout this textbook, we have shown that religions are organic, interactive, and adaptive. The history of the Church of Jesus Christ of Latter-day Saints is a good example. In the days of the founding of the religion, the common goal was to build the Mormon society as the Kingdom of God on Earth. Joining in public works projects for the good of the community was just as important as singing in the choir. By the 1930s, the Mormons yielded to the secular forces that divide religion from other social structures of society.[195] Churches no longer doubled as town halls. Civil courts replaced church courts. Church leaders maintained their religious authority but lost their political clout.

The dramatic modifications to the religion came when the fundamental idea of what it meant to be religious changed. When Mormons began to distinguish religious duties from social duties, worship attendance took priority over social responsibilities. Worship was the primary way to maintain one's religious identity and to take part in the religious community. As a result, worship attendance increased dramatically.

This case shows that though the foundation of a religion may be fixed, a religion will adapt to changing conditions. This response will vary according to the decisions that religious leaders make. It will also depend on intangible factors such as the group spirit and its decisions.

If religions will act as agents, so will individual believers, especially in the future. This chapter showed how globalization leads to religious pluralism. Further, it explained that as people become aware of other religions, they tend to see other sacred ways as personal preferences.

The idea that religion is a personal choice among many options is changing the behavior of many in the global society. We have already cited the Pew research finding that 44 percent of Americans left the faith of their childhood.[196] We also reported that the Pew study found that 12 percent of Americans claims no religious affiliation. This percentage increases when one isolates the younger generations: one in four Americans ages eighteen to twenty-nine have no membership in a religious organization.

Does this mean that the young adults of the nation are not religious? One in four Americans claims they are "spiritual but, so they insist, not 'religious.'" Freed from the restraint of religious institutions, those who say this are likely to prefer their religion à la carte. They want to choose their religious ideas, opinions, and beliefs from different religions according to their inclination. They take the cafeteria of religion for granted. They only need to get in line and fill up their plates from the array of choices that religions, old and new, offer.

As scholars concentrate on measurable data such as demographic statistics, religious membership, religious attendance, and beliefs, they might not notice the larger trend that is shaping the religion of the future. When one steps back, one can see that the basic idea of religion has changed. Sociologist Steve Bruce notes that believers in homogenous cultures have a different sense of the sacred than believers in cultures where individuals are aware of their options. In the global society where beliefs are relativized, people may believe in God. However, they are also aware that it is a choice to believe. Bruce claims that those who have become sovereign consumers in the global religious marketplace can never go back to traditional religion. They know too much and enjoy their choices too much. They choose their religion. The religion does not choose them.[197] In this viewpoint on religion, the "ultimate point of reference" is not the supernatural.[198] It is the individual.

In the end, the "spiritual but not religious" approach to religiosity may not be an enduring form of religion. First, it is not the original and primary form of religion. It is religion in the derived, secondary sense. Spirituality depends on religious traditions for its sources. It takes these sacred ways that it feeds on for granted. It does little to contribute to them. If everyone would feast from the religious cafeteria as customers, there would be no one to serve up the food. Second, a self-chosen religion has no ultimate foundation except the sovereign, deciding self. In terms of the rational choice theory, it lacks a sense of the supernatural that alone can offer convincing compensators to believers. Third, such a religion lacks the support and guidance of a community. Perhaps consumers can support one another on their individual quests. Nonetheless, everyone is on a separate and lonely journey. For these reasons, it may be that invigorated forms of organized religion, driven by the forces of globalization, will be the future of religion.

In conclusion, we have not found a comprehensive theory that would help us forecast the future of religion with confidence. We have shown that religions in the twenty-first century must face the challenge of religious diversity. This means finding ways to interact constructively with other religions. But it also means addressing the latest outcome of globalization, the notion of the believer as religious consumer. Many religions will find ways to deal with such issues of the twenty-first century because neither religions nor their leaders and members are passive. At the turn of the century, the world's religions have shown remarkable resilience and vitality. We can only predict that they will face the challenges of the future with continued resolution and adaptation and that they will redefine themselves as they do so.

KEY TERMS

Compensator: in rational choice theory, a belief that a reward (like heaven) will be obtained in the distant future or some other context that cannot be immediately verified.

Demographics: numerical statistics on the human population and its aspects such as births and deaths.

Fundamentalism: in the narrow sense, the Protestant movement that reacts against modernism by setting out the basic principles that cannot be compromised because they are the foundation of Christianity. The first of these is the literal interpretation of the Bible. In the broader sense, movements like Muslim Salafism that react against modernism by seeking to return to a literal reading of their scriptures and the basic fundamentals of their faith.

Globalization: a constellation of economic, political, communication, and cultural relationships among nations and peoples that are creating a worldwide community.

Jihad: Muslim term for the duty of all Muslims to "strive" to defend Islam and its way of life on a spiritual as well as social level; popularly used for the warfare against the enemies of Islam.

Jihadist: in popular terms, a Muslim who is dedicated to the struggle against the forces of Western modernism for the restoration of Islam and Islamic law in society.

Neosecularization thesis: the renewal of the secularization thesis that limits it to the description of the differentiation of society in which the functions of society like government, education, the courts, medicine, and religion are separated and operate in their own spheres.

Paradigm: a mental framework of rules and procedures about how a subject is to be studied.

Rational choice theory: a market approach to research that assumes that individuals evaluate the benefits and costs of religious rewards in predictable and reasonable ways. The constant in the theory is the demand for intangible religious benefits. The variable is the nature and availability of the supply of religious beliefs and practices to meet this demand.

Salafism: the Islamic movement that seeks to recover the vitality and purity of Islam against the forces of modernism. It hopes to do so by returning to the way of the forebearers, the Islamic prophet Muhammad and his followers, and the strict, literal following of the Qur'an and Sunna (traditions of the example of Muhammad).

Secular: the sphere of public life that is separated from religious influence, especially religious institutions.

Secularism: refers to the ideology that promotes the secularization of society and seeks to purge religion from any role in society.

Secularization thesis: the theory that the processes of modernism that separate religion from government and other functions of society will inevitably lead to the decline of religious influence over society, groups, and individuals.

Shari'ah: Islamic law revealed in the Qur'an and the traditions of the Islamic prophet Muhammad (hadith) binding for all Muslims and covering all aspects of the Muslim way of life whether personal or social.

Sunna: the traditions of sayings and deeds of the Islamic prophet Muhammad that guide Muslims in interpreting the Qur'an and following the way of Islam.

Urbanization: shifts in the human population from the rural areas to cities with the attendant problems such as overcrowding and opportunities such as concentrations of available jobs and workers.

KEY QUESTIONS

1. Secularization Thesis
   a. State the secularization thesis as Comte, Weber, Berger, Stark, and others defined it.
   b. State the secularization thesis as the neosecularization thesis defined it.

   c. What evidence supports the secularization thesis?

   d. What evidence disproves the secularization thesis?

   e. Is the neosecularization thesis useful for speaking about the future of religion? Explain.

2. Statistics of Worldwide Religion

   a. How reliable are the World Christian Database (WCD) statistics? Explain.

   b. In general, what religions are currently growing and what religions are declining?

     (Define what is meant by "growing" and what is meant by "declining.")

   c. What is meant by the *resurgence of religion*? Do the statistics and observations of the change give a convincing case for such a resurgence? Defend your answer.

3. Mass Migrations of Human Populations

   a. What effects is immigration having on religion?

   b. Will these trends continue? What factors might affect these trends?

4. Prediction

   a. What elements are necessary for reliable predictions? Evaluate one prediction in this chapter in terms of these necessary elements.

   b. Name three major factors that will affect the future of religion in the twenty-first century.

5. Europe

   a. Compare the religiosity of Europe and the United States. What factors might explain the difference?

   b. How is the secularity of Europe being challenged? What will the outcome of this challenge be? Defend your answers.

6. The Impact of Globalization on Religion

   a. How does globalization affect religion in a negative way?

   b. How does globalization affect religion in a positive way?

   c. How is globalization changing the nature of religion and religious belief?

7. Fundamentalism

   a. Why do fundamentalists emphasize the certainty of belief?

   b. Compare the *reconquista* (reconquest) and subculture responses to globalization.

8. Rational Choice Theory

   a. List and evaluate the assumptions of the rational choice theory.

   b. What evidence would support the rational choice theory?

   c. What evidence would discount the rational choice theory?

9. The Future of Religion

   a. What critique does the conclusion of this chapter make about how the theories given in this chapter treat religion, religions, and religious believers?

   b. If religions are not passive in the face of the forces of globalization but active, resilient, and adaptable, how should the field of religious studies go about research on the future of religion?

Glossary

Absolute Unitary Being (AUB): Andrew Newberg's term for the experience of being suspended beyond space in a state of "egolessness" and union with everything.

Academic study of religion: the investigation of religion in educational settings dedicated to the advancement of learning. It treats religion as a human endeavor in contrast to theological study that accepts the premises of a particular religion.

Agency detection: a term that evolutionary biologists use to explain why religious people often sense an invisible presence.

Altered states of consciousness: the term for mental states that are different from the ordinary, rational states.

Ambivalence: the condition of being divided in one's thinking and/or having conflicted feelings about something.

Apocalypticism: the belief in the catastrophic end of the world by means of a final confrontation between the forces of good and evil.

Archetypes: according to Carl Jung, the clusters of psychic energy that serve as the templates of the images of dreams and myths.

Arminianism: the reaction to Calvinism in Protestantism championed by Jacobus Arminius that reasserted that humans have a choice of whether to accept the Gospel and be saved from damnation or not.

Association theory of learning: the theory that to learn something new we must fit it into a web of ideas that already exists in our mind.

Belief: the acceptance of a truth claim that is not verifiable by evidence of the senses or inferences from such evidence.

Bliks: a word coined by R. M. Hare suggesting that religious statements are basic ways of looking at the world, not truth statements.

Cambridge Ritualists: members of a movement centered in Cambridge, England, that argued that ritual takes priority over symbols and myths and that ritual is the key to understanding them.

Clash of civilizations: the theory of Samuel Huntington that after the Cold War global hostility will erupt between broad "civilizations" instead of nation-states or empires. There are eight or nine of these civilizations.

Colonialism: principles, policies, and practices of the economic and political control of one country or society over another weaker country or society resulting in exploitation and domination.

Communitas: in the theory of Victor Turner, the quality of the liminal state in which the participants experience the reversal of the normal social order. The participants are bound together by the ordeal of going through this chaotic and hazardous time.

Compensator: in rational choice theory, a belief that a reward (like heaven) will be obtained in the distant future or some other context that cannot be immediately verified.

Constructivism: the philosophy whose central idea is that experience is never separate from its cultural context and that context shapes the experience in various ways before, during, and after the event.

Contextualism: the idea that nothing can be known or understood "in itself" but only in the situation in which it appears.

Contextualists: in the study of religious experience, theorists who reject the idea that there is a "common core" to religious experience. They believe that the (cultural) interpretation of religious experience cannot be separated from that experience.

Cosmic war: the final conflict between the forces of good and evil that believers say will result in the destruction of the universe followed by the creation of a new order of reality.

Critical realism: the philosophy that assumes that we cannot know anything directly. All knowledge is filtered through the human brain. Yet it also assumes that there are "realities" outside the mind that we know indirectly and imperfectly through our mental structures.

Critical thinking: the thoughtful process of reasoning using the skills of logic to reach sound conclusions based on evidence.

Cross-cultural: dealing with more than one culture, usually by comparison or interaction of cultures.

Datasets: a grouping of information arranged in a table of statistics.

Deduction: a conclusion reached by reasoning from a premise. The premise is a statement that is assumed to be true and on which the argument is founded; the process of reasoning from a premise going from a general statement to a specific conclusion.

Demographics: numerical statistics on the human population and its aspects such as births and deaths.

Discursive language: according to Suzanne Langer, the communication of ideas in a serial, linear fashion (one after the other).

Disenchantment: a process of modernization that frees society from the illusions of the supernatural world and its spiritual entities.

Disestablishment of religion: the idea put forth by John Locke (1632–1704) and others that extended Luther's idea of the two spheres of religion and government to the disengagement of religion from political power and government.

Doctrine: the whole of official teachings endorsed by an official authority.

Dualism: the belief that reality is divided into two basic categories that exist side by side; in theories of suffering, the idea of a basic, cosmic struggle between the forces of good and evil.

Eastern Orthodox Christianity: the beliefs, practices, and organization of a family of church bodies united in faith and practice through their bishops originating in the eastern part of the Roman Empire, centered in Constantinople.

Emergence as a character of culture and religion: the theory that the mind is different from the brain because it is a complex but whole system (of systems) that depends on its parts and yet exists as a distinct entity.

Empirical reason: the form of thinking that makes conclusions based on evidence from observation of the senses or scientific experiment.

Empiricism: the ideology that claims that human knowledge comes through observation of the senses and is tested by experimentation.

Enlightenment, the: the period of the 1700s in which the scientific method and human reason replaced religious authority as the standards of truth and knowledge.

Essentialism: the philosophy that each thing has a built-in set of properties that make the thing what it is and distinguish it from all other things.

Essentialists: in the study of religious experience, theorists who posit a "common core" or essence of the religious experience.

Ethnic religious nationalism: ideology that groups whose culture is founded on a common religious identity should also be formed into their own nation-state.

Evidentialism: the idea that sufficient evidence is the only warrant (justification) for belief (see foundationalism).

Exclusivist religions: religions that believe that they alone have the whole truth.

Expressive view of ritual: the view that myth is neither educational nor practical. It is expressive. It helps its participants relive and release the emotions of such primary activities as the hunt or the battle.

Extrovertive mysticism: according to W. T. Stace, the basic type of mysticism that retains a sense of the distinction between the mystic and what the mystic is united to.

Faith: a trust or confidence in something or someone that one deems worthy of such an attitude.

Feminism: a broad set of movements that concern justice for women. These movements regard gender as a major category of analyzing human life and the gender politics of male domination over women as the major dynamic of society.

Fideism: the rejection of any outside tests of belief other than belief itself.

Foundationalism: the idea that beliefs must be founded on ideas that are certain. Evidentialism is a form of foundationalism.

Four Noble Truths: the summary of the teachings of Buddhism concerning the universal human condition of suffering and how it is overcome.

Frames of reference: sets of ideas and attitudes into which we fit facts, information, and experiences and so understand their meaning.

Freedom and destiny: the philosophical problem of the relationship of free will to ideas of a determined outcome of the course of world events or of an individual's life.

Fundamentalism: the Protestant movement that reacts against modernism by setting out the fundamental principles that cannot be compromised because they are the foundation of Christianity. The first of these is the literal interpretation of the Bible.

Globalization: a constellation of economic, political, communication, and cultural relationships among nations and peoples that are creating a worldwide community.

Glossalalia (speaking in tongues): the spiritual practice of uttering syllables that sound like human speech but are unintelligible to the speaker and everyone else except those with the special gift of interpreting them. This is thought to be a sign that one is under the influence of the Holy Spirit.

Group and society religious violence: hostilities that involve social groups without the factor of nationalism. This type of violence includes persecution, discrimination, and segregation of minority groups.

Hadith: refers to the certified traditions of the sayings and deeds of the Islamic prophet Muhammad used for the interpretation of the Qur'an.

Hajj: the Muslim pilgrimage to Mecca, which is an example of Turner's ritual theory of *liminality*.

Halal: permitted for Muslims by Islamic law, in contrast to *haraam*, which is prohibited for Muslims by Islamic law.

Haraam: prohibited for Muslims by Islamic law, in contrast to *halal*, which is permitted for Muslims by Islamic law.

Hierarchy of needs: according to Maslow, the series of levels of human needs that are fulfilled in succession until one reaches the highest state of human fulfillment, the peak experience.

Hijab: head covering, such as a scarf, worn by Muslim women.

Iconoclasm: the practice of destroying symbolic representations (such as icons) because they are seen as "idols." Iconoclasts believe that symbolic representations are material things that are worshipped as if they were the ultimate spiritual reality—that is, God.

Ideological religious nationalism: the ideology that unites the political and the religious in common goals for the formation of a state that is centered in and directed by religion.

Inclusivist religions: religions that believe that they have the truth but others may have at least partial truths.

Ineffable: according to William James, the characteristic of religious experience that describes how the experience is so awesome that it cannot be put into words.

Inference: a conclusion reached by reasoning about what is thought to be true whether it is factual evidence or assumptions of truth.

Inference to the best explanation: a problem-solving method that chooses the most likely explanation or solution to a problem and goes on to test it.

"Insider": a believer who understands a religion from within his or her worldview and way of life.

Intellectualist school: the approach to studying religion that assumes that human beings, whether ancient or modern, have the same brains and mental equipment and so think in the same way; thus myths are primitive attempts to explain realities and how they came to be.

Intrinsic: built in to something's basic nature.

Introvertive mysticism: according to W. T. Stace, the basic type of mysticism in which there is no sense of division or distinction, whether within the mind or without it. All is one.

Islamic law: (see shari'ah)

Jihad: Muslim term for the duty of all Muslims to "strive" to defend Islam and its way of life on a spiritual as well as social level; popularly used for the warfare against the enemies of Islam.

Jihadist: in popular terms, a Muslim who is dedicated to the struggle against the forces of Western modernism for the restoration of Islam and Islamic Law in society.

Karma: in Hinduism and Buddhism the law of consequent action: every action produces a subsequent and corresponding action.

Kashrut: Jewish dietary laws concerning what foods may be eaten and how they must be prepared and consumed.

Kosher: certified fit to be eaten according to the Jewish laws of *kashrut*.

Laïcité: the French form of secularism that enforces a clear-cut and absolute separation of religion and public life.

Likeness: according to C. S. Peirce, a sign that shares the quality of what it signifies (e.g., a diagram).

Liminality: in the theory of Victor Turner, the quality at the heart of ritual that refers to the "in-between" state of the ritual participants where the ritual can transform them.

Logos (opposed to mythos): the rational, practical, and scientific, from the Greek word from which we get the word *logical*.

Madrasa: Muslim school on the primary and secondary levels in Pakistan, Bangladesh, and other Muslim countries that bases its teaching on the Qur'an and its interpretation in hadith. Madrasas provide education, room, and board to children of the lower classes and teach a traditional form of Islam.

Magisterium: the teaching authority of the Roman Catholic Church invested in the pope and the bishops who are in communion with him.

Method of Correlation: a systematic method designed by the theologian Paul Tillich that analyzes and explains beliefs in terms of the ultimate questions that they answer.

Mimesis: in René Girard's theory, the process of imitation that builds up and transmits culture.

Mimetic rivalry: in René Girard's theory, the destructive hostility that begins when two subgroups compete with one another and ends with each trying to wipe the other out.

Modular theory (of the brain): a disputed theory that the brain has different systems (modules), each of which has its own way of operating in specific areas of mental activity. Evolutionary biologists use this theory to explain how religious experience is a product of evolution.

Multidisciplinary: using several distinctive branches of knowledge and scholarship in colleges and universities.

Mysticism: the practice of the direct experience of transcendent realities not accessible to the senses.

Mythic consciousness: according to Cassirer, the awareness in which there is no separation of the symbol from what it stands for. Symbols cannot be explained; their meaning is built in.

Mythos (opposed to logos): the way of thinking that appeals to supernatural realities to preserve, order, and give meaning to human life. From the Greek word from which we get the word *myth*.

Myths: complexes of symbols ordered in story form.

Myths of origin: narratives that tell a sacred history of how certain realities came to be.

Native American Graves Protection and Repatriation Act (NAGPRA): federal legislation of 1990 that mandates that all museums that receive federal funding provide an inventory of human remains, funeral artifacts, sacred objects, and items of cultural heritage. Native American and Hawaiian communities are to be notified so that they can choose to reclaim these objects.

Natural religion: a term for religion that Enlightenment thinkers imagined would be based on reason and not infected by the supernaturalism of existing world religions.

Naturalism: the approach to the study of religion that treats religion as a purely human enterprise and that seeks human explanations for religious phenomena instead of appealing to supernatural causes.

Near death experiences (NDE): awareness of patients as they are undergoing severe trauma that they have died and then are brought back to life again.

Neosecularization thesis: the renewal of the secularization thesis that limits it to the description of the differentiation of society in which the functions of society like government, education, the courts, medicine, and religion are separated and operate in their own spheres.

Neurotheology: the study of the relationship between neurological science and religious phenomena.

Noetic: according to William James, a characteristic of religious experience that fills the subject with profound and deep insight into realities not accessible to the senses.

Numinous: Rudolf Otto's term for the uncanny and unsettling presence and power of the sacred.

Oedipal complex: the ambivalent feelings of a boy's sexual attraction to his mother and rivalry with his father.

Orientalism: the European approach to the study of the Middle East and Far East that treats it as strange, exotic, and captivating in its difference from the advanced and familiar Western world.

Original sin: the Western doctrine based on the teaching of Augustine that the fall of Adam and Eve into sin corrupted human nature. The guilt as well as consequences of that fall are passed down genetically to each person in the human race.

"Other," the: in the theory of Wellman and Tokuno, the alien group that lies outside the boundaries of an ethnic group or society. The ethnic group or society defines itself in contrast to what is considered foreign.

"Outsider": term for a person who studies a religion from outside its worldview and way of life.

Pacifism: ideology that rejects violent conflict in all circumstances as a matter of religion and/or individual conscience.

Paradigm: a mental framework of rules and procedures about how a subject is to be studied.

Paranormal beliefs: beliefs in realities and phenomena that are not sanctioned by traditional and official doctrines.

Patriarchy: various forms of ordering society in which men have power and control over women and children.

Peak experiences: according to Maslow, the highest sense of human fulfillment that is attained once other needs are met.

Perennial Philosophy, the: a term that Aldous Huxley invented to speak of the "common core" of universal concepts of the connection of the "soul" or "higher consciousness" with a transcendent Reality. It is "perennial" because it arises in vastly different cultural contexts.

Phenomenology: the study of subjects as they appear to be without interpretations or explanations. In religion, the study of religious ways from the viewpoint of those who practice them.

Plasticity of the brain: the research finding that the brain is pliable and moldable even after the assumed period of formation in early childhood.

Pluralist religions: religions that recognize that no religion has a claim on the universal truth.

Postcolonialism: a loose set of ideas and theories associated with the aftermath and response to imperialism in lands once held by dominating colonial powers.

Postmodernism: a hard-to-define movement that is unified by its reaction to the modernist assumptions of the objective certainty of scientific, rational, and universal knowledge.

Predestination: the idea of the Protestant Reformer John Calvin and others that whether human persons are to be saved and attain heaven or damned is already determined by the will and foreknowledge of God.

Presentational language: according to Suzanne Langer, the communication of dynamics of our inner life that are not given in linear, discursive fashion.

Primordial time of origins: the mythic time when the foundations of the realities of our world were laid.

Projection: in psychology, the mental mechanism by which humans attribute their feelings, attitudes, or traits to something or someone else.

Protestant Reformation: the movement begun by Martin Luther in 1517 CE that challenged the authority and practices of the medieval Catholic Church.

Protestantism: a form of Christianity originating from the Reformation of the sixteenth century that mounted a lasting protest against the failings of the Roman Catholic Church; a wide variety of beliefs, practices, and denominations that arose from the Reformation churches.

Psychic unity of the human race: the idea that all humans reason in the same basic ways.

Psychological interpretation of myth: the idea that the only way that modern people can interpret myth is to relate it to the inner working of the psyche (e.g., Carl Jung and Joseph Campbell).

Pure Consciousness: according to the Yoga master Patañjali, the state in which there are no longer any divisions or distinctions in awareness. The mind is completely unified in a state without separate thoughts.

Rational choice theory: a market approach to religion that assumes that individuals evaluate the benefits and costs of religious rewards in predictable and reasonable ways. The constant in the theory is the demand for intangible religious benefits. The variable is the nature and availability of the supply of religious beliefs and practices to meet this demand.

Rationalism: the movement originating in the Enlightenment that identified logical reason as the sole source and means of human knowledge instead of either the senses or divine revelation.

Rationalization: the process of founding society solely on human reason and its knowledge and calculations rather than religious belief, superstition, or tradition.

Religionist (approaches): methods of studying religion that seek to understand it according to the ways that religious adherents interpret and explain it.

Religions of resistance: according to Bruce Lincoln, ideologies of dissident groups that are alienated from the government and society and choose to insulate themselves rather than rebel actively.

Religions of revolution: according to Bruce Lincoln, ideologies of dissident groups that choose to break out of their defensive isolation and engage in armed rebellion against the government and society. This type of religious group is involved in what Mark Juergensmeyer calls "ethnic religious nationalism."

Religions of the status quo: according to Bruce Lincoln, ideologies that uphold the power and privileges of the ruling class.

Religious and the secular: in secularization thesis, two spheres of life that must be kept separate in order to avoid religious conflict and coercion.

Religious experience: the justification of belief by the inner feelings, sensations, and apprehensions of the personal, inner life.

Religious studies: a contemporary academic field of scholarship that examines and interprets religion and religions from a wide range of perspectives.

Religious war: a war fought in the name of religion against an opposing religion or ideology.

Renewalist Christianity: a broad term that refers to a contemporary movement in Christianity that emphasizes the direct activity of the Holy Spirit in believers' lives manifested by speaking in tongues, healing miracles, and revelations.

Resurgence of religion: the idea that religion is regaining its influence in public affairs as well as the private lives of believers, especially in contrast to the predictions of secularism about the inevitable decline of religion in modern society.

Retribution: the payment one deserves; in theories of suffering the idea that suffering is deserved.

Ritual system: according to Evans-Pritchard, the complex of interlocking parts of ritual that form the context for understanding the symbols, myths, and actions of rituals.

Rituals: purposeful, repetitive, stylized, and symbolic actions that deal with matters of the cosmic order and/or supernatural presences.

Roman Catholicism: the beliefs, practices, and organization of the Roman Catholic Church headed by the pope in Rome.

Romantic interpretation of myth: the approach to myth that assumes that myth represents a separate reality apart from the ordinary reality of the senses.

Roshi: a title of a master teacher of Buddhism, especially in Zen, who by training and certification is authorized to pass on the traditions of Buddhism.

Sacramental: the quality of certain religious symbols that refers to their ritual function of becoming what they represent so that they convey that spiritual reality to believers in a tangible way.

Salafism: the Islamic movement that seeks to recover the vitality and purity of Islam over the forces of modernism. It hopes to do so by returning to the way of the forebearers, the Islamic prophet Muhammad and his followers, and the strict literal following of the Qur'an and Sunna (traditions of the example of Muhammad).

Samsara: in Hinduism, Buddhism, and so on, the karma-driven endless cycle of birth, life, death, and rebirth.

Sanatana Dharma: the eternal cosmic and social order revealed to the ancient Hindu sages as told in the Hindu scriptures, the Vedas.

Satori: the experience of enlightenment in Zen Buddhism, a deep and personal realization of the nature of reality in the overcoming of illusion.

Scapegoat mechanism: the process of displacement of hostility of mimetic rivalry from the antagonists to a convenient victim. It unites the warring parties in a common release of hostility that results in the sacrificial death of the scapegoat.

Scientific Rationalism: the confidence in the capacity of the human mind using the scientific method to understand reality.

Sectarian: narrowly restricted within the boundaries of a particular religious view or organization.

Secular: the sphere of public life that was separated from religious influence, especially religious institutions.

Secularism: the commitment to the independence of life in society from religion. Secularists believe that knowledge, values, and morality, as well as government have no need for religion. Religion is an unnecessary and potentially harmful element in public life.

Secularization: the ongoing political, social, and religious process of removing the presence and influence of religion and religious organizations from public life while relegating religion to the private sphere of an individual's life and choice.

Secularization thesis: the theory that the processes of modernism that separate religion from government and other functions of society will inevitably lead to the decline of religious influence over society, groups, and individuals.

Shari'ah: Islamic law revealed in the Qur'an and the traditions of the Islamic prophet Muhammad (hadith and sunna) binding for all Muslims and covering all aspects of the Muslim way of life whether personal or social.

Siddhartha Gautama: the birth name of the Hindu prince who became the Buddha, the "Enlightened One" who founded Buddhism.

Smriti: in Hinduism, the scriptures and traditions that are remembered as opposed to shruti, the scriptures directly revealed from divine origins.

Social facts: for Durkheim, the values, morals, customs, and beliefs that society imposes on its members with such force that they seem to be facts.

Sunna: the traditions of sayings and deeds of the Islamic prophet Muhammad that guide Muslims in interpreting the Qur'an and following the way of Islam.

Symbol: according to C. S. Peirce, a sign that conveys abstract meaning by means of the association or convention of the interpreter (e.g., a swastika).

Telepathy: the ability to transmit messages without use of the senses.

Temporal lobe epilepsy (TLE): a disorder of the brain in which there are seizures in the temporal lobe that play key roles in hearing, memory, speech, and smell. In some patients, this condition is associated with interest, even obsession, with religion.

Theodicy: the puzzle of suffering that arises from the twin beliefs of the almighty power and mercy of God: how a merciful God can allow innocent and disproportional suffering.

Theological study: methods of studying religion according to sets of truth claims held by religious believers.

Theoretical knowledge: according to Cassirer, the knowledge that assumes that symbols represent "something else." To understand the meaning of a symbol is to understand the underlying idea that it represents. (Note: In this sense, the important and constant thing is the meaning. The less important and variable things are the symbols that represent it.)

Thick description of a culture: according to Geertz, observation and record keeping of the details of rituals, customs, and relationships in a culture under study with their inconsistencies and contradictions. In contrast, a "thin description" simply skims off selected evidence.

Totem: for Durkheim, the most revered emblem of a society, a concrete representation of the group's life and solidarity.

Ulama: the body of legal experts in several fields of Muslim knowledge, especially Islamic law (shari'ah).

Ultimate concern: a phrase coined by the theologian Paul Tillich that refers to the most serious matters of human existence. In Tillich's view, religious faith deals with matters of ultimate concern.

Ultimate questions: the most profound questions that arise from the "human condition" that every human person faces. These are universal and fundamental, but religious beliefs answer them in different ways.

Univocal statements: statements that have a single meaning that is expressed on the surface level of the grammar and vocabulary of the statement.

Upanishads: a body of Hindu philosophical texts of teachings that were first learned at the feet of ancient Hindu masters and have their center in the relationship of Brahmin (the Absolute) with Ātman (the Self).

Urbanization: shifts in the human population from the rural areas to cities with the attendant problems such as overcrowding and opportunities such as concentrations of available jobs and workers.

Werkzeug: in the Protestant "Community of True Inspiration," which founded the Amana Colonies in Iowa, a person who is an "instrument" of the present-day revealed messages from the Holy Spirit.

Worldview: a total way of looking at reality and all that is in it given by one's culture.

Zen Buddhism: a Japanese form of Buddhism that focuses on the direct experience over doctrines, scriptures, or creeds.

Key Scholars of Religious Studies

al-Ghazzālī, Abu Hāmed Mohammad ibn Mohammad (1058–1111 CE): Muslim legal scholar, theologian, and mystic. He won fame as a renowned legal scholar as head of the Nizamiyyah College in Baghdad. However, a spiritual crisis led him to abandon his career as a scholar when he realized that the Truth could not be found in philosophical reasoning but in mysticism.

Alston, William (1921–2009): American philosopher at Syracuse University, Rutgers University, and the University of Michigan. He was one of the scholars who revived the philosophy of religion in the late twentieth century.

Anselm of Canterbury (1033–1109 CE): Benedictine monk, philosopher, and Archbishop of Canterbury in England. He is famous for his version of the "ontological argument" for the existence of God. Elaborating the theology of Augustine, he argued that the sacrifice of Jesus Christ on the cross was necessary to satisfy the wrath of God.

Appleby, R. Scott: historian and Regan Director of the Kroc Institute for International Peace Studies, Notre Dame University. With American church historian Martin Marty, he headed an eight-year study of fundamentalist movements throughout the world. This thorough study resulted in six volumes of research and insights into the fundamentalist reaction to modernism. He has also explored religious violence in such books as *The Ambivalence of the Sacred: Religion, Violence and Reconciliation.*

Arminius, Jacobus (1560–1609): Dutch theologian at the University of Leiden. His criticism of the Calvinist doctrine of predestination was the basis of a countermovement, Arminianism. In response to Arminius's teaching that God's grace is sufficient for all, the Calvinist called the Synod of Dort (1618–1619) to clarify the tenets of Calvinism. The followers of Arminius answered the synod that salvation is offered to all people and that grace can be resisted. In summary, the Arminians defended the freedom of the human will.

Augustine of Hippo (354–430 CE): bishop of Hippo in North Africa whose teachings laid the foundation for Western Christian theology. He emphasized the grace of God and the inability of the sinner to merit salvation. Augustine influenced practically all aspects of Christian theology, but his doctrine of original sin, his emphasis on redeeming grace without merit, and his "just war" theory of religiously sanctioned violence are especially significant. Among his many works are his personal story in his *Confessions* and the monumental theology of world history, *City of God.*

Benedict XVI, Pope (Joseph Aloisius Ratzinger): German theologian who is the current pope, who heads the Roman Catholic Church. Before his election as pope in April 2005, he was the head of the Congregation for the Doctrine of the Faith, the agency that safeguards church doctrine and morals. He is a conservative leader and prolific writer who has followed in the footsteps of his predecessor, the popular Pope John Paul II.

Berger, Peter: American sociologist who pioneered the sociology of religion. He is the director of the Institute on Culture, Religion and World Affairs at Boston University and is a frequent commentator on religion in American society. With Thomas Luckman, he wrote *The Social Construction of Reality*, a seminal work proposing that life in human society shapes the perceptions of what is real and true for the members of society.

Calvin, John (1509–1564): French theologian who was the founder of Calvinism, a system of Protestant theology at the root of the "Reformed" Protestant tradition. Prominent features of his theology are the absolute sovereignty of God, the sole authority of scripture, the doctrine of predestination, the "Protestant Work Ethic," and the "presbytery," the council of elders that heads the church. A legal scholar, Calvin applied his theology to the governance of the city of Geneva (now in Switzerland) and the leadership of the Protestant church through councils of elders. His *Institutes of the Christian Religion* (in several editions) became a standard theological work for Protestantism.

Campbell, Joseph (1904–1987): American writer and lecturer known for his popular study of mythology, *The Power of Myth*, a PBS television series broadcast after his death. Campbell promoted the theory that myths are versions of the fundamental human quest of the hero. His psychological approach to mythology and his maxim "Follow your bliss!" have been influential in the "New Age" religious movements.

Capps, Walter H. (1934–1997): American politician and professor of religious studies at the University of California, Santa Barbara. He was instrumental in defining and developing the field of religious studies.

Cassirer, Ernst (1874–1945): German philosopher of culture in Germany, England, Sweden, and the United States. He was a neo-Kantian who taught that humans live in the symbolic world of culture and this is the universe in and through which they experience reality.

Clifford, William K.: English mathematician and philosopher at the University College, London. His mathematical work anticipated the work of Albert Einstein.

Coleridge, Samuel Taylor (1772–1834): English poet, philosopher, and literary critic who was one of the principal founders of the romantic movement in England.

Compte, Auguste (1798–1847): French philosopher of science and who founded the movement of *positivism*. Now outdated, this philosophy held that all knowledge is based on the senses or mathematical reasoning from sense data. Compte advocated secular humanism, which he called the *religion of humanity*, in place of religion.

Dawkins, Richard: British evolutionary biologist at New College, Oxford. He is a champion of militant atheism and author of the best-selling *The God Delusion*. He has been in the forefront of debates about religion and violence, creationism, and the evolutionary origins of religion.

Dennett, Daniel: American philosopher who is the codirector of the Center for Cognitive Studies at Tufts University. He is a popular atheist writer and has written many scholarly articles on the philosophy of mind, artificial intelligence, language, psychology and biology.

Derrida, Jacques (1930–2004): French philosopher born in Algeria who developed a theory of "deconstruction" of literary texts. This method of exposing the hidden contradictions of written texts has been applied in many fields of study, especially communications, politics, and the visual arts. His ideas have been a major influence on *postmodernism*.

Durkheim, Émile (1858–1917): French thinker on modernism who developed ways of using the methods of science in the study of human society. Considered the father of sociology, he developed a theory of religion based on its function in society.

Eliade, Mircea: Romanian historian of religion, philosopher, and fiction writer who finished his career at the University of Chicago Divinity School. He played a major role in the development and promotion of the field of history of religions and the phenomenology of the "Chicago school" of religious studies. The core of his thought was the distinction between the *sacred and the profane* and the *hierophany* or manifestation of the sacred that breaks into the ordinary world.

Feuerbach, Ludwig (1804–1872): German philosopher and champion of materialism and humanism. His theory of the origins of religion in human psychology influenced Karl Marx's views.

Flew, Anthony (1923–2010): British analytic philosopher at Oxford, Aberdeen, Keele, and Reading, and at York University, who promoted atheism. At the end of his career, he repudiated his former ideas and embraced deism.

Fox, Jonathan: political scientist at Bar-Ilan University in Ramat Gan, Israel. He has used datasets such as the Religion and State (RAS) project at the Bar-Ilan University to reach conclusions about religious violence based on empirical evidence.

Frazer, James (1854–1941): Scottish anthropologist who was one of the founders of anthropology. He compiled *The Golden Bough*, an encyclopedic twelve-volume comparative study of the world's mythology, magic, and religion.

Freud, Sigmund (1856–1939): Austrian psychiatrist considered the father of psychoanalysis. Freud was a pioneer in the study of the unconscious and developed such concepts as *repression*, and the threefold structure of the psyche: the *id, ego,* and *superego*. He applied his theory of the *Oedipal conflict* to religion, and he held that science has superseded religion in world history.

Geertz, Clifford (1926–2006): American anthropologist at Princeton University who developed a highly influential theory of symbolic anthropology. He prompted attention to complex details (a "thick description") in ethnographic ("field") cultural studies.

Gilkey, Langdon (1919–2004): Protestant theologian at the University of Chicago Divinity School who explored the relationship of religion and science. He was also known for his personal experience in an internment camp in Japan during World War II, where he had been a missionary, and his studies of Reinhold Niebuhr and Paul Tillich.

Girard, René: French literary critic, historian, and philosopher of culture who distilled a weighty theory of violence from a vast collection of sources in myth, literature, art, cultural history, and religion. His theory is founded on the psychology of envy that produces rivalry and results in the tragic abuse of the scapegoat.

Gopin, Marc: Jewish rabbi who is director of the Center for World Religions, Diplomacy and Conflict Resolution at George Mason University. He has applied his theory of conflict resolution to peacemaking in various settings throughout the world. He advocates the role of "citizen diplomacy" in *To Make the Earth Whole: Citizen Diplomacy in the Age of Religious Militancy.*

Habermas, Jürgen: dominant German contemporary philosopher and sociologist whose ideas of the role of reason in human communication have influenced a wide range of academic disciplines including political theory, language philosophy, aesthetics, and the philosophy of religion.

Hamer, Dean: American geneticists and documentary filmmaker whose books and films popularized genetic research. He has proposed that homosexuality, anxiety, and religion are associated with specific, identifiable genes.

Hạnh, Thích Nhất: Vietnamese Buddhist monk, writer, poet, and social activist. He is a major influence in the development of Western Buddhism and invented the term *engaged Buddhism* to refer to the emerging Buddhist activism in social, political, economic, and environmental affairs.

Hare, R. M. (1919–2002): English philosopher who taught at Oxford and the University of Florida. Hare developed the ethical theory that moral principles must be universal and also obligatory. Though this theory seems to rely on the thought of Immanuel Kant, but Hare added that consequences are an important consideration in morality.

Harris, Sam: philosopher, lecturer, and popular writer who is a militant atheist and outspoken critic of religion. His *The End of Faith* is a best seller, and he has lectured in many universities and appeared on many television interviews.

Harrison, Jane Ellen (1840–1928): British Victorian classical scholar, feminist, and member of the Cambridge Ritualists. She applied archeology and visual art to the study of the Greek classics. Her *Prolegomenon to Study of Greek Religion* introduces the seminal idea that myth and religion must be studied in the context of ritual.

Hick, John (1922–2012): philosopher and theologian at various universities including the University of Birmingham, Claremont Graduate University, Princeton University, and Cambridge University. He is considered one the most prominent philosophers of religion of the twentieth century.

Hood, Ralph W.: psychology professor at the University of Tennessee at Chattanooga who has written numerous articles on religion and spirituality. He was an editor of the *Journal for the Scientific Study of Religion*.

Huntington, Samuel (1927–2008): political scientist at Harvard University who stirred controversy with his theory of a "clash of civilizations" after the Cold War. He announced that the conflict of ideologies had ended but now the predominant world conflict is shifting to hostilities between cultures. He identified seven or eight major cultures and outlined the natural conflicts between cultures in a web of interactions.

Huxley, Aldous (1894–1963): novelist, humanist, and pacifist who explored religion, parapsychology, and mysticism. He is known primarily for his novel, *Brave New World*, and for the Perennial Philosophy.

James, William (1842–1910): American philosopher and psychologist who pioneered the study of religious experience and became the father of the *psychology of religion*. He applied the theory of pragmatism to the theory of teaching, psychology, and religion. His *Varieties of Religious Experience* and *The Will to Believe* are classics in the study of religion.

Jenkins, Philip: humanities and religious studies professor at Pennsylvania State University. He has made scholars and the public aware of profound changes in Christianity including the advances of Christianity in the "Third World" and the change in the geographical center of the Christian population.

John of Damascus (676–749 CE): Syrian monk, theologian, and musician who defended the honor given to icons in the Orthodox Church. He worked in Damascus during the reign of the Muslim Umayyad dynasty. His theology of the icon against the iconoclasts applied the belief in the Incarnation, the divine and human natures of Jesus Christ, to the veneration of icons. He is also known for his hymns.

Johnson, Todd: associate professor of global Christianity and the director of the Center for the Study of Global Christianity at the Gordon-Conwell Theological Seminary. He is the editor of the World Christian Database, a comprehensive collection of demographic statistics on current religions throughout the world. He specializes in the empirical study of global religious trends in Christianity and world religions.

Juergensmeyer, Mark: sociology and religious studies professor at the University of California, Santa Barbara. He is an expert in South Asian religions and has specialized in religious violence and conflict resolution. His *Terror in the Mind of God* explored the role of apocalypticism in the promotion of religious violence and sparked a flood of books that probed the causes of religious violence.

Jung, Carl: Swiss psychiatrist who founded the field of analytic (Jungian) psychology. This branch of psychology aims at personal wholeness through the integration of the opposites of the unconscious, the *anima* (feminine) and *animus* (the masculine). Jung developed lasting terms for the study of the human psyche such as the "collective unconscious," "archetypes," and "personality types." He took a positive approach to religion and treated symbols as the language of the unconscious.

Kant, Immanuel (1724–1804): German philosopher of the Enlightenment who shaped the modern worldview. His philosophy influenced all areas of philosophy including ethics and the philosophy of religion.

Katz, Stephen T.: Jewish philosopher and writer who is the director of the Elie Wiesel Center for Judaic Studies at Boston University. Besides his advocacy of the contextualist approach to mysticism, he specializes in the Holocaust, which he considers a singular event in human history.

Kierkegaard, Søren (1813–1855): Danish philosopher and theologian who championed the freedom and responsibility of the individual against modern mass conformity. He countered the idealism of G. W. F. Hegel, criticized the Danish Lutheran Church, and is considered one of the founders of the philosophy of existentialism.

King, Ursala: professor emerita of theology and religious studies, University of Bristol. She has concentrated on the study of the French priest and paleontologist Pierre Teilhard de Chardin and feminist theology.

Krishnamurti, Jiddu (1895–1986): Indian lecturer and writer who was selected and prepared to be the head of the *Theosophical Society* founded by Helena Blavatsky to establish the "Universal Brotherhood of Humanity." Announcing that organizations were a hindrance to the individual's discovery of the Truth, he disbanded the organization that was to prepare for the coming of a World Teacher. He then spent sixty years traveling the world and promoting a revolution in society through the transformation of each individual's psyche.

Langer, Suzanne (1895–1985): American philosopher, teacher, and writer on the arts and culture who wrote the popular study of symbolism, *Philosophy in a New Key*. She was one of the first women to achieve standing as an American philosopher.

Lewis, Bernard: British-American historian and expert on the Middle East and the relationship between Islam and Western society. He countered Edward Said's criticisms of Orientalism. He is a frequent commentator and advisor on Middle Eastern affairs.

Lincoln, Bruce: historian of religion at the University of Chicago Divinity School. He has specialized in developing critical methods of religious studies and exploring the relationship of religion to politics, power, and violence.

Locke, John (1632–1704): British philosopher of the Enlightenment who is considered the father of classical liberalism. His political philosophy influenced the American Revolution and the ideas of the separation of religion from politics and government.

Luther, Martin (1483–1546): German Catholic monk, priest, and professor whose protests against the medieval Catholic Church incited the Protestant Reformation. Luther was a prolific theologian as well as the founder of the Lutheran Protestant church.

Marx, Karl (1818–1883): German philosopher, economist, and sociologist. One of the most influential thinkers of modern times, he developed the theory of *dialectical materialism*. This theory asserts that society develops through the class struggle between the wealthy class and the working class. This struggle would eventually lead to the revolution of the workers and the formation of a "classless" society in which the workers would share equally in the benefits of their labor. His *Communist Manifesto* and *Capital (Das Kapital)* are two of the most significant books of modern times.

Maslow, Abraham (1908–1970): professor of psychology at Brandeis University who developed the theory of the *hierarchy of needs*. His theory is an example of humanist psychology that emphasizes the positives of human potential rather than mental disease.

Mueller, Friedrich Max (1823–1900): German philologist and scholar of India who was one of the founders of the comparative study of religion. He applied the principles of philology (the study of human languages) to develop a "scientific" study of religion, especially concentrating on the sacred scriptures of Hinduism, the Vedas.

Newberg, Andrew: neuroscientist at the Thomas Jefferson University Hospital and Medical College. He has developed the principles of *neurotheology*, the study of the role of the brain in religious and spiritual experience. His principal method is the use of brain imaging while subjects are praying, meditating, or engaging in other religious states.

Nikhilananda (Dinesh Chandra Das Gupta) (1895–1973): Hindu philosopher, writer, and lecturer. He founded the Ramakrishna-Vivekananda Center of New York. He promoted the Vedanta tradition of realizing the divinity of the Self that the Hindu sage Vivekananda brought to the United States in 1893.

Noll, Mark A.: professor of American history at the University of Notre Dame specializing in the history and condition of evangelicalism in America.

Otto, Rudolf (1869–1937): German scholar, theologian, and historian of religion at the University of Marburg. He based his influential conclusions on mysticism and religion on his travels to India, the Middle East, and North Africa. He applied the philosophy of phenomenology to the study of religion in the trend-setting works of *The Idea of the Holy* and *Mysticism East and West*.

Pascal, Blaise (1623–1666): French mathematician, philosopher, and apologist for Catholicism. A genius, he developed mathematical theory in geometry and probability. After a mystical experience, he abandoned mathematics for philosophy and theology. His *Pensées* is one of the most compelling defenses of Christianity.

Patañjali (c. second century BCE): compiler of the *Yoga Sutras*, the chief text of the practice of yoga. Apart from myth, hardly anything is known about this author. But the *Sutras* provide a philosophical basis for *Raja Yoga*, an inclusive form of yoga that involves body, breath, and mind. The *Sutras* are the practical application of the ancient *Samkhya* philosophy of the dualism of mind and matter.

Peirce, Charles Sanders (1839–1914): American logician (study of logical reasoning), philosopher, scientist, and mathematician. He founded the philosophy of pragmatism and the study of "signs" (semiotics). He proposed that *abduction* is the third category of logic. This form of reasoning selects a likely solution or explanation among alternatives, a "guess" that can be tested. Peirce applied the reasoning of pragmatic philosophy to many areas of life including the communication of ideas and religion.

Persinger, Michael: Canadian neuroscientist at Laurentian University, Sudbury, Ontario. He is the inventor of the "God Helmut," which stimulates the temporal lobe with electromagnetic waves. He claims that this technology induces feelings of an invisible presence in a high percentage of experimental subjects. The results of his experiments have not been replicated.

Prothero, Stephen: American religious studies professor at Boston University who is a frequent commentator on religion in the public media.

Proudfoot, Wayne: philosopher of religion at Boston University. He has interests in the contemporary philosophy of religion, mysticism, and the pragmatism of William James and C. S. Peirce.

Raphael-Levine, Melissa: professor of religious studies at the University of Gloucestershire concentrating on religion, gender, and feminist studies. She is a frequent commentator on the media and is a member of several scholarly associations on feminism and Judaism.

Rumi (Jalāl ad-Dīn Muḥammad Rūmī): Persian poet, theologian, legal scholar, and mystic who founded the Sufi *Mevlevi* order of Sufi Muslim mystics in Konya (now in Turkey). The Mevlevi Sufis are known for their ritual dance, whose distinctive feature is whirling on one foot while meditating. Rumi's poetry of passionate longing for union with God has international standing beyond Muslim circles.

Said, Edward (1935–2003): Palestinian-American critic of literature and culture who was a founder of *postcolonialism*. Said championed the cause of Palestinians, and in his seminal book *Orientalism* exposed the Western bias of Orientalism as a way of studying Eastern religions and cultures.

Schleiermacher, Friedrich (1768–1834): German Protestant theologian at the University of Halle. He is considered the father of Protestant liberalism for his attempts to explain and defend religious faith in terms acceptable to the rationalism of the Enlightenment. He found a defensible position against the Enlightenment skeptics in the subjective experience of the individual.

Smart, Ninian (1927–2001): Scottish writer and educator who developed the first Religious Studies department in the United Kingdom at the University of Lancaster and taught at the University of California at Santa Barbara. He considered religion an important aspect of human life that could be studied in an uncommitted academic setting. He developed methods of religious studies that were not founded on the presuppositions of any religion but used many other academic disciplines.

Smith, Huston: the religious studies professor at MIT, Syracuse University, and the University of California, Berkeley, who developed the foremost model of teaching comparative religion. His *The World's Religions* was the classic comparative religions textbook for many years. He reached an even wider audience with his PBS series with Bill Moyers, *The Wisdom of Faith*, and other media products.

Smith, Jonathan Z.: historian of religion and humanities professor at the University of Chicago who has had a major influence on the field of religious studies. He is well known for his claim that religion has no reality other than as a merely convenient abstract concept for the study of the sacred ways of human societies.

Smith, Wilfred Cantwell (1916–2000): Canadian comparative religion professor who was the director of Harvard's Center for the Study of World Religions. He was one of the first to question the concept *religion* as a term that could describe the varieties of the unique sacred ways of human society.

Stace, Walter Terence (W. T.) (1886–1967): British philosopher at Princeton University. He applied the principles of British empiricism to the study of religion and laid the groundwork for the philosophical study of mysticism.

Stark, Rodney: American sociologist at Baylor University who is the major advocate of the Rational Choice Theory of religion. Built on an economic model, this theory proposes that the demand for religion is constant, but people make rational choices about how to fulfill this need among available choices (*supply side*) of religious groups and beliefs. Therefore, religious pluralism is good for religion because it fosters competition for the devotion of potential clients of religious services.

Suzuki, D. T. (Daisetsu Teitaro) (1870–1966): Buddhist author, translator, lecturer, and professor of Zen Buddhism and Japanese culture.

Tillich, Paul (1886–1965): German-American Protestant theologian at Union Theological Seminary, Harvard Divinity School, and the University of Chicago Divinity School. The combination of his popular writings and systematic theology made him one of the most influential theologians of the twentieth century.

Tindal, Matthew (1657–1733): English deist, freethinker, and philosopher.

Tippet, Krista: broadcaster and writer who hosts the American Public Radio program *On Being* (formerly *Speaking of Faith*).

Tokuno, Kyoko: East Asian scholar at the University of Washington specializing in Buddhism.

Tolle, Eckhart: popular Canadian writer of bestselling books on his own brand of spirituality, a mysticism that renounces the ego and its thoughts and lives fully and completely in the present moment. His teaching contains themes of Zen Buddhism, Taoism, Hinduism, and Christianity.

Tutu, Desmond: the first black South African Bishop of Cape Town, South Africa, who was one of the leaders of the fight against South African apartheid. He won the Nobel Prize for his activism for human rights, peace, and relief from AIDS, tuberculosis, and other illness.

Tylor, Edward Burnett (1832–1917): British anthropologist and the first professor of anthropology at Oxford University. He developed an evolutionary view of religion and was one of the founders of social anthropology.

Wahhab (Muhammad ibn 'Abd al-Wahhab) (1703–1792): Muslim legal scholar whose efforts to purity Islam of its alleged decadence resulted in the movement of Wahhabism. Wahhab rejected the historic Muslim theological traditions and did not recognize any authority but the Qur'an and hadith, the certified traditions of the words and deeds of the Islamic prophet Muhammad. He opposed the Sufi mystics, pictures of living things, veneration of the saints and their graves, and anything that rivaled the worship due to the One and Only God.

Weber, Max (1864–1920): social theorist who was a key influence in the development of the discipline of sociology. He applied the developing theories of social science to a broad range of social concerns including law, politics, economics, and religion. He is well known for his *Protestant Ethic and the Spirit of Capitalism* in which he proposed that the origins of modern capitalism can be found in the Protestant Reformation. This theory was an alternative to the dialectical materialism of Karl Marx.

Wellman, James K.: scholar of American religion at the Jackson School of International Studies, University of Washington.

Wittgenstein, Ludwig (1888–1952): philosopher in Austria and England at the University of Cambridge. Despite the fact that he wrote very little, he was one of the most influential philosophers of the twentieth century. Though it was not published until after his death, his *Philosophical Investigations* on language and philosophy was perhaps the most significant philosophical writing of the twentieth century.

Wuthnow, Robert: sociologist at Princeton University who has explored the impact of social and cultural change on religion and religious groups and how they respond.

Notes

NOTES TO CHAPTER 1

1. Larry Loh, "McDonald's Frantic Backpedaling: The Pig Toy Fiasco," *CNNGo. co*, January 25, 2010, www.cnngo.com/singapore/none/mcdonalds-pig-toy-fiasco -371923#ixzz1Z53bIPC4.

2. Loh, "McDonald's Frantic Backpedaling."

3. Loh, "McDonald's Frantic Backpedaling."

4. American Academy of Religion, "The Religion Major and Liberal Education: A White Paper," *Religious Studies News* (2008), www.teaglefoundation.org/learning/ pdf/2008_aar_whitepaper.pdf.

5. Krista Tippett, *Speaking of Faith: Why Religion Matters and How to Talk about It* (Penguin Books, 2008), 41.

6. Tippett, *Speaking of Faith*, 8–9.

7. Jonathan Sacks, *The Dignity of Difference: How to Avoid the Clash of Civilizations*, revised ed. (New York: Continuum, 2003), 40.

8. Sachs, *Dignity of Difference*, 40.

9. Sachs, *Dignity of Difference*, 42.

10. Sachs, *Dignity of Difference*, 39–43.

11. Luis Lugo and Alan Cooperman, "U.S. Religious Knowledge Survey" (2010), 6, 49, http://pewforum.org/uploadedFiles/Topics/Belief_and_Practices/religious-knowledge -full-report.pdf.

12. Lugo and Cooperman, "U.S. Religious Knowledge Survey," 49.

13. Lugo and Cooperman, "U.S. Religious Knowledge Survey," 50.

14. David Waters, "'God Gap' Impedes U.S. Foreign Policy, Task Force Says," *Washington Post*, February 24, 2010.

15. R. Scott Appleby, Richard Cizik, and Thomas Wright, *Engaging Religous Communities Abroad: Report of the Task Force on Religion and the Making of U.S. Foreign Policy* (Chicago: Chicago Council on Global Affairs, 2010), 79.

16. Diane L. Moore, *Overcoming Religious Illiteracy: A Cultural Studies Approach to the Study of Religion in Secondary Education* (New York: Palgrave Macmillan, 2007), 4.

17. Moore, *Overcoming Religious Illiteracy*, 5.

18. John R. Hinnells, *The Routledge Companion to the Study of Religion*, Routledge Religion Companions (New York: Routledge, 2009), 127.

19. William E. Beal, "Why Study Religion?," *Department of Relgious Studies*, www .case.edu/artsci/rlgn/WhyStudy.html.

20. Hinnells, *The Routledge Companion to the Study of Religion*.

21. R. S. Chopp, "2001 Presidential Address, Beyond the Founding Fratricidal Conflict: A Tale of Three Cities," *Journal of the American Academy of Religion* 70, no. 3 (2002): 465–66.

22. Chopp, "2001 Presidential Address," 462.

23. Chopp, "2001 Presidential Address," 472.

24. Quoted in Lisa Miller, "Religious Studies Revival: In Trying Times, a Once Esoteric Major Has Become Increasingly Vital," *Newsweek*, September 18, 2010.

25. Charles Sanders Peirce, "The Neglected Argument for the Reality of God," in *The Essential Peirce: Selected Philosophical Writings, Volume 2*, ed. Peirce Edition Project (Bloomington: Indiana University Press, 1998), 441.

26. Peirce, *The Essential Peirce*, 441.

27. Peirce, *The Essential Peirce*, 441.

28. Wayne C. Booth, Gregory G. Colomb, and Joseph M. Williams, *The Craft of Research*, 3rd ed. (Chicago: University of Chicago Press, 2008), xi–xii.

29. Peter Lipton, *Inference to the Best Explanation*, 2nd ed. (New York: Routledge, 2004).

30. Walter H. Capps, *Religious Studies: The Making of a Discipline* (Minneapolis, MN: Fortress Press, 2000), xi.

31. Tippett, *Speaking of Faith*, Addendum 7, 232.

32. Lisa Miller, "Religious Studies Revival: In Trying Times, a Once Esoteric Major Has Become Increasingly Vital," *Newsweek*, September 18, 2010.

NOTES TO CHAPTER 2

1. Jennifer Golian, "Expressing Their Faith," *South Florida Sun-Sentinel*, October 29, 2007.

2. Scott Keeter and Gregory Smith, *Muslim Americans: Middle Class and Mostly Mainstream* (Washington, DC: Pew Research Center, 2007).

3. Keeter and Smith, *Muslim Americans*.

4. Elizabeth Roberts, "Undercover as a Muslim Woman: Veiled Misconceptions," *USA Today*, December 29, 2011.

5. Roberts, "Undercover."

6. Greg Mills, "Students Challenged to Wear Muslim Head Scarves on Campus," *CBS Los Angeles* (November 9, 2011), http://losangeles.cbslocal.com/2011/11/09/students-challenged-to-wear-muslim-head-scarves-on-campus.

7. Mills, "Students Challenged."

8. Scott Keeter and Gregory Smith, "Muslim Americans: No Signs of Growth in Alienation or Support for Extremism," Pew Research Center, August 30, 2011.

9. Keeter and Smith, "Muslim Americans: No Signs."

10. Walter H. Capps, *Religious Studies: The Making of a Discipline* (Minneapolis, MN: Fortress Press, 2000).

11. Kathleen M. Moore, "Visible through the Veil: The Regulation of Islam in American Law," *Sociology of Religion* 68, no. 3 (2007).

12. Stephen Prothero, "The Muslim Veil: Europe vs. the USA," *USA Today: Opinion* (August 2, 2010), www.usatoday.com/news/opinion/forum/2010-08-02-column02_ST_N.htm.

13. Moore, "Visible through the Veil."

14. Williams Mullen, "Religious Discrimination Cases Brought by EEOC on the Rise," *Resources* (January 18, 2011), www.williamsmullen.com/religious-discriminationarticle-january2011.

15. Moore, "Visible through the Veil."

16. Prothero, "The Muslim Veil."

17. Abdulaziz Addwesh, "The Hijab of Muslim Women," *Sultan Books.org*, www.sultan.org/books/hijab.pdf.

18. "In Graphic: Muslim Veils," *BBC News*, June 15, 2010, http://news.bbc.co.uk/2/shared/spl/hi/pop_ups/05/europe_muslim_veils/html/1.stm.

19. Camille Rustici, "France Burqa Ban Takes Effect: Two Women Detained," *HuffPost*, April 4, 2011, www.huffingtonpost.com/2011/04/11/france-burqa-ban-takes-ef_n_847366.html.

20. Rustici, "France Burqa Ban Takes Effect."

21. Allen W. Wood, "Alienation," in *Routledge Encyclopedia of Philosophy* (London: Routledge).

22. Michael Haggerson, "Netherlands to Propose Burqa Ban," *Jurist Legal News and Research*, September 16, 2011, http://jurist.org/paperchase/2011/09/netherlands-to-propose-burqa-ban.php.

23. Viviane Teitelbaum, "The European Veil Debate," *Israel Journal of Foreign Affairs* 1 (2011).

24. "Belgium the Second European Union Nation to Implement Discriminatory Laws against Muslims," AhlulBayt News Agency, July 24, 2011, http://abna.ir/data.asp?lang=3&id=255306.

25. Teitelbaum, "The European Veil Debate."

26. Maureen Cosgrove, "Italy Lawmakers Approve Draft Burqa Ban Law," *Jurist Legal News and Research*, August 2, 2011, http://jurist.org/paperchase/2011/08/italy-lawmakers-approve-draft-burqa-ban-law.php.

27. Ann Reley, "Spain Lower House Rejects Proposal to Ban Burqa," *Jurist Legal News and Research*, July 21, 2010, http://jurist.org/paperchase/2010/07/spain-lower-house-rejects-proposal-to-ban-burqa.php.

28. Daniel Richey, "Conservative Austria Party Calls for Vote to Ban Minarets, Face Veils," *Jurist Legal News and Research*, August 25, 2011, http://jurist.org/paperchase/2010/08/conservative-austria-party-calls-for-vote-to-ban-minarets-face-veils.php.

29. Jennifer Joan Lee, "International Education: Expulsions over Veil Intensify French Debate on Secularity," *New York Times*, October 21, 2003.

30. "Muslim Leader Says France Has Right to Prohibit Head Scarves," *New York Times*, December 31, 2003.

31. Emma Jane Kirby, "Sarkozy Stirs French Burka Debate," *BBC News*, June 22, 2009, http://news.bbc.co.uk/2/hi/8113778.stm.

32. Catriona McKinnon, *Toleration: A Critical Introduction* (New York: Routledge, 2006), 115–16.

33. McKinnon, *Toleration: A Critical Introduction*, 115–16.

34. Juliane von Mittelstaedt and Stefan Simon, "Religious Provocation or a Woman's Right? Europe's Fear of the Burqa," *Spiegel Online International*, July 19, 2010, www.spiegel.de/international/europe/0,1518,707251,00.html.

35. Pew Forum on Religion and Public Life, "The Future of the Global Muslim Population: Projections for 2010–2030" (January 27, 2011), www.pewforum.org/future-of-the-global-muslim-population-regional-europe.aspx.

36. Jacob L. Vigdor, *Comparing Immigrant Assimilation in North America and Europe* (New York: Manhatten Institute for Policy Research, 2011).

37. von Mittelstaedt and Simon, "Religious Provocation."

38. von Mittelstaedt and Simon, "Religious Provocation."

39. Lorraine Ali, "Behind the Veil," *New York Times*, June 11, 2010.

40. Mona Siddiqui, "When Reconciliation Fails: Global Politics and the Study of Religion," *Journal of the American Academy of Religion* 73, no. 4 (2005): 1148.

41. Pew Forum on Religion and Public Life, "Teaching about Religion in Public Schools: Where Do We Go from Here?" Pew Forum on Religion and Public Life and the First Amendment Center (May 20–22, 2003), 6, 9, 14.

42. C. S. Peirce, "The Fixation of Belief," in *The Essential Peirce: Selected Philosophical Writings, Volume 1*, ed. Nathan Houser and Christian Kloesel (Bloomington: Indiana University Press, 1992), 114–15.

43. Peirce, "The Fixation," 114.

44. Peirce, "The Fixation," 115.

45. William James, "Talks to Teachers on Psychology and to Students on Some of Life's Ideals," in *Talks* (New York: Henry Holt, 1925), www.gutenberg.org/ebooks/16287, 75.

46. James, "Talks to Teachers on Psychology," 76.

47. Cheryl Benard, *Civil Democratic Islam: Partners, Resources, and Strategies* (Santa Monica, CA: Rand Corporation, 2003), 58.

48. James, "Talks to Teachers on Psychology," 42.

49. Jonathan Z. Smith, *Map Is Not Territory: Studies in the History of Religions* (Chicago: University of Chicago Press, 1978): 182.

50. Talal Asad, "Reading a Modern Classic: W. C. Smith's *The Meaning and End of Religion*," *History of Religions* 40, no. 3 (2001).

51. Tomoko Masuzawa, *The Invention of World Religions; or, How European Universalism Was Preserved in the Language of Pluralism* (Chicago: University of Chicago Press, 2005), 61.

52. Peter Harrison, "'Science' and 'Religion': Constructing the Boundaries," *Journal of Religion* 86, no. 1 (2006).

53. This refers to the Thirty Years War (1618–1648) on the continent of Europe and the religious wars in the British Isles (roughly 1547–1559).

54. John Locke, "A Letter Concerning Toleration," 1689, The Constitution Society, www.constitution.org/jl/tolerati.htm.

55. Or "commonwealth."

56. Asad, "Reading a Modern Classic."

57. Talal Asad, *Genealogies of Religion: Discipline and Reasons of Power in Christianity and Islam* (Baltimore: Johns Hopkins University Press, 1993).

58. Locke, "A Letter."

59. Kevin Schilbrack, "Religion, Models of and Reality: Are We Through with Geertz?" *Journal of the American Academy of Religion* 73 (2005): 436.

60. Masuzawa, *The Invention of World Religions*, 47–49.

61. Smith, *Map Is Not Territory*, 186–87.

62. Asad, *Genealogies of Religion*, 41.

63. Immanuel Kant, *Religion within the Boundaries of Reason Alone* (1793; Cambridge: Cambridge University Press, 1999).

64. Lawrence C. Becker and Charlotte B. Becker, eds., "Religion: Kant," in *Encyclopedia of Ethics: Volume 3, P–W*, 2nd ed. (New York: Routledge, 2001), 1473.

65. Paula Dear, "Women Vow to Protect Muslim Hijab," *BBC News*, July 14, 2004.

66. Smith, *Map Is Not Territory*, 184.

67. Robert Alan Segal, ed., *The Blackwell Companion to the Study of Religion*, revised ed. (Malden, MA: Blackwell, 2006), xiv.

68. Segal, *The Blackwell Companion to the Study of Religion*, xiv.

69. Segal, *The Blackwell Companion to the Study of Religion*, xiv.

70. Segal, *The Blackwell Companion to the Study of Religion*, xv.

71. Segal, *The Blackwell Companion to the Study of Religion*, xiv–xv.

72. Stephan Arvidsson, "Aryan Mythology as Science and Ideology," *Journal of the American Academy of Religion* 67, no. 2 (1999): 333.

73. Note that the noun *luna* is not capitalized. But it becomes Luna and is capitalized because it is a proper noun.

74. F. Max Mueller, "Clips From a German Workshop," in *Book Rags Biography on Muller F. Max* (2006).

75. Edward B. Tylor, *Primitive Culture: Researches into the Development of Mythology, Philosophy, Religion, Art, and Custom*, 2 vols. (1871, rprt Nabu Press, 2010), 1:429.

76. James Frazer, "Magic and Religion," in *The Golden Bough: A Study of Magic and Religion* (New York: Macmillian, 1922), 3.

77. Tylor, *Primitive Culture*.

78. For example, in Victorian England of the nineteenth century, the king was ill. People believed that the illness would be fatal because the oldest lion kept by the king in the Tower of London had recently died. (Tylor, *Primitive Culture*.)

79. John Fiske, *Myths and Myth Makers: Old Tales and Superstitions Interpreted* (Boston: James R. Osgood, 1873).

80. Émile Durkheim, Excerpt from *The Rules of the Sociological Method*, ed. Steven Lukes, trans. W. D. Halls (New York: Free Press, 1982), http://media.pfeiffer.edu/lridener/DSS/Durkheim/SOCFACT.HTML, 50–59.

81. Émile Durkheim, *The Elementary Forms of Religious Life*, trans. Karen E. Fields (New York: Free Press, 1995), 111–12.

82. Durkheim, *Elementary Forms*, 112.

83. Durkheim, *Elementary Forms*, 208.

84. Durkheim, *Elementary Forms*, 208.

85. Durkheim, *Elementary Forms*, 236.

86. Durkheim, *Elementary Forms*, 44.

87. They called it "Civil Religion."

88. Kenneth Thompson, *Readings from Emile Durkheim* (New York: Routledge, 2004), 92.

89. Ludwig Feuerbach, "Preface to the Second Edition," in *The Essence of Christianity* (London: Trübner & Co., 1881).

90. Feuerbach, "Preface to the Second Edition."

91. Ludwig Feuerbach and Alexander Loos, *The Essence of Religion* (Amherst, NY: Prometheus Books, 2004), 119.

92. Ludwig Feuerbach, *The Essence of Christianity*, The Library of Religion and Culture (New York: Harper, 1957), chap. 27.

93. D. Z. Phillips, *Religion and the Hermeneutics of Contemplation* (Cambridge: Cambridge University Press, 2001), 103.

94. Wood, "Alienation."

95. Karl Marx, "Theses on Feuerbach," (1976), www.marx2mao.com/M&E/TF45.html.

96. Marx, "Theses on Feuerbach."

97. Karl Marx, "A Contribution to the Critique of Hegel's Philosophy of Right: Introduction," (2005), www.marxists.org/archive/marx/works/1843/critique-hpr/intro.htm.

98. This idea seems to echo the influential but now discredited theory of Ernst Haeckel (1834–1919) that "ontogeny recapitulates phylogeny." This was the idea that the development of the embryo in the womb rehearses the development of the biological species in evolution.

99. Celia Brickman, "Primitivity, Race, and Religion in Psychoanalysis," *Journal of Religion* 82, no. 1 (2002): 53–74.

100. Sigmund Freud, *Totem and Taboo: Resemblances between the Psychic Lives of Savages and Neurotics*, trans. A. A. Brill (New York: Moffat Yard, 1918), 242–55.

101. Phillips, *Religion and the Hermeneutics of Contemplation*, 220.

102. Freud, *Totem and Taboo*, 250.

103. Freud, *Totem and Taboo*, 149.

104. Sigmund Freud, *The Future of an Illusion*, ed. James Strachey (New York: Norton, 1989), 39.

105. Freud, *The Future of an Illusion*, 63.

106. Freud, *Totem and Taboo*, 192.

107. Joas Adiprasetya, "The 1893 World Parliament of Religions," in *The Boston Collaborative Encyclopedia of Modern Western Theology* (2004), http://people.bu.edu/wwildman/bce/worldparliamentofreligions1893.htm.

108. Adiprasetya, "The 1893 World Parliament of Religions."

109. Judith Snodgrass, *Presenting Buddhism to the West: Orientalism, Occidentalism, and the Columbian Exposition* (Chapel Hill: University of North Carolina Press, 2003).

110. Martin Kramer, "Said's Splash," in *Ivory Towers on Sand: The Failure of Middle Eastern Studies in America* (Washington, DC: Washington Institute for Near East Policy, 2001).

111. Kramer, "Said's Splash," 31.

112. Kramer, "Said's Splash," 39–40.

113. Sian Hawthorne, "Feminism: Feminism, Gender Studies, and Religion," in *Encyclopedia of Religion* (Detroit: Macmillan Reference USA, 2005), 5:3203.

114. Ursala King, "Essay: Is There a Future for Religious Studies as We Know It? Some Postmodern, Feminist, and Spiritual Challenges," *Journal of the American Academy of Religion* 70, no. 2 (2002): 372.

115. King, "Essay," 373.

116. Hawthorne, "Feminism," 3024.

117. Rosalind Shaw, "Feminist Anthropology and the Gendering of Religious Studies," in *Religion and Gender*, ed. Ursala King (Oxford: Blackwell Publishers, 2000), 67.

118. King, "Essay," 373.

119. King, "Essay," 373.

120. Stephen K. White, "Postmodernism and Political Philosophy," in *Routledge Encyclopedia of Philosophy*, ed. E. Craig (London: Routledge, 1998).

121. King, "Essay," 382–85.

122. Hawthorne, "Feminism," 3023.

123. Jonathan Z. Smith, *Relating Religion: Essays in the Study of Religion* (Chicago: University of Chicago Press 2004), 194.

124. Smith, *Relating Religion*, 194.

125. Robert A. Segal, "Classification and Comparison in the Study of Religion: The Work of Jonathan Z. Smith," *Journal of the American Academy of Religion* 73, no. 4 (2005): 1178–79.

126. Pew Forum on Religion and Public Life, "Secular Europe and Religious America: Implications for Transatlantic Relations" (April 21, 2005), www.pewforum.org/Politics-and-Elections/Secular-Europe-and-Religious-America-Implications-for-Transatlantic-Relations.aspx.

127. Pew Forum on Religion and Public Life, "Secular Europe and Religious America."

128. Nikki R. Keddie, "Secularism and Its Discontents," *Daedalus* 132, no. 3 (2003): 29.

129. Keddie, "Secularism," 29.

130. Gabriel Abraham Almond, R. Scott Appleby, and Emmanuel Sivan, *Strong Religion: The Rise of Fundamentalisms around the World* (Chicago: University of Chicago, 2003), 1.

131. Almond, *Strong Religion*, 10–11.

132. Dan Lusthaus, "Buddhism, Yogacara School Of," in *Routledge Encyclopedia of Philosophy* (London: Routledge, 1998).

133. Brad Stetson, *Pluralism and Particularity in Religious Belief* (Westport, CT: Praeger Publishers, 1994), 31.

134. N. Ross Reat, "Insiders and Outsiders in the Study of Religious Traditions," *Journal of the American Academy of Religion* 51, no. 3 (1983): 460.

135. Lucy Bregman, "The Interpreter/Experiencer Split: Three Models in the Psychology of Religion," *Journal of the American Academy of Religion* 46, no. 2 (1978): 129–30.

136. Almond, *Rudolf Otto*, 23–24.

137. Almond, *Rudolf Otto*, 17–18.

138. Almond, *Rudolf Otto*, 5.

139. Rudolf Otto, *The Idea of the Holy: An Inquiry into the Non-Rational Factor in the Idea of the Divine and Its Relation to the Rational*, trans. John W. Harvey (London: Oxford University Press, 1958), 8.

140. Bregman, "The Interpreter/Experiencer Split," 131.

141. Otto, *The Idea of the Holy*, 4.

142. *Merriam-Webster Online Dictionary*.

143. Tim Dirks, "Filmsite Movie Review: *Raiders of the Lost Ark*," www.filmsite.org/raid.html.

144. Brad Herling, "Why Study Religion?" *American Academy of Religion: Teaching and Learning Center*, www.aarweb.org.

145. Betsy Hammon, "Oregon Teachers May Get OK to Wear Religious Clothing in Class," *OregonLive.Com*, November 23, 2009, www.oregonlive.com/education/index.ssf/2009/11/oregon_teachers_may_get_ok_to.html.

146. Mona Elgindy, "The End of an Era to Keep Religious Identity Out of Public Schools" (2009), www.luc.edu/law/academics/special/center/child/childed_forum/pdfs/elgindy_end_era.pdf.

147. Elgindy, "The End of an Era."

148. "Coalition Seeks Repeal of Klan-Era Ban on Religious Garb in Oregon Schools," *Catholic News Agency* (2010), www.catholicnewsagency.com/news/coalition_seeks_repeal_of_klan-era_ban_on_religious_garb_in_oregon_schools.

149. Asma T. Uddin, "ACLU, KKK and the Culture of Fear," *On Faith* (February 12, 2010), http://newsweek.washingtonpost.com/onfaith/panelists/asma_uddin/2010/02/aclu_kkk_and_the_culture_of_fear.html.

150. Betsy Hammon, "Governor Signs Repeal on Teachers' Religious Dress; Ban Will Lift in July 2011," *OregonLive.Com*, April 1, 2010, www.oregonlive.com/education/index.ssf/2010/04/governor_signs_repeal_on_teach.html.

151. Brad Avakian and Susan Castillo, "Model Policy Regarding Religious Clothing of Public School Employees," ed. Oregon Department of Education and Bureau of Labor and Industries (2010), www.ode.state.or.us/news/announcements/announcement.aspx?=6961.

152. Avakian and Castillo, "Model Policy Regarding Religious Clothing."

153. David Campbell, "American Grace: How Religion Divides and Unites Us: A Conversation with David Campbell," *Press Luncheon with David Campbell and John Green* (2010), www.pewforum.org/American-Grace--How-Religion-Divides-and-Unites-Us.aspx#1.

154. Smith, *Map Is Not Territory*, 174.

155. Smith, *Map Is Not Territory*, 174.

156. Reat, "Insiders," 467.

157. Reat, "Insiders," 464.

158. Otto, *The Idea of the Holy*, 45.

159. Otto, *The Idea* of the Holy, 31–32.

160. Otto, *The Idea of the Holy*, 31–32.

161. Otto, *The Idea of the Holy*, 133.

162. Gregory D. Alles, "Toward a Genealogy of the Holy: Rudolf Otto and the Apologetics of Religion," *Journal of the American Academy of Religion* 69, no 2 (2001): 323.

163. Russell T. McCutcheon, "A Default of Critical Intelligence? The Scholar of Religion as Public Intellectual," *Journal of the American Academy of Religion* 65, no. 2 (1997).

164. Beth Potier, "Gomes Looks Back, Ahead at Convocation," *Harvard Gazette Archives: Harvard University Gazette*, September 23, 2004.

165. James, "Talks to Teachers."

NOTES TO CHAPTER 3

1. Van Harvey, "The Ethics of Belief and Two Conceptions of Christian Faith," *International Journal for Philosophy of Religion* 63, no. 1–3 (2008): 44.

2. "What Scientists Believe but Can't Prove . . ." *TimesOnline* (2005), www.times online.co.uk/tol/life_and_style/health/features/article782065.ece.

3. William K. Clifford, "The Ethics of Belief (1887)," *The Secular Web*, www.infidels .org/library/historical/w_k_clifford/ethics_of_belief.html.

4. Clifford, "The Ethics of Belief."

5. Clifford, "The Ethics of Belief."

6. Geddes MacGregor, "Doubt and Belief," in *Encyclopedia of Religion*, ed. Lindsay Jones (Detroit: Macmillan Reference USA, 2005), 4:2427.

7. Jeff Jones and Lydia Saad, "Gallup Poll Social Series: Values and Beliefs," *Gallup News Service* (2011), www.gallup.com/poll/File/147890/Belief_in_God_110603percent20.pd.

8. Frank Newport, "More Than 9 in 10 Americans Continue to Believe in God: Professed Belief Is Lower among Younger Americans, Easterners, and Liberals," *Gallup News Service* (2011).

9. Gallup Organization, "Gallup Poll Topics and Trends: Religions," in *Gallup Brain* (2007).

10. Frank Newport, "Americans More Likely to Believe in God Than the Devil, Heaven More Than Hell: Belief in the Devil Has Increased since 2000," *Gallup News Service* (June 13, 2007), www.gallup.com/poll/27877/Americans-More-Likely-Believe-God-Than-Devil -Heaven-More-Than-Hell.aspx.

11. Heather Mason Kiefer, "Divine Subjects: Canadians Believe, Britons Skeptical," *Gallup Brain* (2004). American statistics added to Canadian and British.

12. Pew Forum on Religion and Public Life, "Faith in Flux: Changes in Religious Affiliation in the U.S.," *The Pew Forum Publications* (April 27, 2009), http://pewforum.org/ docs/?DocID=409.

13. Pew Forum on Religion and Public Life, "Faith in Flux."

14. Stanley Presser and Mark Chaves, "Is Religious Service Attendance Declining?" *Journal for the Scientific Study of Religion* 46, no. 3 (2007).

15. Pew Forum on Religion and Public Life, "Many Americans Mix Multiple Faiths: Eastern, New Age Beliefs Widespread," *The Pew Forum: Beliefs and Practices* (December 9, 2009), www.pewforum.org/Other-Beliefs-and-Practices/Many-Americans-Mix-Multiple -Faiths.aspx.

16. Pew Forum on Religion and Public Life, "Faith in Flux."

17. Lilly Fowler, "'Unaffiliated' Show Biggest Change among U.S. Faith Groups," *The Pew Forum: Religion News* (2008), http://pewforum.org/news/display.php?NewsID=15039.

18. David Voas and Alasdair Crockett, "Religion in Britain: Neither Believing nor Belonging," *Sociology* 39, no. 1 (2005).

19. Frank Newport, "Near-Record High See Religion Losing Influence in America," *Gallup* (December 29, 2010), www.gallup.com/poll/145409/Near-Record-High-Religion -Losing-Influence-America.aspx.

20. Dan Cox, Scott Clement, Gregory Smith, Allison Pond, and Neha Sahgal, "Non-Believers, Seculars, the Un-Churched and the Unaffiliated: Who Are Nonreligious Americans and How Do We Measure Them in Survey Research?" (presented at American Association for Public Opinion Research, Hollywood, FL, May 14–17, 2009).

21. Pew Forum on Religion and Public Life, "U.S. Religious Landscape Survey," *The Pew Forum on Religion and Pulic Life* (June 23, 2008), http://religions.pewforum.org/pdf/report2-religious-landscape-study-full.pdf.

22. Pew Forum on Religion and Public Life, "U.S. Relgious Landscape Survey," 36.

23. Pew Forum on Religion and Public Life, "U.S. Relgious Landscape Survey."

24. David W. Moore, "Three in Four Americans Believe in Paranormal: Little Change from Similar Results in 2001," *Gallup* (June 6, 2009), www.gallup.com/poll/117382/Church-Going-Among-Catholics-Slides-Tie-Protestants.aspx.

25. Frank Newport and Maura Strausberg, "Americans' Belief in Psychic and Paranormal Phenomena Is Up over Last Decade," *Gallup* (June 8, 2001), www.gallup.com/poll/117382/Church-Going-Among-Catholics-Slides-Tie-Protestants.aspx.

26. Moore, "Three in Four Americans Believe."

27. Robert C. Fuller, *Spiritual but Not Religious: Understanding Unchurched America* (New York: Oxford University Press, 2001).

28. Abu Hāmed Mohammad ibn Mohammad al-Ghazālī, *The Incoherence of the Philosophers* (Salt Lake City, UT: Brigham Young University, 2002), 3–5, 151–52, 163.

29. Alvin Plantinga, "Reason and Belief in God," in *Faith and Rationality: Reason and Belief in God*, ed. Alvin Plantinga and Nicholas Wolterstorff (Notre Dame, IN: University of Notre Dame Press, 1984), 87.

30. Richard Amesbury, "Fideism," in *Stanford Encyclopedia of Philosphy*, ed. Edward N. Zalta (Fall 2009 edition), http://plato.stanford.edu/archives/fall2009/entries/fideism.

31. Johannes Deninger, "Revelation," in *Encyclopedia of Religion*, ed. Lindsay Jones (Detroit: Macmillan Reference USA, 2005), 11:7773.

32. Jerald D. Gort, ed., *On Sharing Religious Experience: Possibilities of Interfaith Mutuality*, vol. 4, *Currents of Encounter* (Grand Rapids, MI: Eerdmans, 1992), 229.

33. Gort, *On Sharing*, 229.

34. Maulana Muhammad Ali, *A Manual of Hadith* (New York: Taylor & Francis, 1995), 403.

35. Ali, *A Manual*, 12.

36. Bertha Maude Horack Shambaugh, *Amana: The Community of True Inspiration*, Atla Monograph Preservation Program (Des Moines: State Historical Society of Iowa, 1908), 239.

37. Daisetz Teitaro Suzuki, *Essays in Zen Buddhism* (New York: Grove Press, 1961), 229.

38. Suzuki, *Essays*, 230.

39. Suzuki, *Essays*, 250.

40. Victor Gunasekara, "Buddhism and Revelation: Refutation of a Theory," *Vinamasa* 25 (Summer 1988), www.vgweb.org/bsq/revelation.htm.

41. Suzuki, *Essays*, 230.

42. Suzuki, *Essays*, 246.

43. Suzuki, *Essays*, 246.

44. This writer chooses not to name the founders.

45. Irving Hexham and Karla Poewe, "U.F.O. Religion: Making Sense of the Heaven's Gate Suicides," *Christian Century*, May 7, 1997, 440.

46. Catherine Cornille, "Gurū," in *Encyclopedia of Religion*, ed. Lindsay Jones (Detroit: Macmillan Reference USA, 2005), 6:3713.

47. Cornille, "Gurū," 6:3713.

48. Cornille, "Gurū," 6:3714.

49. Theodore M. Ludwig, "Ordination," in *Encyclopedia of Religion*, ed. Lindsay Jones (Detroit: Macmillan Reference USA, 2005), 10:6858.

50. Cornille, "Gurū," 6:3713.

51. William M. Bodiford, "Dharma Transmission in Soto Zen: Manzan Dohaku's Reform Movement," *Monumenta Nipponica* 46, no. 4 (1991): 423.

52. Bodiford, "Dharma Transmission," 423.

53. John Hick, *An Interpretation of Religion: Human Responses to the Transcendent* 2nd ed. (New Haven, CT: Yale University Press, 2005), 213.

54. Hick, *An Interpretation*, 218.

55. Hick, *An Interpretation*, 218–19.

56. Hick, *An Interpretation*, 219.

57. Hick, *An Interpretation*, 216.

58. Hick, *An Interpretation*, 221.

59. Hick, *An Interpretation*, 223–24.

60. Marty Laubach, "The Social Effects of Psychism: Spiritual Experience and the Construction of Privatized Religion," *Sociology of Religion* 65, no. 3 (2004): 252.

61. Laubach, "Social Effects," 252.

62. Alvin I. Goldman, "Religious Belief, Epistemology Of," in *A Companion to Epistemology*, ed. Jonathan Dancy and Ernest Sosa (Cambridge, MA: Blackwell, 2000), 438.

63. This idea is a form of *foundationalism*, the view that beliefs must be founded on what is certain.

64. Thus, evidentialism leans toward empiricism.

65. Peter Forrest, "The Epistemology of Religion," in *Stanford Encyclopedia of Philosophy*, ed. Edward N. Zalta (Fall 2009 edition), http://plato.stanford.edu/archives/fall2009/entries/religion-epistemology.

66. Anthony Flew, R. M. Hare, and Basil Mitchell, *Philosophy of Religion: An Anthology*, ed. Charles Taliaferro and Paul J. Griffiths (Malden, MA: Wiley-Blackwell, 2003), 105.

67. Graham MacDonald, "Ayer, Alfred Jules: Verificationism," in *Routledge Encyclopedia of Philosophy*, ed. E. Craig (London: Routledge, 1998).

68. William Schweiker, "The Varieties and Revisions of Atheism," *Zygon: Journal of Religion & Science* 40, no. 2 (2005): 270.

69. Flew, Hare, and Mitchell, *Philosophy of Religion*, 106.

70. Flew recently changed his mind about religious belief and now considers himself a deist. William Schweiker (University of Chicago) notes that evidently the conclusion that God must exist as the divine designer of such a complicated phenomenon as DNA passes the falsification test.

71. William P. Alston, *Perceiving God: The Epistemology of Religious Experience*, Questia ed. (Ithaca, NY: Cornell University Press, 1993), 103–8.

72. Alston, *Perceiving*, 269.

73. Alston, *Perceiving*, 149.

74. Alston, *Perceiving*, 74–151.

75. Goldman, "Religious Belief," 439.

76. Forrest, "Epistemology."

77. Quoted in Donald S. Kleinefelter, "D. Z. Phillips as Philosopher of Religion," *Journal of the American Academy of Religion* 42, no. 2 (1974): 322.

78. C. Stephen Evans, *Faith Beyond Reason* (Edinburgh, UK: Edinburgh University Press, 1998), 91.

79. Joe Manzari, "Faith and Rationality: A Defense of Plantinga's Reformed Epistemology," www.joemanzari.com/papers/far.pdf, 4.

80. Tom W. Rice, "Believe It or Not: Religious and Other Paranormal Beliefs in the United States," *Journal for the Scientific Study of Religion* 42, no. 1 (2003): 105.

81. Paul Tillich, *Dynamics of Faith* (New York: HarperOne, 2001), 1.

82. Paul Tillich, *Systematic Theology: Volume 3* (Chicago: University of Chicago Press, 1963), 130.

83. Tillich, *Systematic Theology, Vol. 3*, 130.

84. Tillich, *Dynamics*, 20.

85. Paul Tillich, *Systematic Theology: Volume 1* (Chicago: University of Chicago Press, 1963), 61–62; Goldman, "Religious Belief."

86. John Derbyshire, "The Brat Pack of Quantum Mechanics," *New Atlantis: Journal of Theology and Society* (Summer 2008): 96.

87. Armand Nicholai, *The Question of God: C. S. Lewis and Sigmund Freud Debate God, Love, Sex, and the Meaning of Life* (New York: Free Press, 2003), 7.

88. Langdon Gilkey, *Naming the Whirlwind: The Renewal of God-Language* (Indianapolis: Bobbs-Merrill, 1969), 442.

89. Gilkey, *Naming*, 442.

90. William James, *The Varieties of Religious Experience*, ed. Electronic Text Center, University of Virginia (New York: Modern Library, 1902), 499.

91. Note that the origins of Arminianism and the Calvinist response in the Synod of Dort (1619) took place after the Council of Trent (1545–1563).

92. John Meyendorff, *Byzantine Theology: Historical Trends and Doctrinal Themes* (New York: Fordham University Press, 1974), 145.

93. Meyendorff, *Byzantine Theology*, 145.

94. The Recluse Theophan, "An Explanation of Certain Texts of Holy Scripture: Romans 9:11–16, 18," *Gnisios: True Orthodox Christian Resources*, http://gnisios.narod.ru/start.html.

95. Bhikkhu Bodhi, "The Way to End Suffering," *The Noble Eightfold Path* (1984), www.vipassana.com/resources/8fp1.php.

96. Bodhi, "The Way to End Suffering."

97. Bodhi, "The Way to End Suffering."

98. Michael Bersani, "Central New York Personal Injury Lawyer Explains Difference between 'Pain' and 'Suffering,'" *Central New York Injury Blog* (2010), www.centralnewyorkinjurylawyer.com/2010/03/central-new-york-personal-inju-1.html.

99. Jack Bemporad, "Suffering," in *Encyclopedia of Relgion*, ed. Lindsay Jones (Detroit: Macmillan Reference USA, 2005), 13:8804.

100. Rice, "Believe It or Not," 95.

101. F. Carson Mencken, Christopher D. Bader, and Kim Ye Jung, "Round Trip to Hell in a Flying Saucer: The Relationship between Conventional Christian and Paranormal Beliefs in the United States," *Sociology of Religion* 70, no. 1 (2009): 67–68.

102. Mencken, Bader, and Ye Jung, "Round Trip," 68.

103. Alvin Plantinga, "Religion and Epistemology," in *Encyclopedia of Philosophy*, ed. E. Craig (London: Routledge, 1998).

104. Cyril Barrett, ed., *Ludwig Wittgenstein: Lectures and Conversations on Aesthetics, Psychology, and Religious Belief* (Berkeley: Univesity of California Press, 1991), 58.

105. Donal Hudson, *Ludwig Wittgenstein: The Bearing of His Philosophy on Religious Belief* (Richmond, VA: John Knox Press, 1968).

106. Barrett, *Ludwig Wittgenstein: Lectures*, 53, 54.

107. Barrett, *Ludwig Wittgenstein: Lectures*, 54, 55.

108. Barrett, *Ludwig Wittgenstein: Lectures*, 55.

109. John Whittaker, "D. Z. Phillips and Reasonable Belief," *International Journal for Philosophy of Religion* 63, nos. 1–3 (2008): 119.

110. Flew, Hare, and Mitchell, *Philosophy*, 107.

111. Whittaker, "D. Z. Phillips," 119.

112. Linda Lyons, "Paranormal Events Come (Super)Naturally to Some" (2005), www
.gallup.com/poll/19558/Paranormal-Beliefs-Come-SuperNaturally-Some.aspx.

NOTES TO CHAPTER 4

1. Kate Fitz Gibbon, *Who Owns the Past? Cultural Policy, Cultural Property, and the Law* (New Brunswick, NJ: Rutgers University Press, 2005).

2. Jim PathFinder Ewing, "Native American Spirituality" (2006), www.blueskywaters
.com/page_82.pdf.

3. Mac Swackhammer, "A Project to Examine and Compare Experiences with, and Attitudes toward, Repatriation of First Nations Material and Documentary Heritage, in Some Canadian and United States Museums, with the Intent to Develop Models for Repatriation Negotiations and Activities," Smithsonian Institutions, Fellowship Report, 1997.

4. Bambi Kraus, Peter Pino, and Gary Roybal, Panel Discussion: NAGPRA's Newest Rule—43 CFR 10.11 (presented at School for Advanced Research, Santa Fe, New Mexico, February 24, 2011), http://sarweb.org/?iarc_lecture_peter_pino_gary_roybal-p:past_events.

5. NAGPRA Review Committee, *National NAGPRA Program Fy2011 Midyear Report* (Syracuse, NY: U.S. Department of the Interior: National Park Service, 2011), 4.

6. Since 2005, NAGPRA has published a database of items subject to return to native groups. This database includes the remains of 125,671 individuals and 939,385 funerary objects.

7. NAGPRA Review Committee, *National NAGPRA Program Fy2011 Midyear Report*, 3.

8. Robert Gutsche Jr., "Museum Collections Shrink as Tribes Reclaim Artifacts: Problem of Caring for the Items Persists," *Washington Post*, March 9, 2006.

9. Samuel J. Redman, "American Museums in Crisis: A New Thing?" *History News Network* (April 8, 2007), http://hnn.us/articles/37302.html.

10. Samuel J. Redman, "Is NAGPRA Emptying Museums? Native American Tribes Reclaim Museum Collections," *Suite 101* (2006), http://museumhistorystudies.suite101
.com/article.cfm/isnagpraemptyingmuseums.

11. Crispin Paine, "Museums and Religion," in *Encyclopedia of Religion*, ed. Lindsay Jones (Detroit: Macmillan Reference USA, 2005), 9:6243–48.

12. Bridgette Derlon and Marie Mauzé, "'Sacred' or 'Sensitive' Objects," *European Cultural Heritage Online*, www.necep.net/papers/OS_Derlon-Mauze.pdf.

13. Gillian A. Flynn, "Merging Traditional Indigenous Curation Methods with Modern Museum Standards of Care," in *Marie Malaro Award Competition: Museum Studies Program* (Washington, DC: National Museum of Natural History, Department of Anthropology, George Washington University, 2001), 3.

14. Smithsonian Institution, "Traditional Care of Culturally Sensitive Collections: Creating a Box for a Cheyenne Buffalo Skull," Smithsonian National Museum of Natural History, http://anthropology.si.edu/repatriation/projects/buffaloskull.htm.

15. Flynn, "Merging Traditional Indigenous Curation Methods," 5–11.

16. Flynn, "Merging Traditional Indigenous Curation Methods," 8.

17. W. Ford Bell, Comments on the 1024-Ad68 Ruling, www.aam-us.org/getinvolved/
advocate/issues/upload/01_14_2008_AAM_Letter_re_NAGPRA_CUHR-2.pdf.

18. Bruce D. Smith et al., "Letter Re: NAGPRA Disposition of Culturally Unidentifiable Human Remains—Final Rule," www.friendsofpast.org/nagpra/2010NAGPRA/
Smith517.pdf.

19. Robert L. Kelly, "Bones of Contention," *New York Times*, December 12, 2010.

20. Peggy O'Dell, "Statement of Peggy O'Dell, Deputy Director, National Park Service Before the Senate Committee on Indian Affairs Native American Graves Protection and Repatriation Act," www.nps.gov/legal/testimony/112th/NAGPRA-6-16-11.pdf.

21. James Pepper Henry, "Twenty Years and Counting: James Pepper Henry's Multifaceted View of NAGPRA," *Museum* (November–December 2010).

22. GAO, *Summary—Native American Graves Protection and Repatriation Act: After Almost 20 Years, Key Federal Agencies Still Have Not Fully Complied with the Act* (Washington, DC: U.S. Government Accounting Office, 2010).

23. O'Dell, "Statement."

24. G. A. Clark, "NAGPRA, the Conflict between Science and Religion, and the Political Consequences," *SAA Bulletin* 165, 5 (1998), www.saa.org/Portals/0/SAA/publications/SAAbulletin/16-5/index.html.

25. Josie Appleton, "Battle of the Bones: Western Intellectuals, Not Native Peoples, Are Behind Moves to Repatriate Human Remains," *Spiked* (December 12, 2002), www.spiked-online.com/Articles/00000006DB8A.htm.

26. Tiffany Jenkins, "The Censoring of Our Museums," *New Statesman*, July 11, 2005.

27. George Johnson, "Indian Tribes' Creationists Thwart Archeologists," *New York Times*, October 22, 1996.

28. Lynn and Keith Kintigh Goldstein, "Ethics and the Reburial Controversy," in *Repatriation Reader: Who Owns American Indian Remains?* ed. Devon A. Mihesuah (Lincoln: University of Nebraska Press, 2000), 182.

29. Johnson, "Indian Tribes' Creationists," 360–61.

30. James Riding, "Repatriation: A Pawnee's Perspective," in *Repatriation Reader: Who Owns American Indian Remains?* ed. Devon A. Mihesuah (Lincoln: University of Nebraska Press, 2000), 113.

31. Suzanne J. Crawford, "(Re) Constructing Bodies: Semiotic Sovereignty and the Debate over Kennewick Man," in *Repatriation Reader: Who Owns American Indian Remains?* ed. Devon A. Mihesuah (Lincoln: University of Nebraska Press, 2000), 214.

32. Crawford, "(Re) Constructing Bodies," 214.

33. Jenkins, "The Censoring of Our Museums."

34. Ralph W. Hood Jr. et al., "Dimensions of the Mysticism Scale: Confirming the Three-Factor Structure in the United States and Iran," *Journal for the Scientific Study of Religion* 40, no. 4 (2001).

35. John Moses, "An Ethical and Theoretical Background for the Care of Native North American Cultural Materials," *Ethnographic Conservation Newsletter*, no. 16 (October 1997).

36. Moses, "An Ethical and Theoretical Background."

37. Thorkild Jacobsen, *The Treasurers of Darkness: A History of Mesopotamian Religion* (New Haven, CT: Yale University Press, 1976), 166.

38. Jaime Gross, "Prayers at an Exhibition: Bhutan's Art and the Monks Who Protect It," *New York Times*, September 5, 2008.

39. Gross, "Prayers at an Exhibition."

40. Oriental Institute of the University of Chicago, "Research at the Oriental Institute," http://oi.uchicago.edu/research.

41. Carlyn Battilla, "Circles and Straight Lines," *Hohonu: A Journal of Academic Writing* 2, no. 2 (2004).

42. Peter T. Struck and Lindsay Jones, "Symbol and Symbolism," in *Encyclopedia of Religion*, ed. Lindsay Jones (Detroit: Macmillan Reference USA, 2005), 13: 8906.

43. Paul Avis, ed., *God and the Creative Imagination: Metaphor, Symbol, and Myth in Religion and Theology* (New York: Routledge, 1999), 105.

44. Mrs. Pervin J. Mistry, "The Sudreh Kusti" (1996), http://tenets.zoroastrianism.com/sudreh33.html.

45. Jonathan D. Culler, *The Pursuit of Signs: Semiotics, Literature, Deconstruction* (Ithaca, NY: Cornell University Press, 2002), 25.

46. Charles Sanders Peirce, "Sundry Logical Conceptions," in *The Essential Peirce: Selected Philosophical Writings, Volume 2*, ed. Peirce Edition Project (Bloomington: Indiana University Press, 1998), 274.

47. Charles Sanders Peirce, "What Is a Sign?" in *The Essential Peirce: Selected Philosophical Writings, Volume 2*, ed. Peirce Edition Project (Bloomington: Indiana University Press, 1998), 9.

48. Peirce, "Sundry Logical Conceptions," 274.

49. "Crossed Swords: Hindus against Proposed E.U. Swastika Ban," *Spiegel Online International* (January 17, 2007), www.spiegel.de/international/0,1518,460259,00.html.

50. Paul Levesque, *Symbols of Transcendence: Religious Expression in the Thought of Louis Dupre*, vol. 22, Louvain Theological & Pastoral Monographs (Grand Rapids, MI: Wm. B. Eerdmans, 1997, 1997), 73.

51. Levesque, *Symbols of Transcendence*, 73.

52. Levesque, *Symbols of Transcendence*, 73–74.

53. Samuel Taylor Coleridge, *The Statesman's Manual; or, the Bible the Best Guide to Political Skill and Foresight: A Lay Sermon* (Oxford: Oxford University, 1832), 40.

54. Charles Sanders Peirce, "Logical Tracts, No. 2," in *Collected Papers of Charles Sanders Peirce*, ed. Charles Hartshorne and Paul Weiss and Arthur W. Burks (Cambridge, MA: Harvard University Press, 1903), 447.

55. Coleridge, *The Statesman's Manual*, 40.

56. Louis Jacobs, *A Concise Companion to the Jewish Religion* (Oxford: Oxford University Press, 1999).

57. Michael W. Meister and Lindsay Jones, "Temple: Hindu Temples," in *Encyclopedia of Religion*, ed. Lindsay Jones (Detroit: Macmillan Reference USA, 2005), 13:9038.

58. This was the Seventh Ecumenical Council of 787 CE.

59. Annemarie Schimmel and Lindsay Jones, "Iconography: Islamic Iconography," in *Encyclopedia of Religion*, ed. Lindsay Jones (Detroit: Macmillan Reference USA, 2005), 7:4395.

60. Sheikh Imam Muhammad Abdul-Wahhab, ed., *The Book of Tawheed* (Riyadh, Saudi Arabia: International Islamic Publishing House, 1998), chapter 12.

61. Carlotta Gall, "Afghans Consider Rebuilding Bamiyan Buddhas," *New York Times*, November 5, 2006.

62. Noam Cohen, "Wikipedia Islam Entry Is Criticized," *New York Times*, February 5, 2008.

63. Noel Anthony Salmond, *Hindu Iconoclasts: Rammohun Roy, Dayananda Sarasvati, and Nineteenth-Century Polemics against Idolatry* (Waterloo, ON: Wilfrid Laurier University Press, 2004), 134.

64. Dale S. Wright, *Philosophical Meditations on Zen Buddhism* (Cambridge: Cambridge University Press, 1998), 121. (But Wright believes that Westerners have misinterpreted this advice from an individualistic point of view.)

65. Salmond, *Hindu Iconoclasts*, 134.

66. Smithsonian Institution, "Traditional Care of Culturally Sensitive Collections."

67. Charles Honey, "Belief in Hell Dips, but Some Say They've Already Been There," Pew Forum on Religion and Public Life, Religion News on the Web (August 14, 2008), www.pewforum.org/Religion-News/Religion-News-on-the-Web.aspx.

68. Pew Forum on Religion and Public Life, "Religious Beliefs and Practices," in *U.S. Religious Landscape Survey*, February 25, 2008, http://religions.pewforum.org/pdf/report 2religious-landscape-study-chapter-1.pdf.

69. Michael Paulson, "What Lies Beneath: Why Fewer Americans Believe in Hell Than in Heaven," *Boston Globe*, June 29, 2008.

70. Mahidol University, "The Rituals and Traditions of Thai Classical Dance," www .mahidol.ac.th/thailand/classical-dance.html.

71. Mahidol University, "The Rituals and Traditions of Thai Classical Dance."

72. "Yamuna Reaps Toxic Harvest of Immersed Idols," *Thaindian News*, October 12, 2008.

73. K. Seshadri, "The Symbol in Art and Religion," in *Symbolism in Hinduism*, ed. Swami Nityanand (Mumbai: Central Chinmaya Mission Trust, 1971), 67.

74. Eckhart Tolle, *The Power of Now: A Guide to Spiritual Enlightenment* (Novato, CA: New World Library, 1999), 90.

75. Douglas Allen, *Myth and Religion in Mircea Eliade* (New York: Routledge, 2002), 180.

76. Mircea Eliade, *Myth and Reality* (New York: HarperCollins, 1968), 5.

77. Joseph Epes Brown, *The Sacred Pipe: Black Elk's Account of the Seven Rites of the Oglala Sioux* (Norman: University of Oklahoma Press, 1989), 9.

78. Brown, *The Sacred Pipe*, 7.

79. Diana G. Tumminia, *When Prophecy Never Fails: Myth and Reality in a Flying-Saucer Group* (New York: Oxford University Press, 2005).

80. Ed McGaa, *Mother Earth Spirituality: Native American Paths to Healing Ourselves and Our World* (San Francisco: HarperCollins, 1990), 6.

81. James George Frazer, *The New Golden Bough: A New Abridgment of the Classic Work*, ed. Theodor H. Gaster (Garden City, NY: Doubleday, 1961).

82. Mircea Eliade, *The Sacred and the Profane: The Nature of Religion*, trans. Willard Trask (New York: Harcourt Brace Jovanovich, 1959), 12, 211.

83. Eliade, *The Sacred and the Profane*, 97.

84. Eliade, *The Sacred and the Profane*, 101–2.

85. Eliade, *The Sacred and the Profane*, 12, 17.

86. Eliade, *The Sacred and the Profane*, 213.

87. C. G. Jung, *Symbols of Transformation*, trans. R. F. C. Hull, 2nd ed. (Princeton, NJ: Princeton University Press, 1967), 27.

88. Jung, *Symbols of Transformation*, 17.

89. Jung, *Symbols of Transformation*, 390.

90. Joseph Campbell, *The Hero with a Thousand Faces* (Princeton, NJ: Princeton University Press, 1968), 3.

91. Campbell, *The Hero with a Thousand Faces*, 29.

92. Campbell, *The Hero with a Thousand Faces*, 29.

93. Campbell, *The Hero with a Thousand Faces*, 391.

94. Sivasailam Thiagarajan, "Agni Sahasra Namam," Super Audio (Madras) Pvt. Ltd., 2007, compact disc.

95. Ernst Cassirer, *The Problem of Knowledge: Philosophy, Science, and History since Hegel*, trans. William H. Woglom and Charles W. Hendel (New Haven, CT: Yale University Press, 1950), 315.

96. Ernst Cassirer, *The Philosophy of Symbolic Forms: The Phenomenology of Knowledge*, trans. Ralph Manheim (New Haven, CT: Yale University Press, 1977), 78.

97. Allen, *Myth and Religion in Mircea Eliade*, 239.

98. Robert A. Segal, "Jung's Very Twentieth-Century View of Myth," *Journal of Analytical Psychology* 48, no. 5 (2003): 600, 607.

99. Walter Harrelson, "Myth and Ritual School," in *Encyclopedia of Religion*, ed. Lindsay Jones (Detroit: Macmillan Reference USA, 2005): 9:6380.

100. Evan Zuesse, "Ritual," in *Encyclopedia of Religion*, ed. Lindsay Jones (Detroit: Macmillan Reference USA, 2005), 11:7840.

101. Zuesse, "Ritual," 7934.

102. Mary Boyce, *Zoroastrians: Their Religious Beliefs and Practices* (New York: Routledge, 2001), 33.

103. Boyce, *Zoroastrians*, 33.

104. Zuesse, "Ritual," 7841–43.

105. Zeusse, "Ritual," 7843.

106. T. O. Beidelman and Robert A. Segal, "Smith, W. Robertson," in *Encyclopedia of Religion*, ed. Lindsay Jones (Detroit: Macmillan Reference USA, 2005), 12:8452.

107. Beidelman and Segal, "Smith, W. Robertson."

108. Jane Ellen Harrison, *Ancient Art and Ritual* (New York: Greenwood Press, 1969), 41–46.

109. Jane Ellen Harrison, *Themis: A Study of the Social Origins of Greek Religion* (New York: Cambridge University Press, 1927), 45, 329–31.

110. John Middleton, "Evans-Pritchard, E. E.," in *Encyclopedia of Religion*, ed. Lindsay Jones (Detroit: Macmillan Reference USA, 2005), 5:2895.

111. Oscar G. Chase, *Law, Culture, and Ritual: Disputing Systems in Cross-Cultural Context* (New York: New York University Press, 2005), 17.

112. Chase, *Law, Culture, and Ritual*, 15–17, 23.

113. John Middleton, "Magic: Theories of Magic," in *Encyclopedia of Religion*, ed. Lindsay Jones (Detroit: Macmillan Reference USA, 2005): 8:5567.

114. Chase, *Law, Culture, and Ritual*, 18.

115. Middleton, "Magic: Theories of Magic," 8:5567.

116. Chase, *Law, Culture, and Ritual*, 26.

117. Jonathan Z. Smith, *To Take Place: Toward Theory in Ritual* (Chicago: University of Chicago Press, 1987), 104.

118. Smith, *To Take Place*, 63.

119. Sam D. Gill, *Storytracking: Texts, Stories, and Histories in Central Australia* (New York: Oxford University Press, 1998), 183.

120. Jonathan Z. Smith, *Imagining Religion: From Babylon to Jonestown* (Chicago: University of Chicago Press, 1982), 63–64.

121. Smith, *Imagining Religion*, 64–65.

122. Ken Fidlin, "Inside NBC's Super Bowl Coverage," *TorontoSUN.com*, February 4, 2012, www.torontosun.com/2012/02/04/inside-nbcs-super-bowl-coverage.

123. Michael Novak, *The Joy of Sports: End Zones, Bases, Baskets, Balls and the Consecration of the American Spirit* (New York: Basic Books, 1976), 18.

124. Tim Delaney and Tim Madigan, *The Sociology of Sport: An Introduction* (Jefferson, NC: McFarland, 2009), 262–65.

125. Jane Ellen Harrison, "The Influence of Darwinism on the Study of Religions," in *Alpha and Omega* (New York, AMS Press, 1973), 177.

126. Harrison, "The Influence of Darwinism on the Study of Religions," 510.

127. Steven Weitzman, "Reopening the Gates of J. Z. Smith's Temple: *To Take Place* in the Light of New Historicism," *Journal of the American Academy of Religion* 76, no. 3 (2008): 769.

128. Peter N. Jones, *Respect for Ancestors: American Indian Cultural Affiliation in the American West* (Boulder, CO: Bäuu Institute Press, 2005).

129. Jones, *Respect*, 206.

130. Smithsonian Institution, "Traditional Care of Culturally Sensitive Collections."

131. *Lyng v. Northwest Indian Cemetery Protective Association*, 485 U.S. 439 (1988).

132. *Lyng v. Northwest Indian Cemetery Protective Association*.

133. Clifford Geertz, "Religion as a Cultural System," in *The Interpretation of Cultures: Selected Essays* (New York: Basic Books, 1973), 93.

134. Karl W. Luckert and Johnny C. Cooke, *Coyoteway: A Navajo Holyway Healing Ceremonial* (Tucson: University of Arizona Press and the Museum of Northern Arizona, 1934), www.triplehood.com/cw-frontis.htm.

135. Luckert and Cooke, *Coyoteway*.

136. James C. Faris, *The Nightway: A History and a History of Documentation of a Navajo Ceremonial* (Albuquerque: University of New Mexico Press, 1990), 239–40.

137. Geertz, "Religion as a Cultural System," 17.

138. Hans-Günter Heimbrock and H. Barbara Boudewijnse, *Current Studies on Rituals: Perspectives for the Psychology of Religion*, ed. H. Barbara Boudewijnse (Amsterdam, The Netherlands: Rodopi, 1990), 1.

139. Victor W. Turner, *The Forest of Symbols: Aspects of Ndembu Ritual* (Ithaca, NY: Cornell University Press, 1967), 24–26.

140. Turner, *The Forest of Symbols*, 19.

141. Victor W. Turner, "Symbols in African Ritual," in *Perspectives in Cultural Anthropology*, ed. Herbert Applebaum (Albany: State University of New York Press, 1987), 492.

142. Mathieu Deflem, "Ritual, Anti-Structure, and Religion: A Discussion of Victor Turner's Processual Symbolic Analysis," *Journal for the Scientific Study of Religion* 30 (1991): 11.

143. "Pastoring Hispanics," *America: The National Catholic Weekly*, June 18, 2007.

144. Ellie Hidalgo, "Our Lady of Guadalupe Called 'Mother without Borders' in Los Angeles," Catholic News Service, December 5, 2007.

145. Hidalgo, "Our Lady."

146. Hood et al., "Dimensions of the Mysticism Scale."

147. Greg Johnson, "Ancestors before Us: Manifestations of Tradition in a Hawaiian Dispute," *Journal of the American Academy of Religion* 71, no. 2 (2003).

148. NAGPRA Review Committee, *Meeting Minutes*, November 1–3, 1996 (Myrtle Beach, SC: United States Park Service, Department of the Interior, 1996).

149. NAGPRA Review Committee, *Meeting Minutes*, March 25–27, 1997 (Norman, OK: United States Park Service, Department of the Interior, 1997).

150. NAGPRA Review Committee, *Meeting Minutes* (1997).

151. Johnson, "Ancestors," 333.

152. NAGPRA Review Committee, *Meeting Minutes* (1997).

153. NAGPRA Review Committee, *Meeting Minutes* (1997).

154. NAGPRA Review Committee, *Meeting Minutes* (1996).

155. Hui Mālama I Nā Kupuna 'O Hawai'i Nei ("Dispute over a Native Hawaiian Sacred Object," 1996), http://huimalama.tripod.com/index.html.

156. NAGPRA Review Committee, *Meeting Minutes* (1996).

157. NAGPRA Review Committee, *Meeting Minutes* (1997).

158. Johnson, "Ancestors," 332.

159. Johnson, "Ancestors," 333.

160. NAGPRA Review Committee, *Meeting Minutes* (1996).

161. Johnson, "Ancestors," 332.

162. NAGPRA Review Committee, *Meeting Minutes* (1997).

163. NAGPRA Review Committee, *Meeting Minutes* (1996).

164. NAGPRA Review Committee, *Meeting Minutes* (1997).

165. Johnson, "Ancestors," 337.

166. Johnson, "Ancestors," 336.

167. Johnson, "Ancestors," 336–37.

168. Johnson, "Ancestors," 338.

169. Johnson, "Ancestors," 338–39.

170. Johnson, "Ancestors," 330.

171. Carolyn Fluehr-Lobban, Pualani Kanaka'ole Kanehele, and Jennifer Hope Antes, "Repatriation of Indigenous Hawaiian Cultural Property by the City of Providence: A Case Study in Politics and Applied Law," in *Ethics and the Profession of Anthropology: Dialogue for Ethically Conscious Practice*, ed. Carolyn Fluehr-Lobban (Lanham, MD: AltaMira Press: Rowman and Littlefield, 2003), 143.

172. NAGPRA Review Committee, *Meeting Minutes* (1997).

173. Jennifer Hope Antes, "Reflections of Jennifer Hope Antes, Museum Anthropologist, on NAGPRA and the Museum of Natural History & Planetarium," in *Ethics and the Profession of Anthropology: Dialogue for Ethically Conscious Practice*, ed. Carolyn Fluehr-Lobban (Lanham, MD: AltaMira, 2002), 152.

174. Antes, "Reflections of Jennifer Hope Antes," 149.

NOTES TO CHAPTER 5

1. Jeffrey Kluger et al., "Is God in Our Genes?" *Time* 164, no. 17 (2004): 12.

2. Dean H. Hamer, *The God Gene: How Faith Is Hardwired into Our Genes* (New York: Doubleday, 2004), 460.

3. University of California Regents, "What Is Cognitive Science?" http://ls.berkeley.edu/ugis/cogsci/major/about.php.

4. Robert N. McCauley and Harvey Whitehouse, "Introduction: New Frontiers in the Cognitive Science of Religion," *Journal of Cognition & Culture* 5, nos. 1–2 (2005): 2.

5. Michael A. Persinger, "The Neuropsychiatry of Paranormal Experiences," *Journal of Neuropsychiatry and Clinical Neuroscience* 13, no. 4 (2001): 515.

6. Pascal Boyer, *Religion Explained: The Evolutionary Origins of Religious Thought* (New York: Basic Books, 2001), 49.

7. McCauley and Whitehouse, "Introduction," 3.

8. Patrick McNamara, ed., *Where God and Science Meet: The Neurology of Religious Experience* (Westport, CT: Praeger, 2006), 16.

9. A galvanic skin response (GSR) meter.

10. Gregory R. Peterson, *Minding God: Theology and the Cognitive Sciences* (Minneapolis, MN: Fortress Press, 2003).

11. Persinger, "Neuropsychiatry," 515.

12. Persinger, "Neuropsychiatry," 516.

13. Michael A. Persinger, *Neuropsychological Bases of God Beliefs* (New York: Praeger Publishers, 1987), 11.

14. M. A. Persinger, "Religious and Mystical Experiences as Artifacts of Temporal Lobe Function: A General Hypothesis," *Perceptual and Motor Skills* 57, no. 3, part 2 (1983): 1256.

15. Persinger, *Neuropsychological Bases*, 11–12.

16. Persinger, "Neuropsychiatry," 515; "Religious and Mystical Experiences," 1257.

17. Andrew Newberg and Mark Robert Waldman, *Why We Believe What We Believe* (New York: Simon & Schuster; Free Press, 2006).

18. Newberg and Waldman, *Why We Believe*, 175.

19. Newberg and Waldman, *Why We Believe*, 176–79.

20. A. Newberg et al., "Cerebral Blood Flow during Meditative Prayer: Preliminary Findings and Methodological Issues," *Perceptual and Motor Skills* 97, no. 2 (2003): 625–30.

21. Newberg and Waldman, *Why We Believe*, 441, 444.

22. Newberg et al., "Cerebral Blood Flow," 629.

23. Newberg and Waldman, *Why We Believe*, 462–519.

24. Newberg and Waldman, *Why We Believe*, 497–98.

25. Matthew Alper, *The "God" Part of the Brain: A Scientific Interpretation of Human Spirituality and God*, 5th ed. (Brooklyn, NY: Rogue Press, 2001).

26. Steve Connor, "'God Spot' Is Found in Brain," *Los Angeles Times*, October 29, 1997.

27. Jack Hitt, "This Is Your Brain on God," *Wired*, November 1999.

28. Andrew Newberg, Eugene d'Aquili, and Vince Rause, *Why God Won't Go Away: Brain Science and the Biology of Belief* (New York: Ballantine, 2001), 284.

29. David Brooks, "The Neural Buddhists," *New York Times*, May 18, 2008.

30. Brooks, "Neural."

31. Brooks, "Neural."

32. Brooks, "Neural."

33. Michael Persinger, "Dr. Michael A. Persinger," Laurentian University, www.laurentian.ca/Laurentian/Home/Departments/Behavioural+Neuroscience/People/Persinger.htm?Laurentian_Lang=en-CA.

34. Mario Beauregard and Denyse O'Leary, *The Spiritual Brain: A Neuroscientist's Case for the Existence of the Soul* (New York: HarperCollins, 2009).

35. Andrew Newberg, *Principle of Neurotheology* (Burlington, VT: Ashgate Publishing, 2010).

36. Matthew Ratcliffe, "Scientific Naturalism and the Neurology of Religious Experience," *Religious Studies* 39, no. 3 (2003).

37. Matthew Ratcliffe, "Neurotheology: A Science of What?" in *Where God and Science Meet: The Neurology of Religious Experience*, ed. Patrick McNamara (Westport, CT: Praeger, 2006).

38. Henry James, ed., *The Letters of William James* (Boston: Atlantic Monthly Press, 1920), 92.

39. William James, *The Varieties of Religious Experience* (New York: Simon & Schuster, 1997), 42.

40. James, *Varieties*, 299.

41. James, *Varieties*, 299.

42. James, *Varieties*, 309.

43. James, *Varieties*, 24–26.

44. James, *Varieties*, 25–26.

45. Quoted in Elie Kedourie, *Nationalism*, 4th ed. (Malden, MA: Blackwell, 1993), 18.

46. W. T. Stace, *Mysticism and Philosophy* (Philadelphia: J. B. Lippincott, 1960).

47. SkyGazer, "All Is One," http://pub5.bravenet.com/guestbook/395054200/#bn-guestbook-1-1-395054200/next/4.

48. W. T. Stace, *The Teachings of the Mystics* (New York: New American Library, 1960), 14.

49. Ann Taves, "Religious Experience," in *Encyclopedia of Religion*, ed. Lindsay Jones (Detroit: Macmillan Reference USA, 2005), 11:7788.

50. Taves, "Religious Experience," 11:7788.

51. Lucy Bregman, "The Interpreter/Experiencer Split: Three Models in the Psychology of Religion," *Journal of the American Academy of Religion* 46, no. 2 (1978): 131.

52. F. Samuel Brainard, "Defining 'Mystical Experience,'" *Journal of the American Academy of Religion* 64, no. 2 (1996): 365.

53. Brainard, "Defining 'Mystical Experience.'"

54. James, *Varieties*.

55. Alister Hardy Religious Experience Research Centre Archive (Lampeter, Wales: University of Wales: Trinity-Saint David).

56. SkyGazer, "See the Sea Shell," http://pub5.bravenet.com/guestbook/395054200/#bn -guestbook-1-1-395054200/next/4.

57. Association of Religion Data Archives, *General Social Survey* (2006).

58. Association of Religion Data Archives, *General Social Survey* (2004).

59. L. St. Pierre and M. Persinger, "Experimental Facilitation of the Sensed Presence Is Predicted by the Specific Patterns of the Applied Magnetic Fields, Not by Suggestibility: Re-Analysis of 19 Experiments," in *International Journal of Neuroscience* 116 (2006).

60. Alister Hardy Religious Experience Research Centre, "Report on the China Project," The Alister Hardy Trust: University of Wales, Lampeter, www.trinitysaintdavid .ac.uk/en/lrc/librariesandcentres/alisterhardyreligiousexperienceresearchcentre.

61. Alister Hardy Religious Experience Research Centre, "Report on the China Project,"

62. David Lukoff, "Visionary Spirituality and Mental Disorders," in *Altering Consciousness: Multidisciplinary Perspectives*, Vol. 2, ed. Etzel Cardeña and Michael Winkelman (Santa Barbara, CA: Praeger, 2011), 305.

63. James, *Varieties*, 305.

64. Quoted in John Crosley Shaw, *The Brain's Alpha Rhythms and the Mind: A Review of Classical and Modern Studies of the Alpha Rhythm Component of the Electroencephalogram with Commentaries on Associated Neuroscience and Neuropsychology* (Amsterdam, The Netherlands: Elsevier Health Sciences, 2003), 297.

65. This is not to imply that mysticism does not have implications and involvements in public life. See Leigh Eric Schmidt, "The Making of Modern 'Mysticism,'" *Journal of the American Academy of Religion* 71, no. 2 (2003).

66. Bernard Spilka et al., *The Psychology of Religion: An Empirical Approach*, 3rd ed. (New York: Guilford Press, 2003), 511–12.

67. Ralph W. Hood Jr., "The Common Core Thesis in the Study of Mysticism," in *Where God and Science Meet*, Volume 3 of *The Psychology of Religious Experience*, ed. Patrick McNamara (Westport, CT: Praeger, 2006), 131.

68. Nils G. Holm, "Mysticism and Intense Experiences," *Journal for the Scientific Study of Religion* 21, no. 3 (September 1982), 275.

69. Holm, "Mysticism and Intense Experiences," 273–74.

70. Spilka et al., *Psychology of Religion*, 327.

71. James, *Varieties*, 25–26, 38.

72. Michael Grasso, "The Archetype of Death and Enlightenment," in *The Near-Death Experience: A Reader*, ed. Lee Worth Bailey and Jenny L. Yates (New York: Routledge, 1996), 134.

73. Jess Byron Hollenback, *Mysticism: Experience, Response, and Empowerment* (University Park: The Pennsylvania University Press, 1996), 10.

74. SkyGazer, "Searching and Finding God," http://pub5.bravenet.com/guestbook/ 395054200/#bn-guestbook-1-1-395054200/next/4.

75. Ineffable, noetic, passive, and temporary.

76. Alister Hardy Religious Experience Research Centre Archive, "Personal Stories," Lampeter, Wales: University of Wales: Trinity-Saint David, http://alisterhardysociety. weebly.com/personal-stories.html.

77. Abraham H. Maslow, "Appendix A: Religious Aspects of Peak-Experiences," in *Religions, Values, and Peak Experiences* (New York: Penguin, 1964).

78. Or "transcendent" experience.

79. Abraham H. Maslow, *Religions, Values, and Peak Experiences* (New York: Penguin, 1964), 20.

80. Maslow, *Religions*, 19.

81. Maslow, *Religions*, 28.

82. Sarasvati Chennakesavan, "Yoga Sutras," *Asian Philosophy* 2, no. 2 (1992).

83. Swami Satchidananda, *The Yoga Sutras of Pantanjali*, trans. Swami Satchidananda (Yogaville, VA: Integral Yoga Publications, 2003), 4.

84. Charles Johnston, *The Yoga Sutras of Patanjali: The Book of the Spiritual Man* (New York: Charles Johnston, 1912), 24, www.sacred-texts.com/hin/ysp/index.htm#contents, 2:3.

85. Johnston, *The Yoga Sutras of Patanjali*, 2:3.

86. Satchidananda, *Yoga Sutras*, 24.

87. Johnston, *The Yoga Sutras of Patanjali*, 1:45.

88. Johnston, *The Yoga Sutras of Patanjali*, 1:45.

89. Satchidananda, *Yoga Sutras*, 74.

90. "Māṇḍūkya Upaniṣad," in *Upaniṣads*, trans. Patrick Olivelle (Oxford: Oxford University Press, 1996), 289.

91. Satchidananda, *Yoga Sutras*, 76.

92. Chennakesavan, "Yoga Sutras."

93. Johnston, *The Yoga Sutras of Patanjali*, 1:51.

94. B. Alan Wallace, "Vacuum States of Consciousness: A Tibetan Buddhist View" (presented at the 5th Biennial International Symposium of Science, Technics and Aesthetics: "Space, Time and Beyond," Lucerne, Switzerland, January 19, 2003), 3, www.alan wallace.org/Vacuum%20States%20Essay.pdf.

95. Wallace, "Vacuum States of Consciousness," 5, 8.

96. Wallace, "Vacuum States of Consciousness," 10–11.

97. Johnston, *The Yoga Sutras of Patanjali*, 1:45.

98. Aldous Huxley, *The Perennial Philosophy: An Interpretation of the Great Mystics, East and West* (New York: HarperCollins, 2004), vii.

99. Michael F. Palmer, *The Question of God* (New York: Routledge), 80.

100. However, we see the same notion in the Buddhist notion of "dependent origination." In this view, everything has its cause. Nothing springs up or exists independently. In this sense, everything depends on something else.

101. The Christian mystic Meister Eckert distinguishes between the knowable God of the Bible, who reveals himself in the world, and the unknowable "Godhead." This "Godhead" is the ultimate reality—God as existing in the divine nature and knowable only to God. Likewise, Kabalistic Judaism distinguishes between the infinite *Eyn Sof* that is unknowable and the God of revelation. For al-Arabi and other Muslim mystics, there is distinction without separation between the unlimited God and the God revealed in the Qur'an.

102. Huxley, *Perennial*, 3–4.

103. "Chāndogya Upaniṣad," in *Upaniṣads*, trans. Patrick Olivelle (Oxford: Oxford University Press, 1996), 124.

104. Metropolitan of Nafpaktos Hierotheos, *Orthodox Psychotherapy: The Science of the Fathers*, trans. Esther Williams (Levadia, Greece: Holy Monastery of the Virgin Birth, 1994), 140–44.

105. Metropolitan of Nafpaktos Hierotheos, *Orthodox*, 140–54.

106. Eastern Christianity expresses this goal in the thought that because they are made in the "image of God," humans are to become "like God."

107. Reynold A. Nicholson, "The Gnosis," in *The Mystics of Islam* (London: Routledge, Kegan, Paul, 1914), www.answering-islam.org/Books/Mystics/chap3.htm.

108. Boyer, *Religion Explained*, 2–10.

109. Boyer, *Religion Explained*, 2.

110. James W. Dow, "Religions and Evolutionary Theory," *Central States Anthropological Society* (2004), 5, http://personalwebs.oakland.edu/~dow/personal/papers/religion/evolrel1.pdf.

111. David Sloan Wilson, "Testing Major Evolutionary Hypotheses about Religion with a Random Sample," *Human Nature* 16, no. 4 (2005): 436–40.

112. Boyer, *Religion Explained*, 311.

113. Boyer, *Religion Explained*, 65.

114. Justin L. Barrett, *Why Would Anyone Believe in God?* (Lanham, MD: AltaMira, 2004), 31–42.

115. Barrett, *Why Would Anyone Believe in God?* 41.

116. Pascal Boyer, "Why Do Gods and Spirits Matter At All?" in *Current Approaches in the Cognitive Science of Religion*, ed. Ilkka Pyysiainen and Veikko Anttonen (New York: Continuum, 2002), 86.

117. Along with Katz, they include Wayne Proudfoot, Bruce Garside, R. C. Zaehner, Robert Gimello, Peter Moore, Ninian Smart, and Jerry Gill.

118. Robert K. C. Forman, "Paramaartha and Modern Constructivists on Mysticism: Epistemological Monomorphism Versus Duomorphism," *Philosophy East & West* 39, no. 4 (1989): 393.

119. Forman notes that the theory is a form of "social constructionism." Others use the terms "contextualism" and "social constructionism" interchangeably.

120. Bruce Janz, "Mysticism and Understanding: Steven Katz and His Critics," *Studies in Religion* 24, no. 1 (1995): 82.

121. Stephen T. Katz, ed., *Mysticism and Philosophical Analysis* (New York: Oxford University Press, 1978), 26.

122. Forman, "Paramaartha," 393.

123. Wayne L. Proudfoot, *Religious Experience* (Berkeley: University of California Press, 1985), 223.

124. Steven T. Katz, "Language, Epistemology, and Mysticism," in *Mysticism and Philosophical Analysis*, ed. Steven T. Katz (New York: Oxford University Press, 1978), 40.

125. Katz, "Language," 34–35.

126. Katz, "Language," 23–25.

127. Katz, "Language," 38.

128. Katz, "Language," 39.

129. Timothy A. Mahoney, "Contextualism, Decontextualism, and Perennialism: Suggestions for Expanding the Common Ground of the World's Mystical Traditions" (presented at Twentieth World Congress of Philosophy, Boston, MA, August 15–19, 1998), www.bu.edu/wcp/Papers/Reli/ReliMaho.htm.

130. Rita M. Gross, *Feminism and Religion: An Introduction*, 2nd ed. (Boston: Beacon Press, 1996), 22.

131. Gross, *Feminism and Religion*, 164.

132. Ursula King, "General Introduction: Gender-Critical Turns in the Study of Religion," in *Gender, Religion, and Diversity*, ed. Ursula King (London: Continuum International Publishing Group, 2004), 8.

133. Melissa Raphael-Levine, "Feminism, Constructivism, and Numinous Experience," *Religious Studies* 30, no. 4 (1994): 513.

134. Raphael-Levine, "Feminism," 518.

135. Raphael-Levine, "Feminism," 519.

136. Raphael-Levine, "Feminism," 513.

137. Raphael-Levine, "Feminism," 518.

138. Raphael-Levine, "Feminism," 512, 520.

139. Raphael-Levine, "Feminism," 519, 526.

140. Raphael-Levine, "Feminism," 518, 525.

141. Satchidananda, *Yoga Sutras*, 174.

142. Dale S. Wright, "Rethinking Transcendence: The Role of Language in Zen Experience," *Philosophy East & West* 42, no. 1 (1992): 135.

143. Wright, "Rethinking," 125.

144. Huxley, *Perennial Philosophy*, 297.

145. Huxley, *Perennial Philosophy*, 296, 301.

146. Huston Smith, *Beyond the Postmodern Mind* (Wheaton, IL: Quest, 2003), 46.

147. Ilkka Pyysiainen, *How Religion Works: Towards a New Cognitive Science of Religion* (Boston: Brill, 2001), 131–32.

148. Forman, "Paramaartha," 393.

149. Robert K. C. Forman, *The Problem of Pure Consciousness* (New York: Oxford University Press, 1990), 16–17.

150. Larry Short, "Mysticism, Mediation, and the Non-Linguistic," *Journal of the American Academy of Religion* 63, no. 4 (1995): 667–69.

151. Short, "Mysticism," 668, 673.

152. Jerome Gellman, "Mysticism," in *The Stanford Encyclopedia of Philosophy*, ed. Edward N. Zalta (Stanford, CA: Stanford University Press, 2011).

153. Alison Stone, "Essentialism and Anti-Essentialism in Feminist Philosophy," *Journal of Moral Philosophy* 1, no. 2 (2004): 141.

154. Stone, "Essentialism," 140–42.

155. Raphael-Levine, "Feminism," 512.

156. Stone, "Essentialism," 139.

157. Stone, "Essentialism," 142.

158. McNamara, *Where God and Science Meet*, 16.

159. Uffe Schjoedt, Hans Stødkilde-Jørgensen, Armin W. Geertz, and Andreas Roepstorff, "Highly Religious Participants Recruit Areas of Social Cognition in Personal Prayer," *Social Cognitive and Affective Neuroscience* 4, no. 2 (2009).

160. Schjoedt et al., "Highly Religious Participants," 202–3, 205.

161. Schjoedt et al., "Highly Religious Participants," 205.

162. Schjoedt et al., "Highly Religious Participants," 199.

163. Schjoedt et al., "Highly Religious Participants," 205.

164. S. W. Lazar et al., "Meditation Experience Is Associated with Increased Cortical Thickness," *Neuroreport* 16, no. 17 (2005): 5.

165. Lazar et al., "Meditation," 5.

166. Lisa Schirch, *Ritual and Symbol in Peacebuilding* (Sterling, VA: Kumarian Press, Inc., 2005), 106.

167. Gregory R. Peterson, "Species of Emergence," *Zygon: Journal of Religion & Science* 41, no. 3 (2006): 691–701.

168. Peterson, "Species of Emergence," 701.

169. Philip Clayton, *Mind and Emergence: From Quantum to Consciousness* (New York: Oxford University Press, 2004), 100.

170. Peterson, "Species of Emergence," 694.

171. Nancy C. Murphy, *Anglo-American Postmodernity: Philosophical Perspectives on Science, Religion, and Ethics* (Boulder, CO: Westview Press, 1997), 32–33.

172. Henry C. Plotkin, *Darwin Machines and the Nature of Knowledge* (Cambridge, MA: Harvard University Press, 1997), 177.

173. Ursula Goodenough and Terrence W. Deacon, "The Sacred Emergence of Nature," in *The Oxford Handbook of Science and Religion*, ed. Philip Clayton and Zachary Simpson (New York: Oxford University Press, 2006), 863.

174. Terrence W. Deacon, *The Symbolic Species: The Co-evolution of Language and the Brain* (New York: W. W. Norton, 1998), 34, 45–46.

175. Clayton, *Mind and Emergence*, 59.

176. Harry T. Hunt, *On the Nature of Consciousness: Cognitive, Phenomenological, and Transpersonal Perspectives* (New Haven, CT: Yale University Press, 1995), 295.

177. Eugene G. d'Aquili and Andrew Newberg, *The Mystical Mind: Probing the Biology of Religious Experience* (Minneapolis, MN: Fortress Press, 1999), 99–100.

178. d'Aquili and Newberg, *The Mystical Mind*, 99.

179. Nina P. Azari et al., "Neural Correlates of Religious Experience," *European Journal of Neuroscience* 13 (2001): 1649.

180. Azari et al., "Neural Correlates of Religious Experience," 1649.

181. McNamara, *Where God and Science Meet*, 39.

182. Azari et al., "Neural Correlates of Religious Experience," 1651. McNamara, *Where God and Science Meet*, 39.

183. McNamara, *Where God and Science Meet*, 37.

184. Nina P. Azari and Dieter Birnbacher, "The Role of Cognition and Feeling in Religious Experience," *Zygon: Journal of Religion & Science* 39 (2004): 912–13.

185. Azari and Birnbacher, "The Role of Cognition," 911–13.

186. Forman, "Paramaartha," 393.

187. Brainard, "Defining 'Mystical Experience,'" 366.

188. John Hick, *The Fifth Dimension: An Exploration of the Spiritual Realm* (Oxford: Oneworld Publications, 1999), 41.

189. Barbara Bradley Hagerty, "How Our Brains Are Wired for Belief" (paper presented at the Faith Angle Conference on Religion, Key West, Florida, May 5, 2008).

190. Hagerty, "How Our Brains Are Wired for Belief."

NOTES TO CHAPTER 6

1. "Final Statement of Catholic-Muslim Forum: Called to Be Instruments of Love and Harmony," *Zenit*, November 6, 2008.

2. Ian Fisher, "Pope Apologizes for Uproar over His Remarks," *New York Times*, September 17, 2006.

3. "Muslim Fury Grows at Pope Remarks," *CNN.com*, September 16, 2006, www.cnn.com/2006/WORLD/europe/09/16/pope.islam.0750/index.html?section=cnn_latest.

4. "Pope's Apology Rejected by Some, Accepted by Others," *Spiegel Online International*, September 18, 2006, www.spiegel.de/international/0,1518,437636,00.html.

5. Allamah Abd Allah bin Mahfuz bin Bayyah et al., "Open Letter to His Holiness Pope Benedict XVI," *Official Website: A Common Word* (2006), http://ammanmessage.com/media/openLetter/english.pdf.

6. Prince Ghazi bin Muhammad bin Talal et al., "A Common Word between Us and You: Summary and Abridgement," *Official Website: A Common Word* (2007), www.acommonword.com/index.php?lang=en&page=option1.

7. Miroslav Volf et al., "Loving God and Neighbor Together: A Christian Response to 'A Common Word between Us and You,'" *Yale Center for Faith and Culture: Reconciliation Program* (2008), www.yale.edu/faith/about/abou-commonword.htm.

8. Archbishop of Canterbury, "Archbishop Meets Chief Rabbis in Jerusalem," www.archbishopofcanterbury.org/1348?q=jewish+second+meeting+jerusalem.

9. Giorgio Bernardelli, "Islamic Prince to Attend Pope's Interfaith Meeting in Assisi," *Vatican Insider*, July 4, 2011.

10. World Interfaith Harmony Week, http://worldinterfaithharmonyweek.com.

11. Rick Love, Carl Moeller, and Jason Micheli, "Have Muslim-Christian Relations Improved since 9/11?" *A Common Word* (republished from *Christianty Today*, September 14, 2011), www.acommonword.com.

12. "Review of Christian-Muslim Conflict and a Modest Proposal to Counter It" (republished from Reuters), *A Common Word*, November 5, 2010, http://acommonword.com/en/a-common-word-in-the-news/19-new-news-items/439-a-review-of-christian-muslim-conflict-and-a-modest-proposal-to-counter-it.html.

13. "Final Statement."

14. "Final Statement."

15. Allamah Abd Allah bin Mahfuz bin Bayyah et al., "An Open Letter to His Holiness Pope Benedict XVI," http://hatzputra.blogspot.com/2006/09/open-letter-to-his-holiness-pope.html.

16. Daniel C. Dennett, *Darwin's Dangerous Idea: Evolution and the Meanings of Life* (New York: Simon & Schuster, 1995), 519.

17. Daniel C. Dennett, "Teach Our Children Well," *On Faith: A Conversation on Religion with Jon Meacham and Sally Quinn*, March 8, 2007, http://newsweek.washingtonpost.com/onfaith/daniel_c_dennett/2007/03/teach_our_children_well.html.

18. Dennett, "Teach Our Children Well."

19. Daniel C. Dennett, *Breaking the Spell* (New York: Viking, 2006), 97.

20. Dennett, *Breaking the Spell*, 297.

21. Daniel C. Dennett, Alister McGrath, and Madeleine Bunting, "Breaking the Spell: Religion as a Global Phenomenon," March 13, 2006, www.thersa.org/events/audio-and-past-events/breaking-the-spell--religion-as-a-global-phenomenon.

22. Duane L. Cady, "Between Dogmatism and Relativism," *Journal of Religion, Conflict, and Peace* 1, no. 2 (2008), www.plowsharesproject.org/journal/php/article.php?issu_list_id=10&article_list_id=29.

23. J. P. Larsson, *Understanding Religious Violence: A New Framework for Conflict Transformation* (Lampeter: University of Wales, 2002), 75, 76.

24. Bruce Lincoln, *Holy Terrors: Thinking about Religion after September 11* (Chicago: University of Chicago Press, 2003), 79–86.

25. Adapted from Larsson, *Understanding Religious Violence*, 85.

26. Peter Knight, ed., *Conspiracy Theories in American History: An Encyclopedia* (Santa Barbara, CA: ABC-CLIO, 2003).

27. Richard Abanes, "Christian Identity," in *Encyclopedia of Race and Racism*, ed. John Hartwell Moore (Detroit: Macmillan Reference USA, 2008).

28. Larsson, *Understanding Religious Violence*, 86.

29. Center for International Development and Conflict Management, "Assessment for Moros in the Philippines," *Minorities at Risk Project* (2003), www.cidcm.umd.edu/mar/assessment.asp?groupId=84003.

30. Mark Juergensmeyer, "Terror in the Name of God," *Current History* 100, no. 649 (2001): 5.

31. Juergensmeyer, "Terror in the Name," 5.

32. Jonathan Fox, "Religion, Politics and International Relations: The Rise of Religion and the Fall of the Civilization Paradigm as Explanations for Intra-State Conflict," *Cambridge Review of International Affairs* 20, no. 3 (2007): 717.

33. Charles Selengut, *Sacred Fury: Understanding Religious Violence* (Lanham, MD: AltaMira, 2003), 9, 10.

34. Richard Dawkins, *The God Delusion* (Boston: Houghton Mifflin, 2006).

35. Sam Harris, *The End of Faith: Religion, Terror, and the Future of Religion* (New York: W. W. Norton, 2004), 26, 44, 225.

36. Harris, *The End*, 14.

37. Richard Dawkins, *The God Delusion* (Boston: Houghton Mifflin, 2006), 286.

38. Dawkins, *The God Delusion*, 308.

39. Dawkins, *The God Delusion*, 188, 286, 303–4.

40. Harris, *The End*, 16–23, 108–52.

41. Harris, *The End*, 308.

42. Dawkins, *The God Delusion*, 191.

43. Dawkins, *The God Delusion*, 190, 196.

44. Dawkins, *The God Delusion*, 191.

45. René Girard, *Things Hidden since the Foundation of the World*, trans. Stephen Bann and Michael Metteer (Stanford, CA: Stanford University Press, 1987), 17.

46. Girard, *Things Hidden*, 17.

47. René Girard, *The Girard Reader*, ed. James G. Williams (New York: Crossroad Publishing, 1996), 12.

48. René Girard, *Deceit, Desire, and the Novel: Self and Other in Literary Structure*, trans. Yvonne Freccero (Baltimore: Johns Hopkins University Press, 1976), 10–11.

49. Girard, *Things Hidden*, 103.

50. René Girard and Patrick Gregory, *Violence and the Sacred* (New York: Continuum, 2005), 98.

51. S. Mark Heim, "Visible Victim: Christ's Death to End Sacrifice," *Christian Century* (March 14, 2001), 21.

52. Genesis 4:8–17.

53. Charles Bellinger, "René Girard and the Death Penalty" (paper presented at Society of Biblical Literature convened gathering, Brite University, February 23, 2008).

54. René Girard, *I See Satan Fall Like Lightning* (Maryknoll, NY: Orbis, 2001), 160.

55. Girard, *I See Satan Fall*, 159.

56. Henri Tincq, "Interview of René Girard: What Is Occurring Today Is a Mimetic Rivalry on a Planetary Scale," *Colloquium on Violence and Religion* (2001), www.lemonde.fr/article/0,5987,3230--239636-,00.html.

57. James K. Wellman and Kyoko Tokuno, "Is Religious Violence Inevitable?" *Journal for the Scientific Study of Religion* 43, no. 3 (2004): 292.

58. Wellman and Tokuno, "Is Religious Violence Inevitable?" 292.

59. Wellman and Tokuno, "Is Religious Violence Inevitable?" 292–93.

60. Wellman and Tokuno, "Is Religious Violence Inevitable?" 294.

61. Pritam Singh, "The Political Economy of the Cycles of Violence and Non-Violence in the Sikh Struggle for Identity and Political Power: Implications for Indian Federalism," *Third World Quarterly* 28 (2007): 559–60.

62. R. Scott Appleby, "The Unholy Uses of the Apocalyptic Imagination: Twentieth Century Patterns," working paper, MacMillan Center Council on Middle East Studies, Yale University (2002), 2.

63. Samuel Huntington, *Clash of Civilizations: The Remaking of World Order* (New York: Simon & Schuster, 1997), 43.

64. Huntington, *Clash*, 48, 137–54.

65. Samuel Huntington, "The Clash of Civilizations?" *Foreign Affairs* 72 no. 3 (Summer 1993), 25.

66. Huntington, "Clash of Civilizations?" 26, 29.

67. Huntington, "Clash of Civilizations?" 29.

68. Huntington, "Clash of Civilizations?" 25.

69. Mark Juergensmeyer, *Terror in the Mind of God: The Global Rise of Religious Violence*, ed. Mark Juergensmeyer (Berkeley: University of California Press, 2001), 13.

70. Mark Juergensmeyer, "The Worldwide Rise of Religious Nationalism," *Journal of International Affairs* 50, no. 1 (1996), www.questia.com/read/1G1-18623939.

71. Juergensmeyer, "The Worldwide Rise."

72. Arabic: *Haram esh-Sharif.*

73. Mark Juergensmeyer, *The New Cold War? Religious Nationalism Confronts the Secular State* (Berkeley: University of California Press, 1994), 33.

74. Juergensmeyer, *Terror in the Mind*, 165.

75. Juergensmeyer, *Terror in the Mind*, 242.

76. Appleby, "Unholy Uses of the Apocalyptic Imagination," 2.

77. Senate Government Affairs Permanent Subcommittee on Investigations, "Global Proliferation of Weapons of Mass Destruction: A Case Study on the Aum Shinrikyo," (staff statement, October 31, 1995).

78. Senate Government Affairs Permanent Subcommittee on Investigations, "Global Proliferation."

79. Douglas Jehl, "Holy War Lured Saudis as Rulers Looked Away," *New York Times*, December 27, 2001.

80. Jehl, "Holy War Lured Saudis."

81. Jehl, "Holy War Lured Saudis."

82. Jehl, "Holy War Lured Saudis."

83. Juergensmeyer, *Terror in the Mind*, 155.

84. David Cook, "The Apocalyptic Year 200/815–816 and the Events Surrounding It," in *Apocalyptic Time*, ed. Albert I. Baumgarten (Leiden, Netherlands: Brill, 2000), 47–49.

85. Hubert Seiwert, "End of Time and New Time in Medieval Chinese Buddhism," in *Apocalyptic Time*, ed. Albert I. Baumgarten (Leiden, Netherlands: Brill, 2000), 2, 3.

86. Seiwert, "End of Time and New Time in Medieval Chinese Buddhism," 7.

87. For a contrary view, see Regina M. Schwartz, *The Curse of Cain: The Violent Legacy of Monotheism* (Chicago: University of Chicago Press, 1998).

88. Diana L. Eck, *A New Religious America: How A "Christian Country" Has Become the World's Most Religiously Diverse Nation* (New York: HarperCollins, 2001), 1.

89. Diana L. Eck, *Encountering God: A Spiritual Journey from Bozeman to Banaras* (Boston: Beacon Press, 2003), 168–97.

90. Robert Wuthnow, *America and the Challenges of Religious Diversity* (Princeton, NJ: Princeton University Press, 2007), 190.

91. Pew Forum on Religion and Public Life, "Many Americans Say Other Faiths Can Lead to Eternal Life," *U.S. Religious Landscape Survey: Follow-Up* (December 18, 2008), http://www.pewforum.org/Many-Americans-Say-Other-Faiths-Can-Lead-to-Eternal-Life.aspx.

92. Eck, *Encountering*, 96.

93. Eck, *Encountering*, x.

94. Jane Perlez, "Blair Praises the 'Authentic Voices' of Islam," *International Herald Tribune*, June 4, 2007.

95. Laurel Hart, "World Religious Leaders Reject Violence and 'Hijacking of Religion' at Religions for Peace World Assembly," *Religions for Peace: 8th World Assembly*, August 26, 2006, www.wcrp.org/files/PR-Opening-08-26-2006.pdf.

96. Karen Armstrong, "The True, Peaceful Face of Islam," *Time/CNN*, September 23, 2001.

97. Dawkins, *The God Delusion*, 301–8.

98. Harris, *The End*, 199–203.

99. H. Allen Orr, "A Mission to Convert," *New York Times*, January 11, 2007.

100. Dawkins, *The God Delusion*, 278.

101. Harris, *The End*, 206.

102. Dawkins, *The God Delusion*, 308.

103. Robert A. Pape, *Dying to Win: The Strategic Logic of Suicide Terrorism* (New York: Random House, 2005), 36.

104. Fred March, "How to Counter Religion's Toxic Effects," *Humanist* 67, no. 3 (2007).

105. March, "How to Counter Religion's Toxic Effects."

106. Harris, *The End*, 106.

107. Harris, *The End*, 78.

108. Dennett, *Breaking the Spell*, 310.

109. Girard and Gregory, *Violence and the Sacred*, 109.

110. Jan Bremmer, "Scapegoat," in *Encyclopedia of Religion*, ed. Lindsay Jones (Detroit: Macmillan Reference USA, 2005): 12:8145.

111. Tincq, "Interview of René Girard."

112. Tincq, "Interview of René Girard."

113. Tincq, "Interview of René Girard."

114. Bruce Chilton, *The Temple of Jesus: His Sacrificial Program within a Cultural History of Sacrifice* (University Park: Pennsylvania State University Press, 1992), 23.

115. Chilton, *The Temple of Jesus*, 27.

116. For an alternate view, see Schwartz, *The Curse of Cain*, 72.

117. Wellman and Tokuno, "Is Religious Violence Inevitable?" 293.

118. Wellman and Tokuno, "Is Religious Violence Inevitable?" 293.

119. Wellman and Tokuno, "Is Religious Violence Inevitable?" 293.

120. Jonathan Fox, "The Future of Religion and Domestic Conflict" (presented at the Netherlands chapter of the Society for International Development, 2006), 9.

121. Edward Said, "The Clash of Ignorance," *Nation*, October 2, 2001.

122. Said, "The Clash of Ignorance."

123. Bruce M. Russett, John R. Oneal, and Michaelene Cox, "Clash of Civilizations, or Realism and Liberalism Déjà Vu? Some Evidence," *Journal of Peace Research* 37, no. 5 (2000): 13.

124. Russett et al., "Clash of Civilizations, or Realism and Liberalism Déjà Vu?" 3.

125. William T. Cavanaugh, "Behind the Common Question Lies a Morass of Unclear Thinking," *Harvard Divinity Bulletin* 35, no. 2 (2007), www.hds.harvard.edu/news/bulletin_mag/articles/35-23_cavanaugh.html.

126. Huntington, "Clash of Civilizations?"

127. William T. Cavanaugh, "Does Religion Cause Violence?" *Harvard Divinity Bulletin* 35, nos. 2–3 (Spring/Summer 2007).

128. Cavanaugh, "Does Religion Cause Violence?"

129. Juergensmeyer, *The New Cold War?*, 24.

130. Juergensmeyer, *Terror in the Mind*, 10.

131. Terry C. Muck, "Instrumentality, Complexity, and Reason: A Christian Approach to Religions," *Buddhist-Christian Studies* 22 (2002): 115.

132. World Religions Professor Emeritus, Syracuse University.

133. Huston Smith, "Book Review: *Encountering God: A Spiritual Journey from Bozeman to Banaras*," *Christian Century*, March 9, 1994.

134. Russell McCutcheon, "The Category 'Religion' and the Politics of Tolerance," in *Defining Religion: Investigating the Boundaries between the Sacred and Secular*, ed. Arthur L. Greil and D. Bromley (Amsterdam, Netherlands: Elsevier, 2003; reprint available at Russell McCutcheon, University of Alabama, Religious Studies Department), 162.

135. John Esposito, "Islamophobia" (presented at the Prince Alwaleed Bin Talal Center for Muslim-Christian Understanding, Georgetown University, 2006).

136. Joel Kaminsky, "Violence in the Bible," *SBL Forum* (June 2006), http://sbl-site.org/publications/article.aspx?articleId=159.

137. The claim therefore commits the fallacy of suppressed evidence.

138. David A. Hamburg and Cyrus R. Vance, eds., "Chapter 2: When Prevention Fails: How and Why Deadly Conflict Arises," in *Preventing Deadly Conflict: Final Report* (New York: Carnegie Corporation of New York, 1997).

139. R. Scott Appleby, *The Ambivalence of the Sacred: Religion, Violence, and Reconciliation*, Carnegie Commission on Preventing Deadly Conflict (Lanham, MD: Rowman & Littlefield, 1999), 119.

140. Appleby, *The Ambivalence of the Sacred*, 119.

141. Appleby, *The Ambivalence of the Sacred*, 282.

142. Edmund Emeka Ezegbobelu, *Challenges of Interreligious Dialogue: Between the Christian and the Muslim Communities in Nigeria*, European University Studies Series 23 (New York: Peter Lang, 2009), 157–60.

143. Tim Wise, dir., *Soldiers of Peace* (One Tree Films, 2008).

144. Appleby, *The Ambivalence of the Sacred*, 284.

145. Appleby, *The Ambivalence of the Sacred*, 284.

146. Appleby, *The Ambivalence of the Sacred*, 284.

147. Jonathan Fox, "Counting the Causes and Dynamics of Ethnoreligious Violence," *Totalitarian Movements & Political Religions* 4 (2003): 139.

148. Fox, "Religion, Politics and International Relations," 381.

149. Jonathan Fox, "Are Middle East Conflicts More Religious?" *Middle East Quarterly* 8, no. 4 (Fall 2001).

150. Jonathan Fox, "Are Religious Minorities More Militant Than Other Ethnic Minorities?" *Alternatives: Global, Local, Political* 28, no. 1 (2003), www.questia.com/read/1G1-98831068.

151. Jonathan Fox, "The Rise of Religious Nationalism and Conflict: Ethnic Conflict and Revolutionary Wars, 1945–2001," *Journal of Peace Research* 41 (2004): 724–28.

152. Jonathan Fox, "In the Name of God and Nation: The Overlapping Influence of Separatism and Religion on Ethnic Conflict," *Social Identities* 8, no. 3 (2002): 448.

153. Fox, "Religion, Politics and International Relations," 365.

154. Fox, "Counting," 131–32.

155. Fox, "Are Religious Minorities?"

156. Fox, "The Future," 17–18.

157. Appleby, *The Ambivalence of the Sacred*.

158. Marc Gopin, "Dialogue: A Different Model of Peacemaking," *Harvard Divinity Bulletin* 35, no. 4 (2007), 13, www.hds.harvard.edu/news/bulletin_mag/articles/35-4_gopin.html.

159. Marc Gopin, *Holy War, Holy Peace: How Religion Can Bring Peace to the Middle East* (New York: Oxford University Press, 2002), 35–37.

160. Love, Moeller, and Micheli, "Have Muslim-Christian."

161. Douglas Johnston, Azhar Hussain, and Ahmed Younis, "Madrasas and the Global War on Terror," presented at Conflict Prevention and Resolution Forum, sponsored by Search for Common Ground (The Johns Hopkins University, SAIS, September 12, 2006), International Center for Religion and Diplomacy, http://icrd.nonprofitsoapbox.com/index.php?option=com_content&task=view&id=132&Itemid=133.

162. Johnston, Hussain, and Younis, "Madrasas and the Global War on Terror."

163. Christopher M. Blanchard, "Islamic Religious Schools, Madrasas" (2008), www.fas.org/sgp/crs/misc/RS21654.pdf.

164. Blanchard, "Islamic Religious Schools."

165. Johnston, Hussain, and Younis, "Madrasas and the Global War on Terror."

166. Douglas M. Johnston, "How One Organization Is Transforming Pakistani Madrasas," *On Faith: A Conversation on Religion and Politics, Washington Post,* August 11, 2011.

167. Johnston, Hussain, and Younis, "Madrasas and the Global War on Terror."

168. Johnston, Hussain, and Younis, "Madrasas and the Global War on Terror."

169. Johnston, Hussain, and Younis, "Madrasas and the Global War on Terror."

170. Johnston, Hussain, and Younis, "Madrasas and the Global War on Terror."

171. Johnston, Hussain, and Younis, "Madrasas and the Global War on Terror."

172. Johnston, Hussain, and Younis, "Madrasas and the Global War on Terror."

173. Ethan Bueno de Mesquita, "Review of Jonathan Fox's *Religion, Civilization, and Civil War," Studies in Conflict and Terrorism* 28, no. 4 (2005).

174. Appleby, *The Ambivalence of the Sacred.*

175. Fox, "The Future," 24.

NOTES TO CHAPTER 7

1. Center for Inquiry, "The Secular Society and Its Enemies," www.centerforinquiry.net/secularsociety.

2. Center for Inquiry, "The Secular Society and Its Enemies."

3. T. Simon Blackburn, "Paradigm," in *The Oxford Dictionary of Philosophy* (Oxford: Oxford University Press, 2008).

4. John Scott and Gordon Marshall, "Paradigm," in *A Dictionary of Sociology* (Oxford: Oxford University Press, 2009).

5. Bryan R. Wilson, "The Secularization Thesis: Criticisms and Rebuttals," in *Secularization and Social Integration: Papers in Honor of Karel Dobbelaere,* ed. Bryan R. Wilson, Rudi Lermans, and Jaak Billiet (Leuven, Belgium: Leuven University Press, 1998), 48.

6. Max Weber, *Max Weber's Complete Writings on Academic and Political Vocations,* trans. John Dreijmanis (New York: Algora Publishing, 2008), 35, 51–52.

7. Rodney Stark, "Secularization R.I.P.," in *The Secularization Debate,* ed. William H. Swatos and Daniel V. A. Olson (Lanham, MD: Rowman & Littlefield, 2000), 44.

8. Quoted in Stark, "Secularization R.I.P.," 44–45.

9. Jürgen Habermas, "Notes on a Post-Secular Society," *signandsight.com,* June 6, 2008.

10. Peter Berger, "Epistemological Modesty: An Interview with Peter Berger," *Christian Century,* October 29, 1997.

11. David Yamane, "Secularization on Trial: In Defense of a Neosecularization Paradigm," *Journal for the Scientific Study of Religion* 36, no. 1 (1997): 111.

12. Stark, "Secularization R.I.P.," 62.

13. Wilson, "Secularization Thesis," 48.

14. Martin Riesebrodt, "Secularization and the Global Resurgence of Religion" (paper presented at the Comparative Social Analysis Workshop, University of California, Los Angeles, March 9, 2000), 2–3.

15. United Nations Department of Economic and Social Affairs, "Population Estimates and Projections," in *World Population Prospects: The 2010 Revision* (New York: UN Department of Economic and Social Affairs, 2011), http://esa.un.org/unpd/wpp.

16. Central Intelligence Agency, "Introduction-World," in *The World Factbook* (Central Intelligence Agency, 2011).

17. Barney Warf and Peter Vincent, "Religious Diversity across the Globe: A Geographic Exploration," *Social & Cultural Geography* 8, no. 4 (2007): 602.

18. Gregory Scott Paul and Phil Zuckerman, "Why the Gods Are Not Winning," *Edge* (2007), www.edge.org/3rd_culture/paul07/paul07_index.html.

19. Central Intelligence Agency, "Introduction-World."

20. Warf and Vincent, "Religious Diversity," 603.

21. Central Intelligence Agency, "Introduction-World."

22. Timothy Samuel Shah and Monica Duffy Toft, "Why God Is Winning," *Foreign Policy* no. 155 (2006): 40.

23. David B. Barrett, George Thomas Kurian, and Todd M. Johnson, eds., *World Christian Encyclopedia: A Comparative Survey of Churches and Religions in the Modern World* (Oxford: Oxford University Press, 2000).

24. They refer to another WCE table that includes the Orthodox Christians and shows the three largest religions "edging up a more modest 60 to 66%" since 1900.

25. Paul and Zuckerman, "Why the Gods Are Not Winning."

26. Paul and Zuckerman, "Why the Gods Are Not Winning."

27. Paul and Zuckerman, "Why the Gods Are Not Winning."

28. Paul and Zuckerman, "Why the Gods Are Not Winning."

29. Pew Forum on Religion and Public Life, *Tolerance and Tension: Islam and Christian in Sub-Saharan Africa*, Pew-Templeton Global Religious Futures Project (2010), i.

30. Warf and Vincent, "Religious Diversity," 603.

31. *Human Development Report*, "Table 1: Human Development Index and Its Components" (United Nations Development Program, 2011), http://hdr.undp.org/en/media/HDR_2011_EN_Table1.pdf.

32. Phil Zuckerman, "Atheism: Contemporary Rates and Patterns," in *Cambridge Companion to Atheism*, ed. Michael Martin (Cambridge: Cambridge University Press, 2007), 20.

33. *Human Development Report*, "Table 1."

34. Zuckerman, "Atheism," 15–17.

35. *Human Development Report*, "Table 1: Human Development Index and Its Components" (United Nations Development Program, 2004). The 2004 report did not divide the "high" HDI rated countries into "Very High" and "High."

36. Zuckerman, "Atheism," 20.

37. Zuckerman, "Atheism," 13.

38. Paul and Zuckerman, "Why the Gods Are Not Winning."

39. Ruut Veenhoven, "Inequality-Adjusted Happiness in 135 Nations 2000–2009," *World Database of Happiness: Rank Report Inequality of Happiness* (2009), worlddatabaseofhappiness.eur.nl/hap_nat/findingreports/RankReport_InequalityHappiness.php.

40. Zuckerman, "Atheism," 19.

41. Paul and Zuckerman, "Why the Gods Are Not Winning."

42. David Goldman, "2008 Outlook: Fasten Your Seatbelts," *CNNMoney.com* (January 2, 2008), http://money.cnn.com/2007/12/28/markets/2008_predictions.

43. Quoted in Goldman, "2008 Outlook: Fasten Your Seatbelts."

44. "Forecasts from *The Futurist* Magazine" (2009), www.wfs.org/forecasts.htm.

45. "F.A.Q.: What Is the Fastest Growing Religion?" *Adherents.com* (2007), www.adherents.com/adh_faq.html#fastest.

46. United Nations Department of Economic and Social Affairs, "When Is the World Expected to Reach Each Successive Billion?" in *World Population Prospects: The 2010 Revision* (2011), http://esa.un.org/wpp/Other-Information/faq.htm.

47. U.S. Census Bureau, "World Population Growth Rates: 1950–2050 (June Update)," (2011), www.census.gov/population/international/data/idb/worldgrgraph.php.

48. United Nations Department of Economic and Social Affairs, *World Population Prospects: The 2004 Revision, Highlights* (New York: UN Department of Economic and Social Affairs, 2005).

49. "The List: The World's Fastest-Growing Religions," *Foreign Policy*, May 14, 2007, www.foreignpolicy.com/articles/2007/05/13/the_list_the_worlds_fastest_growing_ religions. The article cites the World Christian Database for its statistics.

50. "Religion Statistics by Growth Rate," *ReligionFacts* (2005), www.religionfacts .com/religion_statistics/religion_statistics_by_growth_rate.htm.

51. Barrett, Kurian, and Johnson, *World Christian Encyclopedia*.

52. World Christian Database, www.worldchristiandatabase.org/wcd.

53. Todd M. Johnson, "Demographic Futures for Christianity and the World Religions," *Dialog: A Journal of Theology* 43, no. 1 (2004): 16.

54. Johnson, "Demographic Futures," 15, Scenario 2.

55. Population Reference Bureau, "Population, Health, and Environment Data and Estimates for the Countries and Religions of the World," *World Population Data Sheet* (July 2010), www.prb.org/pdf10/10wpds_eng.pdf.

56. Todd M. Johnson, David B. Barrett, and Peter F. Crossing, "Christianity 2010: Status of Global Mission," *International Bulletin of Missionary Research* 34, no. 1 (2010).

57. Population Reference Bureau, "Population, Health, and Environment Data."

58. Johnson, "Demographic Futures," 15, Scenario 2.

59. Johnson, "Demographic Futures," 15, Scenario 2.

60. Karel Dobbelaere, "Towards an Integrated Perspective of the Processes Related to the Descriptive Concept of Secularization," *Sociology of Religion* 60, no. 3 (1999): 232.

61. Mark Chaves, "Secularization as Declining Religious Authority," *Social Forces* 72, no. 3 (1994): 752.

62. Chaves, "Secularization," 750.

63. Yamane, "Secularization," 115.

64. Dobbelaere, "Towards," 233.

65. According to Karel Dobbelaere, in Belgium and the Netherlands, the Catholic Church established the pillar system. In Belgium, this social and political structure provides a full range of services for the lower classes from cradle to grave under the Catholic Church sponsorship. Examples like this show that the loss of religion's place in society is not inevitable.

66. Peter Beyer, "Secularization from the Perspective of Globalization: A Response to Dobbelaere," *Sociology of Religion* 60, no. 3 (1999): 290.

67. Jason DeParle, "Global Migration: A World Ever on the Move," *New York Times*, June 25, 2010.

68. United Nations Department of Economic and Social Affairs, Population Division, *Trends in International Migrant Stock: 2008 Revision* (POP/DB/MIG/Stock/Rev.2008), www.un.org/esa/population/migration/UN_MigStock_2008.pdf.

69. DeParle, "Global."

70. UN Department of Economic and Social Affairs, *Trends in International Migrant Stock*.

71. DeParle, "Global."

72. Diana Eck, *A New Religious America: How A "Christian Country" Has Become the World's Most Religiously Diverse Nation* (San Francisco: HarperCollins, 2002).

73. Pew Forum on Religion and Public Life, "U.S. Religious Landscape Survey: Religious Composition of the U.S.," (2007), http://religions.pewforum.org/pdf/affiliations-all-traditions.pdf.

74. Steven A. Camarota, "Immigrants in the United States, 2007: A Profile of America's Foreign-Born Population," Center for Immigration Studies (November 2007), 7, www.cis .org/immigrants_profile_2007.

75. Gastón Espinosa, Virgilio Elizondo, and Jesse Miranda, *Hispanic Churches in American Public Life: Summary of Findings*, Chicago Latino Congregations Study, Institute for Latino Studies at Notre Dame University (March 2003), 14, http://latinostudies.nd.edu/ cslr/research/pubs/HispChurchesEnglishWEB.pdf.

76. Robert Suro, Luis Logo, et al., "Changing Faiths: Latinos and the Transformation of American Religion," The Pew Hispanic Project and The Pew Forum on Religion and Public Life, April 25, 2007, 1, www.pewforum.org/Race/Changing-Faiths-Latinos-and -the-Transformation-of-American-Religion.aspx.

77. Carmen M. Cervantes and Ken Johnson-Mondragon, "Pastoral *Juvenil Hispana*, Youth Ministry and Young Adult Ministry," Instituto Fey y Vida Research Publications, 3.

78. Suro, Logo, et al., "Changing Faiths," 7.

79. Suro, Logo, et al., "Changing Faiths," 3.

80. Suro, Logo, et al., "Changing Faiths," 3.

81. Luis Guillermo Pineda, "Parishes Fail to Market Catholicism to Hispanics," *National Catholic Reporter*, January 19, 2007, 5a.

82. Espinosa, Elizondo, and Miranda, *Hispanic Churches in American Public Life*, 15.

83. Suro, Logo, et al., "Changing Faiths," 41.

84. Suro, Logo, et al., "Changing Faiths," 41.

85. "Religious Populations: Christianity Is Main Religion in Britain," *National Statistics Online: UK* (2004), www.statistics.gov.uk/cci/nugget.asp?id=954.

86. David Voas and Rodney Ling, "Religion in Britain and the United States," in *British Social Attitudes: The 26th Report*, ed. A. Park et al. (London: Sage, 2008).

87. British Social Attitudes Survey, "Religion and Beliefs: Some Surveys and Statistics" (2012), www.humanism.org.uk/campaigns/religion-and-belief-surveys-statistics.

88. Lois Rogers, "Britons Are Believers of 'Fuzzy Faith,' Says Survey," *Telegraph* (March 21, 2009), www.telegraph.co.uk/news/religion/5030049/Britons-are-believers-of-fuzzy -faith-says-survey.html.

89. Voas and Ling, "Religion in Britain and the United States," 69.

90. Julie Ray, "Worlds Apart: Religion in Canada, Great Britain, U.S.," *Gallup* (2003), www.gallup.com/poll/9016/worlds-apart-religion-canada-britain-us.aspx.

91. Gallup Organization, "Religion," *Gallup* (2010), www.gallup.com/poll/1690/ religion.aspx.

92. Voas and Ling, "Religion in Britain and the United States," 68.

93. Francis Campbell, "God in a Secular World" (presented at Greenhills Ecumenical Conference, Limerick, Ireland, 2008), http://ukinholysee.fco.gov.uk.

94. Quoted by Francis Campbell, who was the British ambassador to the Holy See (Vatican) from December 2005 to January 2011.

95. U.S. Department of State, *International Religious Freedom Report 2003—Sweden*, www.state.gov/j/drl/rls/irf/2003/24435.htm.

96. Rainer Muenz, "Europe: Population and Migration in 2005," *Migration Information Source* (2006), www.migrationinformation.org/Feature/display.cfm?ID=402.

97. Michael V. Hayden, "Transcript of Director's Remarks at the Landon Lecture Series," *News and Information* (2008), www.cia.gov/news-information/speeches-testimony/ speeches-testimony-archive-2008/landon-lecture-series.html.

98. Islamic Human Rights Commission, "London Muslim's Come Together in Good Faith—Launch of 'London Muslim Coalition,'" press release, March 28, 2003.

99. Adrian Michaels, "Muslim Europe: The Demographic Time Bomb Transforming Our Continent," *Telegraph*, August 8, 2009.

100. Pew Forum on Religion and Public Life, "An Uncertain Road: Muslims and the Future of Europe" (October 19, 2005), 16, www.pcwforum.org/Muslim/An-Uncertain -Road-Muslims-and-the-Future-of-Europe.aspx.

101. Pew Research Center, "Islamic Extremism: Common Concern for Muslim and Western Publics," *Pew Global Attitudes Project* (July 14, 2005), http://pewglobal.org/ reports/display.php?ReportID=248.

102. Pew Forum, "An Uncertain Road," 10.

103. Nick Cumming-Bruce and Steven Erlander, "Swiss Ban Building of Minarets on Mosques," *New York Times*, November 29, 2009.

104. Pew Forum, "An Uncertain Road," 12.

105. Pew Forum, "An Uncertain Road," 6.

106. Pew Forum, "An Uncertain Road."

107. Anne Applebaum, "Portents," *New Republic* 240, no. 21 (2009): 41.

108. Pew Forum on Religion and Public Life, "Is There a Global Resurgence of Religion?" (May 8, 2006), http://pewforum.org/events/?EventID=116.

109. Mary Mederios Kent, "Do Muslims Have More Children Than Other Women in Western Europe?" *Population Reference Bureau* (February 2008), www.prb.org/ Articles/2008/muslimsineurope.aspx?p=1.

110. Pew Forum on Religion and Public Life, *The Future of the Global Muslim Population: Projections for 2010–2030* (January 2011), www.pewforum.org/future-of-the-global -muslim-population-regional-europe.aspx.

111. George Martine, *UNFPA State of the World Population: Unleasing the Potential of Urban Growth*, UNFPA Report (2007), www.unfpa.org/swp/2007/english/introduction .html, chap. 2.

112. Martine, *UNFPA State of the World Population*, chap. 2.

113. Martine, *UNFPA State of the World Population*, chap. 2.

114. Peter L. Berger, "Global Pluralism and Religion," *Estudios Públicos* 98 (Autumn 2005): 3.

115. Peter L. Berger, "Religion and the West," *National Interest* 80 (2005): 114.

116. Pew Forum on Religion and Public Life, "Religion in a Globalizing World," Peter Berger at Faith Angle Conference, Key West, FL (December 4, 2006), http://pewforum.org/ events/?EventID=136.

117. Berger, "Religion and the West," 115.

118. Peter L. Berger, "Reflections on the Sociology of Religion Today," *Sociology of Religion* 62, no. 4 (2001): 449.

119. Berger, "Global Pluralism and Religion," 4.

120. Pew Forum, "Religion in a Globalizing World."

121. Pew Forum, "U.S. Religious Landscape Survey: Religious Composition of the U.S."

122. Pew Forum, "U.S. Religious Landscape Survey: Religious Composition of the U.S."

123. Anne McClintock, Aamir Mufti, and Ella Shohat, *Dangerous Liaisons: Gender, Nation, and Postcolonial Perspectives* (Minneapolis: University of Minnesota Press, 1997), 177.

124. Robert Adam, "Globalisation and Architecture: The Challenges of Globalisation Are Relentlessly Shaping Architecture's Relationship with Society and Culture," *Architectural Review* 223 (2008), 4.

125. Applebaum, "Portents," 39.

126. Adam, "Globalisation and Architecture."

127. Applebaum, "Portents," 39.

128. Edward Farley, "Fundamentalism: A Theory," *Cross Currents* 55, no. 3 (2005), www.crosscurrents.org/farley2005.htm.

129. Farley, "Fundamentalism."

130. Farley, "Fundamentalism."

131. Quoted in Guilain Denoeux, "The Forgotten Swamp: Navigating Political Islam," *Middle East Policy* 9, no. 2 (2002): 58.

132. Denoeux, "Forgotten Swamp," 58.

133. Farley, "Fundamentalism."

134. Mohammed M. Hafez, *Suicide Bombers in Iraq: The Strategy and Ideology of Martyrdom* (Washington, DC: U.S. Institute of Peace Press, 2007), 63–69.

135. Hafez, *Suicide Bombers in Iraq*, 73.

136. Pew Forum, "Religion in a Globalizing World."

137. Hafez, *Suicide Bombers in Iraq*, 70.

138. Pew Forum, "Religion in a Globalizing World."

139. Stephen Vertigans and Philip W. Sutton, "Globalisation Theory and Islamic Praxis," *Global Society: Journal of Interdisciplinary International Relations* 16, no. 1 (2002): 31–32.

140. Bryan S. Turner, "Islam, Religious Revival and the Sovereign State," *Muslim World* 97, no. 3 (2007).

141. Robert Wuthnow and Stephen Offutt, "Transnational Religious Connections," *Sociology of Religion* 69, no. 2 (2008): 209.

142. "Christians and Ancestors," editorial, *Studies in World Christianity* 9 (April 2003).

143. Philip Jenkins, *The New Faces of Christianity: Believing the Bible in the Global South* (New York: Oxford University Press, 2006), 98.

144. Todd Johnson, "Christianity in Global Context: Trends and Statistics," The Pew Forum on Religion and Public Life (2005), www.pewforum.org/uploadedfiles/Topics/Issues/Politics_and_Elections/051805-global-christianity.pdf.

145. Johnson, "Christianity in Global Context."

146. Philip Jenkins, "The Next Christianity," *Atlantic Monthly* 290, no. 3 (2002): 60.

147. Johnson, "Christianity in Global Context."

148. Johnson, "Demographic Futures," 17.

149. Pew Forum on Religion and Public Life, "The Coming Religious Wars? Demographics and Conflict in Islam and Christianity," roundtable discussion (May 18, 2005), www.pewforum.org/Politics-and-Elections/The-Coming-Religious-Wars-Demographics-and-Conflict-in-Islam-and-Christianity.aspx.

150. Johnson, "Demographic Futures," 17.

151. Glenn Masuchika, "Review—*The World Christian Encyclopedia: A Comparative Survey of Churches and Religions AD 30–AD 2200*, 2nd Edition," *Library Journal*, May 1, 2000.

152. Mark Noll, "Review of *World Christian Encyclopedia: A Comparative Survey of Churches and Religions in the Modern World*," *Church History* 71, no. 2 (2002): 449.

153. Some databases count those who do not belong to a religious organization as non-religious. Others only count those who mark "none" when asked about religion.

154. Becky Hsu et al., "Estimating the Religious Composition of All Nations: An Empirical Assessment of the World Christian Database," *Journal for the Scientific Study of Religion* 47, no. 4 (2008).

155. Todd Johnson, "My Journey into the Future: A Personal Essay" (presented at Foresight Conference, Regent University, Virginia Beach, VA, September 2005), www.regent.edu/acad/global/publications/for_proceedings/2005/toddjohnson_essay.pdf.

156. Johnson, "Demographic Futures," 16.

157. Johnson, "Demographic Futures," 16.

158. Richard D. Phillips, "Can Rising Rates of Church Participation Be a Consequence of Secularization?" *Sociology of Religion* 65, no. 2 (2004): 141.

159. Phillips, "Can Rising Rates," 141.

160. Frank Newport, "This Christmas, 78 Percent of Americans Identify as Christian," *Gallup: Well Being* (2009), www.gallup.com/poll/124793/This-Christmas-78-Americans -Identify-Christian.aspx.

161. Kevin J. Christiano and William H. Swatos Jr., "Secularization Theory: The Course of a Concept," *Sociology of Religion* 60, no. 3 (1999): 1.

162. Jeffry S. Passel and D'Vera Cohn, *Mexican Immigration: How Many Come? How Many Leave?* (Washington, DC: Pew Hispanic Center, 2009), i.

163. Pew Forum, "U.S. Religious Landscape Survey."

164. Rodney Stark and Laurence R. Iannaccone, "A Supply-Side Reinterpretation of the 'Secularization' of Europe," *Journal for the Scientific Study of Religion* 33, no. 3 (1994): 232.

165. Stark and Iannaccone, "A Supply-Side Reinterpretation," 232.

166. Stephen Sharot, "Beyond Christianity: A Critique of the Rational Choice Theory of Religion from a Weberian and Comparative Religions Perspective," *Sociology of Religion* (Winter 2002): 4–6.

167. Wikinvest, "Proctor & Gamble," www.wikinvest.com/stock/Procter_%26_ Gamble_Company_(PG).

168. Frank J. Lechner, "Rational Choice and Religious Economics," in *The Sage Handbook of the Sociology of Religion*, ed. James A. Beckford and N. Jay Demerath (Los Angeles: Sage, 2007), 83–84.

169. Lechner, "Rational Choice," 82.

170. Lechner, "Rational Choice," 83.

171. Rodney Stark and William Sims Bainbridge, *The Future of Religion: Secularization, Revival and Cult Formation* (Berkeley: University of California Press, 1986), 6.

172. Andrew Buckser, "Religion and the Supernatural on a Danish Island: Rewards, Compensators, and the Meaning of Religion," *Journal for the Scientific Study of Religion* 34, no. 1 (1995): 3.

173. Lechner, "Rational Choice," 84.

174. Lawrence Alfred Young, *Rational Choice Theory and Religion: Summary and Assessments* (New York: Routledge, 1997), 56.

175. Lechner, "Rational Choice," 87.

176. Lechner, "Rational Choice," 87.

177. R. Andrew Chestnut, *Competitive Spirits: Latin America's New Religious Economy* (New York: Oxford University Press, 2003), 3–4.

178. Stark and Iannaccone, "A Supply-Side Reinterpretation," 233.

179. Rodney Stark, "Catholic Contexts: Competition, Commitment and Innovation," *Review of Religious Research* 39, no. 3 (1998): 199.

180. Stark, "Catholic Contexts," 201.

181. Stark, "Catholic Contexts," 197.

182. Stark and Iannaccone, "A Supply-Side Reinterpretation," 241–44.

183. Stark and Iannaccone, "A Supply-Side Reinterpretation," 234–35.

184. Stark and Iannaccone, "A Supply-Side Reinterpretation," 234.

185. Lynda Barley, "Introduction: The Context for Churches Today," in *Church-Going in the UK*, ed. Jacinta Ashwort and Ian Farthing (Teddington, UK: Tearfund, 2007), 1.

186. Stark and Iannaccone, "A Supply-Side Reinterpretation," 244.

187. J. A. Coleman, "The Bible and Sociology," *Sociology of Religion* 60, no. 2 (1999).

188. Lechner, "Rational Choice," 87–88.

189. Peter Ellway, "Shopping for Faith or Dropping Your Faith," CSA Discovery Guides (May 2005), www.csa.com/discoveryguides/religion/overview.php#con.

190. Lechner, "Rational Choice," 83.

191. Pew Forum on Religion and Public Life, "Faith in Flux: Changes in Religious Affiliation in the U.S." (April 2009), http://pewforum.org/newassets/images/reports/flux/fullreport.pdf.

192. Lechner, "Rational Choice," 83.

193. Buckser, "Religion and the Supernatural on a Danish Island," 4.

194. Buckser, "Religion and the Supernatural on a Danish Island," 4.

195. Phillips, "Can Rising Rates," 145.

196. Pew Forum, "Faith in Flux."

197. Steve Bruce, *Choice and Religion: A Critique of Rational Choice Theory* (New York: Oxford University Press, 1999), 186.

198. Andrew K. T. Yip, "The Persistence of Faith among Nonheterosexual Christians: Evidence for the Neosecularization Thesis of Religious Transformation," *Journal for the Scientific Study of Religion* 41, no. 2 (2002), 210.

Bibliography

Abanes, Richard. "Christian Identity." In *Encyclopedia of Race and Racism*, edited by John Hartwell Moore, 312–15. Detroit, MI: Macmillan Reference USA, 2008.

Abdul-Wahhab, Sheikh Imam Muhammad, ed. *The Book of Tawheed*. Riyadh, Saudi Arabia: International Islamic Publishing House, 1998.

Adam, Robert. "Globalisation and Architecture: The Challenges of Globalisation Are Relentlessly Shaping Architecture's Relationship with Society and Culture." *Architectural Review* 223 (2008).

Addwesh, Abdulaziz. "The Hijab of Muslim Women." *Sultan Books.Org*, www.sultan .org/books/hijab.pdf.

Adiprasetya, Joas. "The 1893 World Parliament of Religions." In *The Boston Collaborative Encyclopedia of Modern Western Theology*, 2004. http://people.bu.edu/wwildman/ bce/worldparliamentofreligions1893.htm.

Ali, Lorraine. "Behind the Veil." *New York Times*, June 11, 2010.

Ali, Maulana Muhammad. *A Manual of Hadith*. New York: Taylor & Francis, 1995.

Alister Hardy Religious Experience Research Centre Archive. "Personal Stories." Lampeter, Wales: University of Wales: Trinity-Saint David.

Alister Hardy Religious Experience Research Centre, "Report on the China Project." The Alister Hardy Trust, University of Wales, Lampeter. www.trinitysaintdavid.ac.uk/en/ lrc/librariesandcentres/alisterhardyreligiousexperienceresearchcentre/research/report onthechinaproject.

Allamah Abd Allah bin Mahfuz bin Bayyah, et al. "Open Letter to His Holiness Pope Benedict X.V.I." http://hatzputra.blogspot.com/2006/09/open-letter-to-his-holiness-pope .html.

Allen, Douglas. *Myth and Religion in Mircea Eliade*. New York: Routledge, 2002.

Alles, Gregory D. "Toward a Genealogy of the Holy: Rudolf Otto and the Apologetics of Religion." *Journal of the American Academy of Religion* 69, no. 2.

Almond, Gabriel Abraham, R. Scott Appleby, and Emmanuel Sivan. *Strong Religion: The Rise of Fundamentalisms around the World*. Chicago: University of Chicago, 2003.

Almond, Philip C. *Rudolf Otto: An Introduction to His Philosophical Theology*. Chapel Hill: University of North Carolina Press, 1984.

Alper, Matthew. *The "God" Part of the Brain: A Scientific Interpretation of Human Spirituality and God*. 5th ed. Brooklyn, NY: Rogue Press, 2001.

Alston, William P. *Perceiving God: The Epistemology of Religious Experience*. Questia ed. Ithaca, NY: Cornell University Press, 1993.

American Academy of Religion. "The Religion Major and Liberal Education: A White Paper." *Religious Studies News*, 2008. www.teaglefoundation.org/learning/pdf/2008_aar_whitepaper.pdf (accessed March 22, 2010).

Amesbury, Richard. "Fideism." In *Stanford Encyclopedia of Philosophy*, edited by Edward N. Zalta, Fall 2009 edition. http://plato.stanford.edu/archives/fall2009/entries/fideism.

Antes, Jennifer Hope. "Reflections of Jennifer Hope Antes, Museum Anthropologist, on NAGPRA and the Museum of Natural History & Planetarium." In *Ethics and the Profession of Anthropology: Dialogue for Ethically Conscious Practice*, edited by Carolyn Fluehr-Lobban, 148–56. Lanham, MD: AltaMira, 2002.

Applebaum, Anne. "Portents." *New Republic* 240, no. 21 (2009): 38–41.

Appleby, R. Scott. *The Ambivalence of the Sacred: Religion, Violence, and Reconciliation*. Carnegie Commission on Preventing Deadly Conflict. Lanham, MD: Rowman & Littlefield, 1999.

———. "The Unholy Uses of the Apocalyptic Imagination: Twentieth Century Patterns." Working Paper, MacMillan Center Council on Middle East Studies, Yale University, 2002.

Appleby, R. Scott, Richard Cizik, and Thomas Wright. *Engaging Religious Communities Abroad: Report of the Task Force on Religion and the Making of U.S. Foreign Policy*. Chicago: Chicago Council on Global Affairs, 2010.

Appleton, Josie. "Battle of the Bones: Western Intellectuals, Not Native Peoples, Are Behind Moves to Repatriate Human Remains." *Spiked*, December 12, 2002. www.spiked-online.com/Articles/00000006DB8A.htm (accessed September 9, 2008).

Archbishop of Canterbury. "Archbishop Meets Chief Rabbis in Jerusalem." www.archbishopofcanterbury.org/1348?q=jewish+second+meeting+jerusalem.

Armstrong, Karen. "The True, Peaceful Face of Islam." *Time/CNN*, September 23, 2001. www.time.com/time/magazine/article/0,9171,1101011001-175987,00.html.

Arvidsson, Stephan. "Aryan Mythology as Science and Ideology." *Journal of the American Academy of Religion* 67, no. 2 (1999).

Asad, Talal. *Genealogies of Religion: Discipline and Reasons of Power in Christianity and Islam*. Baltimore: Johns Hopkins University Press, 1993.

———. "Reading a Modern Classic: W. C. Smith's *The Meaning and End of Religion*." *History of Religions* 40, no. 3 (2001): 205–22.

Association of Religion Data Archives, *General Social Survey*. 2004, 2006.

Avakian, Brad, and Susan Castillo. "Model Policy Regarding Religious Clothing of Public School Employees." Oregon Department of Education and Bureau of Labor and Industries. www.ode.state.or.us/news/announcements/announcement.aspx?=6961.

Avis, Paul, ed. *God and the Creative Imagination: Metaphor, Symbol, and Myth in Religion and Theology*. New York: Routledge, 1999.

Azari, Nina P., et al. "Neural Correlates of Religious Experience." *European Journal of Neuroscience* 13 (2001): 1649–52.

Azari, Nina P., and Dieter Birnbacher. "The Role of Cognition and Feeling in Religious Experience." *Zygon: Journal of Religion & Science* 39 (2004): 901–17.

Barley, Lynda. "Introduction: The Context for Churches Today." In *Church-Going in the UK*, edited by Jacinta Ashwort and Ian Farthing. Teddington, UK: Tearfund, 2007.

Barrett, Cyril, ed. *Ludwig Wittgenstein: Lectures and Conversations on Aesthetics, Psychology, and Religious Belief*. Berkeley: University of California Press, 1991.

Barrett, David B., George Thomas Kurian, and Todd M. Johnson, eds. *World Christian Encyclopedia: A Comparative Survey of Churches and Religions in the Modern World*. Oxford: Oxford University Press, 2000.

Barrett, Justin L. *Why Would Anyone Believe in God?* Lanham, MD: AltaMira, 2004.

Battilla, Carlyn. "Circles and Straight Lines." *Hohonu: A Journal of Academic Writing* 2, no. 2 (2004).

Beal, William E. "Why Study Religion?" *Department of Religious Studies.* www.case.edu/artsci/rlgn/WhyStudy.html.

Beauregard, Mario, and Denyse O'Leary. *The Spiritual Brain: A Neuroscientist's Case for the Existence of the Soul.* New York: HarperCollins, 2009.

Becker, Lawrence C., and Charlotte B. Becker. "Religion: Kant." In *Encyclopedia of Ethics Volume 3: P–W.* New York: Routledge, 2001.

Beidelman, T. O., and Robert A. Segal. "Smith, W. Robertson." In *Encyclopedia of Religion*, edited by Lindsay Jones, 12:8451–53. Detroit: Macmillan Reference USA, 2005.

"Belgium the Second European Union Nation to Implement Discriminatory Laws against Muslims." AhlulBayt News Agency, July 24, 2011. http://abna.ir/data.asp?lang=3&id=255306.

Bell, W. Ford. Comments on the 1024-Ad68 Ruling. www.aam-us.org/getinvolved/advocate/issues/upload/01_14_2008_AAM_Letter_re_NAGPRA_CUHR-2.pdf.

Bellinger, Charles. "René Girard and the Death Penalty." Society of Biblical Literature convened gathering. Brite University, February 23, 2008. http://libnt4.lib.tcu.edu/staff/bellinger/essays/girard_death.htmAccess.

Bemporad, Jack. "Suffering." In *Encyclopedia of Religion*, edited by Lindsay Jones, 13:8804–09. Detroit: Macmillan Reference USA, 2005.

Benard, Cheryl. *Civil Democratic Islam: Partners, Resources, and Strategies.* Santa Monica, CA: Rand Corporation, 2003.

Berger, Peter. "Epistemological Modesty: An Interview with Peter Berger." *Christian Century*, October 29, 1997, 972–78. www.religion-online.org/showarticle.asp?title=240 (accessed December 21, 2009).

———. "Global Pluralism and Religion." *Estudios Públicos* 98 (Autumn 2005).

———. "Reflections on the Sociology of Religion Today." *Sociology of Religion* 62, no. 4 (2001): 443–54.

———. "Religion and the West." *National Interest* 80 (2005): 112–19.

Bernardelli, Giorgio. "Islamic Prince to Attend Pope's Interfaith Meeting in Assisi." *Vatican Insider*, July 4, 2011.

Bersani, Michael. "Central New York Personal Injury Lawyer Explains Difference between 'Pain' and 'Suffering.'" *Central New York Injury Blog*, 2010. www.centralnewyorkinjurylawyer.com/2010/03/central-new-york-personal-inju-1.html (accessed June 23, 2010).

Beyer, Peter. "Secularization from the Perspective of Globalization: A Response to Dobbelaere." *Sociology of Religion* 60, no. 3 (1999): 289.

Bin Talal, Prince Ghazi bin Muhammad, et al. "A Common Word between Us: Summary and Abridgement." *A Common Word*, 2007. www.acommonword.com/index.php?lang-en&page-option1.

Blackburn, T. Simon. "Paradigm." In *The Oxford Dictionary of Philosophy.* Oxford: Oxford University Press, 2008.

Blanchard, Christopher M. "Islamic Religious Schools, Madrasas." 2008. www.fas.org/sgp/crs/misc/RS21654.pdf.

Bodhi, Bhikkhu. "The Way to End Suffering." *The Noble Eightfold Path*, 1984. www.vipassana.com/resources/8fp1.php (accessed June 23, 2010).

Bodiford, William M. "Dharma Transmission in Soto Zen: Manzan Dohaku's Reform Movement." *Monumenta Nipponica* 46, no. 4 (1991): 423–51.

Booth, Wayne C., Gregory G. Colomb, and Joseph M. Williams. *The Craft of Research.* 3rd ed. Chicago: University of Chicago Press, 2008.

Boyce, Mary. *Zoroastrians: Their Religious Beliefs and Practices.* New York: Routledge, 2001.

Boyer, Pascal. *Religion Explained: The Evolutionary Origins of Religious Thought.* New York: Basic Books, 2001.

———. "Why Do Gods and Spirits Matter At All?" In *Current Approaches in the Cognitive Science of Religion*, edited by Ilkka Pyysiainen and Veikko Anttonen, 68–92. New York: Continuum, 2002.

Brainard, F. Samuel. "Defining 'Mystical Experience.'" *Journal of the American Academy of Religion* 64, no. 2 (1996): 359–94.

Bregman, Lucy. "The Interpreter/Experiencer Split: Three Models in the Psychology of Religion." *Journal of the American Academy of Religion* 46, no. 2 (1978): 115–49.

Bremmer, Jan. "Scapegoat." *Encyclopedia of Religion*, edited by Lindsay Jones, 12:8143–46. Detroit: Macmillan Reference USA, 2005.

Brickman, Celia. "Primitivity, Race, and Religion in Psychoanalysis." *Journal of Religion* 82, no. 1 (2002): 53–74.

British Social Attitudes Survey. "Religion and Beliefs: Some Attitudes and Statistics" (2012). www.humanism.org.uk/campaigns/religion-and-belief-surveys-statistics.

Brooks, David. "The Neural Buddhists." *New York Times*, May 18, 2008.

Brown, Andrew. "Dawkins the Dogmatist." *Prospect Magazine*, October 2006. www.prospect-magazine.co.uk/article_details.php?id=7803.

Brown, Joseph Epes. *The Sacred Pipe: Black Elk's Account of the Seven Rites of the Oglala Sioux*. Norman: University of Oklahoma Press, 1989.

Bruce, Steve. *Choice and Religion: A Critique of Rational Choice Theory*. Oxford: Oxford University Press, 1999.

———. "Modernisation, Religious Diversity and Rational Choice in Eastern Europe." *Religion, State & Society* 27, nos. 3/4 (1999): 265.

Buckser, Andrew. "Religion and the Supernatural on a Danish Island: Rewards, Compensators, and the Meaning of Religion." *Journal for the Scientific Study of Religion* 34, no. 1 (1995): 1.

Cady, Duanne L. "Between Dogmatism and Relativism." *Journal of Religion, Conflict, and Peace* 1, no. 2 (2008). www.plowsharesproject.org/journal/php/article.php?issu_list_id=10&article_list_id=29

Camarota, Steven A. "Immigrants in the United States, 2007: A Profile of America's Foreign-Born Population." *Center for Immigration Studies*, 2007. www.cis.org/immigrants_profile_2007 (accessed January 5, 2010).

Campbell, David. "American Grace: How Religion Divides and Unites Us: A Conversation with David Campbell." *Press Luncheon with David Campbell and John Green*, 2010. www.pewforum.org/American-Grace--How-Religion-Divides-and-Unites-Us.aspx#1 (accessed February 15, 2012).

Campbell, Francis. "God in a Secular World." Presented at Greenhills Ecumenical Conference, Limerick, Ireland, 2008. http://ukinholysee.fco.gov.uk/resources/en/pdf/pdf1/080121-Greenhills (accessed January 21, 2012).

Campbell, Joseph. *The Hero with a Thousand Faces*. Princeton, NJ: Princeton University Press, 1968.

Capps, Walter H. *Religious Studies: The Making of a Discipline*. Minneapolis, MN: Fortress Press, 2000.

Cassirer, Ernst. *The Philosophy of Symbolic Forms: The Phenomenology of Knowledge*. Translated by Ralph Manheim. New Haven, CT: Yale University Press, 1977.

———. *The Problem of Knowledge: Philosophy, Science, and History since Hegel*. Translated by William H. Woglom and Charles W. Hendel. New Haven, CT: Yale University Press, 1950.

Cavanaugh, William T. "Behind the Common Question Lies a Morass of Unclear Thinking." *Harvard Divinity Bulletin* 35, no. 2 (2007). www.hds.harvard.edu/news/bulletin_mag/articles/35-23_cavanaugh.html.

———. "Does Religion Cause Violence?" Lecture at the University of Western Australia, Perth, Australia. www.catholicanarchy.org/cavanaugh/Cavanaugh%20-%20Does%20 Religion%20Cause%20Violence.pdf.

Center for International Development and Conflict Management. "Assessment for Moros in the Philippines." *Minorities At Risk Project*, 2003. www.cidcm.umd.edu/mar/assess ment.asp?groupId=84003.

Center for Inquiry. "The Secular Society and Its Enemies." www.centerforinquiry.net/ secularsociety.

Central Intelligence Agency. "Introduction-World." In *The World Factbook*. Washington, DC: Central Intelligence Agency, 2011.

Cervantes, Carmen M., and Ken Johnson-Mondragon. "Pastoral *Juvenil Hispana*, Youth Ministry and Young Adult Ministry." Instituto Fey y Vida Research Publications. http://www.feyvida.org/research/researchpubs.html (accessed January 5, 2010).

"Chāndogya Upaniṣad." In *Upaniṣads*, translated by Patrick Olivelle, 95–176. Oxford: Oxford University Press, 1996.

Chase, Oscar G., and Jerome S. Bruner. *Law, Culture, and Ritual: Disputing Systems in Cross-Cultural Context*. New York: New York University Press, 2005.

Chaves, Mark. "Secularization as Declining Religious Authority." *Social Forces* 72, no. 3 (1994): 749–74.

Chennakesavan, Sarasvati. "Yoga Sutras." *Asian Philosophy* 2, no. 2 (1992): 147.

Chestnut, R. Andrew. *Competitive Spirits: Latin America's New Religious Economy*. New York: Oxford University Press, 2003.

Chilton, Bruce. *The Temple of Jesus: His Sacrificial Program within a Cultural History of Sacrifice*. University Park: Pennsylvania State University Press, 1992.

Chopp, R. S. "2001 Presidential Address. Beyond the Founding Fratricidal Conflict: A Tale of Three Cities." *Journal of the American Academy of Religion* 70, no. 3 (2002): 461–74.

Christiano, Kevin J., and William H. Swatos Jr. "Secularization Theory: The Course of a Concept." *Sociology of Religion* 60, no. 3 (1999): 1

"Christians and Ancestors." Editorial *Studies in World Christianity*, 9 (April 2003), 1–4.

Clark, G. A. "NAGPRA, the Conflict between Science and Religion, and the Political Consequences." *SAA Bulletin* 165, no. 5 (1998). www.saa.org/Portals/0/SAA/publica- tions/SAAbulletin/16-5/index.html (accessed August 24, 2011).

Clayton, Philip. *Mind and Emergence: From Quantum to Consciousness*. New York: Oxford University Press, 2004.

Clifford, William K. "The Ethics of Belief (1887)." *The Secular Web*. www.infidels.org/ library/historical/w_k_clifford/ethics_of_belief.html (accessed September 21, 2009).

"Coalition Seeks Repeal of Klan-Era Ban on Religious Garb in Oregon Schools." *Catholic News Agency*, February 7, 2010. www.catholicnewsagency.com/news/coalition_seeks_re peal_of_klan-era_ban_on_religious_garb_in_oregon_schools. (accessed February 15, 2012).

Cohen, Noam. "Wikipedia Islam Entry Is Criticized." *New York Times*, February 5, 2008.

Coleman, J. A. "The Bible and Sociology." *Sociology of Religion* 60, no. 2 (1999): 125–48.

Coleridge, Samuel Taylor. *The Statesman's Manual; or, the Bible the Best Guide to Politi- cal Skill and Foresight: A Lay Sermon*. Oxford: Oxford University, 1832.

Connor, Steve. "'God Spot' Is Found in Brain." *Los Angeles Times*, October 29, 1997.

Cook, David. "The Apocalyptic Year 200/815–816 and the Events Surrounding It." In *Apoc- alyptic Time*, edited by Albert I. Baumgarten, 41–67. Leiden, Netherlands: Brill, 2000.

Cornille, Catherine. "Gurū." In *Encyclopedia of Religion*, edited by Lindsay Jones, 6:3712–15. Detroit: Macmillan Reference USA, 2005.

Cosgrove, Maureen. "Italy Lawmakers Approve Draft Burqa Ban Law." *Jurist Legal News and Research*, August 2, 2011. http://jurist.org/paperchase/2011/08/italy-lawmakers -approve-draft-burqa-ban-law.php.

Cox, Dan, Scott Clement, Gregory Smith, Allison Pond, and Neha Sahgal. "Non-Believers, Seculars, the Un-Churched and the Unaffiliated: Who Are Nonreligious Americans and How Do We Measure Them in Survey Research?" Presented at American Association for Public Opinion, Hollywood, FL, May 14–17, 2009. http://publicreligion.org/site/wp-content/uploads/2011/06/AAPOR-Paper-Final1.pdf.

Crawford, Suzanne J. "(Re) Constructing Bodies: Semiotic Sovereignty and the Debate over Kennewick Man." In *Repatriation Reader: Who Owns American Indian Remains?* edited by Devon A. Mihesuah, 211–36. Lincoln: University of Nebraska Press, 2000.

"Crossed Swords: Hindus against Proposed E.U. Swastika Ban." *Spiegel Online International*, January 17, 2007. http://www.spiegel.de/international/0,1518,460259,00.html.

Culler, Johathan D. *The Pursuit of Signs: Semiotics, Literature, Deconstruction.* Ithaca, NY: Cornell University Press, 2002.

Cumming-Bruce, Nick, and Steven Erlander. "Swiss Ban Building of Minarets on Mosques." *New York Times*, November 29, 2009.

d'Aquili, Eugene G., and Andrew Newberg. *The Mystical Mind: Probing the Biology of Religious Experience.* Minneapolis, MN: Fortress Press 1999.

Dawkins, Richard. *The God Delusion.* Boston: Houghton Mifflin, 2006.

———. "Is Science a Religion?" *The Humanist*, January/February 1997. www.thehumanist.org/humanist/articles/dawkins.html.

Deacon, Terrence W. *The Symbolic Species: The Co-Evolution of Language and the Brain.* New York: W. W. Norton, 1998.

Dear, Paula. "Women Vow to Protect Muslim Hijab." *BBC News*, July 14, 2004.

Deflem, Matthieu. "Ritual, Anti-Structure, and Religion: A Discussion of Victor Turner's Processual Symbolic Analysis." *Journal for the Scientific Study of Religion* 30, no. 1 (1991): 1–25.

Delaney, Tim, and Tim Madigan. *The Sociology of Sport: An Introduction.* Jefferson, NC: McFarland, 2009.

Deninger, Johannes. "Revelation." In *Encyclopedia of Religion*, edited by Lindsay Jones, 11:7773–79. Detroit: Macmillan Reference USA, 2005.

Dennett, Daniel C. *Breaking the Spell.* New York: Viking, 2006.

———. *Darwin's Dangerous Idea: Evolution and the Meanings of Life.* New York: Simon & Schuster, 1995.

———. "Teach Our Children Well." *On Faith: A Conversation on Religion with Jon Meacham and Sally Quinn*, March 8, 2007, *Washington Post*. http://newsweek.washingtonpost.com/onfaith/daniel_c_dennett/2007/03/teach_our_children_well.html (accessed March 8).

Dennett, Daniel C., Alister McGrath, and Madeleine Bunting. "Breaking the Spell: Religion as a Global Phenomenon." March 13, 2006. www.thersa.org/events/audio-and-past-events/breaking-the-spell--religion-as-a-global-phenomenon.

Denoeux, Guilain. "The Forgotten Swamp: Navigating Political Islam." *Middle East Policy* 9, no. 2 (2002): 56.

DeParle, Jason. "Global Migration: A World Ever on the Move." *New York Times*, June 25, 2010.

Derbyshire, John. "The Brat Pack of Quantum Mechanics." *New Atlantis: Journal of Theology and Society* (Summer 2008): 93–99. www.thenewatlantis.com/docLib/20080813_TNA21Derbyshire.pdf (accessed December 15, 2009).

Derlon, Bridgette, and Marie Mauzé. "'Sacred' or 'Sensitive' Objects." *European Cultural Heritage Online.* www.necep.net/papers/OS_Derlon-Mauze.pdf.

Dirks, Tom. "Filmsite Movie Review: *Raiders of the Lost Ark*." www.filmsite.org/raid.html.

Dobbelaere, Karel. "Towards an Integrated Perspective of the Processes Related to the Descriptive Concept of Secularization." *Sociology of Religion* 60, no. 3 (1999): 229.

Dow, James W. "Religions and Evolutionary Theory." Central States Anthropological Society. http://personalwebs.oakland.edu/~dow/personal/papers/religion/evolrel1.pdf.

Durkheim, Émile. *The Elementary Forms of Religious Life.* Translated by Karen E. Fields. New York: Free Press, 1995.

———. Excerpt from *The Rules of the Sociological Method.* Edited by Steven Lukes. Translated by W. D. Halls. New York: Free Press, 1982. http://media.pfeiffer.edu/lridener/DSS/Durkheim/SOCFACT.HTML.

Eck, Diana. *A New Religious America: How a "Christian Country" Has Become the World's Most Religiously Diverse Nation.* San Francisco: HarperCollins, 2002.

———. *Encountering God: A Spiritual Journey from Bozeman to Banaras.* Boston: Beacon Press, 2003.

Elgindy, Mona. "The End of an Era to Keep Religious Identity Out of Public Schools." 2009. http://www.luc.edu/law/academics/special/center/child/childed_forum/pdfs/elgindy_end_era.pdf (accessed February 15, 2012).

Eliade, Mircea. *Myth and Reality.* New York: HarperCollins, 1968.

———. *The Sacred and the Profane: The Nature of Religion.* Translated by Willard Trask. New York Harvest: Harcourt, 1959.

Ellway, Peter. "Shopping for Faith or Dropping Your Faith." CSA Discovery Guides, May 2005. www.csa.com/discoveryguides/religion/overview.php#con (accessed December 30, 2009).

Espinosa, Gastón, Virgilio Elizondo, and Jesse Miranda. "Hispanic Churches in American Public Life: Summary of Findings." Chicago Latino Congregations Study, Institute for Latino Studies at Notre Dame University (March 2003), 14. www.nd.edu/~latino/pubs/pubs/HispChurchesEnglishWEB.pdf (accessed January 5, 2010).

Esposito, John. "Islamophobia." Presented at Prince Alwaleed Bin Talal Center for Muslim-Christian Understanding, Georgetown University, 2006.

Evans, C. Stephen. *Faith beyond Reason.* Edinburgh, UK: Edinburgh University Press, 1998.

Ewing, Jim PathFinder. "Native American Spirituality." 2006. www.blueskywaters.com/page_82.pdf.

Ezegbobelu, Edmund Emeka. *Challenges of Interreligious Dialogue: Between the Christian and the Muslim Communities in Nigeria,* European University Studies. Series 23: Peter Lang, 2009.

Faris, James C. *The Nightway: A History and a History of Documentation of a Navajo Ceremonial.* Albuquerque: University of New Mexico Press, 1990.

Farley, Edward. "Fundamentalism: A Theory." *Cross Currents* 55, no. 3 (2005). www.crosscurrents.org/farley2005.htm (accessed January 6, 2010).

Feuerbach, Ludwig. *The Essence of Christianity.* New York: Harper, 1957.

———. "Preface to the Second Edition." In *The Essence of Christianity* (London: Trübner & Co., 1881).

Feuerbach, Ludwig, and Alexander Loos. *The Essence of Religion.* Amherst, NY: Prometheus Books, 2004.

Fidlin, Ken. "Inside NBC's Super Bowl Coverage." *TorontoSUN.com,* February 4, 2012. www.torontosun.com/2012/02/04/inside-nbcs-super-bowl-coverage.

"Final Statement of Catholic-Muslim Forum: Called to Be Instruments of Love and Harmony." *Zenit,* November 6, 2008.

Fisher, Ian. "Pope Apologizes for Uproar over His Remarks." *New York Times,* September 17, 2006.

———. "Pope Calls West Divorced from Faith, Adding a Blunt Footnote on Jihad." *New York Times,* September 13, 2006.

Fiske, John. *Myths and Myth Makers: Old Tales and Superstitions Interpreted.* Boston: James R. Osgood, 1873.

Flew, Anthony, R. M. Hare, and Basil Mitchell. *Philosophy of Religion: An Anthology*, edited by Charles Taliaferro and Paul J. Griffiths, 622. Malden, MA: Wiley-Blackwell, 2003.

Fluehr-Lobban, Carolyn, Pualani Kanaka'ole Kanehele, and Jennifer Hope Antes. "Repatriation of Indigenous Hawaiian Cultural Property by the City of Providence: A Case Study in Politics and Applied Law." In *Ethics and the Profession of Anthropology: Dialogue for Ethically Conscious Practice*, edited by Carolyn Fluehr-Lobban, 141–58. Lanham, MD: AltaMira Press, 2003.

Flynn, Gillian A. "Merging Traditional Indigenous Curation Methods with Modern Museum Standards of Care." In *Marie Malaro Award Competition: Museum Studies Program*, 1–22. Washington, DC: National Museum of Natural History, Department of Anthropology, George Washington University, 2001.

"Forecasts from *The Futurist* Magazine," 2009. www.wfs.org/forecasts.htm (accessed January 1, 2010).

Forman, Robert K. C. "Paramaartha and Modern Constructivists on Mysticism: Epistemological Monomorphism versus Duomorphism." *Philosophy East & West* 39, no. 4 (1989): 393–418.

———. *The Problem of Pure Consciousness.* New York: Oxford University Press, 1990.

Forrest, Peter. "The Epistemology of Religion." In *Stanford Encyclopedia of Religion*, edited by Edward N. Zalta, 2009 edition. http://plato.stanford.edu/archives/fall2009/entries/religion-epistemology.

Fowler, Lilly. "'Unaffiliated' Show Biggest Change among U.S. Faith Groups." *The Pew Forum: Religion News*, 2008. http://pewforum.org/news/display.php?NewsID=15039 (accessed October 2, 2009).

Fox, Jonathan. "Are Middle East Conflicts More Religious?" *Middle East Quarterly* (Fall 2001): 31–40.

———. "Are Religious Minorities More Militant Than Other Ethnic Minorities?" *Alternatives: Global, Local, Political* 28, no. 1 (2003): 92. www.questia.com/read/1G1-98831068.

———. "Counting the Causes and Dynamics of Ethnoreligious Violence." *Totalitarian Movements & Political Religions* 4 (2003): 119–44.

———. "The Future of Religion and Domestic Conflict." Presented at the Netherlands chapter of the Society for International Development, 2006.

———. "In the Name of God and Nation: The Overlapping Influence of Separatism and Religion on Ethnic Conflict." *Social Identities* 8, no. 3 (2002): 439–55.

———. "Religion, Politics and International Relations: The Rise of Religion and the Fall of the Civilization Paradigm as Explanations for Intra-State Conflict." *Cambridge Review of International Affairs* 20, no. 3 (2007): 361–82.

———. "The Rise of Religious Nationalism and Conflict: Ethnic Conflict and Revolutionary Wars, 1945–2001." *Journal of Peace Research* 41 (2004): 715–31.

Frazer, James. "Magic and Religion." In *The Golden Bough: A Study of Magic and Religion.* New York: Macmillian, 1922.

Frazer, James George. *The New Golden Bough: A New Abridgment of the Classic Work.* Edited by Theodor H. Gaster. Garden City, NY: Doubleday, 1961.

Freud, Sigmund. *The Future of an Illusion.* Edited by James Strachey. New York: Norton, 1989.

———. *Totem and Taboo: Resemblances between the Psychic Lives of Savages and Neurotics.* Translated by A. A. Brill. New York: Moffat Yard, 1918.

Fuller, Robert C. *Spiritual but Not Religious: Understanding Unchurched America.* New York: Oxford University Press, 2001.

Gall, Carlotta. "Afghans Consider Rebuilding Bamiyan Buddhas." *New York Times*, November 5, 2006.

Gallup Organization. "Gallup Poll Topics and Trends: Religions." In *Gallup Brain* (2007).

————. "Religion." *Gallup*, 2010. www.gallup.com/poll/1690/religion.aspx (accessed June 28, 2010).

Geertz, Clifford. "Religion as a Cultural System." In *The Interpretation of Cultures: Selected Essays*, 87–125. New York: Basic Books, 1973.

————. "Thick Description: Toward an Interpretive Theory of Culture." In *The Interpretation of Cultures: Selected Essays*, 3–30. New York: Basic Books, 1973.

Gellman, Jerome. "Mysticism." In *The Stanford Encyclopedia of Philosophy*, edited by Edward N. Zalta. Stanford, CA: Stanford University Press, 2011.

al-Ghazali, Abu Hamid Muhammad. *The Incoherence of the Philosophers*. Salt Lake City, UT: Brigham Young University, 2002.

Gibbon, Kate Fitz. *Who Owns the Past? Cultural Policy, Cultural Property, and the Law*. New Brunswick, NJ: Rutgers University Press, 2005.

Gilkey, Langdon. *Naming the Whirlwind: The Renewal of God-Language*. Indianapolis, IN: Bobbs-Merrill, 1969.

Gill, Sam D. *Storytracking: Texts, Stories, and Histories in Central Australia*. New York: Oxford University Press, 1998.

Girard, René. *Deceit, Desire, and the Novel: Self and Other in Literary Structure*. Translated by Yvonne Freccero. Baltimore: Johns Hopkins University Press, 1976.

————. *The Girard Reader*. Edited by James G. Williams. New York: Crossroad Publishing, 1996.

————. *I See Satan Fall Like Lightning*. Maryknoll, NY: Orbis, 2001.

————. *Things Hidden Since the Foundation of the World*. Translated by Stephen Bann and Michael Metteer. Stanford, CA: Stanford University Press, 1987.

Girard, René, and Patrick Gregory. *Violence and the Sacred*. New York: Continuum, 2005.

Goldman, Alvin I. "Religious Belief, Epistemology Of." In *A Companion to Epistemology*, edited by Jonathan Dancy and Ernest Sosa, 436. Cambridge, MA: Blackwell, 2000.

Goldman, David. "2008 Outlook: Fasten Your Seatbelts." *CNNMoney.com*, January 2, 2008. http://money.cnn.com/2007/12/28/markets/2008_predictions (accessed January 2, 2010).

Goldstein, Lynn, and Keith Kintigh. "Ethics and the Reburial Controversy." In *Repatriation Reader: Who Owns American Indian Remains?* edited by Devon A. Mihesuah, 181–91. Lincoln: University of Nebraska, 1990.

Golian, Jennifer. "Expressing Their Faith." *Sun Sentinel*, October 29, 2007.

Goodenough, Ursula, and Terrence W. Deacon. "The Sacred Emergence of Nature." In *The Oxford Handbook of Science and Religion*, edited by Philip Clayton and Zachary Simpson, 851–69. New York: Oxford University Press, 2006.

Gopin, Marc. *Between Eden and Armageddon: The Future of World Religions, Violence, and Peacemaking*. Oxford: Oxford University Press, 2000.

————. "Dialogue: A Different Model of Peacemaking." *Harvard Divinity Bulletin* 35, no. 4 (2007). www.hds.harvard.edu/news/bulletin_mag/articles/35-4_gopin.html.

————. *Holy War, Holy Peace: How Religion Can Bring Peace to the Middle East*. New York: Oxford University Press, 2002.

Gort, Jerald D., ed. *On Sharing Religious Experience: Possibilities of Interfaith Mutuality*. Vol. 4 of *Currents of Encounter*. Edited by Rein Fernbout and Anton Wessels. Grand Rapids, MI: Eerdmans, 1992.

Government Accounting Office. *Summary—Native American Graves Protection and Repatriation Act: After Almost 20 Years, Key Federal Agencies Still Have Not Fully Complied with the Act.* GAO-10-768. www.gao.gov/products/GAO-10-768.

Grasso, Michael. "The Archetype of Death and Enlightenment." In *The Near-Death Experience: A Reader*, edited by Lee Worth Bailey and Jenny L. Yates, 409. New York: Routledge, 1996.

Gross, Jaime. "Prayers at an Exhibition: Bhutan's Art and the Monks Who Protect It." *New York Times*, September 5, 2008.

Gross, Rita M. *Feminism and Religion: An Introduction.* 2nd ed. Boston: Beacon Press, 1996.

Gunasekara, Victor. "Buddhism and Revelation: Refutation of a Theory." *Vinamasa* 25 (September 1988). www.vgweb.org/bsq/revelation.htm (accessed October 10, 2009).

Gutsche, Robert Jr. "Museum Collections Shrink as Tribes Reclaim Artifacts: Problem of Caring for the Items Persists." *Washington Post*, March 9, 2006, 1.

Habermas, Jürgen. "Notes on a Post-Secular Society." *signandsight.com*, June 6, 2008. www.signandsight.com (accessed December 21, 2009).

Hafez, Mohammed M. *Suicide Bombers in Iraq: The Strategy and Ideology of Martyrdom.* Washington, DC: U.S. Institute of Peace Press, 2007.

Hagerty, Barbara Bradley. "How Our Brains Are Wired for Belief." Paper presented at the Faith Angle Conference on Religion, Key West, Florida, May 5, 2008.

Haggerson, Michael. "Netherlands to Propose Burqa Ban." *Jurist Legal News and Research*, September 16, 2011. http://jurist.org/paperchase/2011/09/netherlands-to-propose-burqa-ban.php.

Hamburg, David A., and Cyrus R. Vance, eds. "Chapter 2: When Prevention Fails: How and Why Deadly Conflict Arises." In *Preventing Deadly Conflict: Final Report.* New York: Carnegie Corporation of New York, 1997.

Hamer, Dean H. *The God Gene: How Faith Is Hardwired into Our Genes.* New York: Doubleday, 2004.

Hammon, Betsy. "Governor Signs Repeal on Teachers' Religious Dress; Ban Will Lift in July 2011." *OregonLive.Com*, April 1, 2010. www.oregonlive.com/education/index.ssf/2010/04/governor_signs_repeal_on_teach.html (accessed February 15, 2012).

———. "Oregon Teachers May Get OK to Wear Religious Clothing in Class." *OregonLive.Com*, November 23, 2009. www.oregonlive.com/education/index.ssf/2009/11/oregon_teachers_may_get_ok_to.html (accessed February 15, 2012).

Harrelson, Walter. "Myth and Ritual School." In *Encyclopedia of Religion*, edited by Lindsay Jones, 9:6380–83. Detroit: Macmillan Reference USA, 2005.

Harris, Sam. *The End of Faith: Religion, Terror, and the Future of Religion.* New York: W. W. Norton, 2004.

Harrison, Jane Ellen. *Ancient Art and Ritual.* Kila, MT: Kessinger, 1996.

———. *Ancient Art and Ritual.* New York: Greenwood Press, 1969.

———. "The Influence of Darwinism on the Study of Religions." In *Alpha and Omega.* New York: AMS Press, 1973.

———. *Themis: A Study of the Social Origins of Greek Religion.* New York: Cambridge University Press, 1927.

Harrison, Peter. "'Science' and 'Religion': Constructing the Boundaries." *Journal of Religion* 86, no. 1 (2006): 81–106.

Hart, Laurel. "World Religious Leaders Reject Violence and 'Hijacking of Religion' at Religions for Peace World Assembly." *Religions for Peace: 8th World Assembly*, 2006. www.wcrp.org/files/PR-Opening-08-26-2006.pdf.

Harvey, Van. "The Ethics of Belief and Two Conceptions of Christian Faith." *International Journal for Philosophy of Religion* 63, nos. 1–3 (2008): 39–54.

Hawthorne, Sîan. "Feminism: Feminism, Gender Studies, and Religion." *Encyclopedia of Religion*, edited by Lindsay Jones, 5:3023–27 (Detroit, MI: Macmillan Reference USA, 2005).

Hayden, Michael V. "Transcript of Director's Remarks at the Landon Lecture Series." *News and Information*, 2008. www.cia.gov/news-information/speeches-testimony/speeches-testimony-archive-2008/landon-lecture-series.html (accessed January 7, 2010).

Heim, S. Mark. "Visible Victim: Christ's Death to End Sacrifice." *Christian Century* 19 (March 14, 2001).

Heimbrock, Hans-Günter, and H. Barbara Boudewijnse. *Current Studies on Rituals: Perspectives for the Psychology of Religion*. Edited by H. Barbara Boudewijnse. Amsterdam, The Netherlands: Rodopi, 1990.

Henry, James Pepper. "Twenty Years and Counting: James Pepper Henry's Multifaceted View of NAGPRA." *Museum* (November–December 2010).

Herling, Brad. "Why Study Religion?" *American Academy of Religion: Teaching and Learning Center.* www.aarweb.org.

Hexham, Irving, and Karla Poewe. "U.F.O. Religion: Making Sense of the Heaven's Gate Suicides." *Christian Century*, May 7, 1997, 439–40. http://people.ucalgary.ca/~nurelweb/papers/irving/HGCC.html (accessed December 15, 2009).

Hick, John. *The Fifth Dimension: An Exploration of the Spiritual Realm*. Oxford: Oneworld Publications, 1999.

———. *An Interpretation of Religion: Human Responses to the Transcendent.* 2nd ed. New Haven, CT: Yale University Press, 2005.

Hidalgo, Ellie. "Our Lady of Guadalupe Called 'Mother without Borders' in Los Angeles." Catholic News Service, December 5, 2007.

Hierotheos, Metropolitan of Nafpaktos. *Orthodox Psychotherapy: The Science of the Fathers*. Translated by Esther Williams. Levadia, Greece: Holy Monastery of the Virgin Birth, 1994.

Hinnells, John R. *The Routledge Companion to the Study of Religion*. New York: Routledge, 2009.

Hitt, Jack. "This Is Your Brain on God." *Wired*, November 1999. www.wired.com/wired/archive/7.11/persinger.html?pg=5&topic=&topic_set= (accessed March 25, 2009).

Hollenback, Jess Byron. *Mysticism: Experience, Response, and Empowerment*. University Park: Pennsylvania University Press, 1996.

Holm, Nils G. "Mysticism and Intense Experiences." *Journal for the Scientific Study of Religion* 21, no. 3 (September 1982).

Honey, Charles. "Belief in Hell Dips, but Some Say They've Already Been There." Pew Forum on Religion and Public Life, Religion News on the Web, April 14, 2008. www.pewforum.org/Religion-News/Religion-News-on-the-Web.aspx.

Hood, Ralph W. Jr. "The Common Core Thesis in the Study of Mysticism." In *Where God and Science Meet*, Vol. 3 of *The Psychology of Religious Experience*, edited by Patrick McNamara. Westport, CT: Praeger, 2006.

Hood, Ralph W., Jr., et al. "Dimensions of the Mysticism Scale: Confirming the Three-Factor Structure in the United States and Iran," *Journal for the Scientific Study of Religion* 40, no. 4 (2001).

Hsu, Becky, A. M. Y. Reynolds, Conrad Hackett, and James Gibbon. "Estimating the Religious Composition of All Nations: An Empirical Assessment of the World Christian Database." *Journal for the Scientific Study of Religion* 47, no. 4 (2008): 678–93.

Hudson, Donal. *Ludwig Wittgenstein: The Bearing of His Philosophy on Religious Belief*. Richmond, VA: John Knox Press, 1968.

"Hui Mālama I Nā Kupuna O Hawai`i Nei" ("Dispute over a Native Hawaiian Sacred Object," 1996). http://huimalama.tripod.com/index.html.

Human Development Report. "Table 1: Human Development Index and Its Components." United Nations Development Program, 2004. http://hdr.undp.org/en/media/hdr04_complete.pdf.

———. "Table 1: Human Development Index and Its Components." United Nations Development Program, 2011. http://hdr.undp.org/en/media/HDR_2011_EN_Table1.pdf.

Hunt, Harry T. *On the Nature of Consciousness: Cognitive, Phenomenological, and Transpersonal Perspectives*. New Haven, CT: Yale University Press, 1995.

Huntington, Samuel. *Clash of Civilizations: The Remaking of World Order*. New York: Simon & Schuster, 1997.

———. "The Clash of Civilizations?" *Foreign Affairs* (Summer 1993).

Huxley, Aldous. *The Perennial Philosophy: An Interpretation of the Great Mystics, East and West*. New York: HarperCollins, 2004.

"In Graphic: Muslim Veils." *BBC News*, June 15, 2010. http://news.bbc.co.uk/2/shared/spl/hi/pop_ups/05/europe_muslim_veils/html/1.stm.

Islamic Human Rights Commission. "London Muslim's Come Together in Good Faith—Launch of 'London Muslim Coalition.'" Press release, March 28, 2003.

Jacobsen, Thorkild. *The Treasurers of Darkness: A History of Mesopotamian Religion*. New Haven, CT: Yale University Press, 1976.

James, Henry, ed. *The Letters of William James*. Boston: Atlantic Monthly Press, 1920.

James, William. "Talks to Teachers on Psychology; and to Students on Some of Life's Ideals." In *Talks*. New York: Henry Holt, 1925.

———. *The Varieties of Religious Experience*. Electronic Text Center edition, University of Virginia. New York: Modern Library, 1902.

———. *The Varieties of Religious Experience*. New York: Simon & Schuster, 1997.

Janz, Bruce. "Mysticism and Understanding: Steven Katz and His Critics." *Studies in Religion* 24, no. 1 (1995): 77–94.

Jehl, Douglas. "Holy War Lured Saudis as Rulers Looked Away." *New York Times*, December 27, 2001.

Jenkins, Philip. *The New Faces of Christianity: Believing the Bible in the Global South*. New York: Oxford University Press, 2006.

———. "The Next Christianity." *Atlantic Monthly* 290, no. 3 (2002): 53–68.

Jenkins, Tiffany. "The Censoring of Our Museums." *New Statesman*, July 11, 2005. www.newstatesman.com/200507110035 (accessed September 9, 2008).

Johnson, George. "Indian Tribes' Creationists Thwart Archeologists." *New York Times*, October 22, 1996.

Johnson, Greg. "Ancestors before Us: Manifestations of Tradition in a Hawaiian Dispute." *Journal of the American Academy of Religion* 71, no. 2 (2003): 327–46.

Johnson, Todd. "Christianity in Global Context-Trends and Statistics." The Pew Forum on Religion and Public Life, 2005. www.pewforum.org/uploadedfiles/Topics/Issues/Politics_and_Elections/051805-global-christianity.pdf (accessed January 6, 2010).

———. "Demographic Futures for Christianity and the World Religions." *Dialog: A Journal of Theology* 43, no. 1 (2004): 10–19.

———. "My Journey into the Future: A Personal Essay." Presented at Foresight Conference, Regent University, Virginia Beach, VA, September 2005. www.regent.edu/acad/global/publications/for_proceedings/2005/toddjohnson_essay.pdf.

Johnson, Todd M., David B. Barrett, and Peter F. Crossing. "Christianity 2010: Status of Global Mission." *International Bulletin of Missionary Research* 34, no. 1 (2010).

Johnston, Charles. "The Yoga Sutras of Patañjali: The Book of the Spiritual Man." In *An Interpretation by Charles Johnston*. New York: Charles Johnston, 1912.

Johnston, Douglas, Azhar Hussain, and Ahmed Younis. "Madrasas and the Global War on Terror." Presented at Conflict Prevention and Resolution Forum, Washington, DC. Sponsored by Search for Common Ground (The Johns Hopkins University, SAIS, September 12, 2006). International Center for Religion and Diplomacy. http://icrd.non-profitsoapbox.com/index.php?option=com_content&task=view&id=132&Itemid=133.

Johnston, Douglas M. "How One Organization Is Transforming Pakistani Madrasas." *On Faith: A Conversation on Religion and Politics. Washington Post*, August 11, 2011.

Johnston, Douglas M., Azhar Hussain, and Ahmed Younis. "Madrasas and the Global War on Terror." Conflict Prevention and Resolution Forum. Washington, D.C. http://www.sfcg.org/Documents/CPRF/september_2006.pdfAccess.

Jones, Jeff, and Lydia Saad. "Gallup Poll Social Series: Values and Beliefs." *Gallup News Service*, 2011. www.gallup.com/poll/File/147890/Belief_in_God_110603%20.pd.

Jones, Peter N. *Respect for Ancestors: American Indian Cultural Affiliation in the American West*. Boulder, CO: Bäuu Institute Press, 2005.

Juergensmeyer, Mark. *The New Cold War? Religious Nationalism Confronts the Secular State*. Berkeley: University of California Press, 1994.

———. *Terror in the Mind of God: The Global Rise of Religious Violence*. Edited by Mark Juergensmeyer. Berkeley: University of California Press, 2001.

———. "Terror in the Name of God." *Current History* 100, no. 649 (2001): 357.

———. "The Worldwide Rise of Religious Nationalism." *Journal of International Affairs* 50, no. 1 (1996). www.questia.com/read/1G1-18623939.

Jung, C. G. *Symbols of Transformation*. Translated by R. F. C. Hull. 2nd ed. Princeton, NJ: Princeton University Press, 1967.

Kaminsky, Joel. "Violence in the Bible." *SBL Forum* (June 2006). http://sbl-site.org/publications/article.aspx?articleId=159.

Kant, Immanuel. *Religion within the Boundaries of Reason Alone*. 1793; Cambridge: Cambridge University Press, 1999.

Katz, Steven T. "Language, Epistemology, and Mysticism." In *Mysticism and Philosophical Analysis*, edited by Steven T. Katz, 22–74. New York: Oxford University Press, 1978.

Katz, Stephen T., ed. *Mysticism and Philosophical Analysis*. New York: Oxford University Press, 1978.

Keddie, Nikki R. "Secularism and Its Discontents." *Daedalus* 132, no. 3 (2003).

Kedourie, Elie. *Nationalism*. 4th ed. Malden, MA: Blackwell, 1993.

Keeter, Scott, and Gregory Smith. *Muslim Americans: Middle Class and Mostly Mainstream*. Washington, DC: Pew Research Center, 2007.

Keeter, Scott, and Gregory Smith. "Muslim Americans: No Signs of Growth in Alienation or Support for Extremism." Pew Research Center, August 30, 2011.

Kelly, Robert L. "Bones of Contention." *New York Times*, December 12, 2010.

Kent, Mary Mederios. "Do Muslims Have More Children Than Other Women in Western Europe?" *Population Reference Bureau*, February 2008. www.prb.org/Articles/2008/muslimsineurope.aspx?p=1.

Kiefer, Heather Mason. "Divine Subjects: Canadians Believe, Britons Skeptical." *Gallup Brain* (2004).

King, Ursula. "General Introduction: Gender-Critical Turns in the Study of Religion." In *Gender, Religion, and Diversity*, edited by Ursula King. London: Continuum, 2004.

———. "Is There a Future for Religious Studies as We Know It? Some Postmodern, Feminist, and Spiritual Challenges." *Journal of the American Academy of Religion* 70, no. 2 (2002): 365–88.

Kirby, Emma Jane. "Sarkozy Stirs French Burka Debate." *BBC News*, June 22, 2009. http://news.bbc.co.uk/2/hi/8113778.stm.

Kleinefelter, Donald S. "D. Z. Phillips as Philosopher of Religion." *Journal of the American Academy of Religion* 42, no. 2 (1974): 307–25.

Kluger, Jeffrey, Jeff Chu, Broward Liston, Maggie Sieger, and Daniel Williams. "Is God in Our Genes?" *Time* 164, no. 17 (2004): 62–72.

Knight, Peter, ed. *Conspiracy Theories in American History: An Encyclopedia*. Santa Barbara, CA: ABC-CLIO, 2003.

Kramer, Martin. "Said's Splash," in *Ivory Towers on Sand: The Failure of Middle Eastern Studies in America.* Washington, DC: Washington Institute for Near East Policy, 2001.

Kraus, Bambi, Peter Pino, and Gary Roybal. Panel Discussion: NAGPRA's Newest Rule—43 CFR 10.11, presented at School for Advanced Research, Santa Fe, New Mexico, February 24, 2011. http://sarweb.org/?iarc_lecture_peter_pino_gary_roybal-p:past_events.

Larsson, J. P. *Understanding Religious Violence: A New Framework for Conflict Transformation*. Lampeter: University of Wales, 2002.

Laubach, Marty. "The Social Effects of Psychism: Spiritual Experience and the Construction of Privatized Religion." *Sociology of Religion* 65, no. 3 (2004): 239–63.

Lazar, S. W., C. E. Kerr, R. H. Wasserman, J. R. Gray, D. N. Greve, M. T. Treadway, M. McGarvey, B. T. Quinn, J. A. Dusek, H. Benson, S. L. Rauch, C. I. Moore, and B. Fischl. "Meditation Experience Is Associated with Increased Cortical Thickness." *Neuroreport* 16, no. 17 (2005): 1893–97.

Lechner, Frank J. "Rational Choice and Religious Economics." In *The Sage Handbook of the Sociology of Religion*, edited by James A. Beckford and N. Jay Demerath, 81–97. Los Angeles: Sage, 2007.

Lee, Jennifer Joan. "International Education: Expulsions over Veil Intensify French Debate on Secularity." *New York Times*, October 21, 2003.

Levesque, Paul. *Symbols of Transcendence: Religious Expression in the Thought of Louis Dupre.* Grand Rapids, MI: Wm. B. Eerdmans Publishing, 1997.

Lincoln, Bruce. *Holy Terrors: Thinking about Religion after September 11*. Chicago: University of Chicago Press, 2003.

Lipton, Peter. *Inference to the Best Explanation*. 2nd ed. New York: Routledge, 2004.

The List: The World's Fastest-Growing Religions." *Foreign Policy*, May 14, 2007. www .foreignpolicy.com/articles/2007/05/13/the_list_the_worlds_fastest_growing_religions (accessed December 28, 2009).

Locke, John. "A Letter Concerning Toleration." 1689. The Constitution Society. www .constitution.org/jl/tolerati.htm.

Loh, Larry. "McDonald's Frantic Backpedaling: The Pig Toy Fiasco." *CNNGo.co*, January 25, 2010. www.cnngo.com/singapore/none/mcdonalds-pig-toy-fiasco-371923#ixzz1Z53bIPC4.

Love, Rick, Carl Moeller, and Jason Micheli. "Have Muslim-Christian Relations Improved since 9/11?" *A Common Word* (republished from *Christianity Today*, September 14, 2011). http://acommonword.com/en/a-common-word-in-the-news/19-new-news-items/459-have-muslim-christian-relations-improved-since-911.html.

Luckert, Karl W., and Johnny C. Cooke. *Coyoteway: A Navajo Holyway Healing Ceremonial*. Tucson: University of Arizona Press and the Museum of Northern Arizona Co-Publishers, 1979.

Ludwig, Theodore M. "Ordination." In *Encyclopedia of Religion*, edited by Lindsay Jones, 10:6851–60. Detroit: Macmillan Reference USA, 2005.

Lugo, Luis, and Alan Cooperman. "U.S. Religious Knowledge Survey." 2010. http://pew forum.org/uploadedFiles/Topics/Belief_and_Practices/religious-knowledge-full-report .pdf (accessed September 26, 2011).

Lukoff, David. "Visionary Spirituality and Mental Disorders." In *Altering Consciousness: Multidisciplinary Perspectives*, Volume 2, edited by Etzel Cardeña and Michael Winkelman. Santa Barbara, CA: Praeger, 2011.

Lusthaus, Dan. "Buddhism, Yogacara School Of." In *Routledge Encyclopedia of Philosophy*. London: Routledge, 1998.

Lyng v. Northwest Indian Cemetery Protective Association, 485 U.S. 439 (1988).

Lyons, Linda. "Paranormal Events Come (Super)Naturally to Some." 2005. www.gallup.com/poll/19558/Paranormal-Beliefs-Come-SuperNaturally-Some.aspx (accessed December 16, 2009).

MacDonald, Graham. "Ayer, Alfred Jules: Verificationism." In *Routledge Encyclopedia of Philosophy*, edited by E. Craig. London: Routledge, 1998.

MacGregor, Geddes. "Doubt and Belief." In *Encyclopedia of Religion*, edited by Lindsay Jones, 4:2423–29. Detroit: Macmillan Reference USA, 2005.

Mahidol University. "The Rituals and Traditions of Thai Classical Dance." www.mahidol.ac.th/thailand/classical-dance.html (accessed September 13, 2008).

Mahoney, Timothy A. "Contextualism, Decontextualism, and Perennialism: Suggestions for Expanding the Common Ground of the World's Mystical Traditions." Presented at Twentieth World Congress of Philosophy, Boston, MA, August 10–15, 1998. www.bu.edu/wcp/Papers/Reli/ReliMaho.htm.

"Māṇḍūkya Upaniṣad." In *Upaniṣads*, translated by Patrick Olivelle, 288–90. Oxford: Oxford University Press, 1996.

Manzari, Joe. "Faith and Rationality: A Defense of Plantinga's Reformed Epistemology." www.joemanzari.com/papers/far.pdf (accessed October 30, 2009).

March, Fred. "How to Counter Religion's Toxic Effects." *Humanist* 67, no. 3 (2007): 35–37.

Martine, George. *UNFPA State of the World Population: Unleashing the Potential of Urban Growth.* UNFPA Report, 2007. www.unfpa.org/swp/2007/english/introduction.html (accessed January 2, 2010).

Marx, Karl. "A Contribution to the Critique of Hegel's Philosophy of Right: Introduction." www.marxists.org/archive/marx/works/1843/critique-hpr/intro.htm (accessed July 30, 2009).

———. "Theses on Feuerbach." www.marx2mao.com/M&E/TF45.html (accessed July 30, 2009).

Maslow, Abraham H. "Appendix A: Religious Aspects of Peak-Experiences." In *Religions, Values, and Peak Experiences.* New York: Penguin, 1964.

———. *Religions, Values, and Peak Experiences.* New York: Penguin, 1964.

Masuchika, Glenn. "Review—The World Christian Encyclopedia: A Comparative Survey of Churches and Religions AD 30–AD 2200, 2nd Edition." *Library Journal*, May 1, 2000, 104. http://web.ebscohost.com/ehost/pdfviewer/pdfviewer?sid=7fd066a7-6b79-49e0-ad95-4b2f1aa4f66f%40sessionmgr12&vid=2&hid=15 (accessed September 4, 2011).

Masuzawa, Tomoko. *The Invention of World Religions; or, How European Universalism Was Preserved in the Language of Pluralism.* Chicago: University of Chicago Press, 2005.

McCauley, Robert N., and Harvey Whitehouse. "Introduction: New Frontiers in the Cognitive Science of Religion." *Journal of Cognition & Culture* 5, nos. 1–2 (2005): 1–13.

McClintock, Anne, Aamir Mufti, and Ella Shohat. *Dangerous Liaisons: Gender, Nation, and Postcolonial Perspectives.* Minneapolis: University of Minnesota Press, 1997.

McCutcheon, Russell. "The Category 'Religion' and the Politics of Tolerance." In *Defining Religion: Investigating the Boundaries between the Sacred and Secular*, edited by Arthur L. Greil and D. Bromley. Amsterdam, Netherlands: Elsevier, 2003.

McCutcheon, Russell T. *Critics Not Caretakers: Redescribing the Public Study of Religion.* Albany: State University of New York Press, 2001.

——. "A Default of Critical Intelligence? The Scholar of Religion as Public Intellectual." *Journal of the American Academy of Religion* 65, no. 2 (1997).

McGaa, Ed. *Mother Earth Spirituality: Native American Paths to Healing Ourselves and Our World*. San Francisco: HarperCollins, 1990.

McKinnon, Catriona. *Toleration: A Critical Introduction*. New York: Routledge, 2006.

McNamara, Patrick. *Where God and Science Meet: The Neurology of Religious Experience*. Westport, CT: Greenwood Publishing Group, 2006.

Meister, Michael W. "Temple: Hindu Temples." In *Encyclopedia of Religion*, edited by Lindsay Jones, 13:9038–41. Detroit: Macmillan Reference USA, 2005.

Mencken, F. Carson, Christopher D. Bader, and Kim Ye Jung. "Round Trip to Hell in a Flying Saucer: The Relationship between Conventional Christian and Paranormal Beliefs in the United States." *Sociology of Religion* 70, no. 1 (2009): 65–85.

Mesquita, Ethan Bueno de. "Review of Jonathan Fox's *Religion, Civilization, and Civil War. Studies in Conflict and Terrorism* 28, no. 4 (2005).

Meyendorff, John. *Byzantine Theology: Historical Trends and Doctrinal Themes*. New York: Fordham University Press, 1974.

Michaels, Adrian. "Muslim Europe: The Demographic Time Bomb Transforming Our Continent." *Telegraph*, August 8, 2009.

Middleton, John. "Evans-Pritchard, E. E." In *Encyclopedia of Religion*, edited by Lindsay Jones, 5:2895–96. Detroit: Macmillan Reference USA, 2005.

——. "Magic: Theories of Magic." In *Encyclopedia of Religion*, edited by Lindsay Jones, 8:5562–69. Detroit: Macmillan Reference USA, 2005.

Miller, Lisa. "Religious Studies Revival: In Trying Times, a Once Esoteric Major Has Become Increasingly Vital." *Newsweek*, September 18, 2010. www.rowan.edu/colleges/las/departments/philosophy/ReligiousStudiesRevival.pdf.

Mills, Greg. "Students Challenged to Wear Muslim Head Scarves on Campus." *CBS Los Angeles*, November 9, 2011. http://losangeles.cbslocal.com/2011/11/09/students-challenged-to-wear-muslim-head-scarves-on-campus (accessed February 9, 2012).

Mistry, Mrs. Pervin J. "The Sudreh Kusti." 1996. http://tenets.zoroastrianism.com/sudreh33.html (accessed August 24, 2011).

Moore, David W. "Three in Four Americans Believe in Paranormal: Little Change from Similar Results in 2001." *Gallup*. 2009=5. http://www.gallup.com/poll/117382/Church-Going-Among-Catholics-Slides-Tie-Protestants.aspx (accessed October 6, 2009).

Moore, Diane L. *Overcoming Religious Illiteracy: A Cultural Studies Approach to the Study of Religion in Secondary Education*. New York: Palgrave Macmillan, 2007.

Moore, Kathleen M. "Visible through the Veil: The Regulation of Islam in American Law." *Sociology of Religion* 68, no. 3 (2007): 237–51.

Moses, John. "An Ethical and Theoretical Background for the Care of Native North American Cultural Materials." *Ethnographic Conservation Newsletter* no. 16 (October 1997).

Muck, Terry C. "Instrumentality, Complexity, and Reason: A Christian Approach to Religions." *Buddhist-Christian Studies* 22 (2002): 115–21.

Mueller, F. Max. "Clips from a German Workshop." In *Book Rags Biography on Muller, F. Max*, 2006.

Muenz, Rainer. "Europe: Population and Migration in 2005." *Migration Information Source*, 2006. www.migrationinformation.org/Feature/display.cfm?ID=402 (accessed January 2, 2010).

Murphy, Nancy C. *Anglo-American Postmodernity: Philosophical Perspectives on Science, Religion, and Ethics*. Boulder, CO: Westview Press, 1997.

"Muslim Fury Grows at Pope Remarks." *CNN.com*, September 16, 2006. www.cnn.com/2006/WORLD/europe/09/16/pope.islam.0750/index.html?section=cnn_latest.

"Muslim Leader Says France Has Right to Prohibit Head Scarves." *New York Times*, December 31, 2003.

NAGPRA Review Committee. *Meeting Minutes*. Myrtle Beach, SC: United States Park Service: Department of the Interior, 1996.

———. *Meeting Minutes*. Norman, OK: United States Park Service: Department of the Interior, 1997.

———. *National NAGPRA Program Fy2011 Midyear Report*. Syracuse, NY: U.S. Department of the Interior, National Park Service, 2011.

Newberg, Andrew. *Principles of Neurotheology*. Burlington, VT: Ashgate Publishing, 2010.

Newberg, Andrew, Eugene d'Aquili, and Vince Rause. *Why God Won't Go Away: Brain Science and the Biology of Belief*. New York: Ballantine, 2001.

Newberg, A., M. Pourdehnad, A. Alavi, and E. G. d'Aquili. "Cerebral Blood Flow during Meditative Prayer: Preliminary Findings and Methodological Issues." *Perceptual and Motor Skills* 97, no. 2 (2003): 625–30.

Newberg, Andrew, and Mark Robert Waldman. *Why We Believe What We Believe*. New York: Free Press, 2006.

Newport, Frank. "Americans More Likely to Believe in God Than the Devil, Heaven More Than Hell: Belief in the Devil Has Increased since 2000." *Gallup News Service*, June 13, 2007. www.gallup.com/poll/27877/Americans-More-Likely-Believe-God-Than-Devil -Heaven-More-Than-Hell.aspx (accessed February 17, 2012).

———. "More Than 9 in 10 Americans Continue to Believe in God: Professed Belief Is Lower among Younger Americans, Easterners, and Liberals." *Gallup News Service*, 2011.

———. "Near-Record High See Religion Losing Influence in America." *Gallup*, 2010. www.gallup.com/poll/145409/Near-Record-High-Religion-Losing-Influence-America .aspx (accessed February 18, 2012).

———. "This Christmas, 78 Percent of Americans Identify as Christian." *Gallup: Well Being*, 2009. www.gallup.com/poll/124793/This-Christmas-78-Americans-Identify -Christian.aspx (accessed January 9, 2010).

Newport, Frank, and Maura Strausberg. "Americans' Belief in Psychic and Paranormal Phenomena Is up over Last Decade." *Gallup*, 2001. www.gallup.com/poll/117382/ Church-Going-Among-Catholics-Slides-Tie-Protestants.aspx (accessed October 6, 2009).

Nicholai, Armand. *The Question of God: C. S. Lewis and Sigmund Freud Debate God, Love, Sex, and the Meaning of Life*. New York: Free Press, 2003.

Nicholson, Reynold A. "The Gnosis." In *The Mystics of Islam*. London: Routledge, Kegan, Paul, 1914.

Noll, Mark. "Review of *World Christian Encyclopedia: A Comparative Survey of Churches and Religions in the Modern World*." *Church History* 71, no. 2 (2002): 448.

Novak, Michael. *The Joy of Sports: End Zones, Bases, Baskets, Balls and the Consecration of the American Spirit*. New York: Basic Books, 1976.

O'Dell, Peggy. "Statement of Peggy O'Dell, Deputy Director, National Park Service before the Senate Committee on Indian Affairs Native American Graves Protection and Repatriation Act." www.nps.gov/legal/testimony/112th/NAGPRA-6-16-11.pdf.

Oriental Institute of the University of Chicago, "Research at the Oriental Institute." http://oi.uchicago.edu/research.

Orr, H. Allen. "A Mission to Convert." *New York Times*, January 11, 2007.

Otto, Rudolf. *The Idea of the Holy: An Inquiry into the Non-Rational Factor in the Idea of the Divine and Its Relation to the Rational*. Translated by John W. Harvey. London: Oxford University Press, 1958.

Paine, Crispin. "Museums and Religion." In *Encyclopedia of Religion*, edited by Lindsay Jones, 9:6243–48. Detroit: Macmillan Reference USA, 2005.

Palmer, Michael F. *The Question of God*. New York: Routledge.

Pape, Robert A. *Dying to Win: The Strategic Logic of Suicide Terrorism*. New York: Random House, 2005.

Passel, Jeffry S., and D'Vera Cohn. *Mexican Immigration: How Many Come? How Many Leave?* Washington, DC: Pew Hispanic Center, 2009.

"Pastoring Hispanics." *America: The National Catholic Weekly*, June 18, 2007. www.americamagazine.org/content/article.cfm?article_id=10015 (accessed October 21, 2008).

Paul, Gregory Scott, and Phil Zuckerman. "Why the Gods Are Not Winning." *Edge*, 2007 www.edge.org/3rd_culture/paul07/paul07_index.html (accessed December 30, 2009).

Paulson, Michael. "What Lies Beneath: Why Fewer Americans Believe in Hell Than in Heaven." *Boston Globe*, June 29, 2008.

Peirce, Charles Sanders. "The Neglected Argument for the Reality of God," in *The Essential Peirce Volume 2 (1893–1913)*. Edited by the Peirce Edition Project. Bloomington: Indiana University Press, 1998.

—— "The Fixation of Belief." In *The Essential Peirce, Volume 1 (1867–1893)*, edited by Nathan Houser and Christian Kloesel, 107–23. Bloomington: Indiana University Press, 1992.

——. "Logical Tracts, No. 2." In *Collected Papers of Charles Sanders Peirce*, edited by Charles Hartshorne, Paul Weiss, and Arthur W. Burks. Cambridge, MA: Harvard University, 1903.

——. "Sundry Logical Conceptions." In *The Essential Peirce: Selected Philosophical Writings Volume 2*, edited by Peirce Edition Project. Bloomington: Indiana University Press, 1998.

——. "What Is a Sign?" In *The Essential Peirce: Selected Philosophical Writings Volume 2*, edited by Peirce Education Project, 4–10. Bloomington: Indiana University Press, 1998.

Perlez, Jane. "Blair Praises the 'Authentic Voices' of Islam." *International Herald Tribune*, June 4, 2007.

Persinger, Michael. "Dr. Michael A. Persinger." Laurentian University. www.laurentian.ca/Laurentian/Home/Departments/Behavioural+Neuroscience/People/Persinger.htm?Laurentian_Lang=en-CA.

——. "The Neuropsychiatry of Paranormal Experiences." *Journal of Neuropsychiatry and Clinical Neuroscience* 13, no. 4 (2001): 515–24.

——. *Neuropsychological Bases of God Beliefs*. New York: Praeger, 1987.

——. "Religious and Mystical Experiences as Artifacts of Temporal Lobe Function: A General Hypothesis." *Perceptual and Motor Skills* 57, no. 3, part 2 (1983): 1255–62.

Peterson, Gregory R. *Minding God: Theology and the Cognitive Sciences*. Minneapolis, MN: Fortress Press, 2003.

——. "Species of Emergence." *Zygon: Journal of Religion & Science* 41, no. 3 (2006): 689–712.

Pew Forum on Religion and Public Life, "An Uncertain Road: Muslims and the Future of Europe" (October 19, 2005), 16. www.pewforum.org/Muslim/An-Uncertain-Road-Muslims-and-the-Future-of-Europe.aspx.

——. "Faith in Flux: Changes in Religious Affiliation in the U.S.," April 27, 2009. http://pewforum.org/docs/?DocID=409 (accessed October 2, 2009).

——. *The Future of the Global Muslim Population: Projections for 2010–2030*. January 2011. www.pewforum.org/future-of-the-global-muslim-population-regional-europe.aspx (accessed February 11, 2012).

——. "Is There a Global Resurgence of Religion?" (May 8, 2006). http://pewforum.org/events/?EventID=116.

———. "Many Americans Mix Multiple Faiths: Eastern, New Age Beliefs Widespread." *The Pew Forum: Beliefs and Practices*, December 9, 2009. www.pewforum.org/Other-Beliefs-and-Practices/Many-Americans-Mix-Multiple-Faiths.aspx (accessed February 18, 2012).

———. "Many Americans Say Other Faiths Can Lead to Eternal Life," *U.S. Religious Landscape Survey: Follow-Up*, December 18, 2008. www.pewforum.org/Many-Americans-Say-Other-Faiths-Can-Lead-to-Eternal-Life.aspx.

———. "Religious Beliefs and Practices." In *U.S. Religious Landscape Survey*. February 25, 2008. http://religions.pewforum.org/pdf/report2religious-landscape-study-chapter-1.pdf.

Pew Forum on Religion and Public Life. "Religion in a Globalizing World." December 4, 2006. http://pewforum.org/events/?EventID=136 (accessed January 3, 2010).

———. "Secular Europe and Religious America: Implications for Transatlantic Relations," 2005. www.pewforum.org/Politics-and-Elections/Secular-Europe-and-Religious-America-Implications-for-Transatlantic-Relations.aspx (accessed June 20, 2010).

———. "Teaching about Religion in Public Schools: Where Do We Go from Here?" Pew Forum on Religion and Public Life and the First Amendment Center, Conference at Freedom Forum, Arlington, VA, May 20–22, 2003.

———. "The Coming Religious Wars? Demographics and Conflict in Islam and Christianity." Roundtable discussion, May 18, 2005. http://pewforum.org/events/?EventID=82 (accessed January 1, 2010).

———. *Tolerance and Tension: Islam and Christian in Sub-Saharan Africa*. Pew-Templeton Global Religious Futures Project, Pew Forum on Religion and Public Life, 2010.

———. *U.S. Religious Landscape Survey*. June 23, 2008. http://religions.pewforum.org/pdf/report2-religious-landscape-study-full.pdf (accessed October 5, 2009).

———. *U.S. Religious Landscape Survey: Religious Composition of the U.S.* 2007. http://religions.pewforum.org/pdf/affiliations-all-traditions.pdf (accessed January 5, 2010).

Pew Research Center, "Islamic Extremism: Common Concern for Muslim and Western Publics," *Pew Global Attitudes Project*, July 14, 2005. http://pewglobal.org/reports/display.php?ReportID=248.

Phillips, D. Z. *Religion and the Hermeneutics of Contemplation*. Cambridge: Cambridge University Press, 2001.

Phillips, Richard D. "Can Rising Rates of Church Participation Be a Consequence of Secularization?" *Sociology of Religion* 65, no. 2 (2004): 139–53.

Pineda, Luis Guillermo. "Parishes Fail to Market Catholicism to Hispanics." *National Catholic Reporter*, January 19, 2007, 5a. http://search.ebscohost.com/login.aspx?direct=true&db=aph&AN=23804121&site=ehost-live (accessed January 5, 2010).

Plantinga, Alvin. "Reason and Belief in God." In *Faith & Rationality: Reason & Belief in God*, edited by Alvin Plantinga and Nicholas Wolterstorff, 16–93. University of Notre Dame Press, 1984.

———. "Religion and Epistemology." In *Encyclopedia of Philosophy*, edited by E. Craig. London: Routledge, 1998.

Plotkin, Henry C. *Darwin Machines and the Nature of Knowledge*. Cambridge, MA: Harvard University Press, 1997.

"Pope's Apology Rejected by Some, Accepted by Others." *Spiegel Online International* September 18, 2006. www.spiegel.de/international/0,1518,437636,00.html.

Population Reference Bureau. "Population, Health, and Environment Data and Estimates for the Countries and Religions of the World." *World Population Data Sheet*, 2010. www.prb.org/pdf10/10wpds_eng.pdf (accessed September 5, 2011).

Potier, Beth. "Gomes Looks Back, Ahead at Convocation." *Harvard Gazette Archives: Harvard University Gazette*, September 23, 2004.

Presser, Stanley, and Mark Chaves. "Is Religious Service Attendance Declining?" *Journal for the Scientific Study of Religion* 46, no. 3 (2007): 417–23.

Prothero, Stephen. "The Muslim Veil: Europe vs. The USA." *USA Today*, August 2, 2010. www.usatoday.com/news/opinion/forum/2010-08-02-column02_ST_N.htm (accessed February 10, 2012).

Proudfoot, Wayne L. *Religious Experience*. Berkeley: University of California Press, 1985.

Pyysiainen, Ilkka. *How Religion Works: Towards a New Cognitive Science of Religion*. Boston: Brill, 2001.

Raphael-Levine, Melissa. "Feminism, Constructivism, and Numinous Experience." *Religious Studies* 30, no. 4 (1994): 511–27.

Ratcliffe, Matthew. "Neurotheology: A Science of What?" In *Where God and Science Meet: The Neurology of Religious Experience*, edited by Patrick McNamara, 81–104. Westport, CT: Praeger, 2006.

——. "Scientific Naturalism and the Neurology of Religious Experience." *Religious Studies* 39, no. 3 (2003): 323–45.

Ray, Julie. "Worlds Apart: Religion in Canada, Great Britain, U.S." *Gallup*, 2003. www.gallup.com/poll/9016/worlds-apart-religion-canada-britain-us.aspx.

Reat, N. Ross. "Insiders and Outsiders in the Study of Religious Traditions." *Journal of the American Academy of Religion* 51 (1983): 14.

Redman, Samuel J. "American Museums in Crisis: A New Thing?" *History News Network*, April 8, 2007. http://hnn.us/articles/37302.html. (accessed September 9, 2008).

——. "Is NAGPRA Emptying Museums? Native American Tribes Reclaim Museum Collections." *Suite 101*, 2006. http://museumhistorystudies.suite101.com/article.cfm/isnagpraemptyingmuseums (accessed September 9, 2008).

Reley, Ann. "Spain Lower House Rejects Proposal to Ban Burqa." *Jurist Legal News and Research*, July 21, 2010. http://jurist.org/paperchase/2010/07/spain-lower-house-rejects-proposal-to-ban-burqa.php.

"Religion Statistics by Growth Rate." *ReligionFacts*, 2005. www.religionfacts.com/religion_statistics/religion_statistics_by_growth_rate.htm.

"Religious Populations: Christianity Is Main Religion in Britain." *National Statistics Online: UK*, 2004. www.statistics.gov.uk/cci/nugget.asp?id=954.

"Review of Christian-Muslim Conflict and a Modest Proposal to Counter It." (Republished from Reuters.) *A Common Word*, November 5, 2010. http://acommonword.com/en/a-common-word-in-the-news/19-new-news-items/439-a-review-of-christian-muslim-conflict-and-a-modest-proposal-to-counter-it.html.

Rice, Tom W. "Believe It or Not: Religious and Other Paranormal Beliefs in the United States." *Journal for the Scientific Study of Religion* 42, no. 1 (2003): 95–106.

Richey, Daniel. "Conservative Austria Party Calls for Vote to Ban Minarets, Face Veils." *Jurist Legal News and Research*, August 25, 2011. http://jurist.org/paperchase/2010/08/conservative-austria-party-calls-for-vote-to-ban-minarets-face-veils.php.

Riding, James. "Repatriation: A Pawnee's Perspective." In *Repatriation Reader: Who Owns American Indian Remains?* edited by Devon A. Mihesuah, 106–22. Lincoln: University of Nebraska Press, 2000.

Riesebrodt, Martin. "Secularization and the Global Resurgence of Religion." Paper presented at Comparative Social Analysis Workshop, University of California, Los Angeles, March 9, 2000. www.social-sciences-and-humanities.com/PDF/secularization_religion.pdf.

Roberts, Elizabeth. "Undercover as a Muslim Woman: Veiled Misconceptions." *USA Today*, December 29, 2011.

Rogers, Lois. "Britons Are Believers of 'Fuzzy Faith,' Says Survey." *Telegraph*, March 21, 2009. www.telegraph.co.uk/news/religion/5030049/Britons-are-believers-of-fuzzy -faith-says-survey.html.

Russett, Bruce, John Oneal, and Michaelene Cox. "Clash of Civilizations, or Realism and Liberalism Déjà Vu? Some Evidence." *Journal of Peace Research* 37, no. 5 (2000): 583–608.

Rustici, Camille. "France Burqa Ban Takes Effect; Two Women Detained." *HuffPost*, April 4, 2011. www.huffingtonpost.com/2011/04/11/france-burqa-ban-takes-ef_n_847366.html.

Sacks, Jonathan. *The Dignity of Difference: How to Avoid the Clash of Civilizations*. Revised, reprint edition. New York: Continuum, 2003.

Said, Edward. "The Clash of Ignorance." *Nation*, October 2, 2001.

Salmond, Noel Anthony. *Hindu Iconoclasts: Rammohun Roy, Dayananda Sarasvati, and Nineteenth-Century Polemics against Idolatry*. Waterloo, ON: Wilfrid Laurier University Press, 2004.

Satchidananda, Swami. *The Yoga Sutras of Patañjali*. Translated by Swami Satchidananda. Yogaville, VA: Integral Yoga Publications, 2003.

Schilbrack, Kevin. "Religion, Models of and Reality: Are We through with Geertz?" *Journal of the American Academy of Religion* 73 (2005): 23.

Schimmel, Annemarie. "Iconography: Islamic Iconography." In *Encyclopedia of Religion*, edited by Lindsay Jones, 7:4349–52. Detroit: Macmillan Reference USA, 2005.

Schirch, Lisa. *Ritual and Symbol in Peacebuilding*. Sterling VA: Kumarian Press, 2005.

Schjoedt, Uffe, Hans Stødkilde-Jørgensen, Armin W. Geertz, and Andreas Roepstorff. "Highly Religious Participants Recruit Areas of Social Cognition in Personal Prayer." *Social Cognitive and Affective Neuroscience* 4, no. 2 (2009): 199–207.

Schmidt, Leigh Eric. "The Making of Modern 'Mysticism.'" *Journal of the American Academy of Religion* 71, no. 2 (2003): 273–302.

Schwartz, Regina M. *The Curse of Cain: The Violent Legacy of Monotheism*. Chicago: University of Chicago Press, 1998.

Schweiker, William. "The Varieties and Revisions of Atheism." *Zygon: Journal of Religion & Science* 40, no. 2 (2005): 267–76.

Scott, John, and Gordon Marshall. "Paradigm." In *A Dictionary of Sociology*. Oxford: Oxford University Press, 2009.

Segal, Robert Alan, ed. *The Blackwell Companion to the Study of Religion*. Revised edition. Malden, MA: Wiley-Blackwell, 2006.

——. "Classification and Comparison in the Study of Religion: The Work of Jonathan Z. Smith." *Journal of the American Academy of Religion* 73, no. 4 (2005): 1175–88.

——. "Jung's Very Twentieth-Century View of Myth." *Journal of Analytical Psychology* 48, no. 5 (2003): 593–617.

Seiwert, Hubert. "End of Time and New Time in Medieval Chinese Buddhism." In *Apocalyptic Time*, edited by Albert I. Baumgarten, 1–17. Leiden, The Netherlands: Brill, 2000.

Selengut, Charles. *Sacred Fury: Understanding Religious Violence*. Lanham, MD: AltaMira, 2003.

Senate Government Affairs Permanent Subcommittee on Investigations. "Global Proliferation of Weapons of Mass Destruction: A Case Study on the Aum Shinrikyo: Background of the Cult." (Staff statement, October 31, 1995).

Shah, Timothy Samuel, and Monica Duffy Toft. "Why God Is Winning." *Foreign Policy* 155 (2006): 38–43.

Shambaugh, Bertha Maude Horack. *Amana: The Community of True Inspiration*. Atla Monograph Preservation Program. Des Moines: State Historical Society of Iowa, 1908.

Sharot, Stephen. "Beyond Christianity: A Critique of the Rational Choice Theory of Religion from a Weberian and Comparative Religions Perspective." *Sociology of Religion* (Winter 2002).

Shaw, John Crosley. *The Brain's Alpha Rhythms and the Mind: A Review of Classical and Modern Studies of the Alpha Rhythm Component of the Electroencephalogram with Commentaries on Associated Neuroscience and Neuropsychology*. Amsterdam, The Netherlands: Elsevier Health Sciences, 2003.

Shaw, Rosalind. "Feminist Anthropology and the Gendering of Religious Studies." In *Religion and Gender*, edited by Ursala King. Oxford: Blackwell Publishers, 2000.

Short, Larry. "Mysticism, Mediation, and the Non-Linguistic." *Journal of the American Academy of Religion* 63, no. 4 (1995): 659–75.

Siddiqui, Mona. "When Reconciliation Fails: Global Politics and the Study of Religion." *Journal of the American Academy of Religion* 73, no. 4 (2005): 1141–53.

Singh, Pritam. "The Political Economy of the Cycles of Violence and Non-Violence in the Sikh Struggle for Identity and Political Power: Implications for Indian Federalism." *Third World Quarterly* 28 (2007): 555–70.

SkyGazer. "All Is One." http://pub5.bravenet.com/guestbook/395054200/#bn-guestbook-1-1-395054200/next/4.

———. "Searching and Finding God." http://pub5.bravenet.com/guestbook/395054200/#bn-guestbook-1-1-395054200/next/4.

———. "See the Sea Shell." http://pub5.bravenet.com/guestbook/395054200/#bn-guestbook-1-1-395054200/next/4.

Smith, Bruce D., et al. "Letter Re: NAGPRA Disposition of Culturally Unidentifiable Human Remains—Final Rule." Department of the Interior. www.friendsofpast.org/nagpra/2010NAGPRA/Smith517.pdf.

Smith, Huston. *Beyond the Postmodern Mind*. Wheaton, IL: Quest, 2003.

———. "Book Review: *Encountering God: A Spiritual Journey from Bozeman to Banaras*." *Christian Century*, March 9, 1994. http://findarticles.com/p/articles/mi_m1058/is_n8_v111/ai_14900066/pg_2 (accessed November 3, 2007).

Smith, Jonathan Z. *Imagining Religion: From Babylon to Jonestown*. Chicago: University of Chicago Press, 1982.

———. *Map Is Not Territory: Studies in the History of Religion*. Chicago: University of Chicago Press, 1978.

———. *Relating Religion: Essays in the Study of Religion*. Chicago: University of Chicago Press, 2004.

———. *To Take Place: Toward Theory in Ritual*. Chicago: University of Chicago Press, 1987.

Smithsonian Institution. "Traditional Care of Culturally Sensitive Collections: Creating a Box for a Cheyenne Buffalo Skull." Smithsonian National Museum of Natural History. http://anthropology.si.edu/repatriation/projects/buffaloskull.htm.

Snodgrass, Judith. *Presenting Buddhism to the West: Orientalism, Occidentalism, and the Columbian Exposition*. Chapel Hill: University of North Carolina Press, 2003.

Spilka, Bernard Jr., Ralph W. Hood, Bruce Hunsberger, and Richard Gorsuch. *The Psychology of Religion: An Empirical Approach*. 3rd edition. New York: Guilford Press, 2003.

Stace, W. T. *Mysticism and Philosophy*. Philadelphia: J. B. Lippincott, 1960.

———. *The Teachings of the Mystics*. New York: The New American Library, 1960.

Stark, Rodney. "Catholic Contexts: Competition, Commitment and Innovation." *Review of Religious Research* 39, no. 3 (1998): 197–208.

———. "Secularization R.I.P." In *The Secularization Debate*, edited by William H. Swatos and Daniel V. A. Olson, 41–63. Lanham, MD: Rowman & Littlefield, 2000.

Stark, Rodney, and William Sims Bainbridge. *The Future of Religion: Secularization, Revival and Cult Formation*. Berkeley: University of California Press, 1986.

Stark, Rodney, and Laurence R. Iannaccone. "A Supply-Side Reinterpretation of the 'Secularization' of Europe." *Journal for the Scientific Study of Religion* 33, no. 3 (1994).

Stetson, Brad. *Pluralism and Particularity in Religious Belief*. Westport, CT: Praeger Publishers, 1994.

Stone, Alison. "Essentialism and Anti-Essentialism in Feminist Philosophy." *Journal of Moral Philosophy* 1, no. 2 (2004): 135–53.

St. Pierre, L., and M. Persinger. "Experimental Facilitation of the Sensed Presence Is Predicted by the Specific Patterns of the Applied Magnetic Fields, Not by Suggestibility: Re-Analysis of 19 Experiments." In *International Journal of Neuroscience* 116 (2006): 1079–96.

Struck, Peter T. "Symbol and Symbolism." In *Encyclopedia of Religion*, edited by Lindsay Jones, 13:8906–15. Detroit: Macmillan Reference USA, 2005.

Suro, Robert, Luis Logo, et al. "Changing Faiths: Latinos and the Transformation of American Religion." The Pew Hispanic Project and The Pew Forum on Religion and Public Life, April 25, 2007. www.pewforum.org/Race/Changing-Faiths-Latinos-and-the-Transformation-of-American-Religion.aspx.

Suzuki, Daisetz Teitaro. *Essays in Zen Buddhism*. New York: Grove Press, 1961.

Swackhammer, Mac. "A Project to Examine and Compare Experiences with, and Attitudes toward, Repatriation of First Nations Material and Documentary Heritage, in Some Canadian and United States Museums, with the Intent to Develop Models for Repatriation Negotiations and Activities." Smithsonian Institutions Fellowship Report, 1997.

Swatos, William H., William H. Swatos, Jr., and Daniel V. A. Olson. *The Secularization Debate*. Lanham, MD: Rowman & Littlefield, 2000.

Taves, Ann. "Religious Experience." In *Encyclopedia of Religion*, edited by Lindsay Jones, 11:7736–50. Detroit: Macmillan Reference USA, 2005.

Teitelbaum, Viviane. "The European Veil Debate." *Israel Journal of Foreign Affairs* 1 (2011).

Theophan, The Recluse. "An Explanation of Certain Texts of Holy Scripture: Romans 9:11–16, 18." *Gnisios: True Orthodox Christian Resources*, June 23, 2010. http://gnisios.narod.ru/start.html.

Thiagarajan, Sivasailam. "Agni Sahasra Namam." Super Audio (Madras) Pvt. Ltd., 2007, compact disc.

Thompson, Kenneth. *Readings from Emile Durkheim*. New York: Routledge, 2004.

Tillich, Paul. *Dynamics of Faith*. New York: HarperOne, 2001.

———. *Systematic Theology: Volume 1*. Chicago: University of Chicago Press, 1963.

———. *Systematic Theology: Volume 3*. Chicago: University of Chicago Press, 1963.

Tincq, Henri. "Interview of René Girard: What Is Occurring Today Is a Mimetic Rivalry on a Planetary Scale." *Colloquium on Violence and Religion*, 2001. www.uibk.ac.at/theol/cover/girard/le_monde_interview.html.

Tippett, Krista. *Speaking of Faith: Why Religion Matters and How to Talk About It*. New York: Penguin Books, 2008.

Tolle, Eckhart. *The Power of Now: A Guide to Spiritual Enlightenment*. Novato, CA: New World Library, 1999.

Tumminia, Diana G. *When Prophecy Never Fails: Myth and Reality in a Flying-Saucer Group*. New York: Oxford University Press, 2005.

Turner, Bryan S. "Islam, Religious Revival and the Sovereign State." *Muslim World* 97, no. 3 (2007): 405–18.

Turner, Victor W. *The Forest of Symbols: Aspects of Ndembu Ritual.* Ithaca, NY: Cornell University Press, 1967.

———. "Symbols in African Ritual." In *Perspectives in Cultural Anthropology*, edited by Herbert Applebaum. Albany: State University of New York Press, 1987.

Tylor, Edward B. *Primitive Culture: Researches into the Development of Mythology, Philosophy, Religion, Art, and Custom*, 2 vols. (1871; rprt. Nabu Press, 2010).

Uddin, Asma T. "ACLU, KKK and the Culture of Fear." *On Faith*, February 12, 2010. http://newsweek.washingtonpost.com/onfaith/panelists/asma_uddin/2010/02/aclu_kkk_and_the_culture_of_fear.html.

United Nations Department of Economic and Social Affairs. "Population Estimates and Projections." In *World Population Prospects: The 2010 Revision.* New York: UN Department of Economic and Social Affairs, 2011.

———. *Trends in International Migrant Stock: 2008 Revision* (POP/DB/MIG/Stock/Rev. 2008). www.un.org/esa/population/migration/UN_MigStock_2008.pdf.

———. "When Is the World Expected to Reach Each Successive Billion?" In *World Population Prospects: The 2010 Revision.* http://esa.un.org/wpp/Other-Information/faq.htm.

———. *World Population Prospects: The 2004 Revision, Highlights.* New York: UN Department of Economic and Social Affairs, 2005.

United States Census Bureau. "World Population Growth Rates: 1950–2050 (June Update)." 2011. www.census.gov/population/international/data/idb/worldgrgraph.php.

United States Department of State. *International Religious Freedom Report 2003—Sweden.* www.state.gov/j/drl/rls/irf/2003/24435.htm.

University of California Regents. "What Is Cognitive Science?" http://ls.berkeley.edu/ugis/cogsci/major/about.php.

Veenhoven, Ruut. "Inequality-Adjusted Happiness in 135 Nations 2000–2009." *World Database of Happiness: Rank Report Inequality of Happiness*, 2009. worlddatabaseofhappiness.eur.nl/hap_nat/findingreports/RankReport_InequalityHappiness.php.

Vertigans, Stephen, and Philip W. Sutton. "Globalization Theory and Islamic Praxis." *Global Society: Journal of Interdisciplinary International Relations* 16, no. 1 (2002): 31–46.

Vigdor, Jacob L. *Comparing Immigrant Assimilation in North America and Europe.* New York: Manhattan Institute for Policy Research, 2011.

Voas, David, and Alasdair Crockett. "Religion in Britain: Neither Believing nor Belonging." *Sociology* 39, no. 1 (2005): 11–28.

Voas, David, and Rodney Ling. "Religion in Britain and the United States." In *British Social Attitudes: The 26th Report*, edited by A. Park, J. Curtice, K. Thomson, M. Phillips, E. Clery, and S. Butts. London: Sage, 2008.

Volf, Miroslav, et al. "Loving God and Neighbor Together: A Christian Response to 'A Common Word between Us and You.'" *Yale Center for Faith and Culture: Reconciliation Program*, 2008. www.yale.edu/faith/about/abou-commonword.htm.

von Mittelstaedt, Juliane, and Stefan Simon. "Religious Provocation or a Woman's Right? Europe's Fear of the Burqa." *Spiegel Online International*, July 19, 2010. www.spiegel.de/international/europe/0,1518,707251,00.html.

Wallace, B. Alan. "Vacuum States of Consciousness: A Tibetan Buddhist View." Presented at the 5th Biennial International Symposium of Science, Technics and Aesthetics: "Space, Time and Beyond," Lucerne, Switzerland, January 19, 2003. www.alanwallace.org/Vacuum%20States%20Essay.pdf.

Warf, Barney, and Peter Vincent. "Religious Diversity across the Globe: A Geographic Exploration." *Social & Cultural Geography* 8, no. 4 (2007): 597–613.

Waters, David. "'God Gap' Impedes U.S. Foreign Policy, Task Force Says." *Washington Post*, February 24, 2010.

Weber, Max. *Max Weber's Complete Writings on Academic and Political Vocations.* Translated by John Dreijmanis. New York: Algora, 2008.

Weitzman, Steven. "Reopening the Gates of J. Z. Smith's Temple: To Take Place in the Light of New Historicism." *Journal of the American Academy of Religion* 76, no. 3 (2008): 766–73.

Wellman, James K., and Kyoko Tokuno. "Is Religious Violence Inevitable?" *Journal for the Scientific Study of Religion* 43, no. 3 (2004): 291–96.

"What Scientists Believe but Can't Prove." *TimesOnline,* 2005. www.timesonline.co.uk/tol/life_and_style/health/features/article782065.ece (accessed September 21, 2009).

White, Stephen K. "Postmodernism and Political Philosophy." In *Routledge Encyclopedia of Philosophy,* edited by E. Craig. London: Routledge, 1998.

Whittaker, John. "D. Z. Phillips and Reasonable Belief." *International Journal for Philosophy of Religion* 63, nos. 1–3 (2008): 103–29.

Wikinvest. "Proctor & Gamble." www.wikinvest.com/stock/Procter_%26_Gamble_Company_(PG).

Williams Mullen. "Religious Discrimination Cases Brought by EEOC on the Rise." *Resources,* January 18, 2011. www.williamsmullen.com/religious-discriminationarticle-january2011 (accessed February 10, 2012).

Wilson, Bryan R. "The Secularization Thesis: Criticisms and Rebuttals." In *Secularization and Social Integration: Papers in Honor of Karel Dobbelaere,* edited by Bryan R. Wilson, Rudi Laermans, and Jaak Billiet. Leuven, Belgium: Leuven University Press 1998.

Wilson, David Sloan. "Testing Major Evolutionary Hypotheses about Religion with a Random Sample." *Human Nature* 16, no. 4 (2005): 419–46.

Wise, Tim, dir. *Soldiers of Peace.* One Tree Films, 2008.

Wood, Allen W. "Alienation." In *Routledge Encyclopedia of Philosophy.* London: Routledge.

World Christian Database. www.worldchristiandatabase.org/wcd.

World Interfaith Harmony Week. http://worldinterfaithharmonyweek.com.

Wright, Dale S. *Philosophical Meditations on Zen Buddhism.* Cambridge: Cambridge University Press, 1998.

———. "Rethinking Transcendence: The Role of Language in Zen Experience." *Philosophy East & West* 42, no. 1 (1992): 113–38.

Wuthnow, Robert. *America and the Challenges of Religious Diversity.* Princeton, NJ: Princeton University Press, 2007.

Wuthnow, Robert, and Stephen Offutt. "Transnational Religious Connections." *Sociology of Religion* 69, no. 2 (2008): 209–32.

Yamane, David. "Secularization on Trial: In Defense of a Neosecularization Paradigm." *Journal for the Scientific Study of Religion* 36, no. 1 (1997): 109–22.

"Yamuna Reaps Toxic Harvest of Immersed Idols." *Thaindian News,* October 12, 2008.

Yip, Andrew K. T. "The Persistence of Faith among Nonheterosexual Christians: Evidence for the Neosecularization Thesis of Religious Transformation." *Journal for the Scientific Study of Religion* 41, no. 2 (2002): 199–212.

Young, Lawrence Alfred. *Rational Choice Theory and Religion: Summary and Assessments.* New York: Routledge, 1997.

Zuckerman, Phil. "Atheism: Contemporary Rates and Patterns." In *Cambridge Companion to Atheism,* edited by Michael Martin, 47–68. Cambridge: Cambridge University Press, 2007.

Zuesse, Evan. "Ritual." In *Encyclopedia of Religion,* edited by Lindsay Jones, 11:7833–48. Detroit: Macmillan Reference USA, 2005.

Index

Note to index: An *n* following a page number indicates a note on that page; a *t* following a page number indicates a table on that page.

Absolute Unitary Being (AUB), 187–88, 228–29
absolutism, 254, 288
academic study of religion, 9
agency detection system (ADS), 216–17
agnostics, 5, 85. *See also* nonreligious
Ahmed, Hebah, 28
al-Ghazālī, Abu Hāmed Mohammad ibn Mohammad, 89
alienation, 48, 250–51, 283, 286
Alister Hardy Religious Experience Research Centre, 199, 200, 208–9
Almond, Philip C., 57
al-Qaeda, 267
Alston, William, 100–101
altered states of consciousness, 197, 202–3, 228
Amana Colonies, 90
ambivalence, 278–79, 291
American Academy of Religion (AAR), 4, 10, 62
American Catholic Church, 317, 318; rituals in social setting in, 170–71; study of commitment and innovation in, 342
American Civil Liberties Union (ACLU), 24, 63, 64–65
angels, 82, 83*t*, 99, 101
animism, 41–43, 49, 297, 301, 342
anomaly, 22
Anselm of Canterbury, 80–81

Antes, Jennifer H., 178
anthropological approach to religious studies, 41–42
anti-Semitism, 250, 253
anti-structure, 167, 170
apocalypticism, 252, 267–68, 275, 280
apperception, 31
Appleby, R. Scott, 57, 278–80, 284, 285, 286
archetypes, 149–50, 163, 176
Arminianism, 110
Arminius, Jacobus, 110
Armstrong, Karen, 270
Asad, Talal, 35–36
Asahara, Shoko, 266–67
Ashafa, Muhammad, 279
association theory of learning, 31–32, 68
assumption, definition of, 23
astrology, 86, 116
atheists: increase in numbers of, 303, 333; "new atheists," 254, 274; percentage of U.S. population, 85; percentage of world population, 300, 301, 313*t*; and quality of life effects, 303, 304*t*, 305*t*, 305–8, 307*t*; on religious education, 246–48, 272; religious knowledge of U.S., 5; on religious violence, 253–54, 255, 270–72
Augustine of Hippo, 109–10
Aum Shinrikyo terrorist group, 266–67
Australia, 26, 44–46, 51, 127
Austria, 26, 28, 323